COMPARING TORT AND CRIME

The fields of tort and crime have much in common in practice, particularly in how they both try to respond to wrongs and regulate future behaviour. However, despite this commonality in fact, fascinating difficulties have hitherto not been resolved about how legal systems co-ordinate (or leave wild) the border between tort and crime. What is the purpose of tort law and criminal law, and how do you tell the difference between them? Do criminal lawyers and civil lawyers reason and argue in the same way? Are the rules on capacity, consent, fault, causation, secondary liability or defences the same in tort as in crime? How do the rules of procedure operate for each area? Are there points of overlap? When, how and why do tort and crime interact? This volume systematically answers these and other questions for eight legal systems: England, France, Germany, Sweden, Spain, Scotland, the Netherlands and Australia.

MATTHEW DYSON is a fellow in law at Trinity College, University of Cambridge, where he specialises in the relationship between tort and crime. He teaches tort law, criminal law, Roman law, comparative law and European legal history. He has held visiting positions at the Universities of Girona, Valencia, Sydney, Göttingen and Utrecht, and been a visitor at Harvard as well as a Visiting Research Fellow at the Max Planck Institute for Comparative and International Private Law in Hamburg.

COMPARING TORT AND CRIME

Learning from across and within Legal Systems

Edited by

MATTHEW DYSON

CAMBRIDGE
UNIVERSITY PRESS

CAMBRIDGE
UNIVERSITY PRESS

University Printing House, Cambridge CB2 8BS, United Kingdom

Cambridge University Press is part of the University of Cambridge.

It furthers the University's mission by disseminating knowledge in the pursuit of education, learning and research at the highest international levels of excellence.

www.cambridge.org
Information on this title: www.cambridge.org/9781107080485

First published 2015

A catalogue record for this publication is available from the British Library

Library of Congress Cataloguing in Publication data
Comparing tort and crime : learning from across and within legal systems / edited by Matthew Dyson.
pages cm
Includes bibliographical references and index.
ISBN 978-1-107-08048-5 (hardback)
1. Torts 2. Crime 3. Comparative law. I. Dyson, Matthew, 1982– editor.
K923.C65 2015
345 – dc23 2015012527

ISBN 978-1-107-08048-5 Hardback

CONTENTS

CONTRIBUTORS

LORENA BACHMAIER WINTER is Professor of Law at the Universidad Complutense de Madrid, Spain.

JOHN BLACKIE is Emeritus Professor of Law at the University of Strathclyde, Scotland.

KYLIE BURNS is Senior Lecturer in the Griffith Law School, Australia.

JAMES CHALMERS is Regius Professor of Law at the University of Glasgow, Scotland.

MATTHEW DYSON is Fellow in Law at Trinity College, University of Cambridge, England.

SANDRA FRIBERG is Associate Professor in Private Law at the University of Uppsala, Sweden.

IVO GIESEN is Professor of Private Law at the University of Utrecht, The Netherlands.

CARLOS GÓMEZ-JARA DÍEZ is a practising lawyer and Associate Professor of Criminal Law at the Universidad Autónoma de Madrid, Spain.

PHILLIP HELLWEGE is Professor of Private Law, Commercial Law, and Legal History at the University of Augsburg, Germany.

RENÉE KOOL is Associate Professor at the University of Utrecht, The Netherlands.

FRANÇOIS KRISTEN is Professor in Criminal Law and Procedure, at the University of Utrecht, The Netherlands.

ARLIE LOUGHNAN is Associate Professor at the University of Sydney, Australia.

MARK LUNNEY is Professor in Law at the University of New England, Australia.

VALÉRIE MALABAT is Professor of Private Law (Criminal Law) at the University of Bordeaux, France.

JOHN RANDALL QC is a practising barrister, a Bencher of Lincoln's Inn and Adjunct Professor, School of Law, University of New South Wales, Australia.

ALBERT RUDA is Senior Lecturer in Private Law at the Universitat de Girona, Spain.

MARTIN SUNNQVIST is Assistant Professor in Legal History at the University of Lund and a district judge in the Malmö City Court, Sweden.

VÉRONIQUE WESTER-OUISSE is Maître de conférences at the University of Rennes 1, France.

SONYA WILLIS is Lecturer in Law at the University of Sydney, Australia.

PETRA WITTIG is Professor of Criminal Law and Philosophy of Law at the University of Munich, Germany.

FOREWORD

Is there any better way to compare the practices of different legal systems than to look at how they deal with tort and crime? That is exactly what this fascinating book sets out to do. All legal systems share a common problem: how should they react when human behaviour harms another – intentionally or otherwise? Where should the line be drawn between the repression of anti-social behaviour that threatens social order and the compensation of victims? The harm suffered by the victim gives rise to a desire for natural justice. A part of their strength has been taken without justification; it must be given back, and if that is not possible, compensated for. This works as a negative form of the gift and counter-gift (*don contre-don*) logic: just as a gift creates obligations, counter-gift, in return, so does taking from or diminishing an individual create an obligation to restore or compensate.

Who is this victim? In Swedish, the aggrieved party is called '*målsägande*', which means 'the person who *owns* the case'.[1] The victim has to be paid off, otherwise he or she will try to get revenge for the damage – which means violence and risk to social order. There may thus be several victims, different 'bodies' whose interests have been injured. Who is the major victim: the aggrieved party, a public body or the sovereign? According to the old Swedish legal system – all of them! Compensation was divided into three parts – for the king, for the county and for the injured party. That appears to be a most wise solution!

Each legal system has to mark out its own border between tort and crime. All draw a different line – and sometimes no line at all. In England, these two types of law exist in 'splendid isolation' from each other. Sometimes the border is unclear as in France and even more so in Spain – where, as the authors explain, the boundary has been intentionally blurred.

Borders like these have long vexed great minds. Perhaps the border between tort and crime can best be seen in the light of the ancient Greek

[1] Chapter 5.3.A.5.

distinction between inter-family law (*díkē*), and intra-family law (*thêmis*). *Díkē* was the goddess of human justice based on immemorial custom and social norms, as opposed to her mother, *Thêmis*, who ruled over divine justice. *Díkē* is often translated into English as 'justice'. However, that is only one of the roles of justice, aimed at *balancing* social relationships. Justice, as a concept and as belonging to many levels of existence, is a wider concept.

For example, punishment through criminal law is another way to deal with wrongs, and in some cases, thereby compensate the victim (so much so that in the Spanish system the search for compensation distorts criminal justice). In the long term, criminal justice also aims to *pacify* social relations. However, it has a dimension which embodies *thêmis*: a divine touch. In medieval Sweden, a '*bot*', that is, a fine, was both a kind of punishment and a type of compensation because, at that time, no difference was made between criminal and civil law.[2] Therefore, the distinction between criminal and civil law is quite modern for some.

This book sets out for the reader, in great detail, the different aspects of the tensions that arise due to the different approaches of civil and criminal law. Some general trends include:

- criminal law is defendant-centred whereas civil law is victim-centred;
- the starting point for legal intervention is different: the deed in criminal law, as opposed to the consequences of human conduct in civil;
- the criminal law approach focuses on a person and on antisocial behaviour that must fit into a category ('*kategoresthai*' in Ancient Greek: to charge with, to indict). Criminal justice must remain over-shadowed by the Decalogue, a wrongful act in defiance of their terms. Civil justice does not. Being more pragmatic, civil justice aims to put right acts, which are not necessarily unlawful acts.

This difference is reflected in German by two different words: '*Verschulden*' (a human cause which is not necessarily a mistake) and '*Schuld*' (a misdeed leading to a criminal guilt).

All of the contributions to the book are in English, which is now the easiest way to proceed and disseminate the work of a project like this. However, it can result in a possible flaw – mistranslation. Therefore, the reader must pay special attention to the original words. A crucial word such as 'damages' in English does not have an equivalent in Swedish, where it simply means any payment of money. The terms 'tort' and

[2] Chapter 5.2.B.1–5.

'crime' themselves have no direct equivalent in each legal culture: 'crime' and 'delict' in Scotland (with the wonderful expression 'art and part' for expressing aiding and abetting); delictual and criminal liability in Germany; '*faute civile*' (negligence) and '*faute pénal*' (misdeed) in France as in Spain. The French word '*faute*' carries a greater moral weight than 'unlawful behaviour' in the Netherlands. 'Fraud' which is a false friend in French (where it means 'cheating') has different meanings in English in tort and in criminal law. The reader should therefore tread carefully, and pay attention to the specific words used.[3]

One of the first steps, after describing the law, is to see its underlying tensions. For example, in some countries, the distinction between criminal law and civil law is clear-cut, and, in others, less so. In England, tort and crime look like separate countries. This gap perhaps stems from the very nature of the English trial that remains so different from the *procès* on the Continent. The English (and the common law) criminal trial pertains to a 'form of truth' which excludes a joint civil party. In other words, it offers fewer opportunities for *liaison* between tort and crime. In France, as in many countries, the difference between criminal and civil trials not only concerns the standard of proof but the nature of the proceedings. In France, the criminal trial is inquisitorial while a civil hearing is adversarial; and yet it allows for a civil party to join those criminal proceedings, indeed, the state doing most of the work is often why the civil party wishes to join.

However, it is not enough to identify tension. It also has to be analysed: how can these differences be accounted for? Comparative law cannot be confined to listing differences. It has to offer at least tentative explanations. This book also demonstrates common features that encourage legal systems to converge. Tensions exist not only within the systems – between criminal and civil law – but also in their history and legal tradition, and in the evolution of liberal democracies. All of their traditions differ, but all developed societies face common challenges, that are very salient in these chapters.

The national reports do not just focus on doctrinal law but also on culture: historical background, legal professions and general categories. This book therefore gives both the legal solutions and the cultural dynamism that explains them. Every chapter begins with a general presentation of the legal system, which usefully grounds the reader and helps to flag differences early. They then proceed through different perspectives on the

[3] See further, Chapter 1.3.

material: institutional, reasoning, substance and procedure before turning to how and why tort and crime interact in the way they do. There is much of interest for many there, and a specific section at the end of the book which will interest legal practitioners, giving a brief case study where tort and crime might interact in practice.

The explanations of these differences are to be found in history: the common law tradition or the influence of Napoleonic codes, doctrinal tradition or pragmatism (which is perfectly illustrated by the excellent table in the Dutch chapter[4]). It also depends on the importance of fundamental rights, such as in the German case. Perhaps civil justice plays a more important role in a society in which there is no welfare system (at least such as those developed in France and the UK).

The conclusion of the chapter on the English legal system speaks harshly of the separation of tort and crime, calling it 'complex, under-theorised and at times counter-intuitive (to foreign and, at times, even modern English eyes)'. On the other hand, England's 'overriding objective' within its procedural rules may be a useful organisational tool for courts to deal with cases at proportionate costs. In England, reducing the cost of civil litigation has become almost an obsession since the Woolf reforms in 1996. However, this concern could also be a major driver for making systems converge. In many Continental countries, including compensation for the victim in criminal sentences is proving very efficient. Efficiency is the key to understanding the Dutch system, as illustrated by the 'ten minute rule'. According to this, 'if the court is of the opinion that handling the claim will take more than ten minutes, it will be ruled inadmissible."

A successful book is one in which we learn something and which calls into question what we have learnt before. This is just such a book. Before opening it, the distinction between civil and criminal justice was probably obvious in the minds of lawyers in all these countries (obvious, but slightly different in each case); having read it, the reader will doubt what they previously took for granted. This destabilisation is the first step in the training of a comparative lawyer, and this book gives plenty in that respect.

All of the countries analysed have the following in common:

- private insurance is an incredibly significant factor in any form of compensation, and its importance is only increasing. In many cases, it is the primary (and often the only) means for the victims to get

[4] Chapter 8.3.B.

compensation. However, the insurance industry lobby varies in the different legal systems and cultures: it is not as powerful in Spain or France as it is in Australia. Perhaps this is because access to justice is easier in those countries. The intervention of the state is no longer mainly through courts – either criminal or civil – but through victims' compensation schemes. All the countries examined in this book have such schemes.

- the growing importance of victims. Several years ago in France, a wrongful birth claim resulted in an enormous public debate (the case, *Perruche*, has certainly caused much academic, political and medical ink to be spilt). The case is a good example of why there is a perception that the number of tort claims brought to justice is also on the increase. And that injured people are very likely to sue professionals who were previously immune (such as doctors). Is this true? More empirical research is needed.
- over-criminalisation of acts in order to protect victims, except in Germany where the victims' rights movement is less influential. Victims play a major role in all of our societies and all chapters mention that trend.
- criminal offences are growing and criminal sanctions becoming harsher – driven by law and order politics.

Where there is a choice, for the victim, for the legislator, how should that choice be made? Most obviously, the choice between tort and crime may be influenced by the outcome sought, in particular, money. This book does not opt for the simpler law and economics approach as to which is most economically efficient. It does not do so in order not to lose sight of other important considerations, considerations law and economics can sometimes miss. For instance, does money meet all the expectations of victims? Can money do everything? Certainly answering such questions is outside the scope of this book. However, the book does show that the quest for justice goes beyond money. Money is too indeterminate a thing to meet the quest for justice. Today, many victims – and sometimes public opinion – demand more from courts than money.

In this way, the book reveals that tort and crime are not enemies but allies – producing what has been called a 'judicialisation' of liberal democracies.

There is still room for lawyers – and comparative law studies!

Antoine Garapon

PREFACE

This volume is the second outcome of a project to promote scholarship on tort and crime. The first, *Unravelling Tort and Crime*, a collection of essays on English law, was published by Cambridge University Press in July 2014. *Comparing Tort and Crime* is also the first volume dedicated to understanding both areas of law from a comparative perspective, both nationally and across jurisdictions; it will hopefully not be the last. The Chapters in the volume are the evolved states of papers presented at two workshops held at the Faculty of Law and Trinity College, Cambridge, in September 2013 and April 2014. These were wonderful occasions and it was a privilege to work with such a warm, interesting and academically rigorous group of scholars. In particular, national teams were partnered with each other to develop even stronger links between the papers and the teams: England–Sweden, Scotland–France, Australia–The Netherlands, Germany–Spain. It is fitting to recognise here the special assistance each partner team received from working together.

The endeavour has benefitted from being under the aegis of the Cambridge Centre for Private Law, and its Directors, Sarah Worthington and Graham Virgo. The conception of the project owes much to the formative years spent working with David Ibbetson and John Bell. Particular thanks go to Miquel Martín Casals, Jean–Sébastian Borghetti, Reinhard Zimmermann, Michele Graziadei, Demetrio Maltese and Jessica Hudson. In addition, its completion was achieved thanks to the unending support of Janet Thomasson, Michael Dyson and Oliver Dyson as well as colleagues and friends like Catherine Barnard, Jo Miles and Louise Merrett.

The whole project was made possible by the financial support of the Cambridge Humanities Research Grant Scheme, the Newton Trust and Trinity College, Cambridge. The Faculty of the Law has provided logistical support and facilities, with particular thanks owed to Rosie Šnajdr, Laura Smethurst, Elizabeth Aitken and Norma Weir.

Finally, sincere thanks are due to Emma Bickerstaffe, Mathilde Groppo and Max Kasriel for their assistance in the final stages, especially with the completion of the manuscript as well as to the incomparable Finola O'Sullivan and to Richard Woodham and the rest of the staff at Cambridge University Press for making the process so easy.

MND

TABLE OF CASES

TABLE OF LEGISLATION

Spain (*cont.*)
art. 339 237
art. 349 252
art. 386 237
arts. 526ff 254
art. 651 251
art. 760 255
Constitution (Constitución Española, CE)
art. 24.1 234
art. 24.2 256
art. 25 226, 232
art. 25.1 234
art. 81 227
art. 120.3 234
art. 124.1 238
art. 125 239
art. 149.1.6 233
art. 149.1.8 233
art. 163 241
Criminal Code of 1822 225
Criminal Code of 1848 (Código Penal, CP) 225, 437, 471
Criminal Code of 1973 (Código Penal, CP) 232
Criminal Code of 1995 (Código Penal, CP) 226, 231, 247, 250, 258, 262, 263, 265, 269
arts. 1 to 9 232
art. 1.1 232, 234
art. 2.1 234
art. 2.2 234
art. 4.2 234
art. 5 257
Book I (arts. 10 to 137) 232
art. 10 256, 257
arts. 19 and 20 254
art. 19 438
art. 20 255
art. 20.1 255, 261
art. 20.3 261
art. 20.4 264
art. 20.5 231, 264
art. 20.7 264
art. 21.5 268
art. 21.6 244
art. 27 263

1

Introduction

MATTHEW DYSON

The fields of tort and crime have much in common in practice, particularly in how they try to regulate future behaviour and respond to wrongs that have already happened. However, despite this commonality in fact, fascinating questions remain about how legal systems co-ordinate, or leave wild, the border between tort and crime. What is the purpose of tort law and criminal law, and how do you tell the difference between them? Do criminal lawyers and civil lawyers reason and argue in the same way? Are the rules on capacity, consent, fault, causation, secondary liability or defences the same in tort as in crime? How do the rules of procedure operate for each area, and are there points of overlap? Can a criminal court award compensation to a victim and can a victim force a prosecution in order to get it? When tort and crime interact, how and why do they do so? Are there patterns in how legal systems respond to the pressures on tort and crime over time? These questions, and others like them, are what prompted this volume.

Comparing Tort and Crime sets out to do six things. First, it will sketch an outline of the field of tort and crime by cataloguing how tort and crime interact in theory and in practice. Second, the intricate detail on the most significant interactions of tort and crime will be explored. Both these aims are enhanced by the volume's method. Each chapter will present a national story, but all the chapters will cover certain key material to aid in comparative analysis; furthermore, each chapter is co-authored, each is a blending of the perspectives and knowledge of specialists in civil, criminal and, in some cases, procedural law. Third, it will draw out lessons for the application and interpretation of legal rules and doctrine of tort law and criminal law. Fourth, it will discuss the impact of the tort/crime interfaces on the wider content of tort, crime and the law more generally. Fifth, it is the first exploration of how comparative law might shed light not only across legal systems, but also within legal systems.[1] The project's membership has offered the perfect opportunity to test how much lawyers relate across fields of law: such as how much civil lawyers across jurisdictions start from the same approach, and whether that approach is the same as the criminal lawyers, or the procedural specialists. This is then contrasted with how the different specialists from within a legal system relate their law to those outside it. Finally, since the field is vast and under-explored, further lines of research for the future are suggested throughout the book. This introduction will focus on the method underpinning the volume.

The volume is also the second in a series: the first, *Unravelling Tort and Crime*, contained a series of chapters about specific issues, primarily within the law of England and Wales. The preparation of that volume informed the investigations for this.

1. Outline

The book engages in two dimensions of comparative law. On the simplest level, it compares the law connecting tort and crime across eight legal systems. On a more subtle level, it compares, within each legal system, the field of tort and the field of crime. The purpose has been to go beyond one internal (civil, criminal or procedural) perspective on national law just as much as to go beyond one national legal perspective.

Now is not the place for a detailed discussion of the debates within comparative law methodology. However, a brief explanation of the theory, and how the book has attempted to apply that theory, is set out below. The four methodological areas to examine are: the legal systems selected, terminology, the method in theory and the way that theory was put into practice.

2. Legal systems in this work

Comparing Tort and Crime examines the law in eight jurisdictions: England and Wales, France, Germany, Sweden, Spain, Scotland, the Netherlands and Australia. These jurisdictions have been chosen to give

[1] For more detail on this approach, see M. Dyson, 'Ligations Divide and Conquer: Using Legal Domains in Comparative Legal Studies' in G. Helleringer and K. Purnhagen (eds.) *Towards a European Legal Culture* (Baden-Baden: C. H. Beck, Hart and Nomos, 2014). Cf. the discussion in M. Dyson *et al.* 'Symposium on Legal Domains and Comparative Law. Wheels Within Wheels: Using Legal Domains for Domestic Comparative Law' (2013) 17(3) *Edinburgh Law Review* 420.

breadth and depth to the project. There are many reasons why these countries were chosen, but three key reasons about their interaction of tort and crime are particularly important.

First, the systems studied have each structured the institutions of their law very differently. The difference in structure may well represent different theories and value judgments. These differences shape the law generally as well as specifically the overlap between tort and crime. Obviously, amongst the jurisdictions selected are a range of primary sources of law, from the Napoleonic Code or its children (France, Spain), to (more) recent or reformed codes (Germany and the Netherlands) through to a common law system (England and Australia) and a mixed jurisdiction without a code but with a strong link to Roman law (Scotland) as well as a representative of the Nordic systems (Sweden). In fact, while representing that tradition more broadly, Sweden also has a particularly fascinating and individual history to its rules on tort and crime. The work also includes a system, Australia, which is descended from English law but which has evolved differently, particularly by its federal structure and range of regimes, including full and partial codification in different areas of law and in different states.

Second, there is a range of approaches to substantive and normative overlap of tort and crime in the selected jurisdictions: from French law's historic doctrine of unity of civil and criminal fault, through German law's auxiliary or 'adhesion' process and England and Australia's lack of co-ordination even through to the very slight distinction made until recently between the two in Scotland. These arrangements represent different theories and value judgments about the law and the logic of its divisions. The book examines how much these differences affect the law in action. In addition, the work will analyse the impact of such historical frameworks on how legal actors shape the law into the future: how much the patterns of thought and possible legal techniques are conditioned by the framework within which the actor operates.

Third, the jurisdictions selected vary on how much doctrine impacts on how legal actors behave. For instance, the jurisdictions differ on how practically certain their tort/crime rules are and on the extent of the state's involvement (put roughly, high in France, Spain and Sweden, medium in the Netherlands, low in England, Australia, Germany and Scotland). Even once a litigant can gauge the likely effects of a given rule, enforced to whatever extent by the state, its impact can only be understood in connection with a range of other factors. These factors include other legal rules through to cultural approaches to dispute resolution, the extent of state support outside of the legal system, the nature of the insurance market and the wealth of the parties. These practical factors affecting how legal rules play out are particularly important for analysing law falling across significant organisational categories (such as tort and crime).

3. Terminology

In any comparative endeavour, terminology and language more broadly, hold many hidden risks.

To begin with, the volume takes a wide approach to what material is worth comparative study. To express this, certain system-neutral language is required, most particularly the term 'object' for any part of a legal system that is to be examined comparatively. In any given instance, it could be, for instance, a legal rule, a theory, a practice of legal actors, a belief about what the law is doing or should do.

Turning to language more generally, the contributions in this book are all in English, which is not the national language for five of the legal systems covered. Where possible the national reports have included explanations and the vernacular, to keep as much meaning as possible. One example is that many reports refer to 'tort law' even though they do not do so in their national languages. This is obviously useful and the cost may not be too high, but it should be acknowledged that there is in fact a cost in lost nuance. For instance, French and Spanish law tends to refer structurally to this area, describing it as *responsabilité délictuelle* or *extra-contractuelle* (France) or *responsabilidad civil* or *extracontractual* or, slightly more recently, *derecho de daños*, the law relating to harm or loss (Spain). Swedish law also focuses on the outcome, compensation or damages, though translated as 'tort': thus, the skadeståndslag of 1972 is often known as the Tort Liability Act. The Dutch phrase the matter more like the French, talking of 'liability law' as the closest translation of *Aansprakelijkheid*, but the Dutch Civil Code refers more generally in its tort provisions to *onrechtmatige daad*, unlawful act(s). For the Scottish and German chapters, the term 'delict' is preferred, derived from the past participle of *delinquere*, meaning 'to be at fault, offend'. *Delict* is indeed the common term in Scotland, while in Germany, the cognate is *Delikt*, which is used along with more specific references, such as to *Schuldrecht*, the law of obligations, or even more specifically, the fault accompanying the act, such as *Fahrlässigkeit*, negligence.

By comparison, references to criminal law seem rather simple. While 'criminal' might be replaced with 'penal' in some countries, the terms are synonyms with a slight difference in emphasis: the first focuses on the wrong, the second on the consequence of it. However, even here we face some difficulties of nuance. For instance, common law criminal practitioners tend not to refer to 'liability' in the abstract, preferring instead the procedural phase, 'guilty of an offence'; criminal law academics readily refer to 'liability'. For common lawyers, 'accountability' tends to be viewed as a term for abstract theorists, or laypeople, while for German and Dutch lawyers, it is a vital term for everyone for the functions of the criminal law. At times the term also is used more procedurally there, to mean a process of attaching a wrong to an individual (in tort as well),[2] perhaps akin to the term 'imputation', such as discussing when German lawyers hold a child accountable.[3]

Once we move onto more specific terms describing the relationship between tort and crime, we find further difficulties. To begin with, what is the right term for the person who suffers loss through a criminal or tortious action? Most legal systems give hints about how they treat such persons within the criminal justice system by the terms they use. 'Victim' is a substantive statement that a person has suffered recognised harm; until a judicial process has convicted a defendant, technically there is only an *alleged* victim, but most systems gloss over that step, for evident political reasons. On the other hand, claimant (or plaintiff) is a procedural term which describes the person bringing a civil claim. Put another way, the terms 'bookend' proceedings: a 'claimant' *is the starting point of a* civil claim while a 'victim' *is one of the outcomes of* a criminal conviction. While there are crimes which do not need a victim, there are far fewer civil wrongs without there being potential claimants.[4] Indeed, for many systems, a victim must make a complaint or assent to a prosecution for certain crimes, such as some involving personal honour. If a neutral term were sought, perhaps 'person aggrieved' might be used. Something like this has been used in a number of jurisdictions over time,[5] and has the merit of describing this legal actor in more neutral terms, focusing on the perception of the actor as having been wronged. Given the difficulties of nuance in the term, the authors have used whichever term has fitted their

[2] See, especially, Chapter 8.3.A, n. 5. The Dutch Civil Code uses a word best translated as 'accountable' in connection with tort liability, see, e.g., 6:162(3), noted Chapter 8.3.A.

[3] Chapter 4.6.B.3.(c).

[4] A further more neutral claim, 'complainant', is also used in England, particularly for sexual offences.

[5] E.g., cf. Chapter 4.7.B and 4.8 in Germany with Chapter 2.2.C in England and throughout Chapter 5 in Sweden. Spanish law seems to equate 'aggrieved party' with directly damaged party': Chapter 6.3.D.3.

law best depending on the context, having been made aware of the range of implications. As such the term 'victim' or 'aggrieved party' should be offset against more specific terms. For instance, the *partie civile* in France, is a procedural description of the civil party to criminal proceedings, but it includes a range of other parties who it might be difficult to call victims, such as family members, unions defending the collective interests of their members and most recently, even associations.[6] On the other hand, 'damaged party' in Spanish law,[7] is a wide term including at least the victim, his family and some third parties. In the Swedish chapter, the term 'aggrieved party' is used in English, the term is actually *målsägande*, literally translated as 'the person who owns the case', since the *målsägande* has extensive powers.

Other terms of art appear throughout the book, and careful attention to the English used is required. For instance, it is vital in France to distinguish between *civil proceedings*, seeking compensation and which can be joined to a criminal prosecution by a *partie civile*; and *actions with civil ends* (*actions à fins civiles*) such as an action for recovering stolen property which cannot be joined.[8] In Sweden in 2009, payments in response to discrimination were renamed in order to free them from the calculations of quantum that were associated with the traditional term 'damages'. The new payments are called *diskrimineringsersättning*, something like 'discrimination compensation'. However, in Swedish 'damages' does not exist as a term of art in the same way: one word for 'damages', *ersättning*, simply means any payment of money, whilst another similar word, *skadestånd*, could be used equally for a payment of damages based on a contractual relationship as much as a result of criminal or negligent acts.[9]

Even more generally, many common terms hide some difficulties. Each of our systems would use the term 'practical' or 'pragmatic' to describe itself, though not in precisely the same way that other systems use the term. It is important to know what is regarded as practical, or principled, and why it is perceived as such. The particular examples of 'unity' and 'coherence' will be discussed in Chapter 10's conclusion.

4. Method in theory

In theoretical terms, there are four particular techniques that the work uses: functionalism and structuralism on the one hand, and on the other, an understanding of legal culture and legal change or development.

[6] Chapter 3.3.A.2. [7] Chapter 6.3.D.1. [8] Chapter 3.3.A.1. [9] Chapter 5.3.B.5.

Functionalism is a methodology for identifying what should be compared. It is perhaps now the traditional starting point of comparative legal studies, first used by Rabel who was probably inspired by the literature on sociology.[10] In functionalism, an object, such as a legal rule, is compared with whatever performs the same function in the other jurisdiction. This method focuses on action, on the role the rule performs; it does not focus on other conceptualisations of the legal system, like structure, culture and even the names used for rules. It encourages the study of parts of objects which may appear different, revealing any unity of function. This approach has much to commend it, at least in the sense that function is important in working out what to compare. There is, in a sense, a range of functions in each system: any function should be identified first and then, second, the ways different systems use to perform it can be compared. As Zweigert and Kötz influentially put it:

> [T]he legal system of every society faces essentially the same problems, and solves these problems by quite different means though very often with similar results. The question to which any comparative study is devoted must be posed in purely functional terms; the problem must be stated without any reference to the concepts of one's own legal system.[11]

The risk is that if taken too far, too much can be assumed. What is not useful is to move from stating an assumption, to using the assumption as a ground to select material to fulfil it.[12] Therefore this volume did not assume a *praesumptio similitudinis*,[13] or presumption of similarity, especially since the area like the relationship between tort and crime is under-researched.

Functionalism remains the classic starting point for identifying what to compare, particularly in terms of what *rules* to compare. For that reason, many of the questions asked by authors in this volume have searched

[10] E. Rabel, *Aufgabe und Notwendigkeit der Rechtsvergleichung* (Munich: M. Heuber, 1925), 4, E. Rabel, *Das Rechts des Warenkaufs*, vol. 1 (Berlin: de Gruyter, 1938) 67. For more detail on Rabel, see A. Riles, *Rethinking the Masters of Comparative Law* (Hart: Oxford, 2001). On a possible borrowing from sociology, see M. Rheinstein, 'Teaching Comparative Law' (1938) 5 *U Chi L Rev* 617 and R. Cotterell, 'Comparatists and Sociology' in P. Legrand and R. Munday (eds.), *Comparative Legal Studies: Traditions and Transitions* (Cambridge University Press, 2003).

[11] K. Zweigert and H. Kötz, *An Introduction to Comparative Law*, 2nd edn, transl. by T. Weir (Oxford: Clarendon, 1992), 34.

[12] For a similar point, see J. Hill, 'Comparative Law, Law Reform, and Legal Theory' (1989) 9 *OJLS* 101, 107–11.

[13] Zweigert and Kötz, *Introduction*, 40.

for how functions are carried out and avoided national preconceptions. However, the issues functionalism focuses on less should not be forgotten. Key issues like *structure* (what the relationship of one rule to another is, *legal culture*, the way law is perceived and carried out by legal actors or *legal development* (how the rule came to be, why it has remained in place and what its doctrinal or moral significance is), are best explored using other mechanisms.[14]

Structuralism is another way to understand, and thus compare, objects, by considering their position relative to each other within one of a number of larger frameworks. It has been defined as the process 'whereby one fact (A) results from a system of relations with other facts (facts B, C and so on) in which the fact A is not only an element in the structure but is also defined by its relation with the other facts (A, B, etc)'.[15] It requires an understanding of how and why the structures that exist within a legal system have been created. It drives the researcher to understand the importance both of the role of that object within a structure, but also its relation to other objects there. In the context of the relationship between tort and crime, this particular method highlights two key points. First, it highlights that some objects within a legal system have associations with other objects which can strongly affect how both operate. Thus, once an object has been defined as being 'of' tort, or 'of' crime, its relationship with further objects is defined and conditioned. Second, and relatedly, structuralism reminds us that legal actors themselves associate objects within the system and at times even do so without reference to their function. Functionalism is an excellent way to frame certain questions without the constraints of names or associations; however, that narrow focus may miss how functions and objects are bound together. Structuralism can supply some of that understanding. To complete the picture, the action, and nexus, of objects must be understood through the minds and actions of the legal actors who create, sustain and develop the system.

The term 'legal culture' describes the training, mindset and human dimension to the operation of the law. Culture has been described as 'the framework of intangibles within which individuals operate in a given society', with legal culture being a sub-culture constituted within the community of lawyers.[16] It is closer to anthropology than some of the

[14] Cf. Lawrence Rosen, 'Beyond Compare' in P. Legrand and R. Munday (eds.), *Comparative Legal Studies: Traditions and Transitions* (Cambridge University Press, 2003).

[15] G. Samuel, 'Can Legal Reasoning be Demystified?' (2009) 29 *LS* 181, 194.

[16] P. Legrand, 'Comparative Legal Studies and Commitment to Theory' (1995) 58 *MLR* 262, 263.

other ideas in comparative law.[17] It opens the perspective that law exists through the action of legal actors, those legal actors act within a culture and that culture will affect the law's existence.

Legal cultures vary but there is an expectation that within a legal system there is some similarity in approach to law and legal problems. 'Legal culture', like 'legal system', does not have just one meaning. It is typically used to describe the collection of attitudes, practices and approaches to law which are borne by those who deal with the law.[18] As Bell has argued:

> The role that an individual occupies, and the role of other actors, arise from perceptions of the task and from the cultural traditions associated with it. Furthermore, the regularity of any such practice gives rise to professions, which in turn develop their own understandings . . . Although the participant has a personal perspective on legal events, culture is a collective phenomenon where groups use the same language and have a common identity despite other differences.[19]

Bell combines this with a more subtle point. He argues that there are many different legal cultures in France, not just one, seen clearly in the title of his 2001 book *French Legal Cultures*. The possibility that there are different legal cultures within tort law and within criminal law is one of the aspects of the relationship between tort and crime which this volume explores.

The final methodological technique is to appreciate how legal systems change and develop. This is an emerging field. Many individual instances of legal change are tightly bound up with their contexts: the wider questions of how and why law changes are beyond the scope of this work, though interesting examples are littered throughout the book. Two often divergent aspects merit particular attention: the concept of path dependence and how an object might move between different legal systems, or areas of law, commonly known as a 'legal transplant'.

Path dependence is the idea that legal actors, faced with a new problem, avoid the cost and risk of innovative thinking by adapting ideas and techniques they already have.[20] This phenomenon limits creativity. It suggests that the cost of change may be greater than the benefits of change or may only shape the perception that the cost is greater. It can operate both

[17] For a collection of some interesting references on this, see P. Legrand, 'How to Compare Now' (1996) 16 *LS* 232, 233 n. 4.

[18] This is the internal sense of legal culture though arguably there is also an external dimension to it.

[19] J. Bell, *French Legal Cultures* (London: Butterworths, 2001), 5.

[20] See, generally, J. Bell and D. Ibbetson, *European Legal Development: The Case of Tort* (Cambridge University Press, 2012), 24–32.

consciously and sub-consciously. That is, sometimes legal actors know they are restricting their possible choices and approaches, but do so for explicit reasons. At other times, they take for granted certain assumptions about how to deal with legal problems. They tend then to develop the law incrementally, and, in particular, through the use of analogy. By reasoning from a past object to a future one, legal actors will tend to conceive of a new problem in terms of past problems, often without realising it. Many of the issues within path dependence have been explored particularly by social scientists and philosophers for different purposes, and more recently by lawyers:[21] a related term is 'bricolage',[22] meaning 'tinkering' or the 'artful use of what's at hand'.

Path dependence and legal transplants have a complex relationship. In its most common form, a 'legal transplant' is movement from one legal system to another and thus the importation of a new object, rather than the use of an established one. However, using a legal transplant is in fact a method of legal change and our focus could be on the method, rather than the particular object in a given instance. In other words, path dependence may apply to that legal method: legal actors turn to foreign transplants because they typically have in the past. In addition, there is an important difference when considering path dependence and legal transplants *within* a legal system. Within the system it can be harder to distinguish between transplant and more simply drawing from a common source of ideas, techniques and rules. For present purposes, the idea of legal transplants has arisen particularly strongly in the context of tort and crime: both because they share a common root and because there have been exchanges between them right up to the present day. An example of an exchange includes rules on causation in Spain,[23] and an example of a rejection of such exchanges is found in rules of self-defence in England.[24] Three approaches to this are particularly useful for present purposes: legal transplants, legal irritants and legal formants.

The term 'legal transplant' has become the dominant way to express the attempt to adopt an object, most commonly a legal rule, from one legal system to another.[25] Watson has forcefully argued that legal transplants

[21] See, e.g., J. Bell, 'Path Dependence and Legal Development' (2013) 87 *Tul L Rev* 787.

[22] Simone Glanert, 'Method?' in Pier Giuseppe Monateri (ed.), *Methods of Comparative Law* (Cheltenham: Edward Elgar, 2012), 78–81.

[23] Chapter 6.4.C. [24] Chapter 2.2.D.10.

[25] See, generally, David Nelken, 'Legal Transplants and Beyond: Of Disciplines and Metaphors' in Andrew Harding and E. Örücü (eds.), *Comparative Law in the 21st Century* (London: Kluwer, 2002).

are the most common vehicle for legal change,[26] though some contest this claim on less practical grounds, particularly that the object will never truly be the same in the new location, so it cannot really be said to be a transplant.[27] Many other terms could be used, each bringing out different aspects of what appears to be happening in such cases. Thus, if one wanted to highlight that the process involved a bonding of two objects, so that each develop organically and differently than they would otherwise have done, perhaps 'grafting' or 'cross-fertilisation', to stress a link more social or human and less related to plants, perhaps 'borrowing'[28] or to underscore the idea of adjusting the new object to the existing flow and setting of the receiving objects, perhaps 'transposition' and/or 'tuning'.[29] In any case, the use, or non-use, of transplants offers some insights into the relationship between tort and crime.

In attempting to capture the truth of this process, Teubner has focused on understanding how to assess the way an object and the system it joins adjust to each other. He has supplied the idea of 'legal irritants' to explain the process of adoption and mutual adjustment between the new object and its new surroundings.[30] In the present context, once a transplant has been attempted, considering the process of mutual adaption reveals more of how both tort and crime work, whichever gave and whichever received.

An important final alternative looks to the nature of objects themselves, seeking to break down the law into its component parts. Sacco used the term 'legal formants' to unlock the complexities of domestic law and the value of comparative law in examining it. Sacco suggested that lawyers themselves have realised this:

> [L]iving law contains many different elements such as statutory rules, the formulations of scholars, and the decisions of judges – elements that he keeps separate in his own thinking... The jurist concerned with the law within a single country examines all of these elements and then eliminates

[26] Originally, A. Watson, *Legal Transplants*, 1st edn (Edinburgh: Scottish Academic Press, 1974). Cf. W. Ewald, 'Comparative Jurisprudence (II): The Logic of Legal Transplants' (1995) 43 *Am J Comp L* 489.

[27] E.g., Pierre Legrand, 'What "Legal Transplants"?' in Johannes Feest and David Nelken (eds.), *Adapting Legal Cultures* (Oxford: Hart, 2001).

[28] Rodolfo Sacco, 'Legal Formants: A Dynamic Approach to Comparative Law (Installment II of II)' (1991) 39 *Am J Comp L* 293, 397–401.

[29] E.g., Esin Örücü, 'Comparatists and Extraordinary Places' in P. Legrand and R. Munday (eds.), *Comparative Legal Studies: Traditions and Transitions* (Cambridge University Press, 2003).

[30] Gunter Teubner, 'Legal Irritants: Good Faith in British Law or How Unifying Law Ends up in New Divergences' 61 *MLR* 11.

> the complications that arise from their multiplicity to arrive at one rule. He does so by a process of interpretation.[31]

Part of the benefit of a comparative work like this is to show the core of legal objects, whether in tort or in crime, and whether in Spain, Sweden, Scotland or somewhere else.

5. Method in Practice

These four theoretical approaches were woven together in the questionnaire which was used to guide the development of the national chapters. The questionnaire sought to prime the authors with the range of issues that could arise, avoiding national preconceptions but combining an appreciation of the structure of the law as well as the legal culture it operated in and a sensitivity to change, particularly over time. Most importantly, the questionnaire was not to be answered individually as if it contained direct questions. Rather, the chapters tell the tale of that country's relationship between tort and crime as perceived by the authors. They address the questions in the questionnaire, but do so in any order and with the emphasis they think appropriate. Most, if not all, questions find some place in each chapter: some questions might only require a footnote, others might take up pages of text. Some matters not in the questionnaire are included in chapters. The questionnaire is meant to help to make those stories deeper and richer, and (especially) to make them comparatively intelligible.

The final version of the questionnaire, shorn of specific example answers to the questions, appears at the end of this chapter. To introduce its content, a simpler form will suffice.

(1) Where the interactions happen
  (a) Institutions
  (b) Reasoning
  (c) Norms
  (d) Substance
  (e) Procedure
  (f) Outcomes
(2) How the interactions happen
  (a) The extent the two areas are treated as equals, or they are in a hierarchy.

[31] Sacco, 'Legal Formants', 22. See also Bernard Groβfeld, *The Strength and Weakness of Comparative Law*, trans. Tony Weir (Oxford: Clarendon Press, 1990), 45–6.

   (b) The extent that objects can move from one domain to another.
   (c) The extent that influence from one area directly or indirectly affects something in the other area.
(3) Why the interactions happen
   (a) Reasons
   (b) Processes to balance these reasons.
(4) When the interactions happen
   (a) How the relationship between tort and crime changes over time.
   (b) What the factors behind changes or stasis in the relationship are.
   (c) How the legal system responds to pressures to change.

This outline is useful to grasp now, since the book's chapters follow a simple framework: each looks at where, why, how and when the interactions between tort and crime occur. In many instances, the shape of the chapter is given by the discussion of where tort and crime connect, out of which the important points about why, how and where they do are drawn. Because each chapter first and foremost represents a national story of tort and crime, the headings and arrangements vary, but the reader will find this simplified outline represents a good starting point.

A final check on the effectiveness of the methodology adopted is provided by the case study found in the appendix. It tests application of the theory by looking at how a particular case would be resolved in each legal system. The case revolves around two wrongdoers, one of whom wishes to sue the other for harm inflicted during the course of a criminal enterprise.

6. Questionnaire

The final piece of this introduction is therefore to set out the text of the questionnaire.

Where the overlaps between tort and crime happen

(1) Institutions
   (a) How does the legal system construct the relationship between tort and crime?
      (i) Are they separate areas of legal knowledge and legal practice?
      (ii) In the 'map' of the law, what kind of position do they occupy? E.g., tort is part of the law of obligations, and criminal law is part of public law?

(iii) Are tort and crime unusual in any way, compared to other areas of law, like contract law? Are smaller divisions recognised, like construction law, medical law, media law and others?
(iv) Who decides which legal rule will belong to tort law or to criminal law? Is it the legislature in the drafting a statute? Or another institution?
(v) Are there separate courts for the divisions?

(b) Are the places where tort and crime meet discussed in legal literature? Are they controversial?
(c) Are there legal actors who work in both tort and crime?
(i) How specialised are legal actors (for instance, in small towns; cf. the greater specialisation in larger cities)? Is it a national requirement that certain areas of law are studied by everyone? If so, is there a more onerous requirement for judges? Would an academic normally work in both areas?
(ii) Are there reform bodies which look at both?
(iii) What is the role of insurers? Are there instances of specialist insurers dealing with criminal situations?

(2) Reasoning
(a) Are there skills and abilities which could be labelled as particularly important in the exercise of tort, of crime? If so, what are they, and how different are they from each other? For instance, is a 'good tort lawyer' or 'good criminal lawyer' a term recognised in your legal system? If so, what would that person be like?
(b) Are there particular arguments or principles that are commonly favoured by:
(i) tort lawyers
(ii) criminal lawyers
(c) Are there good examples of where differences between the reasoning, culture or values of legal actors would show up?

(3) Norms
(a) Are the same theories used to underpin tort and crime? There are many levels to 'theory', but the first step is to consider the possibilities as abstract as possible and then get more concrete.
(b) Where the same theory is not used in both tort and crime for parallel situations where it could be used, what is used instead and why?
(c) Are the purposes the law is thought to pursue the same in tort and in crime? If not, how and why?

(4) Substance: what is the relationship between substantive rules in tort and in crime?
  (a) How does substantive law fit together across tort and crime? Core examples are:
    (i) Capacity
    (ii) Consent
    (iii) Fault
    (iv) Causation
    (v) Secondary/accessory liability
    (vi) Defences
(5) Procedure
  (a) Jurisdiction
    (i) Can a criminal court deal with a civil claim on the same matter as the prosecution before it?
    (ii) How wide and unified is the jurisdiction of the superior courts?
    (iii) Has jurisdiction shaped the way the boundary between tort and crime has developed?
  (b) Evidence
    (i) What is the standard of proof in civil cases and in criminal cases? If there is a difference in law, how does it apply in practice?
    (ii) Are there other mechanisms to compensate for a difficult procedural position of one of the parties.
    (iii) Are different people or different means of giving evidence possible in tort or in crime?
  (c) Procedure
    (i) If more than one court has jurisdiction over a matter, are the remedies the same, or, for instance, can a criminal court only award compensation or the return of property?
    (ii) Can a civil claim proceed when a criminal prosecution might also take place? The prosecution could be ongoing, beginning, planned, possible or perhaps just speculative. If the civil claim can proceed as a matter of law, does it actually do so, or do practical reasons of the time to make the claim or the effective management of the criminal case etc. make it unlikely? If the civil claim can be affected, how is it affected?
    (iii) Who is able to bring a criminal case (public prosecution, the victim, etc.) and a tort claim before the court?

(iv) If a court has given judgment on a set of facts, what is a later court in the other area of law able to do with that judgment?
(v) What are the powers of investigation in the civil and criminal courts? Are disclosure and compellability of witnesses the same?

(6) Resolutions
   (a) What outcomes are possible in civil and criminal law, both judicial and extra-judicial?
   (b) What are the practical impacts of the different resolutions on an individual?
   (c) Do the resolutions from one domain ever impact on the other?
   (d) Are there other areas which impact the domains of tort and crime, e.g., compensation from schemes run by the government? Have any supranational organisations affected the domains?

How the interactions happen

(1) The extent the two areas are treated as equals or in a hierarchy.
(2) The extent that objects can move from one domain to another.
(3) How direct is any influence from one area to another?

Why the interactions happen

(1) Reasons for the interaction: what are the reasons behind the interactions between tort and crime? In particular, consider this before consulting the list below. Are there other reasons?
   (a) Homogeneity and intelligibility of the legal system: whether the legal system should be one unit in some way: unity of the system cf. coherence/ consistency, sameness, correspondence.
   (b) Fairness, certainty, intellectual robustness
   (c) Competence
   (d) Constitutional values
   (e) Efficiency and regulation
   (f) Power
(2) How are these reasons balanced?
   (a) Internally, they might pull in different directions so how is this managed?
   (b) Externally, how do these reasons compare against other values and principles of a legal system?

When the interactions happen

(1) How has the relationship between tort and crime changed over time? Has it remained stable? If not, when has it changed?
(2) What the factors behind any changes in the relationship are.
  (a) Why did changes happen when they did, and not at some other time?
  (b) What is the relationship between law and non-law: how much are the influences on the links between tort and crime affected by non-legal factors?
  (c) Does the legal system contain explicit or tacit mechanisms for adapting the law?
  (d) What decisions determine the development of tort and crime?
(3) How the legal system responds to pressures to change.
  (a) Shaping areas of law
    (i) Movement into and out of a domain: how is content initially allocated to a domain, and can that allocation change? Do some allocations go against the norm?
    (ii) How are new domains created and filled? Are hybrid domains created from parts of other domains?
  (b) Comparison with the development of other areas of law
    (i) Does the law where tort and crime overlap change in the same way as other areas of law?
    (ii) Does the development of the overlap affect other areas of law?

Case study

Two defendants, D1 and D2 steal V's car and drive off, being chased by the police. D1 tells D2 to drive faster and more dangerously to escape. D2 does, but loses control and crashes the car, injuring D1. D2 has limited financial resources, as does D1. The car is recovered by the police.

Would the situation be any different if D1 and D2 tried to escape on a boat which then crashed in the same way?

Or, would it be any different if D1 and D2 did not commit theft but punched V and broke V's nose, then tried to escape on foot?

2

England's splendid isolation

MATTHEW DYSON AND JOHN RANDALL*

> We have stood here alone in what is called isolation – our splendid isolation[1]

1. Introduction

So spoke an English politician at the end of the nineteenth century describing a splendid isolation from the rest of Europe, but the same might be said of much in its legal, rather than foreign, affairs.

On one level, England has long been proud of the isolation it thinks it has had from civil law influence.[2] That England's common law applied so widely around the world was a reason to think itself splendid, and other legal systems of less importance. This was true in both tort and crime: in general English lawyers disparaged the techniques of the continent, such as the *partie civile*.[3]

Most importantly, there have been just as splendid isolations *within* English law. First, the distinction between procedure and substance has been particularly important. Certainly until the nineteenth century it was procedure that drove the common law, and the procedures were largely made up of isolated systems for each court.[4] The substantive categories we know today were slower to develop than this procedural structure.

* The authors would like to thank Michael Stokes for comments on the text; the usual caveat applies.

1 Lord Goschen, First Lord of the Admiralty, 26 February 1896. See generally J. Charmley, *Splendid Isolation?: Britain, the Balance of Power and the Origins of the First World War* (London: Hodder & Stoughton, 1999).

2 Perhaps most famously, O. W. Holmes, *Collected Legal Papers* (New York: Peter Smith, 1952), 155–7.

3 See, e.g., Winn Committee on Personal Injuries Litigation, Cmnd 3691 (1968), which described the *partie civile* as [393]: 'no faster despatch', [396] 'unworkable' and 'unnecessary'.

4 See, e.g., J. H. Baker, *An Introduction to English Legal History*, 4th edn (London: Butterworths 2002), Ch. 4; Frederick Pollock and F. W. Maitland, *History of English Law*, vol. 2 (Cambridge University Press, 1895), Ch. IX.

The distinction between tort and crime is one division of substantive law that was established relatively early. The forms of action do not permit exactly of being labelled 'civil' and 'criminal' in modern terms, but the core divide between them being aimed at compensation or punishment, is visible from as early as 1200.[5] Once identified, tort and crime operated in splendid isolation from each other.

However, while English lawyers may for the most part have thought this separation of tort and crime was appropriate, there are places where they have been willing for them both to meet. In such places, English law can become incredibly complex. The English lawyer is perhaps most comfortable constructing his case through precise facts and pleadings, and is reluctant to generalise quickly or deal with matters that are not central and could be avoided. The English judge is persuaded by knowing what the results of a proposed rule will be in practice; he fears unintended consequences and being successfully appealed for the illogical implications of his decisions. As a result, once tort and crime do come together, narrow decisions can get built up into intricate structures. Points of interaction are not consciously linked together in the minds of English lawyers. Nonetheless, they can reveal a great deal about how English lawyers think about the law, how they solve problems and what they do when they are forced to decide what English law should be where tort and crime interact.

To describe the many levels of this splendid isolation this chapter adopts the conceptual framework of the questionnaire, even though English lawyers may disagree about how best to express the law.

2. Where tort and crime overlap

A. *Institutions*

> [T]here is no distinction better known, than the distinction between civil and criminal law.[6]

So spoke Lord Mansfield in 1775 when interpreting the rules of evidence for oaths and affirmations in actions on penal statutes in the earlier common law of evidence. At least as a matter of theory, tort and crime are strictly separated in English law. The line between the two is, however, often hard to find.

[5] See, e.g., D. J. Seipp 'The Distinction between Crime and Tort in the Early Common Law' (1996) 76 *BU L Rev* 59, esp. 67.

[6] *Atcheson* v. *Everitt* (1775) 1 Cowp 382, 391; 98 ER 1142, 1147.

Despite some recent cases, English lawyers still tend to see the places where tort and crime grate against each other as isolated incidents, rather than pieces in a broader puzzle. For example, since 2003 an English statute has sought to reduce trespass to the person claims brought concerning the events which led to the claimant's conviction for an imprisonable offence.[7] Such claims are thought to denigrate the criminal justice process and so are restricted: the plaintiff must obtain leave to bring the trespass claim and leave is only granted where the defendant's acts were grossly disproportionate.[8] The House of Lords has also held that the defence of illegality, or *ex turpi causa*, can defeat a claim when a tort had caused the victim to lose full mental responsibility before he killed someone: the plaintiff sought damages for the income lost while he was serving time in prison for the killings and the House of Lords rejected this 'shift' of the criminal law's sanction to the tortfeasor.[9] Further recent examples of intersections between tort and crime have been discoveries,[10] and rediscoveries,[11] of ambiguities in nineteenth century statutes which bridge tort and crime. In these modern cases there has been little analysis of the underlying tensions between tort and crime.

Tort and crime are taught at University as two separate subjects, often in the same year but with little direct comparison. A similar divide can be seen after the academic stage. Civil and criminal procedure are mandatory components of the vocational training courses for practitioners (taken

[7] See Criminal Justice Act 2003 ('CJA 2003'), s. 329(2).

[8] See recently, *Adorian* v. *MPC* [2009] 1 WLR 1859; J. R. Spencer 'Legislate in Haste, Repent at Leisure' [2010] *CLJ* 19, and *Ashley* v. *Chief Constable of Sussex Police (Sherwood intervening)* [2008] UKHL 25, [2008] 1 AC 962.

[9] *Gray* v. *Thames Trains* [2009] 1 AC 1339: the maxim *ex turpi causa* and a line of reasoning based on maintaining the dignity of the criminal conviction defeated a claim for loss of earnings and general damages where a train accident victim, suffering from post-traumatic stress disorder, committed manslaughter by diminished responsibility; on which see J. Goudkamp, 'The Defence of Illegality: Gray v Thames Trains Ltd' (2009) 17 *TLJ* 1 and cf. *Pitts* v. *Hunt* [1991] 1 QB 24, 39 per Beldam LJ.

[10] *Bedfordshire Police Authority* v. *Constable* [2008] EWHC 1375; [2009] Lloyd's Rep IR 39: concerning the Riot (Damages) Act 1886 and the insurability of the Police Authority's liability for the riot at the Yarl's Wood Detention Centre in 2002.

[11] *Wong* v. *Parkside Health NHS Trust and another* [2001] EWCA Civ 1721; [2003] 3 All ER 932 concerning the bar to a later civil action or prosecution after a summary conviction for assault contained in Offences Against the Person Act 1861, ss. 44 and 45. Cf. the contemporaneous CJA 2003, s. 329(2). See also the Regulatory Enforcement and Sanctions Act 2008 discussed by C. Wells, 'Corporate Crime: Opening the Eyes of the Sentry' (2010) 30 *LS* 370, 373–4.

after the University course), done separately. Most practitioners begin as generalists working within broad fields like commercial law (including insurance, shipping, aviation, sale of goods and larger contractual deals), common law (typically being most of tort, contract and restitution, especially 'personal injury' and 'professional negligence'), Chancery (for example, trusts, charities, most of the law relating to land, company, partnership and intellectual property), criminal or family law. There are specialist fields, like money laundering and confiscation, road traffic accidents, economic crime and some other fields which tend to see more work directly on the overlap of tort and crime. A common, though not necessary, pathway resembles an hourglass: increasing specialisation into the middle of a career, but generalisation thereafter, particularly if the practitioner becomes a sitting judge, whether in the Crown Court, County Court, a tribunal (which might be narrower) or the High Court. Many of the more senior barristers will become Recorders (deputy judges), mostly sitting in both the Crown and the County Court (respectively criminal and civil courts), and will commonly hear cases outside their normal field of practice. So do some senior solicitors, though most senior solicitors who undertake part-time judicial work become Deputy District Judges, acting as the lower tier of judge within the civil courts.

Separate courts deal with tort and crime. There tends to be greater specialisation the greater the density of lawyers or the complexity of the transactions. Thus, a regional set of chambers will often have barristers between them dealing with a range of issues crossing divides which would rarely be crossed within any one London chambers. The same is true for a high-street solicitors' practice compared to a 'magic circle' firm. It should be noted that, over the past twenty years or so, there has been a sharp decline in the numbers of practitioners who will undertake work in both fields; now senior practitioners rarely do both.

The legislature has involved itself much more in criminal law than in tort law. A piece of legislation directly or solely on tort law is passed every few years, whereas there are new criminal statutes perhaps every six months. One might look to the number of new offences created, though it appears that not even the executive, which promotes most legislation passed, know exactly how many that is. The Ministry of Justice's statistics for the year May 2010–May 2011, suggest that 174 new offences were created in England; a rigorous academic study has found that the figure is in fact 634, nearly four times as many; while counting methods may vary, it seems difficult to believe *there is* or that *there should be* that much of a difference.[12] Even more troublingly though, the study added:

> The Law Commission estimated that there are 'now over 60 national regulators' with the power to make criminal law, alongside trading standards authorities and 486 local authorities. To put that differently: not only do we not know how many criminal offences there are, we are not even sure how many bodies have the power to create them.[13]

The legislature retains the ability to interfere in doctrinal, procedural and other aspects of both areas of law, but has shown itself far less interested in spending its time on tort, than on crime.

Beyond academics, practitioners and the legislature, other legal actors are involved in both areas of law. Since 1965 the Law Commission of England and Wales has had a remit to propose legislation on both, though the Commission is itself divided into teams, with a criminal law team and a common law team. A few of their projects have covered common ground between the two, such as the Forfeiture Act 1980. Between 1996 and 2014, ten reports have concerned tort law, broadly defined, and twenty (longer) reports have concerned criminal law, out of a total of sixty-nine reports. There are now no longer more specific standing law reform bodies, such as the Criminal Law Revision Committee (responsible for, for instance, the Theft Act 1968 and its provisions on restitution orders), the Advisory Council on the Penal System, or the more civil law focused Law Reform Committee.

Of course, there are other bodies as well, particularly insurers; one insurer in particular, the Motor Insurers' Bureau, covers claims where the wrongdoer is uninsured or untraced (normally a crime).[14] As a broad generalisation, insurers are heavily involved in the litigation of tort law claims, but have little involvement in the criminal courts. In practice, however, the divide is not as clear cut: motorists and employers tend to benefit from their insurers vigorously defending them in serious cases like manslaughter, often funding a higher level of defence than would

[12] J. Chalmers and F. Leverick 'Tracking the Creation of Criminal Offences' [2013] *Crim LR* 543.

[13] Ibid., citing *Law Commission, Consultation Paper on Criminal Law in Regulatory Contexts, Law Com CP No.195 (2010)*, [1.21].

[14] On which, see R. Merkin and J. Steele, 'Policing Tort and Crime with the MIB: Remedies, Penalties and the Duty to Insure' in Matthew Dyson (ed.) *Unravelling Tort and Crime* (Cambridge University Press, 2014) (hereafter '*Unravelling*').

otherwise be available or likely, in order to reduce the chances of a conviction which could then be used against the insured in a later civil claim.

B. *Reasoning*

Legal reasoning in England shows a range of methods and skills, and there is no clear line between a 'criminal' skill and a 'civil' one.

At a high level of abstraction, both areas of law do not like 'bad' people avoiding the consequences of their wrongdoing. Criminal judges might be willing to bend dramatically to achieve this, and some examples will be seen in the course of the chapter. A related issue is the increasing victim-centred discourse, albeit that this is still more political than legal. Tort law, for its part, expresses this focus slightly differently, focusing more on deserving claimants and those wronged:

> The general rule that where there is a wrong there should be a remedy is a cornerstone of any system of justice. To deny a remedy to the victim of a wrong should always be regarded as exceptional . . . any justification must be necessary and [is required to be] strict and cogent . . . [15]

Of course, this kind of argument, the cry for justice in response to a perceived wrong, is just what will be put forward by claimants or prosecutors. The defendant will reply that not every harmful act is criminalised, and nor can or should tort compensate for every wrong. Indeed, intellectually the common law has traditionally had great affinity with asking, in tort, why the loss should not lie where it fell. More recently tort law has seen this balance shift, and it is now relatively easy to provide a plausible answer to why the loss should be shifted elsewhere.[16] In criminal law a similar brake has in practice been applied by the limits of prosecutorial resources.

Above all, the English common law is a supremely practical creature. The ability to solve the problem in front of you is the hallmark of a good lawyer. This also means that if you can solve the present case without dealing with related issues, you will often do so; thus crime and tort are

[15] *Jones* v. *Kaney* [2011] 2 AC 398, [113] per Lord Dyson. See also *X (Minors)* v. *Bedfordshire County Council* [1995] 2 AC 633, 663 per Sir Thomas Bingham MR: 'the rule of public policy which has first claim on the loyalty of the law: that wrongs should be remedied'.

[16] Various factors including the dramatic expansion of the law of negligence, and the generalisation of its conditions into broad rules rather than narrow instances, are behind this.

only dealt with together when they really must be. English lawyers at all levels particularly appreciate the value of analogy in reasoning: students, practitioners and judges will commonly test out propositions through differential factual analysis as a key part of their reasoning process, even if a more normative or theoretical aspect also plays a role. This broadly holds true for criminal lawyers as for civil lawyers. Nonetheless, neither would generate liability by an analogy with an existing tort or crime: that approach is highly unlikely in either case. This can be seen, for instance, by the rules of statutory interpretation known as *eiusdem generis* (earlier items of a list of constituent parts in a definition limit later generalising terms) and *inclusio unius est exclusio alterius* (including one of a group or related set impliedly excludes the others). A related issue is that criminal lawyers are loathe to expunge a criminal offence, even if it is rarely used: the fear that a gap in the law might be created is a strong one. Old offences may be dredged from decades of disutility, though this tends to be kept largely in check by prosecutorial discretion and limited resources; and even if such a charge is brought, the criminal judge can stay it as an abuse of process if it represents an egregious use of the state's coercive power.

More generally though, there is greater flexibility in the shape and internal divisions of tort law than in criminal law. On the one hand, both types of judge will look to construe the law in a way which produces a result which s/he instinctively considers to be a just one. Yet tort law has developed fewer and more general wrongs, largely without strong statutory or procedural limits. The common law can bud new tortious causes of action much more easily than criminal law, which largely cannot now declare new criminal offences.[17] The fact that some torts are to this day known by the name of the case which first recognised them (*Rylands* v. *Fletcher*[18]; *Lumley* v. *Gye*[19]) supports this.[20] Criminal law has not tolerated this level of flexibility for principled reasons of legal certainty. While the tort advocate could adapt and extend his pleadings in the broader statement of claim/particular of claim, vagueness and innovation were not encouraged by the common law's attitude to embarrassingly precise documents like an indictment.

[17] Though there are perhaps seventy torts, few are often used: B. Rudden, 'Torticles' (1991–1992) 6/7 *Tulane Civil Law Forum* 105.

[18] *Rylands* v. *Fletcher* (1868) 3 HL 330.

[19] *Lumley* v. *Gye* (1853) 2 E & B 216; 118 ER 749.

[20] Indeed, it is notable that it has not been felt necessary to give a label to the cause of action that the layman would appreciate, as it would be in criminal law.

Tort law contains relatively few important statutes, perhaps twenty of core importance, and these tend not to be too complex or long. In many cases, such as the Occupier's Liability Act 1957, they are not greatly different to the common law (in that case, negligence). Thus judges have largely been left to develop the law, without legislative intervention on specific issues or even by imposing some general cause for liability. Statutes are much more important in criminal law and so, therefore, is statutory interpretation. In particular, criminal lawyers have shown great skill in 'getting round' the apparently plain words of statute, if necessary in order to avoid a plain injustice. For instance, criminal barristers make as much as they can of judicial discretion to protect the defendant when determining the admissibility of evidence, arguing that the admission of the evidence would make the trial process as a whole 'unfair' and so should be excluded under the much invoked Section 78 Police and Criminal Evidence Act 1984 (PACE). There is no real equivalent in civil proceedings.[21]

It used to be the case that criminal practitioners would have to deal with comparatively little black letter law, and would expect their cases to turn primarily on the quality of evidence (as to guilt) and judicial discretion (as to sentence); civil practitioners would look wherever possible to win tort and other civil cases on legal points, including procedural ones, to avoid being dependent on uncertain judicial resolution of disputed and contradictory evidence. The volume of legislation concerning the criminal law in recent years has changed this: it is far more technical, with less space for judicial discretion, in everything from evidence, procedure and substance through to sentencing.

C. *Norms*

The third place where tort and crime overlap is normative theories: they can draw tort and crime away from each other, or pull them together. There are many theories of law, of punishment and of liability which either do not respect any boundary between tort and crime, or actively seek to re-arrange it as part of a wider conceptualisation of the law. However, it is not a level on which English lawyers have tended to operate, certainly not practitioners and definitely not in respect of tort and crime.

In the common law, perhaps the first modern writer on the matter was William Blackstone, the first Vinerian Professor at Oxford and later a

[21] Notwithstanding the theoretical availability of a general discretion to exclude evidence under Civil Procedure Rules (CPR), 32.1(2); in practice this is rarely used – see commentary on that rule in Civil Procedure (2014).

judge. He argued that criminal penalties for serious crimes 'swallow[ed] up' any parallel civil claim.[22] A number of prominent reformers would later famously disagree, arguing that distinctions between criminal law and civil law are illusory. For Jeremy Bentham, no settled line could be drawn between the civil branch and the penal.[23] Bentham saw all sanctions as 'evils', differing only in degree. The distinction, he argued, came from purpose: it was for the civil law to set out the rights and duties, and criminal law to set out the penalties. Austin also argued that no sensible distinction could be drawn,[24] but did so for different reasons. For him, on the one hand the discretion to enforce the rule varied between tort and crime, between the party aggrieved and the sovereign; on the other hand, a crime is a breach of an 'absolute' duty, whereas torts are violations of 'relative' duties (which have no corresponding 'right').[25] English lawyers struggle to complete the work started over 250 years ago.[26]

Nonetheless, tort and crime seem to have similar normative backbones. We could start at the level of purpose. What are the purposes of tort law and criminal law? There is no consensus on the exact balance of purposes each could achieve, but the range of possible purposes is tolerably clear. Tort law can demarcate and protect rights, compensate those wronged, deter wrongful conduct, allocate the burden of risks, hold wrongdoers to account for their actions, declare the legality of conduct and punish.

Criminal law primarily punishes and thereby express one of four things: retribution or 'just deserts', deterrence (of the individual wrongdoer, known as specific deterrence, and/or of potential wrongdoers at large, known as general deterrence), incapacitation (for instance by imprisonment, restrictions on movement or location, filling time with other activities) or rehabilitation (by changing the offender's decision-making process that led to wrongful conduct in a way other than threatening punishment). In addition, the criminal law is used to reflect and at times, set,

[22] W. Blackstone, *Commentaries on the Law of England*, vol. 4 (Oxford, Clarendon, 1765–1769), 6.

[23] See, generally, J. Bentham, *Of Laws in General* (collected works, substantially completed in 1782), H. L. A. Hart (ed.), (London: Athlone Press, 1970), Ch. 17–18; J. Bentham, *Works*, Bowring (ed.), (Edinburgh: William Tait, 1843), Ch. III.

[24] J. Austin, *Lectures on Jurisprudence*, vol. 1, 3rd edn (R. Campbell, 1869), 520: 'the difference between civil injuries and crimes can hardly be found in any difference between the ends or purposes of the corresponding sanctions'.

[25] Ibid., 518. See further J. Hall 'Interrelation of Criminal Law and Torts. I' (1943) 43 *Colum L Rev* 753, 757–60.

[26] For two recent examples, see R. Stevens, 'Private Rights and Public Wrongs' and R. A. Duff, Torts, Crimes and Vindication: Whose Wrong Is It?' both in *Unravelling*.

standards of conduct, to reduce the risk of wrongs escalating into feuds, and on occasion to compensate victims, despite this being the classic domain of tort law.

There are other more concrete theories which appear to be applied in both tort and crime. For instance, where strict liability is used in either area, one of the justifications for it is administrative convenience: it makes the system simpler to run and for lower level wrongs the cost is not too great. A second justification is that both areas of law have tended to package the risk of liability with the conduct itself: 'enterprise risk' in civil law, and the sentiment that 'if you can't do the time, don't do the crime' in criminal law.

There are examples of theories which are not applied in the same way in tort and in crime. For instance, many tort laws accept that activity which creates a risk can in some situations generate liability even without fault. One example is product liability. Does a theory of risk-taking behaviour creating liability without evidence of fault arise in criminal law? The answer would appear to be yes, but it is difficult to create a list of all such offences. Examples would be road traffic offences related to road safety. Soon, however, these offences blur into inchoate offences which criminal law has, but tort law generally does not. English criminal law recognises taking a risk as a form of fault, in its test for recklessness. Tort law does this, but through the concept of negligence; this, the most common fault standard alleged in tort litigation, makes those who do not take reasonable care liable for the harm they cause, which will often be factually the same as taking unreasonable risks.

There are also examples of theories where the same theory is not used in both tort and crime for parallel situations where it could be used. For instance, 'fair labelling' does not seem to be an important principle in tort law, even though in a number of torts there is a labelling function, albeit clearly not the same as within criminal law.[27]

D. Substance

English law still tends to treat each case on its facts. Each criminal offence and each tort have different substantive components. The default belief in the last 150 years has been that it would cause confusion for one branch

[27] Andrew Ashworth has been the key influence in the development of the principle within criminal law, see most recently, A. Ashworth and J. Horder, *Principles of Criminal Law*, 7th edn (Oxford University Press, 2013), 77–9.

of the law to employ the substantive law of the other.[28] However, there are places where English law does explicitly connect substance across tort and crime. Four examples will suffice.

First, there are some torts and crimes which share the same, or nearly the same, requirements, such as public nuisance[29] or harassment.[30]

Closely related is the second example: that some torts can have the same root as crimes, even though they are then read through a new lens, such as the separate tort of breach of statutory duty. This is a means of creating a tortious claim for harm caused by the (criminal) breach of a duty in a statute where the statute does not itself say whether there is civil liability: the fact that the statute imposes a criminal penalty for breach is one, non-conclusive factor against an implication of liability in tort.[31] Breaches of the Health and Safety at Work etc. Act 1974 duties were for a long time the most significant example of express overlap, but from April 2013, such breaches of such duties have no longer been automatically actionable.[32]

Third, the defence of illegality in tort: a doctrine the law deploys to prevent a claimant making a right out of wrongful conduct. The defence which can prevent this, *ex turpi causa non oritur actio*, is relatively new to English tort law.[33] This might be analysed in a number of different ways, as noted here. One of them is that the criminal law rule is being given force within tort law. Alternative analyses include illegality being a procedural question, or as a matter of personal bars on claimants. The area is highly contentious and few are satisfied with the current position, neither the purpose of any such defence, nor how to apply it in practice. The English Law Commission has recently made recommendations on illegality,[34] but

[28] E.g., on automatism *Mansfield* v. *Weetabix* [1998] 1 WLR 1263, 1266, 1268–9; on the civil law of ownership and theft: *Bentley* v. *Vilmont* (1887) 12 App Cas 471, 477; cf. *R* v. *Hinks* [2001] 2 AC 241, 263–70.

[29] See, e.g., J. R. Spencer 'Public Nuisance – A Critical Examination' [1989] *CLJ* 55; *R v. Rimmington* [2006] 1 AC 459.

[30] Protection from Harassment Act 1997, ss. 1–3.

[31] *Carroll* v. *Barclay & Sons, Ltd.* [1948] AC 477, 489–90, 493; *Biddle* v. *Truvox Engineering Co.* [1952] 1 KB 101, 103; *Cutler* v. *Wandsworth Stadium* [1949] AC 398 and see also A. L. Goodhart (1946) 62 *LQR* 316, 317.

[32] Enterprise and Regulatory Reform Act 2013, s. 69; see J. R. Spencer, 'Civil Liability for Crimes' in *Unravelling*, 305–7.

[33] C. Symmons 'Ex Turpi Causa in English Tort Law' (1981) 44 *MLR* 555; Goudkamp 'The Defence of Illegality'.

[34] Law Commission Report No 320 (February 2010), *The Illegality Defence.*

these have not been legislated and cases,[35] as well as academic[36] and judicial[37] dissatisfaction, continue.

Fourth, there are times when criminal law relies on substantive rules of the civil law.[38] A classic example is the definition of property and who has a right to possess it (on which see Section 9 below).

Many of the same concepts exist, but rarely have exactly the same meaning, in both tort and crime. The following are a number of the more important examples.

1. Capacity

In tort, the general rule is that all persons are entitled to sue or be sued. Historically there were a number of exceptions to this for classes of people but generally these have been removed.[39] A director of a limited company while acting as such will not ordinarily be personally liable for a company's torts,[40] but may become so if he commits the tort personally (for instance, as the negligent driver of a company vehicle), has indicated to the claimant that he assumes personal responsibility for the relevant activity (and the claimant relied on that),[41] has done sufficient to authorise, direct or procure the company's tortious actions as to render himself a joint tortfeasor with the company[42] or has acted fraudulently.[43] Perhaps the leading examples of where immunity in tort persists concern the administration of justice. Thus judges retain a tortious immunity while hearing cases, and things said in court cannot be the subject of an action in defamation.[44]

There is very little developed law about the liability in tort of persons of unsound mind. They are generally considered to be liable in the same way as those unaffected by mental illness or impairment, unless it is so extreme that their actions were not voluntary at all. Hence a driver who becomes

[35] E.g., *Hounga* v. *Allen* [2014] UKSC 47, [24]–[44], [51].

[36] E.g., G. Virgo, 'Illegality's Role in the Law of Torts' in *Unravelling*.

[37] J. Mance 'Ex Turpi Causa – When Latin Avoids Liability' (2014) 18 *Edinburgh L Rev* 175.

[38] E.g., J. C. Smith 'Civil Law Concepts in the Criminal Law' [1972] *CLJ* 197.

[39] See, for examples, the Law Reform (Married Women and Tortfeasors) Act 1935, the Crown Proceedings Act 1947, the Law Reform (Husband and Wife) Act 1962 and the State Immunity Act 1978.

[40] *Williams* v. *Natural Life Health Foods Ltd* [1998] 1 WLR 830.

[41] Ibid., 835–7. [42] *C. Evans Ltd.* v. *Spitebrand Ltd.* [1985] 1 WLR 317.

[43] *Standard Chartered Bank* v. *Pakistan National Shipping Corp.* (Nos 2 and 4) [2003] 1 AC 959.

[44] *R* v. *Skinner* (1772) Lofft 55; 98 ER 529.

unable to control his vehicle due to the onset of a disabling condition will not be liable for resultant injury and damage, unless he chose to drive after he should have been aware of his disabling condition. In *Mansfield* v. *Weetabix*, the leading case, the Court of Appeal expressly disapproved the consideration of criminal cases dealing with equivalent situations, which they suggested 'can only introduce confusion' in a tort case, and criticised the trial judge for having done so.[45] Similarly, intoxication seems not to feature in tort doctrine: if harm is done while intoxicated, it tends to be easier to prove fault[46] and litigation on this, certainly appellate litigation, is rare.

Similarly, while children are liable in tort as if they were adults, in practice children are rarely sued. If you seek money, children are not normally worth suing unless there is an insurance policy somewhere in the background and if you seek to win a point of principle against a child defendant you tend to look foolish. Indeed, as a sign of the rarity of these cases, English law did not know for certain the level of care a child should show until 1998 and the case of *Mullin* v. *Richards*. Two children had been play fighting with rulers when one ruler broke and injured the eye of the claimant. The action failed, as she was held not to have breached the standard of the reasonable fifteen-year-old child.[47] The parallel claim against the teacher also failed as no teacher could maintain perfect control of the classroom at all times.

As a procedural matter, children (i.e. persons below the age of eighteen) may only sue or be sued with – so as to be aided by – another person, known as a 'litigation friend', unless a judge gives permission otherwise.[48] The same rule applies to persons who lack capacity within the meaning of the Mental Capacity Act 2005; such capacity is judged by reference to the claim in question, not globally.[49] Hence an agreement settling a tortious claim brought by a person unaided by a litigation friend who in fact lacked such capacity is voidable on that ground, whether or not the defendant was aware of the claimant's incapacity.[50]

Criminal law deals with capacity in a relatively simplistic fashion: all natural persons have capacity over the age of ten by force of statute, raising

45 [1998] 1 WLR 1263 (CA), esp. 1266.

46 The leading practitioner's text refers to intoxication in the index only in respect of consenting to the risk of a drunk driver's negligent driving: see *Clerk & Lindsell on Torts*, 20th edn (London: Sweet & Maxwell, 2013), 2176 referring to [3–76].

47 *Mullin* v. *Richards* [1998] 1 All ER 920. The same position had been reached much earlier in Australia: *McHale* v. *Watson* (1966) 115 CLR 199.

48 CPR, 21.2.

49 *Dunill* v. *Burgin* [2014] UKSC 18; [2014] 1 WLR 933, [13].

50 Ibid., [18], [34].

the common law age which was originally seven.[51] Children between ten and fourteen had previously benefitted from a rebuttable presumption that they too were *doli incapax*: incapable of committing crime. Legislation in 1998 attempted to remove this possibility[52] but it did so clumsily and it was only in 2009 that a decision of the House of Lords confirmed that it had succeeded.[53] As such, after his tenth birthday, a child is liable as if he were an adult though the trial and sentencing will be tailored to his age.[54]

Other than age, the criminal law recognises a reduction of capacity through doctrines of substantive and procedural insanity as well as specific forms of insanity in specific offences and defences. The two largest headings are the defence of automatism and the special verdict of 'not guilty by reason of insanity'.[55] Automatism does not seem to feature much in civil cases, *Mansfield* v. *Weetabix* being a rare example. In criminal law it requires the complete absence of voluntary control of the body's movements, akin to sleepwalking, sudden reflex motions or some extraneous causes like brain injuries;[56] its use is rare. The special verdict in its current form dates from 1843, where a famous acquittal following an attempt on a politician's life led the judges of the House of Lords to set out the rules they applied in reaching that result; the rules were later recognised by the House of Lords sitting as a court: the defendant must act under a defect of reason, arising from a disease of the mind, so that he did not know the nature and quality of his act or that he did not know what he was doing was wrong.[57] This definition does not follow established medical opinion and is open to some criticism.[58] Some specific offences also exist relevant to the capacity of the defendant, like infanticide contrary to the Infanticide Act 1938, s. 1 which makes it manslaughter rather than murder

[51] See now the Children and Young Persons Act 1933, s. 50, as amended by the Children and Young Persons Act 1963, s. 16 (see generally, s. 44 of the 1933 Act as well).

[52] Crime and Disorder Act 1998, s. 34, and see *R* v. *T* [2009] UKHL 20.

[53] *R* v. *T* [2009] UKHL 20.

[54] For a critical appraisal, see C. Ball, 'Youth Justice? Half a Century of Responses to Youth Offending' [2004] *Crim LR* 167. See, e.g., Practice Direction (Criminal Proceedings: Consolidation), para. III.30 (as inserted by Practice Direction (Criminal Proceedings: Further Directions) [2007] 1 WLR 1790, *DPP* v. *P* [2007] EWHC 946 (Admin). Cf. family law: H. Keating 'The "Responsibility" of Children in the Criminal Law' (2007) 19 *CFLQ* 183.

[55] See recently, Law Commission Discussion Paper (July 2013), *Criminal Liability: Insanity and Automatism.*

[56] *Attorney-General's Reference (No 2 of 1992)* [1994] QB 91.

[57] See, generally, *R* v. *Sullivan* [1984] AC 156.

[58] See D. Ormerod, *Smith and Hogan's Criminal Law*, 13th edn (Oxford University Press, 2011), Ch. 11.1–11.2.

if a mother kills her child within twelve months of giving birth because 'the balance of her mind was disturbed' by the birth or lactation.[59] There are also some specific defences, such as diminished responsibility, a partial defence which reduces a charge from murder to manslaughter where the defendant's recognised medical condition substantially impaired his understanding, rationality or self-control and explains why he killed.[60] Last but not least, for the majority of criminal offences (those of 'basic intent', typically involving recklessness or less, with some offences featuring intention), it is easier to convict a defendant who was intoxicated, with fault essentially being established by the fact of intoxication; it is, however, unclear whether this is a rule of substantive law or of evidence.[61]

Finally, corporate criminal liability is rarer than corporate civil liability. While legal persons can be injuncted and made to pay damages, the sanctions of the criminal law have both required human agency and, beyond fines, have needed a human object. Nonetheless, legal persons can be made liable for criminal wrongs in England, although there are significant difficulties in attributing fault from the legal actors involved to the legal person of the company.[62] It is for that reason that strict liability offences, particularly regulatory ones or those relating to health and safety, are some of the classic offences of which companies are convicted. Significant recent legislation has attempted to broaden the way criminal liability is attributed to companies.[63] Thus the Corporate Manslaughter and Corporate Homicide Act 2007 expanded the criminal law in those offences to look to the way the activities of the company are managed or organised.

Wherever suing one legal person is difficult or impossible, there may be pressure to make another liable instead. In this respect, English law is quite restrictive. For instance, parents are not automatically liable in tort or crime for the acts of their children.[64] What liability there is tends to resolve either around no-fault liability, like vicarious liability, or liability for an omission. A classic example is in the use of firearms before England's strict licensing laws: the parent would have to be negligent in the instructions

[59] Others turn on the mental capacity of the victim, e.g., Sexual Offences Act 2003, ss. 30–37.

[60] Homicide Act 1957, s. 2 as amended by the Coroners and Justice Act 2009, s. 52.

[61] See, e.g., *R* v. *Majewski* [1977] 1 AC 443; A. Simester 'Intoxication is Never a Defence' [2009] *Crim LR* 3.

[62] Ormerod, *Smith and Hogan's Criminal Law*, Ch. 10.1.

[63] See, e.g., Celia Wells, 'Corporate Crime: Opening the Eyes of the Sentry' (2010) 30 *LS* 370.

[64] E.g., *North* v. *Wood* [1914] 1 KB 629.

and use of the gun, s/he could not be directly liable for the child's acts.[65] Of course, this does not only apply to parents: a county council was liable when a school by inattention allowed a four year old boy out, and he predictably ran into a busy road, causing a driver to swerve and suffer injuries.[66] Criminal law is even more restrictive in parental liability. There have been occasional attempts to blame parents for the acts of their children in a legal, rather than a moral sense, most recently with a Private Members Bill in Parliament called the Young Offenders (Parental Responsibility) Bill, which has appeared in 2010 and 2013, but never proceeded beyond a first reading.[67] Criminal law does have offences, often strict liability ones, about the acts of others, such as licensing laws and environmental safety.

In addition, criminal law is far more willing to convict a person as a principal having used someone without capacity, or without fault, as an innocent agent.[68] This doctrine almost never appears in tort law.

2. Liability for others and accessory liability

Both tort and crime can make one person liable for the acts of others.[69] In short: in tort the two mechanisms are vicarious liability and primary non-delegable duties; accessory liability plays a much smaller role. In criminal law, primary duties and accessory liability are both very common.

In tort law, vicarious liability ensures that an employer, often a company, can be made liable for the torts of its employees provided they are committed within the course of employment.[70] The employee's tort could also be a crime and indeed, a crime committed for the employee's benefit and against the employer's interests.[71] However, until recently courts were somewhat restrictive of who was an employee,[72] but more importantly for us, required either some form of authorisation for the tort or that it was an unauthorised mode of doing an authorised act: commonly known as the Salmond Test.[73] This tended to exclude some crimes, particularly sexual assaults, while leaving some assaults and thefts within the scope

65 See, e.g., *Newton* v. *Edgerley* [1959] 1 WLR 1031; cf. *Donaldson* v. *McNiven* [1952] 2 All ER 691.

66 *Carmarthenshire CC* v. *Lewis* [1955] AC 549.

67 Bill 43 of the 2013/14 Parliament; the drafting and purpose are somewhat problematic.

68 E.g., *R* v. *Cogan and Leak* [1976] QB 21.

69 On tort see Spencer, 'Civil Liability for Crimes'.

70 *Dyer* v. *Munday* [1895] 1 QB 742.

71 *Lloyd* v. *Grace, Smith & Co* [1912] AC 716.

72 See now *Various Claimants* v. *Catholic Child Welfare Society* [2012] UKSC 56; [2013] 2 AC 1, [47]; and *E* v. *English Province of Our Lady of Charity* [2013] QB 722.

73 J. Salmond, *Law of Torts* (London: Stevens and Haynes, 1907), 83–94.

of vicarious liability. More recently, in *Lister* v. *Hesley Hall* the House of Lords has extended the test for 'course of employment', holding, in a case concerning sexual assaults by a warden, that a more appropriate test is

> whether the warden's torts were so closely connected with his employment that it would be fair and just to hold the employers vicariously liable.[74]

As such, vicarious liability for criminal acts is, in modern tort law, much easier to establish than it once was, albeit that the new test is rather uncertain.

Tort law also has a number of primary obligations which can be breached by another's action. These are most commonly in negligence, though sometimes under statutory duties. Claims where C simply argues that D created a situation in which it was easy for X to commit the crime are liable to fail on grounds of causation,[75] but this is less likely where the criminal was known to the defendant.[76] These primary obligations are quite extensive, but the law is developing and of uncertain scope: vicarious liability is often the preferred route, though a primary liability will be pleaded in the alternative if available.

In criminal law there is no true vicarious liability at common law. There is liability for others in secondary liability, specific narrow offences, but otherwise only where specified in statute or where the defendant delegated the act to another or that other's act can otherwise be attributed to him.[77]

Another key point is that in tort, the damage caused is an essential part of the cause of action. Accordingly where two different tortfeasors cause separate and distinct damage to a claimant, he must look to each of them separately to be compensated for the distinct loss that each caused him. By contrast, where they cause or contribute to the same damage suffered by the claimant (e.g., a pedestrian injured in a road accident caused by two or more negligent drivers), they are 'jointly and severally' liable to the claimant for that damage, however great or small their respective roles. The claimant may sue one, some or all of them as he chooses (usually depending on who is easier to find and more likely to satisfy the judgment); each is liable to him for his whole loss. English law leaves the problem of quantifying and recovering just proportions of the loss to

74 *Lister* v. *Hesley Hall Ltd* [2002] 1 AC 215, [28] per Lord Steyn (with whose speech Lord Hutton agreed, [52]).

75 E.g., *Topp* v. *London Country Bus (South West) Ltd* [1993] 1 WLR 976.

76 Perhaps most famously, *Home Office* v. *Dorset Yacht* [1970] AC 1004; cf. *Smith* v. *Littlewoods* [1987] AC 241.

77 D. Ormerod, *Smith and Hogan's Criminal Law*, Ch. 10.2.

the multiple tortfeasors, not the claimant. Since 1935, statute has entitled any of multiple tortfeasors liable in tort[78] to bring a claim in contribution against the others.[79]

The wide scope for joint tortfeasorship in English law has reduced the need for separate complicity liability.[80] Tort law requires the accomplice to act according to a 'common design' which criminal law does not, though this limiting concept suffers from having no fixed definition. It has also had an effect on the required mental element, hiding what tort law requires rather than facing it, as criminal law has done.

The approach of criminal law to those who assist or encourage (traditionally known as aid, abet, counsel or procure) another to commit a crime is markedly different from tort law. On the one hand, criminal law treats all such parties as able to be tried and punished as principals. As such, there is no doctrinal advantage for the prosecution to specify into which class they are putting a given defendant, though in practice the prosecution will likely allege specific roles. In fact, substantive criminal law has much lower standards of conduct and fault for an accessory than for the principal. For example, as a principal to murder, D must kill, intending to kill or intending to cause serious bodily harm.[81] As a secondary party, he need only do an act which assists or encourages the principal in killing, which could be as little as offering a knife which the principal then does not use, do that act intentionally and intend to help the principal, foreseeing a risk that the principal would commit that crime, or one of a number of related crimes.[82]

On the other hand, both criminal and tort law incentivise actions against accessories.[83] For the criminal law, the benefit is clear: those the law describes as criminals are being convicted. All are convicted as principals: this is largely to avoid difficulties with proving who was the accessory and who the principal, but also it creates a larger number of people who can be publicly sanctioned for a result, something the system likes the

[78] Or, since Civil Liability (Contribution) Act 1978, under other civil causes of action.

[79] Now by Civil Liability (Contribution) Act 1978, s. 1(1); originally by Law Reform (Married Women and Joint Tortfeasors) Act 1935, s. 6(1)(c).

[80] See, generally, P. S. Davies, 'Complicity' in *Unravelling*; P. S. Davies, 'Accessory Liability for Assisting Torts (2011) 70 *CLJ* 353 and J. Dietrich 'Accessorial Liability in the Law of Torts' (2011) 2 *LS* 231. See most recently, *Sea Shepherd UK* v. *Fish & Fish* [2015] UKSC 10.

[81] *R* v. *Woollin* [1999] 1 AC 82.

[82] *R* v. *Webster* [2006] EWCA Crim 415.

[83] Including, for instance, by the principal's actions not usually breaking the chain of causation between the secondary party's acts and the harm caused: S. Steel, 'Causation in Tort Law and Criminal Law: Unity or Divergence?' in *Unravelling*, 257–8.

public to see (and something much less significant to tort law); thereby prosecutors and governments appear 'tough on crime'. For tort law, the greater benefits of joint and several liability are available to the claimants. However, there is a different consequence here. At a certain point, a claim in tort does not need to add further defendants, but the equivalent point for a criminal action is either non-existent or much further away. Once the total harm caused has been compensated, it is merely a question of the share of the damages each defendant in a tort claim pays. Rarely in criminal law is there a sense that having another accessory charged has a downside other than administrative or trial effort.

3. Consent

Consent can be analysed in a framework of six areas across both tort and crime, but in both fields of law problems are felt at different places.[84]

First, it is unclear exactly what role consent plays in the law. With some wrongs, the lack of consent turns a common everyday act into a crime and a tort, such as holding someone's arm to get their attention.[85] In criminal law, *the lack of consent* is one of the key justifications for intervening in otherwise private affairs; *consent* also grounds a number of rules removing criminal liability.[86] In tort law, consent to harm bars the claim in respect of that harm, and thus in practice can merge into remedial rules like contributory negligence, which reduces a claim according to the contribution the claimant's fault made.[87] Such a concern for the claimant's fault, rather than consent, does not appear in criminal doctrine, though it likely has a strong effect on prosecutorial discretion, particularly in low level offences, and on sentencing.

Second, there is no single answer as to whether *lack of consent* is something that the claimant or prosecution must show or whether *consent* is a defence. Many criminal offences, particularly those drafted more recently, such as sexual offences, specify that lack of consent is constitutive of the offence.[88] There are a few offences where consent, or belief about consent is expressly a defence.[89] More commonly, the law simply has not decided.

[84] On uncommunicated consent and whether consent is scalar or binary, see K. W. Simons, 'Consent and Assumption of Risk in Tort and Criminal Law' in *Unravelling*. For present purposes we have to leave aside questions of implied consent, and medical or other emergencies.

[85] See, e.g., *Collins* v. *Wilcock* [1984] 1 WLR 1172.

[86] Such as duress and a belief in consent under s. 2(1)(b).

[87] See Law Reform (Contributory Negligence) Act 1945, s. 1.

[88] See, e.g., Sexual Offences Act 2003, ss. 1–4.

[89] See, e.g., Criminal Damage Act 1971, s. 5(2).

A famous example of this is in assault and battery.[90] In some other areas, like property offences, the criminal law will ignore the consent that tort would think vital. Tort law generally locates consent as a defence: most torts do not technically allege that the wrong was done without consent, but there will generally be no wrong where the claimant consented. In modern pleadings a defendant who denies an allegation must give his reasons and/or his alternative description of events,[91] and so the existence of an issue about consent should be apparent from an early stage, even though the claimant does not have to plead its absence. It has, for instance, been expressly held so in battery.[92] Hence surgery undertaken with fully informed consent is not even a *prima facie* wrong; but the drunk who takes his drinking companion for a joy ride in his light aeroplane and crashes the same due to his negligent flying,[93] has *prima facie* committed the tort of negligence but is (or, in the leading case,[94] his widow was) entitled to defeat his surviving passenger's claim by raising the defence of *volenti*.

Third, the terminology differs. Criminal law talks about an alleged victim's consent, and often, the defendant's *mens rea* about that consent. Tort law is more varied but nothing turns on the difference: *consent* is normally used for intentional torts, *volenti non fit injuria* for negligence, and *leave* and/or *license* in torts to property; sometimes the distinct but related language of *voluntary assumption of risk* is used.[95]

Fourth, the context of consent can be important, though this question is seriously under-researched. For instance, the law concerning consent under the Offences Against the Persons Act (OAPA) 1861 and related common law offences is entirely judge-made while consent under the Sexual Offences Act (SOA) 2003 is dealt with by that statute, and comprises a general rule, rebuttable presumptions and irrebuttable presumptions.

[90] The majority of the House of Lords in *R* v. *Brown* [1994] 1 AC 212, see, e.g., 231 per Lord Templeman, 246–7 per Lord Jauncey said it was a defence; cf. the minority in *Brown*, e.g., 279 per Lord Slynn.

[91] CPR, r. 16.5(2).

[92] *Collins* v. *Wilcock* [1984] 1 WLR 1172, 1177 per Robert Goff LJ.

[93] There is a special statutory negation of this principle in respect of claims against drivers in respect of road accidents under Road Traffic Act 1988, s. 149; it leaves open the partial defence of contributory negligence and (should the facts be extreme enough to raise it) the defence of *ex turpi causa non oritur actio*.

[94] *Morris* v. *Murray* [1991] 2 QB 6.

[95] On which see K. W. Simons, 'Exploring the Relationship between Consent, Assumption of Risk, and Contributory Fault' in J. Oberdiek (ed.), *Philosophical Foundations of the Law of Torts* (Oxford University Press, 2014).

This can mean that the same acts are consensual for the SOA 2003, but not for the OAPA 1861.[96] Tort law does not expressly have such different tests for consent, but the forms and extent of consent accepted do vary. Sometimes this has been a technique to restrict other doctrines, like a wide law of vicarious liability. For instance, between 1837 and 1948 tort law favoured enterprises over employees through the doctrine of common employment: an employee was deemed to consent to the risk of another employee injuring him.[97] At other times the scope has been more beneficial to claimants, such as seeking to vindicate the right to consent to risks in medical treatment by giving full damages for a particular condition, even though the claimant would have had the operation even if she had known of the risk.[98] Similarly, the Road Traffic Act 1988, s. 149 renders void attempts to constrict or deny claims in negligence for road traffic accidents. Occasionally courts address overlapping regimes of consent. One recent case is *In Re M*,[99] in 2014, where the functional criteria for consent under the Mental Capacity Act 2005, s. 3(1) were contrasted with the regulation of the criminal law. The case concerned the appropriate treatment for a woman with amnesia, including whether she was capable of a sexual relationship with her partner, both having records of addiction and convictions. The 2005 Act specifies such criteria more formally than the criminal law:

> a person is unable to make a decision for himself if he is unable – (a) to understand the information relevant to the decision, (b) to retain that information, (c) to use or weigh that information as part of the process of making the decision, or (d) to communicate his decision (whether by talking, using sign language or any other means).

The Act (in s. 2(1)), the relevant codes of practice and court cases have stressed that functional consent is in regards to a specific act at a specific time, not a general ability to consent.[100] The criminal law had adopted a person- and situation-specific model in 2009[101] and this proved influential in civil law as well, usually in family law, with judges expressly suggesting

[96] See recently, P. Murphy, 'Flogging Live Complainants and Dead Horses: We May No Longer Need to be in Bondage to Brown' [2011] *Crim LR* 758.

[97] Though weakened by statute and case law since the 1880s: see generally P. Winfield, 'The Abolition of the Doctrine of Common Employment' [1949] *CLJ* 191.

[98] *Chester* v. *Afshar* [2004] UKHL 41, an exceptional case: J. Stapleton, 'Occam's Razor Reveals an Orthodox Basis for Chester v Afshar' (2006) 122 *LQR* 426.

[99] [2014] EWCA Civ 37. [100] Ibid., [23].

[101] For an important earlier case, see *R* v. *Cooper* [2009] 1 WLR 1786, esp. [27] per Baroness Hale.

conformity between the two areas was a virtue.[102] Nonetheless, *In re M* highlighted that criminal law is retrospective, determining criminal liability for past events, while civil law looks at capacity first, and consent second, and does so on a wider canvas, particularly one looking to wider future situations: it is therefore less likely to be person- and context-specific.[103] To that extent, some difference in application may exist even if the tests are the same.

Fifth, deciding the exact limits to factual consent can be difficult in both tort and crime. On the one hand, in actual consent cases much will come down to difficult issues of evidence, whether the consent is said to be express or inferred from conduct. Criminal law has had great difficulty in deciding to *what* you must consent: the 'nature and quality' of the act is often referred to as a test, but its application is difficult in practice.[104] One difficulty tort law particularly faces is the form the consent takes. Contracts adjusting tort liability (where the liability is bargained away for some other benefit) and notices which purport to exclude liability operate on the basis of consent, but the law has chosen to intervene in various places to protect the right to consent and, typically, those in a weaker bargaining position.[105]

Finally, even if factual consent exists, both tort and crime set a minimum standard for that consent to be legally effective: the consent must be free, informed and deliberate. The Court of Appeal, Criminal Division, has held that you can consent to the risk of contracting HIV through sexual intercourse (whereas you likely cannot to its deliberate infliction);[106] but if the defendant lies about his HIV status before having sexual intercourse, the complainant's consent to the intercourse does not carry with it any consent to the infliction of the disease (which is equivalent to serious bodily harm).[107] Tort law has a similar requirement that the consent be free, informed and deliberate but only in negligence, not in trespass.[108] Thus a mother is liable in principle in deceit if she obtains money towards the upkeep of a child by telling her co-habiting partner that he is the

[102] *In re M* [2014] EWCA Civ 37, [41]–[45]. [103] Ibid, [46]–[48], [75]–[82].

[104] *R* v. *Richardson* [1999] QB 444 on someone not technically a dentist but performing the services perfectly well; *R* v. *Tabassum* [2000] 2 Cr App R 328 on breast examinations by someone the victims assumed to have been medically trained.

[105] See, e.g., the Unfair Contract Terms Act 1977, Part I; Occupier's Liability Act 1957, ss. 2(1), 2(5), 3, 5.

[106] *Konzani* [2005] EWCA Crim 706. [107] *Dica* [2004] EWCA Crim 1103.

[108] See generally, E. Peel and J. Gourkamp (eds.), *Winfield and Jolowicz on Tort* 19th edn (London, Sweet & Maxwell, 2014) [26–008]–[26–024].

father when he is not.[109] However, English law is loathe to deal with medical cases under trespass, so the level of information supplied tends to get pushed into a calculation in negligence as to whether the defendant doctor took all reasonable care to warn of the risks.[110]

Even if qualitatively valid, the law might still decide that, for reasons of public policy, someone cannot consent to a particular harm. Criminal law famously does so, preventing someone from consenting to more than a mere battery unless they can show they are within one of a group of exceptions based on social customs and public policy, such as medical intervention, tattooing and contact sports. This is the famous decision of *Brown* where a group of sado-masochistic homosexuals were held unable, in law, to consent to the harms they caused one another as part of their sexual gratification. This strong paternalism has been challenged, and in practice, can be distinguished in places.[111] Tort law is more reluctant to resort to paternalism: there seems no reason why the mutual consent of the participating sado-masochists on the facts of *R* v. *Brown* would not have been effective in tort law to preclude any participant injured by conduct within the scope of what all the participants had contemplated might occur from successfully alleging battery against his injurer.[112]

4. Intention

Modern tort law has had its definition of intention strongly affected by the criminal law.[113] An important shift has taken place, whereby the object of the intention in tort and crime has diverged dramatically, leading to intentional tort liability being much easier to establish than intentional criminal liability. In tort, the general position is that D need only intend the act in the sense that he does it voluntarily, rather than intend a particular outcome. Battery, one of the so-called 'intentional torts' requires not that the claimant must show that D intended to cause harm, but only that D must have intended to do a hostile act which interfered with C's bodily integrity. Criminal law varies, depending on whether it is conduct that

[109] *P* v. *B (Paternity: Damages for Deceit)* [2001] 1 FLR 1041.

[110] See, e.g., *Sidaway* v. *Bethlehem Royal Hospital* [1985] AC 871.

[111] See generally, D. Ormerod, *Smith and Hogan's Criminal Law*, 13th edn (Oxford University Press, 2011), [17.2.1].

[112] If the criminal law does prohibit such conduct, the defence of illegality might also bar the claim, in addition to consent. See, e.g., Clerk & Lindsell, [3–90]; cf. *Murphy* v. *Culhane* [1977] QB 94.

[113] See, e.g., P. Winfield, *The Province of the Law of Tort* (Cambridge University Press, 1931), 25.

is prohibited or a result. The more serious result crimes, like murder, require that D intended to kill or cause serious bodily harm to V,[114] not just intended an act which happened to do so.[115]

5. Recklessness

Historically, English law had less space or need for the operation of a notion of recklessness, particularly in the criminal law. However, as the presumptions of the old criminal law passed away, a lower but still significant level of fault was developed: recklessness. Originally, it was unclear what this meant: wickedness, indifference or something else though 'impressionistic and unanalysed'.[116] At the end of the nineteenth century, in the landmark tort case of *Derry v. Peek*, the House of Lords held that to be liable in deceit D needed to make a false statement, knowing it was false or '*recklessly, without belief in its truth*'.[117] The claimant's argument that gross negligence sufficed for recklessness, or perhaps even failure to have a reasonable belief, was rejected.[118] The House of Lords did not expressly refer to foreseeing risks, but the implication is that if you do not care whether a statement is true, you foresee the risk that it might not be true. In the context of a tort where a specific intention is required, namely the intention to bring about a breach of contract, a similar approach has been adopted.[119]

The criminal law was slow to take up this suggestion. It was the House of Lords in *DPP* v. *Andrews* in 1937 which settled on the current use of the term recklessness in criminal law: foreseeing a risk and going on unreasonably to take that risk.[120] It did so without even mentioning

114 *R* v. *Cunningham* [1982] AC 566.

115 Exceptionally, some torts require a high level of intention as a means of restricting the scope of tortious liability, such as the tort of procuring or inducing another's breach of contract: *OBG Ltd* v. *Allan* [2008] 1 AC 1, esp. [39]–[43] per Lord Hoffmann and [191] –[192] per Lord Nicholls.

116 E. Griew, 'Consistency, Communication and Codification: Reflections on Two Mens Rea Words' in P. Glazebrook (ed.), *Reshaping the Criminal Law. Essays in Honour of Glanville Williams* (London, Stevens & Sons, 1978), 62. Cf. K. Smith, 'Criminal Law' in W. Cornish *et al.* (eds.), *Oxford History of the Laws of England* (Oxford University Press, 2010), 224–9; 219–24.

117 *Derry* v. *Peak* (1889) 14 App. Cas. 337, 350, 360.

118 Ibid.

119 *Emerald Constructions Co Ltd* v. *Lowthian* [1966] 1 WLR 691, 700–1 per Lord Denning MR, cited with approval in *OBG Ltd* v. *Allan* [2007] UKHL 21; [2008] 1 AC 1 per Lord Hoffmann, [40]–[41].

120 [1937] AC 576; see now *R* v. *G* [2004] 1 AC 1034, [41] per Lord Bingham, approving Law Commission Report No 177, Draft Criminal Code for England and Wales (1989), cl. 18 (c) and [41]; see also Appendix B, 18 (iii)–(v).

Derry v. *Peek* (splendid isolation in action).[121] The modern criminal law has added a second requirement for criminal recklessness, that the risk you have foreseen was unreasonable.[122] This second limb emerged from a comparison with the law of negligence developed by a leading twentieth-century English jurist, Glanville Williams. Having initially seen recklessness as a branch of the law of negligence, 'that kind of negligence where there is a foresight of consequences',[123] he later separated recklessness from negligence, while retaining the need for the risk to be objectively unjustified.[124]

6. Fraud

The concept of fraud, and the need for any legal system effectively to combat it, is one of significance for tort law as well as the criminal law. In English tort law, 'fraud' as a cause of action takes the form of the tort of deceit. A tort is committed whenever a person makes a false statement of existing fact to another, knowing it to be untrue or being reckless as to its truth or falsity, on which he intends the other to rely, and on which the other does rely, suffering loss as a result.[125] The mental element was determined by the leading case of *Derry* v. *Peek*, dealt with in Section 2.D.5 above. Whilst more difficult to prove than a negligent misstatement or misrepresentation,[126] if proven, all damages directly flowing

[121] Indeed few criminal cases have and then only in dishonest statement situations: *Williams Bros Direct Supply Stores Ltd* v. *Cloote* (1944) 60 TLR 270, *R* v. *Mackinnon* [1959] 1 QB 150, and *R* v. *Staines* (1974) 60 Cr App R 160 being perhaps the three most significant examples.

[122] See, e.g., Law Commission Report No 177, Draft Criminal Code for England and Wales (1989), cl. 18 (c) and [41]; see also Appendix B, 18 (iii)–(v); *R* v. *G* [2004] AC 1034, [41].

[123] See G. Williams, *Criminal Law: The General Part* (London: Stevens & Sons, 1953), 52. His approach to social utility in negligence preceded one of the classic expositions of it by Lord Denning: *Watt* v. *Hertfordshire County Council* [1954] 2 All ER 368, 371.

[124] G. Williams, *Textbook of Criminal Law* (London: Stevens & Sons, 1978), 73. See also the second edition, (London: Stevens & Sons, 1983), 97–9 and G. Williams, 'The Unresolved Problem of Recklessness' (1988) 8 *LS* 74, 76–7. Between 1982 and 2004 there was also a further version of recklessness, inadvertent or objective recklessness, for certain offences like criminal damage and road traffic offences: see *R* v. *Caldwell* [1982] AC 341 and *R* v. *G* [2004] 1 AC 1034.

[125] See, e.g., Peel and Goudkamp (eds.), *Winfield and Jolowicz on Tort*, [12.002]–[12.022]; *Bradford Third Equitable Benefit Building Society* v. *Borders* [1941] 2 All ER 205, 211.

[126] Whilst the civil standard of proof 'on the balance of probabilities' remains applicable, the leading modern reconciliation of these two apparently inconsistent doctrines was given by the House of Lords in *Re H (Minors)* [1996] AC 563.

from it are recoverable not, as in negligence, only those that were reasonably foreseeable.[127]

In criminal law, the concept of fraud has proved considerably more complex. The key term is the mental element of *dishonesty*. This is vital, as in most offences using it the other elements of the offences are very easily satisfied, and dishonesty does all the work of criminalisation.[128] Dishonesty is not statutorily defined, though the Theft Act 1968 does contain a short list of instances where dishonesty is conclusively *not* to be found: the defendant believed he had a right to the property, he would have the consent of the owner or the owner cannot be discovered by reasonable steps.[129] By contrast, a willingness to pay does not make someone honest.[130] To fill this gap, the courts developed a composite test: if the jury need guidance, they should be told to decide what a reasonable person would say was honest and then decide whether the defendant realised that.[131] In the heartland of fraud *per se*, English law recently brought into force simpler and much wider offences in the Fraud Act 2006. The Act essentially criminalises lying.[132]

7. Negligence and reasonableness

'Negligence' is the paradigmatic tort, accounting for the vast majority of claims brought in tort, including those arising out of accidents on the roads and at work.[133] The key component of the tort of negligence is the fault standard of being negligent: failing to take reasonable care (to see that a specified class of persons is not harmed in a specified list of ways). It is an objective test, asking what the reasonable person in the circumstances would do, and is classically expressed in the form:

> Negligence is the omission to do something which a reasonable man, guided upon those considerations which ordinarily regulate the conduct of human affairs, would do, or doing something which a prudent and reasonable man would not do.[134]

By contrast, criminal offences rarely turn on negligence but when one does, the jury is instructed in civil law concepts to the extent necessary.

[127] For a striking modern example, see *Smith New Court Securities* v. *Citibank NA* [1997] AC 254.

[128] See, generally, D. Ormerod, *Smith and Hogan's Criminal Law*, [19–28].

[129] Theft Act 1968, s. 2(1)(a)–(c).

[130] Ibid., s. 2(2).

[131] *R* v. *Ghosh* [1982] QB 1053.

[132] D. Ormerod, 'The Fraud Act 2006 – Criminalising Lying' [2007] *Crim LR* 193.

[133] The latter may well be combined with a claim for a breach of a statutory duty imposed on the employer by health and safety legislation.

[134] *Blyth* v. *Birmingham Waterworks Co.* (1856) 11 Ex 781, 784 per Alderson B.

Negligence is thought to be too low a level of fault for traditional *mens rea*.[135] Thus, only exceptionally do serious crimes have it as the key fault element. For example, there is a homicide offence for failing to look after a vulnerable person, where negligent omissions suffice for liability, but this was designed to cover difficult situations where one of a pair kills and the other should have stopped them.[136] Otherwise it is generally in less serious offences, like driving without due care and attention.[137] One important homicide offence, gross negligence manslaughter, uses civil law notions of duty of care and breach, but then asks the jury

> to consider whether the extent to which the defendant's conduct departed from the proper standard of care incumbent upon him, involving as it must have done a risk of death to the patient, was such that it should be judged criminal.[138]

When it comes to reasonableness more generally, criminal law typically asks the jury to make a decision about what they think is reasonable. It is a key part of many areas of the criminal law, particularly in defences. They tend not to be given detailed formulae for deciding it, such as calculating the likelihood of risk and the severity of harm against the cost of taking precautions. There have been instances of civil and criminal courts disagreeing on what is reasonable for a given set of facts: in one famous example it was a civil case in the House of Lords (then the ultimate court for civil and criminal matters) which effectively decided the matter.[139]

8. Causation

In causation, tort law and criminal law face a very similar problem, and tend to reach similar outcomes, but they go about it in slightly different ways.[140] Both start with 'but for' causation, and both accept that reasonable foreseeability is relevant to determining the extent of responsibility for consequences. Hart and Honoré's verdict in 1985 that 'the general course of decision in the two spheres is strikingly similar' is still true.[141]

[135] See generally, D. Ormerod, *Smith and Hogan's Criminal Law*, Ch. 6.

[136] Domestic Violence, Crime and Victims Act 2005, s. 5.

[137] Road Traffic Act 1988, s. 3.

[138] *R* v. *Adomako* [1995] 1 AC 171, 187 per Lord Mackay LC.

[139] *Thorne* v. *Motor Trade Association* [1937] AC 797; Dyson, 'Disentangling and Organising Tort and Crime', 17–18.

[140] For a detailed analysis, see Steel, 'Causation in Tort Law and Criminal Law'.

[141] H. L. A. Hart and T. Honoré, *Causation in the Law* (Oxford: Clarendon, 1985), 325. See also their remark that the looking in situations 'where difference of policy between civil and criminal law might be expected to make themselves felt, yields a meagre harvest', 362.

However, there are key differences in approach and in the work that causation is made to do.

Most of tort, and large parts of crime, turn on results: the gist of negligence is damage done,[142] and many serious criminal offences are categorised as result crimes, such as criminal damage,[143] where liability turns on bringing about a proscribed outcome. Even those offences which are called conduct crimes, which prohibit the doing of certain acts, often involve immediately apparent harm which just happens not to be the way the offence is phrased, such as rape, where the conduct is penetration (with certain other features, like the lack of consent).[144] Of course the criminal law also prohibits acts where there is no immediate harm. There are general forms of such inchoate offences, like attempt,[145] conspiracy[146] and encouraging or assisting another to commit an offence;[147] there are also specific statutory forms, such as going equipped to steal.[148] In these no causation need be shown. There is also a class of torts where no damage (and thus, no causation) is required to found liability, namely torts actionable *per se*. The classic examples are forms of trespass, whether to the person (assault, battery or false imprisonment) or to land. Claims in such torts are rare and, even when made, are only usually made when harm has been caused, for otherwise only nominal damages are awarded. There is no general inchoate liability in tort law.

In both tort and crime, causation appears to have two sets of questions: first, whether harm was factually caused by the defendant's act; second, whether that harm was within an acceptable scope of liability. However, each resorts to different mechanisms, certainly different language, to do so. Both use an initial test of 'but for' causation, though this may need to be supplemented by further doctrines, for instance for overdetermined causes, where the harm would have happened anyway because of a different cause. The second step is to ask how far such factual causation goes, since it is obviously over-inclusive. After the 'but for' test, tort law asks first about any possible breaks in the 'chain' of causation, such as by a free, informed and deliberate act of the victim or a third party. It then asks whether the harm was too remote from the wrong done, typically asking whether the ultimate harm was reasonably foreseeable. To some extent

142 J. Stapleton, 'The Gist of Negligence, Part 1: Minimum Actionable Damage' (1988) 104 *LQR* 213 and J. Stapleton, 'The Relationship Between 'Damage' and Causation (The Gist of Negligence, Part 2)' (1988) 104 *LQR* 389.

143 Criminal Damage Act 1971, s. 1(1).

144 Sexual Offences Act 2003, s. 1.

145 Criminal Attempts Act 1981.

146 Criminal Law Act 1977.

147 Serious Crime Act 2007, Part II.

148 Theft Act 1968, s. 25.

these are known as 'legal causation' questions. Criminal law eschews such language and instead looks for whether the defendant's wrong was a *substantial* and *operating* cause of the ultimate harm. This frames the investigation differently, and has the effect that omissions tend not to stop the initial event from being 'operative'. Thus in *R* v. *Smith*[149] even 'thoroughly bad' medical treatment did not exclude the defendant's causative role in stabbing the victim as a cause of the victim's death. Here it should be borne in mind that criminal law typically requires intention or recklessness for its serious offences, a higher level of fault, and that may make the role of causation less significant. It is certainly part of the justification for inchoate liability, where, for instance, attempts and conspiracies require that the defendant intended that the substantive crime take place.

This basic pattern of causation is also not the complete story. Both domains have bent their rules of causation, in particular to no longer require 'but for' causation. Some of these problems are inherent in the gaps between different philosophical conceptions of causation and the layperson's everyday ideas of cause and effect. The most significant has been liability for a form of cancer called mesothelioma, where there were multiple possible asbestos causes and there is no way to know which actually caused the harm. Such liability is known by the name of the leading case, *Fairchild.*[150] A statute extended the common law to make this liability joint and several, no matter how small any given defendant's contribution.[151] *Fairchild* itself might seem a valid outcome, but its evolution to *Sienkiewicz*, where epidemiological evidence suggested that only 18 per cent of the risk of contracting mesothelioma came from tortious causes, but the *Fairchild* rule made the defendant liable for 100 per cent of the damages, might seem too far. Compensating an innocent victim, especially one who has had two or more wrongdoers cloud the causal analysis, may no longer be what is happening there. Similarly in criminal law, causation difficulties can be the product of underlying policy rationales, such as statutory offences of causing death while uninsured: the Supreme Court recently prevented this from being an incredibly excessive form of liability, but even then did so by inserting fault into causation rather than inserting standard causation principles.[152] Other difficult examples involve causing other people to act, such as an offender shooting at police

149 [1959] 2 QB 35.

150 *Fairchild* v. *Glenhaven Funeral Services Ltd* [2003] 1 AC 32.

151 Compensation Act 2006, s. 3.

152 *R* v. *Hughes* [2013] UKSC 56, [16], [27], [32], purporting to apply common law reasoning; see too *R v. Robinson-Pierre* [2013] EWCA Crim 2396, [42].

who then shoot back and kill his pregnant sixteen-year-old girlfriend he was using as a human shield,[153] or the shootout where the one shooter kills a bystander but the other is charged with her murder.[154]

That said, English law has not generally turned to one way around difficulties in causation to which some other systems have turned, namely to consider the causation of risk, rather than harm. In tort law, attempts to do this have been phrased in terms of *loss of a chance*: that is, the causal event is reconfigured from actual damage, to the loss of a chance of avoiding that damage. Such claims are typically rejected in tort, particularly in the largest category, personal injury,[155] though one can claim for pure economic losses in some circumstances.[156] Similarly in criminal law, there is no general class of 'endangerment' offences, where increasing a risk is itself criminal. However, a number of criminal offences feature increasing a risk as a component element, such as administering poison thereby endangering life,[157] and in most offences the attendant risks on conduct would go to the seriousness of the offence for the purpose of sentencing.[158]

Occasionally there are ripples in one domain which are picked up in another, but this is typically where an extreme case in one area is used to support a departure in the other. For instance, in *Stansbie* v. *Troman* a decorator has been held liable in negligence for property stolen by a thief when the decorator went to nearby shops but failed to secure the house, despite agreeing to do so.[159] Fifty years later, this was picked up in the criminal law case of *Empress Car*,[160] as evidence of the need to understand the purpose of a prohibition in order to understand how causation operated within it. There the question was whether a third party's opening of a tap led oil to pollute a nearby river. The tap was not locked and the defendants had bypassed other containment mechanisms for operational ease. The defendants were found to have caused polluting material to enter a river, contrary to the Water Resources Act 1991, s. 85(1). There might be some value in taking a purposive approach to environmental

153 *R* v. *Pagett* (1983) 76 Cr App R 279.

154 *R* v. *Gnango* [2012] 1 AC 827. 155 *Gregg* v. *Scott* [2005] 2 AC 176.

156 *Allied Maples Group Ltd* v. *Simmons & Simmons* [1995] 1 WLR 1602.

157 Offences Against the Person Act 1861, s. 23.

158 For other examples of 'endangering' offences see Aviation Security Act 1982, s. 2 (endangering the safety of an aircraft in flight).

159 *Stansbie* v. *Troman* [1948] 2 KB 48.

160 *Environment Agency (formerly National Rivers Authority) v. Empress Car Company (Abertillery) Ltd.* [1999] 2 AC 22, esp. 29–32 (Lord Hoffmann).

legislation. However this line, restricting intervening causes, was later used by the Court of Appeal to convict the person who hands over a syringe of heroine, even though the victim freely self-injected. The House of Lords overturned the conviction, and restricted *Empress Car* to environmental situations and impliedly rejected the scope of *Stansbie* v. *Troman* style reasoning.[161]

9. Property

The criminal law adopts a surprisingly different view of property than civil law, despite purporting to exist to protect those civil law rights. The classic case is *R* v. *Hinks*.[162] The defendant had acquired property from an infirm patron she claimed to have been looking after. The litigation was shaped by the inability of the prosecution to prove that the 'gifts' had been obtained by deception, undue influence or in circumstances where the donor did not have capacity to make them. The defendant was charged with theft and the case went to the House of Lords on whether the defendant appropriated property when taking up a valid gift. The relevant legislation, the Theft Act 1968, clearly referred to civil law norms, particularly the 'owner' of property,[163] proprietary interests at common law and in equity,[164] and the belief in a civil right to property being conclusive evidence of a lack of dishonesty.[165] It might therefore be assumed that no partition could be drawn between the civil and the criminal law. The House of Lords disagreed, the leading speech being given by Lord Steyn:

> The purposes of the civil law and the criminal law are somewhat different. In theory the two systems should be in perfect harmony. In a practical world there will sometimes be some disharmony . . . it would be wrong to assume on a priori grounds that the criminal law rather than the civil law is defective . . . While in some contexts of the law of theft a judge cannot avoid explaining civil law concepts to a jury (e.g. in respect of section 2(1)(a)), the decisions of the House of Lords eliminate the need for such explanations in respect of appropriation. That is a great advantage in an overly complex corner of the law.[166]

161 *R* v. *Kennedy (No 2)* [2007] UKHL 38, [15], [16].

162 *R* v. *Hinks* [2001] 2 AC 241 (hereafter, *Hinks*). The case is about criminal protection of civil law interests broadly, not only those recognised by tort law but also by the law of property. See also, S. Green, 'Theft and Conversion – Tangibly Different?' (2012) 128 *LQR* 564.

163 Theft Act 1968, s. 3(1).

164 Ibid., s. 5(1)–(5).

165 Ibid., s. 2(1)(a).

166 *Hinks*, 252–3.

Lord Steyn posits a normative 'harmony' between the civil and criminal law, but that 'in a practical world' they might be in disharmony, which in that particular context, means that they might have substantively different rules. Lord Steyn grasps for some benefit, citing the potential complexity of the law, such that the jury might be confused by what was 'mine' and 'yours' in practice. The irony is that this was the very distinction that the Criminal Law Revision Committee had been relying on when it drafted the Bill.[167] The difficulty behind this partition is made even more obvious by Lord Hobhouse, in dissent:

> The truth is that theft is a crime which relates to civil property and, inevitably, property concepts from the civil law have to be used and questions answered by reference to that law.[168]

Lord Hobhouse continued, giving examples of famous instances where appellate courts had had to sort out earlier failures to apply civil law concepts properly.[169]

10. Defences

The relationship between criminal and tortious defences has not yet been the subject of careful analysis.[170] Criminal law has much more extensive jurisprudence and theoretical work about its defences. It divides them into excuses and justifications.[171] Excuses seem to be less morally potent defences, whereby the conduct is on some level unlawful but the defendant will not be punished. Justifications mean the conduct is *justified* and so lawful. Criminal law has certain justifications, though there is much

167 'The important element of them all is undoubtedly the dishonest appropriation of another person's property – the treating of "tuum" as "meum"; and we think it not only logical, but right in principle, to make this the central element of the offence'. Criminal Law Revision Committee, Eighth Report, *Theft and Related Offences* (1967) (Cmnd 2977), [33].

168 *Hinks*, 263–4.

169 One, *R* v. *Preddy* [1996] UKHL 13; [1996] AC 815, being particularly famous and leading not only to a number of quashed convictions, but also to a rapid legislative response in the form of the Theft (Amendment) Act 1996. Torts which protect property rights include trespass to land and goods, conversion and reversionary injury, nuisance, passing off and protection of IP rights (albeit now largely statutory torts – e.g. infringement of copyright), and (depending on one's definitions – e.g. are contractual rights or confidential information property?) some of the economic torts (in particular, *Lumley* v. *Gye*) and breach of confidence.

170 See, generally, J. Goudkamp, 'Defences in Tort and Crime' in *Unravelling*.

171 See, e.g., J. C. Smith, *Justification and Excuse in the Criminal Law* (London: Stevens & Sons, 1989).

disagreement about their scope. Examples probably include self-defence and necessity (so far only recognised in a medical context). A further example, use of force to effect an arrest or prevent crime, is set out in a criminal statute but seems to apply to remove all liability in both tort and crime.[172] Tort law also appears to recognise justifications, but has not hitherto talked of them as such. Consider, for example,[173] abatement (stopping a nuisance), defence of one's property, recapture of land and chattels, public necessity (such as tearing down another building to prevent fire[174] or throwing property from a ship to prevent it sinking[175]) and self-defence. On the other hand, it is doubtful that tort law recognises excuses, like loss of self-control and duress in criminal law.[176] There are other instances where the same terminology is used in each field, such as 'partial defence' in criminal law stepping you out of one offence and into a less serious one (e.g., murder down to manslaughter by reason of loss of self-control[177]) whereas in tort law there is no ladder of wrongs to step up or down on; there partial defences reduce liability, though these might better be thought of as remedial rules.[178] Finally, it should be noted that in criminal law there are defences, like insanity, which a court may raise of its own motion; in tort law this is not the case, but in many instances it is an insurance company who holds similar sway, selecting and paying for counsel as well as having a significant role in the conduct of the litigation.

In sum, criminal law defences are more extensively theorised and analysed than tortious ones and only rarely is there significant exchange between the two fields. One rare example is recent: in 2008, the House of Lords had to decide whether the test for self-defence in tort was the same as it was in criminal law. In *Ashley* v. *Chief Constable of Sussex Police*, a police officer had shot an unarmed man during a night raid, having been briefed that a suspect might be armed. The chief constable was sued as vicariously liable for the police officer, and admitted liability in negligence for the organisation of the raid. The trespass claim proceeded in order to establish precisely what happened. The criminal test for self-defence was

[172] Criminal Law Act 1967, s. 3.

[173] See further J. Goudkamp, *Tort Law Defences* (Oxford: Hart, 2013), Ch. 5, who divides all tort defences into justifications and public policy defences.

[174] *Saltpetre Case* (1606) 12 Co Rep 12, 13; 77 ER 1294, 1295.

[175] *Mouse's Case* (1608) 12 Co Rep 63; 77 ER 1341. Cf. *Vincent* v. *Lake Erie Transportation Co* 109 Minn 456; 124 NW 221 (1910) in the USA.

[176] See Goudkamp, 'Defences in Tort and Crime', Section 3.

[177] Coroners and Justice Act 2009, ss. 54–56.

[178] See Goudkamp, 'Defences in Tort and Crime', Section 5.

an honest belief that it was necessary for the actor physically to defend himself, and the use of force limited to what was objectively proportionate to that belief. The House of Lords, settling the question for the first time, held that tort law required the belief to be reasonable as well as honest, together with force used being proportionate. One of the key underlying questions was the 'sameness' or 'consistency'[179] of the law across tort and crime.[180]

E. *Procedure*

The heading of procedure is broken down into four sub-headings: jurisidiction, process, evidence and resolutions.

1. Jurisdiction

The jurisdiction to adjudicate on a question used to vex the courts for two particular reasons: it used not to be clear on many statutory prohibitions whether they were civil or criminal, and there were much more restricted rights to appeal in criminal cases until 1907 (and to this day, a separate track). For these reasons it has been set out for nearly 150 years that no appeal should lie to the Court of Appeal 'in any criminal cause or matter'.[181] A series of cases followed attempting to define what was included. In particular, the matter had to be 'penal', and merely having a penalty was not 'penal'. Many rules have been enforced by *penalties*, the question is whether the object is *punitive*: if the payment of a fine[182] or of imprisonment[183] is possible then the matter is criminal. Thus, an arrest to return a conscript to the Netherlands was a criminal matter because prosecution could follow if deported and therefore a civil court could not hear a writ of *habeas corpus*.[184] This problem has largely disappeared through the slow accumulation of case law on what is criminal and what is civil,

179 *Ashley* v. *Chief Constable of Sussex Police (Sherwood intervening)* [2008] UKHL 25; [2008] 1 AC 962, [17]–[18] cf. [76].

180 Cf. 'coherence': *Gray* v. *Thames Trains* [2009] 1 AC 1339, [29]–[55] and [75]–[87], esp. [82].

181 Judicature Act 1873, s. 47, and it successor, the Judicature Act 1925, s. 31(1)(a). See now Senior Courts Act 1981, s.18(1)(a), recently discussed in *R (Guardian News & Media)* v. *City of Westminster Magistrates Court* [2011] 1 WLR 3253.

182 Courts have acknowledged there are also crimes too trivial to be tried by a jury or visited with imprisonment: *Mellor* v. *Denham* (1880) 5 QBD 467 on breaching by-laws relating to ensuring your children attend school.

183 *Seaman* v. *Burley* [1896] 2 QB 244.

184 *Amand* v. *Home Secretary* [1943] AC 147.

combined with clearer legislative drafting.[185] Some jurisdictional issues remain relevant, such as private international law rules giving preference to the place where a civil action overlaps with a criminal matter.[186]

Sometimes a person will seek to transgress this division for personal advantage. It is difficult to use criminal law for this purpose since a private party has no control over the conduct of prosecutions. By contrast, on occasions, individuals have attempted to use private law remedies to enforce compliance with the criminal law. Where those individuals are not directly caused loss over and above any inconvenience suffered by the public at large,[187] only the Attorney-General, who has a sort of *parens patriae* role in the English legal system, may bring, or authorise the bringing,[188] of such claims.[189]

A more subtle but even rarer attempt is to go to a civil court to seek a declaration (an order that is not available to a criminal court) to set out what the law is on a particular matter, most commonly that proposed conduct would not be criminal. The legal effect of any such declaration is unclear.[190] A related form, and slightly more common recently, is attempting to obtain a declaration that a prosecution would not take place.[191]

The criminal courts also have a jurisdiction which seems to have all of the punitive elements of the criminal law without any of the safeguards: confiscation orders.[192] These controversial powers are relatively

[185] Many were removed by the Common Informers Act 1949 which removed the person most likely to claim for such penalties; e.g., *Brown* v. *Allweather Mechanical Grouting* [1954] 2 QB 443, 448 concerning vehicle excise duty, Vehicles (Excise) Act 1949, s. 13(2). Cf. In 1902 a leading criminal lawyer could do nothing but say that crimes were pardonable by the Crown if it was remissable at all: C. Kenny, *Outlines of Criminal law* (Cambridge University Press, 1902), 1, but that power is now largely obsolete.

[186] Brussels Convention on Jurisdiction and the Enforcement of Judgments, Art. 5(4).

[187] For an example of a case where the claimants' interests were so affected, and they obtained a civil injunction the effect of which was to restrain the defendant from damaging that interest by acting in breach of the criminal law, see *Island Records Ltd* v. *Corkindale* [1978] Ch 122.

[188] Such claims brought with the authority of the Attorney-General are known as 'relator actions'. See generally, Law Commission, Consents to Prosecution, LC 255, 1998.

[189] *Gouriet* v. *Union of Post Office Workers* [1978] AC 435. For discussion of the issues raised, see D. Feldman, 'Injunctions and the Criminal Law' (1979) 42 *MLR* 369.

[190] See, e.g., D. Feldman, 'Declarations and the Control of Prosecution' [1981] *Crim LR* 25; *Financial Services Authority* v. *Rourke* [2002] CP Rep 14, Neuberger, J. Cf. *Imperial Tobacco* v. *Attorney General* [1981] AC 718; *R (Rushbridger)* v. *Attorney General* [2004] 1 AC 357.

[191] See, most recently, on charging guidance in respect of assisting suicide: *R (Nicklinson)* v. *Ministry of Justice* [2014] UKSC 38.

[192] See generally, M. S. Williams, M. Hopmeier and R. Jones (eds.), *The Proceeds of Crime*, 4th edn (Oxford University Press, 2013).

new,[193] created by statute after an attempt to forfeit drug-related property without a specific provision failed.[194] Under the Proceeds of Crime Act (POCA) 2002, Part 2,[195] benefits from offending can be stripped and paid to the state, subject to the defendant still having sufficient assets to do so. A person benefits from an offence if they 'obtain property as a result of or in connection with' that offence according to s. 76(4). This definition is itself very broad, going beyond simple net benefit (benefit less expenses)[196] and, for example, if multiple defendants obtain property together, they are each deemed to have obtained it.[197] A number of presumptions operate to make these powers even broader. For instance, with a number of serious offences, 'a criminal lifestyle' enables the court to assume that everything which has passed through his hands in the six years preceding the institution of proceedings, together with everything he currently owns was derived from criminal activity unless he can prove the contrary or show that 'there would be a serious risk of injustice' if that assumption were made.[198] There are extensive supporting powers, such as restraining the defendant from using assets and requiring him to disclose the full extent and location of all his realisable property.[199]

However, the POCA powers are not systematically used and appear to be largely ineffective in securing money officially confiscated: in 2012 only 2 per cent of outstanding confiscation order debt had been paid off in full after courts imposed a default sentence.[200] There is also a civil Assets Recovery Agency,[201] who can bring civil actions, on the civil standard of proof (s. 6(7)), against a large number of those convicted of property crimes.

These powers obviously affect the defendant's condition within both civil and criminal law. On the one hand, confiscation will reduce the defendant's means to pay compensation: if a compensation order is made, it should be satisfied out of the confiscation order if otherwise it would

[193] Drug Trafficking Offences Act 1986, expanded by the Criminal Justice Act 1988 to any indictable offence and some summary offences.

[194] See *R* v. *Cuthbertson* [1981] AC 470.

[195] Related powers also exist under the Misuse of Drugs Act 1971 or the Terrorism Act 2000.

[196] P. Alldridge 'The Limits of Confiscation' [2011] *Crim LR* 827, 835–42.

[197] *R* v. *Jennings* [2008] UKHL 29; though recovery will not be enforced to the extent that a sum has been recovered from another in respect of the same benefit: *R* v. *Ahmad and Ahmad* [2014] UKSC 36.

[198] POCA, s. 10. [199] Williams *et al. The Proceeds of Crime*, Chs. 2–4.

[200] National Audit Office, 16 December 2013, HC 738.

[201] POCA, parts 1 and 5. Cf. the greater success of the parallel powers in Ireland: Liz Campbell, *Organised Crime and the Law* (Oxford: Hart, 2013), Ch. 7.

not be satisfied,[202] but if no such order is awarded, or no sufficient one, the victim is left to a likely even less effective civil remedy.[203] On the other hand, where confiscation does not follow a conviction, there is no need for any offence ever to have been proven while at the same time the profits of crime are apparently being stripped from him.[204] There are clear fair labelling concerns and burden of proof concerns. While criminal in nature, confiscation proceedings have the civil standard of proof, more permissive rules of evidence (apparently those of a sentencing hearing) and are technically not penal,[205] so defendants do not benefit from the protection of arts 6.2 and 6.3 of the ECHR,[206] even when the 'lifestyle' rules are engaged. However, the ECHR has recently led to a 'sticking plaster' being applied over the 'serious mess'[207] of quantifying the benefit to be removed by the Supreme Court in *Waya.* Essentially Article 1 of the first Protocol of the ECHR was found to require some proportionality between the order and the purpose of the act, which were to strip benefits, not to deter others. It has been described as a seismic shift,[208] generally leading to lower awards but with somewhat uncertain principles.[209]

In its approach to compensating victims of crime, English law demonstrates that it does not necessarily think of itself as being a unified and coherent whole. The award of financial compensation for injuries wrongfully inflicted is a classic domain of tort law, and English law has historically been reluctant to involve criminal courts in awarding compensation.[210] It was not until 1972 that the first general power to order compensation was created. This came in a period of great reform in the criminal law, which began in the 1960s.[211] The power is now found in the Powers of Criminal Courts (Sentencing) Act 2000 (PCC(S)A 2000),

202 POCA, s. 13(5)–(6).

203 See, e.g., *R (Faithfull)* v. *Crown Court at Ipswich* [2008] 1 WLR 1636.

204 A growing trend: Colin King, 'Civil Forfeiture and Article 6 of the ECHR: Due Process Implications for England & Wales and Ireland' (2014) 34 *LS* 371, 372–6 and see *Serious Organised Crime Agency* v. *Gale* [2011] UKSC 49.

205 In the sense that they do not affect the defendant's sentence: POCA, s. 13(4).

206 *HM Advocate* v. *McIntosh (No.1)* [2001] UKPC D 1; [2001] 3 WLR 107, [14]–[28].

207 P. Alldridge, 'Proceeds of Crime Law since 2003 - Two Key Areas' [2014] *Crim LR* 171, 187.

208 *R* v. *Harvey* [2013] EWCA Crim 1104, [38].

209 See, generally, P. Alldridge, 'Proceeds of Crime Law since 2003 – Two Key Areas'.

210 See, generally, M. Dyson, 'Connecting Tort and Crime: Comparative Legal History in England and Spain since 1850' [2009] *Cambridge Yearbook of European Legal Studies* 247, 248–63.

211 E.g., K. Younger, Advisory Council on the Penal System Report on Reparation by the Offender (1970).

ss. 130–134. Under s. 130, criminal courts are able to award a compensation order for 'any personal injury, loss or damage resulting from that offence or any other offence which is taken into consideration by the court in determining sentence'. There are some very important limits for claims related to road traffic events and for crimes which have caused death.[212] There is also a limit on the amount payable, per offence, in the Magistrates' Court, of £5,000, but more may be awarded in the Crown Court. Section 130(12) prioritises paying the compensation order over any fine which is awarded, if both cannot be satisfied. Someone who has received a compensation order can still bring a claim in tort later, and be awarded damages in full, but they will not *recover* any sum already paid under the order.[213]

There are four key ways in which compensation orders differ from tort claims. First, the victim no longer has to be directly involved in the claim: the order is available 'on application or otherwise',[214] as victims had too often missed the opportunity.[215] By trial and error it was realised that the best way for criminal courts to ensure compensation is to inform victims and gather evidence from them[216] and require a judge to give reasons if s/he does not give a compensation order where s/he could.[217]

Second, criminal compensation has recognised different heads of claim from those available in tort. In particular, criminal compensation might be available where no tortious liability exists. This was made clear by the case of *Chappell* in 1985:

> It does not however follow that the criminal remedy is the mirror of an underlying civil remedy. Indeed it plainly is not so, for the Court has a discretion . . . and will take into account factors such as the offender's means and the moral desirability or otherwise of making him pay.[218]

212 *At common law* there is no claim for the death of another human being: see now the Fatal Accidents Act 1976.

213 See s. 134.

214 The application would mean by the prosecuting authority on the victim's behalf, which in practice depends on the victim indicating to the prosecutor that s/he wishes such an application to be made, and providing sufficient information early, as well as the evidence to enable it to be done.

215 Dyson, 'Connecting Tort and Crime', 259–60.

216 See especially PCC(S)A 2000, s. 130(4).

217 See ibid., s. 130(3). Political games led to a new subsection 2A in December 2012: 'A court must consider making a compensation order in any case where this section empowers it to do so', see Legal Aid, Sentencing and Punishment of Offenders Act 2012, s. 63(1). How you could give reasons for not awarding compensation without considering compensation went unexplained.

218 *R* v. *Chappell* (1985) 80 CrAppR 31, 34–5, adding that a lack of 'culpability' would be a reason not to make an order. The case concerned fraudulent VAT payments.

Third, some component parts of the law are different, such as causation. A classic example is a conviction under the Trade Descriptions Act 1968, as in *R* v. *Thomson Holidays*.[219] There the Court of Appeal (Criminal Division)[220] held that civil rules of causation were not to be imported into the criminal law.[221]

Fourth, compensation orders are in many ways narrower than tort claims. On the one hand, the 'valuation' of a victim's injuries will in principle be the same in a civil and a criminal court; indeed, the judge in either court is likely to make reference to the same guidelines, published by the Judicial College, to assist in arriving at an appropriate amount. Yet the means of the defendant will be taken into account in the criminal law,[222] and financial losses are excluded as being too complex.[223] Of course, in tort the defendant's means are largely irrelevant[224] and many financial losses recoverable. Importantly, case law has also developed rules on when compensation should not be given, in particular, where the case before the criminal court is not 'clear' and would require time, effort and expertise to solve uncertain facts or law. In such cases the compensation order is refused and the claimant has to go before a civil court later.[225]

Enforcement differs too. If a civil defendant or his insurer cannot pay he can be bankrupted but not imprisoned or otherwise punished. By contrast, a criminal court must not make any financial order (including any compensation order) against a defendant which he cannot reasonably afford to pay either immediately or by instalments over a reasonable and finite period.[226] This is because they are backed by sanctions of a criminal nature. In practice, few defendants have money so few large compensation orders are made. English compensation orders, in whichever level of court made, are enforced in the magistrates court by basically criminal procedures, to that extent making life much easier for the victim.[227] One

[219] *R* v. *Thomson Holidays* [1974] QB 592.

[220] The successor to the Court of Criminal Appeal.

[221] Ibid., 599. [222] Section 130(11), PCC(S)A 2000.

[223] K. Younger, Advisory Council on the Penal System Report on Reparation by the Offender (1970), [59].

[224] E.g., *Rookes* v. *Barnard* [1964] AC 1129, 1129.

[225] E.g., *R* v. *Crown Court at Liverpool and another, ex parte Cooke* [1996] 4 All ER 589, 595.

[226] Two years or so is the *de facto* maximum; generally orders are not made to run for more than twelve to eighteen months. See J. Richardson (ed.), *Archbold's Criminal Pleading & Practice* (London: Sweet & Maxwell, 2014), [5–707], *R* v. *Olliver* (1989) 11 Cr App R (S) 10 and *R* v. *Yehou* [1997] 2 Cr App R (S) 48; cf. *R* v. *Ganyo* [2012] 1 Cr App R (S) 108.

[227] See, e.g., J. R. Spencer, 'Introduction' in M. Delmas-Marty and J. R. Spencer (eds.), *European Criminal Procedures* (Cambridge University Press, 2002), 36–7.

of the sanctions available for non-payment is imprisonment, although before that is imposed the magistrates court must receive up to date evidence as to the offender's means, so that there can be no question of this being a back-door route to imprisonment for being too poor to meet your legal obligations.

Despite significant academic criticism, tort law textbooks and university legal teaching of both crime and tort has only minimal coverage of compensation orders (indeed, in the latter case often none).[228]

Of greater value to potential civil litigants have been powers to restore specific property.[229] Civil courts have generally found it more convenient to order the value of the property to be paid, particularly given the difficulty of identifying and enforcing orders against specific property where not already held by a court or the police. Criminal courts have, however, had various powers to restore specific property from at least 1529. These have been used extensively, particularly in low-level theft cases. It seems likely that these powers in the Crown Court and magistrates courts have taken the pressure off the need for a civil power to restore specific property since the most obvious instance (identifiable, movable property in the hands of a state agent) were regulated by the criminal law.

2. Process

One key process-related fact is the strong English discourse about 'rebalancing the criminal justice system in favour of victims'.[230] Much of the role of the victim in a criminal proceeding depends on the character of the criminal trial.[231] To those within the common law, the purpose of the criminal proceedings is usually to test the state's case for conviction. The victim's role is therefore primarily as witness, a source of evidence for

[228] See further, M. Dyson, 'Challenging the Orthodoxy of Crime's Precedence over Tort: Suspending a Tort Claim Where a Crime May Exist' in E. Chamberlain, J. Neyers and S. Pitel (eds.), *Challenging Orthodoxy in Tort Law* (Oxford: Hart, 2013).

[229] See, generally, M. Dyson and S. Green, 'The Properties of the Law: Restoring Personal Property through Crime and Tort' in *Unravelling*.

[230] E.g., the Labour government from 1997 to 2010, Justice for All - A White Paper on the Criminal Justice System, CM 5563 (2002) and foreword (line 2), p. 2; recently the language has moved to 'putting the victim first', e.g., the new Victims Code of December 2013, press release from the Ministry of Justice, www.gov.uk/government/news/victims-put-first-in-the-criminal-justice-system (last accessed 17 August 2014).

[231] See, e.g., comparing the US and Germany: W. T. Pizzi and W. Perron, 'Crime Victims in German Courtrooms: A Comparative Perspective on American Problems' (1996) 32 *Stan J Int'l L* 37.

the prosecution's case. Now that victims are rarely prosecutors themselves, the state has not given them a place in the justice system.

Until the end of the nineteenth century, in England it was victims who brought prosecutions for all but the most serious crimes.[232] As a professional police force slowly took over, the victim disappeared as prosecutor, but without any other place set aside for him.[233] Reflecting the public aspect to the criminal law mentioned in Section 2.A above, in most cases decisions whether to institute a criminal prosecution are now made by public bodies. Since 1986 this has predominantly been the Crown Prosecution Service (CPS),[234] of which the Director of Public Prosecutions (DPP) is the ultimate head. The CPS was created so as to separate out the role of reviewing the adequacy of evidence to justify the bringing of a prosecution, and of making decisions as to where the public interest lies, from the investigatory and enforcement roles of the police. A private individual (including but not only a victim) may still commence a criminal prosecution for almost all crimes,[235] though this is rare. In addition, a variety of other public bodies may and do bring prosecutions such as certain charitable bodies to protect animals and other vulnerable groups,[236] local authorities and the Financial Services Authority; they do as private individuals and sometimes under specific statutory powers.[237] The residual right to bring a private prosecution has been described as being 'of questionable value, and can be exercised in a way damaging to the public interest'.[238] The major limitation to private prosecutions[239] is that the DPP has power to take over the conduct

232 M. Dyson, 'The Timing of Tortious and Criminal Actions for the Same Wrong' [2012] *CLJ* 85, 106–8. See generally, J. R. Spencer, 'The Victim and the Prosecutor' in A. Bottoms and J. Roberts (eds.), *Hearing the Victim: Adversarial Justice, Crime Victims and the State* (Portland: Willan Publishing, 2010).

233 See, esp., S. Milsom, *Historical Foundations of the Common Law*, 2nd edn (London: Butterworths, 1981), 409–10.

234 Established under the Prosecution of Offences Act 1985.

235 Unless it is for one of a small number of offences which may only be prosecuted by the DPP or Attorney-General; the right to do so being preserved, ibid., s. 6(1).

236 *R (Virgin Media Ltd)* v. *Zinga* [2014] EWCA Crim 52, [15].

237 *R* v. *Rollins* [2010] UKSC 39, [7]–[31]; now the Prudential Regulation Authority and the Financial Conduct Authority.

238 *Jones* v. *Whalley* [2006] UKHL 41, [16], holding that it would be an abuse of process to bring a private prosecution after a defendant had accepted a caution: the victims should instead have challenged the lawfulness of the caution.

239 There are three others: Law Commission, Consents to Prosecution, Report 255 (1998), [2.01]–[2.21], esp. [2.14]–[2.20].

of the case at any time[240] and in practice, this power is mostly used as a precursor to discontinuing the case.[241] The benefit to the private prosecutor is that the case may well be quicker and cheaper than a civil claim, especially as costs may be easier to obtain upon a conviction,[242] with compensation orders also available. However, in one startling case in 2014,[243] Virgin Media Ltd successfully prosecuted one Mr Zinga for selling devices which evaded paying for subscription television services, Zinga being imprisoned for eight years.[244] The case is surprising because the Metropolitan Police Authority assisted Virgin in obtaining search warrants, without disclosing to the magistrate that the warrants were in aid of a private prosecution. Similarly, the police arrested defendants for Virgin and later used their confiscation investigation powers as accredited financial investigators to look into the defendant's finances and into the financial benefit obtained by the defendant. All of this was underpinned by Virgin agreeing with the police to hand over a quarter of any compensation order.[245] This claim was later abandoned, and the case went to the Court of Appeal on whether a private prosecutor was entitled to bring confiscation proceedings under the Proceeds of Crime Act 2002, even if it had no financial or other personal interest in the outcome; it held that they did, thus on this occasion the benefit of the prosecution (£8.7 million) went entirely to the Crown. It is bad enough that the prosecutor is personally interested in the outcome of the private prosecution, which is not normally the case in state-run prosecutions;[246] here, however, the police were to be paid to share their investigatory powers with a private person. The Court of Appeal were clearly concerned by the deal attempted and the

240 Prosecution of Offences Act 1985, s. 6(2).

241 See now *R (Gujra)* v. *CPS* [2012] UKSC 52; [2013] 1 AC 484 on the CPS's extensive policy, such as requiring a 'reasonable prospect of success'; previously *DPP ex parte Duckenfield* [2000] 1 WLR 55.

242 Practice Direction (Costs in Criminal Proceedings) October 2013, [2.6.1], costs being awarded unless there is a good reason not to do so.

243 *R (Virgin Media Ltd)* v. *Zinga* [2014] EWCA Crim 52; see Leonard Leigh, 'Private Prosecutors and Public Authorities: Co-operation in Law Enforcement' [2014] *Crim LR* 439.

244 Virgin's estimated loss from the fraud had been £380 million.

245 The donation was to be accepted under the Police Act 1996, s 93(1), which provides that a police authority can accept gifts of money or loans in connection with the discharge of its functions; subject to not appearing to benefit the police over the victim of a crime: *R* v. *Hounsham* [2005] EWCA Crim 1366. This amount was a variation on the standard 'incentive scheme' for Serious Fraud Office prosecutions: *Zinga*, [51]–[52].

246 See Richard Buxton, 'The Private Prosecutor as a Minister for Justice' [2009] *Crim LR* 427.

matter was recently discussed in Parliament: further developments are expected.[247] Interestingly, this growth in corporate private prosecutions has occurred as a liberalisation of some involvement of human victims in the criminal justice process.

While the rhetoric of victims' rights has become heavily used by politicians and others in the last sixty years, it is still not the legal reality. For instance, a complaint from, or the consent of, the victim, is not formally required for the prosecution of offences.[248] Of course, in practice the victim's evidence of the crime can be vital to detection and prosecution, but they have no right to prevent a prosecution occurring and can be compelled to give evidence along similar lines to any other witness. Similarly, only very recently has the victim had any concrete ability to appeal the decision of the CPS not to bring a prosecution.[249]

Other process-related points are also important. English law does not apply any general limitation period for the prosecution of crimes, other than the six month limit for summary (low level) offences.[250] Similarly, the criminal nature of facts is usually irrelevant to civil limitation. However, in rare instances it is possible for the criminal character of offences to be relevant to applying the discretion to extend civil limitation, which in most tort cases is either six years or, where the claim is for personal injuries, three. In 2008,[251] the civil limitation period was extended from three to sixteen years to allow a tort claim against the convicted man when he happened to win £7 million on a lottery.[252] Even there, however, much of the discussion was about a sudden increase in wealth as a factor in extending limitation, rather than the criminal nature of the conduct.

English civil law has only allowed criminal convictions to be *admissible*, let alone determinative, since 1968.[253] The Civil Evidence Act 1968 made convictions admissible in respect of the facts upon which they must have been founded, in all claims except defamation. A later civil court has to see what facts from the conviction are useful, and then give the defendant

247 Adam Gersch and David Rosen, 'Proceeds from Pursuing Private Prosecutions' (2014) 3 *Arch. Rev.* 5, 6.

248 The consent of other legal actors may be required, e.g., the Attorney General.

249 *R* v. *Killick* [2011] EWCA Crim 1608, [2012] 1 Cr App R 10, but not implemented until 5 June 2013, see now the CPS's Victims' Right to Review scheme (VRR).

250 Magistrates Courts Act 1980, s. 127(1), subject to some exceptions.

251 *A* v. *Hoare* [2008] UKHL 6; [2008] 1 AC 844; and Limitation Act 1980, ss. 2, 11 and 33.

252 Ultimately, Hoare was required to pay £50,000 in compensation and nearly £800,000 in costs; his costs appeal was also lost: *Hoare* v. *UK* (2011) 53 EHRR SE1, [36].

253 See Dyson, 'Civil Law Responses to Criminal Judgments' 309–29.

to the civil claim the opportunity to rebut the conviction's probative value.[254] The leading case does not give clear guidance, suggesting that the conviction at least shifts the evidential burden to the defendant, but may also be weighty evidence in itself.[255] Recent cases suggest that the fact of a defendant having already been convicted by a criminal court of, in effect, the very act which constitutes the alleged tort will often, though not always, suffice to persuade a court at a procedural hearing that the defendant would have no real prospect of succeeding in his defence were there to be a trial of the claim against him, and therefore to enter judgment against him summarily.[256]

Where actual or potential criminal proceedings have yet to be finally resolved, English law has now moved to the position that a civil court has a discretion, rather than an obligation, to suspend proceedings before it where they suggest a criminal offence.[257]

3. Evidence

One of the most famous differences between civil and criminal litigation in the common law is that the standards of proof are different. The common law tends to require that facts be proven on the balance of probabilities in tortious claims (as with civil claims generally), but to the more onerous standard of 'beyond reasonable doubt' in a criminal prosecution.[258] It is relatively uncommon in criminal law for the *legal* burden of proof to shift from the prosecution to the defendant. Rare examples are (i) where the defendant raises the defence of insanity (an unusual occurrence in practice, given the serious if technically not penal consequences for the defendant), and (ii) offences arising under enactments which prohibit

[254] Section 11(2)(a): 'be taken to have committed that offence unless the contrary is proved'; cf. s. 13, where convictions are conclusive in defamation proceedings.

[255] *Stupple* v. *Royal Insurance* [1971] 1 QB 50, 76 cf. 72. See also *McIlkenny* v. *Chief Constable of West Midlands Police Force* [1980] QB 283, 319–32 per Lord Denning MR (subsequently appealed to the House of Lords *sub nomine Hunter* v. *Chief Constable* [1982] AC 529.

[256] *Brinks Ltd* v. *Abu-Saleh (No. 1)* [1996] 1 WLR 763, 771; *CXX* v. *DXX* [2012] EWHC 1535. For a contrasting judgment, which seems to imply that the judge would have been reluctant to enter summary judgment against the previously convicted defendant had it been sought, see *J* v. *Oyston* [1999] 1 WLR 694.

[257] Civil Procedure Rules (CPR) 1998, *Practice Direction 23A – Applications*, rules 11A.1 to 11A.4. For detail, see Dyson, 'The Timing of Tortious and Criminal Actions'. Criminal courts do not seem to formally stay their proceedings to wait for a civil law determination.

[258] For a useful borderline example, see *In Re H. (Minors) (Sexual Abuse: Standard of Proof)* [1996] AC 563.

the doing of an act but subject to provisos or exemptions.[259] Similarly, tort law does not normally shift the burden of proof. One area which is sometimes said to be an example of a reversed burden of proof is the doctrine of *res ipsa loquitur*, where facts are said to speak for themselves about the existence of fault. However, the better view is that the facts have raised an inference of fault, not shifted the burden of disproving it.[260] As for an *evidential* burden of proof, defendants quite commonly have to raise evidence of a defence before the prosecution has a legal burden to disprove it and the same is particularly true in tort law.

Issues of proof are further complicated by who must be persuaded: in civil law it will usually be trained judges, although for certain limited categories of tort case, notably in the fields of defamation and police misconduct,[261] trial by judge and jury is still possible on application.[262] For the vast majority of (less serious) crimes, the tribunal usually comprises lay magistrates, although a gradually increasing proportion of magistrates court cases are heard by professional District Judges; more serious crimes are tried by judge and jury in the Crown Court.

Similarly, any differences in rules of evidence and procedure may have a significant impact on the reality of tort and crime. In fact, the Criminal Procedure Rules 2013, modelled on the Civil Procedure Rules 1998, have pulled these areas closer together than they previously were. This bears some elaboration, since the two sets of rules, confusingly both called the 'CPR' by their respective users,[263] represent, in effect, codes of procedure in England, a feat of codification not repeated elsewhere in English law.

First, the Civil Procedure Rules represent a single, uniform procedural code applicable across not only the High Court but also the County Court (the civil court which deals with claims of lesser size or importance), each of which had previously operated under its own set of rules.[264] The reasons for the review of the former rules, presided over by Lord Woolf, which led to his Access to Justice Report of 1996, and in due course the preparation and adoption of the 1998 Civil Procedure Rules, were

259 In which case it is not for the prosecution to prove a *prima facie* case of lack of excuse or qualification in order for the onus of proof to shift, but for the defendant to prove that he was entitled to do the prohibited act, as explained in *R* v. *Edwards (Errington)* [1975] QB 27.

260 See, e.g., *Ng Chun Pui* v. *Lee Chuen Tat* [1988] RTR 298, 299–302.

261 Senior Courts Act 1981, s. 69; County Courts Act 1984, s. 66.

262 CPR, 1998, Rule 26.11.

263 In practice the full title is used orally in criminal courts in respect of 'their' CPR.

264 Respectively the Rules of the Supreme Court 1965, and the County Court Rules 1981.

to improve access to justice and reduce the costs of litigation; to reduce the complexity of the rules and modernise terminology; and to remove unnecessary distinctions of practice and procedure. The most striking new feature of the CPR was the inclusion at its outset[265] of an expressly stated 'overriding objective', intended to state the basic principles on which the rules are founded, and to influence civil courts in exercising their numerous discretions thereunder.[266] Its opening statement that the overriding objective is 'enabling the court to deal with cases justly' has recently been pointedly amended by the addition of the words 'and at proportionate cost'.[267] The overriding objective goes on to specify a number of aspects to 'dealing with a case justly', including ensuring that the parties are on an equal footing; saving expense; dealing with the case in proportionate ways, expeditiously and fairly; and allotting to it an appropriate share of the court's resources, taking into account the like needs of other cases. A striking addition to this list in the same 2013 amendments was 'enforcing compliance with rules . . . '. The immediate result has been a flurry of cases in which parties have been subjected to significant restrictions and disadvantages in their conduct of the litigation simply because they have broken some procedural rule, regardless of whether the other party has suffered any unfair prejudice because of it.[268] This change has been highly controversial amongst practitioners, and many judges are known to feel deeply uncomfortable about it. It is too early to say how its application will work out in even the medium term. Quite apart from the overriding objective, the 1998 CPR also embodied a number of innovative suggestions from the Access to Justice Report not found in the predecessor rules, chief among which was the principle of active case management by the court of all proceedings once issued, replacing the previous approach of party control over litigation.

Second, the criminal procedure rules show great influence from the civil ones. The Criminal Procedure Rules 2005 were the first unified set of rules of English criminal procedure, and came into force on 4 April 2005.[269] Rather than spend '3 or 4 years preparing a complete code', the Rule Committee 'decided to draft the overriding objectives and that part of the code relating to case management, and consolidate and tidy up the some 500 individual rules which it had inherited', then turning

[265] CPR, Part 1. [266] Civil Procedure (2014), vol. 2, para. 11–2.

[267] Civil Procedure (Amendment) Rules 2013/262, para. 4(a).

[268] Most notoriously *Mitchell* v. *News Group Newspapers* [2014] 1 WLR 795.

[269] The groundwork had been laid by the Courts Act 2003, ss. 68–74.

to replace individual inherited rules over time.[270] What is immediately apparent, though, is that the criminal rules share much of the civil rules' content. First, much about good case management is the same whatever field of law and the Civil Procedure Rules was clearly used as a model.[271] The general style of the Civil Procedure Rules is followed throughout, although obviously much of the detailed content is different. Second, and importantly for us, the civil rules appear to have been a template for how to draft and approach the relevant issues. For instance, the criminal rules begin with an 'overriding objective', just like the civil rules before them did:

> 1A.1 The presumption of innocence and an adversarial process are essential features of English and Welsh legal tradition and of the defendant's right to a fair trial. But it is no part of a fair trial that questions of guilt and innocence should be determined by procedural manoeuvres. On the contrary, fairness is best served when the issues between the parties are identified as early and as clearly as possible. As Auld LJ noted, a criminal trial is not a game under which a guilty defendant should be provided with a sporting chance. It is a search for truth in accordance with the twin principles that the prosecution must prove its case and that a defendant is not obliged to inculpate himself, the object being to convict the guilty and acquit the innocent.
>
> 1A.2 Further, it is not just for a party to obstruct or delay the preparation of a case for trial in order to secure some perceived procedural advantage, or to take unfair advantage of a mistake by someone else.

This 'overriding objective' 'bears substantial similarities to the equivalent provisions in the Civil Procedure Rules'.[272]

Turning now to that detailed content, there are some key differences between tort and crime. For instance, the practically important rules on disclosure and compellability of witnesses differ. To begin with, disclosure represents an important part of how cases are framed. In criminal law, the defence have to give notice in advance: (a) in general terms, of the case to be advanced (in a Defence Case Statement) and (b) the names and addresses of witnesses of fact to be called (no longer limited to alibi witnesses). Contrast a tort case, where each side has to provide the other with full, signed witness statements (or witness summaries, where

[270] Judicial Studies Board, Criminal Justice Reforms Handbook, November 2004. There is also a Consolidated Criminal Practice Direction issued by the LCJ (as provided for by Courts Act 2003, s.74) sitting alongside the rules.

[271] E.g., Criminal Procedure Rules, Part 3.

[272] Ibid. See also Courts Act 2003, s. 69(4). For a useful insight into the shift in drafting these rules, see *R* v. *Gleeson* [2003] EWCA Crim 3357.

unusually a witness who has not signed a statement is to be called) well in advance of trial.

Compellability is also very important to getting justice. If a witness is able to give evidence which is relevant to a criminal trial, not only can a party to the case obtain a witness summons[273] but the court even has power to issue a warrant for the witness's arrest in advance of the date when the witness is due to appear,[274] and then to remand the witness in custody, if there are sufficient grounds for believing that the witness will not voluntarily attend.[275] In tort proceedings, whilst a witness summons may be obtained[276] and then served, no further pre-emptive powers are available in advance, and non-compliance is dealt with simply by way of a fine in the County Court, and as a contempt of court in the High Court.[277]

In addition, criminal law will go to much greater lengths to assist vulnerable and reluctant witnesses in giving evidence by the use of 'special measures'. Important examples are giving evidence over a television 'live link' from a different room in the court building, and the court receiving a video recorded interview as the evidence in chief.[278] Similarly, complainants in prosecutions for sexual offences, or witnesses in proceedings relating to a variety of violent offences are automatically deemed eligible for special measures.[279] Furthermore, in the case of child witnesses to sexual or a variety of violent offences, the court's discretion not to make an order for special measures is further restricted,[280] and the cases show a clear willingness to ensure that 'those who are competent to give evidence should be assisted to do so'.[281] Nothing like these measures exist in tort cases, though of course, the prosecution will usually precede the civil claim and if a conviction is obtained, it can be admitted as evidence of the facts upon which it must have been grounded.

Some areas of evidence have been coming closer together without the direct influence of the procedure rules. For instance, in hearsay, although the statutory regimes under which hearsay is received are different (tort: Civil Evidence Act 1995; crime: CJA 2003, especially ss. 114–20), and the criteria for admission in criminal cases are more prescribed and somewhat

[273] Criminal Procedure (Attendance of Witnesses) Act 1965, ss. 2 & 2D.
[274] Ibid., s. 4(1), if the witness is over eighteen years old.
[275] Ibid., s. 4(3). [276] CPR, 34.2 and 34.3. [277] CPR, Part 81.
[278] Youth Justice and Criminal Evidence Act 1999 (as amended), Part II, Chapter I.
[279] Ibid., ss. 17(4) and (5) and Schedule 1A. [280] Ibid., ss. 21(1)(b), (4) and (5).
[281] Per *R* v. *Watts (James Michael)* [2010] EWCA Crim 1824, [18]; see also *R (D)* v. *Camberwell Green Youth Court* [2005] 1 WLR 393.

narrower, there is less of a divide here than there was prior to the 2003 Act.

Other areas continue to show differences. In England and many kindred systems, neither criminal convictions nor acquittals bind a later civil court on substantive questions of law. Where convictions are admitted they are admitted as evidence of the facts upon which they must have been founded, albeit that they are weighty evidence. Even if the substantive components of the legal rules in question are the same, which will often not be the case, the civil law requires a lower standard of proof, and imposes far fewer restrictions on the admission of otherwise relevant evidence, than does the criminal law, with its particular concern for the protection of the rights of the accused and the avoidance of wrongful convictions. A jurisdiction to stay, as an abuse of process, later civil cases which challenge earlier findings of a criminal court has developed, but is seldom of practical effect.[282] Famous cases of acquittals in criminal trials, followed by the acquitted defendant being found liable in tort at a subsequent civil trial, reach the media every few years.[283]

4. Resolutions

English tort law tends to monetarise remedies, focusing particularly on awards of damages as the preferred form of remedy. Injunctions are possible, though rare in tort, and seen perhaps most commonly in the law of nuisance, where property and tort meet. In addition, once the Defamation Act 2013 is in force, further powers to order apologies and retractions to be printed will come into being. English criminal law has a range of penalties, including: imprisonment, fines, compensation, community orders, drug rehabilitation orders and being barred from certain offices and professions.

The acknowledgment that the defendant can rarely satisfy either a civil claim or compensation orders is what led to the creation of the Criminal Injuries Compensation Scheme (CICS) in 1964, which had been debated for some time.[284] The scheme is currently governed by the Criminal Injuries Compensation Act 1995.

The scheme provides state funded and administered compensation for physical or mental harm. It only covers 'crimes of violence', which are

[282] See, e.g., *Hunter* v. *Chief Constable of West Midlands* [1982] AC 529, 586–7.

[283] E.g., *Raja* v. *Van Hoogstraten* [2005] EWHC 2890, esp. [110].

[284] Created by written Parliamentary answer: Hansard [697] cols. 89–94 (24 June 1964).

not listed but determined on the facts as offences of violence.[285] The current scheme is in the spirit of the 1964 original, though a series of cost-cutting drives, the most recent being to cut 25 per cent of its annual expenditure means it is now much more narrowly focused.[286] Originally the scheme compensated at tort law levels of damages; from 1995 this became a tariff-based scheme, and now provides only 'a limited degree of financial security (via the lump sum payments for loss of earnings based on statutory sickness pay and for special expenses) for seriously injured victims'.[287] All matters requiring proof need only be proven by the applicant on the balance of probabilities, that is, the civil rather than criminal standard of proof of 'beyond reasonable doubt'.[288] The Scheme was designed to be easy for the applicant to follow the procedure, and it has generally been well publicised to victims.

The probable effect of the scheme has been to *slightly* reduce demand for other modes of compensation. First, the amount the scheme pays out has probably only ever been 'a drop in a bucket' as the vast majority who could apply do not do both.[289] One specific reason is that the scheme has sought to maximise its return on administrative costs by having a minimum award: it began at £50 and by a series of increments is now £1,000.[290] The limit deters applications, though there remains a cost in screening and verifying. Even if an application is made, the Scheme also contains extensive reasons to reduce or withhold awards based on the applicant's conduct, including, for instance, prior convictions.[291] On the other hand, the proportionately few who successfully apply have been disincentivised from bringing a civil action or compensation order because, if successful, the Board is entitled to deduct any such compensation from the Board's award.[292] Therefore, the CICS has not radically changed the landscape of compensation. Instead compensation orders

[285] 2012 Scheme, Annex B.

[286] See most recently, David Miers, 'Compensating Deserving Victims of Violent Crime: The Criminal Injuries Compensation Scheme 2012' (2014) 34 *LS* 242, esp. 277.

[287] Ibid., 277–8. See, generally, www.cica.gov.uk (last accessed October 2014).

[288] Criminal Injuries Compensation Act 1995, s. 3(2).

[289] E. Veitch and D. Miers, 'Assault on the Law of Tort' (1975) 38 *MLR* 139, 148, note 68; note 67 suggests a total of 86,000 potential tort actions based on reported criminal offences to the police in 1973 while note 68 then compares this with 9,000 applications in what appears to be the same year. See also P. S. Atiyah, *Accidents, Compensation and the Law*, 3rd edn (London: Weidenfeld and Nicolson, 1980), 336; cf. P. Cane (ed.), *Atiyah's Accidents, Compensation and the Law*, 4th edn (London: Weidenfeld and Nicolson, 1987), 25 and 292.

[290] 2012 Scheme, [22]. [291] Ibid., [22]–[29]. [292] Ibid., [85].

still have a key role in compensating for minor harms.[293] This is particularly the case in their heartland of property damage.

Finally, it is sometimes stated that some common law countries are exceptional in giving tort law a punitive function, through the award of exemplary damages.[294] Punitive damages are controversial within English law, particularly because they confuse civil and criminal functions; they are also not common in English law in practice.[295]

3. How the interactions happen

English law has examples of just about all the major ways in which tort and crime can interact. First, in terms of hierarchy, there are a number of examples in the past, and a number still current. It is still possible for a tortious (or other civil) claim on a matter which also discloses a crime to be suspended while any prosecution is ongoing. This power is rarely exercised nowadays, especially when it is considered that there was a formal rule requiring such suspensions until it was removed by statute in 1967. It has even been argued that civil claims for serious wrongs, like rape, should not follow failed prosecutions as the criminal sphere's outcome should take precedence.[296] Second, a summary trial of an assault will then preclude the same matter coming before a later court, civil or criminal.[297] Similarly, there are examples of equality between the two. For instance, a criminal court can award compensation in many cases and does so under its own rules, though acknowledging some material from tort law.

Second, objects (institutions, reasoning, norms, substance and procedure) can move from one area of law to another in certain circumstances, though they can be denied in others. As noted above, from 1968 criminal convictions became admissible in civil claims as evidence of the facts upon

[293] Sir Edward Gardiner, HMSO Compensation and Support for Victims of Crime (First Report 1984–85), Evidence of the Home Office, [3.7]; magistrates were aware of this: Evidence of the Magistrates' Association, 75, 76.

[294] E.g., M. L. Rustad, 'The Supreme Court and Me: Trapped in Time with Punitive Damages' (2007–8) 17 *Widener LJ* 783.

[295] *Rookes* v. *Barnard* [1964] AC 1129, 1225–7. See, further, Clerk & Lindsell, [28–137] to [28–151].

[296] Jane Stapleton, 'Civil Prosecutions Part 1: Double Jeopardy and Abuse of Process' (1999) 7 *TLJ* 244 and Jane Stapleton, 'Civil Prosecutions Part 2: Civil Claims for Killing and Rape' (2000) 8 *TLJ* 15.

[297] OAPA 1861, s. 45.

which they must have been founded. This is also an example of equality, in that the criminal court's determinations do not generally bind the civil court, but they are admissible as evidence. In the case of a later libel claim, however, the conviction is determinative of the facts upon which it was founded, so showing the hierarchically greater importance given to the reputation of the criminal justice system in this context. That is, when challenged by implication in a libel claim, public confidence in the criminal justice system is thought to need the protection of the earlier conviction being conclusive evidence. On the other hand, there have also been examples of clear attempts to restrict the passage of component parts of the law, as discussed in respect of the ownership of property and theft. Some resolutions, like imprisonment, are only within the competence of criminal courts. As a general thread, English law prefers to use vague terms like 'coherence' and 'consistency' than requiring that the component parts of tort and crime actually be the same. Such terms are used with or without a definition in the particular instance, but certainly without any general consensus. They engender a great deal of flexibility in interpretation. In some cases, English law also employs something akin to 'correspondence', that is, that the two areas should change at the same rate or in the same way. This will often happen when a criminal rule ties in with a civil rule's changes; for instance, a civil claim to recover half of whatever penalty is set as a criminal punishment for breaking a particular rule: the greater the penalty becomes, the greater the civil recovery automatically becomes.[298]

Third, sometimes the interaction between tort and crime is direct, sometimes indirect. How direct is any influence from one area to another? For instance, a procedural defence of illegality in tort law might arise not from a rule of criminal procedure, but from a substantive criminal law rule prohibiting certain conduct. This will always be hard to be precise about. But it is clear that while some lawyers are happier to move substantive goalposts to achieve a particular result, others prefer to shape legal issues through procedure, such as adjusting costs, rules of evidence or the characteristics of the tribunal which will hear a dispute. For instance, English law often tries to solve a problem of substantive law by changing applicable rules of evidence or procedure. This is an indirect solution in the sense used here, but one English lawyers turn to very readily.

[298] Itself very common in certain statutory duties: a 'moiety' of the fine often went to the person who suffered harm by the breach of duty or to the person who brought the claim to enforce the duty (see, e.g., Cruelty to Animals Act 1835, 5 & 6 W 4 C 59, s. 17).

A further way in which interactions happen is hybridisation. That is, that a new sub-form of legal construct is created which shares characteristics of both its parents, but is not clearly or entirely the same as either. Such is the creation of Anti-Social Behaviour Orders (ASBOs) in England: orders often made by civil courts, breach of which is dealt with by a criminal court.[299] ASBOs effectively tailor the criminal law to individuals, without legislating new rules for everyone. Perhaps the most significant reason why politicians chose the civil law to achieve these ends was because extending the criminal law into such paradigmatically complex areas as 'social behaviour' would have been politically difficult; using civil law at least initially, and forming a 'hybrid', allowed the same process but without the same procedural protections. ASBOs are also made by criminal courts as adjuncts to traditional sentencing, extending the prospective powers of the criminal courts dramatically without apparently having to compromise on the principles of criminal law underpinning them. Professor Andrew Ashworth, who has been a leading commentator on ASBOs, summarises them as:

> [A] hybrid legal order . . . intended to achieve (a) the admissibility of evidence according to rules of civil evidence and procedure; (b) the assessment of the evidence by reference to the civil standard of proof; (c) the making of a civil order, whose terms would not be restricted to desistance from the conduct established in court; (d) the threat of a criminal offence for breach of the civil order, with a substantial maximum penalty; and (e) sentencing on breach that takes account of earlier conduct not proven or admitted in a criminal court.[300]

Other examples of hybridisation are afforded by Sexual Offences Prevention Orders, which may be imposed either as part of a sentence following conviction, or on application to a magistrates court by a Chief Constable without the defendant necessarily having first been convicted of any offence,[301] and by Enforcement Orders under Enterprise Act 2002, Part 8, made in support of consumer protection legislation.

[299] ASBOs were introduced by the Crime and Disorder Act 1998, ss. 1–4. For more detail, see A. Millie, *Anti-Social Behaviour* (Maidenhead: Open University Press, 2009), Ch. 6; E. Burney, *Making People Behave: Anti-social Behaviour, Politics and Policy*, 2nd edn (Devon: Willan, 2005), Ch. 5.

[300] A. Ashworth, 'Social Control and "Anti-Social Behaviour": the Subversion of Human Rights?' (2004) 120 *LQR* 263, 289. See also, A. Ashworth, 'Conceptions of Overcriminalisation' (2007–2008) 5 *Ohio State Journal of Criminal Law* 407, 418.

[301] See the Sexual Offences Act 2003, ss.104–113.

4. Conclusion

The English law on tort and crime is complex, under-theorised, under-researched and at times, counter-intuitive (to foreign, and even modern English eyes). Tort and crime are typically splendidly isolated from each other. The pattern of their interactions has developed only rarely deliberately, and more usually by the impact of many small decisions being made separately to each other across many areas.

The most coherent of these areas has been procedure, the first area where tort and crime had to be co-ordinated for cases to be decided, and thus the longest standing area of consideration. Important English developments here have been compensation orders and restitution orders, the Criminal Injuries Compensation Scheme, the slow acceptance of convictions as evidence and the equally hesitant removal of the rule suspending civil claims while a prosecution is ongoing.

Outside of procedure, tort and crime have had weaker links but some links nonetheless. Thus the substantive comparisons between tort and crime can yield some important and surprising results, both about the understanding of each area alone and in comparison to each other, particularly interesting examples being on consent, causation and the definition of property. Legal reasoning has had some similar traits, with senior judges dealing with both areas of law at the apex of the court system, and with the common law method being similar across the substantive areas of the law. At times it can be surprising how disconnected the reasoning can be, and how haphazard English decisions about whether to criminalise or leave to tortious remedies. For example, some but not all forms of libel, like assault and theft, were potentially both a tort and a crime until seditious libel, defamatory libel and obscene libel were all abolished by the Coroners and Justice Act 2009, s. 73. However, while criminal libel had long been in abeyance, from 1986 to 2014 the Public Order Act, s. 5, made 'insulting' behaviour a criminal offence, without the previous requirement of a risk of a breach of the peace.[302]

Similarly there are many difficult questions about the theories and norms underlying both areas which remain to be explored. Some of the most difficult and largely unanswered questions are about why the interactions have happened across tort and crime. It seems highly plausible that English lawyers are motivated primarily by what they regard as

302 Crime and Courts Act 2013, s. 57 removed the word 'insulting'; cf. Public Order Act 1936, s. 5.

practical considerations specific to each interaction. This tends to mean that wider questions about the homogeneity of the legal system are not fully explored. References to coherence or consistency are made at times, but without depth or, ironically, consistency. There are certainly occasions where English criminal law has asserted its independence from what could be seen as underlying civil law norms, such as in the law of property, and similarly, civil law rules have bent when the reputation of the criminal justice process appears to be doubted.[303]

English law has slowly become willing to link its tort and crime, often striking what it regards as a pragmatic balance. For instance, including compensation within the ambit of the criminal law was a trade-off: if enforced by civil means, it would involve the criminal court making a civil order and require the claimant to do all the work of enforcement; on the other hand, a criminal order would be conceptually and practically simpler to make but would involve the court in enforcing it through potentially penal means. In part for this reason, any compensation order would be set partly based on the defendant's means. In this, it departed from the quantum tort law would set, but thereby limited the use of the state's coercive powers in enforcing compensation. In other ways, compensation orders differed from tort law more for convenience of criminal courts, and in part their competence in determining finer issues of civil law. Conversely, it does not appear that courts have referred to much concern for the defendant's difficulty in contesting a civil component within his criminal trial. In sum, while sometimes legal actors have (rarely) noticed the totality of the effect of civil and criminal rules, such as in the Motor Insurers Bureau, generally English law tends to treat each instance of an overlap as its own problem, as was seen in the 2013 reform to Health and Safety at Work legislation. This is particularly surprising given that the highest court, now called the Supreme Court, is the ultimate court for both civil and criminal matters. English law on tort and crime remains isolated, and only recently has any splendour in that isolation been seriously and broadly questioned.

[303] See, e.g., Dyson, 'Civil Law Responses', 309–29.

3

The quest for balance between tort and crime in French law

VALÉRIE MALABAT AND VÉRONIQUE WESTER-OUISSE

1. Introduction

French law links tort and crime in an elegant way to balance the interests of the victim, of the state and, to some extent, those of the defendant. This sometimes complex quest for balance takes concrete shape particularly in a criminal trial: the victim of an offence can make an application for damages to the criminal court, which has jurisdiction to rule on the existence of a criminal offence and the defendant's liability to pay (civil) damages. This application may also trigger a criminal trial. Because this power is extreme, it comes with certain counterweights: for instance the victim may only claim certain remedies before the criminal court and there are certain safeguards against abuse. For this reason, and others, the French system therefore pays a great deal of attention to the links between tort and crime; it has developed many rules which allow criminal and civil law to interact in a quest for balance between the various interests at stake – a task that is difficult to fulfil.

Some of the very first modern Western law rules on the tort–crime relationship originated in French law; they have since become models for various other legal systems. Three such rules and concepts particularly stand out: that of *partie civile*,[1] which allows the victim to act as a player in the criminal process; the force of *chose jugée* giving precedence to criminal decisions over later civil claims; and the suspension of a civil claim dealing

[1] The notions of victim and civil party (*partie civile*) are separate. The victim of the criminal offence is the person who suffers the damage caused by the offence. The civil party is the person whose (civil) action has been ruled admissible by the criminal court pursuant to Art. 2 and subsequent articles of the Code de procédure pénale (hereafter CPP) (Code of Criminal Procedure). Victims may obviously stand as civil parties but this option is also available to other persons (authorised associations, workers' unions, the victim's next of kin, etc.).

with the same facts as a pending prosecution (*le criminal tient le civil en l'état*). These procedural rules were the first to develop, but in the last hundred years a number of substantive principles followed, such as the unity of fault, the existence of punitive damages, the *sanction-réparation* and other changes to codes and court practice.

One of the interesting aspects of French law is that, despite the well-established tradition of tort/crime in France, there have been a number of important changes since 2000, showing that even apparently stable laws are open to change in the right circumstances.[2]

The chapter will focus on the links between tort and crime in France on the following levels: institutional, procedural and substantive.

2. Institutions

It is necessary to outline the institutional framework within which tort and crime operate in France in order to understand the links between both.

A three-year bachelor's degree is required to become a lawyer. By tradition, ever since a now repealed revolutionary statute,[3] students must learn: civil law, through the Code civil (Civil Code), public law, criminal law and criminal procedure, though they will learn other subjects as well. Many students will also take a Master's degree, whether taught or by research.

In French legal practice, there is some degree of specialisation in roles and in areas of law. The main French legal professions are: avocat,[4] prosecutor, judge (including Advocate-General), academic, legislator and notary.[5] Most solicitors are generalists, certainly at the beginning of their career. In 2012, there were 56,176 solicitors in France and only 11,074 of them mention areas of specialisation (the most common being labour, tax and company law).[6] Some solicitors are specialised in criminal law,

[2] See Section B.1 below.

[3] Loi relative aux Ecoles de droit Paris, 3 January 1804 (22 Ventôse an XII), www.legilux.public.lu/rgl/1804/A/0003/Z.pdf, last accessed November 2014.

[4] There is no distinction in French law between solicitors and barristers: the word *avocat* is used for the lawyer that represents and assists the litigant at trial.

[5] The notary's role relates to official documents, particularly for contracts and property transactions and is not particularly relevant here.

[6] See www.justice.gouv.fr/budget-et-statistiques-10054/etudes-statistiques-10058/statistique-sur-la-profession-davocat-2012–24851.html (last accessed November 2014).

which typically involves lower paid cases, but even in Paris this is less than 14 per cent of them; specialisation in tort law is almost non-existent, except for personal injury lawyers.[7] Tort itself is seen as part of the wider civil law, and deft claims for damages are seen as a general skill needed in most civil claims, such as labour law, real property, tort and the special legislative regime for road traffic accidents.

To become a judge or prosecutor, further studies are required; starting with a national competition to enter the National School for Magistrates (*École Nationale de la Magistrature*). Aspiring judges then follow further courses of lectures, undertake various internships and other forms of training, some of which allows them to specialise in areas of law such as criminal or civil law.[8] However, in practice, there is a slightly blurred distinction between civil and criminal courts, contrary to that which exists between the administrative courts and the general ones. Civil and criminal courts are generally in the same building and administratively are one court (as explained below) with a single president of the jurisdiction but they work separately with their own rules. For example, the 'Tribunal correctionnel' is a part of 'Tribunal de grande instance' but has its own specific rules. Judges are normally assigned to civil or criminal functions but sometimes they can have both (generally for young judges and lower functions) and they do move during their careers. Although one legal actor, the *juge de proximité*, has civil and criminal jurisdiction there are other courts of first instance which do not have this dual jurisdiction. In particular, the 'Tribunal de police', the 'Tribunal correctionnel' and the 'Cour d'assises' have exclusively criminal jurisdiction.

- The Tribunal d'instance (which is competent to settle disputes involving civil claims under €10,000) is also the Tribunal de police (for minor criminal offences called *contraventions*);

[7] And then only if one includes those whose work is predominantly criminal, rather than those who are solely specialised in it. For statistics on Paris, Bordeaux and Rennes bars see, respectively: www.avocatparis.org/annuaire-barreau-paris.html, www.barreau-bordeaux.avocat.fr/annuaire˙index.php and www.ordre-avocats-rennes.com (last accessed November 2014).

[8] In French law, civil law means all matters relating to the rights of individuals and families, contract law, civil liability, matrimonial rules (the choice between a marriage based on joint ownership of property or based on separate ownership of property), succession and other related matters. 'Civil law' is thus distinguished from commercial law and labour law, though they are still close cousins, especially compared to criminal law or administrative law.

- The Tribunal de grande instance (which is competent to settle disputes involving civil claims above €10,000) is also the Tribunal correctionnel (for more serious offences, *délits*);
- For the most serious crimes, such as murder and rape, the judges of the Cour d'assises come from the local Court of Appeal (the regional appellate bodies which hear civil and criminal cases, dividing the claims into separate chambers).

The *Cour de cassation* is divided into chambers, including five civil[9] and one criminal chamber.

Academic lawyers are an integral and important part of the judicial, and to some extent of the legislative law-making process. Academic commentary is important at an appellate level; it is of particular relevance both while a case is being decided since it helps Advocates-General draft their opinions, as well as after the court has given its final decision as it provides an explanation of the judgment. This is because French judgments are very short. For instance, at the level of the Cour de cassation, judgments are on average a terse three pages and do not refer to jurisprudence or academic writing; the case notes from senior academics therefore provide an analysis of the judgment and a vital link to wider materials.

Given what has been noted about the three subjects that students must study, that is civil law, public law and criminal law and procedure, it might be expected that this tripartite division would form part of French academia as well. However, this is not the case: criminal law is part of private rather than public law, and is not technically a separate area of law, as civil and public law are. An illustration of this classification is found in the academic environment. Every academic lawyer is affiliated to a 'section' of the National Council of Universities.[10] There exist three different sections in the law department: private law and criminal sciences, public law and legal history. Public law is strictly restricted to administrative law, constitutional law and fundamental rights. Criminal law's concerns, on the other hand, are linked to public order and society's higher moral values. Some might imagine that the presence of the public prosecutor, who represents the interests of society at large in criminal proceedings, may in some way give those proceedings a public character. Nonetheless, criminal law is part of private law and this does not strike the average

[9] Three strictly civil, one commercial and one *social* (labour and National Insurance disputes).

[10] See www.cpcnu.fr/listes-des-sections-cnu (last accessed November 2014).

French lawyer as strange. Doctoral students and lecturers, affiliated to section 01, are usually specialised in one area: contract law, commercial law, criminal law, tort law, family law, etc. As teaching assistants, however, they are warmly encouraged to teach in any area of the law. Similarly, early career lecturers often teach in different areas in order to fill their university's needs. It is only after a few years that professors and lecturers get more specialised for the purposes of publishing their papers; still, they tend to give few lectures in their area of specialisation. There are a limited number of professorships in each section, with legal history being the smallest section by far.

In France, legal literature is mainly written by academics. Very little such work is done on both tort and crime, and very few tort law books meaningfully discuss criminal liability. Similarly, there are very few conferences, seminars or publications,[11] and only a handful of published doctoral theses,[12] which deal with both areas of the law; this gives a good indication of the level of academic interest in the interrelationship between both. Recently, most of the discussion on the tort/crime overlap has taken place in relation to debates on the nature of punitive damages.

The key legislators in tort and criminal law are the Assemblée Nationale and the Sénat. They produced and are in charge of reforming the principles in the Civil Code and the definitions of nearly all the criminal offences (except for the least serious ones).[13] Criminal law takes up a significant part of their legislative attention, tort law virtually none.[14] At the same time, while the bulk of the Code civil has not changed since 1804, judges have developed tort law so that statutory provisions are no longer interpreted in the way they were in the nineteenth century; it is partly because

[11] For rare examples, see G. Viney, *Introduction à la responsabilité* (Paris: LGDJ 2008), 111–274; 'Responsabilité civile et responsabilité pénale: regards croisés', *Res. civ. et assur. May 2013*; X. Pin, 'La privatisation du procès pénal', *Rev. sc. crim.*, (2002) 245; F. Rousseau, *La fonction réparatrice de la sanction pénale,* Droit penal et autres branches du droit, Regards croisés, Cujas, coll. Actes et Etudes, 2012, 125.

[12] See, recently, S. Carval, *La responsabilité civile dans sa fonction de peine privée* (Paris: LGDJ 1995); see also: B. Stark, *Essai sur la responsabilité civile dans sa double fonction de garantie et de peine privée* (Paris: L. Rodstein 1947); B. Paillard, *La fonction réparatrice de la répression pénale* (Paris: LGDJ 2007); N. Rias, *Aspects actuels des liens entre les responsabilités civile et pénale,* Thèse Lyon III, 2006.

[13] Since the French Constitution of 1958, per its Articles 34 and 37, minor offences ('*contraventions*') are not defined by the law, but by simple regulations ('*réglements*'), from various ministers and local authorities.

[14] The last reform implemented a European Regulation on defective products, and that was twenty years ago.

judges have done so that there is so little legislative intervention in the field of tort law.

Another set of institutional actors worth noting is insurers. Insurers are vital to the functioning of the French system of tortious and non-tortious compensation, and they also play a significant role in the background of criminal law. They often pay damages to the victim of an offence. Having done so, they can then subrogate and bring a claim in the name of the insured victim. Indeed, since 1983,[15] once they have indemnified an insured victim, they can intervene in the *criminal proceedings*, seeking damages in the victim's place before the Cour d'assises or a Tribunal correctionnel for offences of homicide or unintentional injury. In law reform projects, insurers also play a significant role.[16]

In addition, the state sometimes plays the role of insurer. It has created some specific funds to guarantee compensation to the victims of particular kinds of wrongs: for example, ONIAM (Office national d'indemnisation des accidents médicaux, dealing with medical errors or accidents), FGTI (Fonds de garantie des victimes d'actes terroristes et d'autres infractions, dealing with acts of terrorism acts and other specific criminal offences), FGA and FGAO (respectively Fonds de garantie automobile and Fonds de garantie des assurances obligatoires de dommages, which are concerned with car accidents).[17]

3. Procedural links

From a procedural point of view, criminal and tort law are linked because French law authorises the victim of a crime suffering harm to ask for compensation before a criminal judge authorised to handle the case. In what follows we will first outline each principle, and then analyse some specific issues in more depth.

First then, a procedural choice is offered to the victim (Section 3.A below): if the victim at any time selects a criminal court, that court then has jurisdiction to hear a claim for damages; otherwise it is a civil court which

[15] Loi n°83–608 of 8 July 1983 reinforcing the protection of victims of wrongs, *JO*, 9 July 1983, p. 2122; Art. 388–1 CPP.

[16] For instance in the significant *Beteille* project, the list of groups consulted includes Fonds de garantie des assurances obligatoires de dommages (FGAO), the Fédération française des sociétés d'assurance (FFSA) and the Groupement des entreprises mutuelles d'assurance (GEMA): see www.senat.fr/rap/r08–558/r08–55832.html#toc326 (last accessed November 2014).

[17] See vosdroits.service-public.fr/particuliers/F2679.xhtml (last accessed November 2014).

will have that jurisdiction. This requires a co-ordination of the jurisdiction of the civil and criminal judges which is done according to two important principles: the authority of *res judicata* of criminal rulings on civil cases (Section 3.B below) and the necessity to stay any civil proceedings until the criminal judge's work is complete (Section 3.C below).

A. *The victim's role in selecting the procedure*

The victim's power to file a compensatory claim before a civil or criminal judge is obviously a key point of reconciliation between tortious and criminal spheres of French law.

A victim suffering from harm caused by a criminal offence has the option to join criminal proceedings as a civil party (known as an *action civile*, or civil action, it consists in a claim for compensation for the harm suffered) before either a criminal or a civil judge. In theory, the victim is free to make that choice (though a number of exceptions are imposed; e.g., in the law of defamation[18]). There are two ways a victim can file his action before a criminal judge.

First, the victim can join his civil action to a prosecution that has already been filed by the public prosecutor's office: in such a case, the victim is described as acting by means of intervention (*par voie d'intervention*).

Second, the victim can file his civil action before a criminal judge although the public prosecutor's office has not instigated a public action. Prosecutions are discretionary in French law under Article 40–1 of the Code of Criminal Procedure and may be dropped, or not even started, for many reasons, for instance on the ground that there is insufficient

[18] In particular, under Arts. 30 and 31 of the Law of 29 July 1881. These provide that civil actions for damages for the special defamation offences listed cannot be brought separately from public prosecutions. It is therefore mandatory for the victim of these offences to bring his action for damages before the criminal court. Conversely, victims in other cases cannot claim damages before the criminal court. Such is the case, in particular, for special criminal courts as these do not have jurisdiction to rule on the civil action. This concerns, for instance, the Cour de justice de la République (Court of Justice of the Republic). The same solution can be found in matters involving accidents in the workplace. Such accidents generally constitute criminal offences (unintentional acts endangering life or inflicting bodily harm) which may therefore be prosecuted before the criminal court. However, the statute reserves jurisdiction for the award of compensation for damage suffered as a result of an accident at work for the Tribunal des affaires de la sécurité sociale (Social Security Tribunals). The victim in such cases therefore does not have the option of bringing an action before the criminal court or the civil court (in the broad sense). But in those instances where the criminal court does not have jurisdiction to award damages, the case law has nonetheless decided that the victim can initiate the criminal trial.

evidence. It is the victim who might then force the prosecutor to start the criminal proceedings; in which case, the criminal judge gives a decision on both the criminal action and the combined civil claim. In this case, the victim is described as acting through direct action (*par voie d'action*).

In either case, as a question of *justice*, the possibility to join proceedings as a civil party (*partie civile*) in front of a criminal judge is very significant. It is an express link between two otherwise separate jurisdictions, the criminal and the civil, based on the consequences of one act.

But above all, it is interesting from a *political* perspective (political being used in the noble sense of the word): it guarantees the start of a criminal trial by forcing the public prosecutor to act in spite of his inaction or his decision to close the case. The fact that it is the victim who is empowered to safeguard this political value both harnesses his interest in the outcome and benefits him personally.

Exercising the civil claim before a criminal court changes its nature: from a purely civil claim, it becomes at least in part criminal, with a repressive or vindicatory goal.[19] Indeed, given that the victim has the choice whether to bring the application before a civil or a criminal court, his preference for the criminal proceedings expresses his wish to be part of these proceedings and to participate in the prosecution. It is then said that the civil action has two faces, or a double character: it is both an action for damages and 'a civil action brought for extrapatrimonial purposes on the grounds of the victim's wish to corroborate the prosecution and see that the guilt of the defendant is established'.[20] The prosecutorial character of the civil action[21] is especially evident in the case law which states that the civil action sets the prosecution in motion even in those cases where the civil party may not seek damages or where the criminal court (exceptionally)[22] does not have jurisdiction to award compensation.[23]

[19] V. F. Boulan, 'Le double visage de l'action civile exercée devant la juridiction répressive' (1973) 1 *JCP*, 2563.

[20] B. Bouloc, *Procédure pénale*, 24th edn (Paris: Dalloz 2014), 212, n°251.

[21] One consequence of this is that, as the Court of Appeal confirmed in 2003, the application of the victim to join and to instigate proceedings as a civil party interrupts the statute of limitations on the criminal offence. See: Cass. Crim., 1 October 2003, *Bull. crim.* n°178.

[22] See above.

[23] The civil party is admissible and the examining magistrate is bound to report even where the civil action falls within the jurisdiction of the administrative courts (Cass. Crim., 22 January 1953, *D.* 1953, 109, rapport Patin). A subsequent decision of 15 October 1970 clearly stated that the right to stand as *partie civile* under Art. 2 CPP must be distinguished from the right to apply for compensation provided under Art. 418 CPP (Cass. Crim., 15 October 1970, *D.* 1970, 733, note Costa). See, more recently and in the same sense: Cass. Crim., 30 June 2009, *Bull. crim.* n°139.

This double character is a concrete expression of the specificity of the French system, which has conceived those prerogatives granted to the victim as counterweights to the opportunities to prosecute that are open to the public prosecutor. Beyond the private interests of the victim (which are afforded protection through the action for damages), it is also in the public interest that criminal offences be prosecuted.

Finally, this option is interesting in *procedural* terms because there are practical differences in the way the civil claim is processed if it is filed before a criminal court. Significantly, the criminal trial rules may appear more favourable to the victim. For instance, criminal procedure is governed by a principle of 'freedom of proof'[24] and this benefits the victim by allowing a very wide range of evidence, conceivably more than a civil court in practice though this is hard to substantiate. Perhaps even more importantly, there is a difference in the burden of proof as between civil and criminal trials. A civil claim requires the claimant to prove that the defendant's fault did in fact cause him injury. As part of a claim brought by a *partie civile*, by contrast, those elements are established in the course of a criminal trial and it is therefore the criminal actors who bring such proof according to criminal standards. This means that it is the public prosecutor who must prove the elements of the crime, which are then used by the victim to substantiate his tort claim. The criminal court must therefore be convinced of the existence of the offence before it can deduce the consequences of the existence of the conditions of liability. The French examining magistrate (*le juge d'instruction*) may himself seek evidence and often does so in practice.

Evidently, the right of a victim to join the criminal proceeding is very important. But this right is not without some risk. Under Article 392–1 CPP, if the summons is brought before the Correctional Court, the civil party risks a fine, based on his income and capped at 15,000 Euro if his was an abusive or dilatory prosecution; indeed, to bring the claim in the first place he must lodge a deposit to cover any possible fine following an acquittal (unless the civil party is entitled to receive legal aid). In addition, a *partie civile* who has made abusive use of her right to start a prosecution is liable in damages at the suit of the acquitted defendant, and under

[24] In French law, the principle of freedom of proof goes against the evidential rules applicable in civil law, under which evidence may only be presented in a limited number of ways provided by law. Thus evidence of a legal act must in theory be presented in written form (Art. 1341 Civil Code). Conversely, under the principle of freedom of proof all forms of evidence (such as testimonies or written evidence) are allowed, the court being free to assess the value of such evidence.

Article 472 CPP, these damages are ruled on by the Criminal Court before which the prosecution failed.[25]

The approach of the victim in determining whether to become a *partie civile* will be examined below,[26] but this suffices for an outline for the moment.

While the concept of *partie civile* is fundamental to French law and dates back at least to 1809,[27] three particular difficulties in understanding its scope remain: (a) the material scope (what actions can be brought before either judge); (b) the personal scope (who has standing to bring it); (c) its finality (the extent to which a victim is bound, having selected one pathway (*electa una via*)).

1. Material scope

The civil action within a criminal process is not a vehicle for all civil claims, it is primarily for damages. In technical terms it is a form of civil proceedings: it is a claim for compensation arising from the harm caused by the offence. By contrast, 'actions with civil ends' (*actions à fins civiles*) cannot be brought before a criminal judge; they must always be brought before a civil judge.[28] An action with civil ends does not seek to repair the damage caused by the offence but rather to draw certain civil consequences out of the offence or to enforce a right that the offence may have infringed. Examples of actions with civil ends include an action for recovering stolen property or a dismissal action in respect of a donation in cases where an attempt has been made on the life of the donor by the beneficiary. As might be expected, while *civil proceedings* are stayed once a criminal prosecution has begun, *actions with civil ends* are not stayed.[29]

This dissociation is difficult to implement in practice. For example, a victim of domestic abuse can obtain damages in a criminal court by

[25] For instance, an unflattering academic book review, see J. R. Spencer, 'Libel Tourist Ordered to Pay 8,000 Euros' (2011) 70 *CLJ* 317.

[26] On these questions, see Section 3.A.2. below.

[27] It is the case law which acknowledged the victim's right to seize a criminal judge for his compensatory action and to force the start of criminal proceedings. The Court of Appeal first considered that the direct summons before a court delivered at the victim's initiative would automatically start the public action (Cass. Crim., 17 August 1809, *Bull. crim.* n°141). It further extended this rule by holding that an official complaint joined with a civil action presented to the examining magistrate also forced the public action to begin, thus compelling the judge to discuss the alleged facts (Cass. Crim., 8 December 1906, *D.* 1907, I, 207, note R. Demogue, also known after the head clerk's name as *arrêt Laurent-Atthalin*).

[28] Arts. 3 *alinéa* 1 and 4 *alinéa* 1 CPP.

[29] Art. 4 *alinéa* 3 CPP as amended by the Law of 5 March 2007.

filing a civil action before the criminal judge, but cannot obtain a divorce decision from the same judge; he would be forced to go to a civil judge to rule on this request. Similarly, a criminal judge cannot declare a contract invalid because of fraud nor order the restitution of a stolen item, except if the stolen good was seized during criminal proceedings[30] where the criminal judge can rule on the restitution of seized goods.[31] While the victim will therefore have to go before two separate courts to achieve everything he seeks, by joining proceedings as a civil party he receives *compensation* faster, with less effort on his part and, most importantly, he becomes a party in the criminal procedure thus gaining significant rights to participate and be informed.[32]

The limited scope of the civil action exists for sound reasons. Most importantly, the jurisdiction of the criminal judge is strictly delimited by the facts from which the jurisdiction is referred and which can receive a criminal law response. The criminal judge cannot extend his jurisdiction to cover non-criminal law questions, such as divorce. Such an extension would interfere with the civil law's scope and would in turn complicate and slow down the criminal justice too much. Claims for compensation are different, since there the very same act is both a tortious wrong and a criminal offence. By contrast, other matters such as divorce and contractual invalidity require proof of other civil elements and further civil law tests to be applied. In other words, the place of the victim in the criminal trial can only be secondary or accessory to the importance of the crime itself. It is therefore logical to limit the scope of their claims before a criminal judge,[33] and to leave the original route to go before a civil judge untouched, but perhaps delayed.

2. Personal scope

While the benefits of being a *partie civile* should not be granted too widely,[34] criminal courts have steadily increased the scope of those who

[30] In this particular case, since the property is seized during the criminal proceedings, it falls to the court to rule on their fate.

[31] Arts. 373 and 478 ss CPP depending on which court is delivering the judgment (respectively Cour d'assises and Tribunal correctionnel).

[32] See, e.g., Art. 89–1 CPP. In particular, the civil party (*partie civile*) has the right to be informed during the preliminary investigation but also to ask the judge to perform specific investigative acts, the judge's refusal to accomplish them must be justified under Art. 82–1 CPP.

[33] While there has been a steady increase in the victim's prerogatives in criminal proceedings, the victim still remains a *secondary* private party.

[34] In the same vein, see specifically Cass. Crim., 9 November 1992, *Bull. crim.* n°361: 'civil actions brought before criminal courts are an exceptional right which, due to its nature,

have standing to be one. Article 2 Code of Criminal Procedure (CPP) grants the standing to be *partie civile* to any person having, in wide terms, 'personally suffered from damage directly caused by offence'.

Over time courts have expanded the meaning of this provision. Whereas it initially only applied to the victim who suffered harm as a result of the offence, by the end of the 1980s the criminal chamber of the Cour de cassation had extended it to cover family members of the victim for personal damages which 'rebounded' or 'ricocheted', that is, was caused indirectly to them, even those suffered when the victim was still alive.[35]

It had already been extended, in 1913, by judicial recognition of the right of *unions* to defend the collective interests of the profession that they represent,[36] a right now expressly recognised by statute.[37]

The case law seemed to go even further by admitting civil actions brought by *organised professional boards*, where those boards have a collective interest in filing a compensatory action.[38] However, a more recent judgment appears to have limited this right to those boards having received legal authorisation to exercise this action.[39]

Finally, a line of cases even seems to accept the capacity of *associations* to file a civil action in connection with the goal and from the object of their mission.[40] This is surprising in so far as associations do not usually benefit from legal authorisation to act.[41]

3. Finality

There is a tension in how the *partie civile* operates. On the one hand, French law by default requires that the victim is bound by his choice

must be strictly confined within the limits set by Articles 2 and 3 of the Code of Criminal Procedure'. The same formulation was used in Cass. Crim., 25 September 2007, *Bull. crim.* n°220. All translations are the authors' unless otherwise noted.

35 Cass. Crim., 9 February 1989, *Bull. crim.* n°63, *Rev. sc. crim.* 1989, 742; *D.* 1989, 614.

36 Cass. ch. Réunies, 5 April 1913, *D.* 1914, 1, 65.

37 Art. L. 2132–3 Labour Code.

38 There exist special texts for professional bodies that are established by law (e.g., Art. L. 4122–1 Code of Public Health for doctors). However, the Cour de cassation has extended the rule to bodies that do not have a legislative origin: see Cass. Crim., 28 March 1991, *Bull. crim.* n°149; Cass. Crim., 4 November 1991, *Bull. crim.* n°391.

39 Cass. Crim., 2 May 2007, *Bull. crim.* n°111.

40 Cass. Crim., 14 January 1971, *Bull. crim.* n°14 for an association of Resistance fighters; Cass. Crim., 7 February 1984, *Bull. crim.* n°41 for an association protecting the public health, including as regards tobacco; Cass. Crim., 12 September 2006, *Bull. crim.* n°217 for an environmental protection association.

41 See the scenarios considered under Art. 2–1 ss. CPP.

(*electa una via*):[42] once the victim has brought his civil claim before the civil judge, he can no longer change his mind and file his action before a criminal judge (Art. 5 CPP). On the other hand, French law recognises that the civil judge is the 'natural' judge for a civil action and consequently allows a victim who first filed his compensatory claim before a criminal judge to change his mind and file his action before a civil judge.[43] In addition, Article 5 CPP creates an express exit route from a civil claim even after it has been brought in front of a civil judge. The claim can be withdrawn and filed before the criminal court where the public prosecutor initiated the criminal proceedings, so long as the civil judge had not yet given a decision on the substance of the case. The rule is also limited by jurisprudence of the Cour de cassation holding that the claim of the *partie civile* is not part of the *ordre publique*: therefore a plea of non-admissibility under Art. 5 CCP cannot thus be raised *ex officio*.[44] Because the rule is of private interest, only the parties concerned (those placed under judicial examination, accused or the person who is civilly liable) can invoke the rule and not the public prosecutor.

B. *Authority of* res judicata *(claim preclusion) of a criminal judgment on a civil case*

French law recognises that criminal offences produce civil consequences, such as the obligation to pay damages. As shown above, French law allows criminal courts to deal with some, but not all of these consequences. Even where the criminal court does not deal with such consequences, it still imposes some of its determinations on civil courts. The principle is that of the authority of *res judicata* of a criminal judgment on a civil case.[45] This means that a civil judge cannot contradict a decision made by the criminal judge on the elements noted in the criminal decision.[46] Those key elements, which cannot be disputed in a later civil court, are: the existence of a causal link between the defendant's act and the harm to the victim, of

[42] *Electa una via, non datur recursus ad alteram.* [43] Art. 426 CPP.

[44] Cass. Crim., 10 October 2000, *Bull. Crim.* n°290.

[45] The authority of *res judicata* is not grounded in texts but is enshrined in the decisions of the French courts. It was first implemented at the beginning of the nineteenth century but the seminal decision is that of Cass. Civ., 7 March 1855, *D.* 1855, I, 81 (*arrêt Quertier*).

[46] This is because the decision whether or not to prosecute (made by a criminal court) is based on the same elements as that of whether or not to allow the bringing of a civil action (whether this decision is made by a criminal or a civil court).

intentional or negligent misconduct, of the specific harm and of various material facts (as well as consequences to be drawn from such facts).

Conversely, there is no *res judicata* of the civil decision on the criminal court. Of course, in practice, it is unlikely that a civil claim will precede a criminal one since it is in the interest of the victim to become a *partie civile* in a criminal prosecution rather than wait and bring a later civil claim. It is nonetheless possible that a matter be litigated first before a civil court. Some authors who see in *res judicata* a simple rule on the proper administration of justice discuss the possibility of bi-lateralising it.[47] In fact, in other areas of the law, a civil trial precedes criminal proceedings, and the criminal judge is bound by the civil determinations. These are cases of preliminary questions (dealing with property rights in relation to immoveables[48] or citizenship issues),[49] which are discussed further below.

1. The scope of the *chose jugée*

While the rule of *chose jugée* was long stable since its creation by the courts over a hundred years ago, it has more recently been subject to change, particularly legislative change. Since the law of 10 July 2000 the authority of the criminal decision has been curtailed. It changed the law of *chose jugée* not only on a procedural level (in Article 4–1 CPP), but also on a substantive one (changes were made to Article 121–3 Code pénal in respect of non-intentional crimes). Since 2000 indirectly and non-intentionally caused harms in criminal law require one of two higher degrees of fault, *délibérée* (a deliberate breach of a protective rule) or *caractérisée* (misconduct creating a serious risk to another which the defendant must have known about). Therefore although a criminal judge may acquit on the grounds that there is no imprudence (essentially negligence and advertent recklessness), according to Article 4–1, a civil judge may nonetheless subsequently award damages for imprudent conduct under Article 1383 Civil Code. The underlying reasoning is that civil fault has a wider scope than criminal fault. Interpretations of the deeper meaning of this (rather confusing) text vary.

For some, the Law of 10 July 2000 abolished the principle of identity of civil and criminal fault.[50] Under this interpretation, the criminal decision still has the force of *res judicata* over later criminal judges, however it

[47] See A. Botton, *Contribution à l'étude de l'autorité de la chose jugée au pénal sur le civil*, vol. 49 (Paris: LGDJ, Bibliothèque des sciences criminelles, 2010).

[48] Art. 384 CPP. [49] Art. 29 Civil Code.

[50] On the principle of the unity of civil and criminal faults, see below.

can no longer be applicable in cases *imprudence*, since *criminal offences of imprudence* are different from the *civil wrong of imprudence.*

For others, the principle of unity of civil and criminal fault has not been abolished. In this sense, Article 4–1 is an exception to the rule of *res judicata* of criminal judgments on civil cases in matters of simple negligence having caused indirect damage and consequently allows the civil judge to go against the criminal decision only in this specific situation.[51]

Why was the law enacted? The Law came about because of perceived disadvantages for certain types of people who might indirectly be the cause of harm. This is especially pertinent in France given the wide rules of causation. Some of the force for change came particularly from numerous politically important town mayors who feared prosecution, at times driven by *parties civiles*, for accidents and disasters; the majority of these situations involved accidents due to breaches of health and safety rules attributable to senior office holders who had no real ability to prevent them.[52]

2. The basis of the rule

The basis for the *chose jugée* rule is controversial. At first, authors tried to justify this principle on the basis of the rule of civil procedure that requires a civil judge to stay any rulings where a criminal judge had not yet ruled on criminal proceedings.[53] This was difficult to justify, since suspension does not automatically equal subsequent priority. More recently, it has become commonly accepted that the rule stems from the pre-eminence of the criminal decision over the civil one. This pre-eminence would simultaneously attach investigative methods and offered proofs to the criminal judge as well as to the actual object of the criminal trial. The civil judge, who defends private interests, therefore could not contradict the criminal judge, whose duty it is to defend the wider public interest.[54] Yet French law is still unclear, with one author recently arguing that the rule is actually explained entirely by reasons related to the proper administration of justice in that it allows for the harmonisation of decisions and it

51 See A. Botton, *Contribution à l'étude de l'autorité de la chose jugée au pénal sur le civil*, n°403 s.

52 See, e.g. J. R. Spencer and Marie-Aimée Brajeux, 'Criminal Liability for Negligence – a Lesson from Across the Channel?' (2010) 59(1) *ICLQ* 9.

53 On this point, see below.

54 On developments in the basis of the pre-eminence of the criminal *chose jugée* over the civil, see, e.g., B. Bouloc, *Procédure pénale*, n°1181.

accelerates procedures.[55] This author then considered whether the bilateralisation of the rule would be possible. In order to rationalise the procedural process, it would indeed be more logical and effective to consider that the essential points of the decision of the court that first gave its decision will bind the court delivering a later decision. However, the same author dismissed this possibility by pointing out that acknowledging the pre-eminence of the civil *chose jugée* over the criminal would be contrary to the principle of the presumption of innocence, which must prevail in criminal trials.

3. The rule in practice

The rule works out differently depending on whether the defendant was convicted or acquitted in the criminal trial.

a. Consequences of a conviction After a conviction, the key matters described above (the characterisation of the facts, the existence of an offence, the causal link or the attribution of events to the responsible party) will be equally established in a civil court. Whether the civil claim is decided by the criminal judge (through a *partie civile*) or at a later stage in front of a civil judge, the outcome must be the same. One minor difference is that the criminal court dealing with a *partie civile* does not automatically have jurisdiction to deal with those who are jointly liable, while a civil court does.[56]

b. Consequences of an acquittal and discharge First, what can a criminal judge do with the civil party (*partie civile*)'s claim after an acquittal? Historically, where criminal proceedings to which an *action civile* was joined were heard before a Cour d'assises, the court retained the jurisdiction to grant compensation even after an acquittal.[57] However, this used not to be true for lower courts dealing with lower level offences; it is for this reason that Article 470–1 CPP was enacted. This article allows the *Tribunal correctionnel* jurisdiction to give a decision regarding a compensation claim, despite an acquittal on the criminal charge, *unless* the criminal prosecution had been initiated by the victim, *par voie d'action.* Its second paragraph provides protection for third parties who might be

[55] A. Botton, *Contribution à l'étude de l'autorité de la chose jugée au pénal sur le civil*, n°232 et seq.

[56] Cass. Crim., 16 October 2007, *Bull. crim.* n°244; 2 October 2012, *Bull. crim.* n°205.

[57] Article 372 CPP.

affected by such claim. Where third parties must be joined in proceedings, the case is referred to a civil court for a simplified procedure.[58] This is a further example of how French law connects tort and crime on a procedural level.

Second, what about a judge faced with an earlier acquittal in a criminal trial? The same basic position applies after an acquittal but the important issue is the reason why the defendant was acquitted. If the criminal judge acquits the defendant because he finds that the criminal offence was not constituted, or that at least the defendant did not carry it out, a civil judge giving a subsequent ruling on the issue of compensation cannot award damages without contradicting the criminal decision. If on the other hand, the defendant is acquitted because although the acts did occur, they were not in breach of the criminal law, the judge ruling on the civil action can still recognise the existence of a distinct wrongful act giving rise to civil, rather than criminal, liability. Thus, where a defendant is acquitted because neither *intention* nor *criminal negligence* were proven, compensation may nevertheless be awarded on the basis of the commission of a civil wrong such as one based on *civil negligence.* In this respect, criminal and civil negligence might bear slightly different meanings.

The authority of *res judicata* of criminal decisions on civil cases is reinforced by the rules for staying a proceeding, which we turn to next.

C. *Staying a civil claim*

Under Article 4 *alinéa* 2 CPP, a civil claim (including in theory an action with civil ends) before a civil court must be stayed if the same matter is being heard before a criminal court which has not yet reached a definitive verdict. This rule, '*le criminal tient le civil en l'état*', serves to guarantee compatibility between the civil decision on compensation for harm caused by the criminal offence, and the criminal decision ruling on the guilt arising from the commission of that offence.

[58] 'A court seized by the public prosecutor or by an investigatory jurisdiction of proceedings for an unintentional offence as meant by the second, third and fourth paragraphs of Article 121–3 of the Criminal Code, and which orders a discharge, remains competent to grant compensation, at the civil party's or his insurer's request, filed before the conclusion of the proceedings, for any damage resulting from the matters in respect of which the prosecution was brought, pursuant to civil law rules. However, where it is apparent that third parties bearing liability should be joined in the proceedings, the court refers the case to the competent civil court, by a decision that is not open to appeal. The civil court immediately examines the case according to a simplified procedure determined by Decree of the Council of State.'

This suspension rule is often linked to the rule on *res judicata*. Some authors have argued that without the effect of *chose jugée* there would be no point in suspending the civil claim.[59] But this cannot be a complete answer, if only because the *suspension rule* was acknowledged well before the *authority rule*.[60] Thus for other commentators, staying a proceeding can be explained by the 'concern of avoiding any influence of the civil decision on the criminal proceedings' or by 'the superiority of the criminal trial in preliminary matters'.[61] It is arguable that the suspension rule may reinforce the authority rule, but it also has an independent value.[62]

However, the suspension rule is open to abuse. Some *partie civile* claims have been brought for the sole purpose of suspending civil trials that were in progress and thus prolonging them, typically, the claimant hopes, beyond the interest of the other party to carry on.[63] As a consequence, legislation was enacted in order to restrict the effects of the suspension rule. According to the law of 5 March 2007,

> [T]he setting in motion of the public prosecution will not cause the suspension of judgments before the civil court for any actions other than the *action civile*, whatever the nature of such action, even if the decision to intervene at the criminal level is likely to influence, directly or indirectly, the outcome of the civil trial.[64]

What emerges from this text is that the staying of proceedings concerns only civil actions, and no longer applies to actions with civil ends.[65] The civil judge hearing a divorce request can therefore give a decision without having to wait for the criminal judge's ruling on issues of domestic violence. This is because the conditions for divorce are dependent neither on the existence of a criminal offence nor on the conviction of one of the spouses. However, even where the staying of proceedings is not obligatory,

[59] See, e.g., R. Merle and A. Vitu, *Traité de droit criminel*, vol. 2, 5th edn (Paris: Cujas, 2001), 1057; P. Conte and P. Maistre du Chambon, *Procédure pénale* (Paris: A. Colin, 2002), 439.

[60] A. Botton, *Contribution à l'étude de l'autorité de la chose jugée au pénal sur le civil*, n°155.

[61] Ibid., citing the authors defending those ideas. [62] Ibid., 96 s.; 206 s.

[63] A working group on 'Speed and quality of justice' issued a report on 15 June 2004 to the Minister of Justice (known as the Magendie Report after the chairman of the working group). The report stressed that because of the rule '*le criminel tient le civil en l'état*' many applications to join the criminal proceeding as a civil party were aimed to slow down a civil trial (in the broad sense that is to say both civil and commercial court or industrial tribunal). This report directly led to the amendment to Art. 4 CPP.

[64] Art. 4 *alinéa* 3 CPP.

[65] On the distinction between civil actions and actions to civil ends, see above.

the civil judge nevertheless has the option to decide to stay the proceedings in the interest of the proper administration of justice.[66]

The limitation of mandatory stays to civil actions, with an option offered to the civil judge for actions with civil ends, has led some authors to argue that there is a correlative decline of *res judicata*'s authority of criminal rulings on civil cases.[67] Since the civil judge is no longer required to stay proceedings whilst waiting for the criminal decision, some authors have suggested that the civil judge would no longer have to conform with the key elements of the criminal decision relevant to the civil claim. One author has successfully highlighted the unsatisfactory character of such proposition. The 2007 law did in fact reduce the instances in which the *res judicata*'s authority of criminal rulings on civil cases will be applied. Nevertheless, if a final decision has been taken by a criminal court, the civil judge must consider and comply with this decision when giving a decision on an action to civil ends. He cannot contradict an earlier criminal decision or cast doubt on a criminal conviction. For instance, if a defendant is convicted of theft in a final criminal decision, such decision could not be contradicted by the civil judge in a later civil action for the recovery of stolen goods.[68]

4. Substantive links between tort and crime

A. *Conditions of liability*

According to Articles 1382, 1383 and 1384 Civil Code,[69] civil liability arises from the following conditions:

(1) A wrong (in French terminology, an 'abnormal event'), whether it be caused by the defendant's fault, a thing under his custody or a person for whom he is responsible;
(2) which is imputed to a person;

[66] See: Cass. Civ. 1, 30 March 2004, *Bull. crim.* n°95.

[67] See: J.-H. Robert, 'L'autorité de la chose jugée au pénal sur le civil' (August-September 2007) 19 *Procédures*.

[68] On all these points, see A. Botton, *Contribution à l'étude de l'autorité de la chose jugée au pénal sur le civil*, n°369 s.

[69] Art. 1382 Civil Code: Any act whatever of man, which causes damage to another, obliges the one by whose fault it occurred, to compensate it.

Art. 1383 Civil Code: Everyone is liable for the damage he causes not only by his intentional act, but also by his negligent conduct or by his imprudence.

Art. 1384 *alinéa* 1 Civil Code: A person is liable not only for the damages he causes by his own act, but also for that which is caused by the acts of persons for whom he is responsible, or by things which are in his custody.

(3) a loss;
(4) a causal link between the event and the loss.

Conversely, criminal liability is generated only if:

(1) the fault meets the exact provisions of a text criminalising specific acts. The criminal code uses a tripartite classification: *crimes* (serious crimes), *délits* (major offences), *contraventions* (minor offences); for each category, there exist specific penalties;
(2) the text must describe:
    (a) the *actus reus* (the material element of the offence: an illegal behaviour, sometimes coupled with a result and a causal link between the two); and
    (b) the *mens rea* (the moral element of the offence: an intentional or negligent fault, depending on the text).

The apparent differences are deceptive; in practice, both sets of conditions are closely aligned. We will first analyse the similarity between criminal fault and the illicit behaviour. They are so close to the civil notion of abnormal fact, that a principle of unity between civil and criminal fault was once well established; however this principle no longer exists, at least not in its full form (Section 4.A.1.). Then we will study and compare the causal links (Section 4.A.2) and accountability rules (Section 4.A.3).

1. Principle of unity between fault in tort and criminal law?

a. Gradual erosion of the principle of unity between tortious and criminal fault There exists a sharp contrast between the civil law's general definitions of what a civil wrong is in Articles 1382 and 1383 Civil Code, and the criminal law which, according to the principle of legality ('*légalité criminelle*'), must always precisely stipulate the constituent elements of a criminal offence.

Historically, French law used to know a principle of unity between civil and criminal fault. This principle had been established in a 1912 case[70] to facilitate the payment of compensatory damages to victims of accidents, at a time when the number of mechanical accidents (most importantly industrial and road traffic accidents) was growing. The criminal judge would rarely hold that there had indeed been a criminal offence: the negligence or alleged breaches did not appear very serious as criminal offences. But acquittal, following a criminal trial, then prevented any compensation on a civil action, because of the rule of *res judicata* of

[70] Cass. Crim., 18 December 1912, *D.* 1915, I, 17; note L. Sarrut.

a criminal judgment on a civil case. In order to break away from that, the Cour de Cassation meant to compel the criminal judge to base the definition of criminal offences on that of civil wrongs. In that sense, the slightest departure from the ideal behavioural model of the *bon père de famille* (or the reasonable man) would constitute negligent behaviour, which could, under certain conditions, become a criminal offence.

While criminal offences must, in theory, be precisely defined, some of them do resemble the general provisions found in Articles 1382 and 1383 Civil Code. The law of 10 July 2000, discussed above, redefined what counts as recklessness and negligence in Article 121–3 Criminal Code, using a very broad wording. Specific criminal offences refer to the general definitions of Article 121–3: see for example Article 221–6 Criminal Code on manslaughter, which requires carelessness or negligence,[71] or else the law relating to unintentional injuries.[72] The objective components of criminal and civil fault are often defined in broad terms, and similar definitions were adopted for criminal and civil fault.

A few differences remain. By the 1930s, civil judges had adapted tort law to new social needs, because of both the industrialisation process which, by the end of the nineteenth century, had caused a correlative increase in the number of accidents in the workplace, and of the growing number of road traffic accidents in the 1920s and 1930s. The seminal case of *Jand'heur* introduced strict liability in tort law: this new standard of liability is not founded on fault but rather on the mere realisation of an abnormal event caused by a thing. The civil judges based their decision on the broadly worded Article 1384, *alinéa* 1 Civil Code. This new tort law regime, which imposes liability regardless of moral blameworthiness, was expanded and led to the adoption of a new, strictly objective, definition of civil fault.

In fault there were traditionally two components:

- An objective component: the behaviour is inappropriate and deviates from an ideal model of behaviour;
- A subjective, moral component: the judge can impute this behaviour to its author.

[71] Article 221–6 Criminal Code: Causing the death of another person by clumsiness, rashness, inattention, negligence or breach of an obligation of safety or prudence imposed by statute or regulations, in the circumstances and according to the distinctions laid down by Art. 121–3, constitutes manslaughter punished by three years' imprisonment and a fine of 45,000 Euro.

In the event of a deliberate violation of an obligation of safety or prudence imposed by statute or regulations, the penalty is increased to five years' imprisonment and to a fine of 75,000 Euro.

[72] Art. 222–19 Criminal Code.

Since it became possible for liability to arise for a wrong caused by a thing under the defendant's custody with no reference being made to moral liability, it logically also became possible for personal liability to arise with no reference to moral fault.

The civil law took a further step in 1968: the legislator decided that those suffering from a mental disorder should be civilly liable for civil fault.[73] The Cour de cassation handed down a similar decision regarding young children in 1984.[74] Civil fault is now defined only by one objective component: a behaviour deviating from that which would have been adopted under the ideal behavioural model (the prudent man rule: '*good family man*' or 'the reasonable man').[75] In French law, there is no longer an element of imputation to the individual: the subjective component in civil fault has been abandoned.

The same solution cannot be adopted in criminal law: subjective imputation is always required. Consequently, the definition of civil and criminal fault remains slightly different.

While there are breaches in the unity of tortious and criminal fault, tort and criminal law still work together. In practice, the criminal judge very often gives a decision on both the civil and the criminal fault on the basis of the law applicable in the respective areas of responsibility (tort and criminal law) without looking at the possible differences between both.

b. Intention in tort and criminal law The principle of unity of tortious wrongs and criminal offences has been affirmed for the tort of simple

73 Art. 414–3 Civil Code

74 Cass. Ass. Plén., 9 May 1984, n°80–93031, *Bull. crim.* n°2, n°80–93481, *Bull. crim.* n°3, n°82–92934, *Bull. crim.* n°4. See also H. Capitant, F. Terré and Y. Lequette, *Grands arrêts de la jurisprudence civile*, vol. 2, 12th edn (Paris: Dalloz 2008), n°193.

75 A law about equality between men and women is being discussed in Assemblée Nationale and Sénat since January 2014. The expression '*bon père de famille*' will be removed from the texts in the Civil Code and replaced with the concept of the 'reasonable man'. However, the result of this formal change in tort law is uncertain, since the use of the '*bon père de famille*' standard was always based on doctrine, not on the text of the Code. In this sense: 'The easiest way is to say that there is a fault when the conduct was not the one of a very carefull and diligent man' (H. Capitant and A. Colin, *Droit civil français*, vol. 2 (Paris: Dalloz 1948), n°307). Further: 'The fault is nothing more nor less than an error of his way, a defective behaviour – which normally shall be assessed in the light of the abstract model of the righteous man sure of his acts' (F. Geny, 'Risques et responsabilité', (1902) *RTD civ.*, 838). Also in this sense: 'The quasi delictual fault is an error on his part that a prudent person placed in the same external circumstances as the wrongdoer would not have committed', 'that the prudent and wise man' (H. and L. Mazeaud and A. Tunc, *Traité théorique et pratique de la responsabilité civile délictuelle et contractuelle*, vol. 3 (Paris: Sirey 1934), n°428).

negligence and for intentional wrongs, indeed, an intentional criminal fault is obviously a civil fault. But the concept of intention has been largely abandoned in both criminal and civil liability.

The concept of intention in criminal law or in tort law is precisely defined neither by the legislature nor by the judges. Only academics have endeavoured to define it, but they have not reached an agreement on its definitional elements. According to the academics,

- in tort law: intention is the willingness to act in a precise direction;
- in criminal law: intention is the willingness to act with a precise result in mind.

As far as proof of the criminal intention is concerned, case law is content to apply a presumption of intention for all *technical offences* (for offences under the highway code; in tax, planning, environmental, consumer, labour, company laws, etc.): according to the Cour de cassation, 'the crime's intentional element is implied by the report of the breach'.[76] For instance, in one case the treasurers of a workers' council had granted social loans to 182 employees who were on strike. They were charged with misuse of company assets, and were eventually acquitted by the Court of Appeal. The civil party appealed and the Cour de cassation overruled the Court of Appeal's decision; it required them to convict the treasurers, since, given their responsibilities, they were necessarily aware that they had exceeded their powers.[77] This knowledge establishes the *mens rea* element of the crime of misuse of company assets.

These presumptions of intention in criminal law, based exclusively on the establishment of a breach of criminal law, are severe: the defendant's (subjective) intention is effectively substituted by proof of his (objective) action. However, all higher courts (the Cour de cassation, the Conseil constitutionnel) affirm the legality of such presumptions and the European Convention on Human Rights and the principles of a fair trial apparently do not prevent their use.[78]

[76] Cass. Crim., 6 February 2007, n°06–82744.

[77] Cass. Crim., 30 June 2010, *Bull. crim.* n°121.

[78] Cass. Crim., 10 February 1992, *Bull. crim.* n°62, holding that it is not for Art. 6(2) European Convention for the Protection of Human Rights 'to limit the permissible forms of evidence of the domestic law but to require that the guilt is legally proven'; 'it would not bar the presumptions of fact or of law in criminal law, as soon as those presumptions . . . take into account the seriousness of the issue and preserve the rights of the defence.' See also: Cons. const., 16 June 1999, decision n°99–411 DC; *Salabiaku* v. *France* (1991) 13 EHRR 379; *Rev. sc. crim.*, 1989, 167, obs. Teitgen.

Nevertheless, proving subjective intention is still sometimes important elsewhere in the criminal law. The seriousness of the defendant's fault is a determining factor for the choice of the offence on the basis of which he will be prosecuted, and is taken into account by the criminal judge when pronouncing the sentence. On the other hand, the concept of intention has lost its importance in civil law. Civil liability pays little attention to the scale of fault. As a general principle, therefore, the seriousness of the fault does not matter; whether it is caused by intention or negligence, civil liability is the same. For example, the Insurance Code provides that

> [T]he insurer is liable for losses and damages caused by the persons for whom the insured party is held liable under civil law by virtue of article 1384 of the Civil Code, with no consideration being given to the nature and the seriousness of the fault.[79]

There remain a few rare exceptions to this principle, and the link between crime and tort is only relevant in only the first two of these exceptions:

- Under the law of vicarious responsibility, the seriousness of the employee's fault has an influence on the liability of the employer: since 2006, the offender employee who has committed a criminal offence is not afforded immunity against legal proceedings.[80]
- The concept of gross fault ('*faute lourde*') is seldom used in tort law cases. The seriousness of the fault does not depend on the defendant's state of mind, as is the case in criminal law; it is purely objective, being defined by quantitative or qualitative criteria: the number of faults, the seriousness of the risks or the nature of the violated rule (professional or essential rules).[81]
- In the field of contractual liability, the responsible person who has committed an intentional or serious fault will not be exonerated on the basis of the limitation of liability clause contained in the contract. Moreover, the wrongdoer will not be entitled to invoke Article 1150 Civil Code, which limits the liability of contractual parties for damage that was

[79] Art. L. 121–2 Insurance Code.

[80] Cass. Ass. Plén., 14 December 2001 (*arrêt Cousin*); *RTD Civ.* 2002, 109, obs. P. Jourdain: civil liability of an employee, found criminally liable for an intentional offence. Cass. Crim., 28 March 2006, *Bull. crim.* n°91 (*arrêt Etienne R.*), *RTD Civ.* 2007, 135, obs. P. Jourdain, *JCP* 2006, II, 10188, note J. Mouly: civil liability of an employee, found criminally liable for manslaughter, in a case featuring an indirect causal link. See also Figure 3.1.

[81] J. Lagoutte, *Les conditions de la responsabilité en droit privé*, Thèse Bordeaux 2012, n°419.

foreseeable at the time the contract was concluded.[82] Considering these hypotheses, the case law holds that in this situation, the 'seriousness of the behaviour' had to be demonstrated.[83]

- The same notion of serious fault is also used as the minimum level required to engage the liability of an employee to his employer.[84]
- A medical doctor is liable to a patient who is born with a disability, if this disability is linked to the doctor's gross negligence.[85]
- When an accident in the workplace stems from a gross fault committed by the employer, the victims are entitled to additional compensation.[86] The Cour de cassation specified that an employer has an *obligation de résultat* (an obligation to ensure that a given result is achieved)[87] to the employee in relation to the safety of the products made or used at work. The breach of this obligation always constitutes gross negligence when 'the employer was or should have been aware of the danger for the employee, and he did not take the necessary measures to prevent it'.[88] The employer cannot escape liability by proving that he was not at fault.[89]
- There is some degree of uncertainty over the issue of apportionment of liability where multiple wrongdoers are involved. Two options are explored in the case law: apportionment based either on the fault or the causative potency of each party's acts. It has been suggested by commentators that the Cour de cassation has dropped the first criterion,[90] relying solely on the causal link between the wrong and the losses in order to apportion liability. The second civil chamber of the Cour de

[82] Art. 1150 Civil Code: A debtor is liable only for damages, which were foreseen, or which could have been foreseen at the time of the contract, where it is not through his own intentional breach that the obligation is not fulfilled.

[83] Cass. Com., 29 June 2010, *Bull.* 115 (*arrêt Faurecia 2*), *D.* 2010, 1832, note D. Mazeaud: 'a gross fault may result not only from the infringement of a contractual obligation, even an important one, but may also be inferred from the severity of the debtor's misconduct'.

[84] Cass. Soc., 27 November 1958, *D.* 1959, jur. R. Lindon.

[85] Art. L. 114–5 Family and Social Assistance Code.

[86] Art. L. 452–1 Social Security Code.

[87] The French law of contract distinguishes between two types of obligations: *obligation de résultat* (for which a specific result must be achieved) and *obligation de moyens* (under which one must use all available means to achieve a given result; e.g. a doctor has an *obligation de moyens* to cure a disease). Different rules of evidence apply depending on whether the case involves an *obligation de résultat* or an *obligation de moyens.*

[88] Cass. Soc., 28 February 2002, 5 cases, *D.* 2002, jur. 2696, note X. Prétot; *RTD Civ* 2002, 310, note P. Jourdain.

[89] Cass. Soc., 19 October 2011, n°09–68272, *Rev. Droit du travail* 2012, 44, note M. Véricel.

[90] P. Jourdain, *RTD Civ.* 2010, 125.

cassation gave a ruling in this line in 2009, refusing to take into account the seriousness of the defendants' individual fault.[91] In that case, a stab wound victim who was undergoing a life-saving surgery was infused with contaminated blood. The French Blood Donors Organisation was found liable for 80 per cent of the damages resulting from the contamination; the author of the injury was only liable for 20 per cent. The French Blood Donors asked that the seriousness of the fault be taken into account: the author of the injury having stabbed the victim, his fault was much more serious. However, the Cour de cassation approved the judges whose sovereign decision had relied on the causal link criterion to apportion the damages. The Cour de cassation's position, however, has been inconsistent: just two years later, in 2011, it clearly used the fault criterion, asserting that '[i]n case of fault, the contribution of each responsible party is determined according to the gravity of their fault'.[92] The trial court, in its unfettered discretion, determines the size of these damage awards.

c. **Fault: particular cases, influences and porosity** The scope of the criminal law has gradually increased and become a matter of substantial importance since the 1970s: every moral value is protected both by civil means (usually by awarding compensation) and by criminal sanctions. There are a growing number of laws establishing criminal liability in France, for instance in the fields of environmental, planning and consumer law. At the same time, there has been scant decriminalisation: two examples are that of adultery in 1975 and of a few company law offences in 2001. A highly publicised January 2008 report (*rapport Coulon*)[93] argued for the decriminalisation of commercial and company law. While it contained a small note on making civil law more effective and attractive, the main argument was against the criminalisation of the relevant conduct. The report was buried after the summer 2008 financial crisis.

There exist a few direct equivalences between civil and criminal law in French law, but they are not paid much attention. In some instances, judges have set out the scope of each criminal and civil law, or discarded the use of some civil notions or definitions in the criminal field.

[91] Cass. Civ. 2, 19 November 2009, n°08–11622; *Bull.* n°279; *D.* 2009; *RTD Civ.* 2010, 125, obs. P. Jourdain.

[92] Cass. Civ. 2, 9 December 2011, n°09–71196, *Bull.* n°8: 'In case of misconduct, each party's contribution is evaluated only by reference to the severity of their respective misconduct.'

[93] See www.ladocumentationfrancaise.fr/rapports-publics/084000090/#book_sommaire (last accessed November 2014).

One example is the wrong of defamation, defined by Article 29 of the Law of 29 July 1881, which establishes both a tort and a criminal wrong (misdemeanour). However, it faces some definitional issues.[94]

- First, the civil chamber of the *Cour de cassation* ruled that any compensation must be based exclusively on the law of 29 July 1881,[95] and not on the ordinary Article 1382 Civil Code. This does not impact compensation itself, but has important procedural consequences: the prescription period is limited to three months,[96] and the bringing of a civil action is subject to a number of formal rules.
- Second, the criminal chamber of the *Cour de cassation* clearly delimited the line between the law of defamation and ordinary law: defamation is established only where the statement is detrimental to the defamed person's reputation. The judges apply two French law principles: that of '*légalité pénale*' and strict interpretation of the criminal law. The 1881 law on defamation therefore only applies where the person or corporation is named[97] or identifiable in the defamatory statement.[98]
- Most recently, in 2013, the civil chamber of the *Cour de cassation* has specified that claims can only be based on the statute of 1881 if the statement adversely affects the person's 'honour and reputation'; conversely, if it is the person's image that is affected, the action has to be based on ordinary law.[99] After 130 years, the respective fields of the law of 1881 and of Article 1382 seem to be becoming clearly defined.

Another example is the claim for disparagement of product or services. It must not be confused with defamation as it focuses on the product or service, not the company's reputation. Thus when a company seeks compensation for disparagement, the action is based on Article 1382 Civil Code. The defendant journalists or competitors usually claim that they tried to defame the company in order for the law of 1881 to apply,

[94] G. Viney, 'La sanction des abus de liberté d'expression', *D.* 2014, 787.

[95] Cass. Civ. 2, 10 March 2004, n°00–16934, *Bull.* n°114; Cass. Civ. 1, 11 February 2010, n°08–22111.

[96] Article 65 of the law of 29 July 1881.

[97] Cass. Crim., 19 January 2010, n°08–88243: a food critic compared wine to a 'cheap and bitter chemical drink'. The company producing the wine brought an action for public defamation against the editor of the journal. The alleged defamation was found not to be established because there nothing in the text was referring to a legal or a natural person.

[98] Cass. Crim., 5 January 2010, n°09–84328: the published allegations can be defamatory in spite of being presented in a disguised or dubitative format, and even if they are simply insinuated.

[99] Cass. Civ. 1, 27 February 2013, n°11–27751.

thus giving them the benefit of the short three month prescription period. In a similar case, the Cour de cassation adopted a restrictive definition of the wrong of defamation.[100]

Classically in criminal law, the criminal judge does not take into account the subtleties of the civil law. A few examples which might be relevant to a criminal prosecution are:

- the nullity of a marriage contract for the offence of bigamy;
- the nullity of a contract for the delivery of goods in case of later criminal proceedings for '*abus de confiance*' (breach of trust by misappropriating an object temporarily handed over to him);[101]
- the nullity of the security or the seizure which does not prevent the criminal judge from considering that the misappropriation of property that is pledged[102] or attached to secure the rights of a creditor[103] is established.

In all these examples, the criminal statute provides that there is an offence if the criminalised conduct (a bigamous marriage, a contract for the delivery of or the seizure of misappropriated goods) is established. The criminal judge may sentence a person convicted of such an offence even if a civil judge would consider that the criminalised behaviour (for example, the marriage), is invalid. Nevertheless, it would be false to say that the civil law has no impact whatsoever on the criminal law or a criminal sentence. For example, the question of whose property disputed goods are is essential and must be examined as a preliminary issue by the criminal judge, before ruling on any crime of theft (because a person cannot steal his own goods). In cases where the criminal judge is competent to determine this preliminary issue (except in the case of a right *in rem* in immovable property),[104] he gives his decision on the basis of civil law rules. The judge's application of such rules can, however, sometimes be original or at the very least more audacious than that of the civil

[100] Cass. Civ. 1, 5 December 2006, n°05–17710, *Bull.* n°532; *D.* 2008, 672 note V. Valette-Ercole. See also: Cass. Civ. 1, 27 November 2013, n°12–24651; T. Com. Paris, 22 February 2013, RG n°2012076280, where president of mobile network operator 'Free' asserted that the services of its competitors constituted 'fraud', 'racketeering', 'scam', their clients being described as 'cash cows'. This aggressive advertising strategy was in fact a clear disparagement and one of the competitors claimed damages under Article 1382 Civil Code. Free argued that the wrong constituted defamation rather disparagement and that the action was consequently time-barred. The Paris Commercial Court found that it was disparagement.

[101] Art. 314–1 Criminal Code.

[102] Art. 314–5 Criminal Code.

[103] Art. 314–6 Criminal Code.

[104] This is a preliminary ruling (per Art. 384 CPP).

judge. An example is a decision of the criminal chamber of the Cour de cassation which ruled that fraud corrupts everything, which thus causes the invalidity of contracts concluded on the goods subject to the dispute, which in turn establishes the offence of theft.[105]

There are also some situations in which the autonomy of the criminal law is not apparent. This is the case in relation to family immunities in respect of theft, for which the French Criminal Code uses civil categories[106] that are interpreted by the French criminal judge in the same way as they are interpreted by the civil judge. The persons benefitting by those immunities are the spouse (the immunity does not apply to divorced couples), parents in direct line and their spouse, brothers and sisters and their spouse. The fact that the criminal judge adopts restrictive concepts of civil family law is probably due to the fact that the criminal texts on immunities are exceptional, and 'an exception to the general theft statutes and, like all exceptions, have to be restricted to the terms which set it out'.[107] The criminal judge does not take any liberty with the precise notions of civil family law; this family immunity exception only applies to a person who is related to the claimant by a link as described in the statute.[108]

2. Causality between fault and loss

In civil law as well as in criminal law, a causal link must be proven between the wrongful act and the harm alleged. That is, the cause needs to be certain, rather than only potential; it must also be direct. Both these requirements are affirmed by the jurisprudence in both civil and criminal law. However, these clear principles are subject to exceptions and they are implemented in different ways in the two areas of law.

a. Existence of cause: the certainty of the causal link In tort law, the abnormal event (originating in either a person or a thing) must cause the loss complained of. Moreover, causality needs to be certain; a cause

[105] Cass. Crim., 30 October 2012, n°11–81266.

[106] E.g. on theft, Art. 311–12 *alinéa* 1 Criminal Code: No prosecution may be initiated where a theft is committed by a person:
1° to the prejudice of his or her ascendant or his or her descendant;
2° to the prejudice of a spouse, except where the spouses are separated or authorised to reside separately.

[107] Cass. Crim., 3 August 1901, *DP* 1904, 1, 157.

[108] Cass. Crim., 18 April 1857, *DP* 1857, 1, 226.

that is only potential or likely is not sufficient. The fault must have a 'certain and direct' link with the damage; for example, under product liability rules, the event caused by a defective product must have been 'the instrument of the damage, in any manner, even only for a part' in order for causation to be characterised as certain.[109] In cases where multiple causes are involved, when the precise role of each event is unknown or only likely, judges consider that there are 'no serious, precise and consistent presumptions to establish causation' and reject the victim's claim.

This requirement of certainty and directness features in case law across numerous areas of law. Various examples of its application can be cited: cases involving a victim who suffered from physical injuries but could not demonstrate that he subsequently suffered pecuniary damage;[110] in which a bank went bankrupt because it was excluded from a public market;[111] in which a man was wounded by a crowd after a football game because the crowd's evacuation had not been organised well enough by the owner of the underground.[112] In all these cases, the causal link between the wrongful act and the damage was not sufficiently certain. Whenever several facts can explain the origin of the damage, but the role of each is uncertain, judges consider that the causes are not serious, precise and consistent enough for causation to be established. This was so in a case where a fire broke out in a storage area caused by hydrocarbon pollution, because several hypotheses could explain the presence of polluting substances.[113] Another case in which the lack of serious, precise and consistent presumptions prevented causation from being established involved a farmer who noticed weight loss in his crop of lettuces. He argued that his damage was the result of the uncontrolled spreading of weed killer by his neighbour; however, the damage could also be due to drought and bad plantation.[114]

The case law is more flexible only in medical matters: judges have often circumvented the ordinary causation rules in order to allow an unfortunate patient to be granted compensation for his damage. Various

[109] Cass. Civ. 2, 13 September 2012, n°11–19941; 3 February 2011, n°10–13945; 13 October 2005, n°04–15624; 3 April 1978, *Bull.* n°110.

[110] Cass. Civ. 2, 7 February 2013: the functional permanent deficiency of 5 per cent caused by the doctor has marginal repercussions on the victim's profession; it should be attributed to the doctor himself, who acted recklessly.

[111] Cass. Civ. 2, 6 October 2011, n°10–25248: the corporation/bank was already in financial difficulties and even had the somewhat irregular government contract been adhered to, the bank would not have balanced its books.

[112] Cass. Civ. 2, 10 November 2009, n°08–19900, 08–19909.

[113] Cass. Civ. 2, 18 November 2010, n°09–72257.

[114] Cass. Civ. 2, 24 June 1998, n°96–19535.

techniques were used to ground liability in such cases. The judges either asserted that scientific proof of causation is not necessary and that a simple demonstration of 'serious, precise and consistent presumptions is sufficient';[115] or else resorted to the notion of loss of a chance, which is the disappearance of the possibility a favourable eventuality (in that sense, rules on loss of a chance counterbalance the uncertain character of causation since the eventuality it considers is the opposite of the certainty criterion usually used in rules on causation).[116]

There are also exceptions to these general causation rules. For instance, the Law of 5 July 1985 on road traffic accidents and compensation for personal injury establishes a very different system, since the award of compensation does not depend on notions of fault and causation. For this reason, and because compensation solely depends on the implication of a vehicle in a road traffic accident, this statute is not considered a system of liability, but rather as a system of compensation.

In criminal law, any requirement of causation is closely bound up with the precise wording of the provision in question: it must specify that harm being suffered by the victim is a constituent element of the offence. This is an expression of how criminal judges are bound by the texts through the principle of '*légalité pénale*'. There are a number of offences which do not require harm to be suffered. For instance, while the offence of murder[117] requires that the victim's death be reported, that of failing to offer assistance to a person in danger[118] is punishable regardless of whether the victim survived in the absence of any assistance on the part

[115] In the 'Distilbene cases' (Cass. Civ. 1, 24 September 2009, n°08–10081, *Bull.* n°186, *RTC Civ.* 2010, 111, obs. P. Jourdain; *RDSS* 2009, 1161, note J. Peigné; *JCP* 2009, n°44, 381, note S. Hocquet-Berg; *RCA* 2009 études 15, C. Radé; *RLDC* 2010, 3671, B. Parance; *D.* 2010. Pan. 49, obs. P. Brun and O. Gout. Also: Cass. Civ. 1, 6 October 2011, n°10–15759). Likewise, a medicine against gouty arthritis is well-known to cause Lyell syndrome, a serious skin illness (which looks like a generalised burn); moreover judges notice a temporal proximity between the exposure to the substance and the appearance of the damage (Cass. Civ. 1, 5 April 2005, n°02–11947 and 02–12065, *Bull.* n°173, *RTC Civ.* 2005, 607, obs. P. Jourdain; *JCP* 2005, II, 10085, note L. Grynbaum et J.-M. Job et I, 149, n°7, obs. G. Viney; *RCA* 2005, comm. 189, obs. C. Radé; *RDSS* 2005, 498, note A. Laude). In respect of the Isomeride produced by the Servier laboratory (Médiator) the judges' reasoning was based on the same body of serious, precise and consistent presumptions (Cass. Civ. 1, 24 January 2006, n°02–16648, *Bull.* n°34; *RTC civ.* 2006, 323, obs. P. Jourdain; *JCP* 2006, I, 166, obs. P. Stoffel-Munck).

[116] Cass. Civ. 1, 22 March 2012, n°11–10935, *Bull.* n°68; Cass. Civ. 1, 14 October 2010, n°09–69.195, *Bull. civ.* I, n°200, *RTD Civ.* 2011, p. 128, obs. P. Jourdain, *D.* 2010, p. 2682, obs. P. Sargos.

[117] Art. 221–1 Criminal Code. [118] Art. 223–6 Criminal Code.

of the defendant. Various offences do not even require that a potential victim exist (e.g., failure to wear a seat belt, or the failure to declare a construction site under planning law, etc). In fact, the number of so-called 'obstacle offences' has grown in the past decades. These criminal offences are constituted solely by an act; no damage (not even in the form of endangerment) is required.[119]

In the offences for which harm is a constituent element, criminal law enforces stricter standards in relation to causal certainty. Judges must be certain of the cause of the harm, even in cases of gross negligence;[120] any causal uncertainty prevents the defendant from being found guilty. Consider as an example the following case, which involved a prosecution for homicide.[121] A woman went to a clinic to undergo a liposuction. No preoperative tests had been undertaken, and no anaesthetist was present during the operation. The patient got anxious; in order to calm her down the doctor injected her with 20 mg of a sedative, causing her to fall into a coma and eventually die. The doctor was prosecuted on the basis of various faults that he had committed, but was eventually discharged. Indeed, it was impossible to ascertain whether the complication had been caused by the bad conditions in which the injection was realised, or by the patient's hypersensitivity.

Certainty of the causal link between fault and damage is a condition of criminal liability, and the criminal judge refuses to extend liability in the same way the civil judge does. As such, a criminal judge could not sentence a doctor for injury by negligence if the doctor's fault had only caused the victim to lose a chance of recovery; this is because the causal link between the doctor's negligence and the victim's health deterioration is not certain enough. On the other hand, the same judge ruling on the

[119] E.g., Art. 322–4-1 Criminal Code: The act of collectively settling with the aim of establishing residence, even temporarily, on land belonging either to a commune which has conformed to the obligations incumbent on it in accordance with the departmental plan provided for by Art. 2 of Law no. 2000–614 of 5 July 2000 relating to the reception and settlement of travellers or which is not included in this plan, or to any other owner apart from a commune, without being able to prove the owner's permission or the permission of whoever holds the right to use the land, is punished by six months' imprisonment and a fine of 3,750 Euros.

Where the settlement is comprised of motor vehicles, they may be seized, with the exception of vehicles designed for residential purposes, with a view to their confiscation by the criminal courts.

[120] Art. 121–3 Criminal Code

[121] Cass. Crim., 14 May 2008, n°08–80202, *Bull. crim.* n°112. On the requirement of a causal link that is certain, see also: Cass. Crim., 22 March 2005, n°04–84459 or 9 March 2010, n°09–80543, *Bull. crim.* n°49.

victim's civil interests may award compensation based on the lost chance of a better medical outcome.[122]

Even criminal cases sometimes depart from the principle of causal certainty. In particular, a jurisprudential theory has been developed in cases where all the members of a group have assaulted a victim. According to the theory of the 'unique scene of violence', in those cases where the final result cannot be attributed to one participant alone, the Cour de cassation considers all members as authors of the offence, although the causal link between each participant's wrong and the victim's harm cannot be precisely affirmed.[123] This rule has been expanded to other offences such as collective negligence in the medical field[124] and to cases of pollution perpetrated by several authors.

[122] E.g., see Cass. Crim., 3 November 2010, n°09–87.375, *Bull. crim.* n°170, in which a woman ending her pregnancy was allowed to a clinic in November 1998. Her condition suddenly deteriorated. The doctor decided to conduct an emergency caesarean and she was put into reinforced observation by the anaesthesiologist. Her condition kept deteriorating and she was transferred to intensive care. She died three days later. Judges considered that the patient was victim of fulminant HELLP syndrome. The care, as precocious as it could be, does not always allow avoiding a fatal issue. Criminal liability was not characterised: 'it is not demonstrated with certainty that the doings (of the doctors) have provoked the patient a loss of chances to survive', 'as a result there is no certain causation between the reproached acts and the death'. Nevertheless, the doctor's civil liability was characterised 'given the always uncertain prognosis of HELLP syndrome and delays in care of the patient have probably contributed to the loss of chances to survive' and 'the disappearance of the probability of a favourable event constitutes a loss of chances'.

[123] Cass. Crim., 10 April 1975, n°74–92978, *Bull. crim.* n°90: 'when the violence and assault have been voluntarily and simultaneously committed by several defendants during a unique crime scene, the offence can be estimated as a whole. It is not necessary for the judges to precise the nature of the violence perpetrated by each of the defendants on each of the victims.' See also Cass. Crim., 2 September 2005, n°04–87046, *Bull. crim.* n°212, *RSC* 2006, 69, obs. Y. Mayaud: 'The defendants (are) guilty of intentional gang assault; indeed, the offence of violence can be constituted, apart from any material contact with the body of the victim, by any act or behaviour likely to cause an physical or physiological injury on the victim, characterised by an "emotional shock" or a psychological disturbance.' Similarly, Cass. Crim., 12 May 2009, n°08–86734: 'destructions and deteriorations committed by J.R, T. O., W. D., and J. A. have only been possible because they occurred during a gathering attributable to the defendants; given the number of participants, their determination and the throwing of various objects, kept away the police and allowed the facts generating the damage caused to administrative vehicles'.

[124] In the medical field: 'during the post-operative phase, the midwife was free to prescribe or interrupt, under her own responsibility, the administration of ocytocics, comprised in the list of medicines midwifes are allowed to prescribe. Furthermore, existence of the faults attributed to the gynaecologist during the operation of evacuation of the uterus is not sufficient to exclude the eventuality of the faults committed by the midwife during the operations or the surveillance after the delivery': Cass. Crim., 21 Oct. 1998, *Bull. crim.* n°270, *RSC* 1999, 320, obs. Y. Mayaud.

b. Direct or indirect causality At first sight, the existence of a direct causal link between the fault and the damage appears to be a condition of liability in both criminal and tort law. The Code of Criminal Procedure provides that only the person who has personally suffered damage directly caused by the offence can join the criminal proceeding as civil party to claim damages.[125] But the concepts of direct victim and direct causal link between fault and damage differ.

In practice, both the general part of the Criminal Code, and the provisions setting out specific offences, have been held by courts to feature direct, and at times even, indirect, harm. While civil cases repeat the requirement that a direct causal link must be proven, they often do not enforce it.

In criminal matters, the notion of direct or indirect causal link is mostly used in cases involving negligence or recklessness (such as in cases of manslaughter or unintentional injuries). In July 2000, a new statute changed the definition of the criminal fault of recklessness or negligence, and drew a distinction between indirect and direct causal links in Article 121–3 Criminal Code. This novelty, which puzzled academics, was described by one author as *une plaisanterie pour glossateurs à l'imperturbable sérieux*, 'a joke for glossators with unflappable seriousness'.[126] At present it appears very difficult to precisely define the conditions under which a causal link will be characterised as either direct or indirect.

In an effort to decriminalise instances of petty negligence in cases of manslaughter or personal injury, the text provides that where the causal link between the negligence and the loss is indirect, the negligence will not constitute a punishable offence. According to Article 121–3 Criminal Code:

- If the involuntary fault is an indirect cause of the loss, the offender can be condemned only if his actions constitute serious negligence or recklessness in paragraphs 3 and 4 of Article 121–3.
- If the involuntary fault is the direct cause of the loss, the offender can be condemned regardless of the gravity of the fault.

Defining direct and indirect causality proved to be very difficult for judges. The statute's preparatory works reveal that the legislator's intent was

[125] Article 2 CPP: Civil action aimed at the reparation of the damage suffered because of a felony, a misdemeanour or a petty offence is open to all those who have personally suffered damage directly caused by the offence.

[126] P. Conte, *D.* 2004, 1336.

to decriminalise cases of negligent conduct by mayors. The legislator defined direct causal fault as the closest event in the cause and effect relationship, thus suggesting that all other events must be treated as an indirect form of causal fault, dealt with less severely by the judge. Judges, however, rejected this interpretation. The Cour de cassation thus considers that a direct causal link is established where an event is decisive; that is, where it is a determining parameter explaining the harm. Once this direct causal link is established, the judge is free to select other events in the cause and effect relationship; these will be instances of an indirect causal link.

In criminal law, liability can therefore arise whether the causal link between the fault and the loss is direct or indirect. This is illustrated in various statutes. For example, in environmental criminal law the offence of water pollution by discharge of harmful products is condemned regardless of whether the discharge is 'direct or indirect'. A direct discharge is not a necessary condition for liability to arise, and the judge can find the defendant guilty even where the product was released in the immediate vicinity of a river. Some examples are: pesticides sprayed on the riverbank; chemical products being discharged on a land thereby polluting the underground water table; cyanide tailings discharged in factory washbasins, which are in turn released in the sewage treatment plant, eventually polluting a river.[127]

In tort law, while the direct causal link is officially a requirement for liability to arise, in practice it does not add a great deal since the notion of a 'direct' link is similar to that of a 'certain' causal link:[128] what is at stake is the existence of a sufficient causal connection.[129] In other situations, the direct link is related to the question of the existence of harm: cases

[127] Cass. Crim., 24 January 2012, n°11–84564.

[128] E.g., Cass. Civ. 3, 19 February 2003, n°00–13253: a tenant caused a fire which destroyed part of the building's roof. The roof was badly sheeted and another tenant suffers water damage. The fire was not the direct cause of the water damage, whereas the causal link with the bad sheeting was certain. Cass. Civ. 2, 27 January 2000, *Bull. civ.* n°20; *JCP* 2000, I, 241, obs. Viney, II 10363, obs. Conte; *RTD Civ.* 2000, 335, obs. Jourdain: a woman underwent eye surgery after a car accident. During the surgery, her left eye was injured and became blind. Since the surgery was necessary because of the car accident, the car crash was a necessary cause of the blinding of her left eye, as it was a certain and necessary cause. See also: Cass. Civ. 2, 7 December 1988, *Bull. civ.* n°246: a man forgot a company's cheque book in a telephone box. It was later used and three cheques were issued. The first man's negligent act did not have a direct link with the company's loss, therefore the causal link was held to be uncertain.

[129] The connection is made between a direct and certain causal link and the theory of *équivalence des causes*, the French approach to 'but for' causation in Cass. Civ. 2, 27 March 2003, *Bull. civ.* n°76, *JCP* 2004, I, 101, G. Viney.

and academic commentary use the notion of direct link in relation to the issue of non-pecuniary loss suffered by secondary victims ('*par ricochet*'). Some academics consider that the term direct should be removed from the vocabulary of tort law as being effectively useless.[130]

3. Accountability or imputation

The issue of accountability will be examined in three areas: in relation to a very young person or one who suffers from a mental disorder (Section 4.A.3.a); in the context of a claim where a third party other than the defendant caused or contributed to the realisation of the wrong (Section 4.A.3.b); finally, we will look at the conditions under which liability can be escaped on the basis of exonerating circumstances (Section 4.A.3.c).

a. Age and mental disorder French law is based on written statutes and general principles such as the principle of full reparation in tort law or that of '*légalité pénale*' in criminal law; but it does not use concepts such as 'fairness', 'equity' or other similarly imprecise terms. The notion of capacity is used both by the civil and criminal law, but it is not technically a requirement for civil liability to arise.

French tort law does not seek to gauge the relative merits of the two parties. In essence, all citizens are liable for their civil fault, whether their fault is interpreted objectively (rather than morally) as the failure to meet the standard of conduct of the '*bon père de famille*', or is caused by goods that they own or keep. It has already been noted above that in 1968 the legislator decided that people suffering from a mental disorder are liable for civil wrongs causing harm.[131] In 1984, the Cour de cassation extended this regime to children.[132] In practice, there are few cases in which children have been sued, but it has happened in some instances where the children were covered by a form of specific insurance. The victim's own fault or contributory negligence, often in play in such cases,

[130] P. Brun, 'Causalité juridique et causalité scientifique: de la distinction à la dialectique' *D.* 2012, 112: 'We fail to see what could lead the judges to do the complete opposite of the objective and natural observations suggest to do, and to renounce to move up to the end of the chain of cause and effect . . . This requirement is a pathetic attempt to set limits to the causal link concept, in the form of a tribute to science.'

[131] Art. 414–3 Civil Code: A person who has caused damage to another when he was under the influence of a mental disorder is nonetheless liable to compensation.

[132] Cass. Ass. Plén., 9 May 1984, n°80–93031, *Bull.* 2, n°80–93481, *Bull.* 3, n°82–92934, *Bull.* 4: H. Capitant, F. Terré and Y. Lequette, *Grands arrêts de la jurisprudence civile.*

will entail a reduction in the size of the damage award, since his own act was a cause of the damage.

Similarly, French criminal law does not define a minimum age from which an individual can be held criminally responsible. However, in order to convict a child, Article 122–8 Criminal Code requires that the court establish that he was sufficiently aware of the wrongful nature of his actions (that he had the required '*discernement*'). While a few academics have argued that children under the age of eighteen are in fact protected by a 'principle of irresponsibility',[133] this proposition finds no support in statutory provisions. As such, a 1945 ordinance assumes that a child can understand his actions and can therefore be prosecuted before a criminal court, albeit a special one. Article 1–2 of the ordinance, mirroring the language used in Article 122–8, refers to the punishment applicable to a minor who is held 'accountable' for an offence. A 1956 case of the Cour de cassation's criminal chamber noted, in the context of the ordinance, that:

> In accordance with the general principles of law, the minor who is involved in the material act must have understood and wanted this act; all offences, even unintentional ones, presuppose that the perpetrator acted with intelligence and willingness.[134]

If convicted, the minor's punishment will differ from that of an adult. Its primary objective will be educational, thus entailing 'measures of protection, assistance, supervision and education according to the conditions laid down by specific legislation', according to Article 122–8 Criminal Code.

Similarly, a person who is suffering from a mental disorder can be held criminally responsible, as long as he is able to understand the gravity of the act when he did it. Since 1992, Article 122–1 Criminal Code has drawn a distinction between psychological and neuropsychological disorders, depending on the effects of the said disorder:[135]

[133] E.g., G. Stefani, G. Levasseur and B. Bouloc, *Droit pénal général*, (Paris: Précis Dalloz 2000), n°449.

[134] Cass. Crim., 13 December 1956, *B.* 240 (*arrêt Laboube*); J. Pradel and A. Varinard, *Grands arrêts du droit pénal général* (Paris: Dalloz 2012), n°43.

[135] Art. 122–1 Criminal Code: A person is not criminally liable who, when the act was committed, was suffering from a psychological or neuropsychological disorder which destroyed his discernment or his ability to control his actions.

A person who, at the time he acted, was suffering from a psychological or neuropsychological disorder which reduced his discernment or impeded his ability to control

– Where the disorder has entirely removed his ability to understand or control his actions, the defendant cannot be held criminally responsible; however, this does not prevent him from being held civilly liable.
– Where the mental disorder only reduced or impeded his ability to understand or control his actions, the offender remains liable, but the judge has the discretion[136] to reduce the sentence and/or provide for different penalties (such as a suspended sentence, probation, medical treatment, etc.).

b. Vicarious and accessory liability Some of the academic debates about the purposes of French tort law are most fully explored in the context of vicarious and accessory liability. In tort law, while some academics argue that civil liability is based on a theory of risk,[137] others consider that it can only be explained by a theory of '*garanti*'[138] whereby all personal injuries are to be compensated regardless of risk. Yet another group of scholars argue that a citizen has to compensate all losses caused by an abnormal behaviour or abnormal thing that is in his sphere of authority. In that sense, a person is liable for his own conduct, for the things that are in his custody, and for the persons who are under his authority.[139] In criminal law, although the main focus is on the individual's fault, there also exist risk-based liability explicative theories. In particular, the risk-based theory may explain the criminal liability of employers and legal persons.

i. Liability of the employer In tort law, an employer is liable for harm caused by his employees and put more broadly, rules on liability of principals for the acts of their agents require neither the agent's nor the

his actions, remains punishable; however, the court shall take this into account when it decides the penalty and determines its regime.

[136] Cass. Crim., 31 March 1999, *B.* 66; Cass. Crim., 20 October 1999, *B.* 228: 'Article 122–1 *alinéa* 2 does not provide grounds for the reduction of a sentence.'

[137] R. Saleilles, *Les accidents du travail et la responsabilité* (Paris: Libraire Nouvelle de Droit et de Jurisprudence 1897); L. Josserand, *De la responsabilité du fait des choses inanimées* (Paris: A. Rousseau 1897).

[138] B. Stark, *Essai d'une théorie générale de la responsabilité civile considérée en sa double fonction de garantie et de peine privée* (Paris: L. Rodstein 1947).

[139] N. Dejean de la Bâtie, in C. Aubry and C. Rau, *Droit civil français*, vol. 2, 8th edn (Paris: Litec 1989), n°1.

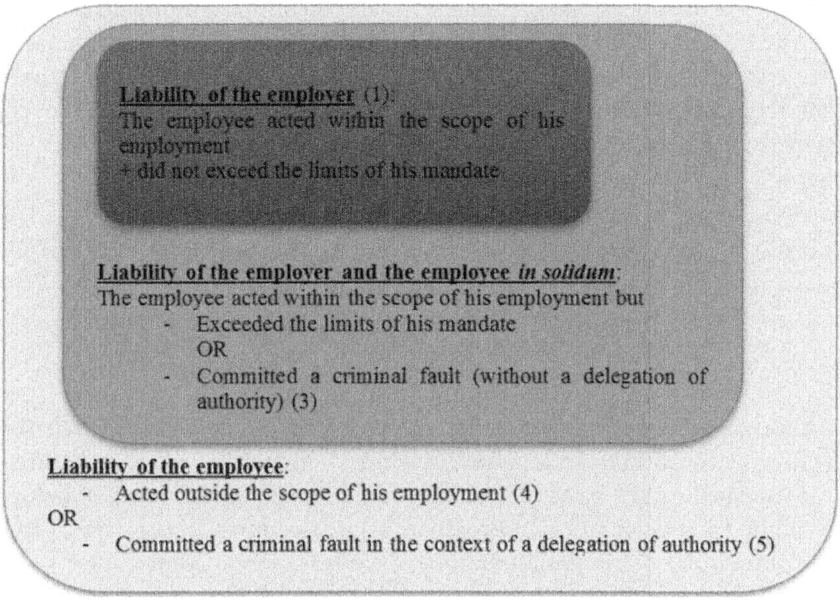

Figure 3.1 Vicarious liability of the employer (or the principal)

(1) Cass. Ass. Plén., 15 February 2000 (*arrêt Costedoat*); Cass. Com., 12 October 1993 (*arrêt Rochas*).
(2) Cass. Civ. 2, 17 March 2011, n°10–14468.
(3) Cass. Ass. Plén., 14 December 2001 (*arrêt Cousin*).
(4) Cass. Crim., 16 February 1999, *Bull.* 23.
(5) Cass. Crim., 28 March 2006, *Bull.* 91.

principal's fault.[140] Depending on the circumstances, liability may be either shared or exclusive (see Figure 3.1). The employee acting within the scope of his employment without exceeding the limits of his mandate is protected by immunity while the principal (employee) remains liable.

In theory, vicarious liability is unacceptable in criminal law. Indeed, Article 121–1 Criminal Code states that '[n]o one is criminally liable

[140] Article 1384 Civil Code: A person is liable not only for the damages he causes by his own act, but also for that which is caused by the acts of persons for whom he is responsible, or by things which are in his custody. . . .

The father and mother, in so far as they exercise parental authority, are jointly and severally liable for the damage caused by their minor children who live with them.

Masters and employers, for the damage caused by their servants and employees in the functions for which they have been employed.

except for his own conduct', and for every criminal offence to be constituted Article 121–3 requires that a form of fault (such as intention or negligence) be established. Nevertheless, since the 1950s at least, case law has recognised a form of vicarious criminal liability of employers (whether they be company managers or legal persons):

> [W]hile in principle, no person shall be punishable except for his own conduct, criminal liability may however arise vicariously in those exceptional cases where statutory duties impose that direct action be exercised on the acts of an assistant or a subordinate... Particularly in those industries subject to health and safety regulations, criminal liability lies primarily with the managers because the operating conditions and the exploitation methods of the industry are personally imposed on them.[141]

Although academics suggest that the employer is only liable when the employee committed an involuntary fault,[142] in many cases, their liability was engaged on the basis of their employee's wilful misconduct in failing to abide by official rules and regulations. Cases most illustrative of this phenomenon raise issues in relation to environmental regulations,[143] the pharmaceutical sector[144] and the award and use of bars and pubs' liquor licences.[145]

How can this form of criminal liability be reconciled with Article 121–1 Criminal Code? For one thing, it is not true vicarious liability. If the employer cannot prove that the employee had the power and the necessary skills to fulfil the employer's obligations, he is found guilty. It might even be said that the manager is *ex officio* responsible for the business's operational aspects and that he must consequently take all the measures necessary to comply with the applicable regulatory standards. He is held criminally responsible for a prior objective misconduct of the employee. In this sense, it is not really a form of vicarious liability, but it is rather one of criminal responsibility to ensure sound operations which was breach by another person's material act. The moral fault (which is essential for criminal liability to arise) lies with the employer. In addition,

141 Cass. Crim., 28 February 1956, *JCP* 1956, II, 9304.

142 H. Matsopoulou, 'La "faute pénale" du préposé' *RCA* March 2013, 16.

143 Most importantly in relation to issues of pollution of a river by spilling: Cass. Crim., 28 February 1956, *JCP* 1956, II, 9304, de Lestang; *D.* 1956, 391, Grands arrêts n°37; Cass. Crim., 27 July 1970, *Bull. crim.* n°250; Cass. Crim., 3 April 2001, n°00–84176 and n°00–84190. On the perperator's liability: Article L. 160–1 s. Environmental Code.

144 Cass. Crim., 8 February 2012, n°11–80495; Cass. Crim., 5 May 2009, n°07–88598.

145 Cass. Crim., 5 April 2006, n°05–85031.

the liability presupposes the involvement of the employer in that task. The employer's criminal liability is based on a presumption that can be rebutted by proving that he delegated authority to the employee:

> Unless otherwise provided by the law, the manager who did not personally take part in the infringement can avoid his criminal responsibility if he proves that he had delegated his powers to a person who had skills, authority and necessary means.[146]

ii. Liability of legal persons An explicative theory similar to that based on risk taking can also explain the fact that criminal liability is imposed on legal persons. This was one of the major changes brought about by the 1992 Criminal Code, which also introduced more general changes to criminal liability. According to Article 121–2, '[l]egal persons are criminally liable for the offences committed on their account by their organs or representatives'.[147] However, a legal person is merely the result of an organisational technique, whereas one of the key elements of criminal liability is moral accountability, or the consciousness of relative values of 'right' and 'wrong'. As a result, moral accountability in cases involving legal persons can only be established by referring to its managers' actions.

It is therefore necessary to establish an intentional or negligent material act committed by a natural person as part of the legal person's enterprise, although the identity of the said natural person may be difficult to ascertain. As such, in a recent case of corporate manslaughter, the Cour de Cassation ruled that it was not necessary to indicate the identity of the natural person who had been reckless about the victim's death.[148] What must be established is that the wrong was committed by an organ or representative, and on account, of the legal person.[149] The criminal liability of legal persons can be analysed as a form of vicarious liability. The Cour de cassation's criminal chamber has long stated that '[e]very penalty is personal, except for the cases expressly excluded by law; it cannot be imposed on a legal being, which can only be civilly liable'.[150]

[146] Cass. Crim., 11 March 1993, *Bull. crim.* n°112.

[147] Article 121–2 Criminal Code: Legal persons, with the exception of the State, are criminally liable for the offences committed on their account by their organs or representatives . . .
The criminal liability of legal persons does not exclude that of any natural persons who are perpetrators or accomplices . . .

[148] Cass. Crim., 18 June 2013, n°12–85917.

[149] Cass. Crim., 11 April 2012, n°10–86974.

[150] Cass. Crim., 10 Jan. 1929, *Bull. crim.* n°14; Cass. Crim., 6 July 1954, *Bull. crim.* n°250.

iii. Complicity The notion of complicity is specific to the criminal law. While the accomplice is sometimes described as a 'secondary participant', his is never described as a form of 'secondary responsibility'. One reason for this may be that in French criminal law the instigator of an offence is treated as an accomplice, but can at times be more dangerous than the main wrongdoer. The legislator thus created some statutes incriminating specific forms of provocation in order to strengthen the penalties applicable to dangerous forms of instigations.[151]

The French law of civil liability, on the other hand, ignores the notion of 'complicity'. In some cases, an accomplice is possibly already a wrongdoer: for example an incitor in criminal law is an accomplice, while in tort law he is treated as a wrongdoer that contributed to the damage. However, all defendants sharing responsibility for the wrong are held jointly and severally liable and must pay damages (as per the principle of responsibility *in solidum*). Each defendant is liable up to the full amount of the damages award regardless of the basis of each defendant's liability (one may be liable for a wrong caused by a thing under Article 1384, and another under the ordinary fault liability rule of Article 1382). Where the claimant receives payment from one of the defendants, that defendant may request that the other defendants contribute to their share of liability. That share is divided in equal sums where liability is based on Article 1384, and is proportional to each defendant's relative wrongdoing where liability is based on Article 1382. It is the trial court, in its unfettered discretion, which determines these amounts.

c. **Defences** There exists a body of defences that are common to civil and criminal law. Known as '*faits justificatifs*' in criminal law, they can also impact civil liability. Such defences include the existence of a legal directive or the command of a legitimate authority, the state of necessity, self-defence and duress (the equivalent of the civil law concept of '*force majeure*'). These defences are considered in determining the existence of civil fault. Unlike in criminal law, the existence of a defence in tort does

[151] Art.227–19 Criminal Code on the direct provocation of a minor to regular or excessive consumption of alcoholic beverages. See also Arts. 227–18, 227–18–1 and 227–21 of the same Code on the direct provocation of a minor to make unlawful use of drugs, to transport, keep, offer or give controlled drugs, or to commit a felony or a misdemeanour. Further, Art. 221–5-1 which involves making another person offers or promises, or offering him gifts, presents or benefits of any kind to induce him to commit an assassination or a poisoning. Finally, we can note the provisions relating to provocations through the press and audio-visual means (Art. 24 of the Law 29 July 1881).

not necessarily prevent liability from arising; in particular, they may not be applicable in cases involving no-fault civil liability.

Self-defence may appear as a mechanism similar to exemption of liability due to the victim's own fault. However, the reasoning differs in criminal and civil law. In criminal law, self-defence is an objective ground of exemption: its effect is that no liability arises because no offence was established (for academics, the offence was in fact committed but cannot be punished). In civil law on the other hand, the reasoning is more balanced. The defendant is not found to have committed a *faute* (because he acted as a '*bon père de famille*'), whereas the victim is found to have been at fault by attacking first; the judge can therefore decide not to award damages. In other cases, the judge may reduce the size of the damage award and/or rule that liability was shared between the parties if the response was disproportionate[152] or delayed;[153] these two factors prevent liability from being escaped under the rules of criminal law.

There is therefore a substantial link between the defences in tort and criminal law; however they operate differently within each area of law. That is, '*faits justificatifs*' are used for their appropriate effect and as specific concepts in criminal law whereas the components of tort law themselves ask the questions that are answered by discrete defences in criminal law.[154]

B. *Damages and punishments*

The purposes of criminal law (punishment, social rehabilitation, preventing recidivism) and tort law (compensation for losses) are in a state of confusion. Parallels may be drawn between both, leading to further confusion as to the consequences sought by bringing either civil or criminal proceedings.

1. When damages reach punishments

There exist junction points between the purposes of civil and criminal liability and the consequences of civil and criminal proceedings; in particular, it appears that modern French tort law is not restricted to compensatory goals, but can also be used to punish a defendant.

[152] Cass. Civ. 2, 3 November 1972, *Bull.* 184.

[153] CA Paris, 22 June 1988, *D.* 1988, IR, p. 244.

[154] For more details, see G. Viney, P. Jourdain and S. Carval, *Les conditions de la responsabilité*, 4th edn (Paris: LGDJ, 2014), n°556 s.

The concept of punitive damages is debated in France. Three draft reform projects proposed to integrate punitive damages in the Civil Code; part of the damage award would go to the victim, the other part to the state.[155] In 2010, the Cour de Cassation accepted the principle of punitive damages by recognising a punitive damage award granted by an American court.[156] However, the American judgment was held not to be enforceable since the damage award was 'manifestly disproportionate' to the losses and to the breach of contract. There are several indications that punitive damages are in fact a criminal penalty, applied by a civil judge.

The first indication is the court's reference to the principle of proportionality, which arises from Article 8 Declaration of the Rights of Man and of the Citizen 1789, and according to which '[t]he law shall provide for such punishments only as are strictly and obviously necessary'.[157] This is a criminal law principle, but which the Cour de cassation nonetheless referred to in a civil case. The award of punitive damages thus depends on compliance with criminal principles. Recently, the Cour de cassation stated that the principle of proportionality is a matter of international public policy, and extended its scope to civil sanctions.[158] The case in 2010 just mentioned confirmed such expansion. Although punitive damages are a form of civil sanction, the enforcement and execution of the foreign judgment awarding them was subject to its conformity with the principle of proportionality, itself part of the wider public policy. This position was confirmed by the European Court of Human Rights, whose judges considered that the principle of proportionality is a matter of civil law, and applied it to property law, stating that 'there should exist a reasonable relationship of proportionality between the means employed and the aim sought by any measure which deprives a person of its property'.[159] The European Rome II Regulation also provides that the principle of proportionality of punitive damages can be a relevant public interest

155 P. Catala, *Avant-projet de réforme du droit des obligations, Rapport au Garde des sceaux*, 22 September 2005, Art. 1371; A. Anziani and L. Béteille, Proposition de loi n°657 portant réforme de la responsabilité civile, Sénat, 9 July 2010, Art. 1386–25; F. Terré, *Pour une réforme du droit de la responsabilité civile* (Paris: Dalloz 2011), Art. 54.

156 Cass. Civ. 1, 1 December 2010, n°09–13303, *RCA* 2011, n°3, Etude n°5; V. Wester-Ouisse and T. Thiede, 'Punitive Damages in France: A New Deal?' (2012) 3 *JETL* 115; Cass. Civ. 1, 7 November 2012, *Bull.* 228.

157 See also Cons. const., decision n°86–215 DC of 3 September 1986.

158 Cass. 1re civ., 28 January 2009, n°07–11729, D. Martel, Précisions sur les conditions de l'exequatur, JCP 2009, II 10086.

159 *Pressos compania Naviera* v. *Belgium* (1996) 21 EHRR 301; *Hamer* v. *Belgium*, 27 November 2007 (ECHR), *D.* 2008, 884, note J.-P. Marguénaud.

consideration.[160] In Europe, each time a civil sanction has the character of a punishment, the principle of proportionality must be applied. Punitive damages probably fall within the area of criminal law, in what the European Court of Human Rights refers to as '*matière pénale*' (criminal matters). In recent decades, the legislator excluded whole parts of criminal law from criminal procedure: independent administrative authorities, and sometimes even private persons, have been granted the power to prosecute and sanction.[161] The European Court of Human Rights, however, was not mistaken: in an effort to safeguard essential criminal procedural aspects, it analysed these alternative systems as being part of the '*matière pénal*'[162] thus requiring that fundamental criminal principles (such as *non bis in idem*, the right to fair trial, the rights of the defence, the principle of proportionality, the presumption of innocence) be complied with.

Further indications that punitive damages are a criminal penalty applied by a civil judge are found in the *Catala*[163] and *Béteille* reform projects, which suggest that:

- Punitive damages should be awarded only for wilful misconduct: this is the same minimum standard for criminal liability (subject to statutory exceptions allowing mere negligence to establish the defendant's fault);[164]
- Punitive damages are not automatically awarded to the victim. It is within the trial judge's discretion whether or not to award such damages, and a portion of the award can be due to the treasury;
- Punitive damages, just like criminal fines, cannot be covered by insurance.

A question that consequently arises is whether an award of nominal damages could be analysed as serving a punitive, rather than a compensatory function in the law of civil liability.

160 Regulation (EC) No 864/2007 of the European Parliament and of the Council of 11 July 2007 on the law applicable to non-contractual obligations (Rome II), §32.

161 For instance the banks can prosecute a defendant who has issued a cheque in the absence of sufficient funds. More recently, professional associations have been granted similar investigatory and sanctioning powers in relation to illegal downloading under Art. L. 331–2 Intellectual Property Code.

162 *Jamil* v. *France* (1996) 21 EHRR 65, *JCP* 1996, II, 22677, obs. G. Bourdeaux; Cass. Crim., 29 February 1996, *Bull.* n°100: '*mesure à caractère pénal*'.

163 S. Carval, *La responsabilité civile dans sa fonction de peine privée.*

164 Art. 121–3 Criminal Code.

More generally, while in theory conventional damage awards are purely compensatory, in practice they may include a punitive element. In some cases, the award is explained by reference to somewhat abstract or unclear criteria, thus suggesting the existence of an underlying retributive function. One example is that of damage awards for non-pecuniary loss suffered by an indirect victim (a victim '*par ricochet*'): an award for the pain and suffering of the primary victim's family is probably retributive in essence,[165] since the harm they suffer is immeasurable. This is also true of damage awards for a company's trouble in commercial operations, which are also immeasurable. Another atypical but significant example is the case involving rogue trader Kerviel who fraudulently engaged in trading operations with 50 million Euros belonging to French bank Société Générale. Kerviel was sentenced to a five-year prison term (three immediate and two suspended) and to pay a stratospheric damage award of 4.9 million Euros. This civil award was *much more oppressive than the punishment.* The Cour de cassation therefore overturned the appellate decision stating that the Société Générale's lack of effective control mechanisms was a fault that should be taken into account when determining the size of the damage award[166] (which will in any case remain huge). Conversely, when the judges award one symbolic Euro as damages, it is obviously a vindicatory *symbol*; the aim is not to compensate since there is nothing that needs to be compensated.

On the other hand, the defendant's financial ability to contribute, his personal circumstances and the gravity of his fault are not taken into account when determining the amount of damages to be awarded. This is because French law applies a principle of '*réparation intégrale*' (full compensation). This principle is only tempered by the fault of the victim: both issues in play in the Kerviel case.

2. When punishments reach damages

There is a similar expansion of the use of civil law rules in criminal law. In particular, the victim's role is becoming more and more significant in French criminal procedure. His exact role is unclear, but we can note some relevant rights of action that the victim is granted, which may influence the punitive sentence given by the criminal court. Criminal law's function

[165] Cass. Ch. Mixte., 27 February 1970, *Bull.* 1, recognised damages for indirect pain and suffering suffered by a concubine; this decision was extended to brothers and sisters as well as uncles and aunts in Cass. Civ. 2, 16 April 1996, *Bull.* 94.

[166] Cass. Crim., 19 March 2014, *JCP* G 2014, 449, note V. Wester-Ouisse.

becomes more and more centred on two goals: compensating the victim and preventing new offences from being committed. Both the public prosecutor (Section 4.B.2.a) and the judge (Section 4.B.2.b) have been given the powers necessary to enforce payment of the damages awarded.

a. The public prosecutor and the victims The district prosecutor receives complaints and denunciations and decides how to treat them. Where he considers that facts brought to his attention constitute an offence, he can either initiate a prosecution or resort to alternative proceedings, which feature (more or less strong) links with the goal of compensating the victim.

First, the prosecutor may resort to mediation[167] where this measure is likely to either secure reparation of the victim's harm, or to end to the disturbance resulting from the offence. The mediator stimulates discussion between the victim and the author of an offence. The main goal is to make the offender aware of the victim's losses. If the mediator succeeds in this discussion and obtains an agreement, the prosecution is suspended until the offender pays the agreed amount of compensation. If compensation is paid, the criminal action is discontinued.[168]

The prosecutor may also resort to a *composition*,[169] which involves a direct discussion between him and the offender, who pleads guilty and accepts a sanction such as a mediatory fine or the surrender of his vehicle. Where the victim is identified, the district prosecutor must propose to the offender that he compensate the losses caused by his offence, and inform the victim of such proposal. While both mediation and *composition* close the criminal case, the victim may still bring a civil action before a civil court after a composition.

b. The criminal judge and victims There is a further form of remedy between the offender and the victim which is part civil and part criminal: the '*sanction-réparation*'. While being a form of compensation, it is a criminal penalty, introduced in the Criminal Code[170] by the law of 5 March

[167] Art. 41–1 CPP (in force since 1993). [168] Art. 41–1 and 6 *alinea* 3 CPP.

[169] Art. 41–2 CPP (in force since 1999).

[170] Art. 131–8-1 Criminal Code: Where a misdemeanour is punishable by imprisonment, the court may, as an alternative to or at the same time as imprisonment, impose a *sanction-réparation (order for compensation/reparations).* The same shall apply where a misdemeanour is punishable by a single fine only.

Where the misdemeanour is punishable solely by a fine, the court shall only set the total sum of the fine, which shall not exceed 15,000 Euros, which may then be enforced.

2007. The convicted defendant must compensate the victim's losses, either by paying him damages within a limited timeframe, or by making good the damage in kind. The victim must approve this sanction and the chosen form of reparation. The public prosecutor or his deputy/representative then certifies that the defendant has complied with his obligation to compensate or repair. When imposing a *sanction-réparation*, the court also sets a default maximum term of imprisonment (which cannot exceed six months), or the total sum of the fine (which cannot exceed 15,000 Euros). Should the convicted defendant not comply with his obligation, the sentencing judge may order that the set penalties be enforced, in full or in part, subject to the conditions set out in Article 712–6 CPP. This new form of penalty is available for any *délit* (major offences, not crimes), and can either replace or be added to a fine or prison sentence. The *sanction-réparation* is the most recent and definite victim-friendly policy in criminal law, since the victim and his wishes are central to the determination of the defendant's obligations.

Furthermore, the Criminal Code has long provided in Article 132–59 that:

> An exemption from penalty may be granted where it appears that the reintegration of the guilty party has been achieved, that the damage caused has been made good and that the public disturbance generated by the offence has ceased.

Compensating harm suffered by the victim is a necessary condition for the granting of a penalty exemption or of the reduction of the prison sentence. It is also a condition for the judge to be able to defer the sentence: if the damage is in the process of being repaired, the judge can rule on the punishment in another later hearing.[171] The criminal judge is also in some instances given the means to force the convicted defendant to pay civil damages,[172] to order that he pay the costs of the civil party[173] (except in situations where equity does not call for it).

Finally, the state is involved to some extent in compensating victims of crime. A Compensation Commission was created in 1977 to guarantee

The presiding judge shall inform the convicted person of the same once the decision has been handed down.

[171] Article 132–60 CPP.

[172] Since 2008, Article 474–1 CPP has allowed the judge to inform the defendant about the consequences of not making a voluntary payment.

[173] Article 475–1 CPP.

that victims of some criminal offences be compensated.[174] The victims who do not fall within this category can request assistance for the satisfaction of the claim,[175] however their fault can reduce or even exclude their right to recovery under this scheme.[176]

5. Conclusion

French law has developed advanced theories both on tort and crime. It attempts to balance the principles and purposes of the criminal law with supporting victims and, to some extent, using those victims to provide some oversight of the criminal justice system.

On the one hand, tort and crime each have their own distinct character in France. Academics have worked hand in hand with the Cour de cassation to develop two systems, each highly coherent within itself: an objective system in tort law, a subjective and moral system in crime law. French tort law became very generous towards victims: tort law awards damages whether there is moral fault or not. The *partie civile* is a way to take into account the purposes of the penal law while at the same time giving an opportunity to undo harm, even harm done without moral fault. Criminal law, through its procedure, takes into account the victims while at the same time the judges apply the rules of tort law; they even sometimes suggest new solutions for tort law itself.

On the other hand, while doctrine and judges are specialised whether in tort law or in criminal law, and few look to the other field of law, many influences and interactions do exist. Most famously the *partie civile* is an important link between civil and criminal law, as are a number of substantive doctrines and some theoretical perspectives. French law, by some standards, goes a long way to give civil law interests an impact on criminal law procedure. But to the French, this system is a practical and principled way to achieve justice, balancing by restrictions on the types of actions brought and the risk of costs and prosecution if a *partie civile* is wrongfully brought.

In the future, the ways of tort law and criminal law could cross more and more. Draft tort law reforms currently on the table propose to add the punitive damages in tort law, and thereby include a penal or punitive

[174] Article 706–3 of CPP. [175] Article 706–15–1 CPP.

[176] Article 706–3 CPP provides that compensation may not be awarded or may be reduced where the victim was at fault.

element to civil law. Similar adjustments from the other direction can already be seen in criminal law. The most recent reform of criminal procedure, of 15 August 2014, inserted the notion of 'restorative justice' in the French procedure Code. Mutual influences between tort law and criminal law are a trend that has no end in sight.

4

Delictual and criminal liability in Germany

PHILLIP HELLWEGE AND PETRA WITTIG*

1. Introduction

This chapter will analyse the relationship of the law of delict and criminal law in German law. It will show where both interact and where they do not.

A. *Two points of departure: the principle of the unity of the legal system and the division of the legal system*

Our discussion has two starting points which, *prima facie*, conflict with each other. First, there is the principle of the unity of the legal system. The principle of unity follows from the rule of law,[1] and both the rule of law and the principle of unity have constitutional status. According to this principle the entirety of the legal norms forms a consistent system. The consistency of the legal system is not merely a theoretical assumption or a guideline for the legislator. It is of practical importance for statutory interpretation. The principle of unity requires that each legal norm is interpreted in such a way that the consistency of the legal system is preserved.[2] One would assume that, as a consequence, the same legal questions, as for example those relating to fault, receive uniform answers across the legal system and are answered in the same way in the law of

* Translations of statutory provisions are taken from www.gesetze-im-internet.de (last accessed 15 June 2014).

[1] H. Schulze-Fielitz, in H. Dreier (ed.), *Grundgesetz*, 2nd edn (Tübingen: Mohr Siebeck, 2006), Art. 20 (Rechtsstaat) para. 141; F. Ossenbühl, 'Gesetz und Recht' in J. Isensee and P. Kirchhof (eds.), *Handbuch des Staatsrechts der Bundesrepublik Deutschland* vol. 5 (Heidelberg: Müller, 2007) para. 100.85–6; BVerfGE 98, 106 (1998); BVerfGE 108, 169 (2003).

[2] M. Kloepfer, *Verfassungsrecht* vol. 1 (Munich: Beck, 2011), para. 10.141; R. Zippelius, *Juristische Methodenlehre*, 11th edn (Munich: Beck, 2012), 43; R. Zippelius and T. Würtenberger, *Deutsches Staatsrecht*, 31st edn (Munich: Beck, 2005), 101–2.

delict and in criminal law. After all, different answers to the same questions seem to result in inconsistencies.

Anybody familiar with the German legal system will immediately sense that such an assumption is misleading: as with many legal systems, the German system is divided into private, public and criminal law, with constitutional law overarching all three.[3] This division is our second starting point. It is reflected in academia, education and practice. If the same legal questions were to receive identical answers across private, public and criminal law, then this division would be superfluous. Division implies difference.

How can this conflict be resolved? According to the German understanding, the unity principle demands consistency. It does not call for sameness. Whenever different answers to similar questions are policy based they do not conflict with this principle.[4] German lawyers are in agreement that the theoretical foundations of, and the policy considerations underlying, the law of delict and criminal law are different and that both may therefore develop different solutions to similar problems.[5] Indeed, the relationship of the law of delict and criminal law is discussed in the German legal literature without being a matter of controversy: both are distinct.[6] The distinction between private law and criminal law is even said to be one of the great achievements of the nineteenth century.[7] Consequently, this chapter will deal to a great extent with the differences between the law of delict and criminal law and explain why they do not conflict with the principle of unity.

B. *Setting the scene I: the substantive perspective*

Both the law of delict and criminal law share a common historical root.[8] Both are also bound together by the fact that delictual and criminal

[3] G. Robbers, *An Introduction to German Law*, 5th edn (Baden-Baden: Nomos, 2012), para. 6–10.

[4] Kloepfer, *Verfassungsrecht*, para. 10.141; H. Schneider, *Gesetzgebung*, 3rd edn (Heidelberg: Müller, 2002), para. 58.

[5] See E. Deutsch, *Haftungsrecht* vol. 1 (Cologne: Heymanns, 1976), 89–97.

[6] D. Medicus, *Allgemeiner Teil des BGB*, 10th edn (Heidelberg: Müller, 2010), para. 1.

[7] C. Roxin, 'Strafe und Wiedergutmachung' in Th. Rauscher and H.-P. Mansel (eds.), *Festschrift für Werner Lorenz* (Munich: Sellier, 2001), 61 (himself critical as to the importance of the distinction).

[8] Deutsch, *Haftungsrecht*, 89; G. Wagner, in *Münchener Kommentar zum Bürgerlichen Gesetzbuch* vol. 5, 6th edn (Munich: Beck, 2013), Vor § 823 para. 2, 62; H. Stoll, 'Schadensersatz und Strafe' in E. von Caemmerer *et al.* (eds.), *Ius Privatum Gentium. Festschrift für Max Rheinstein* vol. 2 (Tübingen: Mohr Siebeck, 1969), 569–90.

liability are often triggered by the same facts. Thus, there are points of contact between them which make it worthwhile to reflect on their relationship and to compare the substantive law of delict and the substantive criminal law.

However, we have to keep in mind that the law of delict and criminal law only overlap, they are not congruent.[9] The law of delict is a two-tier system:[10] fault-based liability for wrongs and strict liability (*Gefährdungshaftung*). Strict liability, the second tier, requires neither a wrong nor fault. Somebody who lawfully opens, maintains or controls a source of risk may be held liable for damages if the risk eventuates and causes damage. The prime example is the liability of motorcar owners. The idea of strict liability is alien to criminal law. Criminal liability always requires wrongfulness and guilt – or as many criminal lawyers would say: the punitive powers of the state are ultimately restricted by the principle of individual guilt.[11] One could say that in a comparative project on tort and crime, the German chapter should, thus, focus on the delictual fault-based liability for wrongs to the exclusion of strict liability because it is only the delictual fault-based liability for wrongs which finds a direct counterpart in criminal law. However, fault-based liability for wrongs and strict liability interact with each other in many ways and this has to be kept in mind when comparing the fault-based liability for wrongs with criminal liability.

There are other areas of law which one has to consider when analysing the law of delict. One of them is breach of contract. German law does not know the rule of *non-cumul*:[12] in Germany, a claim for breach of contract and a claim in delict may be raised on the basis of the same facts. There are

[9] Deutsch, *Haftungsrecht*, 91–2.

[10] J. Esser, 'Die Zweispurigkeit unseres Haftpflichtrechts' (1953) *JZ*, 129–34; D. Looschelders, *Schuldrecht. Besonderer Teil*, 9th edn (Munich: Vahlen, 2014), para. 1166; H. Kötz and G. Wagner, Deliktsrecht, 12th edn (Munich: Vahlen, 2013) para. 5–8; D. Medicus and S. Lorenz, *Schuldrecht II. Besonderer Teil*, 16th edn (Munich: Beck, 2012), para. 1228–9; M. Wandt, *Gesetzliche Schuldverhältnisse*, 5th edn (Munich: Vahlen, 2012), para. 14.2; M. Fuchs and W. Pauker, *Delikts- und Schadensersatzrecht*, 8th edn (Berlin: Springer, 2012), 6. There are other tiers which we will neglect: E. Deutsch and H.-J. Ahrens, *Deliktsrecht*, 4th edn (Cologne: Heymanns, 2002), para. 5–10; K. Larenz, 'Die Prinzipien der Schadenszurechnung' (1965) *JuS*, 373–9. There is a definitional discussion whether the law of delict comprises fault-based liability for wrongs, only: B. S. Markesinis and H. Unberath, *The German Law of Torts*, 4th edn (Oxford: Hart, 2002), 24.

[11] C. Roxin, *Strafrecht Allgemeiner Teil Band I*, 4th edn (Munich: Beck, 2006), para. 3.51; J. Wessels *et al.*, *Strafrecht Allgemeiner Teil*, 44th edn (Heidelberg: Müller, 2014), para. 396; T. Fischer, *Strafgesetzbuch*, 62nd edn (Munich: Beck, 2015), Vor § 13 para. 47.

[12] Wagner, in *Münchener Kommentar*, Vor § 823 para. 67; Deutsch, *Haftungsrecht*, 80–4.

differences between breach of contract and delict. They are again policy based and, thus, do not contradict the unity principle. Yet, there are also interactions: both are, for example, directed at damages, the amount of which is calculated on the basis of the same provisions, §§ 249 ff BGB (Bürgerliches Gesetzbuch – the Civil Code).[13]

Furthermore, one has to keep insurance law and practice in mind when analysing the law of delict.[14] In many cases, the injured party will have insurance coverage: with personal injuries, the injured party's loss will be made good by health and social insurances. And often the injurer will equally be covered by liability insurance. In practice, the damage will be adjusted between the two insurers and this adjustment will, for reasons of commercial ease, not necessarily follow the rules of the law of delict.

Thus, we should not focus on fault-based liability for wrongs to the exclusion of all other areas of law but we have to be aware that it interacts with such other areas. We will specifically point out where this is of importance to our reflections. Turning to criminal law we have to distinguish criminal offences from minor regulatory offences. The latter do not form part of criminal law but are treated separately and belong to administrative law.[15] Like criminal offences, minor regulatory offences involve a wrong and they will inflict a monetary fine only if the offender acted with intent or, with special enumerated offences, if he acted negligently. Thus, there is no strict liability for regulatory offences. The one distinguishing feature is said to be that the wrong involved is of a different quality. It is a minor wrong which is said not to involve something ethically wrong or – to put it in different terms – a social danger that makes punishment necessary. Examples of regulatory offences are crossing a red light, renting out an apartment without presenting the energy effeciency pass of the building or advertising for prostitution. Another distinguishing feature is that in the law of minor regulatory offences a monetary fine is not a criminal sanction but simply an administrative fine. However, we can overlook them in the present chapter.

[13] G. Wagner, 'Schadensersatz' in E. Lorenz (ed.), *Karlsruher Forum 2006* (Karlsruhe: Verlag Versicherungswirtschaft, 2006), 5, 11.

[14] J. Hager, in *Staudingers Kommentar zum Bürgerlichen Gesetzbuch*, 13th edn (Berlin: Sellier–de Gruyter, 1999), Vorbem zu §§ 823 para. 7–8; M. Makowsky, *Der Einfluss von Versicherungsschutz auf die außervertragliche Haftung* (Karlsruhe: Verlag Versicherungswirtschaft, 2013), *passim*; C. von Bar 'Das 'Trennungsprinzip' und die Geschichte des Wandels der Haftpflichtversicherung' (1981) 181 *AcP*, 289–327.

[15] Foremost, they are treated in the Act on Regulatory Offences (Gesetz über Ordnungswidrigkeiten – OWiG).

C. *Setting the scene II: the procedural perspective*

Turning to procedural law the picture is a different one. Even though the difference is quite obvious, it is important for methodological reasons. The division into private and criminal law is mirrored in the division into civil and criminal procedure. Yet, whereas substantive private law is subdivided with the law of delict being one specific area of the law of obligations, there are – and this is the important difference which we are referring to – no separate rules that govern the procedure of actions based on delictual liability.

Why is this difference important? When analysing the relationship between the substantive law of delict and substantive criminal law, we have two distinct sets of statutory provisions which we can compare even though these distinct set of rules interact with many other areas of law. When analysing the relationship between the law of delict and criminal law from a procedural perspective, we have to analyse the relationship of the general rules on civil procedure and the law of criminal procedure even though our focus will be on the rules of civil procedure as they apply to delictual cases.

It is not sufficient to compare civil and criminal procedure as there are other forms of interaction on the procedural level and these forms of interactions are important. Delictual and criminal liability are often triggered by the same facts. As a rule, criminal and civil proceedings are tried separately. Does it follow that the respective courts can answer the same question of fact differently? Or is one court bound by the findings of the other court? Can one court stay its proceedings until the other court has reached a judgment? With these forms of interaction our focus shifts away from a mere comparison of legal rules.

D. *Overview*

The theoretical foundations of the law of delict and criminal law and the policy considerations underlying them are central to this chapter. They will be discussed first (Section 2 below) followed by constitutional, institutional and methodological reflections (Sections 3 to 5). Our focus will be on the differences and interactions between the substantive law of delict and criminal law as well as between civil and criminal procedure (Sections 6 to 7) followed by some further remedial reflections (Section 8).

2. The policy-based perspective: the theoretical foundations of the law of delict and of criminal law

Whenever the law of delict and criminal law depart from each other, the resulting differences are supported by divergent theoretical foundations of each area of law and by differing policy considerations that underlie them. Having said that, we run immediately into problems. The discussions of these foundations and policies by criminal and private lawyers do not always correspond and in any case are controversial.

A. *Different concepts and different focal points*

If you ask a German lawyer why there are differences between tort and crime, he would likely respond that the functions of the two areas of law are different: the purposes which each area should serve are different. However, for two reasons, the reference to different functions would seem to be inexact.

First, private lawyers primarily discuss the functions of the law of delict.[16] The discussion in the criminal law sphere has a slightly different spin to it. Criminal lawyers do not only speak of the functions of criminal law or punishment but, at the same time, also discuss the legitimisation of criminal law and any limitations to it resulting from such legitimisation.[17] Thus, criminal lawyers are not only concerned with the purposes of criminal law and of punishment but also with the question of why a society should be allowed to punish.

Second, the discussions have different focal points. Criminal lawyers draw a distinction between the general and the specific: between the general legitimisation and function of criminal law and the functions of punishing in a single case.[18] The abstract legitimisation of criminal law is to protect legal interests (*Rechtsgüterschutz*).[19] This concept helps to identify which acts can legitimately be penalised and which acts simply infringe moral standards.[20] Some private lawyers, too, distinguish between the abstract function of the law of delict and the function of an award of damages in a single case.[21] Yet, this distinction does not play a prominent role. Nevertheless, any private lawyer would

16 See Looschelders, *Besonderer Teil*, para. 1167.

17 C. Roxin, 'Sinn und Grenzen staatlicher Strafe' (1966) *JuS*, 377–87.

18 Roxin, *Strafrecht*, para. 3.1. 19 Ibid., para. 2.7. 20 Ibid., para. 2.43.

21 Kötz and Wagner, *Deliktsrecht*, para. 56–8.

agree that the function of the law of delict as such is to protect legal interests.[22]

The idea of *Rechtsgüterschutz* in a broad sense is common to both the law of delict and criminal law and is therefore not able to justify any differences between the two. However, the discussions in the criminal law sphere and in the private law sphere use slightly different concepts and certainly have different focal points.

B. *Discussion in the law of delict*

Most private lawyers will argue that the law of delict has two functions.[23] First, it aims to compensate a loss (*Ausgleichsfunktion*).[24] Second, the existence of the law of delict is said to regulate future behaviour; German lawyers say that the existence of the law of delict 'prevents' future damage (*Präventionsfunktion*).[25] An award of damages for pain and suffering (*Schmerzensgeld* and *Geldentschädigung*) is said to have a third function: it provides personal satisfaction for the injured (*Genugtuungsfunktion*).[26] These three functions are common to claims for damages regardless of whether they are based on delict or breach of contract.[27] And these functions are common to claims for damages regardless of whether they stem from fault-based liability for wrongs or from strict liability.[28] There is thus no separate discussion of the function of fault-based liability for wrongs which one could directly compare to the discussion in criminal law. Rather, the discussion in private law has to be seen in a broader

[22] K. Larenz and C.-W. Canaris, *Lehrbuch des Schuldrechts* vol. 2/2, 13th edn (Munich: Beck, 1994), 350.

[23] H. Koziol, *Grundfragen des Schadensersatzrechts* (Vienna: Sramek, 2010), 75–91; G. Brüggemeier, *Haftungsrecht* (Heidelberg: Springer, 2006), 9–12; M. Staake, *Gesetzliche Schuldverhältnisse* (Heidelberg: Springer, 2014), para. 7.1–2.

[24] Looschelders, *Schuldrecht. Allgemeiner Teil*, 11th edn (Munich: Vahlen, 2013), para. 873; R. Wilhelmi, *Risikoschutz durch Privatrecht* (Tübingen: Mohr Siebeck, 2009), 62–3.

[25] G. Wagner, 'Neue Perspektiven im Schadensersatzrecht' in *Verhandlungen des 66. Deutschen Juristentages* vol. I (Munich: Beck, 2006), A20–1, A77–83; G. Wagner, 'Haftung und Versicherung als Instrumente der Techniksteuerung' (1999) VersR, 1441–3; H. Kötz, 'Ziele des Haftungsrechts' in J. F. Baur *et al.* (eds.), *Festschrift für Ernst Steindorff* (Berlin: de Gruyter, 1990), 643–66; Looschelders, *Besonderer Teil*, para. 1167; M. Rohe, 'Gründe und Grenzen deliktischer Haftung' (2001) 201 *AcP*, 117, 125.

[26] BGHZ 18, 149, 155–68 (1955); H. J. Hirsch, 'Zur Abgrenzung von Strafrecht und Zivilrecht' in P. Bockelmann *et al.* (eds.), *Festschrift für Karl Engisch* (Frankfurt: Klostermann, 1969), 304–27.

[27] Looschelders, *Allgemeiner Teil*, para. 873.

[28] Hager, in *Staudinger*, Vorbem zu §§ 823 para. 9, 28.

context. A fourth function, discussed only with respect to delictual liability, is to punish the injurer (*Straffunktion*) but it has been predominantly rejected by academia and practice.[29] As a consequence, the concept of punitive damages is, generally speaking, rejected.[30] This was a brief and simplistic account of a complex and controversial discussion and the purpose of the following three paragraphs is to give an impression of this complexity and these controversies.

We have already noted that private lawyers, too, at times distinguish between the abstract function of the law of delict as such and the reason why damages are awarded in a single case. Many say that the function of the law of delict is to compensate. Yet, the idea of compensation seems to be the reason why damages are awarded in a single case. Or to put it differently, the compensatory function seems to be limited to the remedial side of the law of delict. Some point out that compensation cannot be the abstract function of the law of delict because such function should also help to answer the question when no compensation is given.[31] However, not every loss will be compensated for. In many cases the maxim *casum sentit dominus* applies[32] – the loss lies where it falls. One could say that the abstract function of the law of delict as such is to decide who should bear a loss, but it has been pointed out that this is so vague as to be meaningless.[33] In particular, it does not make explicit why the legislator decides when compensation should be granted.

The preventive function has become ever more important in the academic discussion.[34] However, there is a divergence of views, particularly on its relationship to the compensatory function. Traditionally, prevention is said to be a secondary function, only.[35] Others say that regulating future behaviour is not the function of the law of delict but a mere side effect[36] – it is argued that the questions of when compensation should be given and when the loss should lie where it falls cannot be answered by referring to such preventive function. Again others argue the opposite: the

[29] Hager, in *Staudinger*, Vorbem zu §§ 823 para. 11; BGHZ 118, 312, 338 (1992).

[30] Wagner, in *Karlsruher Forum*, 16–8.

[31] Wagner, in *Münchener Kommentar*, Vor § 823 para. 38.

[32] Deutsch and Ahrens, *Deliktsrecht*, para. 1.

[33] Kötz and Wagner, *Deliktsrecht*, para. 57.

[34] G. Wagner, 'Prävention und Verhaltenssteuerung durch Privatrecht' (2006) 206 *AcP*, 352–476; G. Wagner, 'Die Aufgaben des Haftungsrechts' (1991) *JZ*, 175, 176; R. Möller, *Das Präventionsprinzip des Schadensrechts* (Berlin: Duncker & Humblot, 2006).

[35] Deutsch, *Haftungsrecht*, 73; P. Marburger, 'Grundsatzfragen des Haftungsrechts' (1992) 192 *AcP*, 1, 30–1.

[36] Hager, in *Staudinger*, Vorbem zu §§ 823 para. 10.

abstract function of the law of delict is to regulate future behaviour only.[37] They claim that the question of when compensation should be given can be answered by referring to the preventive function if one applies the concepts of law and economics. Indeed, law and economics reasoning has some followers in German legal writing on the law of delict[38] but they are not uncontested.[39]

Finally, even though the rejection of the penal function is commonly accepted some argue in favour of it.[40] Central to the discussion are awards of damages for pain and suffering (*Schmerzensgeld* and *Geldentschädigung*) which are said to provide personal satisfaction (*Genugtuungsfunktion*), especially in cases of an infringement of the general right to privacy (*allgemeines Persönlichkeitsrecht*).[41] Some argue that the *Genugtuungsfunktion* is akin to a penal function.[42] Others argue for slightly less, saying that damages for pain and suffering have a punitive side effect albeit not a penal function.[43] Yet others deny that an award of such damages has any penal element at all.[44] Indeed, German law allows damages for pain and suffering in the case of strict liability[45] and it is wrong to punish a person who acts without fault.[46] As a consequence the dominant view is that the *Genugtuungsfunktion* is only applicable to fault-based liability. In the case of strict liability, the *Schmerzensgeld* is said to compensate for immaterial losses only,[47] and the

[37] Kötz and Wagner, *Deliktsrecht*, para. 59. Compare also T. Dreier, *Kompensation und Prävention* (Tübingen: Mohr Siebeck, 2002); K. Sailer, *Prävention im Haftungsrecht* (Frankfurt: Lang, 2005).

[38] Wagner, in *Münchener Kommentar*, Vor § 823 para. 41; H.-B. Schäfer and C. Ott, *Lehrbuch der ökonomischen Analyse des Zivilrechts*, 4th edn (Berlin: Springer, 2005), 121; M. Adams, *Ökonomische Analyse der Gefährdungs- und Verschuldenshaftung* (Heidelberg: Decker, 1985), 8–35.

[39] Hager, in *Staudinger*, Vorbem zu §§ 823 para. 14–8; J. Taupitz, 'Ökonomische Analyse und Haftungsrecht' (1996) 196 *AcP*, 114–67.

[40] I. Ebert, *Pönale Elemente im deutschen Privatrecht* (Tübingen: Mohr Siebeck, 2004), 409–566, 576–8; M. Körner, 'Zur Aufgabe des Haftungsrechts' (2000) *NJW*, 241–6; P. Müller, *Punitive Damages und deutsches Schadensersatzrecht* (Berlin: de Gruyter, 2000); B. Großfeld, *Die Privatstrafe* (Frankfurt: Metzner, 1961), 75–124.

[41] G. Wagner, 'Geldersatz für Persönlichkeitsverletzungen' *ZEuP* 8 (2000), 200–28. For other cases see: Dreier, *Kompensation*; Müller, *Punitive Damages*; Möller, *Präventionsprinzip*.

[42] Deutsch, *Haftungsrecht*, 89, 91; Stoll, in *Festschrift Rheinstein*, 579–83.

[43] Hager, in *Staudinger*, Vorbem zu §§ 823 para. 11.

[44] Wagner, in *Münchener Kommentar*, Vor § 823 para. 44.

[45] C. Grüneberg, in *Palandt. Bürgerliches Gesetzbuch*, 74th edn (Munich: Beck, 2015), § 253 para. 7.

[46] Wagner, in *Münchener Kommentar*, Vor § 823 para. 44.

[47] Grüneberg, in *Palandt*, § 253 para. 4.

question of fault is important for the amount of damages for pain and suffering.[48]

C. Discussion in criminal law

Criminal lawyers will argue that the private lawyers' rejection of the *Straffunktion* is wrong footed as it gives the impression that punishment is a function in itself:[49] in criminal law there is an extensive discussion on why we punish – a discussion with a long history.[50] Mainly three theories have developed.[51] The *Vergeltungstheorie* (retribution theory) argues that punishing is about retribution. It has prominent philosophical roots in German idealistic philosophy[52] but still has some adherents arguing for example that by punishing the offender he is taken seriously in his status as a citizen.[53] The *Theorie der Spezialprävention* (special prevention theory) claims that punishing is about preventing the individual offender from committing another offence in the future. Most importantly, F. von Liszt and the modern school of criminal law developed this theory distinguishing between deterrence, rehabilitation (or – as F. von Liszt put it – 'bettering') and incapacitation of the individual offender.[54] Nowadays the focus is on rehabilitation.[55] Finally, the *Theorie der Generalprävention* (general prevention theory) argues that punishment should not deter the individual offender but the general public. In a negative version it says that the mere threat of punishment should prevent anybody from committing a crime. This conception was forcefully developed by P. J. A. Feuerbach[56] and today is often linked with the model of a *homo oeconomicus*.[57] In its

[48] BGH, NJW 1993, 1531; Grüneberg, in *Palandt*, § 253 para. 15–17; H Oetker, in *Münchener Kommentar zum Bürgerlichen Gesetzbuch* vol. 2, 6th edn (Munich: Beck, 2012), § 249 para. 48.

[49] From a private lawyer's perspective Wagner, in *Münchener Kommentar*, Vor § 823 para. 43.

[50] See, e.g., R. von Hippel, *Deutsches Strafrecht* vol. 1 (Berlin: Springer, 1925), 459–65.

[51] R. Rengier, *Strafrecht. Allgemeiner Teil*, 6th edn (Munich: Beck, 2014), para. 3.10–26; T. Weigend, in *Strafgesetzbuch. Leipziger Kommentar*, 12th edn (Berlin: de Gruyter, 2007), Einleitung para. 58.

[52] See, e.g., I. Kant, *Die Metaphysik der Sitten*, in W. Weischedel (ed), *Werkausgabe* vol. 8, 1st edn (Frankfurt: Suhrkamp, 1977) para. 46 E I.

[53] This is the position of M. Pawlik, *Person, Subjekt, Bürger* (Berlin: Duncker & Humblot, 2004), 90.

[54] F. von Liszt, 'Der Zweckgedanke im Strafrecht' (1883) *ZStW*, 1–47.

[55] Roxin, *Strafrecht*, para. 3.41.

[56] P. J. A. Feuerbach, *Lehrbuch des gemeinen in Deutschland gültigen peinlichen Rechts* (Giessen: Heyer, 1847), 39.

[57] Roxin, *Strafrecht*, para. 3.48.

positive version the general preventive theory argues that the punishment should stabilise the trust in the existence and force of the legal order and it should ensure that everybody is law-abiding. This model is based on the assumption that persuasion, not threat, has better preventive effects.[58]

The retribution theory has mainly been criticised because it fails to explain why one *malus* (the crime) can be equalised by another *malus* (the punishment). Retribution can therefore not be regarded as an end in itself. The purpose and legitimisation of punishment can only lie in the future – that is the position of the preventive theories. Yet, these future related theories have the problem of how to limit criminal sanctions proportionally to the gravity of the past crime and the degree of personal guilt. If the individual offender is only 'used' for preventive purposes these theories even face problems with human dignity. Many authors therefore follow a theory that combines all three functions.[59] Others believe that only the preventive functions may explain why we punish and they reject the *Vergeltungstheorie* altogether.[60] With these theories the principle of guilt is only of secondary importance.[61]

In recent times, academia has argued that the idea of compensation should be (re-)integrated into criminal law: if compensation is ordered as a result of criminal proceedings, the reasons why we punish may be met especially with small offences. Furthermore, the interests of both the victim and the general public will be met, and the offender will be forced to think about the consequences of his wrongdoing. There is also a discussion as to whether punishment has a victim related purpose, for example, as a symbolic act.[62] Yet, from a German perspective, these aspects are not the reasons which can legitimise punishment. They only add further aspects to the remedial perspective and we will return to them later.

Apart from these discussions the compensatory idea does appear in the criminal law sphere in a different context: criminal law is not about compensating the victim for a loss suffered. Yet, the punishment should relate to the personal guilt of the offender and it should not go beyond his personal guilt.

[58] W. Hassemer, *Einführung in die Grundlagen des Strafrechts* (Munich: Beck, 1990), 323.

[59] Rengier, *Strafrecht. Allgemeiner Teil*, para. 3.21–2; Weigend, in *Leipziger Kommentar*, Einleitung para. 59–60.

[60] Roxin, *Strafrecht*, para. 3.44–50; Rengier, *Strafrecht. Allgemeiner Teil*, para. 3.24.

[61] Roxin, *Strafrecht*, para. 3.51; L. Greco, *Lebendiges und Totes in Feuerbachs Straftheorie* (Berlin: Duncker & Humblot, 2009), 247–52.

[62] T. Hörnle, *Straftheorien* (Tübingen: Mohr Siebeck, 2011), 37–41.

D. Comparison

Comparing the discussions in the criminal and private law spheres yields interesting results. For instance, it seems that private lawyers, when they say that an award of damages does not have a penal function, are rejecting the retribution theory.[63] In fact, private lawyers probably only mean that an award of damages should, in general, not go beyond compensation when they reject a penal function.

Furthermore, criminal and private lawyers locate the function of regulating future behaviour on different levels of abstraction: private lawyers argue that this is the abstract function of the law of delict; criminal lawyers say that this is why we punish in a single case. The special prevention theory can indeed legitimise punishment in a single case. However, the general prevention theory, at least in its 'negative' version, is only dependent on the threat of punishment as in theory the mere threat will regulate future behaviour. But a threat which is not carried out is hollow.[64] Punishing is necessary to enforce the threat. Nevertheless, the primary focus is on the threat. The punishment itself is only of secondary importance. Thus, general prevention relates to the threat of punishment, special prevention to the enforcement of the threat.[65] Private lawyers do not explicitly draw the distinction between special and general prevention but implicitly refer to general prevention when they argue that the function of regulating future behaviour is rather the abstract function of the law of delict and not the function of an award of damages in a single case.

Thus, the discussions of the policy considerations underlying the law of delict and criminal law do not fully correspond but we can see two functions, prevention and compensation which appear in both spheres. Are the policy considerations underlying both criminal law and the law of delict after all identical? The answer is in the negative. There are a number of differences from a theoretical and policy based perspective: the primary function of the law of delict is to decide who should bear a loss. Should it lie where it falls or is there a reason to shift it? The answer to this question depends on a number of considerations – prevention being one of them – none of which is able to explain the law of delict in its entirety. The idea common to all awards of damages is that they compensate and

63 Wagner, in *Verhandlungen*, A77-A78; idem, in *Karlsruher Forum*, 19.

64 P. J. A. Feuerbach, *Revision der Grundsätze und Grundbegriffe des positiven peinlichen Rechts* (Erfurt: Henningsche Buchhandlung, 1799), 50.

65 Roxin, *Strafrecht*, para. 3.42.

that they do not, in principle, go beyond compensation. According to the (preferable) preventive theories, the primary function of criminal law and of punishment is to protect legal interests through punishment and the threat of punishment. The punishment and the threat of it are primarily justified by the idea of regulating future behaviour. Compensation in the meaning that the victim is to be compensated for his loss is in the criminal sphere only an appropriate punishment if it meets this function. Thus, while comparable functions exist in both spheres they are arranged in a different hierarchy.

3. The constitutional perspective

The constitutional perspective allows a German lawyer to draw another sharp line between the law of delict and criminal law. To those outside of Germany a key point must be borne in mind: in some countries, like England, questions as to the influence of human rights on substantive and procedural law have first been asked in connection with the European Convention on Human Rights (ECHR) and the Human Rights Act 1998, but this is not the case in Germany. In Germany, the corresponding questions have first been discussed with reference to the Constitution (Grundgesetz – GG) and the fundamental rights contained therein. As a consequence, the introduction of the ECHR did not have the same impact in Germany as it had in, say, England. In private law, for example, it did not result in any theoretical questions which had not already been discussed in relation to the GG. Indeed, this constitutional perspective still dominates the discussion.[66] We will concentrate on the constitutional perspective, too, leaving aside the ECHR.

Constitutional law overarches private, public and criminal law. The law of delict is part of private law. Criminal law forms part of public law but is traditionally treated as a separate subject. The criteria for deciding whether something belongs to private or public law have long been disputed.[67] However, we have already seen reasons for why criminal law belongs to public law and why delict belongs to private law.

Delict deals with the question of when a claimant – normally a private individual or private entity but where it is a public body it is treated the

[66] See J. Basedow, 'Europäische Menschenrechtskonvention und Europäisches Privatrecht' (1999) 63 *RabelsZ*, 409–13; R. Ellger, 'Europäische Menschenrechtskonvention und deutsches Privatrecht' (1999) 63 *RabelsZ*, 626–64.

[67] See Medicus, *Allgemeiner Teil*, para. 7–10.

same as a private individual – has a right to ask for compensation from another private individual or private entity.

In criminal law, it is the state who claims the right to punish. If the state starts criminal proceedings against an accused, the constitutionally guaranteed fundamental rights of the accused are engaged. These rights are thus directly applicable both on the level of procedural and substantive law.[68] However, they are not merely applicable, they are of greatest importance in the context of criminal law: criminal procedure has been called the 'seismograph of constitutional law'[69] and criminal law as a whole has been referred to as the 'Magna Charta for the offender'.[70] By reason of the fundamental rights of the accused and the constitutional principle of proportionality, it is undisputed that criminal law can only be the *ultima ratio*, the last resort.[71] As a consequence, the legislator is constitutionally bound to penalise acts only if alternative measures in the private or public law sphere are not sufficient to protect legal interests; similarly, on the level of sentencing, judges should only use prison sentences if other criminal sanctions are inadequate.[72] In contrast, the victim's rights are not of the same importance in German law as in other European legal systems even though they are discussed.[73] A duty of the state to penalise certain behaviour is only accepted in very special circumstances, e.g., in the case of abortion[74] and even this is highly controversial.[75]

Turning to private law we are able to see that the fundamental rights are not of the same importance. The whole discussion follows different patterns than in criminal law and there are different layers to it. The question as to the effect of fundamental rights within the sphere of substantive private law in general[76] – and the question as to the effect of

[68] C. Roxin and B. Schünemann, *Strafverfahrensrecht*, 27th edn (Munich: Beck, 2012), para. 2.9.

[69] Ibid., para. 2.1.

[70] F. von Liszt, *Strafrechtliche Vorträge und Aufsätze* vol. 1 (Berlin: Guttentag, 1905), 80.

[71] Roxin, *Strafrecht*, para. 2.97; J. Kaspar, *Verhältnismäßigkeit und Grundrechtsschutz im Präventionsstrafrecht* (Nomos: Baden-Baden, 2014), 243.

[72] Kaspar, *Verhältnismäßigkeit*, 243.

[73] See W. Holz, *Justizgewähranspruch des Verbrechensopfers* (Berlin: Duncker & Humblot, 2007).

[74] BVerfGE 88, 203 (1993).

[75] R. Merkel, in U. Kindhäuser *et al.* (eds.), *Strafgesetzbuch*, 4th edn (Baden-Baden: Nomos, 2013), Vor § 218 para. 13–22.

[76] See, e.g., C.-W. Canaris, *Grundrechte und Privatrecht* (Berlin: de Gruyter, 1999); J. Hager, *Grundrechte und Privatrecht* (Berlin: Humboldt Universität, 1995); U. Diederichsen, 'Das Bundesverfassungsgericht als oberstes Zivilgericht' (1998) 198 *AcP*, 171, 199–239.

constitutional law on the law of delict in particular[77] – has generated an extensive and controversial discussion. Nevertheless it is safe to make the following statements.

First, the decision of the legislator to introduce a ground of delictual liability will affect the rights of anybody who is so liable. Consequently the legislator cannot arbitrarily introduce a ground of liability.[78] Similarly, the legislator has to safeguard the legal interests by the means of law of delict,[79] and therefore cannot arbitrarily abolish a ground of liability. In terms of deciding when to introduce delictual liability, the legislator is not bound by the *ultima ratio* principle. And when applying the law of delict to a single case, the courts may grant, and generally speaking must grant, damages even if only very minor legal interests are infringed. Again, the *ultima ratio* principle does not apply.

Second, a delictual claim usually involves two private parties. Article 1(3) GG states that the 'following basic rights [those in the articles following Art. 1 GG] shall bind the legislature, the executive and the judiciary as directly applicable law'. The fundamental rights as guaranteed by the constitution are, thus, not directly applicable between two private individuals,[80] however, they do have significance. They have an indirect effect, a so-called *mittelbare Drittwirkung*: the courts, who adjudicate the private dispute, are bound by the fundamental rights and have to observe them when applying the provisions of the BGB.

Third, the rights of the *accused* in criminal procedure as guaranteed by the constitution are of no importance in civil procedure,[81] but of course this does not mean that constitutional rights in general are of no importance for the parties at all.

4. The institutional perspective

We now turn to the institutional perspective of comparing tort and crime. This will include questions concerning legal education, the structure of legal practice and courts. We will again see that the law of delict and criminal law are clearly separated in principle but that there are certain forms of interaction between the two.

[77] See, e.g., C. von Bar, 'Der Einfluß des Verfassungsrechts auf die westeuropäischen Deliktsrechte' (1995) 59 *RabelsZ*, 203–28; Hager, in *Staudinger*, Vorbem zu §§ 823 para. 68–71.

[78] Hager, in *Staudinger*, Vorbem zu §§ 823 para. 68.

[79] Wagner, in *Münchener Kommentar*, Vor § 823 para. 64.

[80] BVerfGE 7, 198 (1958).

[81] Wagner, in *Karlsruher Forum*, 17–18.

A. *Legal education and legal academia*

In law schools, private, public and criminal law are separated from each other for teaching and research. Professors teach private, public or criminal law. There are hardly any chairs combining two of the three subjects together. This separation does not mean that German lawyers ignore certain thematically arranged areas of law which cut across private and criminal law as, for example, medical law. Medical malpractice cases often raise problems in criminal law, the law of delict and contract law. This is reflected in the law school curriculum. Law schools which offer a specialisation in medical law will teach the relevant private, public and criminal law components.[82] Furthermore, German legal education ensures that all fully trained lawyers have a grasp of both private and criminal law. Law students who want to become practising lawyers have to attend lectures in both areas of law and will have to sit exams on both areas in their first and their second state examinations.[83] During their *Referendariat*, the two years of practical training which leads to the second state examination, trainees have to serve some time in courts working on private law and some time either in courts working on criminal law or in the public prosecution service.[84]

B. *Legal practice*

Practitioners – in Germany no distinction is made between solicitors and barristers – will often specialise in certain subjects and build up a special expertise, as they do in every legal system. However, in Germany, there is a formal title to show such specialisation to potential clients: *Fachanwalt* ('specialised legal practitioner'). It is not necessary to become *Fachanwalt* in order to work in that field of specialisation. Nevertheless, it is of great importance:[85] nearly a quarter of all German practitioners have acquired the title of *Fachanwalt*.[86] The right to use the title is granted by the Association of Legal Practitioners (Rechtsanwaltskammer).

According to § 43c(1)(1) BRAO (Bundesrechtsanwaltsordnung – Federal Act of Legal Practitioners) 'the right to call oneself *Fachanwalt* can

[82] See, e.g., § 5(3)(f) of the Curriculum and Examination Regulations (Studien- und Prüfungsordnung) of Augsburg Law School.

[83] See, e.g., §§ 18, 23, 58 of the Bavarian Curriculum and Examination Regulations for Lawyers (Ausbildungs- und Prüfungsordnung für Juristen – JAPO).

[84] See § 48(2)(1) JAPO.

[85] S. Peitscher, *Anwaltsrecht* (Baden-Baden: Nomos, 2013), para. 310.

[86] M. Kilian, *Developments in the German Legal Profession 2000–2010* (Bonn: Deutscher Anwaltverlag, 2012).

be granted to any legal practitioner if he has proven special knowledge and experience in a certain field of practice'.[87] In order to acquire and prove special knowledge the practitioner has to attend courses and sit exams.[88] The Regulations for the Specialisation of Legal Practitioners (Fachanwaltsordnung – FAO) which are passed by the Regulatory Assembly at the Association of Legal Practitioners[89] defines for each specialisation a catalogue of subjects which the courses have to cover. In order to prove the special experience the practitioner has to confirm that he has counselled a certain number of cases within the last three years in the relevant field of specialisation.[90] Each practitioner can acquire the title of *Fachanwalt* in up to three fields of specialisation. To retain a title, once it has been acquired, the practitioner must attend further courses each year.[91]

There is only a limited number of specialisations for which the title of *Fachanwalt* can be granted, criminal law being one of them.[92] There are specialisations in the private law sphere, but none specifically for the law of delict. It seems that practitioners who have acquired the title in criminal law (*Fachanwalt für Strafrecht*) will concentrate almost exclusively on this area of law (but there are no statistics on this point). Thus, we again see some kind of separation between the criminal law sphere and other areas of law including private law and the law of delict. However, the fact that there are certain areas of law which cut across private and criminal law, is again reflected in the requirements of becoming a *Fachanwalt*. Practitioners who, for example, want to specialise in medical law (*Fachanwalt für Medizinrecht*) are required to attend courses on the private, public and criminal law side of medical law in order to acquire and prove his or her specialised knowledge.[93]

C. *Court structure*

The division into private, public and criminal law is partly reflected in the court structure. There are the *ordentliche Gerichtsbarkeit* (ordinary jurisdiction) and the special jurisdictions for administrative, financial,

87 Authors' translation.

88 W. E. Feuerich, in W. E. Feuerich and D. Weyland (eds.), *Bundesrechtsanwaltsordnung*, 7th edn (Munich: Vahlen, 2008), § 59b para. 32–3.

89 K. von Lewinski, *Grundriss des Anwaltlichen Berufsrechts*, 2nd edn (Baden-Baden: Nomos, 2008), 197–8.

90 Feuerich, in *Bundesrechtsanwaltsordnung*, § 43c para. 34.

91 Peitscher, *Anwaltsrecht*, para. 339–40.

92 § 1 Regulations for the Specialisation of Legal Practitioners (Fachanwaltsordnung – FAO).

93 § 14b FAO. On the details A. Vossebürger, in *Bundesrechtsanwaltsordnung*, § 14b para. 2–10.

labour and social law.[94] There are no special courts for criminal law but the ordinary jurisdiction includes private and criminal law: § 13 GVG (Gerichtsverfassungsgesetz – Federal Judicature Act). However, even though the ordinary jurisdiction includes both private and criminal law within the courts of this jurisdiction, each field of law is treated separately. Each Amts-, Land-, Oberlandesgericht and the Bundesgerichtshof have a number of divisions, chambers and senates which specialise and, as a consequence, there are separate divisions, chambers and senates for criminal law.

Whereas it is unusual for judges to change between the different jurisdictions (ordinary, administrative, financial, labour and social law jurisdiction), judges within the ordinary jurisdiction will most probably sit during their career both in divisions, chambers and senates on private and criminal law and they might even do so at the same time. Furthermore, in some German states, like Bavaria, every judge of the ordinary jurisdiction has to serve some time at the public prosecution service.[95] Even though the details of how a judge's career develops differ in each state and according to his or her field of specialisation, it is safe to say that most of them will work during their career both in criminal and private law. However, after becoming a judge at the Bundesgerichtshof (BGH – Federal Supreme Court of Ordinary Jurisdiction) judges will have reached a degree of specialisation which makes it unlikely for them to change between criminal and private law thereafter.

D. *Preserving the unity of the legal system*

This raises the question of how – in a system with distinct jurisdictions and with specialised divisions, chambers and senates – the principle of the unity of the legal system is preserved in practice. The tools are the Great Senates (Große Senate), the United Great Senates (Vereinigte Große Senate) and the Joint Senate of the Federal Supreme Courts (Gemeinsamer Senat der obersten Gerichtshöfe des Bundes). If a senate of the BGH on private law wants to answer a question of private law differently from how another private law senate has already decided it, then, according to § 132 GVG,[96] the matter must be heard by the Great Senate on Civil Matters.

[94] Art. 95(1) GG.

[95] Cf. www.justiz.bayern.de/justiz/berufe-und-stellen/richter-und-staatsanwaelte/ (last visited November 2014).

[96] W. Zimmermann, in *Münchener Kommentar zur Zivilprozessordnung* vol. 3, 4th edn (Munich: Beck, 2013), § 132 GVG para. 1–20.

This Great Senate consists of the President of the BGH and judges from each senate on civil matters. For criminal law there is the corresponding Great Senate on Criminal Matters. If a senate on civil law wants to answer a question of law differently from a senate on criminal law, or *vice versa*, the United Great Senates of the BGH will hear the matter. It comprises the judges of both Great Senates. Finally, there is the Joint Senate of the Federal Supreme Courts which ensures that the BGH and the Federal Supreme Courts of the other jurisdictions do not answer the same question of law differently. The details of this Senate are regulated in Art. 95 GG and in the Federal Act on the Preservation of the Uniformity of the Jurisprudence of the Federal Supreme Courts (Gesetz zur Wahrung der Einheitlichkeit der Rechtsprechungder obersten Gerichtshöfe des Bundes).[97] However, in the context of the present chapter it is clear that these senates are only of little practical importance.

5. The methodological perspective

The constitutional differences between tort and crime have a number of implications. One of these is a methodological one: since criminal proceedings affect the fundamental rights of the accused, German law has adopted the principle of *nulla poena sine lege*, as have other European legal systems.[98] On a European level this principle is laid down in Art. 7(1)(1) ECHR[99] and in Art. 49(1) Charter of Fundamental Rights of the European Union.[100] German law has further specified this principle to mean *nullum crimen, nulla poena sine lege scripta*, *sine lege certa*, *sine lege praevia* and *sine lege stricta*: the penal provision needs to be in writing, it needs to be certain, it needs to be in force when the offence is committed and it needs to be applied strictly. These principles have constitutional status (see Art. 103(2) GG[101]) but are also acknowledged in § 1 StGB.[102] German lawyers have deduced from these principles that it is forbidden

[97] M. Schulte, *Rechtsprechungseinheit als Verfassungsauftrag* (Berlin: Duncker & Humblot, 1986).

[98] See the comparative survey of Schulze-Fielitz, in *Grundgesetz*, Art. 103 II para. 9.

[99] J. Meyer-Ladewig, *Europäische Menschenrechtskonvention*, 3rd edn (Baden-Baden: Nomos, 2011), Art. 7 para. 1.

[100] H. D. Jarass, *Charta der Grundrechte der Europäischen Union*, 2nd edn (Munich: Beck, 2013), Art. 49 para. 10–21.

[101] Schulze-Fielitz, in *Grundgesetz*, Art. 103 II para. 11–62.

[102] R. Schmitz, in *Münchner Kommentar zum Strafgesetzbuch* vol. 1, 2nd edn (Munich: Beck 2011), § 1 StGB para. 1–10.

to apply a provision by way of analogy in order to justify a conviction; the wording of a penal provision ultimately delimits statutory interpretation in criminal law. Furthermore, the legislator has to be exact when drafting penal provisions: the elements which constitute a *crimen* have to be put into precise and clear language, as does the *poena*.[103]

The same principles do not apply to the law of delict. Delictual provisions may be, and in fact are, drafted in a way which would be unacceptable in the criminal law sphere, even though German law does not accept a general clause of delictual liability as French and Austrian law do.[104] § 823(1) BGB states that a 'person who . . . injures the life, body, health, freedom, property or another right of another person is liable to make compensation'. The words 'or another right' are rather unspecific as the legislator leaves open what kind of rights fall under § 823(1) BGB and in a criminal provision such a phrase would be regarded as problematic. § 826 BGB simply states that a 'person who, in a manner contrary to good morals, . . . inflicts damage on another person is liable . . . to make compensation'.[105] The reference to good morals would not be in line with the principle of certainty if it appeared in a criminal provision. Finally, even though there is a reluctance to apply delictual provisions by way of analogy, to do so would not contradict any constitutional principles.[106]

6. The substantive perspective

The principle of the unity of the legal system does not call for sameness but demands consistency only. Different answers to similar questions need to be supported by different policy considerations in order not to conflict with this principle. In the following section, we will turn to the substantive law and identify examples where the law of delict and criminal law coincide and where they do not.

A. *The three 'small' general clauses of fault-based liability for wrongs*

Before doing so, it is necessary to introduce the so-called three 'small' general clauses of fault-based liability for wrongs in the law of delict. Unlike Austrian and French law, German law does not know a general

103 Schulze-Fielitz, in *Grundgesetz*, Art. 103 II para. 38–49.

104 H. G. Leser, 'Zu den Instrumenten des Rechtsgüterschutzes im Delikts- und Gefährdungshaftungsrecht' (1983) 183 *AcP*, 568, 576–9.

105 Authors' translation.

106 See Hager, in *Staudinger*, Vorbem zu §§ 823 para. 29.

clause. § 823(1), § 826 and § 823(2) BGB are, however, referred to as the three small general clauses.[107] In addition, there are other residual grounds of fault-based liability for wrongs. Of the 'small' general clauses, academia focuses on § 823(1) BGB and many problems relating to delictual liability have been discussed with reference to this provision. It reads:

> A person who, intentionally or negligently, unlawfully injures the life, body, health, freedom, property or another right of another person is liable to make compensation to the other party for the damage arising from this.

Under § 823(1) BGB the tortfeasor is liable even if he acted negligently. However, to be liable for a particular damage, it must flow from injury to one of the specific rights set out. Thus, for instance, it does not cover pure economic losses to the injured party as economic interests are not amongst the named rights. One could argue that the words 'another right' could be interpreted widely enough to include such economic interests. Yet, this is not how the BGB has been interpreted. Life, body, health, freedom and property are so called absolute rights and the words 'another right' are understood to include only other absolute rights, for example, the *allgemeines Persönlichkeitsrecht* (general right to privacy) and the *Recht am eingerichteten und ausgeübten Gewerbebetrieb* (right of an established and operating business enterprise), but not the assets.[108] Thus, in the case of § 823(1) BGB, it is necessary to establish the injury of an absolute right on the one hand and a resulting loss on the other hand. § 826 BGB then states:[109]

> A person who, in a manner contrary to good morals, intentionally inflicts damage on another person is liable to the other person to make compensation for the damage.

Under § 826 BGB, negligence will not do. The tortfeasor must have acted intentionally. However, pursuant to § 826 BGB, it is enough if the tortfeasor causes a pure economic loss to the injured party. It is not necessary that the tortfeasor has injured an absolute right that results in a damage.

107 Wandt, *Schuldverhältnisse*, para. 15.7. See also R. Zimmermann and D. A. Verse, 'Die Reaktion des Reichsgerichts auf die Kodifikation des deutschen Deliktsrechts (1900–1914)' in U. Falk and H. Mohnhaupt (eds.), *Das Bürgerliche Gesetzbuch und seine Richter* (Frankfurt: Klostermann, 2000), 319, 321; G. Schiemann, in M. Schmoeckel *et al.* (eds.), *Historisch-kritischer Kommentar zum BGB* vol. 3/2 (Tübingen: Mohr Siebeck, 2013), §§ 823–30 para. 20–5.

108 For further examples, see Deutsch and Ahrens, *Deliktsrecht*, para. 175.

109 Authors' translation.

Finally, there is § 823(2) BGB:

> The same duty [the duty to make compensation] is held by a person who commits a breach of a statute that is intended to protect another person. If, according to the contents of the statute, it may also be breached without fault, then liability to compensation only exists in the case of fault.

§ 823(2) BGB requires a breach of a statutory provision which is intended to protect another person, itself requiring fault at least in the form of intent or negligence.

B. *Differentness*

The starting point is similar in both private and the criminal law. *Casum sentit dominus* is the point of departure in the law of delict:[110] the damage lies where it falls. A claim for damage is only granted when there is special justification for doing so. Shifting the loss is justified in the accepted cases of fault-based liability for wrongs and of *Gefährdungshaftung*. Equally, in the criminal law sphere, we need a special justification for punishing. These justifications are enumerated under the criminal provisions.

Turning to the requirements of delictual and criminal liability, we are able to see that both have the same general requirements. Or to put it differently: both private and criminal lawyers group the different detailed requirements of delictual and criminal liability together, and these groups of requirements are similar: *Tatbestandsmäßigkeit*, wrongfulness and guilt/fault.[111] Each of these general requirements involves a different value judgment.[112]

The distinction between these requirements becomes apparent from the wording of § 823(1) BGB. For a private lawyer, the *Tatbestandsmäßigkeit* describes the *objective* elements of delictual liability. Under § 823(1) BGB, there are three such objective elements: the injury of an absolute right of another person; the act of the tortfeasor ('a person who . . . injures'); and the causal nexus between this act and the injury. In addition, § 823(1) BGB requires that all of this needs to have been unlawful. And finally, the tortfeasor must have acted intentionally or negligently: he must have been at fault.

[110] Deutsch and Ahrens, *Deliktsrecht*, para. 1.

[111] Larenz and Canaris, *Schuldrecht*, 362; P. Wittig, *Wirtschaftsstrafrecht*, 3rd edn (Munich: Beck, 2014), para. 5.1.

[112] Roxin, *Strafrecht*, para. 14.1–3, 19.1–9.

While criminal lawyers speak of the same three general requirements, they understand them slightly differently. For a criminal lawyer, *Tatbestandsmäßigkeit* describes the *objective* and *subjective* elements of a criminal offence. The objective elements of a criminal offence are to be found in the many provisions of, for example, the StGB. The difference from the law of delict is that the subjective elements are already of relevance in the first general requirement of *Tatbestandsmäßigkeit* (and in addition in the third requirement of guilt) whereas in delict subjective elements only appear in the third general requirement, that is, fault. This difference results from the criminal law's acceptance of the so-called *finale Handlungslehre* according to which every prohibited act must be supported by a will for there to be liabilty.[113]

We may conclude that both criminal and private lawyers use similar concepts. We turn now to examples where these similar concepts are applied differently.

1. The elements of delictual and criminal liability

We will start with the elements of delictual and criminal liability (*Tatbestandsmäßigkeit*). Before turning to more subtle differences, we will point out some very obvious ones.

(a) Legislative style. There are obvious differences in how the elements of delictual liability and the elements of a criminal offence are drafted. In the law of delict, we find the three small general clauses which are drafted in a style to cover very diverse cases. The legislative style in the criminal law sphere is different. The StGB, as you would expect from the foregoing constitutional and methodological discussions, provides us with many individual provisions which define the elements of an offence very specifically.

(b) Attempt. If an attempt does not result in damage, the law of delict will not step in.[114] Nevertheless, it may be a criminal offence as is, according to § 223(2) StGB, the case with an attempt to physically assault or to damage the health of another. The different policy considerations – the importance of the compensatory function in the law of delict and the importance of the preventive function in criminal law – justify criminal law's intervention even though no injury has occurred.

[113] H. Welzel, 'Die deutsche strafrechtliche Dogmatik der letzten 100 Jahre und die finale Handlungslehre' (1966) *JuS*, 421, 424; H. Welzel, *Das deutsche Strafrecht*, 11th edn (Berlin: de Gruyter, 1969), 30, 33, 35.

[114] Deutsch, *Haftungsrecht*, 90.

(c) Injury of a protected legal interest versus damage. A criminal lawyer is concerned with the injury of protected legal interests (*Verletzungsdelikte*) and with putting such interests at the risk of being injured (*Gefährdungsdelikte*). In both cases the focus of a criminal lawyer is on the protected interest: has it been injured, interfered with or put at risk?

The law of delict is concerned with protecting legal interest, too. However, a delict lawyer has a different focus. The crucial question in his mind is whether the victim has suffered damage. At first sight, the difference seems to be minor. We have just seen that in the case of § 823(1) BGB we actually need both, the injury of an absolute right and damage. In other cases, the injury of the protected interest and the damage are identical, as is the case with fraud. The protected interest of the criminal provision relevant to fraud, § 263 StGB, are the assets (*Vermögensdelikt*);[115] the damage suffered may be recoverable under §§ 823(2) BGB, 263 StGB.

The different focus in criminal and private law becomes clear when we consider cases in which the damage is remote from the injury of the protected interest. A case of the Imperial Supreme Court (RG – Reichsgericht) serves as an example:[116] in 1903 the claimant was run over by a carriage. The carriage was out of control because the defendant's train intimidating the coachman's horses, causing them to bolt. As a result the claimant lost a leg. In the first action in 1907 the court awarded him damages in form of a sum to be paid annually thereafter. In 1925, the claimant fell, broke his shoulder and his right arm became disabled. This accident was caused by the fact that the claimant only had one leg and was not able to move properly with his prosthesis. In 1927, the RG awarded the claimant further damages in form of an annual sum. If the defendant had been criminally liable under § 229 StGB for causing a bodily harm to the victim by acting negligently he would have been convicted once. Later damages resulting from the act that only appear after conviction are irrelevant. In contrast, in private law courts are concerned with the question of allocating all the loss resulting from the act and they may return to the case when further loss appears. This difference relates to the different functions of the law of delict and criminal law. The law of delict has a compensatory function and the wrongful act is simply the vehicle to attribute the loss to the tortfeasor. In criminal law the wrongful act is not simply the vehicle to attribute the loss to the wrongdoer but the very reason for punishing him.

[115] Wittig, *Wirtschaftsrecht*, para. 14.4.

[116] RGZ 119, 204 (1927).

(d) Protecting different legal interests. Furthermore, we find legal interests to be protected in criminal law which are not, and should not be, protected in the law of delict. According to § 90a StGB it is, for example, a criminal offence to publicly disparage the German flag. § 90a StGB is not without problems and there is controversy over which legal interests are protected by § 90a StGB.[117] Irrespective of these problems, it is clear that such act does not, according to modern legal reasoning, constitute a tort in the private law sphere.

(e) Defining the legal interests differently. In many cases the protected legal interest is phrased differently in delict than in crime and this leads to a different understanding. § 823(1) BGB speaks of 'A person who . . . injures . . . the . . . property . . . of another person.' Private lawyers understand this phrase broadly: even the interference with the use of the property may count as an injury of the property.[118] The so-called *Fleetfall* of the BGH may serve as an example:[119]

> The defendant Federal Republic of Germany was the owner of a navigable channel [a *Fleet*] which connected a mill with the port of B. During the night of 21 October 1965, part of the wall forming the bank collapsed bringing down part of the external wall of a dwelling house based on it. In order to prevent a further collapse of the house, its owner, acting in accordance with an order of the competent authority . . . inserted beams as support. Two of these were inserted between the two banks of the channel . . . Thus the channel was effectively closed . . . As a result the plaintiff's motor vessel *Christel* was immobilised at the mill; nor could the plaintiff approach the mill with his other vessels, as he was contractually bound to do, in order to carry goods to and from the mill. He claimed damages . . . for loss of earnings.

The BGH held that the defendant injured the plaintiff's property rights with regard to the vessel *Christel* but not with regard to the other vessels, as only *Christel* could not be used as a means of transport at all.[120] No criminal liability would exist on these facts. The appropriate provision, § 303 StGB, phrases the legal interest in terms of damage or destruction, not use: 'Whosoever unlawfully damages or destroys an object belonging to another shall be liable to imprisonment not exceeding two years or a fine.' According to § 303 StGB, it is not an offence to interfere with the use

117 H.-U. Paeffgen, in: Kindhäuser *et al.* (eds.), *Strafgesetzbuch*, § 90a para. 2.

118 Wandt, *Schuldverhältnisse*, para. 16.30–4.

119 BGHZ 55, 153 (1970). The translation of the facts is taken from Markesinis and Unberath, *Torts*, 219.

120 On the further details Medicus and Lorenz, *Besonderer Teil*, para. 1288–90.

of the property of another.[121] In any case, in those cases where it has been held that the tortfeasor is liable under § 823(1) BGB for such interference he acted negligently;[122] § 303 StGB, on the other hand, requires intent. The requirement of intent does not appear on the face of § 303 StGB but follows from a provision in the general part of the StGB, § 15. But even if the wrongdoer acted intentionally he is not criminally liable under § 303 StGB. Nevertheless, he might be so liable for the injury of another legal interest. § 240(1) StGB may apply: 'Whosoever unlawfully with force or threat of serious harm causes a person to commit, suffer or omit an act shall be liable to imprisonment not exceeding three years or a fine.'

We may also find similarities when comparing the legal interests which are protected both in delict and criminal law. Both § 823(1) BGB and § 223(1) StGB speak of an injury of the body of another. The question of what counts as a body injury is answered identically in private and criminal law.[123] Nevertheless, there are also differences and one of them relates to who may be a victim. Private lawyers do not see a problem to apply § 823(1) BGB to unborn babies or babies who are not as yet conceived, thus to acts happening before conception and causing later injuries to a baby. If through medical malpractice the mother of a child, the child having at the time of the medical malpractice not as yet been conceived, is injured and later the baby is born with a medical condition caused by the medical malpractice done to the mother, the medical doctor is directly liable for the damage to the baby.[124] The problem is that one cannot, strictly speaking, say that the baby has been injured because it was never without the medical condition. By comparison, the only criminal law provision relevant to the unborn baby is § 218 StGB which penalises (intentional) abortion.[125] The unborn baby cannot be the victim of § 223(1) StGB. The reader might wonder whether this difference does not conflict with the principle of the unity of the legal system. A German lawyer would answer this question in the negative. § 1 BGB states that the 'legal capacity of a human being begins on the completion of birth'. One would assume that in the criminal and the private law sphere, one is only able to be the holder of a protected legal interest on completion of birth.

[121] J. Wessels and T. Hillenkamp, *Strafrecht Besonderer Teil 2*, 37th edn (Heidelberg: Müller, 2014) para. 141.

[122] BGHZ 55, 153 (1970); BGHZ 105, 346 (1988); BGH, NJW 1994, 517.

[123] Medicus and Lorenz, *Besonderer Teil*, para. 1272.

[124] Wandt, *Schuldverhältnisse*, para. 16.10–1; BGHZ 124, 128 (1993).

[125] A. Eser, in A. Schönke and H. Schröder (eds.), *Strafgesetzbuch*, 19th edn (Munich: Beck, 2014), § 218 para. 1–3.

Criminal lawyers argue that they are not bound by § 1 BGB and may autonomously define when somebody may be the holder of a protected legal interest. They say that the legal capacity begins with the beginning of birth that is the point of time when the first stage pains start. Thus, a child will be criminally protected under § 223(1) StGB once the mother has gone into her first stage pains even though at that point of time the child does not have the legal capacity of a human being under § 1 BGB. However, in the present context, even the law of delict departs from § 1 BGB by holding that somebody who has not been born can be injured in an absolute right.[126]

(f) Causation. There are further differences concerning causation. According to the prevailing opinion in criminal law one starts off with the *Äquivalenztheorie* (theory of equivalence): the act must have been a *conditio sine qua non*:[127] English lawyers speak of a 'but for' test. The theory is called *Äquivalenztheorie* because it treats all acts which are a *conditio sine qua non* as equivalent conditions to the result.[128] It follows that the infinity of the *Äquivalenztheorie* has to be limited by additional criteria – since, for instance, the act of giving birth to a murderer 'causes' the murder decades later. Large parts of literature argue that this problem can already be solved on the level of the *objektiver Tatbestand* by applying the principles of *objektive Zurechnung* (objective attribution).[129] Accordingly, a result is not attributable to the wrongdoer if it was, for example, objectively unforeseeable, objectively unavoidable or if it was not covered by the protective ratio of the infringed norm.[130]

Equally, the private lawyer starts out with the *Äquivalenztheorie* and he, too, has to restrict its infinity.[131] Yet, there is a distinction which is of great importance in private law but of no importance in criminal law: under § 823(1) BGB, private lawyers distinguish between two forms of causation.[132] According to the wording of § 823(1) BGB, the tortfeasor must have injured an absolute right of the victim by his actions, and will

[126] There is a controversy how this departure from § 1 BGB can be explained: see Staake, *Gesetzliche Schuldverhältnisse*, para. 8.25.

[127] Compare BGHSt 1, 332 (1951); Wessels, *Allgemeiner Teil*, para. 156.

[128] Wittig, *Wirtschaftsrecht*, para 6.36–38; Roxin, *Strafrecht*, para. 11.6–19; D. Medicus and S. Lorenz, *Schuldrecht I. Allgemeiner Teil*, 20th edn (Munich: Beck, 2012), para. 636.

[129] BGHSt 32, 262 (1984); Wessels, *Allgemeiner Teil*, para. 178.

[130] On the details, see Roxin, *Strafrecht*, para. 11.44–105; Rengier, *Strafrecht. Allgemeiner Teil*, para. 13.38–99.

[131] Oetker, in *Münchener Kommentar*, § 249 para. 103.

[132] Wandt, *Schuldverhältnisse*, para. 16.123–4.

be liable for any loss of the victim resulting from the injury. Thus, there is the *haftungsbegründende Kausalität*, liability generating causation. It describes the nexus between the tortfeasor's act and the injury. A medical practitioner commits malpractice and causes bodily harm to a patient. Then there is the *haftungsausfüllende Kausalität*, liability fulfilling causation. It describes the nexus between the injury and the damage. The injured patient has to incur costs for his treatment, he has loss of earning and he suffers considerably from pain. For the common lawyer, the problems surrounding the *haftungsausfüllende Kausalität* are discussed under the heading of remoteness of damage.[133]

The distinction between the two forms of causation is only of importance for § 823(1) BGB. § 826 BGB does not require the injury of an absolute right and, thus, there is only one form of causation involved. However, even though § 826 BGB does not distinguish between two forms of causation, a difference arises under criminal law which flows from the point we identified above: the criminal lawyer's focus is on the injury of a protected interest and the private lawyer's focus is on the damage. § 826 BGB requires a nexus between the tortfeasor's act and the damage.[134] In contrast, criminal lawyers are concerned with what a private lawyer calls *haftungsbegründende Kausalität*, the causation between the act and the injury of the protected legal interest.

Criminal lawyers limit the infinity of the *Äquivalenztheorie* when discussing the causal nexus between the offender's act and the resulting injury. Private lawyers often say that there is no need to restrict causality on the level of the *haftungsbegründende Kausalität*.[135] This relates to another difference between criminal and private law: under § 823(1) BGB, the *haftungsbegründende Kausalität* is part of the objective elements of delictual liability. The tortfeasor has to act intentionally or negligently and the intent or negligence has to relate to the *haftungsbegründende Kausalität*. However, according to the wording of § 823(1) BGB, the tortfeasor need not have acted intentionally or negligently with respect to the damage resulting from the injury. Thus, the infinity of the *Äquivalenztheorie* may on the level of the *haftungsbegründende Kausalität* be restricted by the requirement of fault:[136] an injury of one of the named protected legal interests which was neither foreseeable nor avoidable will not lead to any

[133] Markesinis and Unberath, *Torts*, 106. [134] Looschelders, *Allgemeiner Teil*, para. 893.

[135] Deutsch and Ahrens, *Deliktsrecht*, para. 47, 420. For a different perspective, see Oetker, in *Münchener Kommentar*, § 249 para. 108.

[136] Deutsch and Ahrens, *Deliktsrecht*, para. 420.

liability. The same is not possible on the level of the *haftungsausfüllende Kausalität*, the liability fulfilling causation between the injury and the damage.

There is a further difference between private and criminal law in terms of causation: the infinity of the *Äquivalenztheorie* is restricted in criminal law by applying the principles of *objektive Zurechnung*. Private lawyers also speak of *objektive Zurechnung*[137] yet under this heading they apply the *Adäquanztheorie*[138] – a theory which criminal lawyers do not follow. According to the *Adäquanztheorie*, a damage which is highly unusual and which could not have been foreseen by an ideal observer will not count.[139] In addition, private lawyers also refer to the protective ratio of the infringed norm.[140] The relationship of the protective ratio to the *Adäquanztheorie* is still unclear.[141]

The most important difference between causation in private law and criminal law is that in criminal law the infinity of the *Äquivalenztheorie* is restricted further than in private law. Two academics, E. Deutsch and H. J. Ahrens, analysed the relevant case law and came to the conclusion that private lawyers rarely negate causality by use of the *Adäquanztheorie*.[142] That private lawyers do not do so is not actually a consequence of the structural differences which we just have pointed out: rather it is a consequence of applying the substantial requirements of foreseeability and also of the protective ratio of the infringed norm differently.

A case of the BGH will exemplify what we mean:[143] after an accident, a surgeon removed a kidney of a thirteen year old girl without noticing that she was born only with one kidney. The removal of her only kidney constituted medical malpractice. The girl's mother agreed to donate one of her kidneys to her daughter. Subsequently the mother suffered harm from living with only one kidney and she claimed damages from the surgeon. She relied on § 823(1) BGB. It was not sufficient to argue that the damage was still attributable to the surgeon: § 823(1) BGB requires

[137] Looschelders, *Allgemeiner Teil*, para. 901–9.

[138] Deutsch and Ahrens, *Deliktsrecht*, para. 52, 420; Medicus and Lorenz, *Allgemeiner Teil*, para. 638; Wandt, *Schuldverhältnisse*, para. 16.133–5; BGHZ 3, 261 (1951); BGH, NJW 2012, 2964.

[139] BGHZ 3, 261–70 (1951); BGH, NJW 2002 2232–4.

[140] Looschelders, *Allgemeiner Teil*, para. 906–9; Wandt, *Schuldverhältnisse*, para. 16.136.

[141] See the discussion and case law cited in Medicus and Lorenz, *Allgemeiner Teil*, para. 640.

[142] Deutsch and Ahrens, *Deliktsrecht*, para. 53–5. See also the analysis of Oetker, in *Münchener Kommentar*, § 249 para. 114–15.

[143] BGHZ 101 215 (1987). See also Looschelders, *Allgemeiner Teil*, para. 927.

that the malpractice caused the mother's injury (*haftungsbegründende Kausalität*) and that she suffered damage as a result of her injury (*haftungsausfüllende Kausalität*). The first form of causation was problematic in the present case but ultimately the BGH held that the mother's injury was still attributable to the surgeon's medical malpractice. She succeeded with her claim. However, would the surgeon have been criminally liable under § 229 StGB for negligently causing harm to the mother? The BGH did not have to answer this question but it would most probably be in the negative: the protective purpose of § 229 StGB is said not to include indirect harm to third persons.[144] The mother's donation of a kidney is such an indirect harm. Furthermore, it was deliberate self-harming behaviour by the mother. Thus, the indirect harm to the mother as third person was in her control. To hold the surgeon criminally liable for negligently causing harm to the mother would provide her the power to 'create' the surgeon's criminal liability by donating a kidney. The 'psychological pressure' under which the mother acted, thus, leads in the present case to delictual, but not to criminal liability.

In summary, there are structural differences between the discussion of causation in criminal and private law. Apart from these structural differences, criminal and private lawyers use similar, substantial criteria to answer the question whether the injury or whether the damage is still attributable to the wrongdoer. However, when applying these criteria, private lawyers are more ready to answer questions of attribution in the affirmative than criminal lawyers are. The reasons for these substantial differences are clear: private law is about compensation. Criminal law is about whether the state has a right to punish because the offender has done a wrong. Private lawyers more readily see a justification to shift a loss to a tortfeasor whereas criminal lawyers require more to see a legitimate reason to punish the wrongdoer.

2. Wrongfulness

Turning to the second general requirement, wrongfulness (or unlawfulness), we find again differences between the law of delict and criminal law. In criminal law, an act which is *tatbestandsmäßig* – which fulfils the objective and subjective elements of crime – is unlawful unless it is justified. It may, for example, be justified under § 32 StGB in the case of

[144] C. Roxin, 'Zum Schutzzweck der Norm bei fahrlässigen Delikten' in K. Lackner (ed.), *Festschrift für Wilhelm Gallas zum 70. Geburtstag* (Berlin: de Gruyter, 1973), 241, 256; M. Burgstaller, *Das Fahrlässigkeitsdelikt im Strafrecht* (Vienna: Manz, 1974), 126.

self-defence. Criminal lawyers say that the wrongfulness follows from the *Tatbestandsmäßigkeit*. This means that a court does not have to positively ascertain the wrongfulness. There are only rare exceptions in which the wrongfulness has to be ascertained positively. They are specifically set out in the StGB, for example in § 240(2) StGB:

> (1) Whosoever unlawfully with force or threat of serious harm causes a person to commit, suffer or omit an act shall be liable to imprisonment not exceeding three years or a fine.
> (2) The act shall be unlawful if the use of force or the threat of harm is deemed inappropriate for the purpose of achieving the desired outcome.

The protected legal interest in § 240(1) StGB is very open textured: it is the personal autonomy to form a free will and to act freely.[145] The protection of such an open textured legal interest is said to need further restriction on the level of wrongfulness.[146]

In the private law sphere the matter is more complicated. We have to distinguish between two types of cases.[147] The first encompasses those in which the wrongfulness follows from the *Tatbestandsmäßigkeit*, too (*Lehre vom Erfolgsunrecht*) and all one has to do is see whether the act is justified. The *Lehre vom Erfolgsunrecht* covers most cases of a direct injury of an absolute right. However, in case of an injury by omission and in case of an indirect injury, the wrongfulness has to be ascertained positively (*Lehre vom Handlungsunrecht*). It is positively ascertained by constructing a duty of care (*Verkehrspflicht*), though the details of this technique are hotly contested. The 'duty of care' within § 823(1) BGB has a different function than in the English tort of negligence. In particular, in German law not every damage resulting from a breach of a duty of care must be compensated. § 823(1) BGB always requires that the breach of the duty of care must first have infringed an absolute right.[148] *Prima facie*, we do not have similar discussions on the criminal law side. However, on closer

[145] A. Eser and J. Eisele, in Schönke and Schröder (eds.), *Strafgesetzbuch*, § 240 para. 1.

[146] R. Rengier, *Strafrecht. Besonderer Teil II*, 14th edn (Munich: Beck, 2013) para. 23.57–62.

[147] Medicus and Lorenz, *Besonderer Teil*, para. 1240–3; Wagner, in *Münchener Kommentar*, § 823 para. 4–27; G. Hager, 'Zum Begriff der Rechtswidrigkeit im Zivilrecht' in D. Bickel *et al.* (eds.), *Recht und Rechtserkenntnis. Festschrift für Ernst Wolf* (Cologne: Heymanns, 1985), 133–42; K. Larenz, 'Rechtswidrigkeit und Handlungsbegriff im Zivilrecht' in E. von Caemmerer *et al.* (eds.), *Vom Deutschen zum Europäischen Recht. Festschrift für Hans Dölle* vol. 1 (Tübingen: Mohr Siebeck 1963), 169–200.

[148] For the details Deutsch and Ahrens, *Deliktsrecht*, para. 254.

examination, it seems that the differences are again only structural: they relate to how we analyse the problem. Take the case of omissions: private lawyers say that it is wrongful to cause the infringement of a protected legal interest by omission if there is a duty to act. The most important examples are the control of a source of danger, the exercise of a dangerous activity and antecedent dangerous activity.[149] Criminal lawyers apply exactly the same criteria on the level of *Tatbestandsmäßigkeit* when asking whether an omission may be sufficient to trigger criminal liability.[150]

Other than omissions, there are further cases in which wrongfulness has to be ascertained positively and does not simply follow from the *Tatbestandsmäßigkeit.* These cases concern certain absolute rights such as the *allgemeines Persönlichkeitsrecht* (general right to privacy) and the *Recht am eingerichteten und ausgeübten Gewerbebetrieb* (right of an established and operating business enterprise). These rights count as absolute rights within the meaning of § 823(1) BGB. The concept of the general right to privacy is known to the reader from other jurisdictions and there is no need to explain it here.[151] The right of an established and operating business enterprise is a little more distinctive and requires explanation. Such a right may be infringed, for example, if another person publicly calls for a boycott of a certain business. The background of both rights is to be found in the shortcomings of § 823(2) BGB and § 826 BGB.[152] For example, with respect to the general right to privacy it was considered inadequate to grant claims for damages only in the case of defamation. In such a scenario, § 823(2) BGB would apply and the statutory provision which is intended to protect another person, would be §§ 185–8 StGB. Both the right to privacy and the right of an established and operating business enterprise are, just like § 240(1) StGB in criminal law, very open textured. This was why it was felt that the wrongfulness in respect of them has to be ascertained positively by balancing out the involved legal interests.

Finally, there are some substantial differences in wrongfulness. The most significant of which is a matter that appears only in private law, and which we can only note briefly here: insurance. In private law only, questions of whether the injurer or the injured party had insurance coverage or could have received such coverage might influence the question of

[149] Medicus and Lorenz, *Besonderer Teil*, para. 1244–9.
[150] Rengier, *Strafrecht. Allgemeiner Teil*, para. 48.
[151] On the details Wandt, *Schuldverhältnisse*, para. 16.49–72.
[152] Zimmermann and Verse, 'Reaktion des Reichsgerichts', 326–9.

wrongfulness.[153] To give just one example: an injurer does not act wrongfully if the injured party had consented to the injury or to his absolute right being put at the risk of being injured. In some cases we might have an express consent. But under what circumstances can we say that the injured party has given an implied consent? – One relevant point is who was able to insure against the risk materialising.[154]

3. Fault and guilt

Turning to the next requirement of delictual and criminal liability, we are able to see fundamental differences: in criminal law the offender must be personally guilty.[155] Personal guilt is a purely subjective concept. In private law, personal guilt is not necessary.[156] The tortfeasor must be at fault. Fault is an objective concept. The differences are reflected in a different terminology. Whereas private lawyers speak of *Verschulden* (fault), criminal lawyers use the term *Schuld* (guilt).

(a) The Schuldprinzip *and the* Verschuldensprinzip *compared.* In the criminal law sphere we speak of the principle of guilt (*Schuldprinzip*): there is no punishment without personal guilt – *nulla poena sine culpa.*[157] This is an absolute principle without exceptions. Furthermore, the punishment has to be proportionate to the offender's personal guilt.[158] The higher the degree of personal guilt, the more severe the penalty will be. Private lawyers speak of the principle of fault (*Verschuldensprinzip*): delictual liability requires fault.[159] However, this is not an absolute principle. German private law knows instances of strict liability. Furthermore, the degree of fault does not have any influence on the measure of damages. The tortfeasor will be liable to compensate the full loss, and nothing more, irrespective of whether he was acting negligently only or whether he was acting with intent. There are two exceptions: the measure of damages for pain and suffering is said to depend on the degree of fault.[160] And, of course, § 826 BGB requires intent.

(b) Defining negligence. Fault and guilt both comprise intent and negligence. Intent is, in general terms, defined similarly in the law of delict and in criminal law as *Wissen und Wollen*, as acting with knowledge and

[153] See von Bar, (1981) 181 *AcP*, 324–5.
[154] Hager, in *Staudinger*, Vorbem zu §§ 823 para. 43–6.
[155] Rengier, *Strafrecht. Allgemeiner Teil*, para. 24, 1; Roxin, *Strafrecht*, para 19.
[156] Deutsch and Ahrens, *Deliktsrecht*, para. 123.
[157] Rengier, *Strafrecht. Allgemeiner Teil*, para. 24; BVerfGE 20, 323 (1966).
[158] Roxin, *Strafrecht*, para. 19.1–9.
[159] Looschelders, *Allgemeiner Teil*, para. 227–8.
[160] Ibid., para. 973.

wilfully with respect to the elements of the delictual and criminal liability as defined above and, in the law of delict, with respect to wrongfulness. However, the subjective approach to guilt in the criminal law sphere and the objective approach to fault in the private law sphere become obvious when comparing the definitions of negligence. In criminal law, negligence is both an objective and subjective concept. Negligence is understood objectively in the *Tatbestandsmäßigkeit*. The accused is objectively negligent if he has not observed the degree of diligence, prudence and foresight that is reasonably and ordinarily exercised by a person under the same or similar circumstances and conditions. A subjective concept of negligence is considered on the level of guilt. If the accused personally was not able to foresee and to avoid committing the offence, he will not be punished. In the private law sphere, negligence is not discussed on the level of *Tatbestandsmäßigkeit* but only in terms of fault and here it is a purely objective concept. The wrongdoer will be liable in damages if a person in the position of the wrongdoer would have been able to foresee and to avoid the wrongdoing.[161] The wrongdoer will not be able to escape his delictual liability by arguing that he subjectively was not able to foresee the injury of the other party. This is what is meant when German lawyers speak of an objective notion of negligence.

The objective approach to negligence in private law is sometimes justified by reasons of the 'protection of transactions' (*Verkehrsschutz*, on which more below).[162] However, this justification is not of strong force in the law of delict and one could, as some authors do, argue in favour of a subjective approach in the delictual setting. It is argued that the objective approach is rather justified in a contractual setting. For instance, if somebody undertakes to carry out medical treatment, the other party should be protected in his expectation that the treatment provider will have the expertise of an ordinary treatment provider. The treatment provider should be unable to escape liability by arguing that his expertise is so below that of an average treatment provider that he was subjectively unable to foresee and to avoid the injury. Thus, it is justified to use an objective notion of negligence in a contractual setting. In tort law this reasoning does not have equal force.[163] For instance, it is questionable that somebody

[161] BGH NJW 2000, 2737, 2740; Wandt, *Schuldverhältnisse*, para. 16.172.

[162] Looschelders, *Besonderer Teil*, para. 1192. For a detailed discussion Wagner, in *Münchener Kommentar*, § 823 para. 36–41.

[163] H. Koziol, 'Objektivierung des Fahrlässigkeitsmaßstabes im Schadensrecht?' (1996) 196 *AcP*, 593–610.

injured in a car accident should be protected in his expectation that every participant in motor traffic, and consequently also the tortfeasor, will have the ability of a reasonable car driver. There is no reason to protect such an expectation as everybody knows that there are rather incompetent drivers on the road. Thus, one could adopt a subjective notion of negligence in the delictual setting. Yet, private lawyers feel that it is preferable to define negligence the same way across private law. This uniform approach is supported by the fact that we find one definition of negligence in § 276(2) BGB which applies equally to the law of contract and the law of delict. It is even said[164] that the definition of § 276(2) BGB has an objective spin to it: 'A person acts negligently if he fails to exercise reasonable care.' 'Reasonable care' is not the best translation for the German phrase '*im Verkehr erforderliche Sorgfalt*'. There is no good English translation for the word '*Verkehr*'. In the beginning of this paragraph we have translated it as transaction (protection of transaction – *Verkehrsschutz*). However, it refers more broadly to interacting with everything externally. And negligence is defined as the care which is required ('*erforderlich*') in the course of such interaction.

(c) Age of accountability. A further difference between the law of delict and criminal law exists with respect to the age of accountability. It is important to note that somebody who has not reached the age of accountability is able to commit a wrong. However, in criminal law he cannot be punished because his personal guilt is excluded. Equally, in the law of delict, anybody who has not reached the age of accountability is understood to have the ability to act wrongfully but he can nevertheless not be liable in damages if he was not able to discern that he acted in a way that attracts accountability.

In private law, under § 828(1) BGB, a person under the age of seven years is not liable in delict.[165] He does not have delictual capacity. According to § 828(3) BGB, a person between the age of seven and seventeen years has limited delictual capacity. He needs to have the ability to discern that he is responsible for his action. It is not a requirement of liability that the underage tortfeasor was able to understand in the concrete situation that he acted wrong and that he was, in the concrete situation, able to act differently. The capacity of discernment is determined in the abstract. There is a further provision in § 828(2) BGB which is not relevant now. What is important is that, according to § 829 BGB, a minor who is not

[164] Medicus and Lorenz, *Allgemeiner Teil*, para. 368.

[165] On the following, Looschelders, *Besonderer Teil*, para. 1194.

liable under § 828 BGB may be liable out of reasons of equity. § 829 BGB states:

> A person who, for reasons, cited in sections 827 and 828, is not responsible for damage he caused in the instances specified in sections 823 to 826 must nonetheless make compensation for the damage, unless damage compensation can be obtained from a third party with a duty of supervision, to the extent that in the circumstances, including without limitation the circumstances of the parties involved, equity requires indemnification and he is not deprived of the resources needed for reasonable maintenance and to discharge his statutory maintenance duties.

§ 829 BGB does not only apply to an underage tortfeasor in the meaning of § 828 BGB but also to those who commit a wrong 'in a state of unconsciousness or in a state of pathological mental disturbance precluding free exercise of will' who are not liable under § 827 BGB.

Liability under § 829 BGB requires that (a) the minor would, apart from his lacking full delictual capacity, be liable under §§ 823 to 826 BGB, (b) the injured party does not have a claim against a third party (e.g., against the parents under § 832(1) BGB[166]) and (c) equity requires liability of the underage tortfeasor irrespective of him lacking full delictual capacity. This last requirement of equity applies, for example, where the underage tortfeasor has considerable means whereas the injured party does not or where the damage is covered by the minor's compulsory liability insurance.[167]

It might come as a surprise to a non-German lawyer that there are a number of cases concerning § 829 BGB. Who would sue a minor? And why would one do so? In a case decided by the OLG Köln, for example, the seven-year-old defendant panicked when seeing a wasp, tried to defend himself with a knife and thereby hurt the six-year-old plaintiff.[168] The reason why anyone would sue a minor is to be found in the fact that (a) the parents are not strictly liable under § 832(1) BGB and (b) insurance coverage is so widespread in Germany.

[166] 'A person who is obliged by operation of law to supervise a person who requires supervision because he is a minor . . . is liable to make compensation for the damage that this person unlawfully causes to a third party. Liability in damages does not apply if he fulfils the requirements of his duty to supervise or if the damage would likewise have been caused in the case of proper conduct of supervision.'

[167] On the details, E. Lorenz, 'Einfluß der Haftpflichtversicherungen auf die Billigkeitshaftung nach § 829 BGB' in V. Beuthin *et al.* (eds.), *Festschrift für Dieter Medicus* (Cologne: Heymanns, 1999), 353–65.

[168] OLGR Köln 2000, 293.

Turning to criminal law, pursuant to § 19 StGB, a person under the age of fourteen cannot be held criminally liable. The StGB takes the position that children under that age lack the capacity to be guilty. Every criminal proceeding against a person under the age of fourteen must be terminated without judgment. There is no exception for reasons of equity as in § 829 BGB. Furthermore, for juveniles between the age of fourteen to seventeen (*Jugendliche*) and for young adults of the age of eighteen to twenty (*Heranwachsende*), the Youth Courts Act (Jugendgerichtsgesetz – JGG) provides special provisions. With regards to juveniles, the capacity to be guilty must be examined by the court and, in its judgment, it must state such capacity individually (§ 3 JGG). Such a finding must cover whether the juvenile was mature enough to understand the unlawfulness of the deed he committed and whether he acted according to that appreciation. Young adults on the other hand have criminal capacity. However, in case the young adult lacks maturity or is delayed in his personal development, the provisions concerning juvenile wrongdoers will be applied regardless of the age.[169] Again, in private law, there is no special treatment of young adults between the ages of eighteen to twenty in the same fashion as the JGG.

(d) Conclusion. There are many other differences between the substance of delict and crime. In the law of delict we have, for example, some special grounds of liability in which it is presumed that the tortfeasor acted with fault.[170] In the criminal law sphere, a presumption of guilt is regarded as unconstitutional and in contrast there is a presumption of innocence.[171] All such differences are explicable by reference to the general differences between the law of delict and criminal law: criminal law is about the state punishing an individual for committing a wrong. The law of delict is about allocating a loss between two private individuals.

C. Sameness across the legal system

In the previous subsections we looked at structural and substantive differences between criminal law and the law of delict. However, there are also examples of provisions of private, public and criminal law applied across the whole legal system that allow us to observe instances of uniformity of crime and delict. The prime examples are reasons which exclude

169 B.-D. Meier, D. Rössner and H. Schöch, *Jugendstrafrecht*, 3rd edn (Munich: Beck, 2013), para. 5.1–31.

170 On these grounds of liability Deutsch and Ahrens, *Deliktsrecht*, para. 316–40.

171 BVerfGE 9, 167, 169 (1959); BVerfGE 74, 358, 370–1 (1987).

wrongfulness as, for example, self-defence. We find such reasons both in the BGB and the StGB. Those reasons which justify a wrongdoing and are regulated in the BGB, will, in general,[172] be applied in criminal law; those in the StGB similarly apply in civil law.[173] It is said that anything else would contradict the principle of the unity of the legal system.

D. Tort law looking to criminal law

The next two subsections are concerned with cases in which tort law makes reference to criminal law or *vice versa*. Let us first turn to cases in which tort law looks to the criminal law. The prime example is § 823(2) BGB. Provisions of the StGB are often statutory provisions that are 'intended to protect another person', even though not every provision of the StGB has such a protective purpose, as we have seen above.[174] If criminal provisions are applied within § 823(2) BGB, courts generally speaking follow the criminal law concepts.[175]

E. Criminal law looking to private law

There are also cases in which criminal law looks to private law. An important example is § 242(1) StGB:

> Whosoever takes chattels belonging to another away from another with the intention of unlawfully appropriating them for himself or a third person shall be liable to imprisonment not exceeding five years or a fine.

The phrase 'belonging to another' means that somebody else must be the owner of the chattel. The phrase thus refers to ownership in the meaning of private law.[176]

However, there are also limits to the criminal law looking to private law. We have already seen instances where the law of delict and criminal law define the protected legal interest differently – where the purposes of criminal law demand that criminal courts define legal concepts autonomously and without reference to the private law sphere. For example, the word chattel is defined differently in private law and in criminal law. According

[172] Deutsch and Ahrens, *Deliktsrecht*, para. 93, point to exceptions to this general principle.
[173] Medicus and Lorenz, *Besonderer Teil*, para. 1250–4.
[174] On the details, see Looschelders, *Besonderer Teil*, para. 1282–3.
[175] On the details, E. von Olshausen, 'Über die Verwendung strafrechtlicher Normen im Zivilrecht' in J. Schulz and T. Vormbaum (eds.), *Festschrift für Günter Bemmann* (Baden-Baden: Nomos, 1997), 125–58. On the exceptions, see Deutsch and Ahrens, *Deliktsrecht*, para. 227.
[176] Fischer, *Strafgesetzbuch*, § 242 para. 5

to § 90 BGB, it is every corporeal object. Criminal lawyers agree.[177] Yet under § 90a BGB, animals do not count as chattels. § 90a BGB nevertheless states that provisions applying to chattels are applicable to animals with necessary adaptations. Criminal law does not follow this restriction of the definition of chattels but holds animals to be things. Thus the same term, 'chattel', one that might be thought to be civil, is thought to be public when used in § 242 StGB.

This rather simple example shows that criminal lawyers do not blindly follow private law concepts but that they modify them where they deem it necessary. A rather complex example relates to the requirement of wrongfulness. It is said that 'what is lawful according to private law, cannot be punishable'.[178] Criminal breach of trust is dealt with in § 266 StGB. § 266(1) StGB reads:

> Whosoever abuses the power accorded him by statute, by commission of a public authority or legal transaction to dispose of assets of another or to make binding agreements for another, or violates his duty to safeguard the property interests of another incumbent upon him by reason of statute, commission of a public authority, legal transaction or fiduciary relationship, and thereby causes damage to the person, whose property interests he was responsible for, shall be liable to imprisonment not exceeding five years or a fine.

In many cases the fiduciary duty is grounded in private law ('power accorded him by... legal transaction'). Anybody acting in accordance with his duties flowing from such a private law relationship cannot be punished.[179] Thus, criminal law follows private law thinking. However, it does not follow that every violation of private law can be criminalised; this would not be in accordance with the *ultima ratio* principle.[180] The liability of members of the management board may serve as an example.[181] § 93(1)(1)–(2) AktG (Stock Corporation Act – Aktiengesetz) states:[182]

177 H. Kudlich, in H. Satzger *et al.* (eds.), *Strafgesetzbuch*, 2nd edn (Cologne: Heymanns, 2014), § 242 para. 5, 7; Fischer, *Strafgesetzbuch*, § 242 para. 3.

178 C. H. Seibt and S. Schwarz, 'Aktienrechtsuntreue' (2010) *AG*, 301–15; M. Lutter, 'Zivilrechtlich korrekt und doch strafbar?' (2010) *NZG*, 601–3.

179 F. Saliger, in Satzger *et al.* (eds.), *Strafgesetzbuch*, § 266 para. 31.

180 V. Ibold, *Unternehmerische Entscheidungen als pflichtwidrige Untreuehandlungen* (Berlin: Duncker & Humblot, 2011), 94.

181 Compare the discussion of Wagner, in *Münchener Kommentar*, Vor § 823 para. 62.

182 Translation from www.nortonrosefulbright.com/files/german-stock-corporation-act-2010-english-translation-pdf-59656.pdf (last visited 5 May 2014).

> In conducting business, the members of the management board shall employ the care of a diligent and conscientious manager. They shall not be deemed to have violated the aforementioned duty if, at the time of taking the entrepreneurial decision, they had good reason to assume that they were acting on the basis of adequate information for the benefit of the company.

If a board member does not comply with the duty under § 93(1)(1) AktG, he is liable for damages under § 93(2)(1) AktG. And he will be so liable even if he did not act intentionally.[183] In the criminal law sphere, not every breach of § 93(1) AktG is relevant. Of course, criminal liability under § 266 StGB requires an intentional breach of duty; negligence will not do.[184] This follows again from the general provision on the requirement of intention in criminal law, § 15 StGB. A more important restriction is exemplified in a criminal case of the BGH:[185] the accused, S, was chairman of the Organisation of Independent Employees (Arbeitsgemeinschaft Unabhängiger Betriebsangehöriger – AUB). The AUB was financed in essence by Siemens AG. The payments were authorised by the second accused F, who was a senior manager with Siemens. The underlying idea was that AUB should be an employer friendly organisation which should diminish the influence of the labour union IG Metall, especially in elections to the Siemens' works council. F was accused of breach of trust to the detriment of Siemens under § 266 StGB, and S was accused of assisting F. The first senate on criminal law of the BGH held that F was in breach of his duty under § 119(1)(1) BetrVG (Betriebsverfassungsgesetz – Works Constitution Act). § 119(1)(1) BetrVG reads:

> The following offences shall be punishable by a term of imprisonment not exceeding one year or a fine, or both: 1. interfering with an election to the works council . . . or influencing such elections by inflicting or threatening reprisals or granting or promising incentives . . .

It followed that F was also in breach of his duty under § 93 AktG, a duty flowing from a private law relationship. The BGH then had to answer the question whether this breach of duty was sufficient to trigger criminal liability under § 266 StGB. The BGH came to the conclusion that there was no room for a criminal liability under § 266 StGB in this case. Not

[183] H. Fleischer, in G. Spindler and E. Stilz, *Kommentar zum Aktiengesetz* vol. 1, 2nd edn (Munich: Beck, 2010), § 93 Rn. 10 u. 205.

[184] W. Perron, in Schönke and Schröder (eds.), *Strafgesetzbuch*, § 266 Rn. 49.

[185] BGH, NJW 2011, 88. The facts are taken from M. Jahn, 'Pflichtverletzung bei Untreue' (2011) *JuS*, 183–5.

every breach of duty under § 93 AktG will result in criminal liability under § 266 StGB. It needs to be a duty which aims at protecting the victim's assets and this is not the case under § 119(1)(1) BetrVG.[186] With explicit reference to the *ultima ratio* principle, the BGH thus restricted the applicability of § 266 StGB.[187]

7. The procedural perspective

A. *Procedural differences*

Civil procedure and criminal procedure are fundamentally different. First, the parties have different functions. In civil procedure they will only produce those facts which support their case. In criminal procedure the duty of the public prosecution service is not limited to producing evidence which will support the conviction of the accused. It is also its duty to produce any evidence in favour of the accused.[188] Second, the function of the court is different. Civil procedure is governed by the *Beibringungsgrundsatz*, according to which the burden rests with the parties to produce any evidence which support their case.[189] The court may only consider such facts which have been produced by the parties. In contrast, in criminal procedure we have the *Amtsermittlungsgrundsatz*, pursuant to which the court may initiate investigations in order to find relevant facts which have neither been produced by the accused nor the public prosecution service.[190]

Furthermore, both private and criminal lawyers have to answer the question of what happens if something cannot be proven. Even though the problem is identical, private and criminal lawyers address the question in a fundamentally different way. A private lawyer would speak of the burden of proof. Criminal lawyers do not speak of the burden of proof. Indeed, to use the phrase 'burden of proof' in criminal procedure would not make any sense; it would only prove that the person using that phrase has not understood the function of the parties and of the court in criminal proceedings: all the evidence against the accused and

[186] BGH, NJW 2011, 88 at 92; Kudlich, in Satzger *et al.* (eds.), *Strafgesetzbuch*, § 266 para. 32c.

[187] BGH, NJW 2011, 88 at 92.

[188] Roxin and Schünemann, *Strafverfahrensrecht*, para. 9.11; R. Griesbaum, in R. Hannich (ed.), *Karlsruher Kommentar zur Strafprozessordnung*, 7th edn (Munich: Beck, 2013), § 160 para. 22.

[189] O. Jauernig and B. Hess, *Zivilprozessrecht*, 30th edn (Munich: Beck, 2011) para. 25.11–14.

[190] Roxin and Schünemann, *Strafverfahrensrecht*, § 15 para. 3; T. Fischer, in *Karlsruher Kommentar*, Einleitung para. 12.

in his favour has to be produced by the public prosecution service and the court. And according to the principle of *in dubio pro reo* the accused can only be convicted if it is proven beyond doubt that he is guilty.[191] In the civil law sphere the principle of *in dubio pro reo* is not applicable. In civil procedure each party has the burden of proof for those facts which are advantageous to his case. Consequently, the party claiming damages has to prove that all requirements of the claim are met. If the defendant wants to rely on a defence – on a reason which would exclude the wrongfulness, as for example self-defence – it rests with him to prove the relevant facts.[192] In contrast, in criminal procedure, the defendant is not required to prove that he has acted in self-defence. It is the responsibility of the prosecutor and the court to prove that this ground for excluding wrongfulness is not applicable. If this cannot be proven then, according to the principle of *in dubio pro reo*, the accused cannot be convicted.

The criminal law principle of *in dubio pro reo* is a strict one. Conversely, in civil procedure the burden of proof may shift to the other party. Often the legislator will make explicit when the burden of proof is so shifted. In the law of delict we find, for example, cases of liability for presumed fault and it is accordingly on the defendant to exculpate himself.[193]

Finally, in criminal procedure there are procedural rules which are constitutionally guaranteed. The presumption of innocence and the *in dubio pro reo* principle follow directly from the constitutional principle of the rule of law.[194] These procedural rules do not find any equivalent in civil procedure.

In summary: civil procedure and criminal procedure are fundamentally different. As a consequence, the same case heard before a civil court and a criminal court may produce two different results. For a German lawyer this is unproblematic.

B. Procedural interactions

Having pointed out these fundamental differences we also have to note overlaps. A first hint of the overlaps is found in the title of part five of the

[191] W. Schluckebier, in H. Satzger *et al.* (eds.), *Strafprozessordnung* (Cologne: Heymanns, 2014), § 261 para. 49; U. Eisenberg, *Beweisrecht der StPO*, 8th edn (Munich: Beck, 2011), para. 116

[192] Deutsch and Ahrens, *Deliktsrecht*, para. 89.

[193] See on these cases, ibid., para. 316–40.

[194] BVerfGE 74, 358, 371 (1987); Roxin and Schünemann, *Strafverfahrensrecht*, para. 11.1.

Code of Criminal Procedure (Strafprozessordnung – StPO): 'Participation of the Aggrieved Person in Proceedings'.[195]

1. The *Adhäsionsverfahren* in criminal procedure

From a procedural perspective, the most intense form of interaction between the law of delict and criminal law is found in the procedure of adhesion (*Adhäsionsverfahren*). According to §§ 402–6 StPO, it is possible for the victim to claim compensation within criminal proceedings. The *Adhäsionsverfahren* is rarely made use of. Judges and practitioners apparently have reservations against it. In 1986 and in 2004, the legislator tried to enhance its importance.[196] The options for a judge to reject the procedure were restricted. Under § 406(1)(3)–(5) StPO, such rejection is possible if the claim for compensation is 'inadmissible or insofar as it appears unfounded. In all other cases the court may dispense with a decision only if the application is not suitable to being dealt with in criminal proceedings . . . An application will be unsuited to being dealt with in criminal proceedings particularly where its further examination . . . would considerably protract the proceedings.' The rejection has no effect on a possible lawsuit in civil court.

The advantages of the *Adhäsionsverfahren* are obvious: lawsuits are run more efficiently, and the victim will save time and costs. Furthermore, contradictory decisions can more easily be avoided.[197] Furthermore, the victim has the advantage that he may appear as a witness in his own lawsuit. This is at least theoretically important because the evidence of a 'witness' is given more weight than a party to the proceedings. Finally, the court has to apply the Amtsermittlungsgrundsatz and therefore has to inquire and investigate the case.[198]

Nevertheless, the *Adhäsionsverfahren* remains practically unimportant: in 2010 it was conducted in only 0.59 per cent of all criminal proceedings.[199] Practising lawyers fear that the complexities of the law

[195] Still inspiring H. Schöch, 'Die Rechtsstellung des Verletzten im Strafverfahren' (1984) *NStZ*, 385–91.

[196] See L. Meyer-Goßner, in *Strafprozessordnung*, 56th edn (Munich: Beck, 2013), Vor § 403 para. 1; Roxin and Schünemann, *Strafverfahrensrecht*, para. 65.1–2; K. Spiess, *Das Adhäsionsverfahren in der Rechtswirklichkeit* (Berlin: Lit, 2008), 5.

[197] H. Schöch, in Satzger *et al.* (eds.), *Strafprozessordnung*, Vor §§ 403 para. 1.

[198] K. Haller, 'Das 'kränkelnde' Adhäsionsverfahren' (2011) *NJW*, 970–4; V. Greiner, 'Zivilrechtliche Ansprüche im Strafverfahren' (2011) *ZRP*, 132–4.

[199] Schöch, in Satzger *et al.* (eds.), *Strafprozessordnung*, Vor §§ 403 para. 7.

of delict will overwhelm judges who are specialised in criminal law.[200] Furthermore, the fees which a practising lawyer may charge his client are lower in comparison to an additional pure civil law suit.[201] Finally, the question as to the binding force of a judgment may arise. If the victim's claim against the offender is denied in the *Adhäsionsverfahren* then this judgment will have binding force in relation to the offender's compulsory insurance. The victim cannot raise a second claim against the insurer.[202] On the other hand the binding force of a judgment which awards damages is restricted as against the offender's insurer for a number of reasons:[203] first, in civil procedure the insurer as a third party can participate in the procedure in a number of ways and thereby influence the outcome of the case while in the *Adhäsionsverfahren* he cannot do so. Second, in criminal proceedings it might be advantageous for the offender to admit certain facts – to the detriment of the insurer. Finally, a criminal court might leave it open whether the offender acted with intent. For determining whether the offender has insurance coverage, the question as to the offender's intent is essential. Thus, the *Adhäsionsverfahren* might be of little help to the victim if he wants to claim damages directly from the insurer. However, it should be noted that a number of these points are hotly contested in the literature.[204]

2. The *Klageerzwingungsverfahren*

In principle the public prosecution service is in charge of all criminal investigations: §§ 152, 160 StPO. After all, it is only the state which has the right to punish. At the same time – following the rule of law – the state has an obligation to prosecute if a crime has been committed: § 152(2) StPO.[205] Even though the victim is not in charge of the prosecution

200 Spiess, *Adhäsionsverfahren*, 161; H. O. Höher, 'Keine haftungsrechtliche Bindungswirkung der im Adhäsionsverfahren ergangenen Entscheidung' (2013) *NZV*, 373–5.

201 Spiess, *Adhäsionsverfahren*, 221; Schöch, in: Satzger *et al.* (eds.), *Strafprozessordnung*, Vor §§ 403 para. 1.

202 See F. Schwartze, in D. Looschelders and P. Pohlmann (eds.), *VVG-Kommentar*, 2nd edn (Cologne: Heymanns, 2011), § 124 para. 5–9.

203 BGH, JZ 2013, 1166.

204 The discussions have been intensified following BGH, JZ 2013, 1166: see M. Foerster, 'Das Verhältnis von Strafurteilen zu nachfolgenden Zivilverfahren' (2013) *JZ*, 1143–8; Höher, 'Bindungswirkung', 375; U. Knappmann, 'Bindungswirkung einer Entscheidung im Adhäsionsverfahren' (2013) *StRR*, 235–6.

205 For the details, see Roxin and Schünemann, *Strafverfahrensrecht*, para. 12.1–16, 13.1–9, 14.1–4.

it has, in case the victim for example assesses the facts or the law differently than the public prosecution service, the possibility to force the public prosecution service to act: the victim may file a complaint with the superior authority of the acting public prosecution office and if the superior authority does not revise the decision, raise a court action to compel public charges (*Klageerzwingungsverfahren*: §§ 172–7 StPO).[206] But the victim does not by way of the *Klageerzwingungsverfahren* become party to the criminal proceedings against the accused.

3. The *Nebenklage*

The victim has further rights: he can join the public prosecution and become a private accessory prosecutor. The victim can only do so in respect of specific, listed offences which in general are those that cause severe injury to the victim: § 395(1)(2) StPO. The *Nebenklage* allows the victim to oversee the public prosecution office and to safeguard his personal interest.[207] The private accessory prosecutor has his own procedural rights, for example the right to ask questions or to apply for evidence to be taken: § 397(1) StPO.[208] Moreover he has a (limited) right to appeal. So, on the one hand the private accessory prosecutor is a normal witness – as the victim of the crime always is – but on the other hand he is able to influence the proceedings much more actively than a normal witness who is (more or less) only a 'means of evidence'. He can play an active part of the proceedings without becoming, strictly speaking, a party to them. Moreover the right to join as a private accessory prosecutor has absolutely no formal influence on proceedings of adhesion and on later civil proceedings.

4. The *Privatklageverfahren*

Finally, even though it is the state who claims to have the right to punish and even though it is the public prosecution service which has the authority to initiate public charges, German law recognises the concept of the *Privatklageverfahren*, which permits the victim to initiate criminal proceedings and take the role of the public prosecution service with respect to specifically enumerated criminal offences. By introducing

[206] For more details, see ibid., para. 41.

[207] Meyer-Goßner, in *Strafprozessordnung*, Vor § 395 para. 1; Roxin and Schünemann, *Strafverfahrensrecht*, para. 64.1.

[208] Schöch, in Satzger *et al.* (eds.), *Strafprozessordnung*, § 397 para. 1; Meyer-Goßner, in *Strafprozessordnung*, Vor § 395 para. 2.

the *Privatklageverfahren*, the legislator did not intend to improve the victim's procedural position but to relieve the states institutions in the field of minor crimes.[209] In contrast to the *Nebenklage*, the victim does not merely assist or control the public prosecutor; he takes the position of the public prosecutor. Thus, a private person can initiate public charges but this appears not to happen very often.

5. Suspending proceedings and the binding force of judgments

In civil proceedings as well as in criminal proceedings, the court has to 'decide the dispute in the light of all relevant legal aspects': § 17(2)(1) GVG. Nevertheless, there is the possibility to suspend the proceedings. For civil procedure, § 149(1) ZPO states:[210]

> If the suspicion arises in the course of a legal dispute that a criminal offence has been committed, the investigation of which will influence the court's decision, the court may direct that the hearing be suspended until the criminal proceedings have been dealt with and terminated.

For a civil court to suspend its proceedings, the related criminal prosecution must bear on the factual elements of the civil action, not just the legal elements.[211] The court has a wide discretion to suspend; it has to compare the advantages of awaiting the criminal judgment with the disadvantages, especially the delay.[212] If it does suspend, the civil court is not bound by the criminal court's judgment on the relevant matter.[213] The judge in the civil procedure has to consider the legal relevance of the criminal judgment himself: § 286 ZPO.[214] However, if the civil court does not have serious doubts about the accuracy of the judgment and especially the facts that it is based on, it must adopt the findings of the criminal court.[215] Consequently a civil judge will normally follow his colleagues from the criminal court.

209 R. Jofer, in Satzger *et al.* (eds.), *Strafprozessordnung*, Vor §§ 374 ff. StPO, para. 2.

210 See A. Stadler, in H.-J. Musielak (ed.), *Zivilprozessordnung*, 11th edn. (Munich: Vahlen, 2014), § 149 para. 1; critically C. Wagner, in *Münchner Kommentar zur Zivilprozessordnung* vol. 1, 4th edn (Munich: Beck, 2013), § 149 para. 1.

211 Wagner, in *Münchner Kommentar ZPO*, § 149 para. 5.

212 Stadler, in Musielak, *Zivilprozessordnung*, § 149 para. 3.

213 Ibid., § 149 para. 1; Wagner, in *Münchner Kommentar ZPO*, § 149 para. 2. Monographically, see M. Foerster, *Transfer der Ergebnisse von Strafverfahren in nachfolgende Zivilverfahren* (Tübingen: Mohr Siebeck, 2008).

214 BGH, NJW 2012, 1659; OLG Zweibrücken, NJW-RR 2011, 496.

215 U. Foerste, in Musielak, *Zivilprozessordnung*, § 286 para. 9.

In criminal proceedings, too, the court decides the case in the light of all relevant legal aspects even if it depends on a legal relationship not regulated under criminal law.[216] § 262(1) StPO states:

> If the criminal liability for an act depends on the evaluation of a legal relationship under civil law, the criminal court shall also decide thereon according to the provisions applicable to procedure and evidence in criminal cases.

This implies that the criminal court is – with few exceptions – not bound by a civil court's judgment.[217] Thus, both courts can rule differently on the same issue. However, the criminal court is, according to § 262(2) StPO, entitled to suspend the proceedings:

> The court, however, shall be entitled to suspend the investigation and to set a time limit within which one of the participants is to bring a civil action, or to await the judgment of the civil court.

This exception aims at promoting the efficiency of criminal proceedings. The criminal court shall not be blocked by difficult questions concerning civil law, especially because one of the parties involved could be tempted to make use of the criminal procedure to clarify his civil claims as this involves a number of advantages: for example, in criminal proceedings the court has to find the relevant facts itself.[218] The criminal court may, but does not have to, base its judgment on the civil court's judgment.[219] One should note that there are exceptions in which there is binding force, as is, for example, the case with judgments which change the legal status of a person.[220]

8. The remedial perspective

Finally, there is the remedial perspective. As a rule, it is the task of a court in civil proceedings to award damages. However, we also find in both the StGB and the StPO some provisions which relate to the victim's interests. First, there is § 153a StPO. § 153a(1) StPO reads:

> In a case involving a misdemeanour, the public prosecution office may, with the consent of the accused and of the court . . . dispense with preferment

[216] J.-D. Kuckein, in *Karlsruher Kommentar*, § 262 para. 1.

[217] Meyer-Goßner, in *Strafprozessordnung*, § 262 para. 2; Kuckein, in *Karlsruher Kommentar*, § 262 para. 3.

[218] U. Franke, in Satzger *et al.* (eds.), *Strafprozessordnung*, § 262 para. 1.

[219] Meyer-Goßner, in *Strafprozessordnung*, § 262 para. 14.

[220] P. Gottwald, in *Münchener Kommentar ZPO*, § 325 para. 6.

> of public charges and concurrently impose conditions and instructions upon the accused if these are of such a nature as to eliminate the public interest in criminal prosecution and if the degree of guilt does not present an obstacle. In particular, the following conditions and instructions may be applied: 1. to perform a specified service in order to make reparations for damage caused by the offence;... 5. to make a serious attempt to reach a mediated agreement with the aggrieved person (perpetrator–victim mediation) thereby trying to make reparation for his offence, in full or to a predominant extent, or to strive therefore;...

The amount of damages under § 153a(1)(2)(1) StPO is calculated on the basis of private law rules and immaterial losses can be taken into account.[221] It is important to note that the victim may raise further private law actions for damages.[222] The serious effort to reach a settlement with the victim under § 153a(1)(2)(5) StPO is not so much about compensation as about interpersonal conciliation between the offender and the victim.[223]

Second, there is the possibility of a so called *Täter-Opfer-Ausgleich* (offender–victim reconciliation) in § 46a StGB which reads:

If the offender

> (1) in an effort to achieve reconciliation with the victim, has made full restitution or the major part thereof for his offence, or has earnestly tried to make restitution; or
> (2) in a case in which making restitution for the harm caused required substantial personal services or personal sacrifice on his part, has made full compensation or the major part thereof to the victim,
>
> the court may mitigate the sentence pursuant to section 49(1) or, unless the sentence to be imposed on the offender is imprisonment of more than one year or a fine of more than three hundred and sixty daily units, may order a discharge.

The *Täter-Opfer-Ausgleich* has its origin in the criminal law relating to young people under the JGG which strongly follows educational ends. It is intended to bring the victims interests into focus[224] but also

[221] H. Diemer, in *Karlsruher Kommentar*, § 153a para. 14; R. Schnabl and H. Vordermayer, in Satzger *et al.* (eds.), *Strafprozessordnung*, § 153a StPO para. 13; B. Schmitt, in Meyer-Goßner, *Strafprozessordnung*, § 153a para. 16.

[222] Schmitt, in Meyer-Goßner, *Strafprozessordnung*, § 153a para. 15.

[223] H. Achenbach, 'Obligatorische Zurückgewinnungshilfe?' (2001) *NStZ*, 401, 403; Diemer, in *Karlsruher Kommentar*, § 153a para. 20.

[224] BT-Drucks. 12/6853 (1994), p. 21; BGHSt 48, 134, 137 (2002); R. Eschelbach, in Satzger *et al.*, *Strafgesetzbuch*, § 46a para. 1a.

provides the possibility for the judge to mitigate the (criminal) sentence or to suspend the sentence or to order a discharge. § 46a StGB is aimed at giving the offender an incentive to come to terms with the victim, to compensate the victim and to make good the wrong which the offender committed.[225] Especially in terms of small offences, the criminal punishment is, for that purpose, only of secondary importance as it may be mitigated.[226] The hope is that the victim will come to his rights quicker and that at the same time the offender will be forced to think about the consequences of his wrongdoing and take responsibility for its consequences.[227] Thus, the reasons why we punish, especially under the theory of special prevention, may be met by such reconciliation.[228] For the present project it is important to note that only § 46a(2) StGB aims at compensating the victim's damage.[229] The offender must have compensated at least half of the victim's damage owed according to private law if he wants to fall under § 46a StGB.[230] § 46a(1) StGB goes beyond: the offender has to make a personal sacrifice; it involves a communicative process with the victim in which the offender takes responsibility for his wrongdoings.[231]

Finally, according to § 56 StGB the court has the power to suspend imprisonment. § 56(1) StGB reads:[232]

> If a person is sentenced to a term of imprisonment not exceeding one year the court shall suspend the enforcement of the sentence for a probationary period if there are reasons to believe that the sentence will serve as sufficient warning to the convicted person and that he will commit no further offences without having to serve the sentence. The court shall particularly take into account the character of the convicted person, his previous history, the circumstances of his offence, his conduct after the offence, his circumstances and the effects to be expected from the suspension.

225 Eschelbach, in Satzger *et al.* (eds.), *Strafgesetzbuch*, § 46a para. 1b.

226 Fischer, *Strafgesetzbuch*, § 46a para. 2. Cf. R. Hamm, '"Täter-Opfer-Ausgleich" im Strafrecht' *(1995) StV*, 491–6.

227 BT-Drucks. 12/6853 (1994), p. 21.

228 W. Theune, in *Leipziger Kommentar*, § 46a para. 2; Critically Fischer, *Strafgesetzbuch*, § 46a para. 3.

229 Eschelbach, in Satzger *et al.* (eds.), *Strafgesetzbuch*, § 46a para. 31. Slightly differently the case law; compare BGH, NStZ 2002, 29; BGH, NStZ 2000, 205.

230 Eschelbach, in Satzger *et al.* (eds.), *Strafgesetzbuch*, § 46a para. 32; BGHSt 48, 134, 144 (2002).

231 Theune, in *Leipziger Kommentar*, § 46a para. 42; BT-Drucks. 12/6853 (1994), p. 21; BGHSt 48, 134, 142 (2002); BGH, NStZ 2012, 439, 440; Eschelbach, in Satzger *et al.* (eds.), *Strafgesetzbuch*, § 46a para. 24.

232 For further details, see § 56b and § 56f StGB.

The 'conduct after the offence' includes efforts by the convicted to make compensation to the victim.[233]

9. Conclusion

The purpose of this chapter was to analyse the relationship of the law of delict and criminal law in German law. What has become obvious is that criminal law and the law of delict have developed a number of differences on the methodological level, the level of substantive law and on the level of procedural law. The fact that these differences have evolved is not an historical accident or the result of a degree of specialisation in academia and practice which renders lawyers blind to their existence. Quite the opposite is true: German lawyers are very well aware of these differences. They are said to follow from the different theoretical foundations of, and differing policy considerations underlying, criminal law and the law of delict. And to a great extent, they can be attributed to the special importance of constitutional guaranteed rights in the criminal law sphere. Consequently, these differences do not conflict with the principles of the unity of the legal systems. Nevertheless, there are also examples where criminal and private lawyers follow similar rules and there are examples of other forms of interaction, primarily on the procedural level which aim at strengthening the victim's rights in criminal proceedings.

[233] J. Hubrach, in *Leipziger Kommentar*, § 56 para. 26; Fischer, *Strafgesetzbuch*, § 56 para. 8.

5

Crime and tort in Sweden

Theoretical distinction, practical connection

SANDRA FRIBERG AND MARTIN SUNNQVIST

1. Introduction

When comparing tort and crime in Swedish law, three distinguishing features stand out. First, the relationship between tort and crime – both in legislation and in practice – is strongly affected by historical events, rather than normative forces or forces limited to tort and crime themselves. Second, although tort and crime belong to two different areas of law that are governed by different theories and principles (private law and public law), there are places of both legal substance and procedure where tort and crime – particularly for practical reasons – are treated jointly. This joint treatment clearly affects the outcome of litigation. Finally, Swedish tort law is part of a greater framework of compensation which includes a publically funded welfare system, private and public insurances and a government-funded scheme for victims of crime. The government has also provided ample opportunities for crime victims to participate in the criminal trial and bring forward their claims with the assistance of governmental-funded counsel. This support is both a legacy from earlier Swedish legal history and a more modern ambition to strengthen victim rights.

In the following, we will describe a number of areas where tort and crime overlap or interact in Swedish law, and explain why and how this has occurred. Particular focus is on such damage that is caused by a criminal act, and how these cases are regulated and tried in the Swedish system. First of all, we will give a brief overview of the historical background to the present legislation in tort law and criminal law.

2. Historical background

A. *Introduction*

The history of the material and procedural connection between tort law and criminal law in Sweden is not well known at the international level. The literature in English is sparse, if it even exists at all. There are two Swedish articles written in 1934 to mark the 200-year anniversary of the 1734 Law Code. That Law Code was a law of the realm – *Sveriges rikes lag* – and replaced the mediaeval law codes, one for the towns and one for the countryside. The Law Code of 1734 is still – in both Sweden and Finland – the framework for civil, criminal and procedural law, even if most parts of it have been replaced by new legislation. Attempts made in Sweden in the early nineteenth century to replace it with one Civil Code and one Criminal Code, modelled on the French codifications, failed.

While the relationship between tort and crime is practically very important, the discussion in legal scholarship is surprisingly scarce, leaving us reliant on work done sometime in the past. In 1934, an anthology was published, with articles on the history and development of the law in the various parts of the Law Code, written by renowned Swedish and Finnish scholars.[1] Two of these pieces are, to this day, the leading academic works on the history of the relationship between tort and crime. The first, written by Ivar Strahl, then associate judge of appeal and later professor of criminal law at Uppsala University, was on the development of the Swedish law of tort.[2] The second work was by Hjalmar Granfelt, former justice of the Supreme Court of Finland and professor of procedural law at Helsinki University. It concerned the development of the principle that civil claims were joined with criminal cases, i.e. the principle of adhesion.[3] In the same anthology, the proposals for law reform of the nineteenth century – highly relevant for the procedural and material connection between tort and crime – were discussed by Erik Marks von

[1] *Minnesskrift ägnad 1734 års lag av jurister i Sverige och Finland* (Stockholm: Svensk juristtidning, 1934). It has three parts, I - general essays on the legal development (549 pages), II - more specific essays (1,154 pages) and III – a reprint of the 1734 Law Code.

[2] I. Strahl, 'Utvecklingen av den svenska skadeståndsrätten på det utomobligatoriska området' in *Minnesskrift ägnad 1734 års lag*, II, 874–912. Swedish lawyers divide damages into *inomobligatoriska skadestånd* (damages to be paid based on a contractual relation) and *utomobligatoriska skadestånd* (damages to be paid outside contractual relations, e.g. based on crimes and negligence etc.); Strahl concentrated on the latter.

[3] O. Hj. Granfelt, 'Adhäsionsprincipen. Dess tillämpning enligt rättegångsbalken i 1734 års lag med särskilt beaktande av finländsk processpraxis' in *Minnesskrift ägnad 1734 års lag*, II, 1005–22.

Würtemberg, former Justice of the Supreme Court and President of the Svea Court of Appeal.[4]

B. *The connection between crime and tort in legislation*

1. Mediaeval background: no distinction between crime and tort

In mediaeval times, one category of wrongs was seen as committed primarily towards society as such, and another category to be committed primarily against other individuals. The first category was more serious and could not be compromised by deals between the victim and the wrongdoer. In the second category, a fine (*bot*) was a common punishment. This *bot* – an order to pay money to the injured party – was both a type of punishment and a type of reparation; there was no distinction between criminal law and tort law. There was no general rule to the effect that compensation should be paid for whatever damage the wrongdoer caused. Instead, there was a tariff system: every type of wrong was enumerated together with the fine to be paid for that damage. In some cases, such as assault, there could be one fine for wounds (*sårabot*), one for disabilities (*lytesbot*) and one for costs for medical treatment (*läkarbot*).[5] For example, if the defendant had intentionally cut the hand or the foot off the injured party, he should pay twelve marks to the injured party for the disability and twenty marks to be divided into three for the wound.[6] The three parts of the payment for the wound went to the King, the county and the injured party respectively. If the defendant had done the same thing unintentionally, including by accident, he should pay three marks for the disability and three marks for the wound.[7]

2. Law Code of 1734: still no distinction between crime and tort

In the Law Code of 1734, the old connection between crime and tort that was immanent in the *bot* was retained. At the same time, however,

[4] E. Marks von Würtemberg, 'Blick på den svenska lagstiftningen alltifrån adertonhundratalets början' in *Minnesskrift ägnad 1734 års lag*, I, 143–202.

[5] Strahl, 'Utvecklingen av den svenska skadeståndsrätten', 878–9, 883–4. See also Hj. Karlgren, *Skadeståndsrätt* (Stockholm: Norstedt, 1952), 8–9.

[6] 'Såramålsbalken I, sår med vilja' [Book on wounds I, wounds caused intentionally], Ch. II, *Magnus Erikssons allmänna landslag* [Law Code of King Magnus Eriksson], ed. Åke Holmbäck and Elias Wessén (Lund: Institutet för Rättshistorisk Forskning, 1962), 252.

[7] 'Såramålsbalken II, sår av våda' [Book on wounds II, wounds caused by accident], Ch. I, *Magnus Erikssons allmänna landslag* [Law Code of King Magnus Eriksson], ed. Holmbäck and Wessén, 262.

a tendency towards a division between tort and crime can be seen in the scholarly literature. This is due mainly to the fact that David Nehrman Ehrenstråle, the most important Swedish law scholar of the eighteenth century, wrote separate books about Swedish civil law, civil procedure, criminal law and criminal procedure and thus needed to distinguish between these topics.[8] There is a connection in time between this division and an increased focus on the degree of culpability of the accused: *culpa*, negligence, was introduced as a requirement for responsibility, whereas the older laws had regulated accidents, too. Thus, the amount of the *bot* was related to the degree of culpability of the accused, which shows that the *bot* remained both a punishment and a way to repair damages. There was still no general rule to the effect that compensation should be paid for caused damage. In addition, every type of damage continued to be enumerated together with the fine to be paid for that damage.[9]

In the legal literature, David Nehrman Ehrenstråle argued that damages, as a compensatory remedy, were different from punishment. For Ehrenstråle, compensation should flow from serious wrongs, regardless of the positive law, whereas he did not think the same about punishment. He formulated a general rule to the effect that compensation should be paid for damage caused intentionally (by *dolus*), even in cases where there was no applicable rule in the law code.[10] This position was adopted, and expanded: in the literature of the nineteenth century, this rule was extended also to cases of gross negligence.[11]

3. Reform projects of the early nineteenth century: a distinction is established

When the Swedish state had been constitutionally reorganised in 1809, it was apparent that civil and criminal legislation needed to be updated. Thus, in the early nineteenth century, a series of proposals for new civil and criminal codes were made. None of the proposals were enacted as drafted, though a highly amended Criminal Law Code was finally promulgated in 1864. Nonetheless, the nineteenth century proposals have had great influence on Swedish legal thinking.

[8] See, e.g., D. Nehrman (Ehrenstråle), *Inledning till den svenska jurisprudentiam civilem* (Lund: Ludwig Decreaux, 1729), 152–4.

[9] Strahl, 'Utvecklingen av den svenska skadeståndsrätten', 886–9.

[10] D. Nehrman (Ehrenstråhle), *Inledning till den svenska jurisprudentiam criminalem* (Lund: Carl Gustav Berling, 1756), 85.

[11] F. Schrevelius, *Lärobok i Sveriges allmänna nu gällande civilrätt*, vol. II (Lund: Fr. Berling, 1847), 399.

A committee was appointed, which presented a draft Civil Code in 1826. The government could not prepare a proposal for the 1828 parliamentary session and wished to wait for the committee to finish the draft Criminal Code.[12] At this time, parliamentary sessions were held every sixth, and later every third, year. Sessions were held in the four estates: nobility, clergy, burghers and peasants. The king needed parliamentary consent to change civil and criminal law.

The committee then took up the work on the Criminal Code. Whilst the draft Civil Code could at least build on the structure of the Law Code of 1734, the Criminal Code could not. Both the definitions of the different crimes, and the types of punishments, were antiquated. After having co-operated with its Norwegian counterpart, the committee was in a position to present a draft Criminal Code in 1832.[13]

The 1826 proposal for a Civil Code featured recognisably civil law rules on damages as a remedy. A general rule was formulated to the effect that someone who had suffered harm from another's culpable acts, whether or not the acts causing the harm had been specifically prohibited in legislation, should be compensated.[14] This shows that the connection between punishment and damages was loosened.[15] This loosening is even clearer in the 1832 proposal for a Criminal Code. The *bot* – as a punishment by way of a fine to be paid to the injured party – was to be abolished. The fines – then and to this day called *böter* – were to be pure criminal sanctions, to be paid to the state.

However, while separating the conceptual and remedial aspects of tort and crime, the 1832 draft Criminal Code actually took a remarkable step towards the practical coupling of these two areas of law. A specific chapter in the Criminal Code concerned damages. The most important rule therein provided that the just mentioned general rule in the Civil Code was also applicable in criminal cases.[16] This was an attempt to turn things round: instead of understanding compensation as part of the punishment, it should be a civil law claim based on a criminal act.

[12] Marks von Würtemberg, 'Blick på den svenska lagstiftningen', 143–68.

[13] Ibid., 169–72.

[14] 1826 draft Civil Code, Ch. 15 § 5 handelsbalken, *Förslag till Allmän Civillag* (Stockholm: Georg Scheutz, 1826), 148. See also 1838 draft Civil Code, Ch. 15 § 5 handelsbalken, *Förslag till Allmän Civillag*, 2nd edn (Stockholm: Hörbergska Boktryckeriet, 1838), 148.

[15] Strahl, 'Utvecklingen av den svenska skadeståndsrätten', 890.

[16] 1832 draft Criminal Code, Ch. 8 § 1 straffbalken, *Förslag till Allmän Criminallag* (Stockholm: Johan Hörberg, 1832), 14. See also 1839 draft Criminal Code, Ch. 8 § 1 straffbalken, *Förslag till Allmän Criminallag*, 2nd edn (Stockholm: Bernh. M. Bredberg, 1839), 14.

In 1833, the Supreme Court – a body which was required by the Constitution to give its opinion on the proposals for new civil, criminal and procedural legislation – criticised the drafts since they deviated too much from the Law Code of 1734. The committee that prepared the new codes had been highly influenced by the French codifications. At the parliamentary session of 1834, the drafts were discussed without any formal proposal from the government. The conclusion reached was that the parliament wanted the proposals summarised in a way that made them easy to understand. The Supreme Court took its time to review the drafts, and no proposal was made at the 1840 parliamentary session. The government hoped to be able to put forward a proposal at the next parliamentary session.[17]

At the extra parliamentary session in 1844, when King Oscar I acceded to the throne, the government put forward a proposal for a Criminal Code. The estates did not have enough time to discuss its details but approved the main principles regarding the punishments. After this, the committee assumed the work on different parts of the draft Civil Code.[18]

The 1844 draft Criminal Code adopted the same rule on damages as the version of 1832, but with one important formal difference: this rule was now to be inserted in the Criminal Code not as a reference to a rule in the Civil Code but as a stand-alone rule.[19] The reason for this was that it was foreseen that the difficult negotiations over the Civil Code might delay that Code coming into force. If that happened while the Criminal Code had removed the compensatory function of the *bot*, it was unclear what rules would be used to determine compensation.[20] This was also what happened: a Criminal Code was enacted in 1864, but a Civil Code was never enacted. In other words, in 1844, the law committee had realised that the Criminal Code would have a chance to be approved before the Civil Code. The fact that criminal law was so antiquated made reform necessary, and the new king, Oscar I, had an interest in the issues of criminal law, which made reform possible.

By the mid-nineteenth century, the draft Civil and Criminal Codes were more or less ready for approval but other issues had gained importance.

17 Marks von Würtemberg, 'Blick på den svenska lagstiftningen', 172–9.

18 Ibid., 179–82.

19 1844 draft Criminal Code, Ch. 8 § 1, *Förslag till Straff-Balk* (Stockholm: Norstedt, 1844), 18.

20 Strahl, 'Utvecklingen av den svenska skadeståndsrätten', 890–1.

Johan Gabriel Richert – district judge, member of the law committee and leading liberal proponent for law reform – also engaged in the discussion of parliamentary reform. He wanted the four estates to be abolished and replaced by a modern parliament. This caused suspicion among the conservative forces in the nobility and clergy, and this suspicion also affected consideration of the draft Civil and Criminal Codes.[21]

Thus, the reason for the failure to enact the Civil Code was a clash between liberal, reform-orientated forces in society, and conservative forces. The first mentioned group – which was well represented in the committee that worked with the proposals – wanted reform. The last mentioned group – which was well represented in the Supreme Court – wanted to keep the traditions of the 1734 Law Code and thus the historical approach to criminal and tort law. Even if they realised the need for reform in specific areas, they did not want it through codification, which threatened the historic legal culture. The positions resemble those of Thibaut and Savigny in the German *Kodifikationsstreit*.[22]

At the parliamentary session of 1853, parts of the draft Criminal Code were actually approved. Members of parliament put forward a proposal for legislation about theft and robbery, which the parliamentary committee on legislation approved. This led to the enactment of legislation in 1855, with new punishments (imprisonment with labour) and a system of latitudes instead of fixed punishments. This meant that some crimes were sentenced according to modern principles and others according to old. The reforms continued in the same way, with partial reforms in 1857 (forgery and fraud) and 1861 (murder and manslaughter).[23] It seems that these first reforms were of the material that was least controversial and/or where the reforms had already been sufficiently drafted.

The partial reforms made the need for a total reform of criminal law evident. A proposal put forward at the 1862 parliamentary session built on the draft Criminal Code of 1844 and the partial reforms, but excluded some parts of the draft that concerned general issues such as attempt. This proposal was approved, and the Criminal Code was enacted in 1864.[24]

[21] Marks von Würtemberg, 'Blick på den svenska lagstiftningen', 182–5.

[22] C. Peterson, 'Debatten om 1826 års förslag till en allmän civillag – en svensk kodifikationsstrid?' in *Norden, rätten, historia – Festskrift till Lars Björne* (Helsinki: Soumalainen Lakimiesyhdistys, 2004), 245–63; Kj. Å Modéer, *Historiska rättskällor i konflikt. En introduktion i rättshistoria* (Stockholm: Santérus, 2010), 152–9.

[23] Marks von Würtemberg, 'Blick på den svenska lagstiftningen', 186–7.

[24] Ibid., 187. See also R. Bergendal, 'Strafflagen' in *Minnesskrift ägnad 1734 års lag*, I, 318–40.

On the other hand, the draft Civil Code was never approved. Partial reforms of civil law were made, but the government did not make an effort to realise the total reform. In 1872, the government formally decided to no longer work on the draft Civil Code.[25] The effect of this was that legislation on tort in civil law was not realised, and therefore the only rules on tort were the ones placed in the Criminal Code, which was an 'odd' result.[26]

On the one hand, this was well in line with the historical tradition, if punishment and compensation are seen as emanating from the *bot*. On the other hand, it was not in line with the planned system of law, in terms of creating a division between civil and criminal law, which was one of the core aims of the reforms. It is an odd half-way house, but as time showed, a practical one.

4. The Criminal Code of 1864: a general rule about tort based on crime

The Criminal Code of 1864 (*strafflagen*) was applied from 1 January 1865 and replaced the Criminal Code in the 1734 Law Code and the partial reforms of 1855–61. Punishments and payment of damages were made into two parallel systems but administered by the same court at the same time. This finalised the separation of punishment and damages materially, but not procedurally. In particular it was acknowledged that the sanctions had separate functions. Punishment aimed to correct the wrongful, dangerous volition, while the award of damages was supposed to repair the damage. In Chapter 6 § 1 of the Criminal Code, a general rule was enacted that compensation should be paid for damages, such as costs for medical treatment, loss of income, suffering and disability, caused by crimes, committed with *dolus* or *culpa*. A similar rule about damages based on non-criminal acts was never enacted because a Civil Code was never approved, but that did not mean that such compensation could not be ordered.[27]

During the hundred years when the tort rules remained in the Criminal Code – between 1864 and 1972 – important legal developments in tort law took place in court practice. There was a great need to elaborate on questions of principal importance, such as the basis of liability outside the

[25] Marks von Würtemberg, 'Blick på den svenska lagstiftningen', 186–9.

[26] Karlgren, *Skadeståndsrätt*, 11 ('*den underliga placeringen av den svenska rättens skadeståndsregler i strafflagen*').

[27] Strahl, 'Utvecklingen av den svenska skadeståndsrätten', 891–2.

scope of the existing (quite rudimentary) provisions, the limits of liability, the definition of recoverable damage etc. The courts were, however, rather cautious and restrictive when it came to deviating from long honoured principles. At the same time, they were faced with new challenges resulting from technical and socio-economic developments, which demanded a functional system for compensation of new types of damages. The legal discussion therefore came to focus mainly on the possibility to impose liability without fault.[28] This clearly marks the separation of tort law from penal law since the latter did not consider strict liability at this time (or since).

5. The resurgence of tort law

The Criminal Code of 1864 lasted a hundred years. A new Criminal Code (*brottsbalken*) was enacted in 1962 and was applied from 1 January 1965.[29] In this code, there are no rules about damages.[30] Chapter 6 of the 1864 Criminal Code remained in force during the preparations for new legislation until the Tort Liability Act (*skadeståndslagen*) was enacted and came into force in 1972.[31] That law is generally applicable to the issue of damages even though specific rules in, for instance, contract law, have precedence over the general rules set out in the Tort Liability Act. The historical background to the tort rules remains evident, for instance, where the existence of a criminal offence is specified as a prerequisite for tort liability.

The most significant changes in tort law after 1972 have been the expansion of private and general insurance systems. These systems, and other governmentally funded compensation schemes, are of great importance since they usually are brought to the fore as the primary (and sometimes, only) means for the injured party to receive compensation for damages. You could say that the hierarchy between tort law damages, insurances and social security systems has shifted since 1972. Both private insurance and governmentally funded compensation schemes (for specific types of damage) have increased in importance.

If one were to generalise, the system of compensation can now be portrayed as a pyramid. Social security system is on the bottom, widest level; the system is designed to cover the basic needs for all citizens and

[28] Ibid, 893–909.

[29] SFS (Svensk författningssamling) 1962:700 with later amendments.

[30] In Ch. 1 § 8, there is, however, a reference to tort law, just to notify that a crime can have other effects outside of criminal law.

[31] SFS 1972:207 with later amendments.

does not require that someone involved in causing the harm eventually pay. At the next level, there is the private, optional insurances that people can buy. These cover both pure accidents and damage that someone could be held liable for. At the top layer we would find tortious damages. At each level we find different provisions and compensation limits, and these different levels are functionally related to each other. Since provisions, sums and rules of evidence in the bottom two levels continuously change according to debates within society and the practice of insurers, and amendments of the law are often politically motivated, the willingness and need to use tort law is affected. If, for instance, an injured person no longer will get his or her medical expenses fully covered by social insurance, the need to claim (either from private insurance compensation or in tort), higher up the pyramid, will increase. What makes this distinctive in Sweden is that the base of the pyramid is so broad: the coverage afforded by the state scheme is extensive, even if it rarely amounts to full compensation. Indeed, since the basic level through the social security system only covers things like loss of income (up to a certain limit) and costs for necessary medical care, damage such as pure economic loss, pain and suffering or violation will have to be met on the other two levels. At the same time, private insurance schemes are limited in their coverage; hence tort law still plays an important part in compensating (particularly personal) damage.[32]

Since this framework was set up, legislation has rarely intervened in Swedish tort law. However, the Supreme Court has acted when deemed necessary to meet the demands in society. The latest examples concern damages as remedy for violations of human rights where legislation has not been able to keep up with demands from the European Court on Human Rights.[33]

6. Development in criminal law after 1965

For its part, criminal law has been a hot topic in society and in the political debate since not long after 1965. Even today, the legislator often wants to show decisiveness by using criminal law as a tool to address unwanted behaviour in society to an extent that perhaps is not always motivated

[32] See S. Friberg, *Kränkningsersättning. Skadestånd för kränkning genom brott* (Uppsala: Iustus, 2010), 400–42.

[33] See, e.g., ibid., 497–514 and M. Sunnqvist, *Konstitutionellt kritiskt dömande. Förändringen av nordiska domares attityder under två sekel* (Stockholm: Institutet för Rättshistorisk Forskning, 2014), 1012–15.

when considering principles for criminalisation.[34] At the same time, the legislator has had to deal with new types of crime that the previous legislation does not clearly address. Apart from this, perhaps national approach, criminal law is also highly influenced by what happens within the European Union when it comes to criminalisation.

3. The overlap of tort and crime today

A. *Institutions and actors*

1. Courts

There are a number of institutions and actors where matters regarding tort and crime overlap or interact. One reason for this could be what seems to be a distinguishing feature from a comparative perspective, namely that there are no separate *civil and criminal courts* in Sweden. This means that all criminal trials and tort claims are tried by the same courts. Criminal and civil issues are tried either jointly or separately.

The key division in Sweden is between (a) general courts and (b) general administrative courts, with administrative courts dealing only with appeals against decisions of state or municipal authorities. Within these two court systems, there are three kinds of courts, hierarchically organised, in Sweden: (a) the general courts comprise district courts (*tingsrätt*), courts of appeal (*hovrätt*) and the Supreme Court (*Högsta domstolen*), while (b) the general administrative courts are divided into administrative courts (*förvaltningsrätt*), administrative courts of appeal (*kammarrätt*) and the Supreme Administrative Court (*Högsta förvaltningsdomstolen*). Apart from these courts, there are a few special courts, which determine disputes within special areas, for example, the Labour Court and the Market Court. The Market Court (*Marknadsdomstolen*) is a specialized court that handles cases related to the Competition Act as well as cases involving the Marketing Act and other consumer and marketing legislation. The same court tier, the general courts, handle both criminal law cases and tort law cases.

In Sweden, there are a number of actors and institutions, which deal with matters of both tort and crime, although in some areas there is a high degree of specialisation. In the following, we will describe the most central actors and institutions relevant to the areas of tort and crime.

[34] Friberg, *Kränkningsersättning*, 111–18.

2. Law clerks, judges and lay judges

It is common for a lawyer to work at a court as a law clerk after obtaining his or her law degree. It is a two-year appointment, and the law clerk prepares cases for the judges and decides minor cases. Usually, when applying to become a law clerk you choose if you want to do your training in general courts or in general administrative courts.

Historically, it is these law clerks who go on to become judges, first by serving their two years at a district or administrative court, and then at the court of appeal for a year of preparing cases. Then the law clerk will come back to a district court as a deputy district judge for two years and then be an extraordinary associate judge of appeal for one year. If these six years are served successfully, the lawyer will get 'approval' as an associate judge of appeal (*hovrättsassessor, kammarrättsassessor*), which is the basis for an application to be an ordinary judge with a constitutionally guaranteed tenure. Whilst this system remains the most important way of educating and recruiting judges, in the last few decades, it is increasingly the case that prosecutors, advocates and lawyers employed in the civic administration are also appointed as judges.

Judges within the general courts are not normally specialised in certain areas of law, but must be capable of delivering judgments on all cases that come before the court. Thus, judges in the general courts normally hear both civil and criminal cases. That being said, there are some specialisations within court structures, which indicate the type of work a particular judge primarily does, for instance, economic crime or intellectual property law. It is fair to say that this kind of specialisation is more common in larger cities, but it should be noted that the Supreme Court does not have any particular sections for different areas of law; the sixteen judges, the Justices of the Supreme Court, deliver judgments on all cases that have received a leave to appeal, whatever area of law they concern. Leave to appeal is granted by the Supreme Court itself and basically only in those cases where it is important to establish a judgment to provide guidance for the Swedish district courts and courts of appeal. The court grants leave to appeal in approximately 140 out of 5,100 applications per year.[35] Since 1874, the judgments and decisions of the Supreme Court are published in the series *Nytt juridiskt arkiv, NJA* (*New Juridical Archives*).

Apart from legally trained judges, there are *lay judges* in most criminal law (and many family law) cases tried in the district courts and the court

[35] See www.hogstadomstolen.se, last accessed November 2014.

of appeal, but not in the Supreme Court. To give an example, in the main hearing of a criminal case at a district court, the court consists of one professional judge and three lay judges.[36] In the court of appeal, there are three professional judges and two lay judges.[37] If during the deliberations there are different opinions that cannot be resolved, a vote is taken in which the vote of each lay judge carries the same weight as that of the professional judge.[38] Lay judges are not jurors; they are nominated by the political parties and appointed for four years by the municipal assembly. Their role is not to put forward political views but to apply the law and represent the general sense of justice. Conversely, juries in Swedish law only sit in cases concerning breaches of the constitutional laws on freedom of press and freedom of expression.[39]

3. Academy

When it comes to *academic lawyers*, it is fair to say that it was more common earlier (especially at the end of the nineteenth and beginning of the twentieth century) to pay attention to the relationship between tort and crime.[40] Nowadays, within academia one usually specialises in either tort or crime but very rarely studies or does research in both subjects.[41]

All law students study criminal law and tort law in different years, with no direct comparison made between the subjects. They take their exams once or more every semester, and the exam can be in either a particular subject (e.g., tax law, tort law or European law) or private law, which could include questions concerning tort law, contract law and labour law. Not much attention is paid to the connection between crime and tort.

4. Prosecutors

A description of the role of the prosecutor, and of the aggrieved party, requires some historical background. Through the instrument of government of 1634, the central and the local administration were reshaped. Besides the courts of appeal, collegia were organised for the central administration. For the local administration, county chiefs or lord lieutenants (*landshövding*) were appointed, as a representative of the government in

[36] Code of Judicial Procedure, Ch. 1 § 3b.

[37] Code of Judicial Procedure, Ch. 2 § 4.

[38] Code of Judicial Procedure, Ch. 29 § 3.

[39] Freedom of the Press Act (Tryckfrihetsförordningen), Ch. 12 § 2, and Freedom of Expression Act (Yttrandefrihetsgrundlagen), Ch. 9 § 1.

[40] E.g. Professors Ivar Strahl (1899–1987), Hjalmar Karlgren (1897–1978), and Hans Thornstedt (1917–2010).

[41] See, exceptionally, Friberg, *Kränkningsersättning*.

each county. The *landshövding* was the head of an office divided into two parts, one for general administrative issues and one for tax revenue. Under the offices of the *landshövding*, there were bailiffs (*kronofogde, kronolänsman*) who were responsible for taking up taxes, keeping peace and order, prosecuting crimes and enforcing judgments of courts. In the towns, there was a *stadsfiskal* who was responsible for police and prosecution.

Through the Criminal Code of 1864, the task of the bailiffs to prosecute was defined more tightly to specify which crimes the bailiff should prosecute and which were left to the aggrieved party. The bailiff prosecuted and presented evidence, but the judge – as the only lawyer in the courtroom aside from the law clerk – still took an active part in the trial. The reform movements in procedural law that led to the Code of Judicial Procedure of 1942 meant that the adversarial principle was strengthened and the activity of the judge restrained, prompting a need for prosecutors with a law degree.[42]

In 1948, the office of Prosecutor of the Realm (*riksåklagare*) was introduced. The office of Chancellor of Justice (*justitiekansler*) was divided in two: his tasks as chief prosecutor were transferred to the Prosecutor of the Realm, and he kept the tasks of being prosecutor in freedom of press cases and handling claims for damages against the state. Under the Prosecutor of the Realm were the local prosecutors. Through this reform, some important steps were taken towards setting up one professional organisation of prosecutors. To become a prosecutor, it is necessary to have a law degree and to have served as a law clerk at a district court or administrative court.

Prosecutors have a rather different role in Swedish law compared to other legal systems. To begin with, the prosecutor has an absolute duty to prosecute for most crimes.[43] The key threshold is that the prosecutor must decide that there is sufficient evidence to prove that a crime has been

42 B. Westerhult, *Kronofogde, häradsskrivare, länsman. Den svenska fögderiförvaltningen 1810–1917* (Lund: Gleerup, 1965), 73–5.

43 Code of Judicial Procedure Ch. 20 § 6. – Exceptions are made for certain offences where it may be felt that the interests of the general public in instigating legal proceedings are not strong enough. Examples of such offences are breach of domiciliary peace and crimes of unlawful appropriation, or stealing, within the family (i.e. theft etc.). The prosecutor may prosecute in these cases if there 'for special reasons is deemed necessary in the public interest'. This requirement is proposed to be struck out in one particular area where the government at present thinks there is a need for powerful actions, namely defamation – particularly on internet. If the bill is accepted by parliament, the prosecutor will to a large extent have to assist citizens who have been exposed to defamation.

committed and that a certain person has committed it.[44] The prosecutor is also under an obligation to prepare a lawsuit (to be brought as part of the criminal procedure) and represent a victim of a crime who has requested damages: such a person has the status of 'aggrieved party'.[45]

5. Aggrieved parties (*målsägande*)

The aggrieved party, the *målsägande,* literally translated as 'the person who owns the case', has a specific status in criminal procedure. He or she can prosecute cases, which the prosecutor decides not to put forward, support the prosecution, appeal an acquittal against which the prosecutor does not appeal and act as a party claiming damages.[46]

In the Law Code of 1734, there was no rule that defined the aggrieved party. David Nehrman Ehrenstråle defined the aggrieved party as someone who had suffered a loss and thus had reason to claim damages and take the initiative to prosecution.[47] A definition was incorporated into the procedural part of the 1832 draft Criminal Code: the aggrieved party was the person towards whom the crime had been committed or who had suffered from the crime.[48] A similar definition is found in the 1844 draft.[49] The rule was finally set out in the 1864 Criminal Code in the chapter on damages.[50] The purpose of the rule was to define who the aggrieved party was in order to stipulate who had the right to prosecute and to claim damages. The position of the rule in the chapter on damages

[44] Code of Judicial Procedure Ch. 23 § 2. – There are exceptions, e.g. if a person has recently received sentence for another offence and the crime in question would not result in the punishment being increased. An example of this is when a person is sentenced to a long period of imprisonment for grand theft and it transpires that he/she was also guilty of shoplifting immediately before being found guilty of theft. Since the period of imprisonment would in all probability not have been longer if charges had also been brought against the suspect for shoplifting, the prosecutor may grant a waiver of prosecution. Waiver of prosecution is also common in the case of young people under the age of eighteen. If the person in question is a first offender and it is a question of a minor offence, the idea is that he or she should be given another chance. A basic precondition for granting a waiver of prosecution is that it does not conflict with any important private or public interest. See the Code of Judicial Procedure Ch. 20 § 7. A side effect of granting a waiver of prosecution is that a damages claim from the victim would have to be brought forward as a civil claim without the assistance of the prosecutor. However, if the claim is more substantial in sum, it would probably be considered as such an important private interest that a waiver of prosecution would not be granted.

[45] See Section 4 below.

[46] Code of Judicial Procedure, Ch. 20 §§ 8–9 and Ch. 22.

[47] D. Nehrman (Ehrenstråle), *Inledning till den svenska processum criminalem* (Lund: Carl Gustav Berling, 1759), 27.

[48] 1832 draft Criminal Code, procedural part, Ch. 2 § 8.

[49] 1844 draft Criminal Code, Ch. 8 § 9.

[50] 1864 Criminal Code, Ch. 6 § 8.

could lead to the misunderstanding that the rule only governed that part of the aggrieved party's rights relating to damages; in fact it also governed what were, in effect, private prosecutions. Prosecution solely by the aggrieved party is now very rare: it receded in importance from 1864 to 1948, when the new Code of Judicial Procedure came into force with the state taking over prosecutions. Nevertheless, the rule that the aggrieved party is the person towards whom the crime has been committed or who has suffered from the crime[51] is today still specified in a chapter concerning the right to prosecution by the state prosecutors and aggrieved parties.[52]

6. Counsel for the aggrieved party and for the defence

An aggrieved party has the right to require the prosecutor to bring forward his or her civil claim. However, in addition to this right, the court can appoint a state funded *aggrieved party counsel*,[53] usually an attorney (*advokat*),[54] who will assist the aggrieved party. In certain cases (mostly sexual offences and assault), the court *must* appoint an aggrieved party counsel, unless the victim already has a counsel and objects to any other counsel being appointed. In more serious cases concerning assault, unlawful deprivation of liberty and robbery, the court will appoint such counsel if it can be assumed that the victim is in need of counsel due to, for instance, the relationship with the defendant. The aggrieved party counsel protects the interests of the victim and, for example, can bring an action for damages in the criminal trial if the prosecutor does not do so. It is fair to say that in those cases where the court has appointed an aggrieved party counsel, the presumption is that counsel rather than the prosecutor will assist the plaintiff regarding the civil claim.[55] It is not uncommon that

[51] Code of Judicial Procedure, Chapter 20 § 8 ss. 4.

[52] L. Heuman, *Målsägande*, (Stockholm: Norstedt, 1973), 19–20.

[53] See SFS 1988:609, Act on aggrieved party counsel.

[54] See Code of Judicial Procedure, Ch. 8.

[55] See Th. Bring and Ch. Diesen, *Förundersökning*, 4th edn (Stockholm: Norstedts Juridik, 2009) 101 and Statens Offentliga Utredningar (SOU) (Swedish Government Official Report) 2007:6. See also a report from the National Council for Crime Prevention (Brottsförebyggande rådet) 2009:4, where the question is raised whether such a system is fair, where aggrieved parties who have received counsel thereby automatically will get state funded assistance with their damages claims in contrast to those aggrieved parties who do not benefit from an aggrieved party counsel. The question has not been discussed further. The underlying reason to this difference in treatment between victims is probably the need to find a balance in a legal system with limited financial resources, where victims of more serious crimes have greater need of legal assistance than victims of lesser crimes with regard to the type of crime suffered. The right to aggrieved party counsel is not income-related.

an attorney who takes on work as an aggrieved party counsel has broad practice and experience that extends outside that one field, and also takes on assignments as defence lawyer, although not in the same case of course.

7. Advocates

As will be obvious from the foregoing section, advocates working on criminal cases before district courts and courts of appeal need knowledge and experience in both criminal and tort law. However, they rarely deal with tort issues other than those that have a connection to crime. It is probably fair to say that in general, the knowledge of other areas of tort law (for instance environmental or medical damage) is very limited for this category of lawyers. Practising lawyers who specialise in tort law, on the other hand, may also engage in contract, family, real estate or insurance law. One could say that the degree of specialisation depends on the size and profile of the law firm. In smaller cities, lawyers often have to be quite versatile, but the larger the city, the more specialised the lawyers are. Apart from the advocates appearing both as counsel for aggrieved parties and defendants, there are some advocates that focus on working only with clients on one of these sides.

8. Insurance

Insurance companies are nowadays large and important actors when it comes to the overlap of tort and crime. Somewhere around 90 per cent of the Swedish population has insurance that covers claims of compensation for personal injuries caused by some intentional crimes (*överfallsskydd*),[56] as well as insurance against liability for damages (*ansvarsförsäkring*). Insurance against liability for damages applies only if the damage is not caused by intentional acts. The scope of the first type of insurance (*överfallsskydd*) is subject, however, to certain limitations both in coverage and sums, which means that a claim sometimes is not met in full. For instance, cover might well not include damage caused by a member of the insured person's household or if the damage is self-induced. Furthermore, the amount of compensation paid to an injured party is more often than not predetermined according to a tariff scheme, which means that there is a risk of both over and under compensation.[57] Where the victim is under-compensated for any of these reasons, she might make a subsequent tort

[56] E.g. assault, sexual offences and robbery.

[57] Almost all of the large insurance companies apply such a pre-determined tariff scheme instead of trying each insurance case individually.

claim against the tortfeasor, the claim being for the amount not covered by the insurance company. As might be expected, insurers can also bring a litigation claim: when an insurance company has paid compensation to the insured party, it can subrogate the claim against the tortfeasor. It should also be mentioned in this context that the regular home insurance that most people have also covers costs (up to 200,000 SEK) for hiring an attorney if the insured person wishes to sue for damages as a civil claim separate from the criminal trial.[58]

9. The Crime Victim Compensation and Support Authority

Finally, one last institution particularly worth mentioning in this context is the Crime Victim Compensation and Support Authority (*Brottsoffermyndigheten*).[59] The authority was founded in 1978 (then called *Brottsskadenämnden*) although there had been a system of financial compensation to crime victims since the budgetary year 1948–9. To begin with, the compensation was limited to damage caused by fugitives from prisons, institutions for care of young persons and mental hospitals. The reason for providing compensation was 'societal planning'. Since the people living in close vicinity of the institutions were the ones most at risk of suffering damage it was arguably inequitable if they did not have any right to compensation when such damage occurred. It was also to avoid the anxiety and reluctance that the location of such institutions could otherwise arouse among local residents. Finally, the costs for damage caused by fugitives were considered to be less than what it would cost to minimise the risk of prisoners breaking out. The political ambition at the time was to have less coercion and control in institutions, an ambition, which was consistent with economic policy. Since 1971, legislation has extended to crime victims a general right to damages for personal injuries, violation and in a small number of cases, damage to property.[60]

Nowadays, the authority's overall aim is to look after the rights of all crime victims and to draw public attention to their needs and interests. It has three nationwide functions: to administer the crime victim

[58] Friberg, *Kränkningsersättning*, 401–13.

[59] See J. Mikaelsson and A. Wergens (eds.), *Repairing the Irreparable. State Compensation to Crime Victims in the European Union* (Umeå: Brottsoffermyndigheten, 2001), 133–46, and Friberg, *Kränkningsersättning*, 415–34. See also www.brottsoffermyndigheten.se, last accessed November 2014.

[60] A proposal to introduce such a compensation system, funded by the state, was put forward already in 1950 but was flatly rejected.

fund,[61] to work as a centre of knowledge and to process cases concerning crime injuries compensation. The authority can, after any legal process is concluded, pay governmentally funded compensation, so-called 'crime injuries compensation', for injuries. Not all forms of damage are eligible, for example, property and economic losses can only be compensated for under certain special conditions. The most important types of damages with the authority are the non-pecuniary damages for pain and suffering (*sveda och värk*) and violation (*kränkning*). All other possibilities for compensation (for instance, damages and insurance) must be exhausted before it is possible to obtain compensation from the Crime Victim Compensation and Support Authority. If the offender is unknown, the authority makes a decision based on police reports and medical statements as to whether the alleged victim is entitled to compensation. Some of the more significant decisions concerning violation damages granted by the authority are published in a booklet.[62] These decisions are indicative for the courts, who give them great importance; this is something the Supreme Court has also accepted.[63] Many times, it is the authority who has taken the initiative to increase the compensation level for violation damages for different types of crimes, and the courts have followed suit.

A payment by the Crime Victim Compensation and Support Authority gives it a right of recourse against the offender: the offender becomes liable to pay back the money to the authority instead of the crime victim, after the compensation has been paid out. About one third of the amount paid from crime victim compensation in a given year is financed by recourse revenue. During the last thirty years, there has been a shift in attitude regarding recourse. Previously, the legislator thought that the possibility to bring a recourse action should be used sparingly so that the convicted person's reintegration into society would not be hampered by burdensome claims. Nowadays, it is deemed important from a crime

[61] The fund's aim is to give financial support to different kinds of crime victim oriented activities, which can range from simpler information campaigns to large-scale research projects. The goal is to improve the situation for crime victims through increased knowledge and understanding. The Crime Victim Fund is primarily built up through a special fee of 800 SEK, which every person convicted of a crime that is punishable by a prison sentence has to pay. The Fund is also open for donations. Every year, the Fund distributes approximately 30–35 million SEK.

[62] See most recently *Brottsoffermyndighetens referatsamling 2014* (Umeå: Brottsoffermyndigheten, 2014). It is also available on the Internet, see www.brottsoffermyndigheten.se/ersattning/referatsamling (last accessed November 2014).

[63] NJA 1997, 315; see Friberg, *Kränkningsersättning*, 429–32.

victim perspective that the convicted person has to face full responsibility for the damage that his or her crime has caused.

B. *Norms*

1. Introduction

While both punishment and damages can be said to be sanctions against conduct that is unwanted in society, and at least historically had the purpose of attributing blame to the person who had committed a wrong, the separation of the two legal institutes has rendered the differences clear (although there still are similarities as well). Criminal law punishes the wrongdoer, and it is basically a destructive sanction (although within criminal law, there are elements of rehabilitation, for instance). It could be said that punishment presupposes that the offender is a moral agent with capacity to receive the message of blame. If the offender lacks mental capacity (is seriously mentally ill), he or she still committed the crime but cannot be punished (with a few exceptions) and will undergo involuntary psychiatric treatment instead. Children are considered capable of committing crime, but they cannot be sentenced for what they might have done before the age of fifteen.[64] Thus, in criminal law there is not really a minimum age of responsibility (although it is difficult to imagine a child who cannot walk and talk conducting a prohibited act), but it would probably be fair to say that it would be the same assessment as in tort law, where you do not acknowledge responsibility before the age of three or four. More practically relevant in such situations, a parent who arranges for a five-year old to steal would be liable as at least an accessory or – more likely – as a perpetrator.[65]

In comparison, it cannot be said that awarding damages presupposes that the tortfeasor is a moral agent with whom the court communicates a moral message. For instance, within tort law it is possible to apply strict liability to an extent that is not possible in criminal law, and children and people with mental insufficiencies are held liable although they do not understand what they have done.[66] Then again, damages are not about attributing blame anymore, but rather serve as an instrument of risk sharing.

[64] Criminal Code, Ch. 1 § 6.

[65] See P. Asp, M. Ulväng and N. Jareborg, *Kriminalrättens grunder*, 2nd edn (Uppsala: Iustus, 2013), 432–35.

[66] See Ch. 2 §§ 4 and 5 Tort Liability Act. In these cases, the amount of damages can be mitigated.

Under this heading, it is useful to distinguish between the following three different levels:[67]

(1) The purposes of tort law and criminal law, i.e. which functions can we say that the two areas of law have on an overarching level? How do we justify the existence of a publicly sanctioned system of distributing loss or why should the burden of the loss be attributed to someone other than the injured party?
(2) What distinguishes a crime and a tort?
(3) How do we punish when someone is convicted of a crime, and how do we determine the level of damages?

Within each level, one can find a multitude of normative theories that are more or less generally accepted, some of which will be sketched below. Some of them have relevance to both criminal law and tort law, while others clearly illustrate the difference between the two areas of law.

2. The purpose of tort law and criminal law

The purpose of criminal law is to deter undesirable conduct and to get people to behave in a certain way. It is needed to preserve a society in order, a society where demands for justice are met and where private retaliation is suppressed. A criminal law system is also needed because it is necessary as an expression and an affirmation of a moral point of view: prohibited actions require responses that involve blame.[68]

The purpose of tort law can be said to keep society in order, to – through deterrence – get people to act in a certain way, to create economic efficiency

[67] Cf., e.g., H. L. A. Hart, *Punishment and Responsibility. Essays in the Philosophy of Law* (Oxford: Clarendon, 1970) 3–6, T. Honoré, *Responsibility and Fault* (Oxford: Hart, 1999), 67, N. Jareborg, *Straffrattsideologiska fragment* (Uppsala: Iustus, 1992) 135–8, A. Ross, *Skyld, ansvar og straf* (København: Berlingske, 1970), 68–9. See also Friberg, *Kränkningsersättning*, 79–82, for further references regarding this division into different levels with different questions and answers, and why the author believes it to be relevant to make a comparison between criminal and tort law in this sense.

[68] Legal doctrine is vast in this area. See, e.g., I. Agge, *Straffrättens allmänna del*, 4th edn (Stockholm: Juristförlaget, 1984), 50–3, P. Asp, M. Ulväng and N. Jareborg, *Kriminalrättens grunder*, 49–50. See also J. Hagströmer, *Svensk straffrätt* (Uppsala: A&W, 1901–5), 16–27, R. A. Duff, *Punishment, Communication and Community* (Oxford University Press, 2001) xiv–xv; Hart, *Punishment and Responsibility*, 4, M. Ulväng, 'Criminal Law and Civil Peace' in Maksymilian Del Mar (ed.), *Law as Institutional Normative Order* (Farnham: Ashgate, 2009), 134.

and security in a sense that those who are injured know that they will be compensated.[69] Tort law can protect rights by awarding compensation where no other means are available. It deals with the allocation of the burden of risk and can declare what is a tolerable creation of risk.[70] Through its threat of liability to pay for harm caused, tort is forward-facing; through the same requirement it also looks back to the harm caused and seeks to put the victim back in the position as if the wrong had never occurred.[71] An award of damages is more constructively focused than punishment since it compensates the injuries.[72]

These underlying purposes of tort law and criminal law as systems and the sanctions of punishment and damages are obviously relevant for how standards in the respective systems are designed and applied. However, while in general terms, it can be said we have systems of tort law and criminal law to discourage people from certain behaviour, it cannot automatically be said that this reason should be decisive in determining the level of punishment or damage. If so, we would, for example, have levels of damages that do not correspond to the degree of harm but to the amount of money needed to deter.[73]

[69] See, e.g., B. Bengtsson, 'Det skadeståndsrättsliga reformarbetet' in *Uppsala universitet* (Uppsala 1976), 105, J. Hellner, 'Skadeståndsrättens Reformering' (1967) *Svensk Juristtidning*, 698–700 and 'Värderingar i skadeståndsrätten' in *Festskrift till Per Olof Ekelöf* (Stockholm: Norstedt, 1972), 328, J. Hellner and M. Radetzki, *Skadeståndsrätt*, 8th edn (Stockholm: Norstedts juridik, 2010), 43 and 46–7, I. Strahl, 'Skadeståndsrättens framtid' in *Rättsvetenskapliga studier ägnade minnet av Phillips Hult* (Stockholm: Almqvist & Wiksell 1960), 435. Cf. V. Lundstedt, *Grundlinjer i skadeståndsrätten. I. Culparegeln* (Uppsala: Norblad, 1935), 104–6 and *Grundlinjer i skadeståndsrätten II:2. Strikt ansvar* (Uppsala: Norblad, 1953), 208–10.

[70] H. Andersson, *Skyddsändamål och adekvans. Om skadeståndsansvarets gränser* (Uppsala: Iustus, 1993), 252–5 and 321, Friberg, *Kränkningsersättning*, 111.

[71] Cf. A. Agell, *Samtycke och risktagande. Studier i skadeståndsrätt* (Stockholm: Norstedt, 1962), 75, G. Astrup Hoel, *Risiko og ansvar. Utviklingslinjer i forsikrings- og erstatningsret* (Oslo: Gyldendal, 1929), 18, fn 1, P. O. Ekelöf, *Straffet, skadeståndet och vitet. En studie över de rättsliga sanktionernas verkningssätt* (Uppsala: Lundequist, 1942), 77, K. Grönfors, *Om trafikskadeansvar utanför kontraktsförhållanden : studier över skadeståndsproblem vid trafik till lands, till sjöss och i luften* (Uppsala 1952), 90 with foot note 8, J. Hellner and M. Radetzki, *Skadeståndsrätt* 39, Hj. Karlgren, 'Den allmänna skadeståndsläran' (1938 *Svensk Juristtidning* 356 and Hj. Karlgren, *Skadeståndsrätt*, 5th edn (Stockholm: Norstedt, 1972), 14–16, F. Stang, *Erstatningsansvar* (Oslo: Aschehoug, 1927), 47–9. See also H. Andersson, *Skyddsändamål och adekvans*, 323 with further references.

[72] A. Serlachius, *Straff och skadestånd* (Helsingfors, 1901), 64 and 70: 'punishment aims to harm, while damages aims to repair' (author's translation), Stjernberg, *Den positiva straffrättens allmänna del, I* (Uppsala: Almqvist & Wiksell, 1920), 28–30.

[73] Friberg, *Kränkningsersättning*, 78–101.

3. Distinguishing features of a crime compared to a tort?

A distinguishing feature for criminal law compared to tort law is what follows from the principle of legality defined as *nulla poena sine lege* and *nullum crimen sine lege*: no one can be sentenced for an act (or omission) that was not criminalised at the time

A 'crime' is defined in the Criminal Code (Ch. 1 § 1) as an act that is *ex ante* defined and regulated by law, described in the Criminal Code or in other legislation, for which a punishment is defined. This means that no other behaviour or consequences of an act than those described in the criminal provisions are criminalised. 'Punishment' is defined as imprisonment (which can be replaced by, e.g., probation) or fines.[74] Normally, criminal intent is also required for considering an act as criminal,[75] but there are several crimes which only require negligence. The Criminal Code consists of chapters with different categories of precisely defined acts. Besides the Criminal Code, there are other Acts, which have the character of criminal legislation, such as Acts on the use of drugs, traffic crimes and smuggling. As a third category, Acts concerning almost all areas of law can have some final provisions criminalising specified acts within that area of law.

The legislation on tort is much more open in its texture and the general rule is that the limitations of liability have to be established on a case by case basis, effectively allowing much greater flexibility (and less certainty). There is no definition of a tortious act, which resembles the definition of crime. In the Tort Liability Act, there are general rules stating that 'anyone who intently or negligently causes damage to persons or things shall compensate for the damage',[76] that 'anyone who causes pure economic loss (that is, economic loss without any connection to damage to persons or things) through a crime shall compensate for the damage'[77] and that 'anyone who seriously violates someone else through a crime which consists of an attack against his or her person, liberty, peace or honour shall compensate for the damage which lies in the violation'.[78] Deriving from this, one could say in general terms that a tortious act is when a person intentionally or negligently harms someone else or their property in a situation where there is a duty not to cause harm. As might be expected, the general rules in the Tort Liability Act have given rise to many more Supreme Court cases than the general rules of criminal law.

[74] Criminal Code, Ch. 1 §§ 1 and 3. [75] Criminal Code, Ch. 1 § 2.
[76] Tort Liability Act, Ch. 2 § 1. [77] Tort Liability Act, Ch. 2 § 2.
[78] Tort Liability Act, Ch. 2 § 3.

The historical connection to criminal law is however clear in that the two last mentioned categories explicitly refer to crime and the first – intently or negligently causing damage to persons or things – in most aspects correspond to criminalised behaviour.[79] There are, however, also areas in tort law where the definition of tortious liability is much more precise and *ex ante* defined in law, namely areas of typically 'dangerous' activities such as railway or car traffic, electrical installations, nuclear power stations. In those cases, strict liability is often applied and is defined in other legislations outside the general Tort Liability Act.

4. Sentencing and assessment of damages

When a court has found a defendant guilty of a crime, and a punishment is to be decided, the court applies the latitude defined in the legislation for each crime. Assault, for example, is liable to imprisonment from fourteen days to two years. Petty assault is punishable by a fine or imprisonment for a maximum of six months. There are two classes of gross assault, one which is liable to one to six years of imprisonment and the other from four to ten years of imprisonment.[80]

When the court has decided which of these four classes the crime corresponds to, the court should decide the so-called penal value (*straffvärde*). Whilst the degree is chosen mainly on the basis of the objective facts, the subjective factors are given more weight in determining the penal value. The penal value is decided according to the damages, violation or danger that the act caused, what the defendant knew or should have known about this and his reasons for committing the act.[81] After taking the aggravating and mitigating circumstances into account, the court uses the penal value to choose the appropriate sanction. The penal value is expressed in an amount of fines or a term of imprisonment. If the term of imprisonment is one year or above, or the defendant has committed similar crimes recently, the sentence will most likely be imprisonment. If the penal value is on the level of imprisonment but not above one year, the sentence will still often be imprisonment but only for certain types of crime, such as perjury. For some types of crime, such as thefts or frauds, a conditional sentence combined with a fine is considered adequate, while for crimes, such as assault, conditional sentence or probation with societal service

[79] There is an exception as regards negligent damage to property, see Section 3.C below.

[80] Criminal Code, Ch. 3 §§ 5–6.

[81] Criminal Code, Ch. 29 § 1.

is considered sufficient if the penal value is less than approximately six months.[82]

Despite legal theory suggesting that damages seek to undo the harm the wrongdoer has caused, damages can in some cases be *perceived* (by the defendant, the victim, media, general public) as a punitive sanction, particularly in those instances of non-pecuniary damage where it is difficult to define what constitutes the damage, namely violation damages.[83] In such circumstances, the level of damages will be decided according to the facts concerning the act causing the damage, and in some cases even the tortfeasor's degree of guilt. For instance, when deciding on how much damages a victim of assault is to be awarded, the court takes into account the degree of violation that a person typically experiences during an assault, if there are any aggravating circumstances concerning the criminal act that can be said to affect the degree of violation and whether the accused acted with intent or gross negligence. Negligent acts typically result in recovery of lesser damages than intentional crimes. In this sense, the process of measuring damages has a lot in common with sentencing and especially determining the penal value.

The legislation on how to determine the amount of damages for violation has great similarities with the legislation on how to calculate the penal value; the fact that civil claims are most commonly brought before the court in the context of a criminal case can be said to reinforce these similarities and when such a similarity is well established, it feeds back as a reason to continue the joint proceedings. Taking again a case of assault as an example, the court will mainly rely on the same facts when deciding the penal value and the damages for violation. It is possible for the damages claimant to refer to further or other facts than the prosecutor has put forward in the criminal case, but this is more often seen in the cases where the criminal case and the civil claim on damages are tried in separate proceedings. However, there are also divergences that have to do with the different headings of damages in Swedish tort law. On the one hand, the penal value and the level of damages for violation do not derive directly or solely from the evidence, but are determined by precedent,

[82] See in detail M. Borgeke, *Att bestämma påföljd för brott*, 2nd edn (Stockholm: Norstedt, 2012), 119–402. There are many details in the system e.g. for youths which are not discussed here.

[83] See H. G. Hartmann, 'Noen refleksjoner omkring erstatningskrav i strafferettspleien' in *Rett og rettssal* (Oslo: Aschehoug, 1984), 301–3, and, for further examples, Friberg, *Kränkningsersättning*, 233–4.

comparing the facts of the given case with the facts of earlier cases.[84] On the other hand, in a case of assault the court will often have to assess the amount of damages for pain and suffering (determined as standard sums on the basis of how many weeks the aggrieved party has not been able to work) and costs and loss of income (most often based on what has been proven through receipts and other documents), factors which are more closely bound to their facts rather than precedent.

5. 'Blurring' the picture

One thing meriting mention in this context is the difficulties that sometimes arise in determining whether or not to qualify a sanction as criminal. Since the normative theories that motivate and support a criminal sanction are somewhat different from the purpose of administrative or private law sanctions and the rationale behind how the sanctions are to be measured differs, the question of defining a sanction is important. By way of introduction, it should be understood that the term 'damages' does not exist in the simple way it does in English. In Swedish, one word for 'damages', *ersättning*, simply means any payment of money, whilst another similar word, *skadestånd*, means the payment of damages both in contractual relationships and as a result of criminal or negligent acts that have no relationship with contracts.

First, there are a number of ways in which the legislator seeks to promote or deter certain behaviour using the criminal law. On the one hand, there are of course a range of what might be thought pure punishments, including imprisonment and orders to undergo certain treatments like drug rehabilitation orders. On the other hand, there are other measures, including penalties, fees, company fines and prohibition to do business. Some of these sanctions can be defined as belonging to criminal law, but they are not punishments according to Swedish legal thought, others are defined as administrative sanctions but are still governed by the criminal heading of Article 6 ECHR. However, in respect of these measures the rules regarding evidentiary standards in criminal law, requirements of intent or fault and procedural safeguards concerning crimes are not always applied. Thus, the legislator can decide to make use of such alternative sanctions to

[84] Important tools are, for the penal value and the violation respectively, M. Borgeke, C. Månsson, G. Sterzel *et al.*, *Studier rörande påföljdspraxis med mera*, 5th edn (Stockholm; Jure, 2013) and *Brottsoffermyndighetens referatsamling 2014* (Umeå: Brottsoffermyndigheten, 2014).

punishment in order to create an opportunity for more effective actions against certain behaviour.

Second, there are compensatory orders within certain areas of law, which can be thought of as 'damages' or a sanction on the border of criminal law, for instance, discrimination compensation, general damages in labour law and violation damages. These are sometimes defined as damages although the characteristics can differ from other, and more 'traditional', types of damages, for example, physical injuries, property damage and financial loss. Here, violation damages (described briefly above) and general damages in labour law are also pertinent. Criminal law theories concerning, for instance, sentencing and prevention, can be seen in the application of the rules on damages.

Related to these damages is compensation for discrimination, with discrimination on grounds of race, gender and many other reasons prohibited by the Discrimination Act 2008.[85] Since 2009 this is no longer called 'damages', but what might loosely be called 'discrimination compensation' (*diskrimineringsersättning*). The name was changed in order to distance it from typical tort law principles, especially to provide an opportunity to award higher damages than previously possible under tort and thereby achieving a more punitive kind of sanction. This is so even though the word in Swedish does not sound more 'penal' to the Swedish ear. These awards now have two purposes: to compensate the discriminated person for both pecuniary and non-pecuniary harm and to award damages that will deter further discriminatory behaviour. It is of course difficult to tell if the compensation is set to a higher level than would be justified to be purely compensatory, and thus the extent of its punitive element, since it is impossible to value the non-pecuniary damage by some objective, factual measure.[86] The legislator's idea was to ensure that the courts do not compare the non-pecuniary harm suffered by a person who has been discriminated against, with the non-pecuniary harm of a crime victim. Such kinds of comparisons tend to result in compensation levels that, according to the legislator, cannot deter discrimination. One can therefore observe the resemblance with criminal law theories when discussing

[85] SFS 2008:567.

[86] It has been discussed if the courts in practice first decide the non-pecuniary damages that should be awarded and then decide the amount of damages that could suffice to deter from further discriminatory behaviour. See e.g. Friberg, *Kränkningsersättning*, 488–9. See also H. Andersson, 'Diskrimineringsjuridikens ersättningsrättsliga diskurs – en argumentativ inventering' (2013) Svensk Juristtidning, 779–806. This method has later been confirmed by the Supreme Court in NJA 2014, 499.

both the purpose of why certain acts are and should be prohibited and the adjudication of compensation for discrimination.

Swedish law therefore has an overlap of normative theories that blur the picture of tort law and criminal law as being two entirely separate legal areas. While we can intellectually separate (1) the purpose of tort law and criminal law, (2) what distinguishes a tort and what distinguishes a crime, and (3) how we punish crimes and determine the level of damages, we cannot do so completely in practice. This is particularly clear as regards the determination of penal values and damages for violation.

C. *Substance*

1. Introduction

Tort liability will very often be mirrored in criminal liability, at least in theory. This is because most of frequent harms caused have also been criminalised with one clear exception being negligent damage to property.[87] In other aspects, however, the two forms of liability do not coincide. For instance, criminal law has higher evidentiary requirements than tort law, which can have great practical importance. Nonetheless, in this section, we will focus on similarities and difference in substance.

As will be evident from above, there is a very general rule that committing a crime creates liability for the damages caused by the crime. There are however, a number of exceptions. First, when the purpose behind the criminalisation is to protect interests other than those of the injured party, a claim for damages cannot be based solely on the crime. A classic example is that criminal punishment for smuggling does not create a right to damages for those business competitors who have suffered financially from the smuggler selling the smuggled goods at a low price (hence receiving a greater profit than the competitors); the purpose of criminalising smuggling is not to protect the financial interests of the smuggler's competitors. Another example is that littering is a crime in the Environmental Code, protecting the general interest but not the property owner – he can be sentenced for littering on his own property. If the littering has also caused damage on the property, the claim for damages will have to be based not on littering as a crime but on the tortious damage. The relevant question to ask, when facing the issue of a crime and a potential tort, is whether the criminal provision protects the interests of a party who is injured by the offence. One could say that the offence may serve as a starting point

[87] See Criminal Code, Ch. 12 §§ 1–3 *e contrario*.

for the assessment of whether the claimant has a right to damages, and in the most common crimes it is easily satisfied.

Second, justifications like self-defence, distress or consent can be assessed differently when judging a tort claim and a criminal prosecution (on which, see Section 3.C.2 below). This means that the defendant could be held criminally liable yet the aggrieved party is not awarded damages. One example is assault: criminal law allows individuals to consent only to a low level of harm, roughly between the crimes of petty assault and assault; tort law allows consent to preclude liability for a much wider range of harms, so that if the claimant brings a claim after the events, she is unlikely to be awarded damages, either at all or only partial compensation.[88]

Third, for some types of damages the Tort Liability Act draws some distinctions that are not relevant in criminal law. For instance, a person who commits murder, manslaughter or involuntary manslaughter is liable to pay damages to the victim's family. However, under the heading of non-pecuniary damage (pain and suffering), only certain family members are entitled, namely spouses, grandparents and children provided that they lived together at the time of death. Adult siblings who do not live together are for instance not entitled to damages, even though they have suffered the same loss.

2. Crime as a prerequisite in tort law

In two situations, tort liability requires that the damage has been caused by a crime. This is a remnant of the previous legislation, under which tort liability was intimately associated with criminal liability (see Section 2).

The first situation is pure economic loss (a loss that occurs without connection to a personal injury or property loss), although there are a number of exceptions to this rule. The requirement that the acts constitute a crime is of course not applicable within contractual cases and there are provisions where liability is stipulated under other circumstances. In court practice, damages have been awarded although no crime has been committed, but in those cases the underlying conduct was reprehensible, bordering on criminal, in order for the court to find the defendant liable in tort.[89]

The second situation where tort liability requires that a crime is committed is a particular kind of non-pecuniary damages – violation damages.

[88] Friberg, *Kränkningsersättning*, 162–4. [89] See NJA 1987, 692, cf. 2001, 878.

A person who seriously violates another person by a crime containing an assault on his or her person, liberty, peace or honour, must pay compensation for the damage that the violation involves. One must distinguish between damages for pain and suffering and violation damages; they are two different headings of damages in Swedish tort law. Violation damages aim solely to compensate the victim for the fact that he/she has been assaulted – it is a purely non-pecuniary harm to the person's integrity – and has nothing to do with physical or psychological damage to the person. If the defendant is acquitted by the court, the claim for damages is dismissed. However, if the defendant is found guilty, the claimant might still not be awarded damages for violation since there are other prerequisites that must be complied with. For instance, as mentioned above (Section 3.C.1), the questions of justificatory factors like consent or self-defence can be judged in one way in the criminal case and another in the tort case. Criminal liability is excluded if, for example, the defendant acted in *self-defence*, whilst damages for violation is excluded if the aggrieved party acted in a way that makes clear that he or she did *not protect his or her integrity*. The results of these assessments are often the same but not always. If the allegedly aggrieved party in some way provoked the defendant which gave the defendant a right to self-defence, but he/she acted outside the scope of what can be deemed reasonable in response to the provocation, the defendant can be held criminally liable. In such a situation it is possible that the provocateur will not be awarded damages, since he/she 'started it' and thereby can be said not to have protected his/her integrity. Furthermore, not all criminal violations are considered to be serious enough to result in a right to damages for violation. A less grave offence, for instance molestation or a petty crime of assault, might not be considered sufficiently serious to result in tort liability.

A consequence of the latter legislation, that is, damages for violation, is that other offensive or invasive – though non-criminalised – conduct does not confer a right to damages. For instance, infringements of the rights stipulated in the European Convention of Human Rights (ECHR) have been problematic to deal with in the Swedish courts where there is no criminal provision that prohibits the kind of acts which constitute a violation. The solution has been to use the ECHR as a direct legal basis for a tort claim when it is obvious that a violation has occurred. However, this solution is only possible when the tortfeasor is the state – the ECHR is not applicable between private citizens. Accordingly, it was not previously possible to award damages for the violation of integrity that a person experiences when someone else secretly takes pictures of him or her in an intimate or private situation (e.g., in a dressing room, on a toilet or with a hidden camera in the bedroom), since that kind of behaviour was not criminal until 1 July 2013.[90] There are other examples of non-criminalised behaviour where one can question why there is no right to damages despite the fact that the victim's integrity clearly has been violated. However, the prerequisite of a crime remains absolute.

When assessing the level of damages in violation cases, the reasoning is very similar to the one in determining punishment for the same act. Since it is impossible to name a monetary value of a person's integrity and the harm done to it, the gravity of the offence functions as a starting point in the court's reasoning in how to assess the degree of violation. The important thing is to weigh different violations against each other, so that a victim of, for instance, an attempted murder receives a higher level of damages than someone who has been assaulted.

3. Substantive, civil law requirements in criminal statues

Often, tort law and criminal law rely on the same substantive components. However, there are times when statutes in criminal law have their own definition of concepts, which is separate from how the same concepts are understood in civil law. This is particularly common in property crimes, where criminal law is built up from a concept of possession that deviates from how civil law would treat possession of property. According to criminal law, one can for instance possess funds in a bank account; in civil law this would be a claim against the bank for a certain amount, rather than possessing the money in the account.[91] The concept of possession in criminal law then defines the difference between theft, embezzlement and fraud in a way that is not fully compatible with civil law distinctions. Another example where it is difficult to tell whether criminal and civil law share the same view, is in conveyance of real estate, particularly what impact conveyance has on the criminal liability for an assault on someone else's property.[92] A civil lawyer might say that a conveyance has

[90] Cf. the judgment of the European Court of Human Rights 12 November 2013 in case no. 5786/08 *Söderman* v. *Sweden*.

[91] See NJA 1994, 480, cf. NJA 2011, 524, especially the opinion of Justice Lindskog.

[92] E.g., liability for arson (Criminal Code, Ch. 13 § 1) requires that the starting of a fire entails danger to another person's life or health or extensive destruction of *another's property*. The question on when property is conveyed is therefore central to the application of the paragraph.

happened at a different time from a criminal lawyer; legal doctrine is unclear on this point and the question has yet to be tried by the Supreme Court.

The meaning of more general concepts is often the same in tort law and criminal law although the significance may vary. Some specific points of contact are considered further in the next headings.

4. Capacity

According to Swedish law, there is no *accountability* requirement, that is, all persons can commit crimes and tortious acts. Although a person has to be over the age of fifteen and mentally sane to be punished in criminal law, individuals not meeting this threshold can still commit crimes. This means that a twelve-year old who has damaged a person's car or assaulted an individual will not be sentenced, but will be held liable to pay damages for the damage caused by the crime. The same applies for persons who suffer from serious mental disorder.

The first step in such situations is almost always that the victim applies to his insurance company. The insurance companies have certain rules when it comes to young tortfeasors and persons with serious mental disorders who cause damages through criminal acts. Up to the age of twelve, the insurance covers any tort claims made, even if the child acted intentionally (for mentally insane persons there is no age limit). Otherwise, such claims are dismissed since it is considered un-ethical to be able to insure yourself against liability for damages that arise from your own intentional crimes.

Since the rules of the insurance companies may not cover the harm, or more likely, not cover it in full, these cases can go to court. The claim will be handled by a general court, who applies both criminal law and tort law using the evidentiary standards for civil cases. When deciding on a tort case in court where the tortfeasor lacks capacity in the now discussed sense, there are special rules to apply.[93] According to these rules, the tortfeasor (up to the age of eighteen, or when the damage is caused under the influence of a serious mental disorder or any other mental disorder which is not self-induced and temporary) should only be held responsible for damages caused to the extent that is reasonable with respect to his age and development/state of mind, the nature of the act, if there is an insurance in effect, other financial factors together with any

[93] Tort Liability Act, Ch. 2 §§ 4–5.

other circumstances. These rules stipulate requirements for both liability and mitigation of damages.

5. Causation

The concept of causation is more or less the same in tort law and criminal law. All justifications for liability (intent, negligence and strict liability, the last only existing in tort law) presuppose a causal link between the act and the effect.[94] That link must at least be at the level of 'but for': that the effect would not have happened without the act.

There is, however, a difference in how causation works in detail. In criminal law, each offence is defined in narrow terms, with the exact causal link required being a matter of statutory interpretation. This also means that inchoate crimes can be and are recognised: crimes where no causal link to a harm is required. Instead, in such cases necessary effect is often described as a state of risk or danger of injury, and of course a causal relation between this condition and the act is required. In tort law, there is a general requirement that the causality is adequate, that is, that the effect is foreseeable to an optimal observer, a rule derived from German law.[95]

There are also 'exceptional' situations in tort law more than in criminal law. In particular, certain evidentiary difficulties concerning causality can arise for example, with environmental damages or medical injuries. While Swedish law does not normally change the substantive rules of causation here, there are principles and statutory rules that stipulate that the standard of proof is lowered to a question of balance of probabilities; it is deemed sufficient evidence that the party that bears the burden of proof shows that it is 'clearly more likely' or even only 'more likely' that factor A caused the damage than factor B.[96] This is compared with the normal situation, which is that a relevant fact must be 'proven' (a higher standard than 'clearly more likely than not' but lower than 'beyond reasonable doubt'), on which see Section 4.C below.

6. Negligence and intent

Since liability for personal injuries and property damage requires only negligence, not intent, tort law textbooks do not normally discuss intent

[94] P. Asp, M. Ulväng and N. Jareborg, *Kriminalrättens grunder*, 2nd edn (Uppsala: Iustus, 2013), 78–89

[95] Friberg, *Kränkningsersättning*, 147–52.

[96] See, e.g., the Environmental Code Ch. 32 § 3; NJA 1992, 113, where the three standards of proof in civil cases are defined; see also NJA 1977, 176, 1981, 622, 1984, 501 I-II, 1986, 3, 1986, 358, 1986, 470, 1990, 93, 1991, 481, 1994, 449 I-II, 2006, 721.

in detail. A similar approach applies in the courts, who rarely have to deal with it in the context of a civil claim, since there is no advantage in proving the details of intentional conduct, rather than merely negligent conduct. Instead, if necessary, reference is made to criminal law literature for definitions.[97] One exception, where intent is of great significance to a civil claim, is non-pecuniary damages – violation damages and compensation for pain and suffering to relatives when a person has been killed (*anhörigersättning*). Adjudication of damages for violation and *anhörigersättning* is also affected by if the crime or tortious act was committed with intent or negligence; intentional crimes are considered to involve a higher degree of violation or pain and suffering to the victim than (gross) negligence.[98]

The definition of negligence is similar in criminal law and tort law. The joint question is whether the defendant should have acted differently in the current situation. It was proposed in older legal literature that the threshold for criminal negligence is higher than for tort liability, but there is no evidence or examples of such a difference in modern court practice. One difference does exist, however, in respect of the doctrinal structure in each area. Criminal law and tort law have two different theoretical formulations for assessing which consequences a defendant can be held liable for. Whereas criminal law has an inherent limitation through the formulation of the statues, tort law's limitations are on a case by case basis. However, since most acts causing damage of one sort or another are criminalised, the outcome of an assessment of fault in a criminal case would be more or less the same in substance as in a tort case. The main difference would evolve in the application of different evidentiary standards (discussed below).

7. Secondary/accessory liability

Swedish law has a much more developed set of rules on complicity in criminal law than in civil law.

There are two types of participation in crime – acting as a principal and acting to further a crime through complicity. Generally one can say that a principal is a person who fulfils the prerequisites of a certain offence (the one who kills when it comes to murder, the one who steals when it

[97] Friberg, *Kränkningsersättning*, 165–72, J. Hellner and M. Radetzki, *Skadeståndsrätt* 128.

[98] As a general rule, violation damages pre-supposes an intentional crime. See NJA 1997, 315 and NJA 1997, 572. See also Friberg, *Kränkningsersättning*, 533–49, with further references concerning both violation damages and *anhörigersättning*.

comes to theft and so on), while an accomplice is a person whose actions as such do not fall within the definition of the offence but whose acts have furthered the act of the principal in one way or the other.[99]

In addition, a person may fulfil the prerequisites of a certain offence not only by performing the acts or bringing about the consequences him- or herself, but also by causing another person to perform it (making use of another person more or less as a tool). A person can be considered as such an innocent agent if he is unaware of the significance of his actions or that he does not embark on the crime voluntarily (because of, for instance, coercion, deceit or misuse of his youth). The result has been arranged by someone in the background, who used the other person to bring about the *actus reus*. In situations like these, it would obviously be unjustified to blame the one who has perpetrated the act personally, since he or she has acted, without fault and under the control of another. In the same way it would be inappropriate to punish the *hinterman* (principal acting through an innocent agent) only as an aider or instigator of the offence. This latter person is usually the one who controlled the other person and will therefore be seen as the perpetrator while the agent will not be liable.

It should also be observed that it is not a necessary requirement that the principal carries out the offence alone. According to Swedish law it is possible to be a principal by embarking on a crime together with others. Two or more persons can be principals (co-perpetrators) as long as every party carries out the act that fulfils the prerequisites of the offence. Two or more persons can also be considered to be principals in cases where they have performed the act as a common endeavour, but have had slightly different tasks. Consider, for example, a robbery, where A has threatened the victim, B has taken the victim's wallet and C has been acting as a lookout at the place of the robbery: all are co-perpetrators.[100]

According to the Swedish Criminal Code, Chapter 23 § 4, each accomplice shall be judged according to the intent or the negligence attributable to him. An accomplice is normally, so to speak, further from the actual causing of harm; his intent focuses on furthering someone else's act rather than on causing the harm himself. Being an accomplice does not, however, automatically imply lesser responsibility or blameworthiness (and thereby, a lower sentence), but parties to a crime who have participated after being subjected to strong influence by someone are thought to

[99] P. Asp, M. Ulväng and N. Jareborg, *Kriminalrättens grunder*, 2nd edn (Uppsala: Iustus, 2013), 432–5.

[100] See, e.g., NJA 2006, 535.

be less blameworthy. Correspondingly, inducing another person to take part in a crime by coercion, deceit or misuse of that person's youthfulness, lack of understanding or dependent status are circumstances that aggravate the offence.[101] If a perpetrator's participation in the completion of a crime could be said to be minor (relatively speaking, in comparison with other parties' actions), his sentence will be reduced. Under exceptional circumstances, a party to a crime can be discharged from criminal liability altogether, namely if his contribution to the crime (a) was induced by strong influence, or (b) was of minor importance, and (c) the circumstances in the case were such that the crime is judged to be a petty offence.[102]

By comparison, in tort law, accomplice liability is simpler. First, there is no difference in the degree of liability between principal and accomplice as regards the initial attribution of liability. The general principle is instead that in relation to the claimant all tortfeasors are jointly liable for the whole damage, which means that the claimant can address his claim against any one of the tortfeasors. This is of course a great advantage for the claimant since he does not have to sue for damages against more than one person. The more tortfeasors there are, the greater the risk that some of them would not be solvent to pay the damages. Instead, the claimant can choose to address his claim against the most solvent one.

Second, every defendant is liable in tort for every contribution to harm. While criminal law may discharge someone who played a minor role, tort law does not, not even where a person's contribution to the damage caused was induced by strong influence, of minor importance and the damage is less significant (cf. above). Anyone who can be held accountable for taking part in causing the damage will be held liable. It is possible, however, to consider every tortfeasor's contribution separately if the damage is severable into different parts that can be derived from the different actors. This rarely occurs in Swedish tort law. Instead, the different tortfeasors' degrees of participation and whether they have acted with intent or negligence can be a matter of importance in recourse actions between the tortfeasors: each and every joint wrongdoer is liable for the full loss, but they then have recourse actions between them.

For a long time, Swedish law was of the opinion that there was no right of recourse between wrongdoers when the damage had been caused by

[101] Criminal Code, Ch. 29 § 2 subsection 5.

[102] The criteria of a petty offence relates to the penal value. Any crime that would amount only to a fine would be rendered a 'petty' offence.

a crime. That is, whoever had to pay the damages lacked the possibility to claim any share from the other tortfeasors, at least with the help of the judiciary system.[103] It was not considered proper that the courts should assist criminals to realise justice between them. However, through a plenary case in 1937,[104] where a right to recourse between criminally liable tortfeasors was acknowledged, the previous view changed, and there are nowadays no such difference between cases where the damage is caused by a criminal act and cases where it is not. This right of recourse exists only as a principle of law, is has not been fleshed out in any legislative provision.

4. Procedure

A. *The historical development: tort tried in criminal cases*

1. Before the Law Code of 1734: adhesion in the courts of first instance

During the seventeenth century, procedural rules developed so that a division between civil and criminal procedure was made. Civil cases were appealed from the court of first instance (a district court, *häradsrätt*, on the countryside or a magistrates' court, *rådhusrätt*, in the towns) to the regional court (*lagmansrätt*)[105] and from there to the Court of Appeal (*hovrätt*).[106] Criminal cases were appealed from the court of first instance directly to the Court of Appeal (*hovrätt*).

In his commentary of 1726 to the mediaeval law code for the countryside, much amended through various statutes and ordinances, district judge Petter Abrahamsson discussed the procedure when one part of the case at the court of first instance was criminal and another part civil. He said that the *lagmansrätt* should try the civil claims, even when they were based on criminal acts, but not try the criminal parts of the case, since they belonged to the jurisdiction of the *hovrätt*.[107] A judgment in a criminal case in which there was a civil claim based on the crime thus

[103] See, e.g., Schrevelius, *Lärobok i Sveriges allmänna nu gällande civilrätt*, 399–400.

[104] NJA 1937, 264. The Supreme Court sits in plenary when there is an issue about deviating from established case law and establishing new doctrines.

[105] There was one lagmansrätt in each of the historical provinces.

[106] At first, from 1614, there was only one hovrätt, Svea hovrätt in Stockholm, but more were soon established: 1623 in Turku (Åbo), 1630 in Dorpat (Tartu), 1634 in Jönköping (Göta hovrätt) etc. Today, there are six hovrätter in Sweden and six in Finland.

[107] P. Abrahamsson, *Swerikes Rijkes Lands-Lag... med Anmärkningar uplagd*, 2nd edn (Stockholm: Johan Henrich Werner 1726), 603–4.

could be appealed to the *hovrätt* in relation to the criminal part and to the *lagmansrätt* (and thereafter to the *hovrätt*) with regards to the civil part. But, as Granfelt has concluded, this means that the principle of *adhesion*, connecting criminal and civil claims to be tried in the same trial, was already established in the courts of first instance, since the division between civil and criminal consequences of an act was relevant only on appeal. In this last respect, there was a development in the early eighteenth century to the effect that minor civil claims related to major criminal claims were decided under criminal procedure and *vice versa*.[108] Nehrman, however, made a distinction between criminal cases and civil cases based on whether any punishment was involved or not. He noted that a civil claim in a criminal case did not change the nature of the criminal process.[109]

2. Law Code of 1734: claims based on crimes were always tried under criminal procedure

Although there were some different interpretations when the Law Code was prepared,[110] the principle of adhesion was a clear fundamental principle of the Code of Judicial Procedure in the 1734 Law Code. There was no clear rule to that effect, but, again, the rules of appeal give clear indication of how the system worked. Chapter 25 set out the rules on appeals of first instance judgments. In § 5, it was made clear that an appeal against a judgment in a criminal case could also concern costs and damages that the appellant had been ordered to pay. On the other hand, minor criminal sanctions such as fines were tried in civil cases if they were based on civil wrongs.[111]

In 1849, the *lagmansrätt* was abolished in Sweden.[112] Thus, the *hovrätt* was the court of appeal in all cases, which paved the way for applying the principle of adhesion in all instances. According to Fredrik Schrevelius, a professor of procedural law writing in the 1850s, the difference between civil and criminal procedure was defined by the fact on which the claim was based. If it was based on behaviour, for which a punishment was prescribed, the procedure was criminal. This could be understood as if a claim for compensation would *per se* be decided in a criminal procedure if it were based on a criminal act, but in terms of damages, Schrevelius specifically opined that a claim for compensation was properly a civil case,

[108] Granfelt, 'Adhäsionsprincipen', 1008–10.
[109] D. Nehrman (Ehrenstråle), *Inledning till den svenska processum civilem* (Lund: Gottfried Kiesewetter, 1751), 13.
[110] Granfelt, 'Adhäsionsprincipen', 1010–11.
[111] Ibid., 1016–19. [112] In Finland, it was abolished in 1868.

even though it followed the criminal case as an *accessorium*.[113] That the claim for compensation was properly a civil case was also the opinion of Wilhelm Uppström, associate judge of appeal and author of a comparative study of criminal procedural law on behalf of a committee working with law reforms. He thought that civil and criminal consequences of an act should in principle be tried in different procedures, but that this principle was not so strong that it excluded adhesion.[114]

Similarly Ernst Kallenberg, a professor of procedural law in Lund, made this distinction between the principle that a civil claim should be tried in civil procedure and the reality that civil claims based on crimes were tried in criminal procedure. Whilst the other authors had maintained the original civil procedural character of the civil claim, Kallenberg abandoned this fiction and admitted that Swedish law did not follow the principle: 'According to Swedish law, every case, where the action aims towards a remedy based on a criminal act, whether it be punishment, compensation or another remedy, has the nature of a criminal case.' Thus, the basis of the claim, not the type of claim, was the determining factor.[115]

B Jurisdiction

1. Adhesion after 1948

In the Code of Judicial Procedure of 1942, which entered into force in 1948, there are different rules for civil and criminal cases. One difference concerned the composition of the court: in the first instance, civil cases (except family cases) are tried only by legally trained judges, whilst criminal cases are tried with one legally trained judge and – nowadays – three lay judges. Another distinction is manifest in the preparation of the case: it is the prosecutor who prepares the criminal cases (except cases where the injured party puts forward a claim for criminal responsibility[116]) in accordance with the police investigation. Civil cases are prepared before the court, through the exchange of documents and preparatory hearings. A third difference, which has developed after 1948, is a difference in the standards of proof.

[113] F. Schrevelius, *Lärobok i Sveriges allmänna nu gällande civilprocess* (Lund: Berling, 1853), 13–14.

[114] W. Uppström, *Öfversigt af straffprocessrätten enligt främmande och svensk rätt* (Stockholm: Norstedt, 1884), 5–6.

[115] E. Kallenberg, *Svensk civilprocessrätt* (Lund: Håkan Ohlsson, 1917), 28–47; quotation in translation from p. 29.

[116] This happens rarely, most often when the prosecutor has decided not to put forward charges but the injured party wants the criminal case tried anyway.

Chapter 22 of the Code of Judicial Procedure of 1948 is conceived of as a criminal procedure rule and concerns civil claims based on criminal acts. Such claims may be brought in criminal cases and usually will be. Prior to 1948, as evidenced in the preparatory words to the Code, and based on Kallenberg's writings, civil claims based on criminal acts were tried as criminal cases for the purpose of evidence and procedure, regardless of whether or not they were tried with the criminal case. In the 1948 Code, the normal rule is that the principle of adhesion shall apply and the civil claim be brought with the criminal case. However, a change was made to the effect that if a civil claim was brought separately from the criminal case, it should be tried as a civil case. This is also the case if only the civil part of the case is appealed. Strong practical reasons were invoked for adhesion, since in both actions the evidence was to a great extent the same. In most cases, the extra evidence needed, for instance, to determine the amount of damages, was not so onerous that it caused problems or delays in the criminal trial. Where problems or delays were caused, it was possible to refer the civil claim to a separate civil case.[117]

Normally, in a Swedish criminal trial, the district court sits with one professional judge as chairman, three lay judges and one law clerk taking minutes. To the right from the view of the court sit the prosecutor, the aggrieved party and the counsel of the aggrieved party, if there is one. To the left are the defendant and his or her counsel. The prosecutor reads his or her indictment, and if there is a civil claim, it is read by the prosecutor or the counsel of the aggrieved party. The counsel of the defendant tells the court whether the defendant pleads guilty or not guilty and whether he accepts or rejects the civil claim. When written evidence has been presented, the aggrieved party, the defendant and witnesses are heard. In the judgment, the court will assess both the criminal and the civil issues in the case.

2. What connection is required between crime and civil claim?

In the 1938 draft Code of Judicial Procedure, Chapter 22 concerned only 'private claims *based on* crime'.[118] Such claims could be tried in the

[117] Processlagberedningens förslag till rättegångsbalk, *SOU* 1938:43, 277–9, 281–2, Governmental Propostition for a new Code of Judicial Procedure, *Prop.* 1941:5, 201–3 and 503, and N. Gärde *et al.*, *Nya rättegångsbalken jämte lagen om dess införande med kommentar*, (Stockholm: Norstedt, 1949), 274. See R. Nordh, *Enskilt anspråk. Om handläggning av civilrättsliga anspråk i samband med åtal för brott*, 2nd edn. Praktisk Process III (Uppsala: Iustus, 2010).

[118] '*Om enskilt anspråk på grund av brott*'.

criminal case, or, alternatively, as a civil case. In its proposal, however, the government slightly widened the possibility to put forward civil claims in a criminal case, and parliament accepted this. This is marked in Chapter 22 in a way that is not clearly accessible even in Swedish: the wider category is called 'private claims *caused by* crime'[119] and the smaller 'private claims *based on* crime'.[120]

The smaller category, 'private claims based on crime', comprises the cases where the criminal act, as described by the prosecutor, is the sole basis of the claim. A common example is that the defendant is accused of having destroyed, or stolen and consumed, property, and the injured party wants damages, or wants the court to declare that he, and not the defendant, is the owner of the stolen goods. Another example is that the defendant has assaulted the injured party, who wants damages for wounds, violation and lost income. In cases concerning destroyed or stolen property, it is not uncommon that the claimant is an insurance company, who has taken over the injured party's right to claim compensation through subrogation.

The wider category, 'private claims caused by crime', extends the scope to a type of case, which has some connection with the crime but where more issues need to be tried. Typical examples are where the criminal act gave rise to a claim for damages but where it is not the accused but his employer, who is liable, or where the stolen goods are kept by a third person who is not accused of a crime. In these cases, the injured party needs to put forward more facts as the basis of his claim than the ones defined by the prosecutor.[121] Cases where the prosecutor has only prosecuted an intentional crime but where the injured party bases his claim for damages first on the intentional crime, and second on negligence (e.g., where there is no applicable negligent crime), also belong to this category. So too do cases where the court finds that the allegedly criminal act was not criminal but can serve as a basis for damages.[122] Theoretically, the person putting forward this type of claim could be seen as a plaintiff rather than a *målsägande* (aggrieved party). However, it is court practice that all persons bringing forward civil claims in criminal cases will be referred to as *målsägande*, as part of an approach which downplays any theoretical differences between the two types of *målsägande*.

119 '*Om enskilt anspråk i anledning av brott*'.

120 '*Om enskilt anspråk på grund av brott*'. See Nordh, *Enskilt anspråk*, 33–6.

121 Gärde, *Nya rättegångsbalken*, 275.

122 See to the last category Code of Judicial Procedure, Chapter 22 § 7.

These latter type of claims, outside the ones 'based on crimes', could not originally be brought by the prosecutor. However, in 1994, the Supreme Court held that if a claim is based first on the crime and second, on other circumstances closely related to the crime, it should be seen as a claim 'based on' the crime.[123] The claim was about the right to a boat. The alleged crime was that the accused had dealt with stolen goods, and the second basis for the claim was that the defendant, even if he had not committed a crime, had obtained the boat in a way that did not confer ownership on him. An important reason for the decision was that the second basis for the claim was so close to the crime that the judgment on the first claim would preclude a trial based on the other circumstances. The intent behind the rules compelled the Supreme Court to accept that the prosecutor brought the claim, on the two alternative bases, as based on the criminal allegation.

In both these categories, the civil claim may be brought within the criminal case, but may also be brought as a separate civil claim.[124] More common than not, the civil claim is brought in the criminal case by adhesion. For example, in most cases concerning assault, there is a civil claim that the court tries.

The extent of the judgment on damages is only limited to what the injured party has claimed. For instance, it is possible to receive damages for medical care and pain and suffering in one trial, and then sue the offender for damages regarding the personal violation. It is the different headings of damage, as defined by tort law, which sets the boundaries of what has been tried by the previous court trial; these claims are seen as different cases which can – but do not have to – be merged with each other and with the criminal case. A previous criminal trial has very strong evidentiary value for a subsequent tort trial.[125] The parties can settle the civil claim. In this part the rules of civil procedure are applied to the civil claim.[126]

3. The duty of the prosecutor to put the claim forward

If the claim is a 'based on crime', the prosecutor normally has to bring the civil claim before the court that deals with the criminal prosecution. The exceptions are cases where it would cause problems or the claim is unfounded. The prosecutor has to, where relevant, inform the injured

[123] NJA 1994, 306. [124] Code of Judicial Procedure, Ch. 22 § 1.
[125] Nordh, *Enskilt anspråk*, 125–7.
[126] Gärde, *Nya rättegångsbalken*, 276–7, see also Nordh, *Enskilt anspråk*, 68–71.

party about this possibility[127] and put forward the claim in connection with the indictment or after.[128] Thus, normally, in a case of theft or assault, the prosecutor will ask the injured party if he has a claim on the stolen goods or on damages. If the injured party has a claim, the prosecutor presents the claim before the court. If the injured party sends the claim to the court, the court normally presumes that the prosecutor will represent the injured party also in that part.

If the claim is 'clearly unjustified' or if there is a 'significant inconvenience' for the prosecutor putting it forward, for example, if it requires evidence that is difficult for the prosecutor to obtain (such as loss of income) or otherwise needs investigation beyond what is required for the prosecution, the prosecutor will use the exception and not bring the claim. The court cannot decide whether or not the prosecutor shall bring the claim.[129] A claim for damages is normally deemed 'clearly unjustified' when the claim is legally unfounded, when the plaintiff wants to put forward a claim that is unprecedented or when the prosecutor finds that there is not enough evidence to support the claim. Some situations where a claim could be considered a 'significant inconvenience' are where the investigative work that is necessary to support the claim is extensive, or if a question of law is difficult to determine, for example, whether or not the plaintiff has the legal status of aggrieved party. Yet another example is when there is a conflict of interest between the prosecutor and the plaintiff. This can happen where the prosecutor wants the crime to be classified in one way and the plaintiff in another because his or her right to damages requires that classification. Another instance is when there are two or more plaintiffs who claim compensation from one another; then it may be unsuitable that the prosecutor represent them both in their claim for damages.[130]

A decision by the prosecutor not to represent the victim in the matter of damages (which is rare) can be subject to review by a superior prosecutor, if the plaintiff so requests. If the prosecutor decides not to prosecute, due to for instance lack of evidence, the aggrieved party has – under certain circumstances – a right to bring a private prosecution. This right also involves a right to appeal to a higher court if the prosecutor withdraws the prosecution or decides not to appeal. However, in practice private prosecutions are rare, in part perhaps where the public prosecutor initially

[127] Code of Judicial Procedure, Ch. 22 § 2.

[128] Code of Judicial Procedure, Ch. 45 §§ 4–5. See Nordh, *Enskilt anspråk*, 40–5.

[129] Gärde, *Nya rättegångsbalken*, 278.

[130] Nordh, *Enskilt anspråk*, 37–8.

does not prosecute, that decision is open to effective review, providing a back-up to catch cases with merit.[131]

4. Cumulating and separating cases

If the civil case is already brought before the court, the court can merge it with the criminal case.[132] If the civil case is brought in the criminal case, the court can decide that it should be taken out of the criminal case and be tried as a civil case. This happens, for example, if the prosecutor withdraws the prosecution but the injured party wants the civil claim tried.[133] It happens also if it would cause substantial problems if the civil claim were to be tried in the criminal case,[134] for example, when the civil case requires evidence, which is not needed in the criminal case. There is, however, no rule of thumb as to how much time the civil part of the criminal case is allowed to consume. If the civil case is taken out of a criminal case, which continues, the prosecutor can no longer represent the injured party in the civil case.[135] The court will usually wait for the criminal case to be decided before dealing with the civil case.[136]

If the prosecutor decides not to prosecute, it is possible to sue for damages although the alleged crime has not been tried in court. The court will then have to, applying the civil law procedural and evidentiary rules, decide whether it is proven that the defendant has committed a crime so that the claimant is entitled to damages caused by the crime. This is of course only true in those cases where tort liability presupposes that a crime has been committed (claims of violation damages and – broadly speaking – damages for pure economic loss).

C. Evidence

In criminal cases, the prosecutor bears the burden of proof. This is regarded as an effect of the presumption of innocence – it would be

[131] Per O. Ekelöf and R. Boman, *Rättegång II,* 8th edn (Stockholm: Norstedt, 1996), 59–60.

[132] Code of Judicial Procedure, Ch. 22 § 3. See to this section Nordh, *Enskilt anspråk,* 72–7. Swedish lawyers use *adhesion* for attaching a civil case to a criminal but *cumulation* as a wider concept. Adhesion is most often used for the principle that the criminal and the civil cases are cumulated, and cumulation is used when discussing the actual cases taken up together.

[133] Code of Judicial Procedure, Ch. 22 § 6.

[134] Code of Judicial Procedure, Ch. 22 § 5.

[135] Gärde, *Nya rättegångsbalken,* 279.

[136] Code of Judicial Procedure, Ch. 32 § 5.

contrary to that presumption to put a burden of proof on the defendant.[137] In civil cases, the burden of proof is distributed in a different way. For every directly legally relevant fact, it can be placed on the plaintiff or defendant, but there is a vivid discussion as regards the grounds on which this is made. Different principles have been introduced, but the one that seems most important nowadays is that the party typically able to secure evidence the easiest and at the least cost shall have the burden of proof.[138]

The standard of proof is different in civil and criminal litigation. In a criminal prosecution, the requirement is formulated as 'beyond reasonable doubt'. In a civil claim, it is required that the facts are 'shown' or 'proven' (a higher standard than 'clearly more likely than not' but lower than 'beyond reasonable doubt'). It is therefore possible that an acquittal can be followed by liability in a later civil action, although it is not a common feature. This is rare particularly because most claims for damages are considered in conjunction with the criminal trial. In the eventuality of a subsequent civil action, the ruling in the criminal prosecution is not binding for the court although it has a very strong influence on the court's consideration of the evidence.[139]

In cases where the same circumstances are relevant for deciding the criminal and the civil claim, the way the court reaches its finding in relation to the crime will determine how the court decides the civil claim.[140] Thus, it is not possible for the court to decide that the criminal act is not proven beyond reasonable doubt, whilst the civil claim is proven according to the standard in civil procedure.[141] This means that there is one disadvantage for the injured party: a civil claim, which if tried separately, would have met the standard of proof in civil procedure, will be dismissed if the criminal case is not proven beyond reasonable doubt. In that situation no civil claim can be brought afterwards where the criminal case also gave final judgment on the accompanying civil claim.

[137] See, e.g., Roberth Nordh, *Bevisrätt B*, Praktisk Process VII (Uppsala: Iustus, 2011), 35.

[138] See, especially, NJA 2001, 177 and 2005, 205, and to the discussion, see, e.g., P. Westberg, 'Processtaktik och bevisbörda i dispositiva tvistemål' in *Festskrift till Per Henrik Lindblom* (Uppsala: Iustus, 2004), 731–54, L. Heuman, *Bevisbörda och beviskrav i tvistemål* (Stockholm: Norstedt, 2005) and C. Diesen and M. Strandberg, *Bevisprövning i dispositiva tvistemål. Teori och praktik*, Bevis 9 (Stockholm: Norstedt, 2012).

[139] P. Fitger, 'Om brottmålsdomens bevisverkan', in *Skrifter av fakultetens hedersdoktorer* (Uppsala: Iustus, 1992) 357. See also Friberg, *Kränkningsersättning*, 328–30.

[140] Code of Judicial Procedure, Ch. 29 § 6.

[141] R. Nordh, 'Bevisbörda och beviskrav vid kumulation av åtal och enskilt anspråk', in *Festskrift till Per Henrik Lindblom*, (Uppsala 2014), 539–573 and Nordh, *Enskilt anspråk*, 89–110.

There are three exceptions: first, the claim for damages also (i.e. as an alternative to the prosecution) is based on negligence when the defendant is on trial for an intentional crime, the court's judgment in the criminal part is not binding when trying the civil claim. Instead, the court has to try the civil claim applying the procedural rules for civil cases. The same applies if the defendant has admitted civil liability but not criminal liability: if the court finds the defendant not guilty, it will still have to award damages according to the admission from the defendant. Lastly, if the prescription period for the criminal offence has passed, it is still possible to award damages to the claimant as long as the tort claim itself has not been prescribed and all other prerequisites for tort liability are met.[142]

Finally, Swedish law does not recognise rules of 'disclosure' but there are rules to the effect that you can force your opponent to show documents that you know that he has.

D. *Advantages and disadvantages*

All in all, this means that there are some great benefits for – particularly – the injured party to the Swedish system. Many small claims for property and damages in ordinary criminal cases would probably never have been tried by a court if the injured party had not had the assistance of the prosecutor and the possibility to try the issue in the criminal court session that takes place anyway.

There are many purposes behind the rule on coalescing civil claims in criminal procedure. One reason as to why damages claims should be tried in conjunction with the criminal prosecution relates to procedural economy considerations. By dealing with both cases at the same time, you save costs of evidence, the parties' appearance, the hearing in court etc. Another reason is that a joint process reduces the risk of conflicting decisions. A criminal–political aspect of the possibility to claim damages in conjunction with the criminal trial has to do with the standing of the victim; a long-stated ambition has been to strengthen the victim's position in the trial. By combining the claim with the prosecution, a real opportunity for the aggrieved party to have his or her claim examined is created. This is perhaps the single most important reason behind the rule of conjunction.

There are a number of other advantages in trying claims for damages in conjunction with the criminal prosecution. First, the claimant

[142] See Friberg, *Kränkningsersättning*, 298–301.

can benefit from the investigatory responsibility of the prosecutor so that evidence that otherwise would be hard to obtain can be presented to the court. Second, the prosecutor also has to a large extent a duty to represent and assist the claimant in putting forward the claim. In a number of cases, the claimant is also entitled to have an aggrieved party counsel. Neither of these publically-funded sources of legal assistance (the prosecutor and the aggrieved party counsel) would be available in a civil trial: the claimant would instead represent him- or herself, but would often at his or her own expense hire a lawyer. The defendant also benefits in the sense that he or she only will have to appear before court once and have the right to a publically funded defender.[143] Finally, one clear advantage from the claimant's point of view has to do with the system of compensation as a whole. If the defendant is found liable to pay damages to the claimant but has no means to do so, the claimant can apply to the Crime Victim Compensation and Support Authority for compensation. Such an application can only be granted if all other possibilities to obtain compensation have been exhausted. This means that the claimant has to have sued the defendant in a civil trial if the claim is not tried in conjunction with the prosecution. The actual difficulties, cost risks and emotional effort to litigate on one's own would probably deter many claimants from seeking compensation from the tortfeasor, which as a consequence would lead to a loss of possibility to obtain crime victim compensation.[144]

So far it is obvious that clear efficiency and cost benefits are to be won in treating both cases at the same time, but there are also a number of disadvantages. First of all, it is clear that the tort claim is not as thoroughly tried as it would be in a civil trial, since the focus – for obvious reasons – is on the question of criminal liability and penalty issue.[145] Worth mentioning in this context is that the court at any given time in the trial can *ex officio* decide to separate the two cases – the tort claim and the prosecution – if deemed beneficial to the furtherance of the criminal trial, for instance because the tort claim turns out to be complex. The civil trial will then most likely be stayed until the criminal case is decided before the trial resumes.[146] For the claimant, a second disadvantage is that the evidentiary standard in a criminal procedure makes it more difficult to find the defendant liable. This has direct consequences on the outcome of

[143] If the defendant is sentenced, he or she will have to pay for – at least a part of – the costs of the counsel, the amount depends on the income of defendant.

[144] As an alternative, the rules could be made so that a civil judgment would not be required but that would probably increase the costs of the state.

[145] See, critically, Nordh, *Enskilt anspråk*, 13–17.

[146] See ibid., 73–4.

the tort claim when the claimant has based his or her claim on the prosecution. Tort claims that have another legal basis will be tried according to civil procedural rules (together with or separate from the criminal case), although the court's judgment on the facts of the criminal case – where they are of significance to the tort case as well – will have direct bearing on the assessment of the tort claim.

Another aspect of the merger of cases, not entirely good or bad *per se*, is that in the eye of the public, damages awarded by the court at the same time as the judgment in the criminal case can be perceived as having a punitive character. Sometimes, media reporting confuses questions of punishment and damages to a point where, for example, it sounds like the defendant is sentenced more leniently on appeal (with regard to either choice of sanction or length of incarceration) when in fact it is the amount of damages, which has been reduced in the court of appeal compared to what the court found in the district court. This can of course affect public perception of what constitutes tort and crime, or damages and punishment, which in turn can lead to pedagogical problems in explaining why a certain amount of damages is awarded (or not at all) and how sentences are measured.[147]

However, from the perspective of the courts there is a clear advantage in being able to handle both the tort claim and the prosecution at the same time. This is especially important as the same judge, or another judge at the same court, would otherwise handle the other case, re-hearing the same evidence and wasting time and money. In addition, the outcomes open to the court can be more carefully balanced. When measuring the sentence or choosing sanction, the court can take into consideration whether the judgment as a whole (punishment together with any other sanction, e.g., deportation or dismissal from duty) is too severe in relation to the gravity of the offence. If so, the length of incarceration or the number of day fines can be lowered. In exceptional cases – for example, when a defendant has committed a minor offence through which considerable damage has been caused – the court can consider liability to pay damages as a mitigating factor when measuring the sentence. Of course, this would not be possible to do if the two cases were tried separately, typically with the criminal trial preceding the civil trial.[148]

[147] See for the pros and cons of the system, Friberg, *Kränkningsersättning*, 227–35.

[148] Somewhat surprising is that the fact that the defendant has already compensated the victim will very rarely be taken into consideration when measuring the sentence or choosing sanction: see NJA 2008, 359, cf. NJA 1997, 652.

On the other hand, the problem of co-ordination between different sanctions for the same act has occurred between criminal and administrative law instead. The system of parallel sanctions – punishments and tax surcharges – for tax fraud has recently been set aside,[149] and there are other similar issues under discussion.[150]

5. Resolutions

In Swedish tort law, financial remedies are really the only ones that occur. There are also orders to restore stolen property, and in defamation cases, the person who has been convicted of the crime can be obliged to finance the printing of the judgment if the claimant puts forward such a claim.[151] There is also a seldom (if ever) used possibility in criminal law to order compensation in kind; when a crime has caused damage to property, the defendant can be ordered to assist the claimant with certain tasks that are designed to mitigate or remedy the damage, if such an order is deemed suitable to promote the offender's re-adaptation in society.[152] The order can only be made with consent from the claimant.

In criminal law, different penalties are available such as the two types of punishment – imprisonment and fines – and probation, protected supervision and surrender for special care. Some of these penalties can be combined and an obligation to perform community service can be added to a conviction of probation. It is also possible to impose other types of sanctions related to criminal law (that is, with special legal effects) on a person convicted of a crime. For example, he can lose his driving licence or weapon licence (depending on what crime he is convicted of), be banned from business activity and property can be confiscated.

6. Conclusion

In Swedish law, there is a clear distinction between tort and crime, manifested in the fact that they belong to different areas of law and are treated separately in legal education and, to a great extent, in legal research. But

[149] See plenary cases NJA 2013, 502 and HFD 2013 ref. 71, following the judgment of the ECJ 26 February 2013 in C-617/10 *Åkerberg* v. *Fransson* [2013] 2 CMLR 46.

[150] See M. Sunnqvist, 'Klart stöd'-doktrinens historia och dubbelförfarandeförbudets framtid' (2014) *Europarättslig tidskrift*, 389–99.

[151] Freedom of Press Act 1949 Ch. 7 § 6 subsection 2, Freedom of Expression Act 1991 Ch. 5 § 4 subsection 3 and Tort Liability Act Ch. 5 § 6 subsection 2.

[152] Criminal Code, Ch. 27 § 5 subsection 2.

in Swedish law there is also a close connection between tort and crime, manifested in the facts that compensating and punitive effects of a wrong have a common historical origin and go together in legal practice.

The distinction between crime and tort has its roots in the eighteenth century, but the connection between them has its roots further back in history. The distinction has a theoretical background, whilst the connection works well in practice. Is this then an example of Nordic legal pragmatism? Jan M. Smits has argued that Nordic pragmatism is not the exception from normal theoretical systematisation of law but rather German theoretical systematisation of law is the exception of normal legal pragmatism.[153]

Against this background, the distinction between crime and tort could be dismissed as an eighteenth century transfer of theory, ill adapted to the practical needs of law. But such a conclusion would go too far. There are important and necessary practical implications in remembering that there are theoretically based differences between the two areas of law. One important difference is the principles *nullum crimen sine lege* and *nulla poena sine lege* applicable in criminal law in contrast to the more open texture of tort law. Another is the different evidentiary standards in criminal and civil law, which are important for a plaintiff who is about to decide whether to bring a tort claim as a civil case or to report the matter to the police in order to put forward a civil claim in the criminal trial. This means that there is – when dealing with tort and crime in Swedish law – reason to keep in mind many different aspects at the same time, so that neither the theoretical distinction nor the practical connection is exaggerated to the detriment of the opposing interest.

[153] J. M. Smits, "Nordic Law in a European Context: Some Comparative Observations" in J. Husa, K. Nuotio and H. Pihlajamäki (eds.), *Nordic Law – Between Tradition and Dynamism* (Antwerp–Oxford: Intersentia, 2007), 55–64.

6

Blurred borders in Spanish tort and crime

LORENA BACHMAIER WINTER, CARLOS GÓMEZ-JARA DÍEZ AND ALBERT RUDA-GONZÁLEZ*

1. Introduction

The dominant development in substantive criminal law has been the disappearance of any clearly definable line between civil and criminal law.[1] This blurring of the border between tort and crime results not only in injustice, but ultimately weakens the efficacy of criminal law as an instrument of social control.[2] Some have attempted to define the proper sphere of the criminal law by resorting to how its purposes and methods differ from tort law. Although it is easy to identify distinguishing characteristics of the criminal law – the greater role of intent, the relative unimportance of actual harm to the victim, the special character of incarceration as a sanction and the criminal law's greater reliance on public enforcement – none of these have been ultimately decisive in defining criminal law, or separating it from tort law.[3]

While this seems to be happening in many modern legal systems, the Spanish legal system positively fosters the eradication of any clear divide between tort and crime. The fact that victims can directly intervene as

* Albert Ruda's contribution has been written within the framework of the research project R+D+I (Ref Der2013-40613-R) 'Modernization and Harmonization of the Law of Tort: Boundaries of Responsibility, Compensable Damage and Assessment', funded by the Ministry of Science and Innovation of Spain for the period 2014-2016 (main researcher: Professor Dr. M. Martin-Casals and Dr. Josep Solé-Feliu).

[1] This is not uncommon in legal systems: see generally, D. Husak, *Overcriminalization* (Oxford Univerity Press, 2008); J. Silva-Sánchez, *La Expansión del Derecho Penal*, 2nd edn (Madrid: Civitas, 2001).

[2] This has been especially criticised by Spanish scholars. See J. L. Díez Ripollés, 'The "Law and Order" Approach in Spanish Criminal Justice Policy', *ReAIDP / e-RIAPL*, 2007, A-02:1.

[3] See generally J. C. Coffee, 'Does "Unlawful" Mean "Criminal"? Reflections on the Disappearing Tort / Crime Distinction in American Law', (1991) 71 *BULR* 201. For a thorough analysis see M. Dyson 'Tort and Crime', in M. Bussani and A. Sebok (eds.) *Comparative Tort Law*, (Cheltenham: Edward Elgar, forthcoming).

private prosecutors (even against the position of the public prosecutor) and that civil damages are awarded in the criminal judgment by the criminal court certainly makes it tougher to argue in practice that there is a foundational difference between tort and crime.

Because of the peculiar structure of the Spanish legal system, many cases that would traditionally be considered torts end up in the criminal jurisdiction. Therefore, as we shall see below, whether a specific wrongdoing is considered a crime or a tort depends to a great extent on the decision by the victim to press charges and to be active in the criminal procedure. Also, the fact that not only the victim him/herself can initiate criminal proceedings, but any third party that is affected by the wrongdoing,[4] increases the possibility of dealing with civil wrongdoings as part of the criminal justice system.

One of the most famous cases in Spanish criminal law, the *Colza Oil* case, shows how the distinction between tort and crime works, especially in class action cases.[5] The defendants commercialised industrial oil as regular oil for human consumption. Dozens of people died, hundreds suffered severe injuries and thousands were harmed (with more not yet fully diagnosed).[6] The so-called National Court, as a first instance decision, and then the Supreme Court in a landmark decision, convicted the defendants and awarded millions of Euros in compensation to thousands of victims. An important nuance for civil liability claims was the conviction of a State officer for a misdemeanour, which triggered civil liability for the Spanish state itself.

2. Overview of the Spanish system of torts and crime

A. *A tale of two codes*

The present Spanish system of torts and crime is more the result of historical accident than of rational thinking. Spanish criminal law was first

[4] The Spanish rules of criminal procedure clearly distinguish between the victim and any other person affected by the wrongdoing, as will be seen below. Although the distinction between both of them sometimes becomes blurry, the increased number of legal actors that can actually initiate criminal proceedings on their own increases the odds of torts being treated as crimes.

[5] See P. Gutiérrez de Cabiedes Hidalgo, *Group Litigation in Spain. National Report* (2007), (globalclassactions.stanford.edu/) and P. Salvador Coderch (ed.), *Civil Liability for Defective Products. Green Paper* (Barcelona: Universitat de Girona-Universitat Pompeu Fabra-Cuatrecasas Abogados, 1999).

[6] Children were born with severe anomalies and the effects on the genetic code are still to be determined.

codified in 1822, during the wave of codifications to sweep over Europe and without much controversy. Conversely, the codification of private law during the nineteenth century was a long and difficult process. Due to the political tension between those regions (such as Catalonia and the Basque Country) with a different private law and the central government in Madrid, the Civil Code was not passed until 1889.

This difference between criminal and civil codes has been of great importance in Spain. The second Criminal Code, of 1848 (Código Penal, hereafter, CP) included a set of rules on tort liability arising from crime, since no Civil Code had been able to be passed and a need was felt to have such rules without further delay. When the Civil Code (Código Civil, hereafter CC) was finally passed the rules in the Criminal Code were nonetheless maintained. The CC reflected this status quo in Art. 1092: *civil obligations deriving from crimes or misdemeanours will be governed by the Criminal Code provisions.* The Criminal Code has continued to contain these rules; the current Criminal Code[7] is wholly in keeping with that tradition when it lays down several provisions on tort deriving from crime (Arts. 109–122). For practical reasons, it was considered better for legal practitioners to keep the rules related to crime (including tort liability deriving from it) in the code where they had always been. Obviously, in those cases where – according to rules which will be explained further on – it is the civil judge who has to deal with this issue, the judge will have to leave the tort law provisions set in the Civil Code (Arts. 1902–1910) aside and apply the rules in the Criminal Code in a civil procedure.

B. The relationship between tort and crime

1. Several codes, one single system?

Criminal law is generally seen as the field of the law which responds to the most serious infringements of the law, according to the principle of minimal intervention, subsidiarity or *ultima ratio.* On this basis, the legislature is bound in a double sense: (a) it must address conduct which deserves the most rigorous response (even though, of course, many criminal penalties are very minor), and (b) whereas the commission of intent crimes will always be punishable, not every wrong committed in a negligent manner

[7] Ley Orgánica 10/1995, de 23 de noviembre, del Código Penal (*Boletín Oficial del Estado (BOE)* No. 281, of 24 November 1995).

will also bring about criminal liability, but only those which affect fundamental legal interests (life, physical integrity, health).[8] Therefore in theory there is some continuity with regard to other fields such as administrative law (*Derecho administrativo*) and private law (*Derecho civil*), which may provide responses to the very same facts, which trigger criminal sanctions. From a very broad perspective, administrative law and criminal law may be grouped under the heading of public law (*Derecho público*) and are governed by some common principles. The most important connections between the codes, and the practice of the law itself, will be discussed in the rest of the chapter. However, it should be noted early that some of the rules which might reach across the codes do not in fact do so. For instance, Spanish law recognises the principle that the same act or omission should not be punished twice (*ne bis in idem*) as an implied part of the broader principle of legality as enshrined by the Spanish Constitution (Constitución Española, hereafter CE, Art. 25; affirmed by the Constitutional Court (Sentencia del Tribunal Constitucional, hereafter STC), 2/1981 of 30 March). However, this principle does not apply to the interplay between private law and criminal law, since civil remedies are not seen as a punishment. This is particularly evident where it is the liability insurer who pays compensation to the victim in lieu of its insured.[9] As a result, if someone harms another and the requirements laid down by the law are met, an act or omission may give rise to consequences both in private law (pursuant to Art. 109 ff. CP) and either administrative or criminal law. Indeed it may be suggested that the statutory rules on tort derived from crime laid down by the Criminal Code are private law rules in a statute, which for the remaining part happens to be public in nature. Strictly speaking, punishment is a consequence of crime, whereas compensation of damage is a consequence of damage, not crime.[10] Liability in tort is of an economic or patrimonial nature, but criminal liability is personal.[11] Therefore, it may be possible to construe the tort law provisions in both Codes as a whole.

[8] See F. Muñoz Conde and M. García Arán, *Derecho Penal. Parte general*, 6th edn (Valencia: Tirant, 2004), 282.

[9] See F. Sánchez Calero, 'Artículo 73' in F. Sánchez Calero (ed.), *Ley de contrato de seguro* (Cizur menor: Thomson Reuters Aranzadi, 2010), 1599.

[10] See M. Yzquierdo Tolsada, *Sistema de responsabilidad civil, contractual y extracontractual* (Madrid: Dykinson, 2001), 28–9.

[11] See E. Font Serra, *La acción civil en el proceso penal. Su tratamiento procesal* (Madrid, La Ley, 1991), 10.

Furthermore, criminal law provisions have to be passed by way of an Organic Act (Ley Orgánica), which requires a qualified majority of the Lower Chamber of Parliament (Art. 81 CE).[12] However, given that the tort provisions of the Criminal Code lack a true criminal character, they could have been passed – or could be modified in the future – through an ordinary Act.[13] By the same tenet, tort provisions in the Criminal Code, which lack an equivalent in the Civil Code, could be applied on an analogical basis (provided that a rule to be applied by analogy does not itself provide for a specific set of facts, but it does provide for a similar set and the two sets are united by common purposes or reasons, pursuant to Art. 4.1 CC).[14]

This peculiar feature of the Spanish system entails that it is usually the criminal court which deals with liability in tort when the same facts also concern criminal liability. By default, it is the criminal judge who has to decide on tort liability arising from the criminal act (Art. 742 para. 2 Criminal Procedure Act, Ley de enjuiciamiento criminal, or LECrim).[15] This is because the action in tort is deemed to have been filed together with the action in crime unless the victim renounces his or her claim or makes a reservation to file a separate claim before a private law court at a later stage (Art. 109.2 CP and Art. 112 LECrim). This procedure tallies with the substantive rules as well: the commission of a crime (*delito*) or misdemeanour (*falta*) obliges the culprit to restore damage caused (Art. 109.1 CP). Therefore, the aggrieved party (*perjudicado*) may choose to claim damages before a civil court in a subsequent procedure (if a victim, pursuant to Art. 109.2 CP) but is not allowed to do so while the criminal procedure is pending (Art. 111 LECrim).

The decision to bring a separate tort liability claim before the civil judge or let the criminal judge deal with both crime and tort is much of a personal choice, where strategy may play a role. In particular, counsel may take into account whether there are differences between the approaches adopted between the courts of the different jurisdictional orders (criminal/civil) as regards the particular case on which he is advising.

[12] As construed by STC 140/1986, of 11 November. See J. Córdoba Roda, 'Artículo 1' in J. Córdoba Roda and M. García Arán (eds.), *Comentarios al Código Penal (Parte general)* (Madrid: Marcial Pons, 2011), 14.

[13] See Yzquierdo, *Sistema de responsabilidad civil, contractual y extracontractual*, 31.

[14] See L. Díez-Picazo, *Derecho de daños* (Madrid: Civitas, 1999), 279–81.

[15] Real decreto de 14 de septiembre de 1882 por el que se aprueba la Ley de Enjuiciamiento Criminal (*BOE* No. 260, 17 September 1882).

From a social point of view, the fact that a criminal procedure is started is perceived differently from when a merely civil action is filed, which is discussed further below. It is certainly no secret that in some cases recourse is made to the criminal procedure with the sole purpose of obtaining compensation. However, the gains from the point of view of procedural economy – since the need for a subsequent claim in tort disappears once the criminal case is closed – may offset such an inconvenience.

In comparison with some other countries, the number of cases, which reach the Supreme Court, is extremely high; the balance of those cases between tort and crime is interestingly of a similar order. For instance, in 2012 a total of 4,238 cases were filed before the Civil Chamber of the Supreme Court, whereas the number of cases decided was 3,580 (of which 792 were final decisions, *sentencias*). Similarly, 4,224 cases reached the Criminal Chamber of the same Court, and 4,236 cases were decided (of which 977 were final decisions).[16]

Finally, there are several devices in order to solve conflicts of jurisdiction, including a Special Chamber of Conflicts of Jurisdiction (pursuant to Art. 42 Organic Act of the Judicial Power (LOPJ)),[17] which solves such conflicts that arise between courts with different jurisdictions.

2. Different or same purposes?

There has been a lot of discussion as to the purposes of the law in both fields. Criminal law has to do with liability of the individual towards the state. Tort law, however, is about the compensation of damage suffered by the victim.[18] Tort liability should not punish the wrongdoer and therefore punitive damages would be contrary to the principles of the Spanish tort law system.[19] Nonetheless, in recent times the number of legal scholars in favour of punitive damages has increased.[20] Apart from that, there is

16 See Consejo General del Poder Judicial, *La justicia dato a dato: año 2012* (Madrid: CGPJ, 2013), 34–5, www.poderjudicial.es/stfls/CGPJ/ESTAD%C3%8DSTICA/JUSTICIA%20DATO%20A%20DATO/FICHERO/20130621%20Justicia%20Dato%20a%20Dato%20A%C3%B1o%202012.pdf (all websites last accessed November 2014).

17 Ley Orgánica 6/1985, de 1 de julio, del Poder Judicial (*BOE* No. 157, of 2 July 1985).

18 See Muñoz Conde and García Arán, *Derecho Penal. Parte general,* 595, 605 and P. Salvador Coderch and T. Castiñeira Palou, *Prevenir y castigar* (Madrid: Marcial Pons, 1997), 10–11.

19 SSTS 1st Chamber, 19.12.2005 [RJ 2006/295] and 12.1.2009 [RJ 2009/544]; R. de Ángel Yágüez, *Daños punitivos* (Madrid: Thomson Reuters, 2012), *passim.*

20 See S. Muñoz Machado, 'Información y derecho al honor: la ruptura del equilibrio' (1992) 74 *Revista Española de Derecho Administrativo* 175, and M. Gómez Tomillo, 'Los daños punitivos. Análisis desde una perspectiva jurídico-penal' in M. Gómez Tomillo (ed.),

also a recent trend to insist more on the effects of tort liability in terms of deterrence along the lines of economic analysis of law.

3. Reciprocal influences

It seems difficult to think that a private law court will not feel affected by the criminal implications of a case. A few examples give a flavour of these implications. To begin with, the court may give notice to the Public Prosecutor in case there may be any such implications. Apart from that, several statutory rules take into account whether there is a criminal deed in order to provide a solution to a private law conflict. This is for instance the case with regard to acquisition of property from a non-owner (*a non domino*). Although the general rule is that through the mere transfer of possession the buyer becomes owner of the good, there is an exception to the rule, namely that the good at stake has been the object of an 'illegal deprivation', for example, a theft (Art. 464 CC). Therefore, the same action by which a person acquires the rights to property cannot make her a thief of that property. In this regard, the relationship between criminal law and private law is one of co-ordination.

4. Readiness to change

It is evident that major changes have taken place in criminal law many more times than in tort law. Notably, there has been only one Civil Code in Spanish history, whereas there have been nine different Criminal Codes. Criminal law seems therefore more malleable to political change, although not always for good reason.[21] As for change in the areas where crime and tort overlap, it has already been mentioned that the Spanish approach is deeply rooted in history and may thus not change easily. However, this seems an area which may be much affected by some social phenomena and therefore minor changes may occur rapidly. For instance, in recent times a statutory reform was passed so criminals may not enrich themselves (or their relatives) by explaining intricacies of their crimes in the media. To that end, the legislature empowered the victims to claim disgorgement of the benefits.[22]

Límites entre el Derecho sancionador y el Derecho privado (Valladolid: Lex Nova, 2013), 21–64, 54.

[21] See G. Quintero Olivares, *Parte General del Derecho Penal*, 2nd edn (Cizur Menor: Thomson Reuters Aranzadi, 2007), 208–9.

[22] Ley Orgánica 5/2010, de 22 de junio, por la que se modifica la Ley Orgánica 10/1995, de 23 de noviembre, del Código Penal (*BOE* No. 152, of 23 June 2010).

5. Legal education and legal actors

In Spain the legal profession is not seen as a single 'entity', because usually, once the choice for a specific legal career has been made, the majority follow it, without changing to other activities.[23]

As in other Continental European civil law systems, in Spain, legal science comes mainly from legal scholars and the role of the judges is more restricted than the judge in a common law system. Although it is no longer true that civil law is a law of the professors, and case law (in particular of the Constitutional Courts) has strongly contributed to the changing of the sources of law, it is still true that the scholars still play a significant role in shaping the Spanish legal system.

The University plays a key role in the Spanish legal education, as the law degree obtained in a law faculty has long been an absolute requirement for exercising any legal profession in Spain. The education in law faculties has been traditionally focused on theory rather than practice. Practical legal training really begins once the University is finished. This approach has been changing during the last decade, giving more importance to the study of cases and the active involvement of students in the classroom.

Specialisation may take place at postgraduate level if students chose to take a substantive Masters course or similar.[24] During the last years, however, even if there are still a number of subjects which are mandatory in every programme, there is the possibility of choosing between a major specialisation in public or private law. Within the law programmes, civil law and criminal law are mandatory subjects and usually there is no connection between them. They are frequently taught by different professors, who have specialised in their topic and as a rule, do not pay much attention to one another.[25] This does not favour a comprehensive approach to legal problems when there are interactions between different legal areas when teaching to the students. Moreover, those topics that have implications for different legal fields tend to be side-lined in the teaching practice. This has been sometimes the case of civil actions *ex delicto*.

However, in legal scholarship, increasing attention has actually been paid to the interplay of both areas, coinciding with the growing

[23] See J. H. Merryman, *The Civil Law Tradition* (Stanford University Press, 1985), 101.

[24] Nevertheless, most students take a general Masters course in Advocacy, the only one giving access to the legal profession (Ley 34/2006, de 30 de octubre, sobre el acceso a las profesiones de Abogado y Procurador de los Tribunales (*BOE* No. 250, 31 October 2006)).

[25] See C. López Beltrán de Heredia, *Efectos civiles del delito y responsabilidad extracontractual* (Valencia: Tirant, 1997), 15.

importance of accident law in practice in the last decades.[26] Also, after the Civil Chamber of the Supreme Court has adopted causal criteria elaborated by the Criminal Chamber, there seems to be an increasing interest regarding issues such as state of necessity (which is specifically provided for by the Criminal Code, Art. 20.5, and not by the Civil Code) and causation. Moreover, professors who are at the same time practising lawyers may pay more attention to the interactions between legal fields.

6. Specialisation in practice

The peculiarities of the Spanish crime/tort system has some consequences from the point of view of specialisation of the lawyers involved with tort. A tort lawyer has to be ready to file a criminal action if the victim decides to follow that path, as is usually the case. Therefore, he or she will have to be well-versed in the intricacies of both the criminal procedure (governed by the above mentioned LECrim) and the civil procedure (Ley de enjuiciamiento civil, hereafter LEC).[27] They may regard themselves as sufficiently expert in criminal law, though of course they are not as specialised as the lawyers working only in criminal law. In practice, the fact that the public prosecutor is 'on-board' with the prosecution means that less-experienced counsel need only deviate, if they wish, when requesting a greater sanction or greater compensation than that which the state seeks. The same is often true in reverse: criminal lawyers may have to be prepared to deal with the tort law consequences of a criminal act.

7. Sources

Tort and crime are some of the most dynamic areas of Spanish law. Undoubtedly, tort is nowadays one of the most important areas both in legal scholarship and legal practice, even though it had received very little attention by the Spanish codification process. Notably, a few statutory provisions are devoted to tort law (both in the CP and the CC). From this point of view, one of the most salient features of tort law in its present state is that it has had to be shaped by case law to a much greater extent than other areas of private law. This is also in contrast to criminal law, which holds to the principle of legality, that is, *nulla crimen sine lege*

[26] On this evolution, see M. Martin-Casals and A. Ruda, 'The Development of Legal Doctrine on Fault in Spanish Tort Law' in N. Jansen (ed.), *The Development and Making of Legal Doctrine* (Cambridge University Press, 2010), 183–211.

[27] Ley 1/2000, de 7 de enero, de Enjuiciamiento Civil (*BOE* No. 7, 8 January 2000).

(Art. 25 CE and Art. 1.1 CP) and therefore judicial developments play a less extensive role. Should a particular conduct fall outside the precise terms of a criminal provision, it could not be punished by the state due to the legality requirement, whereas it could still trigger liability in tort under the general clause of liability for fault (Art. 1902 CC).

As a rule, initiatives for reform run quite separately in the two areas. Although a general reform body does exist (the Comisión General de Codificación),[28] the sections devoted to civil law (the first one) and to criminal law (the third) are separate.

8. Divisions

Both areas of law are divided into smaller areas. As for criminal law, it is usually divided into substantive (or material) and formal (or procedural) criminal law,[29] but the main division is between the general and the special parts. Book I of the Criminal Code (Arts. 10 to 137) deals with the 'General Provisions on Crimes and Misdemeanours, Liable Persons, Punishments, Safety Measures, and Other Consequences of the Criminal offence', preceded by a 'Preliminary Title' (Arts. 1 to 9 CP) on the 'Criminal Guarantees and the Application of Criminal Law'. On the other hand, specific 'Crimes and Punishments' are included in Book II (Arts. 137 to 616 *quater*), and misdemeanours in a much shorter Book III (Arts. 617 to 639). Textbooks and university courses usually follow such a general/special divide. Legal practitioners have to keep this dual structure in mind, since it determines where the rules to a problem may be found in the Code. As for tort law, legal scholarship usually distinguishes between a general part, which typically includes the purposes of tort law, conditions of liability, damages, etc., and a special part which refers to the special statutory regimes and other particular areas which may lack a specific statutory regulation.

It is the legislature which decides whether a type of act or omission deserves to be punished by way of criminal law on the basis of considerations of criminal policy and the criterion of *ultima ratio*. For instance, the 1989 reform[30] of the previous Criminal Code (1973) suppressed the crime of negligent causation of damage because, as a matter of fact, tort

[28] Its website can be found at www.mjusticia.gob.es/cs/Satellite/es/1215198250496/EstructuraOrganica.html.

[29] See Quintero, *Parte General del Derecho Penal*, 36.

[30] Ley Orgánica 3/1989, de 21 de junio, de actualización del Código Penal (*BOE* No. 148, 22 June 1989).

law was enough to deal with such damage.[31] Indeed, quite often the criminal offence and the civil wrong may not be different in essence. In fact, the differences, if at all, may be imperceptible, as in the case of the deception amounting to fraud (Art. 248 CP) and intent on which a contract may be voidable (Art. 1269 CC).[32] Obviously the initiative to criminalise conduct may originate in the government, which then brings it to parliament. In Spain, it is only the central state, which may legislate on criminal law issues (Art. 149.1.6 CE), and therefore not the regional or 'autonomous' communities (*Comunidades Autónomas*). In civil law, regions may have legislative competence in private law (pursuant to Art. 149.1.8 CE and their Statutes of Autonomy). For instance, there is a separate Civil Code in the region of Catalonia, although it has not tackled tort liability yet, with the exception of prescription.[33]

Legal scholars tend to be very critical of the inclusion of tort liability rules within the Criminal Code, underlining that these double divergent set of rules have given rise to different and confusing interpretations.[34] It has also been pointed out many times in the Spanish discourse that the language adopted by the legislature ('tort liability arising from crime') is incorrect, since tort liability does not properly speaking derive from crime but from an act or omission, which at the same time happens to be a crime or misdemeanour. It has also been discussed why very similar situations may give rise to a different legal treatment or response (for instance, joint and several liability in one case, and separate liability in the other) depending on whether the fact at stake amounts to a crime or not.

9. Legal reasoning and principles

Legal reasoning is more or less the same in the two areas at stake, although it is also true that the outcomes of criminal cases can channel, or even determine, civil liabilities, reasoning and resources.[35] This sameness is due to the fact that there are some common principles which govern both

[31] See C. M. Romeo Casabona, 'Los delitos culposos en la reforma penal' (1990) 43 *Anuario de derecho penal y ciencias penales* 491. Another example of decriminalisation (1995) is abortion (Art. 417 *bis* CP). A reverse development (2003) is the criminalisation of the failure to pay alimony (Art. 227.1 CP).

[32] See Muñoz Conde and García Arán, *Derecho Penal. Parte general*, 596.

[33] See Llei 29/2002, de 30 de desembre. Primera Llei del Codi civil de Catalunya (*BOE* No. 32, 6 February 2003).

[34] See A. Arnaiz Serrano, *Las partes civiles en el proceso penal* (Valencia: Tirant, 2006), 53–70.

[35] See M. Dyson, 'Civil Law Responses to Criminal Judgments in England and Spain' (2012) 3 *Journal of European Tort Law* 329 and, Section 3.B, below.

areas, such as the need to give reasons for the decision reached by the judge. So, for example, a court is bound to explain the criteria upon which the compensation award is established (Art. 115 CP) just as much as it must explain criminal convictions: both stem from the constitutional duty to motivate court decisions (Art. 120.3 CE). Such a duty is connected with the constitutional right to a fair trial (*tutela efectiva*) and the prohibition of helplessness (*indefensión*, Art. 24.1 CE).[36] Arguments based on the protection of fundamental rights have had an impact in both areas.[37] It has also been mentioned that in case of doubt, criminal law must find in favour of the accused (*pro reo* principle). Similarly, it is the claimant in the civil procedure who bears in principle the burden of proof (Art. 217 LEC).

However, the focus of both areas obviously differs to some extent. For instance, certainty is a major concern in criminal law due to the principle of legality (Art. 25.1 CE and Art. 1.1 and 2.1 CP). It is for instance for this reason that some of the techniques of legal reasoning available to a tort lawyer may be out of reach of the criminal lawyer. Notably, criminal law provisions cannot be construed on an analogical basis – and the same applies to exceptional or temporary rules (Art. 4.2 CP). Analogical application *in bonam partem* is however explicitly accepted in connection with mitigating circumstances (*atenuantes*).[38] In contrast to that, analogy is permitted in private law on a general basis as mentioned above (Art. 4.1 CC). The same is true in chronological terms: criminal law provisions may be applied retrospectively provided that the result is more favourable to the culprit (Art. 2.2 CP), whereas private law provisions will not have a retroactive effect unless provided otherwise (Art. 2.3 CC).

Apart from that, some arguments (such as fairness or proportionality) may be common to both areas, although proportionality may play a larger role in criminal law. It may be the case that a criminal response to a case seems excessive from the perspective of criminal policy or another consideration, whereas in principle compensation will always be limited to the damage caused. Due to the principle of *ultima ratio*, criminal law theory seems more prone to discuss whether criminal law has to intervene at all or there is an alternative.[39] As is well known, determination of the compensation award is unrelated to the seriousness of the criminal

[36] See, e.g., STC 192/2003 of 27 October. [37] See Section 3.B, below.

[38] Beyond that the debate seems unsettled. Cf. Muñoz Conde and García Arán, *Derecho Penal. Parte general*, 124 (in favour) and Quintero, *Parte General del Derecho Penal*, 128 (against).

[39] See Quintero, *Parte General del Derecho Penal*, 34, 75.

offence, unlike the criminal punishment.[40] Pardon (*indulto*) may be issued by the government in some cases (Art. 130.1.4 CP). However, it frees the culprit from criminal liability only (thus leaving tort liability unaffected).[41]

3. Courts, procedure and evidence

A. *Judicial organisation*

According to the Spanish Constitution, the principle of unity governs the exercise of judicial power. This does not mean that the jurisdiction is not divided into branches, but refers to the prohibition of exceptional courts not subject to the general rules and principles of the judiciary. For reasons of efficiency and to foster specialisation, the courts are divided into four branches: civil, criminal, labour and administrative courts (Arts. 22–25 LOPJ). The modern division represents long-standing practice in the courts, with separate courts existing since the seventeenth century for commercial matters and courts for treasury and public finances claims, but with common courts (*Audiencias*) for civil and criminal matters, in addition to the courts of general jurisdiction with jurisdiction over civil and criminal matters.[42] In short, historically the interaction between torts and crime was favoured by the judicial organisation, being the same courts, although split across courtrooms, competent to hear both civil and criminal cases.

Despite this high-level separation, several courts are unified and the same judge exercises functions in both jurisdictions. This is the case of the Justice of the Peace (Juzgados de Paz), the Courts of First Instance and Investigation (Juzgados de Primera Instancia e Instrucción) and the Regional Superior Courts (Tribunal Superior de Justicia), where the same section has competence over criminal and civil subject-matters. In addition, there are the 'Courts for cases of violence against women', a specific type of court created in 2004 that deals with certain crimes related to domestic violence, where the victim is a woman, and that have also jurisdiction to decide provisionally on family and civil matters.[43]

[40] See Muñoz Conde and García Arán, *Derecho Penal. Parte general*, 596.

[41] See B. Mapelli Caffarena, 'Artículo 130' in Gómez Tomillo (ed.), *Comentarios al Código Penal*, 521.

[42] On the history of these courts, see J. Sánchez Arcilla, *Historia de las instituciones político-administrativas contemporáneas* (Madrid: Dykinson, 1994), 409–11.

[43] Pursuant to Ley Orgánica 1/2004, de 28 de diciembre, de Medidas de Protección Integral contra la Violencia de Género (*BOE* No. 313, 29 December 2004).

First Instance Courts merit closer attention as a relevant example of mutual interactions and influence between the field of civil and criminal law. In smaller judicial districts, the court is made of a single judge, who serves as investigating judge, petty offences judge and as civil first instance court. In practice this is organised the following way: some weekdays the judge holds civil trials, other days petty offences trials, and every day deals with the pre-trial stage investigating criminal offences. It goes without saying that these judges with manifold functions tend to have a similar approach to torts and crime, regardless of whether they are deciding the issue of damages through a civil or a criminal procedure.

Added to this, the recruitment and examination to become a judge in Spain is based on the knowledge of the whole legal system so that every judge can at the beginning of his/her career sit in any jurisdiction. In practice, the first destination of a young judge is usually a first instance and investigating court, which explains and accentuates the tendency to have a similar approach to torts and crime.

B. *Overview*

1. Principles and structure of civil and criminal proceedings

In Spain, the Laws of Alfonso X the Wise, known as *Las Partidas de Alfonso X el Sabio,* dated between 1256 and 1265 contain a complete regulation of the proceedings before the courts of Castille,[44] with a differentiated set of rules for civil and for criminal proceedings (*Partida* number 3). This does not mean that until then the two procedures were unified in one: it only states that precise legal regulation is to be clearly found since the thirteenth century. The *Partidas* – the name comes from the seven parts it was divided into – is the most famous Hispanic legal text, which strongly influenced its successor procedural laws.

At present and since the nineteenth century, Spanish civil and criminal procedure are governed by different principles, mainly due to the influence of the concept of liberalism as developed in Spanish jurisprudence. Civil procedure is conceived as a tool or channel to deal with conflicts of a private nature, whilst the criminal procedure is meant to handle the sanctioning of crimes, performing therefore a public function and seeking to solve a conflict that goes beyond the interest of two private parties.

[44] See F. Tomás y Valiente, *Manual de historia del derecho español* (Madrid: Tecnos, 1996), 237–42.

2. Civil procedure

In part following the French codification but still maintaining its own historical roots, Spanish civil procedure is grounded on the so-called *principio dispositivo*: the parties decide whether to initiate the proceedings, delimit the subject-matter of the proceedings and when to put an end to them. This 'dispositive' principle makes the claimant the *dominus litis* and places on him the burden to prove the facts that underpin the lawsuit. In short, civil procedure is purely adversarial, with only a very limited evidentiary initiative on the side of the court, where the court is bound to decide exclusively upon the facts and evidence presented by the parties.[45] In cases of torts, there is no civil procedure involving a state official and no judicial investigation because the courts do not assume the function of finding the truth of the facts, but only assessing the evidence presented by the parties. As a general rule there is no discovery procedure, and no discovery orders as such are issued by the courts. The admissibility of the complaint and the progress of the proceedings are not subject to the prior showing of a cause of action or *prima facie* evidence of the existence of the right claimed. There is no closed list of the means of proof – neither in civil nor in criminal proceedings – except the exclusion of evidence obtained in a way that directly or indirectly infringes human rights (Art. 11 LOPJ).

In civil law, the claimant has to prove the constituent elements of the rights claimed, while the defendant bears the burden of proving those facts that extinguish, exclude or hinder the effectiveness of the facts proved by the claimant. There is no legal rule on the assessment of evidence, except for the notorious facts,[46] which can be considered as proved without evidence being presented at trial. Those facts that are admitted by both parties are not subject to evidence and the court must consider them proven. Each of the parties has to take a stance on the facts alleged by the opposing party, because those facts that have not been denied by the opposing party can be considered by the court as tacitly admitted. Tort law has eased the proof of fault in many ways, including a reversal of the burden of proof (see Sections 4.B and D below). Proof by presumptions (Art. 386 LEC) could also be applied to the proof of the causal link,

[45] However, the court has certain evidentiary initiative (Art. 282 LEC), the witnesses will be summoned by the court and are obliged to appear subject to sanction for not appearing in court (Art. 292 LEC) and in limited circumstances, the court may appoint an expert to present evidence and shed light upon the disputed facts (Art. 339 LEC).

[46] In civil law theory on procedure, 'notorious facts' are those that are generally known as existing and thus do not need to be proved to be considered as certain by the court.

although it is not common. The standard applied by the courts as to the degree of certainty to be achieved is very high both in tort and in crime.[47] The Civil Chamber of the Supreme Court has sometimes stated that an absolute complete certainty is not required. By contrast, absolute certainty is required as regards crime due to the presumption of innocence.[48]

3. Criminal procedure

While civil procedure may be classified as the judicial channel for solving private legal conflicts, criminal procedure can be defined as the channel for the state to investigate possible criminal conduct and once proved, apply the *ius puniendi* within a framework of legal guarantees as a way to contribute to the social peace. Public prosecution and courts are strictly bound by the principle of legality, which is defined as the principle by which the commencement, scope and continuation of a criminal procedure are strictly regulated by the law and not subject to criteria of criminal policy, or any discretionary powers. This principle should mean that every time a crime has been committed, the state has to react and the mechanisms to provide the criminal response have to be activated.

If traditionally the criminal procedure has been understood as a framework of safeguards with the aim of finding out the truth and imposing a sanction if the criminal facts were proved, the increasing role of plea agreements (now in evidence in approximately 60 per cent of all criminal cases)[49] might have changed the meaning and the aims of the procedure itself. In practice, it is open to doubt that all offences reported are thoroughly investigated in order to search for the truth, since some minor offences with an unknown offender are closed without a proper pre-trial investigation.

The main task of the public prosecutor consists in 'promoting the justice in the defence of the rule of law, the rights of the citizens and of the public interest safeguarded by the law' (Art. 124.1 CE and 534 LOPJ), most often by bringing a criminal prosecution. However, they may also oppose the charges pressed by another accusing party (Art. 3.4 Law on

47 See S. García-Cuerva García, 'Las reglas generales del onus probandi', in X. Abel Lluch and J. Picó i Junoy (eds.), *Objeto y carga de la prueba civil* (Barcelona: J. M. Bosch, 2007), 60.

48 See, e.g., Judgment of the Constitutional Court 44/1989, 20 February.

49 See Memoria Consejo General Poder Judicial 2012, www.poderjudicial.es/cgpj/es/Poder_Judicial/Consejo_General_del_Poder_Judicial/Actividad_del_CGPJ(last accessed November 2014).

Public Prosecution). The public prosecutor is also obliged to claim damages for the victim (*ex delicto*) together with the criminal action, as outlined above and discussed further below.

The victim can freely decide if she wants to become a party in the proceedings. By allowing the victim to act as accusing party, the Spanish criminal justice system implicitly recognises that the criminal procedure protects both a public interest and an individualised private interest based on harm suffered by the victim.

It is essential to know that the public prosecutor does not have a monopoly of the prosecution: every Spanish citizen, in addition to the victim, can constitute themselves as an accusing party and is given standing to represent the public interest in prosecuting public crimes (Art. 125 CE). This so-called popular action (*acción popular*) requires a security deposit to be lodged to cover costs and damages. In practice, only in a very few criminal proceedings is a popular accuser present (not more than 3 per cent of all criminal cases), but it has proved to be useful as a means of controlling the State's actual exercise of its *ius puniendi*.

As to the principles of evidence, the right to presumption of innocence, the right to cross-examination and the principle of *in dubio pro reo* apply to the criminal cases.

The presumption of innocence entails that the accusing party must prove the facts alleged in the indictment and the guilt of the defendant, who is not bound to prove his innocence. The rules for the distribution of the burden of proof in a formal sense are not strictly applicable to the criminal process because the public prosecutor, being an impartial official, has to produce evidence both on the facts that can lead to the conviction of the defendant as well as those other facts that could justify his acquittal.

Spanish criminal procedure follows the principle of free evaluation of evidence ('according to the judge's conscience' reads Art. 741 LECrim). This principle must be interpreted in light of the case law of the Constitutional Court on the presumption of innocence, from which the following criteria can be derived: (1) there must be substantial evidence; (2) it must have been produced respecting the procedural safeguards – mainly, the confrontation clause and the right to a public hearing; (3) evidence has to be legally obtained; and (4) the court is bound to provide reasoning for its assessment of the evidence.[50] Therefore, the standard of proof may

[50] See STC 34/1996, 11 March and J. Vegas, *Presunción de inocencia y prueba en el proceso penal* (Madrid: La Ley, 1993), 77–105.

differ when assessing the same facts, depending on the kind of procedure (criminal/civil). However, in practice the standard of proof applied to the facts in the criminal procedure for criminal and civil liability will be the same.[51]

C. *Preliminary issues: interaction between civil and criminal courts*

Preliminary issues (*cuestiones prejudiciales*) arise when a jurisdiction has to decide on a subject-matter, which falls within the competence of another jurisdictional division, in order to make a decision on their own subject-matter. Traditionally in these cases the proceedings had to be suspended and the court had to remand the preliminary question to be decided by the competent jurisdiction. This general rule changed in 1985 to the opposite one: each jurisdiction can decide on issues that do not fall within their powers, but only as far as this is needed to decide on the merits of the principal case (Art. 10.1 LOPJ). Thus a civil court, for example, will be able to apply and decide over an administrative or a labour law question if this is necessary to decide on the civil suit. The decisions over preliminary issues belonging to another jurisdiction do not have effects out of that procedure: they lack a *res judicata* effect. However, as will be explained below, the general principle applicable to criminal preliminary issues is that *le pénal tient le civil en l'état.*

1. Criminal matters in civil proceedings

Once the general rule on preliminary issues is defined, Art. 10.2 LOPJ sets out the special rule for criminal questions: if in a civil procedure facts appear that might constitute a criminal offence, and a decision on these facts is essential to decide on the civil suit, the criminal question has to be sent to the criminal courts, and the civil proceedings will be suspended until the criminal court takes a decision (Art. 40 LEC). This is an exception to the general rule in Art. 10.1 LOPJ ('Exceptions for certain civil proceedings'). Depending on the type of criminal issue, the civil procedure will be suspended immediately (in case of an offence of falsehood of documents relevant for the civil outcome), or once the procedure is ripe for sentence (all other cases where there is a relevant criminal issue that affects the civil case).

The regulation set out in the civil procedure is complemented by Art. 114 LECrim, which states that once a criminal procedure has commenced, it is not possible to bring a civil procedure regarding the

[51] See Font, *La acción civil en el proceso penal*, 107.

same facts. If the civil procedure on those same facts is pending, it will be suspended immediately. This rule appears to conflict with the rule established in the LEC, in that it orders the immediate suspension of the civil procedure once the criminal procedure has been initiated (Art. 114 LECrim), while Art. 40 LEC allows the civil procedure to continue, ordering the suspension before the rendering of the sentence. This contradiction may be solved by understanding that the rule in the LEC is applicable to proceedings dealing with 'the same facts', while Art. 40 LECrim refers to a strict preliminary issue.[52]

2. Civil matters in criminal proceedings

The criminal court has been accorded jurisdiction to decide on non-criminal issues if this is necessary for the assessment of the criminal liability,[53] but the decision within the criminal judgment on non-criminal issues will not produce *res judicata* effect.[54] At present, the existence of preliminary questions in the criminal procedure can be decided by the criminal court, and does not cause the suspension of the criminal procedure, except in two cases: (1) when the preliminary question is raised before the ECJ with regard to economic crimes[55] and (2) when a constitutional preliminary question (Art. 163 CE) is raised within the criminal proceedings.[56]

D. The civil action in criminal proceedings

1. Civil action in criminal proceedings: jointly deciding criminal and civil liability

The basic substantive rules across tort and crime are explained in Section 4, but an important feature of Spanish criminal procedure is the so-called 'civil action *ex delicto*'.

[52] See A. Del Moral Martín and A. Del Moral García, *Interferencias entre el proceso civil y el proceso penal* (Granada: Comares, 2002), 31–6.

[53] On case law regarding preliminary questions and civil issues within the criminal procedure, see Del Moral and Del Moral, *Interferencias entre el proceso civil*, 231–82.

[54] A. De la Oliva, *et al.*, *Derecho Procesal Penal* (Madrid: CERA, 2007), 255.

[55] See Decision of the ECJ 23 Feb. 1995, regarding a prejudicial question raised by the Spanish Audiencia Nacional in a case related to monetary crimes.

[56] Organic Law of the Constitutional Court, Art. 35.3 provides for the provisional suspension of the judicial proceedings until the Constitutional Court renders a decision over the question raised by the judge with regard to the constitutionality of the statutory rule that is to be applied in the criminal case. Both this, and a reference to the ECJ must be made by the judge, and he is unlikely to do so readily.

Special protection is granted to the aggrieved party (*perjudicado*) in the Spanish system. The public prosecutor is obliged to file the civil suit for damages together with the criminal action,[57] except when the damaged party explicitly renounces his rights (Art. 108 LECrim and Art. 3.4 of the Law on Public Prosecution) or expresses his preference to sue before the civil courts once the criminal procedure has ended (Art. 112 LECrim). In such cases, it is not possible to exercise the civil action until a final judicial decision has put an end to the criminal proceedings.

This is a peculiarity of the Spanish criminal procedure, by which a public institution, the same institution duty-bound to prosecute crimes, files the civil claim for the person who suffered damages derived from an offence, even though the latter did not ask that institution to do so. It must be noted that the public prosecutor does not act as a representative of the damaged party, for he must exercise the civil action even if the damaged party himself files the civil action and acts as a civil party in the criminal procedure. Nor is he acting in substitution of the damaged party, for he is not claiming a third party's right on his own behalf and in his own interest.[58] In addition, the public prosecutor cannot dispose (for instance, withdraw) of the civil action.

Deciding on the civil liability within the criminal procedure is usually explained by the factual connection between those two legal consequences, for the civil liability derives from the same facts that are judged in the criminal procedure. Thus, the criminal court acquires jurisdiction 'by adhesion' (*competencia por adhesión*) to decide on the civil action, but its competence is granted *secundum eventum litis*: that is, the court is competent to decide on the civil issues only if it renders a criminal conviction. This does not necessarily exclude civil liability, but this will have to be decided in the civil jurisdiction.

It has long been discussed whether civil actions should be decided within a criminal procedure or separately. The fact is that most continental European legal systems allow certain civil claims (damages and restitution) to be raised within the criminal procedure, which entails advantages and disadvantages. The arguments for allowing the decision

[57] This was first introduced in the Spanish system with the LECrim of 1882, being a forerunner of the present European directives regarding the protection of victims. See A. Arnaiz Serrano, *Las compañías aseguradoras en los procesos penal y contencioso-administrativo* (Madrid: Mapfre, 2008), 23.

[58] J. Montero Aroca *et. al.*, *Derecho Jurisdiccional III. Proceso Penal* (Valencia: Tirant, 2012), 94.

in the same procedure can be summarised as judicial economy, preventing conflicting decisions and aiding the victim.[59]

Judicial economy seeks to prevent a later civil procedure on the same – or almost the same – facts. On the one hand, dealing with compensation and restitution may delay the criminal proceedings. On the other hand, the administration of justice and the parties will avoid the expenses of engaging in subsequent proceedings. The relative priority of fast and simpler criminal justice and only having one set of proceedings, continue to divide scholars.[60] Most remarkably, Spanish law has no rules to reject a complex civil claim as being too time-consuming or inappropriate for the criminal courts.

Spanish law is also highly concerned to prevent conflicting judicial decisions to the extent that is reasonably possible. From the point of view of the rule of law, coherence and legal certainty, it is undesirable that a civil court can declare that certain facts, already declared as proved by a criminal court, are deemed as not having existed. Spanish law reduces this risk by determining both obvious claims together by default, by suspending a reserved civil claim and then binding any such reserved action by the facts decided earlier by the criminal judge (on which, see below). However, the risk is not completely excluded in cases where the offender has caused damages to a number of persons, some of which decide to claim damages in the criminal proceedings, while others prefer to sue before the civil courts.[61]

Of course, the system also better protects the rights of the victim, so that she does not have to commence another procedure to get the restitution or the compensation for the damages.

2. The victim's decision on whether to reserve his civil claim

While the victim can choose to reserve his civil claim from the criminal prosecution, there are at least four reasons why he typically does not.

First, the criminal route is easier than the civil. The criminal prosecutor will do all the work of the prosecution and the civil claim. Indeed, the criminal jurisdiction is now the only jurisdiction in which the (criminal)

[59] See, e.g., Arnaiz, *Las partes civiles en el proceso penal*, 86–105.

[60] See E. De Llera, 'La responsabilidad civil en el proceso penal', in G. Quintero Olivares, S. Cavanillas Múgica and E. De Llera, *La responsabilidad civil ex delicto* (Navarra: Aranzadi, 2002), 177–233, 177.

[61] See STS 846/2000, of 22 May 2000, cited by C. Granados Pérez in X. O'Callaghan Muñoz (coord.), *Responsabilidad civil ex delicto* (Madrid: La Ley-Wolters Kluwer, 2010), 43.

plaintiff does not have to pay court fees.[62] A victim, having already suffered harm from wrongdoing, should not have to suffer further economic costs or other obstacles. Also, the fact that criminal law is part of public law and that the state is seeking the traditional goals of punishment, that is, deterrence, rehabilitation and retribution, plays a great role in exempting plaintiffs from paying court fees.[63] Similarly, in criminal cases, victims can obtain preliminary injunctions without giving security (which is normally required in civil proceedings).[64] Freezing of assets, posting bonds and other matters are easier and less costly to achieve in criminal matters than in civil matters.

Second, a criminal vehicle for the civil claim is faster. Although Spain does not have a right to a speedy trial *per se*, criminal cases are handled more expeditiously than civil cases.[65] A normal victim in a criminal case will obtain compensation faster than in a civil case.

Third, there is little risk. In the case of an acquittal, the victim is not required to pay costs. For the private prosecutor to be liable for the defendant's legal costs, the court has to establish malicious prosecution. For this to happen, the public prosecutor must have considered that the case should be dismissed (at the investigation stage) or the defendant has been acquitted (at the trial phase). More often than not, the public prosecutor prosecutes whenever a victim lodges a criminal complaint. Thus the court will normally hold that the prosecution was not malicious. Similarly, the risk of a conviction for the crime of a false prosecution is very low.[66] In order for a plaintiff to be convicted of this charge, the criminal complaint must contain false statements or forged documents; in practice, the victim within the criminal trial tends only to make arguments, not produce documents. A second requirement, that the criminal

[62] Court fees were established by Act 10/2012, of 20 November, for civil, labour and administrative law. By some estimates, about 70 per cent of the cases are criminal.

[63] Yet, the currently proposed reform of the CP will eliminate misdemeanour offences, which will result in less cases exempted from court fees, see J. M. Hernández Carrillo, 'La reforma en curso del Código penal cierra el círculo que abre la ley de tasas' (2013) 7998 *Diario La Ley*.

[64] It was intended that certain procedures require security. Thus Art. 764 LECrim establishes that preliminary injunctions for so-called 'abbreviated' trials i.e., speedy trials, must abide by the requirements of the rules of civil procedure. These latter rules normally require giving security in case of preliminary injunctions. Yet, this is almost never done in practice.

[65] Unjustified delays in criminal proceedings will be considered as an attenuating circumstance (Art. 21.6 CP).

[66] A notable exception has been the conviction of the former CEO of Banco Santander: STS of 24 February 2011.

prosecution must have been dismissed, also makes the victim's position less risky.

Fourth, it is more effective in securing compensation. To begin with, in certain complex cases, the private prosecutor has the opportunity to obtain from the judge search and seizure warrants that would be technically impossible in a civil case.[67] The fact that the criminal discovery procedure in Spain does not have the stringent obligations that, for instance, are present in the American system, that is, the duty of the defendant in a civil trial to produce certain records and testimonies, makes criminal jurisdiction the ideal 'battleground' to obtain certain pieces of evidence that could be decisive in the final result of the case. In addition, enforcement of the order by a criminal court is more effective. For instance, where a defendant is required to post bail to avoid pre-trial detention, the monies posted for such purpose will go towards satisfying the victim's award of compensation. And in addition to all that, criminal prosecutions are also an effective means to force a settlement. Spanish legal slang has developed a concept for those criminal complaints that are filed just to coerce the opposing party to a monetary settlement: 'Catalonian criminal complaints'. Even the Supreme Court uses this language.[68]

On the other hand, there are some possible downsides to the criminal pursuit of a civil claim. First, the standard of proof is higher in criminal law, and this may make the prosecution fail, thereby ending that civil claim brought as part of it. The precise rules of evidence in civil and criminal law are also uncertain, leaving the extent of this problem unknown. In practice as well, if the claim fails outright, the victim has lost nothing and can always sue again in a civil court. That said partial success may be no success at all. If the public prosecutor does not quantify and prove damage correctly and the court awards lower damages than were really suffered, the victim will not be able to claim later in a civil suit, nor ask for review of the judgment. Second, the flipside of the victim not paying for the prosecution is that he is not in control of the proceedings, and may disagree with the approach taken by the public prosecutor. However, even this drawback is not that serious. Even when the public prosecutor brings the civil claim, the damaged party can appear as a civil party in the criminal proceedings, presenting the same claim. It may even occur that the damages claimed by the victim are higher than those claimed by the public prosecutor on his/her behalf. This is somewhat illogical, given

[67] Without the support of the public prosecutor, such requests will almost always fail.

[68] See, e.g., STS 7 April 2006.

the protective nature of the activity of the public prosecutor. It might be argued that, if present and represented, the victim is in a better position to plead and prove his own losses.[69]

There are cases where the victim does not have a meaningful choice. The most important example is where a single wrongdoing creates multiple victims, a paradigm instance being a widespread defective product. The lack of specific civil rules which enable victims of the same misconduct to work together towards the same goal, results in hundreds or thousands of criminal complaints filed before the criminal courts that are then aggregated in a single criminal proceeding.

In particular, Spain has a special criminal court, the National Court, for dealing with cases in which groups of victims of various Spanish regions have been harmed by the same alleged misconduct. Though the nature of this 'ad hoc' court has been heavily questioned,[70] it has established itself as a court of last resort for multiple victims that wish to proceed in the same case. When local courts get notice that the national court has initiated a criminal investigation regarding an alleged misconduct that is similar to some pending cases within their jurisdiction, they immediately transfer their cases to the National Court to be merged with it.

Some famous large-scale wrongs have involved criminal rather than civil courts. The relevance of the *Colza* case has already been mentioned in the introduction. More recently, in the aftermath of the financial crisis, thousands of non-sophisticated investors, mostly average retirees, housewives, teenagers, filed criminal complaints alleging that certain financial institutions sold them toxic financial products. Although the final decision in this case will take several years – the complaints were mainly filed in 2012 –, the underlying juxtaposition of tort and crime remains clear. Case management of these cases is extremely difficult and adds an additional workload to the already overloaded criminal justice system.

In other words, certain areas of class action suits, such as consumer finance/mortgage banking, securities and derivative suits, environmental or toxic tort, consumer protection and product liability are common features of the criminal justice landscape in Spain. As noted before, this is not out of arbitrary decision, but out of necessity given the procedural rules in civil law. But for the pressure from civil claimants, Spanish prosecutors would not be in a position to prosecute these offences as they currently

[69] See, e.g., Arnaiz, *Las partes civiles en el proceso penal*, 221–2.

[70] It was originally created to deal with terrorism cases and then expanded its reach to organised crime cases, complex white-collar crime cases and multi-jurisdiction cases.

do. While reform has been discussed, no proposal currently looks set to solve this problem.

3. Who can sue: the 'damaged party' as civil party in the criminal proceedings

The 'damaged party', the person who, as a consequence of an offence, has suffered harm or been deprived of property, can exercise in the criminal procedure the action for compensation or for restitution of that property. This category explicitly includes the victim, his family and some third parties, but this is only an illustrative list of potential claimants. In fact, the unclear legal regulation on this point – the provisions in the LECrim differ from those in the CP, and both are unclear – has raised various interpretations as to who should be allowed to file a civil suit in the criminal procedure.[71] In practice, every person who has suffered harm directly derived from the acts, which are judged to be criminal through a criminal prosecution, can act as civil party in that prosecution. The victim can constitute himself as civil claimant not so much for being offended by the crime but for being the person that suffered a civil damage or tort. The victim's relatives are deemed a directly damaged party (*perjudicados*) if the victim has died. Among the relatives, the Spanish courts have decided that you are only a damaged party if you are closely related to the victim (i.e. those living in the same domestic environment or dependent on the victim): typically, the widow or widower – except in cases of separation – and the children.[72] If the damage is covered by insurance, the insurer is not deemed damaged by the offence, as the possible damage is not considered to derive from the offence but from contract.

The victim and other persons who have suffered damages will be informed as to their right to present a civil claim for compensation or restitution in the criminal case at the very beginning of the procedure, when first appearing before the investigating judge. The damaged party can participate in the preliminary investigation, proposing certain investigative measures related to his claim (Art. 320 LECrim), and, specifically, he may apply for provisional and protective measures to secure the offender's civil liability. The judge, according to the LEC, can order seizure and confiscation of the property of the defendant. He also will inform the damaged party as to the right to be assisted by legal counsel, or get one appointed if he is entitled to legal aid.

[71] Arnaiz, *Las partes civiles en el proceso penal*, 178–83.

[72] Font, *La acción civil en el proceso penal*, 27.

As a rule the civil claimant – that is the damaged party who is not the victim – is not allowed to appeal independently from the prosecutor or accusing party. Only when the public prosecutor files an appeal will the civil party be able to appeal the civil part of the judgment. This represents a disadvantage in relation to the possibilities to appeal in the civil proceedings, but as the civil claim is considered as ancillary, it seems reasonable that the civil party may not appeal when the criminal decision is not challenged.

As all persons who have suffered damage directly derived from the crime may claim damages in the criminal procedure, this often leads to proceedings with multiple civil claimants, who can be victims or not.[73] This caused huge problems in the *Colza oil* affair already mentioned, one of the first criminal cases which involved a large number of damaged parties. The case concerned fraud and food poisoning of oil resulting in more than 20,000 people being affected, many of them killed.[74] Obviously the amount of damages was enormous and the question of the civil liability was all but clear. There is no way to separate such complex civil action from the criminal procedure, except when all the damaged parties explicitly express an intention not to exercise the civil claim for damages before the criminal court. This not only caused delays and increased complexity of the criminal proceedings, but it made it clear that the rules of the criminal procedure were not apt to deal with such macro-cases. In that occasion the protection of their rights was assumed by the public prosecutor and the consumer protection association was granted the right to represent the group of victims, adding to the criminal case a sort of class actions procedure. The specific amount of damages and the identification of all the persons entitled to compensation were established afterwards in the enforcement procedure. Since then, many other criminal proceedings with multiple damaged parties have faced similar difficulties.

4. Who can be sued: the defendant, civilly liable third parties and others

The defendant to the civil claim is the person who, according to the claimant (and/or the public prosecutor), must be held as civilly responsible. Four categories exist.

First, there is *the offender*. Every person who has committed an offence is criminally responsible for it and liable for damage caused (Art. 116 CP).

[73] The LECrim lacks special rules to deal with these multiple-parties cases.

[74] STS 26 September 1997 (RJ 6366/1997).

In case of joint offenders they will be also jointly liable for the damage done. The extent of the liability of each one will be established by the judge. As to the accomplices, they are jointly liable among themselves, and are subsidiary liable in respect to the principal offenders.

Second, *insurance companies* both indemnify defendants and can be sued directly. The relevant statutory provisions and their judicial interpretation have been greatly criticised. Most significantly, Art. 117 CP holds that insurers are directly responsible for damage resulting from criminal wrongdoing, while Art. 764.3 LECrim states that insurers may not act as parties in the criminal proceedings, but they will be requested to post a surety for damages covered by the insurance. The best approach is to distinguish between the cases where the insurance is mandatory (*seguro obligatorio*, like third-party liability insurance for motor vehicle accidents) and where it is not (*seguro voluntario*).

In cases of mandatory insurance, the general stance is that the insurance company cannot act as a party in the criminal proceedings, although there is not a uniform practice in the criminal courts.[75] Some courts consider that the obligation of the insurer to compensate for damage arises from the contract and not from the offence, so the insurer should not intervene in the criminal case. And in those cases where the insurer posts the bond in advance, there is no civil claim against the insurer, and thus there is no need to allow the company to be party to the proceedings. However, the prevailing opinion holds that, since insurers can be ordered to pay damages in the criminal judgment, they should be allowed to intervene as civil party in order to preserve their right to be heard. However, their position in the criminal case opposing the public prosecutor and possibly the victim as private accuser may not be adequate for the aims of the criminal proceedings.

Where the insurance was not mandatory, the insurer can sue and be sued directly in the criminal proceedings. The civil claim is dealt with in the criminal proceedings but separately and the insurer can only act in respect of the civil issue (Art. 764.3 LECrim). This restricted intervention of the insurance company, limited to civil liability, has been affirmed by the Supreme Court and confirmed by the Constitutional Court,[76] although sharply criticised by scholars on the basis that the insurer will be directly

[75] See Arnaiz, *Las compañías aseguradoras en el proceso penal y contencioso-administrativo*, 50–56.

[76] STC 90/1988, 13 May 1988, cited by Arnaiz, *Las compañías aseguradoras en los procesos penal y contencioso-administrativo*, 57.

affected by the outcome of the criminal case and therefore should also be heard with regard to the criminal responsibility.[77]

Third, criminal law may, for reasons of *capacity*, reduce the liability of one party but this tends to be balanced out in some way. For example, wrongful acts committed under the influence of alcohol or other drugs may not amount to crimes because of a lack of capacity, but the wrongdoer will still be liable in civil law. More interestingly, sometimes further possible defendants to civil claims are added. Thus, Art. 118.1 CP makes anyone in charge of or with custody over the insane, subsidiarily liable, so long as they were at fault under their supervision.

Fourth and finally, *any person who has unknowingly benefited* from the crime is obliged to give restitution and/or compensation within the criminal proceedings (Art. 122 CP).[78] This person will not be criminally liable, but the fact that the wrongdoing has provided him/her with certain benefits, imposes a duty give restitution and/or compensate the victim to an equal extent. This is not considered to be secondary civil liability but as direct civil liability. For example, if the victim of a fraud transfers 10,000 Euros to the bank account of the offender, and the bank account has two different account holders – say, the offender and his wife – the wife will be considered as directly civilly liable for the benefits of the wrong and must compensate the victim with 5,000 Euros even if she did not know of or act in connection with the fraud scheme.

This type of civil liability is joint and several, but limited to the amount of his/her receipt of the benefits of the wrongdoing. Also, the type of civil liability derives theoretically from receiving benefits from a wrong, not from the fact that that wrong is also a crime. The confusion of crime and tort at this stage is unhelpful: despite being dealt with in the same section of the CP, this is not civil liability *ex delicto*, but another breed of civil liability. In simple terms, the underlying logic of this institution is that the individual has obtained an illicit benefit. Saying more is difficult since the nature of this type of liability is somewhat unclear. Some Supreme Court rulings tend to assign the 'civil' label to this restitution order; others feel more inclined to conceive of this institution as a weapon to fight

[77] In this sense, see V. Cortés Domínguez in V. Moreno Catena and V. Cortés Domínguez, *Derecho Procesal Penal* (Valencia: Tirant, 2012), 331.

[78] On this rule see I. Segrelles de Arenaza, 'El partícipe por título lucrativo: Un aspecto de delincuencia patrimonial y económica' (2000) 5 *Diario La Ley* 1918; J. M. Torras Coll, "El partícipe a título lucrativo en el proceso penal" (2013) *El Derecho Revista de Jurisprudencia*, available at www.elderecho.com/penal/participe_a_titulo_lucrativo-proceso_penal-titulo_lucrativo_en_el_proceso_penal_11_573055003.html.

organised crime. The cause of action is a criminal law projection of the well-established principle in civil law that business transactions declared void and without cause result in both parties reciprocally restoring to each other the amounts of their contributions. Finally, it is also worth noting that the rights assisting a civil 'accessory' are similar to those held by defendants in a case. They can appear before court and contest the allegations. However, they do not have to be served until the trial phase is opened. Therefore, there can be an on-going investigation without the civil accessories being present and represented before the investigating court.

5. Rules applicable to the claim for damages and/or restitution of property in criminal proceedings

The claim for damages or restitution is usually filed together with the indictment (Art. 651 LECrim) and being a pure civil claim, the rules and principles of the civil procedure apply despite the fact that it is presented within a criminal procedure.[79] It must state the damage caused, the sum claimed, the identification of the civil defendants and the fact or facts that caused damage. As in other civil cases, the parties sued can settle, leaving the criminal proceedings to continue to decide on the criminal liability. However, if the defendant is finally acquitted, the prior admission of the civil liability has no effects in the criminal proceedings, since the criminal court only has jurisdiction on the civil liability if it renders a conviction sentence. In such a case, the damaged party would have to sue before the civil courts, and the statement of the defendant admitting the civil liability could only be presented as evidence in the civil procedure.

The civil party can propose and present evidence, and the judge will decide on its admission. For matters relating to criminal liability, the evidence rules that apply are those established for criminal causes. Those criminal procedure rules also apply to evidence of facts which also ground the civil liability. This means that the evaluation of evidence is more strict than in a civil procedure, as mentioned above. But the civil party profits from the evidence gathering done by the prosecutor, who is also an expert at getting that evidence. This is an example of how the joining of these actions will also cause a modification of the principles applicable to civil cases.[80] Criminal procedure gives greater protection to the defendant, but this is off-set by advantages to the civil party.

[79] See De Llera, 'La responsabilidad civil en el proceso penal', 207–9.

[80] See Font, *La acción civil en el proceso penal*, 105–9.

E. *The effects of criminal judgments on civil claims*

As regards the effect of criminal judgments on civil claims we shall distinguish three possible situations, as the consequences will differ:

(1) Joint actions and criminal conviction.
(2) Joint actions and criminal acquittal.
(3) Separate actions, because the damaged party expressed his will not to file the civil claim in the criminal procedure.

In addition, when the accused is acquitted by reason of an exonerating circumstance but the criminal facts and their author have been proved, the criminal court can render judgment on the issue of civil responsibility (Art. 119 CP).

1. Joint actions and criminal conviction

Where the civil claim has been joined to the prosecution, and the defendant is convicted, the judgment must then decide the defendant's civil liability: compensation and/or restitution. The criminal court has to establish who is civilly liable and determine the amount of damages to be awarded.[81] This judgment granting or denying damages, once it is final, will have *res judicata* effect, so that a second procedure on the same facts and same parties is excluded.[82] With regard to the civil action it means that there cannot be a second procedure to dispute the civil liability based on the same facts and with the same parties before a civil court. In the event such a suit should be presented, the parties sued should allege the *res judicata* effect and the civil court would close the proceedings and impose the costs on the claimant upon the general rules on shifting the cost onto the party who loses the claim (Art. 394 LEC). However, in practice it is not always easy to identify the elements to establish the *res judicata* effect.

2. Joint actions and criminal acquittal

When the offender has been acquitted of the offence, the criminal court does not have jurisdiction to decide over any civil action joined to the prosecution. Exceptionally, as noted above, in those cases where the acquittal

[81] As regards loss arising from road traffic accidents, the general policy is that the victim should recover from the offender's insurers up to the amount of the mandatory insurance. For the rest of damages, the damaged party should recover from the offender himself.

[82] See I. Nadal Gómez, *El ejercicio de acciones civiles en el proceso penal* (Valencia: Tirant, 2002), 203–7.

is based on the lack of responsibility of the accused because of its insanity or another cause of exemption, the criminal court will decide on the subsidiary civil liability. As a rule, the acquittal of the accused does not have any effects on the civil liability and does not prevent the civil party from filing the claim before the civil courts.

However, when the criminal acquittal sentence has declared that the facts that underpinned the accusation did not exist or that the accused did not take part in them, this statement has a binding effect on the civil courts (Art. 116 LECrim). The reason is that non-existent facts cannot cause any damage and thus, they cannot cause any civil liability. This is the only case where the acquittal in the criminal case will ban a later civil suit because such criminal judgment extinguishes the civil action.[83] In practice, this does not occur often as usually the acquittal sentence results from the lack of sufficient evidence, rather than enough evidence to prove that the acts never happened or, more narrowly, that the defendant did not do them.[84]

In those cases where the offender has absconded and therefore the criminal trial cannot take place, the criminal court has to suspend the criminal proceedings.[85] The damaged party will be able to file the civil lawsuit for damages before the civil jurisdiction, without having to wait until there is a criminal decision. This is also the solution established when the criminal proceedings have to be suspended. If pending the civil proceedings, the criminal proceedings can be resumed, because the offender has been found and brought to court, the civil procedure will have to be suspended and the civil suit transferred back to the criminal proceedings (Art. 114 LECrim).[86]

3. Separate actions, because the damaged party expressed his will not to file the civil claim in the criminal procedure

When the damaged party has expressed his/her will to try the civil action separately before the civil courts, the criminal court will only decide on the criminal responsibility. The civil action cannot be filed until the criminal case is decided and a final sentence is passed.

[83] See E. Gómez Orbaneja, 'Eficacia de la sentencia penal en el proceso civil' (1946) 355 *Revista de Derecho Procesal* 207–46, 238.

[84] That an acquittal based on evidentiary insufficiency does not conflict with a later judgment granting damages for the same facts, was recognised by the STC 59/1996, 15 April 1996, cited by Nadal, *El ejercicio de acciones civiles en el proceso penal,* 194.

[85] See Del Moral and Del Moral, *Interferencias entre el proceso civil,* 546.

[86] See Arnaiz, *Las partes civiles en el proceso penal,* 157.

The question of the effects of the criminal conviction sentence in a subsequent civil procedure has been controversial for some time, but it is now recognised that, although the criminal sentence does not have a strict *res judicata* effect, it has binding effects as to the facts.[87] Therefore, the civil court deciding on the civil liability *ex delicto* cannot change the facts already established as certain in the sentence by the criminal court.

4. Enforcement of the judgment

The enforcement of the civil part of the judgment rendered in a criminal case will be made according to the LECrim. There is only one difference compared with a criminal order. Whereas the enforcement of the civil sentences only can take place after a written application of the party, the civil liability decision rendered in a criminal case will be enforced without the need of application by the beneficiaries. The criminal court will order the enforcement *ex officio*. The criminal courts have jurisdiction to carry out the execution of the damages and this decision can be provisionally enforced (Arts. 526 ff. LEC). In case that property or assets had been found and frozen or secured at the beginning of the criminal procedure, the execution will usually be speedy. However, the vast majority of offenders convicted in Spain, with the exception of those convicted of economic crimes, are insolvent and no enforcement procedure is carried out. When the offender sentenced to pay damages has also been punished to pay a fine, Art. 126 CP states the order in which the property of the sentenced person will be distributed: the property seized will first cover the amount of damages; second, the reimbursement to the state of costs of the proceedings; in third place the reimbursement of costs of the private accuser, if the sentence imposes the payment of them; and only after the reimbursement of costs, the seized property will be dedicated to pay the fine.

4. Substance of tort and crime

A. *Capacity*

Liability requires capacity but tort and crime interpret this requirement differently (see generally Art. 19 and 20 CP and 200 CC).

87 See M. Yzquierdo Tolsada, *Aspectos civiles del nuevo código penal* (Madrid: Dykinson, 1997), 67 and Nadal, *El ejercicio de acciones civiles en el proceso penal*, 202.

According to criminal law, a person lacks capacity where she has any psychic anomaly or alteration which prevents her from understanding that her deed was illicit or from being able to act according to such understanding at the moment when the crime or misdemeanour occurred (Art. 20.1 CP). Criminal law cannot motivate such a person not to commit a crime or misdemeanour and therefore a preventative effect cannot be achieved.[88]

In contrast, the Civil Code focuses on the long-term status of the individual and sets out to decide how to regulate all the interests of someone without capacity (Art. 200 CC). Such a person can, on application to a judge, be declared to be without capacity: tutor(s) will then be appointed by the judge (Art. 760 LEC). The test used is similar to the criminal law: permanent illnesses or deficiencies either of a physical or psychological nature, which prevent a person from governing herself.[89] However, a substantial proportion of mentally ill people have not been subject to any such judicial declaration of incapacitation[90]

In addition, a declaration under Article 200 CC does not make the bearer immune to liability in tort.[91] It is tort law's own rules about lack of tortious capacity (or imputability) which are important, not the Article 200 CC declaration. It is all the more surprising then, that the Civil Code lacks a provision equivalent to Article 20 CP. In spite of that, legal scholarship agrees that such liability cannot be established where the defendant lacks the ability to understand the injustice of her conduct and behave accordingly, or to realise the effects of her acts and foresee their consequences. Without such ability there cannot be fault.[92] There lies the difference between criminal law and tort law, since the first is not possible without – at least – fault, whereas the second may be established without regard to fault in instances of strict liability.

Finally, the tort provisions in the CP actually use a wider test for capacity than the tests developed by civil courts. That is, where criminal law, and tort law in a civil court would both decide there was no capacity, the tort rules in the CP might nonetheless be content to award damages against that person (Art. 118.1.1 CP). This liability is apparently based on considerations of equity of fairness which do not exist in the Civil Code.

[88] See Muñoz Conde and García Arán, *Derecho Penal. Parte general,* 94 and 357.

[89] STS 1st Chamber, 28 July 1998 [RJ 1998/6134].

[90] See S. de Salas Murillo, *Responsabilidad civil e incapacidad* (Valencia: Tirant, 2003), 21.

[91] Again, Salas, *Responsabilidad civil e incapacidad,* 71, 95.

[92] See M. Martín-Casals and J. Solé Feliu, 'Fault under Spanish Law' in P. Widmer (ed.), *Unification of Tort Law: Fault* (The Hague / London / New York: Kluwer, 2005), 237.

However, some scholars have – after having criticised such disparity in treatment – argued for an analogous solution under tort law, provided that the parents or guardians cannot be held liable.[93] In any case, according to the Criminal Code, the non-imputable person will be held liable in tort together with her guardians – provided that that person has behaved in a negligent manner (Art. 118.1.1 CP). The burden of proof of fault on their side lies on the claimant, such fault cannot be presumed.[94] The guardians will be liable on a direct and solidary basis.[95] As for the liability of the guardians themselves, the Civil Code (Art. 1903 para. 3) remains silent as to any *de facto* guardians (only the guardians appointed by a court are mentioned by the rule). Moreover, fault on their side is presumed (Art. 1903 *in fine*).[96]

B. *Fault and intent*

Only the Civil Code defines fault or *culpa* (Art. 1104 CC). It consists in a lack of care according to the circumstances of time, space and the persons involved. Intention, however, is not defined in either the CC or CP. The Criminal Code expressly requires for a crime or misdemeanour to exist that the defendant behaved with fault (*imprudencia*) or intent (*dolo*) (Art. 10 CP). Therefore there is no 'liability for the mere result' – that is, no strict liability – under criminal law (*nullum crimen sine culpa*).[97] This requirement is known as subjective attribution (*imputación subjetiva*). In this regard, criminal law sets a very high standard in order to find the culprit guilty, as a result of the presumption of innocence (Art. 24.2 CE),

93 See F. Pantaleón Prieto, 'Comentario a la Sentencia de 10 de marzo de 1983' (1984) 2 *Cuadernos Civitas de Jurisprudencia Civil (CCJC)* 447–58, esp. 455 and Salas, *Responsabilidad civil e incapacidad*, 325.

94 See Muñoz Conde and García Arán, *Derecho Penal. Parte general*, 601.

95 See M. Alastuey Dobón 'Artículo 120' in M. Gómez Tomillo (ed.), *Comentarios al Código Penal*, 2nd edn (Valladolid: Lex Nova, 2011) 478, 468; see also M. García-Ripoll Montijano, *Ilicitud, culpa y estado de necesidad* (Madrid: Dykinson, 2006), 80.

96 These differences are pointed out by Salas, *Responsabilidad civil e incapacidad*, 98 and López Beltrán de Heredia, *Efectos civiles del delito y responsabilidad extracontractual*, 34, among others. There is a separate statutory criminal regime for dealing with minors, on which see Section 4.D below.

97 See Muñoz Conde and García Arán, *Derecho Penal. Parte general*, 94, 293 and Quintero, *Parte General del Derecho Penal*, 75. Criminal lawyers also usually speak of guilt (*culpability*) to express the reproach towards the culprit. See F. Muñoz Conde and J. A. Martos Gómez, 'Culpabilidad (D. penal)', in *Enciclopedia Jurídica Básica* (Madrid: Civitas, 1995), vol. 2, 1870.

whereas a lower standard may apply in tort law. The latter requires fault as a rule to establish liability (pursuant to Art. 1902 CC).

However, the civil courts have traditionally had much leeway in this regard and for several decades they have systematically reversed the burden of proof of fault in tort. Moreover, they have applied a very demanding standard of care. Even the slightest negligence will be deemed sufficient in order to establish liability (*in lege Aquilia et levissima culpa venit*), whereas it may not be enough as regards criminal liability.[98] Indeed, some crimes require at least gross negligence (*imprudencia grave*), although slight negligence (*imprudencia leve*) may also be punishable when it affects human life or physical integrity.[99] In addition to that, a higher standard of care is applied in tort in case of liability of professionals, whereas there are some instances of punishable negligence which are imaginable only if its author is a professional (e.g., genetic manipulation, Art. 159.2 CP).[100] Finally, in some cases the courts have concluded that the mere occurrence of damage proves that the defendant was negligent. All in all, this brings liability in fault under the Civil Code very close to strict liability.[101] More recently there has been a counter-movement, case law seeming to have demanded more as to the proof of fault.[102] Apart from that, obviously there are several instances of strict liability both in the Civil Code (e.g., liability for damage caused by animals in Art. 1905 CC or by toxic fumes in Art. 1908.2 CC) and outside of it (for instance, in case of nuclear damage, or damage caused by hunting in Art. 33.5 LC).

While Articles 5 and 10 CP make clear that some fault is required for every offence, no consensus exists about exactly what that fault is. For most of the twentieth century, psychological theory has dominated the case law and academic landscape. According to this theory the offender must have knowledge of and volition in respect of the consequences of his/her behaviour.[103] Yet, the legal evolution in the late twentieth century mainly resulted in the suppression of the element of volition (or willingness)

[98] See Font, *La acción civil en el proceso penal*, 14.

[99] See Muñoz Conde and García Arán, *Derecho Penal. Parte general*, 292.

[100] Again see Muñoz Conde and García Arán, *Derecho Penal. Parte general*, 288.

[101] As noted by Miquel Martin-Casals *et al.* 'Strict Liability under Spanish Law' in B. A. Koch and H. Koziol (eds.), *Unification of Tort Law: Strict Liability* (The Hague: Kluwer, 2002), 281.

[102] For further details, see J. Ribot and A. Ruda, 'Spain' in Helmut Koziol and Barbara C. Steininger (eds.), *European Tort Law 2007* (Berlin / Boston: De Gruyter, 2008), 555.

[103] For a psychological interpretation of *mens rea*, see S. Mir Puig, *Derecho penal Parte General*, 258–70.

and a focus on the intellectual element (knowledge). This resulted in a normative perspective of *mens rea* in which the fundamental issue is whether the offender was aware of the risk he was creating and of the possibility of that risk resulting in the actual harm.[104] The leading case was the decision of the Spanish Supreme Court of 23 April 1992, where it was impossible to determine that the defendants had the willingness to kill hundreds of people and injure thousands of them. But it was certainly possible, and the Court convicted on those grounds, to establish that they were aware and had knowledge of the risk they were creating by introducing industrial oil for human consumption purposes.[105]

To be sure, that does not mean that volition plays no role in the interpretation of criminal law statutes. Some offences do refer to terms such as intent, for example, Articles 270.2, 275, 277, 408, 605 CP or malice, such as in Article 459 CP. When addressing these specific issues, the court and academia refer to long-established classifications that have some resemblance to the Model Penal Code's four-tier distinction between purpose, knowingly, recklessness and negligence:

(1) first degree *dolus* (intent): the offender desires the final outcome of his criminal action;
(2) second degree *dolus* (knowledge): the offender knows the consequences of his actions, and he accepts them;
(3) *dolus eventualis* (recklessness): the offender is aware that his actions might bring some criminally relevant consequences;
(4) negligence, the offender should have known the harmful consequences of his behaviour.

All these definitions are not in the CP, but have been constructed by a notable body of scholarship and jurisprudence.[106]

C. *Causation*

1. Causation in criminal law

The CP gives no rules for determining causation. It has been the task of the Spanish courts and scholarship to develop a set of rules in order

[104] See E. Bacigalupo, *Principios de Derecho penal. Parte General*, 5th edn (Madrid: Akal, 1998), 223–32.

[105] STS 23 April 1992 (RJ 1992\6783).

[106] For a comprehensive research and exposition, see J. M. Ragués i Vallés, *El dolo y su prueba en el proceso penal* (Barcelona, J.M. Bosch, 1999).

to determine that the actor's conduct caused the prohibited result. For most part of the twentieth century, the jurisprudence followed the easy-to-use rule of the 'but for' cause of the result or *conditio sine qua non* rule. However, just relying on this test may lead to unfair results, especially when dealing with complex cases with concurring causes and regulated risk levels. The complexity of modern social life stimulated the development of a more nuanced 'but for' theory. Adopting the German law, the so-called 'adequate' cause theory requires an *ex ante* prognosis from the actor's perspective, that is, not only from a reasonable man's view but also including the knowledge that this particular individual might have, as to the foreseeability of causing the result.[107]

Notwithstanding the achievements of this development, another step was needed in order to determine the relevance of specific conduct within the wider complexities of human interactions. Therefore in addition to the factual cause, criminal law scholarship and jurisprudence developed the so-called *objective imputation theory*.[108] As the name reveals, it is not so much centered on causation but on imputation, that is, a normative assessment of certain facts and their association to an individual. According to this theory, the actor's conduct must create a non-permitted risk, a first level of imputation, and that precise risk must produce the result a second level of imputation.[109] To a certain extent, objective imputation is a kind of proximate (legal) cause theory that, nevertheless, forbids the punishment of some cases that are normally punished in common law jurisdictions.[110]

2. Causation in tort law

The criteria concerning causation which had been formulated by the Criminal Chamber of the Supreme Court have recently been adopted by the Civil Chamber as well, following their adoption by civil law scholars.[111] Therefore and in contrast to other countries, it is civil law which followed

[107] See Mir Puig, *Derecho penal Parte General*, 242–54.

[108] See M. Cancio Meliá, 'Victim Behavior and Offender Liability: A European Perspective' (2004) 7 *Buffalo Criminal Law Review* 513, 541–4.

[109] See Mir Puig, *Derecho penal Parte General*, 254–59.

[110] For an in-depth analysis, see L. E. Chiesa and C. Gómez-Jara, 'Spain', in J. Jon Heller and M. D. Dubber (eds.), *The Handbook of International Comparative Criminal Law* (Stanford University Press, 2011), 505–7.

[111] See J. Ribot and A. Ruda, 'Spain' in B. Winiger *et al.* (eds.), *Essential Cases on Natural Causation* (Wien/New York: Springer, 2007), 41–4.

criminal law and not the other way round.[112] Recently some tort law scholars have criticised this on the basis that it is a blanket reception of a doctrine which may make sense in criminal law but not – or only to a much more limited extent – in tort law.[113] It has also been suggested that some of the problems tackled by the doctrine of objective imputation could be solved by other means, such as the concepts of fault or state of necessity.[114] Nevertheless, on balance, the shift in the stance of the Civil Chamber has brought some clarity to the approach to causation, at least in a broad sense.

As regards the contributory activity of the victim, unlike the Civil Code, which does not mention it (cf. Art. 1902 ff.), the Criminal Code provides that if the victim has contributed to the production of harm suffered by her, the courts may reduce the amount of damages accordingly (Art. 114). However, such a rule is found in other statutes which lay down a tort liability regime, in particular where liability is strict (e.g. Art. 33.5 Hunting Act [LC];[115] Art. 145 Consumers Protection Act;[116] Art. 1.1 para. 2 Motor Vehicle Liability Act [LRCSCVM]).[117] This does not mean that contributory activity of the victim only reduces or excludes liability of the tortfeasor if liability of the latter is strict. While the Civil Code is silent, the courts apply the defence in practice; indeed, it is actually the most common defence on which defendants rely in practice.[118]

[112] The evolution is described by A. Ruda, 'Spain' in K. Oliphant and B. C. Steininger (eds.), *European Tort Law 2010* (Berlin/Boston: De Gruyter, 2011), 583. See also C. Díaz-Regañón García-Alcalá, *Responsabilidad objetiva y nexo causal en el ámbito sanitario* (Granada: Comares, 2006), 7.

[113] See F. Peña López, *Dogma y realidad del derecho de daños: imputación objetiva, causalidad y culpa en el sistema español y en los PETL* (Cizur Menor: Thomson-Reuters-Aranzadi, 2011), 22.

[114] See M. García-Ripoll Montijano, *Imputación objetiva, causa próxima y alcance de los daños indemnizables* (Granada: Comares, 2008), 20.

[115] Ley 1/1970, de 4 de abril, de caza (*BOE* No. 82, 6 April 1970).

[116] Real Decreto Legislativo 1/2007, de 16 de noviembre, por el que se aprueba el texto refundido de la Ley General para la Defensa de los Consumidores y Usuarios y otras leyes complementarias (*BOE* No. 287, 30 November 2007).

[117] Real Decreto Legislativo 8/2004, de 29 de octubre, por el que se aprueba el texto refundido de la Ley sobre responsabilidad civil y seguro en la circulación de vehículos a motor (*BOE* No. 267, 5 November 2004).

[118] See L. F. Reglero Campos, 'El nexo causal' in J. M. Busto Lago and L. F. Reglero Campos (eds.), *Lecciones de responsabilidad civil*, 2nd edn (Cizur menor: Thomson Reuters Aranzadi, 2013), 126.

D. *Liability for others*

As has been said before, the fact that two separate sets of statutory rules deal with tort liability, depending on whether or not the damaging act or omission is criminal, may cause similar cases to be solved differently. For instance, under Article 120.1 CP, the parents or guardians are liable on a subsidiary basis for damage caused by crimes or misdemeanours committed by adults aged eighteen who are under their parental authority or guardianship and living with them, provided that the parents or guardians have behaved negligently.[119] This is a problematic rule, since if the son or daughter is an adult (mostly commonly we are talking about a disabled adult) she will be liable as an author herself (Art. 116 CP), and whether or not she lives with her parents will be irrelevant – since the parental authority will have finished on her reaching majority. For this reason, Article 120.1 CP may seem absurd.[120] Even if the rule was applied to disabled adults upon whom the parental authority has been extended (Art. 171 CC), they would very likely escape criminal liability. While the relationship between Articles 120 and 116 CP is highly problematic, it seems there would be no criminal liability for the criminal procedure from which to start. The relevant forms of exoneration include, for example, Article 20.1 CP on mental disorder and Article 20.3 CP on serious alteration of the conscience of reality. Another opinion suggests that the rule may still be applicable to persons who have been judicially incapacitated but have nevertheless tortious capacity.[121]

The picture is even odder when compared with the full detail of the civil and criminal law rules. If damage is caused by a minor, and it amounts to a crime or misdemeanour, the minor will be held liable in tort – on a solidary basis with her parents, guardians, keepers or custodians – but only if she is over fourteen (Art. 61.3 and Art. 1.1 Organic Act on the Criminal Liability of Minors (LORPM)).[122] If minors are under fourteen their liability will have to be established according to the general provisions.[123] In contrast, if there is no crime or misdemeanour, liability of the parents

[119] See Muñoz Conde and García Arán, *Derecho Penal. Parte general*, 602.

[120] See Yzquierdo, *Sistema de responsabilidad civil, contractual y extracontractual*, 64.

[121] See Salas, *Responsabilidad civil e incapacidad*, 103.

[122] Ley Orgánica 5/2000, de 12 de enero, reguladora de la responsabilidad penal de los menores (*BOE* No. 11, of 13 January 2000), Final Disposition 2.1. This Act will be tackled later in this report.

[123] See Martin-Casals *et al.* 'Strict Liability under Spanish Law', 287.

or the guardians is a direct one (Art. 1903 paras. 2 and 3 CC). Moreover, and in contrast to the tort liability rules in the CP, the Civil Code reverses the burden of proof of fault of the parents. The special statutory regime on the criminal liability of minors seems rather a harsh one and its rules are in contradiction with those in the Civil Code.[124] In particular, if the minor is criminally liable, her guardians – in a broad sense – will be held liable in any case. Only if the guardians succeed in proving that they acted with only slight negligence may the court reduce their liability – though they will not reduce the liability of the minor herself (Art. 61.3 LORPM). This draws liability of the guardians close to strict liability.

As regards public authorities, tort liability for others is subsidiary provided that damage ensues from a criminal deed (Art. 121 CP). Therefore, if a teacher has negligently contributed to damage being caused and that amounts to a crime, a public authority (such as a local education authority, i.e. the municipality on which the school depends) will be held liable on a subsidiary basis. By contrast, the general rule of tort liability of public authorities is that they are strictly, directly and vicariously liable for the torts of their employees (Art. 139 Act on the Legal Regime of public administration and general administrative procedure (LRJAP)).[125] Whether the victim may also file a claim against the staff member of the public administration directly is a matter of controversy.[126] However, the public authority has a recourse action against the member of its personnel, at least where she behaved with intent or at least gross negligence (Art. 145.2 LRJAP). Concerning tort liability of public education institutions, it is governed by the latter regime – one of strict liability – inasmuch as it is caused as a result of a public service provided by the state. In this regard, it is immaterial whether the damaging act or omission of the student amounts to a crime or misdemeanour.[127]

Regarding tort liability of the entrepreneur for damage caused by their auxiliaries (e.g., employees), it is subsidiary according to the CP (Art. 120.4) and direct under the CC (Art. 1903.4). The same happens in

[124] See M. L. Atienza Navarro, *La responsabilidad civil por los hechos dañosos de los alumnos menores de edad* (Granada: Comares, 2000), 152, and M. R. Ornosa Fernández, *Derecho penal de menores* (Barcelona: Bosch, 2001), 445.

[125] Ley 30/1992, de 26 de noviembre, de Régimen Jurídico de las Administraciones Públicas y del Procedimiento Administrativo Común (*BOE* No. 285, 27 November 1992).

[126] See J. A. Moreno Gómez, *Responsabilidad de centros docentes y profesorado por daños causados por sus alumnos* (Madrid: McGraw-Hill, 1996), 49–50, 210.

[127] See Atienza, *La responsabilidad civil por los hechos dañosos de los alumnos menores de edad,* 248.

connection with the liability of teaching institutions below higher education (Art. 1903.5 CC). Moreover, the tort liability of the entrepreneur for the act of others according to the CP is strict.[128] In contrast to that, Art. 1903.4 is based on presumed fault.[129]

E. *Secondary/accessory liability*

Both the principals and accomplices can be criminally liable (Art. 27 CP). Principals are those who commit the crime alone, jointly with others, or by means of another who is used as an instrument (Art. 28.1 CP). Direct inducers and necessary co-operators – that is, those without whom the execution of the criminal deed would have been impossible – are equated to the principals (Art. 28.2 CP). Accomplices are those who are not included in the categories above but have co-operated to execute the criminal deed with acts before or during it (Art. 29 CP). As has been seen, both the authors and the accomplices will be liable in tort (Art. 116.2 CP).

In cases of subsidiary liability under the Criminal Code, it is enforced first against the property of the principals and then those of the accomplices (Art. 116.2 para. 2 CP). The Civil Code lacks an equivalent regime. Therefore a possible solution could be applying the tort law rules in the Criminal Code on an analogical basis.[130] Nonetheless, the justification of the solidary liability rule down by the Criminal Code may be the purpose to deal with the guilty persons in a more severe way, which would make such an analogical application impossible.[131] It may result that the Civil Code already provides a solution, since the general rule on liability of a plurality of persons is separate liability (*parciariedad*) as opposed to solidarity (Art. 1137 CC).[132] Finally, it has been suggested that context should not be lost between the differing tort and crime provisions: it would be better, this view argues, that each group of cases – i.e. alternative causation, joint causation, etc. – should be analysed on their own merits.[133]

[128] See Alastuey Dobón, 'Artículo 120', 478.

[129] See J. Solé Feliu, *La responsabilidad extracontractual del principal por hechos de sus auxiliares: principios y tendencias* (Madrid: Reus, 2012), 31.

[130] As suggested by J. Santos Briz, *La responsabilidad civil. Derecho sustantivo y procesal* (Madrid: Montecorvo, 1993), 512.

[131] See Yzquierdo, *Sistema de responsabilidad civil, contractual y extracontractual*, 405.

[132] See Á. Cristóbal Montes, *Mancomunidad o solidaridad en la responsabilidad plural por acto ilícito común* (Barcelona: Bosch, 1985), 112.

[133] See J. Solé Feliu, 'Pluralidad de causantes del daño y solidaridad' (2008) *Revista de Derecho Privado* 3–42.

F. *Defences*

Another of the most remarkable differences between criminal and tort law relates to defences. As has been mentioned, some of them (such as contributory activity of the victim) are provided for by the Criminal Code but not by the Civil Code, although they operate the same way in practice.

Something similar happens with regard to the state of necessity defence. According to the Criminal Code, the person who behaves in such a state will be exonerated from liability if certain conditions are met (Art. 20.5 CP). Some of these are exonerating circumstances (*eximentes*) which exclude wrongfulness: such as self-defence (*legítima defensa*) and having fulfilled a duty or the legitimate exercise of a right, profession or position (Art. 20.4 and 7 CP). As a result, the accused will not be liable either criminally or in a tort claim within the criminal process (cf. Art. 118 CP *a sensu contrario*).[134] With regard to the specific defence based on the exercise of a right, the final decision may depend on what private law or administrative law provide on the right at stake, if that is the case. This way, the unity or coherence of the whole legal system is achieved.[135]

The Civil Code remains silent so it is open to debate whether analogical application of the aforementioned provisions is possible or not. The prevailing scholarly opinion holds that the criminal law provisions may be taken into account even in private law cases where there is no direct relationship with a criminal deed.[136] This is rejected by another opinion, according to which the criminal law provisions have an exceptional nature, which prevent them from being applied outside the criminal arena.[137] Moreover, it has been suggested that both Codes rely on different principles.[138]

G. *Assessment of damages*

Another interesting example where the interplay between tort and crime may be seen is the application of criteria concerning assessment of damages to criminal law cases. We have already seen that in practice much will depend on how the public prosecutor presents the criminal case and quantifies the civil claim. However, the substantive law is not that clear

[134] See Salas, *Responsabilidad civil e incapacidad*, 100.

[135] See Quintero, *Parte General del Derecho Penal*, 83, 483.

[136] See J. M. Busto Lago, *La antijuricidad del daño resarcible* (Madrid: Tecnos, 1998).

[137] See Yzquierdo, *Sistema de responsabilidad civil, contractual y extracontractual*, 230.

[138] As regards state of necessity, see García-Ripoll, *Ilicitud, culpa y estado de necesidad*, 86 and 193.

either. The Criminal Code does not contain any rule on assessment of damages. Therefore it is usually accepted that the issue is left to the discretion of the courts. The only statutory determination is that compensation of damage has to include both pecuniary and non-pecuniary damage as well as damage both to the victim herself and to her relatives and third parties (Art. 112 CP). Therefore the court will be bound by any objective elements which the parties put forward during the evidentiary stage of the procedure.[139] The same is true of civil procedure, although the Civil Code does not mention any persons as beneficiaries of the compensation other than the victim. Only exceptionally does the criminal legislature refer to the criteria laid down by a private law statute, as for instance happens with regard to crimes against intellectual property (Art. 272 CP, which refers to the Intellectual Property Act).

Leaving that aside, it may be worth paying some attention to the statutory regime on tort liability for motor vehicle accidents. It is an important regime in practice, laying down a statutory tariff of compensation for damage caused by motor vehicles. The tariff provides on an explicit basis that its rules should not be applied in criminal cases, where the crime was committed with intent (Art. 1.1 of the Annex to the Act). This is consistent with the statutory rule according to which the use of a motor vehicle as an instrument to commit an intentional crime cannot be deemed a 'traffic-related event' (*hecho de la circulación*), that is, does not trigger liability pursuant to the special statutory regime (Art. 3.3 LRCSCVM). Damage caused by a crime committed intentionally also falls outside damage insurance (Art. 19 LCS), so the insured person who intentionally destroys his own property will not be able to recover anything against the insurer. However, there has been some debate as to whether the insurer may rely on such intent *vis à vis* a third person affected by such damage.[140] The issue was partly solved by a statutory reform according to which the use of the motor vehicle as an instrument for the commission of an intentional crime against the persons or the goods will not be considered a 'fact of the circulation', that is related to road traffic (Art. 1.4 LRCSCVM).[141] Nevertheless doubts may arise where a vehicle is used as a transport means

[139] See R. Juan Sánchez, *La responsabilidad civil en el proceso penal* (Madrid: La Ley, 2004), 205.

[140] See L. F. Reglero Campos, 'Responsabilidad civil y seguro en la circulación de vehículos de motor' in Reglero (ed.), *Tratado de responsabilidad civil*, II, 4th edn (Cizur menor: Aranzadi Civitas, 2008), 149.

[141] This was added to the LRCSCVM in 2000. See Art. 71 of the Ley 14/2000, de 29 de diciembre, de Medidas fiscales, administrativas y del orden social (*BOE* No. 313, of 30 December 2000).

and because of some sudden desire it is used as a means to assault a third person.[142]

In any case, it is worth noting that criminal courts which, as has been said, cannot apply the statutory tariff to assess damages in cases of intentional crimes, have stated that the tariff may be taken into account anyway on the basis of its objective and detailed character, in spite of the clear exclusion mentioned above. Nevertheless, case law leaves the tariff aside in particularly serious cases.[143] Apart from that, the fact is that the statutory tariff is nowadays applied as an orientation guide to many other types of accidents, such as medical malpractice.

H. *Insurance issues*

Criminal liability is not insurable under Spanish law and therefore insurers do not deal with it directly. Therefore, if the culprit is fined or sent to jail, this is a punishment that he has to bear personally. Such liability may be distinguished from the costs of litigating it, which may be covered by an insurance of legal defence, which may be contracted for separately or linked to liability insurance. Legal defence insurance (Art. 76.a) to f) Insurance Contract Act (LCS))[144] usually includes the costs of litigating both criminal liability and tort liability, amongst other things, although it may exclude one of them.[145]

Tort liability is insurable irrespective of whether or not it derived from a damaging act or omission amounting to a crime or misdemeanour (Art. 73 LCS). The victim will have a direct action against the insurer (Art. 117 CP and 76 LCS). The impact of insurance on tort litigation is unclear, but quite possibly very important. In particular, the development of liability insurance may have had an impact on tort practice: (a) courts have been influenced by the availability of insurance, which has on average increased the compensation awards, and (b) insurance has also fostered the spread of strict liability, either by way of statute or in practice.[146]

[142] See Reglero, 'Responsabilidad civil y seguro en la circulación de vehículos de motor', 153.

[143] See L. F. Reglero Campos, 'Valoración de daños corporales. El sistema valorativo de la ley de responsabilidad civil y seguro de vehículos a motor', in Reglero (ed.), *Tratado de responsabilidad civil*, I, 4th edn (Cizur menor: Aranzadi Civitas, 2008), 451.

[144] Ley 50/1980, de 8 de octubre, de Contrato de Seguro (*BOE* No. 250, of 17 October 1980).

[145] See A. J. Tapia Hermida, 'Artículo 76.a)' in F. Sánchez Calero (ed.), *Ley de contrato de seguro. Comentarios a la Ley 50/1980, de 8 de octubre, y sus modificaciones* (Cizur menor: Thomson Reuters Aranzadi, 2010), 1876–7.

[146] See Sánchez Calero, 'Artículo 73', 1596.

Apart from that, first party insurance also plays some role, such as victims having insured some goods against the risk of being stolen (Art. 51 LCS).

A public compensation scheme called *Consorcio de compensación de seguros* provides limited compensation for some victims of accidents where the author is unknown (and therefore there is no one to be sued) or uninsured (as the defendant is likely unable to satisfy the claim).[147] The *Consorcio* has a recourse action against, amongst others, the owner or the driver of the uninsured vehicle, as well as against the author or accomplices of the theft of the vehicle which caused the accident. It should be borne in mind that compulsory insurance regarding motor traffic accidents does not cover damage caused by stolen vehicles (Art. 5.3 LRCSCVM). Therefore the purpose of the *Consorcio* is to provide some relief to victims of personal injuries who would otherwise be probably left empty-handed. Moreover there are some statutory regimes providing public aid to victims of specific kinds of criminal deeds, such as terrorist attacks,[148] as an expression of public solidarity, not as a true compensation.[149]

1. Practical impact of the different resolutions on an individual

The practical impact of the different resolutions on an individual may obviously depend on the kind and extent of the measures adopted by the court. According to the Criminal Code, the convicted defendant will be held liable to compensate damage. This means: (a) restitution, (b) restoration of damage caused and (c) pecuniary compensation (Art. 110 CP). Restitution may be impossible whenever a third party acquired the good at stake in good faith and she is protected against the vindication of the good (Art. 111.2 CP). Leaving aside the fact that restitution may not properly belong to liability, this is an instance where recourse to the civil law concepts is required in order to apply a criminal provision.[150] With regard to criminal liability, the culprit may also be sent to prison or fined depending on the crime and the circumstances of

[147] See Real Decreto Legislativo 7/2004, de 29 de octubre, por el que se aprueba el texto refundido del Estatuto Legal del Consorcio de Compensación de Seguros (*BOE* No. 267, of 5 November 2004); J. L. Gayo Lafuente and A. Estella López, *El Consorcio de Compensación de Seguros y la responsabilidad civil de la circulación* (Granada: Comares, 1997), 13.

[148] Ley 29/2011, de 22 de septiembre, de reconocimiento y protección integral a las víctimas del terrorismo (*BOE* No. 229, of 23 September 2011).

[149] See A. Ruda, 'Spain' in K. Oliphant and B. C. Steininger (eds.), *European Tort Law 2011* (Berlin / Boston: De Gruyter, 2012), 632–5.

[150] See Muñoz Conde and García Arán, *Derecho Penal. Parte general*, 599.

the case. Compensation is the general remedy pursuant to the Civil Code (Art. 1902).

A monetary fine may have little effect for a culprit who has plenty of financial resources whereas it may be crushing for others. Such responsibility will not be transferred to the heirs of the culprit, due to its personal nature (Art. 130.1.1 CP). However, the civil law duty to compensate is transferable by death (Art. 659 CC).

Resolutions from one domain may impact the other. For instance, if the defendant and a victim settle the claim between them, the prosecutor is fully entitled to prosecute, but in many cases will choose not to do so. They might justify that decision to drop the case on the basis of a criminal law-related rationale such as the lack of intent by the defendant. If the prosecution goes forward, the criminal sanction may be reduced by the judge where the criminal has paid compensation to the victim already (Art. 21.5 CP). Such a payment can be made at any moment during the court procedure but at any rate not later than the moment in which the oral hearing takes place. Whether the culprit repents is irrelevant in this regard[151] and it is also not required that the victim has claimed any tort liability.[152] The mitigating circumstance will be applicable on the condition that compensation is paid on the initiative of the culprit[153] and that she has obtained the money paid lawfully.[154] Moreover, case law states that compensation has to be relevant and satisfactory from the victim's perspective.[155] Compensation has to be paid to the victim either directly or indirectly such as by a payment into the court.[156] Similarly, in order to suspend a prison sentence, 'civil liability deriving from the offence must have been satisfied in full, except if the court determines that the felon lacks financial resources' (Art. 81.3 CP). In addition, in order to substitute an imprisonment sentence by a fine or community service, the court must pay special attention to the fact of whether the felon 'has made a significant effort to make the victim whole' (Art. 88.1 CP).

A different issue is the relationship of hierarchy or equality in case of plurality of debtors as a result of the criminal judgment. Should the judge impose a fine and establish tort liability, the state and the victim may

[151] STS 2nd 12 May 2005 [RJ 2005/5140].

[152] See J. Córdoba Roda, 'Artículo 21.5ª' in Córdoba and García Arán (eds.), *Comentarios al Código Penal (Parte general)*, 249.

[153] STS 2nd Chamber, 27 December 2007 [RJ 2007/9067].

[154] See J. Goyena Huerta, 'Artículo 21.5ª' in Gómez Tomillo (ed.), *Comentarios al Código Penal*, 190.

[155] STS 2nd Chamber, 12 May 2005.

[156] STS 2nd Chamber, 13 November 2007 [RJ 2007/9115].

concur as creditors of the culprit. According to the Insolvency Act,[157] the state enjoys a general preference to recover tax debts and any other debts governed by public law (Art. 91.4). The victim of a tort enjoys the same general preference but is ranked after the state (Art. 91.5). However the claims for non-insured personal injury are ranked on par with the claims of the state referred to (Art. 91.5 2nd part). Tort liability claims derived from a crime against the Treasury and the Social Security have the same prority as the claims of private tort victims (Art. 91.5 para. 2).

6. Conclusion

Spanish law intentionally blurs any distinction between tort and crime. The rules for compensating wrongs, which are both torts and crimes are contained in the Criminal Code, not the Civil Code. Prosecutors bring civil damages claims within the criminal prosecution automatically, unless victims reserve or renounce their claim. Victims can directly intervene as private prosecutors (both where the public prosecutor is against the prosecution, and where he wishes to conduct it differently). As a matter of principle, every crime which causes damage generates civil liability.

One of the most troubling results of this blurring is the trend towards over-criminalisation. Criminal law does so many of the tasks of civil law, and does them more easily, faster, with less risk and in a more effective fashion. The only short-term problem for the victim arises when, as often happens, the public prosecutor evaluates the damages much lower than the civil party would and there is then nothing the civil party can do.

Part of this over-criminalisation can be seen in Spanish law incentivising the prosecution of non-criminal, or barely criminal, conduct. Cases typically addressed by tort law or civil law in other countries end up in criminal courts because the claimant registers a criminal complaint, regardless of the position of the public prosecutor. Breach of contracts, excessive executive compensation, environmental damage and defective products are regularly addressed by criminal courts. Combined with the low level of real prosecutorial discretion and the ability of investigating judges to institute cases of their own motion, a vast number of cases reach the criminal courts. In addition, the lack of a civil class action drives large multi-victim wrongs into the criminal court. The closest the courts have

[157] Ley 22/2003, de 9 de julio, Concursal (*BOE* No. 164, 10 July 2003), as amended by Ley 38/2011, de 10 de octubre, de reforma de la Ley 22/2003, de 9 de julio, Concursal (*BOE* No. 245, 11 October 2011).

come to criticism is of the 'Catalonian complaints' but that is in effect to blame the victim for filing a complaint to use the system, a system which actually has no way to reject that complaint.

Also, perversely enough, criminal courts tend in some instances to produce a conviction in order for the victim to obtain restitution. Because civil liability awarded by a criminal court must derive from the offence, there are signs that courts assert the existence of a criminal misconduct just to be able to provide the victim with the necessary compensation. Being conscious of the potential injustice of such decisions, if the courts impose a prison term it is typically one which can be either suspended or substituted by a fine or community service.

The exercise of a civil action in a criminal proceeding is fully appropriate when there is no doubt about the offender's liability to compensate. In other cases, it is obvious that it will entail an additional complexity of the criminal procedure. This causes delay in the resolution of criminal liabilities and is not a tenable position for Spanish law.

In a sense, this blurring of tort and crime has led to the 'monetarisation' of criminal justice and thus, the weakening of its ability to regulate society. In particular, the expressive function of criminal law is wasted. If criminal law should only deal with the most egregious violations of community values, then rubberstamping the 'criminal' label to decisions that deal with civil matters dents the expressive function of criminal law. If anything is criminal law, then nothing is criminal law.

7

Mixing and matching in Scottish delict and crime

JOHN BLACKIE AND JAMES CHALMERS

Scots law provides a distinct perspective on the relationship between tort and crime: it is a small jurisdiction with big neighbours. Reliant on case law, but producing a relatively small volume of it given the size of the jurisdiction, the development of Scots law is characterised by flexibility, innovation – and, often, uncertainty. The result has been a mixing of different concepts and traditions, creating a distinctive system but one which still keeps pace with developments elsewhere. It might come as a surprise that within the boundaries of its legal system Scots law has not seen tort and crime running together.

1. Locating criminal law and delict: practical and organisational observations

In Scots law, delict is typically and uncontroversially regarded as part of private law, and more specifically part of the law of obligations. The position of criminal law is theoretically clear but more ambiguous in practice. The leading student text on criminal law correctly reminds students at the outset that criminal law is part of public and not private law. That position is uncontroversial and reflects the commonly understood nature of crimes as public wrongs,[1] but the sharp-eyed student might note the oddity that one of the authors was (before retirement) employed as a lecturer in private law.[2]

[1] See R. A. Duff and S. E. Marshall, 'Public and Private Wrongs', in J. Chalmers, F. Leverick and L. Farmer (eds.), *Essays in Criminal Law in Honour of Sir Gerald Gordon* (Edinburgh University Press, 2010), 70.

[2] T. H. Jones and M. G. A. Christie, *Criminal Law*, 5th edn (Edinburgh: W. Green, 2012), para 1–02. Christie was a lecturer in private law at the University of Aberdeen prior to his retirement, teaching criminal law and Scottish legal history. Jones is currently Professor of Public Law at the University of Swansea, a title which reflects his broader interests in constitutional law and legislation.

A. Academic organisation and structure

Until recently,[3] a typical law faculty might be divided into four departments, including a 'private law' or 'Scots law' one.[4] The terms 'private law' and 'Scots law' were often treated as near synonymous. While criminal law, as a core part of the law degree,[5] was invariably taught out of these departments, it occupied a somewhat uncertain position even when taught within the department described as Scots law.[6] Gloag and Henderson's *Introduction to the Law of Scotland* – for many years the core text for Scots law students,[7] and in practice a private law text despite its main title – included for most of its history a chapter on criminal law, but this was excised in 1995.[8] The current absence of departmental demarcations within Scottish law schools means that criminal law is typically regarded as somewhat free-standing and not belonging to any particular domain, with most academic criminal lawyers teaching almost exclusively in the areas of criminal law, criminal justice and evidence. Those who teach delict generally combine this with other areas of private law.

In research terms, there would appear to be no academic writer who has made major contributions to both fields of study. Some criminal lawyers have written on delictual issues,[9] but it has not been common for private

[3] Most Scottish university law faculties became unitary law schools in the 1990s, without formal departmental divisions. This reflected a general trend in university administration whereby small academic departments were amalgamated into larger units over this period.

[4] E.g. Edinburgh had four departments: Scots Law, Constitutional Law, Civil Law and International Law: see J. W. Cairns and H. L. MacQueen, *Learning and the Law: A Short History of Edinburgh Law School* (Edinburgh Law School, 2013), Ch. VI. Aberdeen operated with departments of Private Law, Public Law, Jurisprudence, and Conveyancing and Professional Practice.

[5] Students who wish to enter legal practice must pass courses in both criminal law and delict. Both subjects are also (but with rare exceptions) compulsory components of the LLB degree in Scotland.

[6] See J. Chalmers, 'Resorting to Crime' in R. Anderson, J. Chalmers and J. MacLeod (eds.), *Glasgow Tercentenary Essays: 300 Years of the School of Law* (Edinburgh: Avizandum Publishing Ltd, 2014), 70.

[7] The first and most recent editions are W. M. Gloag and R. C. Henderson, *Introduction to the Law of Scotland* (Edinburgh: W. Green, 1927) and Lord Eassie and H. L. MacQueen, *Gloag and Henderson: The Law of Scotland*, 13th edn (Edinburgh: W. Green, 2012). Although this remains an important work of reference, students will normally rely on specialist texts corresponding to modules in individual areas of law.

[8] W. A. Wilson and A. D. M. Forte (eds.), *Introduction to the Law of Scotland*, 10th edn (Edinburgh: W. Green, 1995), ix.

[9] See, e.g., P. R. Ferguson, *Drug Injuries and the Pursuit of Compensation* (London: Sweet & Maxwell, 1996); J. Chalmers, 'Remedies' in G Cameron *et al.*, *Delict* (Edinburgh: W. Green, 2007), Ch. 10; F. Leverick, 'Counting the Ways of Becoming a Primary Victim" (2007) 11 *EdinLR* 258.

lawyers to write on criminal law except where the interaction of private and criminal law is concerned.[10] There is little evidence of reference to delict in writing on criminal law,[11] or *vice versa.*[12]

B. *Judicial organisation and structure*

Within Scotland, all judges have jurisdiction over both criminal and civil matters, with the exception of lay justices in the Justice of the Peace court, which deals with minor criminal matters, There is, however, no procedure which allows criminal and civil matters to be heard in a single action.[13]

The supreme courts within Scotland are the Court of Session (for civil cases) and the High Court of Justiciary (for criminal cases). Both of these courts have first instance and appellate jurisdiction. While the courts are formally separate, judges are appointed simultaneously to both of them, and are referred to as Senators of the College of Justice. Approximately two-thirds of days on which these courts sit are to deal with criminal business, and one-third to deal with civil business.[14] The proportion of civil business may reduce substantially as a result of recent legislation which will significantly raise the minimum sum which must be disputed.[15] All Senators are competent to deal with all civil and criminal business, although the specialist knowledge of individual judges may be taken into account in the allocation of business. This is formalised in the context

[10] D. M. Walker, 'The Interaction of Obligations and Crime', in R. F. Hunter (ed.), *Justice and Crime* (Edinburgh: T&T Clark, 1993), 15; J. Blackie, 'Unity in Diversity: The History of Personality Rights in Scots law', in N. R. Whitty and R. Zimmermann (eds.), *Rights of Personality in Scots Law: A Comparative Perspective* (Dundee University Press, 2009), 31; J. Blackie, 'The Protection of Corpus in Modern and Early Modern Scots Law', in E. Descheemaeker and H. Scott (eds.) *Iniuria and the Common Law* (Oxford: Hart Publishing, 2013), 155; J. Blackie, 'The Interaction of Crime and Delict in Scotland', in M. Dyson (ed.), *Unravelling Tort and Crime* (Cambridge University Press, 2014), 356.

[11] The leading modern text on criminal law contains no index entry for either 'delict' or 'tort': G. H. Gordon, *The Criminal Law of Scotland*, 3rd edn by M. G. A Christie (Edinburgh: W. Green, 2000–1).

[12] A significant number of criminal cases are cited in D. M. Walker, *The Law of Delict in Scotland*, 2nd edn (Edinburgh: W. Green, 1981) but the number is small in the context of the book as a whole. Cf E. C. Reid, *Personality, Confidentiality and Privacy in Scots Law* (Edinburgh: W. Green, 2010), who does discuss criminal cases in the context of assault.

[13] It is, however, possible for a criminal court to make a compensation order following conviction for a criminal offence: see below.

[14] See the 2008–9 figures at Lord Gill, *Report of the Scottish Civil Courts Review* (2009), 276 table 2.

[15] At present, most civil cases brought in the Court of Session must have a minimum financial value of £5,000. Section 39 of the Courts Reform (Scotland) Act 2014, when brought into force, will raise this to £100,000.

of special arrangements in place for commercial business – sometimes referred to as the 'Commercial Court', although this is a shorthand reference to the use of particular procedures rather than a separate court – the result is simply that a number of judges have been informally designated as 'commercial judges' for practical purposes.[16]

The other tier of Scotland's court system is the Sheriff Court. Sheriffs have jurisdiction over both civil and criminal cases.[17] Approximately the same number of civil and criminal cases are raised in the Sheriff Court each year.[18] There is at present no formal system of judicial specialisation in the Sheriff Court, although the Courts Reform (Scotland) Act 2014 permits the Lord President (the head of the Scottish judiciary) to create such a system.[19]

As for courts outside of Scotland itself, the UK Supreme Court has jurisdiction over civil appeals from Scotland.[20] Only a handful of such cases are heard each year. In criminal cases, the same court has a limited jurisdiction to consider what are termed 'devolution issues' (questions relating to the competence of the Scottish Government or Parliament) or 'compatibility issues' (questions relating to the compatibility of official action with human rights). It has, however, no power to rule on matters

[16] See Scottish Court Service, 'Commercial Actions', www.scotcourts.gov.uk/the-courts/court-of-session/taking-action/commercial-actions, all websites last accessed November 2014. At the time of writing three judges (Lord Malcolm, Lord Woolman and Lord Tyre) were designated 'commercial judges'.

[17] But see *Davenport* v. *Corinthian Motor Policies at Lloyds* 1991 SC 372, where it was held that the Sheriff Court, in hearing a criminal case, was not the 'same court' as the Sheriff Court in hearing a civil one. The consequence of this was that Art. 5 Brussels Convention, which provides that a person domiciled in one contracting state may be sued in another 'as regards a civil claim for damages or restitution which is based on an act giving rise to criminal proceedings, in the court seised of those proceedings, to the extent that that court has jurisdiction under its own law to entertain civil proceedings', does not allow a criminal prosecution to found any basis for a civil action, and certainly not for the two to be combined. See also G. Maher and B. J. Rodger, *Civil Jurisdiction in the Scottish Courts* (Edinburgh: W. Green, 2010), para. 4–31.

[18] Compare Lord Gill, *Report of the Scottish Civil Courts Review* (2009), 286 table 1 (124,039 civil actions initiated in 2008) with Crown Office figures stating that 127,418 criminal cases were disposed of by court action in 2007–8. This Review produced more detailed figures than are routinely published.

[19] Courts Reform (Scotland) Act 2014, ss. 34–37. Specialisation must be taken into account in the allocation of judicial business, but will not bar sheriffs from hearing any particular category of case. The Act also creates 'summary sheriffs' who will have jurisdiction in both civil and criminal matters, but to a limited extent in both.

[20] See, generally, J. Chalmers, 'Scottish Appeals and the Proposed Supreme Court' (2004) 8 *Edin LR* 4; N. Walker, *Final Appellate Jurisdiction in the Scottish Legal System* (Edinburgh: Scottish Government, 2010).

of criminal law beyond the scope of these issues.[21] It has been said that civil courts should not pronounce on criminal matters because – aside from any general question of principle about the appropriateness of a civil court pronouncing on a criminal matter, or *vice versa* – the structure of the Scottish court system means that this would raise a conflict between the right of appeal to the UK Supreme Court in civil cases and that court's limited jurisdiction in criminal matters.[22]

C. *Professional and educational requirements*

The Scottish legal profession is split into two branches: solicitors, who make up by far the largest part of the profession; and advocates, who have exclusive rights of audience in the higher courts.[23] Admission to both branches requires a pass in examinations in, amongst other subjects, both criminal law and delict, normally at university but possibly in a professional examination. There is no additional academic qualification required for judicial office, although judges must participate in training offered by the Judicial Institute once appointed. Senators are normally appointed from the Faculty of Advocates, and there is an expectation that an advocate seeking such an appointment will have spent a period as an 'advocate depute', commissioned by the Crown to prosecute criminal cases. This is not, however, essential. Historically it would also have been normal for judges to have had some experience of personal injury work as practitioners, but that may no longer be universal given that such work now forms a lesser part of the caseload of members of the Faculty of Advocates.[24]

Both advocates and solicitors are appointed as generalists and are not limited to any one area of legal practice. It is common, however, for solicitors to specialise (especially in urban areas). Since 1990, the Law Society of Scotland has operated a 'specialist accreditation' scheme. Solicitors can apply for accreditation as specialists in a number of areas, including

[21] Criminal Procedure (Scotland) Act 1995, s. 124(2).

[22] *Law Hospital NHS Trust* v. *Lord Advocate* 1996 SC 301 (the case refers to appeals to the Appellate Committee of the House of Lords, which preceded the Supreme Court, but the principle is the same).

[23] That is the High Court, the Court of Session and the Supreme Court. It is now possible for solicitors to qualify for 'extended rights of audience' in these courts; such solicitors are commonly referred to as 'solicitor advocates'.

[24] A trend which is likely to become even more pronounced as a result of the Courts Reform (Scotland) Act 2014, noted earlier.

medical negligence law, personal injury law and professional negligence law.[25] There is no specialist accreditation available in criminal law. Advocates, on the other hand, will list a number of specialist areas in the Faculty of Advocates' directory.[26] In February 2014, 109 advocates were listed as having a specialism in personal injury law, 104 in criminal trials. Seventeen advocates appeared on both these lists, with only two of the seventeen being QCs (senior advocates).

D. Formal distinctions

The question of whether a rule is a criminal or civil one should be specified in legislative drafting, and in modern practice it is rarely left unclear. Some legislative offences remain on the statute book which are less than clear. In particular, breach of statutory provisions can sometimes result in 'civil penalties': these are awkward and may not really belong to either area.

It is, of course, for the courts to decide on the scope of a common law rule. Historically, summary criminal procedure was a convenient method for recovering 'penalties' for breach of statute law[27] without it being particularly clear whether such 'penalties' were really criminal or civil matters.[28] This problem seems to have disappeared in modern practice, perhaps due to changes in drafting technique, but its disappearance seems not to have been clearly documented.

The Scottish Law Commission, as a standing law reform body,[29] can examine both criminal and civil law, although it did not do much criminal law work until relatively recently.[30] The recent shift to include criminal law has tended to be because a commissioner has been appointed to focus on criminal law work[31] rather than by someone crossing boundaries in their area of expertise.

[25] As of February 2014, there were six accredited specialists in medical negligence law, eight in medical negligence law (defender only), seventy in personal injury law, and seven in professional negligence law. See www.lawscot.org.uk/wcm/lssservices/find_a_solicitor/Core/directory.aspx.

[26] This is available online at www.advocates.org.uk/stables/index.html, where fifty different specialisms (from Admiralty to Valuation and Rating) are listed. It follows on from an earlier hard copy publication: Faculty of Advocates, *Directory* (1992).

[27] See, e.g., T. Trotter, *Summary Criminal Jurisdiction According to the Law of Scotland* (Edinburgh: W. Hodge, 1936), 4–7.

[28] A problem also in English law: see, e.g., *Brown* v. *Allweather Mechanical Grouting Co Ltd* [1954] 2 QB 443.

[29] Law Commissions Act 1965.

[30] C. H. W. Gane, 'Criminal Law Reform in Scotland' (1998) 3 *SLPQ* 101.

[31] Initially Gerry Maher, then Patrick Layden.

E. *The purposes of criminal law and delict*

It is difficult to discern any distinctively Scottish articulation of the purposes of criminal law. The absence of any clear statement of these may in part be a consequence of the absence of any attempt to systematise and codify this area of law.[32] The courts have frequently worked by analogy or even assertion rather than by reference to principle,[33] while the standard student text offers an account of general Anglo-American theory rather than a distinctively Scottish statement, although it notes one Scottish case where it was said that the victim's views on sentencing were not a matter to be taken into account by a criminal court.[34] Statutory provision has been made for a Scottish Sentencing Council which will, amongst other things, produce guidelines on 'the principles and purposes of sentencing' in criminal cases.[35] The commencement of these provisions was delayed due to financial constraints, but it is now understood that the Council will commence its work in late 2015.[36]

It is easier, perhaps, to identify the purposes of the law of delict, which can be discerned from the Scottish approach to damages. The purpose of an award of damages is *restitutio in integrum*: the wronged party should be put as nearly as possible into the position which they would have been but for the delict.[37] The degree of fault on the part of the wrongdoer is irrelevant to the damages which should be awarded.[38] So, for example, in a successful action for defamation, the damages awarded will be the same regardless of whether the publication of the defamatory material was in good faith or malicious.[39] Scots law does not recognise any form

[32] Cf. E. Clive, P. Ferguson, C. Gane and A. McCall Smith, *A Draft Criminal Code for Scotland with Commentary* (2003), 5: the authors note that their work was based on 'procedural' values of accessibility, comprehensibility, consistency and certainty and that they had not consciously addressed 'political' values.

[33] Gordon, *The Criminal Law of Scotland*, vol. 1, paras. 1.44–1.45.

[34] Jones and Christie, *Criminal Law*, paras. 1.16–1.20, citing *HM Advocate* v. *McKenzie* 1990 JC 62.

[35] Criminal Justice and Licensing (Scotland) Act 2010, s 3(3)(a). A non-statutory Sentencing Commission for Scotland existed between 2003 and 2006; its work addressed a number of specialist topics rather than questions of general principle.

[36] Cf. Criminal Justice Act 2003, s. 142, which provides a statutory statement of the purposes of sentencing in English law. The Bill which led to the 2010 Act did, as introduced into the Scottish Parliament, include a statement of the principles of sentencing (s. 1) but this was removed following a critical response from the Justice Committee: *Stage 1 Report on the Criminal Justice and Licensing (Scotland) Bill* (18th Report, 2009 (Session 3)), paras. 34–8.

[37] See J. Chalmers, 'Remedies' in Cameron *et al.*, *Delict*, para. 10.19.

[38] The case law is reviewed by Chalmers, 'Remedies'.

[39] *Stein* v. *Beaverbrook Newspapers Ltd* 1968 SC 272, although cf. the earlier case of *Cunningham* v. *Duncan and Jamieson* (1889) 16 R 383.

of 'punitive', 'aggravated' or 'exemplary' damages.[40] The only wrinkle in Scots law's rigid adherence to a restitutionary approach seems to be damages for assault, which may be reduced if the pursuer provoked the defender's conduct.[41]

2. Procedural aspects

It might reasonably be expected that Scots law would have something analogous to the 'timing rule'[42] in English law, whereby a party to a civil action (most likely the defender) could apply for an action to be suspended ('sisted') pending the outcome of a criminal case. However, the position is unclear. It is certainly true that one writer, perhaps the only one to address it expressly, has denied the existence of any such rule.[43] That claim, however, proceeds on a misreading of the authority cited, which states merely that civil and criminal remedies are independent and so the imposition of a penalty does not defeat a civil claim.[44] Beyond this the matter seems simply not to have been addressed. Discussions of the power of a civil court to order a sist simply do not advert to the possibility of this being justified by reference to a concurrent criminal case.[45] Given the broad discretion of courts to sist civil cases, there seems to be no reason why an application for a sist could not be founded on the existence

40 *Black* v. *North British Railway Co* 1908 SC 444.

41 See *Ross* v. *Bryce* 1972 SLT (Sh Ct) 76 and subsequent cases, see Section 3.F below.

42 M. Dyson, 'The Timing of Tortious and Criminal Actions for the Same Wrong' (2012) 71 *CLJ* 86.

43 Walker, *The Law of Delict in Scotland*, 16.

44 G. J. Bell, *Principles of the Law of Scotland*, 10th edn (Edinburgh: T&T Clark, 1899), §§ 548, 551.

45 See, e.g., Æ. J. G. Mackay, *The Practice of the Court of Session*, vol. 1 (Edinburgh: T&T Clark, 1877), 506–11; J. Dove Wilson, *The Practice of the Sheriff Courts of Scotland in Civil Causes*, 4th edn (Edinburgh: Bell & Bradfute, 1891), 259–60; W. Wallace, *The Practice of the Sheriff Court of Scotland* (Edinburgh: W. Green, 1909), 257–9; T. A. Fyfe, *The Law and Practice of the Sheriff Courts of Scotland* (Edinburgh: W. Hodge, 1913), para. 466; G. R. Thomson, 'Practice and Procedure', in *Encyclopaedia of the Laws of Scotland*, vol. XI (Edinburgh: W. Green, 1931), § 1299; W. J. Dobie, *Law and Practice of the Sheriff Courts in Scotland* (Edinburgh: W. Hodge, 1948), 176–8; D. Maxwell, *The Practice of the Court of Session* (Edinburgh: Scottish Courts Administration, 1980), Ch. 10; I. Macphail, *Sheriff Court Practice*, 3rd edn by T. Welsh (Edinburgh: W. Green, 2006), paras. 13–71 to 13–80; C. Hennessy, *Civil Procedure and Practice*, 3rd edn (Edinburgh: W. Green, 2008), para. 15–04; D. Sheldon, 'Sisting of the Action and Wakening', in N. Macfadyen (ed.), *Court of Session Practice* (Haywards Heath: Tottel, 2005), Ch. 5 para. 502; 'Civil Procedure' in *The Laws of Scotland, Stair Memorial Encyclopaedia* (Edinburgh: Law Society of Scotland), § 170.

of a parallel criminal prosecution, but there does not appear to be any reported case on the point.

This is not as surprising as it might seem at first glance. Historically, one justification offered for the English rule was that an injured party should not be allowed to 'abstain from prosecuting' or 'waive the felony' and seek a civil remedy instead; instead, he had a public duty to bring the offender to justice through the criminal courts.[46] That justification was absent in Scotland, given the extreme rarity of private prosecution.[47] More recent English cases have approached the issue of timing from the perspective of the defendant's interests: asking, for example, whether it is fair that a defendant in a civil case might be compelled to disclose his likely defence to any future criminal prosecution.[48] While that argument of principle would be (almost) as strong in Scotland as in England,[49] the longstanding separation of public criminal prosecution and private civil remedy – alongside a relatively strict approach to the prevention of delay in criminal trials, particularly in serious cases[50] – may have deprived any potential timing rule of a foundation from which to develop.

Given these observations, it is perhaps not surprising that one case where the timing issue did receive some attention is the 1909 decision in *J & P Coats Ltd* v. *Brown*,[51] where C sought permission to bring a private prosecution against B, whom they alleged to have committed fraud. The Lord Advocate had declined to prosecute, but suggested that C should bring a civil action against B and that if this were successful he would reconsider his decision and might bring a prosecution at that stage. The court granted permission for a private prosecution,[52] and the Lord Justice-Clerk commented that:[53]

46 See the authorities canvassed by Swinfen Eady LJ in *Smith* v. *Selwyn* [1914] 3 KB 98, 105.

47 An issue discussed immediately below.

48 See *Jefferson* v. *Bhetcha* [1979] 1 WLR 898; Dyson, 'The Timing of Tortious and Criminal Actions', 99–103, 110–12.

49 But not quite, as Scots law has historically been more receptive to recognising obligations of disclosure by the defence in criminal cases: see J. Glynn, 'Disclosure' [1993] *Crim LR* 841, 842–3.

50 See J. Chalmers and F. Leverick, *Criminal Defences and Pleas in Bar of Trial* (Edinburgh: W. Green, 2006), Ch. 16.

51 1909 SC (J) 29.

52 B was convicted and admonished (that is, a conviction was recorded but no further punishment was imposed), a sentence which the prosecutor expressly requested: see 1909 2 SLT 370.

53 1909 SC (J) 29, 36.

> It is quite contrary to the order of procedure in criminal law administration that the whole circumstances of a case should first be thrashed out in a civil Court, with possibly a succession of proceedings of review, ending, it may be, in the House of Lords after a litigation extending over years, and that then the question of criminal prosecution should be finally determined ... civil proceedings might be seriously hampered by a defender being able to decline to give evidence which might incriminate him, if he was in the position of knowing that a future criminal prosecution was hanging over his head. Both sides might be hampered by such a course being taken.

A. *Private parties in the criminal courts*

Private prosecution for criminal offences is practically unknown in Scotland. In solemn procedure (that is, jury trial) a private prosecution can only be brought with the consent of the Lord Advocate or the High Court of Justiciary. There appears to have been only one such prosecution over the last century, and that was in a case where the public prosecutor would clearly have wished to prosecute had he not barred himself from doing so.[54] There has been no political pressure to expand the right of private prosecution, which is generally treated as a curious anomaly of some interest but little real significance.[55] While the Scottish prosecutor is never legally obliged to prosecute,[56] and has a broad discretion to pursue alternatives to prosecution or take no action at all,[57] recent legislation will give victims (or alleged victims) of crime a formal right to request review of decisions not to prosecute.[58]

In summary procedure, prosecutions may only be brought by the procurator fiscal unless another enactment expressly provides.[59] The only

[54] *X* v. *Sweeney* 1982 JC 70. The last case prior to this was *J & P Coats* v. *Brown* 1909 SC (J) 29, discussed above.

[55] See, e.g., P. Duff, 'The Prosecution Service: Independence and Accountability' in P. Duff and N. Hutton (eds.), *Criminal Justice in Scotland* (Aldershot: Ashgate, 1999), 115, 117. The difference between English and Scottish practice is significant here, but English developments mean that the two systems appear slowly to have converged towards something closer to the Scottish model. See most recently *R (Gujra)* v. *Crown Prosecution Service* [2012] UKSC 52, [2013] 1 AC 484; F. Stark, 'The Demise of the Private Prosecution?' (2013) 72 *CLJ* 7.

[56] Unless, perhaps, a failure to prosecute might violate obligations to a victim under the ECHR: cf. most recently app no 5786/08 *Söderman* v. *Sweden*, ECtHR, 12 November 2013.

[57] S. Moody and J. Tombs, 'Alternatives to Prosecution: The Public Interest Redefined' [1993] *Crim LR* 357.

[58] Victims and Witnesses (Scotland) Act 2014, s. 4. This will give effect to Art. 11 of Directive 2012/29/EU of the European Parliament and of the Council of 25 October 2012 establishing minimum standards on the rights, support and protection of victims of crime.

[59] Criminal Procedure (Scotland) Act 1995, s. 133(5).

significant example of such a power is the right of an education authority to prosecute parents for offences of failing to secure education for their children.[60] Other statutes may in theory confer a right of private prosecution (although it is unclear whether any such provisions are still in force).[61]

B. *Overlap between civil and criminal proceedings*

As a general rule, decisions in criminal cases are not binding in civil cases, and *vice versa*.[62] Even when facts have been proven beyond reasonable doubt in a criminal case, this represents only the judgment of the court on the evidence presented before it, and the verdict will have no validity outside of those proceedings.[63]

By statute, however, a criminal conviction is now admissible in civil proceedings as evidence that a person committed the offence concerned.[64] It is not conclusive evidence, except in defamation cases.[65] That provision duplicates an English one[66] which was introduced following a report of the Law Reform Committee[67] and a number of English cases where plaintiffs brought actions for libel, claiming that they were not guilty of the offences of which they had been convicted.[68] There is no record in the law reports of any such action having been attempted in Scotland.[69]

[60] Education (Scotland) Act 1980, ss. 35–43.

[61] The only example cited in G. Gordon and C. H. W. Gane (eds.), *Renton and Brown's Criminal Procedure*, 6th edn (Edinburgh: W. Green, 1996), para. 3–15 n. 6 is the Game (Scotland) Act 1832, but this has recently been repealed: Wildlife and Natural Environment (Scotland) 2011, Sch. 1(2), para 1. Notably, the 1832 Act provided that *either* civil or criminal proceedings could be taken, but not both.

[62] See M. L. Ross and J. Chalmers, *Walker and Walker: The Law of Evidence in Scotland*, 4th edn (Haywards Heath: Bloomsbury, 2015), para. 11.5.3.

[63] So, in *Howitt* v. *HM Advocate; Duffy* v. *HM Advocate* 2000 JC 284, it was held that where A had been tried and for offences allegedly committed with B and acquitted, B (who had been out of the country at the time of the first trial) could nevertheless be prosecuted at a later date for committing the offences along with A.

[64] Law Reform (Miscellaneous Provisions) (Scotland) Act 1968, s. 10.

[65] Ibid., s. 12. [66] Civil Evidence Act 1968, s. 13.

[67] Fifteenth Report of the English Law Reform Committee, Cmnd 3391. See I. D. Macphail, *Evidence* (Edinburgh: Law Society of Scotland, 1987), para. 11.15.

[68] Principally *Hinds* v. *Sparks* [1964] *Crim LR* 717; *Goody* v. *Odhams Press* [1967] 1 QB 333. See further M. Dyson, 'Civil Law Responses to Criminal Judgments in England and Spain' (2012) 3 *JETL* 308, 320–2.

[69] The matter appears to receive no attention in A. G. Walker and N. M. L. Walker, *The Law of Evidence in Scotland* (Edinburgh: W. Hodge, 1964). In *Shaw* v. *Johnston* (1894) 2 SLT 324, the defender was permitted to rely on extract convictions in support of a plea of

C. *Overlaps between criminal and civil cases: compensation and sentencing issues*

1. Private compensation

While the payment of compensation would in principle be a relevant factor in mitigation of sentence,[70] there is no statutory obligation on the court to take this into account,[71] nor does it appear to have featured prominently in the practice of the courts.[72] A court may defer sentence 'on such conditions as the court may determine',[73] which may include the payment of compensation (more commonly, 'the amount involved in an offence of dishonesty').[74]

2. State compensation

The report of a 1961 working party, which led to the creation of a British criminal injuries compensation scheme, remarked that the 'common law right to bring an action for damages is practically useless in relation to crimes of violence',[75] because offenders were 'as a rule' either unknown or had no means and were therefore not worth suing.[76] The Criminal Injuries

veritas, but the defamatory statement in that case was specifically that the pursuer was a 'returned convict'.

70 Subject to caveats such as those identified in the English case of *R* v. *Crosby and Hayes* (1974) 60 Cr App R 234, offenders should not be sentenced differently on the ground of means alone. It may be that compensation is therefore only relevant insofar as it evidences remorse (cf. A. Ashworth, *Sentencing and Criminal Justice*, 6th edn (Cambridge University Press, 2010), 181–2).

71 See the list of matters which the court is statutorily obliged to take into account in *Renton and Brown's Criminal Procedure*, para. 22–19.

72 See C. G. B. Nicholson, *Sentencing: Law and Practice in Scotland*, 2nd edn (Edinburgh: W. Green, 1992), paras. 9–12 to 9–40 and *Renton and Brown's Criminal Procedure*, paras. 22–27 to 22–35. Both texts review the (non-statutory) matters which have been considered by the courts to be of relevance; the payment of compensation is not mentioned in either instance.

73 Criminal Procedure (Scotland) Act 1995, s. 202. Cf. the English provisions on deferred sentence, which expressly highlight the possibility of the offender making reparation to the victim: Criminal Justice Act 2003, Sch. 23, para. 1. Beyond the possibility offered by the deferred sentence procedure, the criminal courts have no power to order restitution of property. In the unusual case of *Chief Constable of Strathclyde* v. *Sharp* 2002 SLT (Sh Ct) 95 the police resorted to the civil courts to establish ownership of a car they had taken possession of in the course of a criminal investigation, but where no criminal proceedings had resulted.

74 *Renton and Brown's Criminal Procedure*, para. 23–153.

75 *Compensation for Victims of Crimes of Violence* (Cmnd 1406: 1961), para. 9.

76 Ibid., para. 4. For a more recent expression of the same view, see *Criminal Injuries Compensation Board: Seventeenth Report* (Cmnd 8401: 1981), para. 53.

Compensation Board mentioned in its 1970 report that if it had the power to take recourse against offenders to repay compensation payments which it had made, there would only have been nineteen cases – out of 5,614 awards made by the Board – where they could usefully have exercised that power.[77]

Establishing the extent to which victims of crime resort to suing the offender in tort is difficult,[78] but empirical research on personal injury actions in court suggests that it is very rare. Court action based on criminal activity simply does not feature to any significant extent in such work.[79] Even in cases which might clearly involve criminal liability, such as vehicular accidents where road traffic offences are likely to have been committed, the commission of a crime is not a significant factor for the lawyer pursuing a case on behalf of the injured party. Instead, their work will focus on establishing negligence on the part of the defender, along with questions of causation and quantum;[80] any criminal liability on the part of the defender is not of assistance in answering these questions.

There have been two stages in the development of compensation for victims of crime in Scotland which might have resulted in a degree of integration between criminal and delictual liability.[81] In both instances, the opportunity was not taken up.

[77] *Criminal Injuries Compensation Board: Sixth Report* (Cmnd 4494: 1970), para. 13 and Appendix A. See also *Criminal Injuries Compensation Board: Tenth Report* (Cmnd 5791: 1974), para. 19, noting that there had been four instances that year of the Board having been 'repaid by victims from damages they recovered in civil actions against their assailants'.

[78] In 1999, Peter Cane claimed that such recourse had 'definitely increased in recent years': P. Cane, *Atiyah's Accidents, Compensation and the Law*, 6th edn (Cambridge University Press, 1999), 249, n 1; this was subsequently revised to the more cautious 'apparently increased': 7th edn (Cambridge University Press, 2006), 300, n. 1; 8th edn (Cambridge University Press, 2013), 299, n. 1.

[79] See, e.g., H. Genn and A. Paterson, *Paths to Justice Scotland* (Oxford: Hart Publishing, 2001), 22, noting that 'situations where violence raised the possibility of civil actions' were included in the study; it does not however feature significantly in the subsequent analysis. It is significant that in identifying the 'justiciable events' which formed the basis of the study, the researchers unhesitatingly distinguished between 'civil matters' and 'criminal matters' subject to this minor caveat. See also E. Samuel, *In the Shadow of the Small Claims Court: The Impact of Small Claims Procedure on Personal Injury Claimants and Litigation* (Edinburgh: Scottish Office, 1998).

[80] See H. Genn, *Hard Bargaining: Out of Court Settlement in Personal Injury Actions* (Oxford: Clarendon Press, 1987), Ch. 4.

[81] In England and Wales, the Winn Committee had in the 1960s considered the possibility of 'dual jurisdiction' whereby a criminal court might deal with compensation issues, and emphatically rejected it: *Report of the Committee on Personal Injuries Litigation* (Cmnd 3691: 1968), paras. 380–96.

The first of these is the creation of a national scheme for criminal injuries compensation, resulting from the report of a working party in 1961.[82] This followed earlier work suggesting that modern criminal law had 'almost completely lost sight' of reparation from the offender to the victim, something which had been the 'basis of early law', and that punishment could not be regarded as sufficient satisfaction of any claim which the victim might have.[83]

While this background might hint towards a restoration of the link between delict and crime, that was not the basis on which the working party approached its task. It saw criminal injuries compensation as being an example of the state making provision for one of the 'accidents and mischances of life',[84] in the same manner as national insurance for industrial injuries. It noted that offenders were in principle delictually liable to their victims, but only to comment on the practical uselessness of this remedy.

As for procedural integration, the working party appears to have given no serious consideration to the possibility that an order for compensation might be made by the criminal court on conviction, but the reasons why are clearly apparent from its report. It did not think that the conviction – or even apprehension – of an offender should be a pre-requisite to compensation. Offenders might be unidentifiable; even if they were identifiable their conviction might be prevented by a 'legal technicality' or evidential deficiency which should not stand in the way of state compensation.[85]

The working party did consider making the right of civil action against the offender meaningful, by placing the state in the position of insurer, so that the victim could obtain a civil judgment against the offender and obtain satisfaction from the state if the offender were unable to pay the damages awarded. It rejected this for a variety of reasons: first, the state should not be seen to 'underwrite criminal violence'; second, this would not deal with the situation where an offender was unknown or out of the jurisdiction of the courts; third, an offender, particularly one without means, would have little interest in the civil proceedings and might not trouble to defend them or assist the state if it were placed in

[82] *Compensation for Victims of Crimes of Violence* (Cmnd 1406: 1961).

[83] *Penal Practice in a Changing Society: Aspects of Future Development (England and Wales)* (Cmd 645: 1959), para. 24.

[84] *Compensation for Victims of Crimes of Violence* (Cmnd 1406: 1961), para. 9. See also paras. 17–18. The justification for such schemes is a complex matter: see further P. Duff, 'Criminal Injuries Compensation: The Symbolic Dimension' 1995 *JR* 102.

[85] *Compensation for Victims of Crimes of Violence* (Cmnd 1406: 1961), para. 29.

the (undesirable) position of having to defend them on his behalf.[86] The possibility was therefore not considered further.

3. Compensation orders in the criminal courts

The second instance which might have led to a degree of integration is compensation orders. Scottish courts have had the power to make compensation orders against convicted offenders since 1980.[87] If the extent of the injured party's loss is not clear from the proceedings prior to conviction and is a matter of dispute, the court may hear evidence on the matter.[88] Recent legislation obliges the court to consider making a compensation order in any case where it is competent to do so.[89] The injured party does not enforce the order as if it were an award of damages in a civil action. Instead, compensation orders are enforceable only by the court, which will account for the money received to the injured party.[90]

Although there is no limit on the sum which can be awarded by way of a compensation order,[91] the practical scope of the power to make such orders is limited because of their interaction with imprisonment.[92]

[86] Ibid., paras. 136–40.

[87] Criminal Justice (Scotland) Act 1980, Part IV. See now the Criminal Procedure (Scotland) Act 1995, ss. 249–253. The provisions of the 1980 Act follow from the recommendations of the Dunpark Committee: *Reparation by the Offender to the Victim in Scotland* (Cmnd 6802: 1977), which were themselves influenced by the powers conferred on the English courts by the Criminal Justice Act 1972. Prior to 1972, there were some limited statutory powers on the part of the English criminal courts to order a convicted person to pay compensation for loss of or damage to property, dating back to 1870, but there seem to have been few if any analogous provisions in Scotland. See *Compensation for Victims of Crimes of Violence* (Cmnd 1406: 1961), para. 6; G. Maher and C. J. Docherty, *Compensation Orders in the Scottish Criminal Courts* (Edinburgh: Scottish Office, 1998), 2.

[88] *Shaw* v. *Donnelly* 2003 SLT 255.

[89] Victims and Witnesses (Scotland) Act 2014, s. 24. The Dunpark Committee had recommended (Ch. 9) that the court have the power to grant a 'compensation certificate' enabling a victim to seek legal aid in order to table a full statement of his or her claim for compensation at a later date, but this was not implemented.

[90] Criminal Procedure (Scotland) Act 1995, s. 249(9)–(10).

[91] Ibid., s. 249(7). A compensation order for £11,000 (in favour of the Benefits Agency) was made in *Downie* v. *HM Advocate* 1999 SCCR 375 but quashed on appeal. This unlimited power, however, is only available in solemn proceedings. In summary proceedings, the maximum compensation order is limited in line with the maximum fine which can be imposed by the court: s. 249(8).

[92] Nicholson, *Sentencing: Law and Practice in Scotland* notes at para. 10–54 that though it is competent to combine a compensation order with a sentence of imprisonment, '[i]n practice this is seldom done'. See also Maher and Docherty, *Compensation Orders*, 22; P. Duff, 'Compensation Orders in the Sheriff Court' 1982 *SLT (News)* 171.

In imposing a compensation order, the court should take into account the offender's means *excluding* any earnings contingent on his obtaining employment after release.[93] The limited means of most offenders, particularly those sentenced to imprisonment, restricts the ability of the courts to impose compensation orders in serious cases and may often rule it out altogether.[94] The High Court has suggested that compensation orders are primarily a form of punishment rather than a substitute for damages in a civil case.[95]

3. Crime and tort: interactions in the substantive law

Comparing substantive law rules of delict and crime in Scotland today can fruitfully be done by identifying issues that are common to both. As will be seen, in the early formative period of Scots law there was a single body of law, which can be for convenience described as crime/delict where the interest protected was life, bodily physical integrity, sexual integrity and physical liberty. To a limited extent, in those contexts that origin continues to affect the rules of the substantive law. Notwithstanding this, writers on the law, courts, the legislator and law reform bodies have rarely focused on the two bodies of substantive law together. The rules have thus developed separately, and by the courts. The core of criminal law and intentional delict remain Scottish common law, including, for instance, homicide, assault, theft and fraud. A recent statutory reform of the whole of the criminal law of sexual offences is a significant exception to this situation.[96] The developments in criminal law have been driven by a large body of case law through the nineteenth century up to the present. While the law of negligence (and also at least in the nineteenth century, defamation) has similarly been developed through a large body of case law, the case law on civil liability arising where a crime is committed, other than in the area of statutory health and safety law, has been limited.

[93] Criminal Procedure (Scotland) Act 1995, s. 249(5)–(6). This follows a recommendation of the Dunpark Committee (para 8.09), which disapproved of the contrary approach taken by the English courts in *R* v. *Kneeshaw* [1975] QB 57, taking into account the offender's capacity to earn money after release from borstal training.

[94] See, e.g., *Clark* v. *Cardle* 1989 SCCR 92, although cf. *Collins* v. *Lowe* 1990 SCCR 605.

[95] See *Notman* v. *Henderson* 1992 SCCR 409, holding (in quashing compensation orders imposed by the sentencing judge) that as the sentences of detention adequately reflected the seriousness of the offences, it was 'unnecessary to increase the punishment' by imposing compensation orders. This approach seems wrong in principle: cf. the contrary view correctly expressed in *R* v. *Bewick* [2008] 2 Cr App R (S) 31.

[96] Sexual Offences (Scotland) Act 2009. See further Section 3.C.2 below.

A. *Capacity*

The question of mental capacity in crime and, it seems, in delict arises as a 'defence'. Nonage in criminal law is also treated as a defence. But it is appropriate to deal with it first. As a result of recent change the age of criminal responsibility is now twelve.[97] No consideration was given to civil actions against children under the age of twelve in the work of the Scottish Law Commission that ultimately[98] resulted in this change. The general legislation on capacity in civil law does not deal with it either.[99] It has recently been stated that 'a child under the age of 16 can, theoretically at least, be sued if the child has committed a delict'.[100] However, we do not know whether there is a test for a particular child. For instance, it might be that there is a particular age, or an age combined with another factor, or a test based on what a particular child's characteristics were. The only modern case law on delict and children is concerned with contributory negligence where the child, as a pedestrian, is injured by a negligent driver.[101] The question is determined on considering the maturity and background experience of the child. It is one step removed, but probably correct in theory that this also means that a child could on this basis be himself or herself liable for negligently causing an accident. However, there are obvious problems in applying it to delicts in contexts where, but for the child being under twelve, a crime or offence would have been committed. In early modern Scots law when there was a close identification of crime and delict, the approach in criminal law would have been applicable. A judge today, it may be predicted, however, would not be happy in applying either of the reported decisions, both sixteenth century 'spuilzie' cases, that appear to conflict,[102] on whether there is any

[97] In the sense that no child can be prosecuted for a crime which allegedly occurred before they reached that age. Criminal Procedure (Scotland) Act 1995, s. 41A inserted by Criminal Justice and Licensing (Scotland) Act 2010, s. 52.

[98] For changes between the Scottish Law Commission's earlier recommendations and this see J. Chalmers and F. Leverick, *Criminal Defences and Pleas in Bar of Trial* (Edinburgh: W. Green, 2006), 9.05.

[99] The general legislation on nonage in civil law, the Age of Legal Capacity (Scotland) Act 1991, does not deal with delict.

[100] J. M. Thomson, *Delictual Liability*, 5th edn (Haywards Heath: Bloomsbury Professional, 2014), para. 13.1.

[101] The first case reported case formulating this test is *Campbell* v. *Ord and Maddison* (1873) 1 R 149, where it was taken that a four-year-old child could be contributorily negligent, although not on the facts of the case in question.

[102] *Somerville* v. *Hamilton* (1541) Mor 8905 and *Bryson* v. *Somerville* (1565) 1703, discussed in W. J. Stewart, *Delict and Related Obligations*, 3rd edn (Edinburgh: W. Green, 1998), 182.

age limit that is relevant. Indeed, those cases are influenced by the fact that spuilzie functions principally as a property law remedy for the return of possession, not a delictual gateway to compensation. The whole problem of the civil liability of children in delicts of intention is a particularly obvious one, justifying further study of the relation of delict to crime, and ripe for law reform.

B. Conduct

1. Intention, recklessness, negligence etc

Scottish criminal law cases and literature devote considerable attention to the concept of intention and recklessness and the literature is informed by extensive Anglo–American scholarship.[103] Scottish delict cases and literature have not devoted much attention to what is meant by conduct described by the terms intention and recklessness. An important exception is the discussion of 'intention' in a leading recent work,[104] as discussed further below, and the meaning of 'reckless' in the context of nuisance,[105] where the meaning is different from that in criminal law. Scottish delict case law and literature naturally considers negligence in depth; negligence and 'carelessness' is also considered in the literature on criminal law, the latter particularly in Road Traffic cases. Nonetheless, conscious contrast with concepts of conduct in civil law is rare in criminal cases,[106] and absent in civil cases.

2. Breach of statute

The law of civil liability for breach of statute inevitably raises difficulties of integration in a system of civil liability, except in the case of statutes that expressly create civil liability.[107] It was, as elsewhere in the United Kingdom, industrial safety legislation of the nineteenth and twentieth centuries[108] which prompted a consideration of the implications of legislation which if breached could give rise to criminal prosecution is to be integrated in the law of delict. The integration of breach of statutory

[103] Gordon, *The Criminal Law of Scotland*, paras. 7.13–7. 68.

[104] Reid, *Personality, Confidentiality and Privacy in Scots Law.*

[105] N. Whitty, 'Nuisance' in *Stair Memorial Encyclopaedia* (Reissue), 89.

[106] An instance is *Transco* v. *HM Advocate (No. 1)* 2004 JC 29, [6] (Lord Maclean) – considering voluntary culpable homicide.

[107] Notably the Occupiers Liability (Scotland) Act 1960 (negligence) and Animals (Scotland) Act 1987 (strict liability).

[108] For a recent move away from this in UK legislation, see J. Spencer, 'Civil Liability for Crimes', in M. Dyson (ed.), *Unravelling Tort and Crime* (Cambridge University Press, 2014), 304.

duty was authoritatively stated: '[s]tatutory negligence is none the less negligence. It infers that breach of duty which underlies every common law action for *culpa*.'[109] There still, however, remains a question as to just exactly what the reach of the concept of *culpa* is. It has very recently been relied on, as discussed further below, in holding a solicitor liable for fraud committed by a client.[110] What *culpa* embraces has been considered in the context of neighbourhood law.[111] But that consideration is not necessarily easily adaptable to questions that arise at the interface of crime and delict.

C. *Intentional invasions of protected interests*

1. Invasions and threatened invasions of bodily physical integrity

The relationship of the rules and principles of the law of delict today in cases of invasions of bodily physical integrity to the rules and principles applicable in a criminal prosecution is complex. Until the late eighteenth century, the law of crime/delict utilised an elaborate set of subcategories, which had been developed in the *ius commune*. Functionally they operated not to add a level of sophistication to the overarching concept of the crime/delict of *iniuria* as it applied in cases of bodily physical injury caused by acts (as opposed to words), i.e. '*iniuria realis*', 'real injury'. The general law of *iniuria* was simple. The requirements were an intention to injure (*animus iniuirandi*) by causing affront. The difficult conceptual questions hidden in both of these requirements were not addressed in Scotland nor, it seems, elsewhere. The focus of the subcategories was on the seriousness of the particular impact on the injured party's body, as a way of determining both the nature of the criminal sentence and as a factor in determining the extent of a sum awarded as damages for non-patrimonial loss. These categories in descending order of seriousness were: demembration (removing a distinct functioning part of the body – such as a leg), mutilation (permanently causing such not to function, though still attached), beating wounding, invasion and a few others.[112]

[109] *William Hamilton & Co Ltd* v. *WG Anderson & Co. Ltd* 1953 SC 129, 137 and so the decision in a negligence claim is *res judicata* to bar a subsequent statutory claim (*Matuszczyk* v. *National Coal Board (No. 2)* 1955 SC 418).

[110] *Frank Houlgate Investment Co. Ltd.* v. *Biggart Baillie LLP* [2014] CSIH 79.

[111] *Kennedy* v. *Glenbelle Ltd* 1996 SC 95.

[112] See Blackie, 'Unity in Diversity', 94–101; J. Blackie, 'The Protection of Corpus in Modern and Early Modern Scots Law' in E. Descheemaeker and H. Scott (eds.), *Iniuria and the Common Law* (Oxford: Hart Publishing, 2013), 155.

From the eighteenth century onwards, Scotland has used one single organising category for all actual or threatened invasions of bodily physical integrity by acts: assault (though that can be 'aggravated'). There are some situations where in absence of the requirement in the modern criminal law of assault of a deliberate attack, the accused has nonetheless acted recklessly in a way that has caused bodily physical injury or could have resulted in that and is criminally liable. The terminology used is confused and various. In one high profile case,[113] where the accused was convicted of having supplied kits for sniffing glue to children, the charge was of 'causing real injury'. However, in so far as this is the right term for this category of crime, or as part of a wider term for it, which it almost certainly is not,[114] it does not reflect the early concept 'real injury', where the 'real' denoted the mechanism used: acts as opposed to words. The use of the phrase in modern criminal cases is to describe the consequent invasion of bodily integrity, or potential invasion of bodily integrity, and was adopted in complete ignorance of the law of *iniuria* as historically part of crime/delict, and arguably in some respects still part of delict.

The core crime relevant to intentional invasions of the person and acts such as raising a fist is today 'assault'. The law of delict also categorises these as 'assault'. The question remains, how far the approach of the criminal law to the crime of assault, as it has developed in the last two hundred years or so since it was likewise invented as a *nomen iuris*, is the same as or different to the private law of assault. The emergence of assault in both criminal and civil law was associated with the general crime/delict of *iniuria* ceasing to be developed, and its connected nominate categories relating to the seriousness of the impact on the victim's body being tacitly abandoned. The process whereby this happened has been traced in detail.[115] In essence the word assault, having at one time in Scotland only the military meaning of assaulting a building, came in ordinary language to be used in the general sense that it is used today. That development provided a background where, probably by influence from English legal terminology, at the turn of the eighteenth and nineteenth century it became the term for the legal category in Scotland. This was at the very time when the principles of delict relevant to claims of

[113] *Khaliq* v. *HM Advocate* 1984 JC 23.

[114] The correct term may be 'recklessly causing injury'. A useful accessible discussion is P. R. Ferguson and C. McDiarmid, *Scots Criminal Law: A Critical Analysis* (Dundee University Press, 2009), para. 10.12.

[115] Blackie, 'Unity in Diversity', 104–10.

this sort and those of criminal law under the same head began to develop (separately) on a new basis. The number of reported civil claims of this type was at least in the early part of the nineteenth century considerably larger than it has been since. By contrast, of course, numerous assault prosecutions have continued since that time to be a very significant part of routine criminal business. This contrast has meant that there has been ample opportunity through case law to determine the requirements for establishing a crime of assault, whereas the requirements of delict have remained in some important respects unclear.

Moreover, the requirements as they currently exist in criminal law reflect the public interest in discouraging particular types of conduct. As a result of nineteenth-century case law the crime of assault requires an 'attack . . . with evil intent'[116] to have taken place. These requirements enable the courts in particular to reject the possibility that a defence of consent of the victim is relevant in a criminal assault case. The absence of the required *mens rea* of 'evil intent' has been an unconvincing way of explaining why in contact sports, the crime of assault is committed where the 'attack' is outside the parameters of the sport.[117]

What lies behind these *actus reus* and *mens rea* requirements for the crime of assault are not only the general policy goals of criminal law, but also the requirement for criminal law to distinguish crimes and offences according to some hierarchy of relative moral blameworthiness. These requirements are not readily transferable to the law of delict. One feature the delict of assault has in common with the crime is that it does not require an actual invasion of the victim's bodily integrity; it, too, can occur through, for example the raising of a fist or spitting at someone where the spit failed to hit that person.[118] However, the *actus reus* requirement of 'attack' is not necessary to comprehend this kind of thing within the delict of 'assault'.[119] The delict comprehends such acts because they are a form of 'affront'. That approach was carried over from old law of *iniuria,* out of which 'assault' emerged as a nominate delict by the nineteenth century. (Similarly, other affronting acts that were actionable on that basis are – following much more recent developments – considered under the specific delictual categories of breach of privacy or dignity.)[120] The

116 *Smart* v. *HM Advocate* 1975 JC 30, 33.

117 *Lord Advocate's Reference (No. 2 of 1992)* 1993 JC 43.

118 *Ewing* v. *Earl of Mar* (1851) 14 D 314.

119 As in Reid, *Personality, Confidentiality and Privacy in Scots Law*, paras. 2.15–2. 18.

120 See ibid., para. 2.20 commenting on *Henderson* v. *Chief Constable of Fife Police* 1988 SLT 361: 'such conduct is more logically characterised as infringing privacy alone'.

mens rea requirement of criminal law, 'evil intention', was not adopted nor suggested as relevant in the only civil assault case since the emergence of the delict from the old law of *iniuria* where the facts called for clarification of the elements of the delict. The context in which the pursuer was injured was skylarking in a haystack.[121] However, the case did not lay down what the test is. Nor did the standard general works of the nineteenth and twentieth centuries on delict. It is inevitable, therefore that the law will draw on insights from Anglo–American scholarship, and the approach taken in modern English cases. Recent detailed work has put forward the following as being the requirements for the delict of assault: 'liability may be found if and only if: (a) the defender acted deliberately; and (b) (i) with the purpose of causing harm; or (ii) knowing that harm of some kind was likely to occur, even if he or she did not positively desire that outcome; or (iii) with reckless disregard to the possibility of causing harm'.[122] This comes close to the position taken in some recent Anglo–American literature[123] that the civil law of assault is in sense an area of strict liability. As such it is very much wider in its reach than the criminal law, though situations that constitute the crime come within reach.

2. Invasions and threatened invasions of sexual integrity

The identification of crime and delict existed where there was a sexual element in just the same way as with invasions of bodily integrity more generally. What was different was that there were specific subcategories used, which in contrast to those for bodily injury, were not based on the nature of the impact on the victim but on the quality of the conduct involved in the invasion of the right. Also the categories had to be fitted into categories that appeared as relevant in certain Roman texts which from the late Middle Ages in Canon law are interpreted in the light of the goals of Christian sexual morality as they were then understood.[124] From the nineteenth century through to the late twentieth century, Scottish criminal law developed really different categories, except in so far as rape, meaning at that time having penetrative sex through overbearing the will of the victim, had existed in that earlier scheme, as 'deforcement of a woman'. ('Rape', following the dominant *ius commune* doctrine, had

[121] *Reid* v. *Mitchell* (1885) 12 R 1129.

[122] Reid, *Personality, Confidentiality and Privacy in Scots Law*, para. 2.10.

[123] As in A. Beever, 'The Form of Liability in the Torts of Trespass' (2011) 40 *CLWR* 378.

[124] Blackie, 'Unity in Diversity', 64–70.

required abduction, or on one view abduction *libidinis causa* (with the aim of having sex.)

In 2009, the whole of the criminal law of sexual offences was reformed and considerably recast[125] as a result of recommendations of the Scottish Law Commission. That work was carried out without any consideration of the law of delict's treatment of claims for invasions of sexual integrity. The relationship in this area of the law of delict to crime even before this happened required a view to be taken as to whether there is a distinct protected interest of sexual integrity or whether, rather, the interest invaded where a sexual act impacting on the body is simply that of bodily integrity and the sexual dimension then is relevant only to the amount of non-patrimonial damages that would be payable. On this view the applicable category in the law of delict is now simply assault, as considered above. The leading modern work[126] does not adopt any special categories for cases involving sexual contact nor give such cases any particular treatment as instances of assault. Another recent work starts by expressly bringing such delictual actions into the category of assault: 'the delictual actions of rape and indecent assault provide the individual with protection for their bodily integrity that also respects the individual's autonomy by allowing the right to be waived by consent'.[127] Yet the author then proceeds to use (pre 2009) criminal cases for details of rape, as 'an aggravated assault'.[128] Additionally,[129] it is asserted that there is a nominate delict named 'seduction' where consent to sexual intercourse 'with the virgin [is obtained] by fraud, circumvention, guile misrepresentations or other persuasive practices'. (This suggested nominate delict of seduction is a direct descendant of the *ius commune* category, developed particularly by the canonists of the crime/delict '*stuprum*', which was also available to chaste widows.[130] It is at least doubtful whether a court would recognise a seduction claim as relevant today. The last reported instance was in 1919[131] and it appears that no later ones have been attempted.)

There is then a difficult question as to whether it is appropriate for the law of delict simply to categorise a claim arising from sexual contact as assault or even 'aggravated assault'. In the pre-2009 criminal law, 'indecent assault' was classified as an 'aggravated assault' while other sexual

[125] Sexual Offences (Scotland) Act 2009.

[126] Reid, *Personality, Confidentiality and Privacy in Scots Law*, paras. 2.01–2.41.

[127] A. MacLean, 'Autonomy, Consent and the Body in Delict' in J. M. Thomson (ed.), *Delict* (Edinburgh: W. Green, 2007), 11.79

[128] As in Walker, *The Law of Delict in Scotland*, 498–9.

[129] As in ibid., 698–702.

[130] Blackie, 'Unity in Diversity', 65–7, 125.

[131] *MacLeod* v. *MacAskill* 1920 SC 72.

offences, for instance rape, were nominate crimes. But since the reform of sexual offences the category of indecent assault itself has been removed from the criminal law, and several new statutory crimes have been introduced. This reform raises a particular issue about the relationship of crime and delict. Reform of the criminal law was needed to reflect social and cultural changes, and the fact that the prosecution of sexual cases is of great concern to the public. Civil claims arising out of these facts do not occupy the same public attention. It would be clearly inconsistent, however, for the law of delict to utilise case law from the unreformed common law sexual offences in giving precision to the requirements in a civil claim since they are no longer in force. This could be a reason for treating civil claims involving sexual contact as assault claims reflecting the sexual element only in the quantum of non-patrimonial damages. However, to plead what the general public would see as a claim in respect of rape under the heading 'assault' risks not giving sufficient prominence to the fact that sexual integrity can reasonably be classified as an additional protected interest to that of bodily physical integrity. Further, public expectation may be better met by using categories that map on to the current law sexual offences. Delict may require 'fair labelling' as does criminal law, though for this different reason of meeting public expectation.[132]

3. Invasions of other personality rights

Any criminal dimensions to other invasions to dignity, privacy and reputation in the common law disappeared in the nineteenth century with the abolition of the separate system of Commissary Courts. In so far as these invasions could give rise to proceedings in ordinary criminal courts that had already ceased in practice at some time in the eighteenth century.[133] There is extensive UK statute law protecting privacy and giving rise to criminal offences. It is an area where crime and delict certainly may interact, but there is no particular Scottish dimension.

4. Invasions of assets

The protection of the interest in corporeal property, except in cases of intentionally or negligently caused damage and nuisance, is part of

[132] See further, Blackie, 'The Protection of Corpus', 162–7.

[133] For a detailed treatment of these changes see J. Blackie, 'Defamation' in K. Reid and R. Zimmermann (ed.s) , *A History of Private Law in Scotland*, 2 vols. (Oxford University Press, 2000), vol. II, 631, 686.

property law, and where it can no longer be restored to the person entitled, part of the law of unjustified enrichment. The interface with crime occurs at the practical level of remedies, and accordingly is discussed below in considering the interaction of criminal investigation and criminal process with civil remedies.

As with the law of delict generally there is an issue whether there is an underlying principle, *culpa*, on which particular economic delicts have been built, and, which is capable of extending the law by creating new categories. Fraud is the one economic delict with a long history. It is definitely wider than in criminal law. It goes beyond where there is actual dishonesty, to extend also to where a person making an assertion 'entertains no belief in its truth'.[134] This is derived from a nineteenth-century Scots case,[135] though the English tort of deceit has also had an influence. Very recently it has been held, in *Frank Houlgate Investment Co. Ltd.* v. *Biggart Baillie LLP*[136] that, irrespective of a question of accessory liability (discussed further below) a solicitor, having become aware that his client was committing a crime in connection with obtaining a loan, was liable to the client's creditor, for losses incurred as a result of the fraud after he, the solicitor, became aware of it, and had not taken steps to contact the creditor. Two distinct analyses are given in the judgements as to the basis of this liability. One is that liability arises because there is a 'continuing implied representation'.[137] The other is that liability follows from *culpa*, the fundamental principle of the law of delict which is capable then of developing the law so that a form of duty of care for omission arises.[138] These two analyses were suggested as being different ways of expressing the same thing.[139] However, they are really different. The former in truth recognises a new economic delict. This analysis expressly distinguishes the obligation 'from a *Caparo* type duty of care; it arises not as a result of any delictual duty, nor from considerations of foreseeability, proximity, or other familiar in the law of delict'.[140] The latter extends the concept of duty of care. Whatever the basis of liability on the defender's part, his or her relationship with the party committing the delict is necessarily central to

134 *H & J M Bennet (Potatoes) Ltd* v. *Secretary of State for Scotland* 1986 SLT 665, 671(Lord Davidson).

135 *Lees* v. *Tod* (1882) 9 R 807.

136 2014 SLT 1001.

137 [33]–[39] (Lord Menzies).

138 [73]–[74] (Lord Malcolm).

139 [91] (Lord McEwan): agreeing 'for either the reasons given by Lord Malcolm or your Lordship in the chair'; [43] Lord Menzies: 'we reach the same result by essentially the same means'.

140 [36] (Lord Menzies).

liability being established. It seems unlikely that this new economic delict will extend beyond that of lawyers, and other professionals.

This new development may also be consistent with some extension of the delict of fraud itself, even though this new development goes even further than an expanded delict of fraud. There is an argument that fraud as a delict may be extended to cover a range of behaviour in bad faith given the understanding of fraud as found in Scots private law generally.[141] One example might be fraud in this wider sense as forming the basis of liability for an action of damages by a pursuer with a contractual right to be conveyed the right of ownership of property, or some other real right, against a third party who knew of that prior contractual right but had obtained the real right from the current owner.[142]

The remainder of the law of economic delicts consists of a recent direct importation of the rules of English tort law,[143] as set out in *OBG Ltd* v. *Allan*[144] and as further developed since that case.[145] A consequence is that the tort of conspiracy, including the understanding of what constitutes 'unlawful means', is part of Scots law. There is no distinct Scottish dimension to the interface with criminal law.[146]

D. *'Art and part', 'joint wrongdoing' and 'accessory liability'*

In criminal law, the broad heading for joint liability is 'art and part' and additionally in some situations the crime of conspiracy[147] may be committed. But 'art and part' is not a generic term for all joint criminal liability. A distinction is made between a party who carries through the *actus reus*, for example, who delivers a lethal blow in a homicide case, as an 'actor' and others who did not but are liable solely because of being

141 For this understanding, see D. Reid, *Fraud in Scots Law*, (unpublished PhD thesis, University of Edinburgh, 2012), *passim*.

142 For a view that damages may be an alternative remedy to reduction of the third parties real right may be available in such an 'offside goals' case, see J. MacLeod, *Fraud and Voidable Transfer: Scots Law in European Context* (unpublished PhD thesis, University of Edinburgh, 2014), 236. It may be that where there are consequential losses, it is also available additionally to a decree of reduction. For similarities and contrasts between 'offside goals' cases and cases of inducing breach of contract, see J. MacLeod, 'Offside Goals and Induced Breaches of Contract' (2009) 13 *Edin LR* 278.

143 *Global Resources Group Ltd* v. *Mackay* 2009 SLT 104 (Lord Hodge – inducing breach of contract); *MacLeod* v. *Rooney* 2010 SLT 499.

144 [2008] 1 AC 1.

145 Thomson, *Delictual Liability*, para. 2.8.

146 *Customs and Excise Commissioners* v. *Total Network SL* [2008] 1 AC 1174.

147 In practice conspiracy is charged where a plan was not carried through to completion.

'art and part'. The distinction is old and reflects the civilian concept of liability *ope et auxilio* (by help and advice).[148] It needs emphasis for two reasons. First it highlights the fact that 'art and part' liability exceptionally treats a person as criminal where he or she did not carry out the *actus reus*, nor sometimes even have the necessary *mens rea*.[149] Second, there is a pragmatic reason for the distinction. It assists juries in their analysis of evidence, even though its use can give rise to difficulty where on the evidence it is unclear which party or parties did carry through the *actus reus*.[150]

In delict, the generic heading 'joint wrongdoing' is correct, though the term describing the result, 'joint and several liability', that is, that each defender found liable is liable for the whole, subject to a right of relief against the others found liable, has often been used routinely to cover also the basis of liability.[151] Very recently the term 'accessory liability', which occasionally appeared in earlier cases,[152] has become prominent. It is used throughout the very recent case[153] holding a solicitor who became aware of his client's fraud liable, discussed in the preceding section. The case is the first appellate level decision on accessory liability for a century. It approved, as giving the law today, a passage in the seventeenth century institutional writer, Stair: '[a]ccession to delinquence is either anterior, concomitant, or posterior to the delinquence itself'.[154]

One way in which art and part can be established in criminal law is where parties agree to commit a crime. However, the concept of a combination between parties extends much further than this. The concept is that of 'a common criminal purpose'. A distinction is made between where there is some sort of plan beforehand ('antecedent concert') and where there is a coming together in an event, typically a fight ('spontaneous concert'). Both are determined by an objective test. But the precise

148 Sir George Mackenzie, *The Laws and Customs of Scotland in Matters Criminal* (Edinburgh: Swintoun, 1678), 35.2.

149 F. Leverick, 'The (Art and) Parting of the Ways: Joint Criminal Liability for Homicide' 2012 SLT (News) 227.

150 *Gardener* v. *HM Advocate* 2010 SCCR 116; *HM Advocate* v. *Igoe* 2010 SCCR 759.

151 E.g. the heading used in Walker, *The Law of Delict in Scotland*, 111.

152 Instances of the use of 'accessory' can also be found in one earlier fraud case, *Cairns* v. *Harry Walker* 1914 SC 51, referred to in the very recent case, and the terminology 'principal' and 'accessary' (*sic*) in an early nineteenth century civil assault case, *Bannerman* v. *Fenwicks* (1817) 1 Mur 249, where the defenders agreed '. . . to pick a quarrel with the pursuer'.

153 *Frank Houlgate Investment Co. Ltd* v. *Biggart Baillie LLP* 2014 SLT 1001.

154 Stair, *Institutions*, 1.9.5.

form of the test and its application is clear in cases of 'antecedent concert', while there some lack of clarity with regard to the position in cases of 'spontaneous concert'.[155]

Where there was 'antecedent concert', whether a particular party was involved can be inferred from facts. So acts that in one context may not infer being part of such a purpose, such as driving a person who was subsequently murdered to a spot near where the murder occurred, will give rise to art and part criminal liability if it can be reasonably inferred that it was part of a plan with others, who carried out the killing.[156] Whatever the plan really was, objective foreseeability is used to determine its potential ambit. This is normally illustrated by reference to robbery cases where it is foreseeable that one of the parties would use lethal violence, which then gives rise to art and part guilt for murder on the part of the other with no need to establish *mens rea* on his or her part.[157] In that context the rule has been summarised as: 'whether there was evidence entitling the jury to find that it was objectively foreseeable to [the party in question] that such violence was liable to be used as carried an obvious risk of life being taken'.[158] But the approach is not confined to homicide. For instance, in a case[159] where a trailer lorry of cigarettes and other tobacco products was stolen as part of a concerted plan, an accused, who provided premises for transferring the trailer to another vehicle, but who was not present at the taking of the trailer, which in the event involved a violent assault on the driver, was found guilty of the assault. It was foreseeable because extensive precautions, including locking the doors while driving, are standard in the transport of such material.

In cases of 'spontaneous concert', there is a certain lack of clarity. In the literature two possibilities have been canvassed,[160] namely, that to be art and part it must be shown that the party had the *mens rea* for the crime, or perhaps, if it is not just putting the same idea in other words, to have in contemplation that the other party would act in a way constituting the crime in question. Very recent authority puts it that 'what matters . . . is what the particular accused knew or agreed to, what was the nature of the criminal enterprise to which he became a party, and what

155 Leverick, 'The (Art and) Parting of the Ways'.

156 *Ryan* v. *HM Advocate* [2011] HCJAC 83.

157 *McKinnon* v. *HM Advocate* 2003 JC 29; Leverick, 'The (Art and) Parting of the Ways', 230.

158 *Poole* v. *HM Advocate* 2009 SCCR 577, [11] (Lord Kingarth).

159 *Cameron* v. *HM Advocate* 2008 SCCR 669.

160 Leverick, 'The (Art and) Parting of the Ways', 230, discussing *Crawford* v. *HM Advocate* [2012] HCJAC 40 and *Brown* v. *HM Advocate* 1993 SCCR 382.

degree of violence was to be expected during the carrying out of that enterprise'.[161] This formulation seems to include at least an element of objective foreseeability in referring to 'to be expected'. However, in that case it was in fact used to uphold a direction to the jury that the party acting in 'concert' could be found guilty of the lesser crime of culpable homicide while the other party was convicted of murder. It is, thus, consistent with focusing on the *mens rea* of each party separately. Indeed, the court emphasised this in holding that 'it does not hold that the *mens rea* [of the party who delivered the fatal blow] was necessarily' that of the party liable on the basis of concert.

Until the very recent fraud case, *Houlgate Investment*,[162] and a first instance decision in 2013 discussed in it, where Greenpeace was held on the facts not liable for activities of certain protesters,[163] there was very little case law on civil joint and several liability as it arises from facts that constitute a crime. There were, of course, cases of personal injury or death based on breaches of safety legislation. In that context the law, however, focuses on whether the parties' contributions were material or gave rise to a material increase of risk. The law is the same as in England,[164] and for better or for worse, the limitations on joint and several liability[165] in cases of 'material increase of risk' apply. A similar approach was also taken in one Scottish common law pollution case.[166] The approach in these cases is not directly relevant to other types of civil case where a crime was committed. There were civil fraud cases, one of which[167] is referred to *Houlgate Investment*, as supporting the approach taken in it. However, that earlier case is better read as one where there was some active participation by the accessory in the fraud committed by the principal,[168] as there was in the other earlier fraud cases.[169] Not referred to in *Houlgate*

161 *Parfinowski* v. *HM Advocate* 2014 SCCR 30, [22] (Lady Dorrian) and *Stewart* v. *HM Advocate* [2012] HCJAC 126, [11] (Lady Paton).

162 *Frank Houlgate Investment Co. Ltd.* v. *Biggart Baillie LLP* 2014 SLT 1001.

163 *Cairn Energy Plc* v. *Greenpeace Ltd* 2013 SLT 570.

164 The line of authority in England culminating in *Barker UK Ltd* v. *Corus* [2006] 2 AC 572 goes back to a Scottish decision on breach of safety legislation *Wardlaw* v. *Bonnington Castings* [1956] 2 WLR 707; [1956] SC (HL) 26.

165 *Barker UK Ltd* v. *Corus* [2006] 2 AC 572.

166 *Fleming* v. *Gemmill* 1908 SC 340, 350 (Lord President Dunedin).

167 *Cairns* v. *Harry Walker* 1914 SC 51.

168 *Frank Houlgate Investment Co. Ltd* v. *Biggart Baillie LLP* 2014 SLT 1001, [66] (Lord Malcolm, dissenting): 'a classic example of direct participation in another party's unlawful operation'.

169 E.g. *R. H. Thomson & Co* v *Pattison Elder & Co* (1895) 22 R 432.

Investment were three early nineteenth century civil assault cases,[170] only one of which is of some help.[171] Not directly referred to in it are several defamation cases,[172] but two of these are to be found in the literature[173] which was held[174] to state the law correctly. There are relevant *obiter dicta* in the defamation cases, one of which makes an analogy with civil assault.[175]

On the basis of this material the law of accessory liability in delict is:

(1) separate delicts by different parties do not give rise to joint and several liability,[176] however close the interval between them;
(2) one (but not the only) form of accessory liability is where there was 'common design',[177] variously referred to in other cases as 'acting in concert',[178] 'preconcert'[179] 'combination' or 'conspiracy';[180]
(3) it is not necessary for an accessory to have the same intent as the principal;[181]
(4) intent is to be assessed objectively;[182]
(5) foreseeability is relevant.[183]

In addition, a party can be liable as an accessory in certain situations of a close relationship with a person committing a delict, and having become

170 *Smith* v. *O'Reilly* (1800) Hume 605; *Bannerman* v. *Fenwicks* (1817) 1 Mur 249; *McLauchlan* v. *Monach* (1823) 2 S 390.

171 *Bannerman* v. *Fenwicks* (1817) 1 Mur 249.

172 *Turnbull* v. *Frame* 1966 SLT 24; *Hook* v. *McCallum* (1905) 7 F 528; *Taylor* v. *McDougall* (1885) 12 R 1304; *Barr* v. *Neilsons* (1868) 6 M 651.

173 Walker, *The Law of Delict in Scotland*, 111–12.

174 *Frank Houlgate Investment Co Ltd* v. *Biggart Baillie LLP* 2014 SLT 1001, [20] (Lord Menzies).

175 *Hook* v. *McCallum* (1905) 7 F 528.

176 *Barr* v. *Neilsons* (1868) 6 M 651, 654 (Lord President Inglis); *Turnbull* v. *Frame* 1966 SLT 24.

177 *Frank Houlgate Investment Co Ltd* v. *Biggart Baillie LLP* 2014 SLT 1001, [44] (Lord Menzies).

178 *Leslie* v. *Lumsden* (1856) 8 D 1046; *Jack* v. *Fleming* (1891) 19 R 1 – single issue allowed for jury where defamatory statements averred to be made 'in concert'. Two dogs that worried sheep together were treated as their separate owners combining in the Scottish House of Lords decision *Arneil* v. *Paterson* [1931] AC 560, referred to in *Barker* v. *Corus UK Ltd* [2006] 2 AC 572, [69] per Lord Rodger (dissenting) and [122] per Baroness Hale.

179 *R H Thomson & Co* v. *Pattison Elder & Co* (1895) 22 R 432.

180 *Turnbull* v. *Frame* 1966 SLT 24 (Lord Fraser). Conspiracy has a quite different meaning as the name of an economic delict, as outlined above.

181 *Frank Houlgate Investment Co Ltd* v. *Biggart Baillie LLP* 2014 SLT 1001, [43] (Lord Menzies).

182 Ibid. 183 Ibid.

aware of it, for loss arising after that time if he or she has not taken appropriate steps to alert the victim.

Direct reference to criminal law was held to be appropriate in *Houlgate Investment*,[184] and in one of the earlier fraud cases.[185] It is also implied in the *dicta* in the defamation cases.[186] However, there still remains a question as to whether all of the criminal law is directly applicable to a civil case or just some of it.

The distinction in criminal law within joint liability, where two or more parties are actors, or where there is only one actor, has a counterpart in a civil case where it is used to distinguish 'accessory liability' from joint liability where the parties acted together but none is an accessory. The generic heading 'joint wrongdoing' is thus still useful in delict, to cover that as well as accessory liability. Stair himself distinguished accessory liability from the form of joint wrongdoing 'where the delinquence is equally and principally committed by more [than one person]'[187] as did the eighteenth century institutional writer, Erskine.[188] Obvious modern instances are in road accident cases where more than one driver is liable, personal injury or death based on breaches of safety legislation, and pollution cases, referred to above. However, making the distinction is also helpful in considering joint liability in the contexts, such as assault, where criminal law distinguishes liability as an actor, and liability as being art and part. While the pragmatic advantage in assisting juries is of limited significance in a civil case,[189] the distinction nonetheless serves to highlight that in such a case there is no need to apply the approach to intent and foreseeability that are relevant to case of accessory liability. An *obiter dictum* in one of the defamation cases with reference to civil assault may support making distinction in a civil case arising from such facts: the parties 'may . . . be jointly and severally liable for the whole injuries, although it may be quite uncertain what specific part of the injuries was due to each, yet as the whole *res gestae* come together when both are present, each is responsible for

[184] Ibid., [44] (Lord Menzies).

[185] *Cairns* v. *Harry Walker* 1914 SC 51 (Lord Skerrington at first instance).

[186] *Leslie* v. *Lumsden* (1856) 18 D 1046 ('concert'); *R. H. Thomson & Co* v. *Pattison Elder & Co* (1895) 22 R 432 ('preconcert').

[187] Stair, *Institutions* 1.95.

[188] J. Erskine, *An Institute of the Laws of Scotland* (Edinburgh: John Bell, 1773), 3.1.15.

[189] Civil jury trials can occur in Scotland but they are rare, and defenders may submit that cases involving complex questions, which would be the case with accessory liability, should be heard before a judge sitting alone. See Court of Session Act 1988, s. 9(b).

the whole'.[190] However, this may have been intended to refer to accessory liability, and there is an early nineteenth century civil assault case where this approach was taken in a case of accessory liability where there was alleged to be 'concert'.[191]

Particularly in the light of *Houlgate Investment* it does now look as if the criminal law of 'antecedent concert' may in the future be drawn on in a civil case of 'concert' to determine the ambit of the enterprise. Thus, for instance a party to a planned theft would be liable as an accessory for personal injury or death when he or she was not involved in the carrying out of the theft and not present at the time of the violence. Indeed, it has been held that the intent of a party liable as an accessory need not be the same as that of the principal, that it is tested objectively and that foreseeability is relevant. Furthermore, foreseeability, as determining the ambit of the enterprise in a case of antecedent concert, can be traced back to the period when there was still an identification of crime/delict in Scots law as it applied to the protection of bodily physical integrity.[192] Moreover there is an early civil assault case dating from shortly after the time when the delict of assault became distinct from the crime, where foreseeability was held to be sufficient.[193] It now seems likely, too, that in a civil case of accessory liability where there was 'concert' the same approach will be applied as in criminal law with respect to the liability of a party who dissociated himself from it before the other party or parties carried it out. The criminal law is:

> [i]f a crime is merely in contemplation and preparations for it are being made, a participator who then quits the enterprise cannot be held to act in concert with those who may go on to commit the crime because there will be no evidence that he played any part in its commission. If on the other hand the perpetration of a planned crime or offence has begun, a participant cannot escape liability for the completed crime by withdrawing before it has been completed unless, perhaps, he also takes steps to prevent its completion.[194]

The word, 'perhaps' leaves it possibly open for some future decision to determine whether a participator remains criminally liable or not, even

190 *Hook* v. *McCallum* (1905) 7 F 528, 531 (Lord Justice-Clerk Macdonald).

191 *Bannerman* v. *Fenwicks* (1817) 1 Mur 249

192 D. Hume, *Commentaries on the Law of Scotland, Respecting Crimes*, vol. 1 (Edinburgh: Bell & Bradfute, 1819), 268–9: 'an obvious and not unforeseen consequence'.

193 *Bannerman* v. *Fenwicks* (1817) 1 Mur 249 – the concert was 'to pick a quarrel with the victim'. It is possible, however, that at that time this meant to assault the person.

194 *MacNeil* v. *HM Advocate* 1986 JC 146, 148 (Lord Justice General Emslie).

despite having taken steps to prevent the crime's completion. In a civil claim, the participator who had withdrawn and taken such steps would seem to escape liability. On the facts of *Houlgate Investment*, having been a participator in the enterprise may be argued to be *a fortiori* of the relationship of solicitor to client that was held to result in accessory liability for failing to alert the creditor of the client's fraud when the solicitor became aware of it: as such where such steps were taken there would be no liability.

The category of 'spontaneous concert' in criminal law, however, may not be of significance in civil cases. The question of proof of *mens rea* in the criminal law in a 'spontaneous concert' case would not be likely to arise in delict since there will be liability to compensate whatever the classification of the wrongdoing.

Accessory liability is an area where the identification of crime and delict up to the nineteenth century most obviously impacts on delict today. This follows particularly from the use of Stair's formulation, '[a]accession to delinquence is either anterior, concomitant, or posterior to the delinquence itself'[195] in *Houlgate Investment*. But two questions need to be considered. The first requires legal historical work to done to determine precisely what Stair meant. As observed in the dissenting judgment[196] in *Houlgate Investment* manifestly limited approaches are found in the eighteenth century institutional writers: Bankton defines 'accessaries (*sic*) to a delinquency, whence damage ensues' as 'properly such as have a real influence in the fact by command, advice or concurrence'.[197] Erskine, in a passage quoted in the dissenting judgement, speaks of 'concurred in committing the wrong'.[198] The context in which this statement is found, admittedly, was in his giving the rationale for why there is joint and several liability for the whole damage, whether the defender was accessory or one of two or more persons liable as principals. Nonetheless, in a later passage, dealing with crime/delict, which was not referred to in *Houlgate Investment*, he states the law as: 'being an accessory to or abetting

[195] Stair, *Institutions* 1.9.5.

[196] *Frank Houlgate Investment Co Ltd* v. *Biggart Baillie LLP* 2014 SLT 1001, [66] (Lord Malcolm)

[197] Lord Bankton, *An Institute of the Laws of Scotland in Civil Rights: With Observations upon the Agreement or Diversity between them and the Laws of England*, vol. 1 (Edinburgh: Fleming, 1751–3), 1.9.46. Bankton, at 1.10.1–1.10.8 (not referred to in *Houlgate Investment*) outlines the contemporary English (criminal law) of 'accessaries' (*sic*) but does not expressly make any comparison with it.

[198] J. Erskine, *An Institute of the Laws of Scotland* (Edinburgh: John Bell, 1773), 3.1.15,

it . . . art and part', and that art and part can take the form of 'a warrant or mandate [or] giving counsel or advice . . . or assistance'.[199] Stair, likewise, wrote 'at a time when the distinction been criminal liability and civil liability was less clear than it is now'.[200] He may have meant in his formulation to encapsulate the same approach as is found in these institutional writers, who cannot but have been aware of what he said. However, it will be necessary to consider whether a particular *ius commune* doctrine is being followed by Stair, and with respect to accessory liability for fraud the relationship of this to the concept of liability as a *particeps fraudis*.[201]

The second question is whether it is desirable to follow an approach developed when there was a close identification of crime and delict. Obviously the law of delict has greatly developed since that time. Nonetheless, there has been no consideration by Scottish courts in civil case as to whether the policies that underpin the treatment in today's criminal law, or those when there was a close identification of crime and delict may differ from policies underpinning today's law of delict. The approach to accessory liability taken by the English courts, as well as the debates in the literature in England have been highlighted by Elspeth Reid in her extensive consideration of *Houlgate Investment* when it was at first instance.[202] The dissenting judgment in the case at appellate level, having pointed out the lack of Scottish authority, as well as the problem of determining the meaning of Stair's statement, approves the view taken by the Court of Appeal in England.[203] This approach is also found in the first instance case in Scotland in 2013 where it was held that Greenpeace was not accessorily liable on the facts for acts taken by protesters which it had not been agreed to or instigated by it.[204] The dangers of an over expansive doctrine of accessory liability have been stressed by Elspeth Reid,[205] but though reference was made by one of the judges in the majority in the appeal[206]

199 Erskine, *Institute*, 4.9.10.

200 As emphasised in the dissenting judgement in *Frank Houlgate Investment Co Ltd* v. *Biggart Baillie LLP* 2014 SLT 1001, [67] (Lord Malcolm).

201 See D. Reid, *Fraud in Scots Law*, (unpublished PhD thesis, University of Edinburgh, 2012), ch. 7.

202 Reid, 'Accession to Delinquence': *Frank Houlgate Investment Co Ltd* v. *Biggart Baillie LLP*' (2013) 17 Edin LR 388, 389–92.

203 Referring to *Credit Lyonnais* v. *Export Credits Guarantee Department* [1998] 1 LL Rep 19.

204 *Cairn Energy plc* v. *Greenpeace* 2013 SLT 570, [24]–[28] (Lord Glennie).

205 Reid, 'Accession to Delinquence', 392–3.

206 *Frank Houlgate Investment Co Ltd* v. *Biggart Baillie LLP* 2014 SLT 1001, [44] (Lord Menzies).

to her plea for a 'cautious steer'[207] it is not clear just where the limits have been or will be set.

E. *Causation and remoteness*

The distinction between factual causation (whether something is a cause at all) and legal causation (whether, if it is, it is a cause of sufficient to give rise to liability) and the associated idea of remoteness is not stressed in criminal law. One single test for causation is employed, that of 'significant contribution',[208] which is applied to the circumstances by utilising 'common sense'.[209] The approach is principally derived from English criminal law.[210] The reason expressed in Scotland for using a common sense principles for causation in criminal cases is both 'the importance of avoiding undue elaboration in the directions on causation that are given to a jury', and that a jury does not require an explanation of the 'ordinary moral notions that they reflect'.[211] Recent instances of the approach being used in cases where the issue was factual causation are where there were two accused not acting in concert and the question was whether blows from one or both were a cause of the death of the victim,[212] and where the question was whether the accused's acts were a cause of death or whether death was from natural causes alone.[213] A recent instance where it was used where the question was legal causation, was in holding that the action of a drug user in taking drugs does not necessarily break the chain of causation to prevent a conviction for culpable homicide by the supplier of the drugs.[214] It is conceivable that there could arise a criminal case in which it would be necessary to consider whether though it could not be shown that the accused's acts were a 'significant contribution' they

[207] Reid, 'Accession to Delinquence', 394. [208] *Johnston* v. *HM Advocate* 2009 JC 227

[209] Ibid. [210] Starting with *R* v. *Smith (Thomas Joseph)* [1959] 2 QB 35.

[211] Ibid. This approach is supported in *Johnston* v. *HM Advocate* 2009 JC 227, [56] per Lord Reed by reference to the extrajudicial statement in Lord Hoffmann, 'Causation' (2005) 121 *LQR* 592, 593–4: 'The great achievement of Hart and Honoré was to unpack the concept of causation when it is used, as the law uses it, to attribute responsibility for things that happen. They showed that when judges say that it is a matter of common sense, they usually mean that it accords with ordinary moral notions of when someone should be regarded as responsible for something which has happened . . . They demonstrated that when the judges spoke of applying common sense, they were appealing to moral notions of what would fairly delimit the events for which a . . . defendant should be responsible.'

[212] *Johnston* v. *HM Advocate* 2009 JC 227.

[213] *McDade* v. *HM Advocate* [2012] HCJAC 38.

[214] *MacAngus* v. *HM Advocate* 2009 SLT 137.

did 'materially increase' the risk of occurrence of the harm that the victim has suffered. If such a case should arise there is an indication that the court could draw on the extensive consideration in civil case law and literature of factual causation.[215]

In the context of civil cases of negligence or breach of statutory duty the distinction between factual causation and legal causation is identical to that in England. The applicable law is also identical. Given this, the leading modern work on the factual causation in this context is as much a contribution to English as to Scots law.[216] Questions of factual causation have never been addressed in a case of intentional delict. Nor have they been specifically considered in the literature as they might arise in that context. There is no distinct Scottish doctrine for determining legal causation questions, such as what type of act or event will breach a chain of causation as *novus actus*, in negligence and breach of statutory duty cases. 'Remoteness' is used in negligence law as the term for foreseeability of the injury that occurred. There is a tradition in the literature[217] that once some injury that meets that criterion is established, the question about liability for further consequences is a separate issue distinguished as 'remoteness of damage'. This distinction is not readily supported by the case law, and in negligence cases the test is anyhow 'foreseeability'.

Whether the 'significant contribution' test and the 'common sense' approach to its application in criminal law will apply equally in a civil case of intentional delict in circumstances amounting to a crime has never been considered. There is no civil case considering legal causation (or remoteness) in this context. Just one author has propounded a test for remoteness where the delict is intentional, namely that the wrongdoer 'is also liable for consequences, which not intended, are the natural and direct consequences of his conduct . . . even though unforeseen.'[218] However, the (criminal) case cited for this does not support the proposition,[219] and the civil case cited is about negligence in creating a situation where others

[215] *Johnston* v. *HM Advocate* 2009 JC 227, [56] per Lord Reed: 'Although the correct identification of the causal connection required by the law can in some contexts be a matter of difficulty (as has been illustrated, for example, by cases in the law of negligence concerned with industrial diseases), in the present context the law's requirement – that the wrongful act of the accused should have materially contributed to the death of the deceased – is not in doubt.'

[216] M. Hogg, 'The Role of Causation in Delict' 2005 *JR* 89; M. Hogg, 'Re-establishing Orthodoxy in the Realm of Causation' (2007) 11 *Edin LR* 8.

[217] Stemming from Walker, *The Law of Delict in Scotland*, 231–3, 242–83.

[218] Ibid., 167.

[219] Ibid.: cf. *Bird* v. *HM Advocate* 1952 JC 23 (the point was not causation but whether on the facts the crime of voluntary culpable homicide was committed).

naturally came to cause damage.[220] Furthermore, what has been said about the inadequacy of this sort of approach in the criminal context is equally applicable to the civil: 'whatever the philosophical implication of using directness as an exclusive causal criterion, such a use would be clearly impractical . . . Somewhere along the line there comes a point at which the effect of A's act must be deemed to cease.'[221] It may be predicted that the criminal law approach would be adopted. One factor that might support this is that, while there have been no civil intentional delict cases considering the question, the criminal law has developed partly through drawing on civil (negligence) cases dealing with legal causation and remoteness.[222] On the other hand the criminal approach may require further elaboration if applied in an intentional delict case. As noted above, in criminal law the approach has not only been justified by the need to avoid elaboration when instructing juries, but also because the law 'reflects ordinary moral notions' which do not require to be explained to them. Such an ordinary moral notion was expressed by the author propounding a 'natural and direct consequences' test for remoteness: 'there would seem no injustice' if the wrongdoer should be held responsible for instance for the death of a person assaulted.[223] However, the question in a civil intentional delict case would be dealt with by a judge rather than a jury.[224] A judge would need to be more explicit with regard to 'moral notions' or 'justice' than that. In providing support for his or her approach to what the test is and its application the most readily usable material would be examples of the application of the criminal law in criminal cases.

F. *Defences*

General considerations of legal policy may play a part in determining what defences are available as well as a part in the development of the

[220] *Scott's Trustees* v. *Moss* (1889) 17 R 32.

[221] Gordon, *The Criminal Law of Scotland*, 4.14.

[222] *Blaikie* v. *British Transport Commission* 1961 SC 44 at 49 (Lord Justice-Clerk Thomson), cited in *Johnston* v. *HM Advocate* 2009 JC 227, [56] (Lord Reed) and in *MacAngus* v. *HM Advocate* 2009 SLT 137, [45] (Lord Justice-General Hamilton) and *McKew* v. *Holland & Hannen & Cubitts (Scotland) Ltd* 1970 SC (HL) 20, cited in *MacAngus* v. *HM Advocate* 2009 SLT 137, [45] (Lord Justice-General Hamilton).

[223] Walker, *The Law of Delict in Scotland*, 167.

[224] As noted above with respect to accessory liability, civil jury trials can occur in Scotland but they are rare, and defenders may submit that cases involving complex questions, which would be the case with accessory liability, should not be heard by a jury. See Court of Session Act 1988, s. 9(b).

requirements for any defences that are available. Such considerations may differ between crime and delict. A striking contrast is that consideration of legal policy is almost entirely absent from both the case law and literature on defences in the law of delict, but is clear in criminal law. That contrast is apparent first in the structure of the literature on defences. Defences are treated in detail in the 'General Part' of the modern authoritative work on Scottish criminal law,[225] and are now covered comprehensively in work devoted to them that includes analysis of the theory of criminal defences.[226] The tradition in the literature on delict has been to deal with particular defences in the context of particular subcategories of delict.[227] An important departure from this tradition is the chapter in a large ongoing multi-author work on delict.[228]

Where until the nineteenth century there was identification of crime and delict, the defences and their detailed requirements were, inevitably the same. Given the considerable development of defences in the modern criminal case law and literature, it is extremely unlikely that this is true at all today, although the lack of Scots case law on the delictual equivalents makes it generally uncertain what the requirements in the context of delict are. Before the nineteenth century, it was also the case that overriding defences barring any sort of claim, notably prescription at common law and 'personal bar' (the defence where a right holder has acted unfairly and inconsistently with asserting the right)[229] were applicable in the same way. However, since a majority decision in the 1930s,[230] clearly based on a consideration of the goals of criminal justice and a perception of the public's view of them,[231] but in the teeth of the historical evidence,

225 Gordon, *The Criminal Law of Scotland*, paras. 10.01–13.35.

226 Chalmers and Leverick, *Criminal Defences and Pleas in Bar of Trial.*

227 E.g. A. T. Glegg, *The Law of Reparation in Scotland*, 4th edn (Edinburgh: W Green, 1955); Walker, *The Law of Delict in Scotland*; Thomson, *Delictual Liability.*

228 B. Rodger, 'Defences to Delictual Liability' in Thomson (ed.), *Delict*, 8.01–8.55. Cf. the English, US and Australian focus: J. Goudkamp, 'Defences in Tort and Crime', in M. Dyson (ed.), *Unravelling Tort and Crime* (Cambridge University Press, 2014), 208.

229 The defence has similarities to aspects of the law of estoppel in Anglo-american law. But there are fundamental differences. E. C. Reid and J. Blackie, *Personal Bar* (Edinburgh: W. Green, 2006), paras. 1.35–1.37, 5.18–5.25.

230 *Sugden* v. *HM Advocate* 1934 JC 103.

231 Ibid., 112 (Lord Justice-Clerk Aitchison): [Whatever was the old law it] 'was laid down in times that are far distant from our own, and under social and political conditions affecting the purity of prosecutions, that have long since passed away. I cannot regard a rule so laid down 160 years ago as fixed and unalterable, and so sacrosanct that it is beyond the power of this Court to declare that the rule no longer exists. I think it should be so declared. This appears to me to be in accordance with justice and expediency. . . . It

there has been no general prescription of crime, while there are general limitations and prescriptive periods for claims on the basis of delict.[232]

The starkest contrast today is with respect to the effect of 'mental disorder'[233] and some other states of mind. The criminal law is detailed; the law of delict lacks material and is largely uncertain. Criminal law contains detailed analysis of insanity and automatism, which are classified as 'defences',[234] and also of diminished responsibility, that is not a complete defence but in cases of homicide operates to reduce the crime from murder to culpable homicide. Most of the literature on delict does not mention these issues at all. It is accepted that 'a voluntary act'[235] is required for negligence. But that is treated not as a 'defence' but as relevant to whether there was a 'breach of duty'[236] or as an example of 'inevitable accident'.[237] The only Scottish material relied on in the literature for the 'voluntary act' approach is a case where a driver of a vehicle as a result of a coronary thrombosis had lost control or was dead at the time the vehicle crashed. A case that he was driving negligently at that moment of the crash was rejected in the Court of Session.[238] Walker, separately, and uniquely, addresses 'insanity', treating it as a 'defence' to delict generally. He notes the question is 'very difficult',[239] includes a melange of material, ranging from cases on divorce for cruelty, testamentary capacity, and criminal law and ultimately produces no clear rule. It is implied in the literature that there is no relevant Scots delict case law. In fact, there is an unreported first instance decision on a property damage claim from the 1970s where the issue arose as the property was damaged by fire by someone who

requires no effort of the imagination to figure a notorious crime committed twenty years ago, in which, were the criminal allowed to walk abroad with impunity merely because twenty years had run, such a liberty would be against the public conscience, and contrary to the community sense of what is just, upon which the law and respect for the law must ultimately be based'.

232 Now statutory: Prescription and Limitation (Scotland) Act 1973 as amended. As in England and Wales there is a default three-year limitation period for personal injury and defamation. The default period for other delictual actions is five years, with a long stop of twenty years.

233 Including in this term 'learning difficulties'.

234 For an exhaustive treatment, see Chalmers and Leverick, *Criminal Defences and Pleas in Bar of Trial.*

235 Walker, *The Law of Delict in Scotland*, 33; Thomson, *Delictual Liability*, para. 5.2.

236 Thomson, *Delictual Liability*, para. 5.2.

237 Walker, *The Law of Delict in Scotland*, 506.

238 *Waugh* v. *James K Allan Ltd* 1963 SC 175. The alternative case that he was negligent in deciding to drive was rejected on appeal to the House of Lords (*Waugh* v. *James K Allan Ltd* 1964 SC (HL) 102) on the basis that on the facts that was a reasonable decision.

239 Walker, *The Law of Delict in Scotland*, 90.

committed suicide by that means.[240] It, however, was decided applying a very imprecise rule found in the institutional writer, Erskine[241] from the eighteenth century, adopting the medical categories of the time,[242] and was the criminal/delict test of that period. It cannot be that the test common for crime/delict of the eighteenth century is the law today. But it seems unlikely that today's criminal law test is either. Essentially there is a void in the modern law of delict, which if it ever arises is likely to be filled with English and Commonwealth material.

There is another void in the law of delict: there is no consideration in Scottish material of the role, if any, of coercion as a defence. Nor is there any Scottish case law on necessity as a defence. Where the act was by a public officer in one modern case it was assumed that it was necessary to show malice and lack of probable cause, an analysis where there would be almost no need for a defence of necessity. Since no malice or lack of probable cause was shown, the police were held not liable for injuries to members of the public when charging into a crowd on police horses.[243] However, the malice and lack of probable cause requirement is better understood as not even applying to such a situation.[244] If a true case of necessity or coercion of any sort were to arise it may be assumed that the position would be the same as in England.[245]

Consent, at least on the current authorities is not a defence in a criminal prosecution. The reasoning of the Court for its inapplicability has been on the one hand to admit it is not in the public interest,[246] and on the other, that consent does not remove the *mens rea* of evil intent to assault,[247] nor the *mens rea* for murder or culpable homicide.[248] This latter aspect of the reasoning has been convincingly criticised in the English Court of Appeal.[249] There is a very recent indication judicially that the absolute position that there are no situations where consent is a defence in

240 *Redgates Caravan Parks* v. *Thomson* 17 December 1975, unreported.

241 J. Erskine, *An Institute of the Laws of Scotland* (Edinburgh: John Bell, 1773), 4.4.7

242 Ibid.: 'Idiots and furious persons must be . . . incapable . . . of committing crimes since a malicious intention cannot be charged against either of them [the "either" in this refers to pupils, who have been omitted by an ellipsis] . . . but a lesser degrees of fatuity or furiosity, which darken reason without totally obscuring it, afford not a total defence'.

243 *Ward* v. *Chief Constable of Strathclyde* 1991 SLT 292.

244 Reid, *Personality, Confidentiality and Privacy in Scots Law*, paras. 2.35–2.36.

245 Rodger, 'Defences to Delictual Liability', 8.55.

246 *Smart* v. *HM Advocate* 1975 JC 30, 34 (Lord Justice-Clerk Wheatley).

247 Ibid., 32 (Lord Justice-Clerk Wheatley).

248 *HM Advocate* v. *Rutherford* 1947 JC 1.

249 *Attorney General's Reference (No. 6 of* 1980) [1981] QB 715, 719 (Lord Lane CJ).

the criminal law of assault may be reconsidered.[250] Any reconsideration may be predicted to focus on the public interest dimension and follow developments in English case law.[251]

Consent is a defence at least in some contexts in a civil case. The question has arisen in delict in the case trespass to land.[252] It has been tentatively submitted that it is a defence to a civil assault claim.[253]

Illegality can operate to exclude a civil claim. There is a lack of appellate level authority. Some first instance judges have analysed the matter as relating to whether there is a duty of care, others as a defence.[254] The most recent decision clearly, and correctly, indicates the law is identical to English law.[255]

In the context of invasions of bodily physical integrity and homicide, owing to the identification of crime/delict up to the nineteenth century, the requirements of the defence of self-defence were inevitably the same whether there was a claim for damages combined with a prosecution or not. Reflecting different approaches to due process and fair trial there is a difference with regard to burden of proof of facts relevant to defences. In a civil case the burden of proof lies on the accused, whereas in a criminal case there is only an evidential burden on the defender.[256] There are also some wrong-specific differences. For instance, such limited Scottish case law as there is on self-defence in civil claims today focuses on a requirement that, to constitute self-defence, the response must be proportionate. In the context of an occupier asserting the right to take self-help measures with respect to an intruder on property, a defence of having acted reasonably

250 *Stewart* v. *Nisbet* 2013 SCL 209, [38] (Lord Justice-Clerk Carloway).

251 *R* v. *Brown* [1994] 1 AC 212 (sado-masochism) and *R* v. *Wilson* [1997] QB 47 (branding with consent) are discussed in Ferguson and McDiarmid, *Scots Criminal Law: A Critical Analysis,* paras. 10.2.5–10.2.6.

252 K. G. C. Reid, *The Law of Property in Scotland* (Edinburgh: Law Society of Scotland, 1996), para. 181.

253 Reid, *Personality, Confidentiality and Privacy in Scots Law*, para. 3.02.

254 See Rodger, 'Defences to Delictual Liability', para. 8.32.

255 *McLaughlin* v. *Morrison* 2014 SLT 111, [40] (Lord Jones) following *Gray* v. *Thames Trains Ltd* [2009] 1 AC 339.

256 In civil cases, the burden of proof generally rests with the pursuer, and the case must be proved on the balance of probabilities. The burden of proof in criminal cases lies on the prosecutor, and guilt must be established beyond reasonable doubt. The accused in a criminal case may be required to discharge an evidential burden before raising certain issues such as self-defence, but this requires no more than the identification of some evidence which raises the issue. If the issue is raised, the prosecution must disprove the defence beyond reasonable doubt.

was developed for that context.[257] In a civil assault or homicide case it is almost certain that the approach of the English courts to self-defence in a civil case would be applied, whatever that exactly is,[258] and, as in England, the requirements are not exactly the same as for the defence in criminal law.

One distinctive feature of criminal law is that in the context of homicide and crimes against the person there is a defence, provocation, that operates not as a complete defence but as one that in the context of homicide reduces the crime from murder to culpable homicide and in the context of assault is relevant to the sentence passed. In the context of a civil case where the requirements of a criminal charge of culpable homicide could be established in the context of provocation, provocation has no effect since the death is wrongfully caused. At the period when there was identification of crime and delict cases of invasions of bodily physical integrity, the defence of provocation was a complete defence, applying the principle of *compensatio iniuriae*, so long as the provocation was by acts not words. There is late nineteenth century authority treating it still as a complete defence in a civil assault case[259] though at a time when it had by case law development become a partial defence in criminal cases. However, in three modern first instance civil assault cases,[260] it was held that it operates to reduce damages. The doctrinal basis for treating provocation as a partial defence lowering damages in civil cases has never been fully explored. One suggestion has been that it reflects the concept *culpa*.[261] Treating provocation as a partial defence may have the effect of encouraging the adoption of doctrine from criminal cases on the details of the requirements for the defence of provocation,[262] though the lack of civil case law leaves this uncertain. On the other hand, while accepting

[257] *Bell* v. *Shand* (1870) 7 SLR 267.

[258] *Ashley* v. *Chief Constable of Sussex* [2008] 1 AC 962.

[259] *Aitchison* v. *Thorburn* (1870) 7 SLR 347.

[260] *Ross* v. *Bryce* 1972 SLT (Sh Ct) 76; *Ashmore* v. *Rock Steady Security Ltd* 2006 SLT 207; *McLaughlin* v. *Morrison* 2014 SLT 862 (sequel to *McLaughlin* v. *Morrison* 2014 SLT 111).

[261] *Ross* v. *Bryce* 1972 SLT (Sh Ct) 76, 77 (Sheriff Principal Kidd) referred to in Reid, *Personality, Confidentiality and Privacy in Scots Law*, para 2.31.

[262] See Reid, *Personality, Confidentiality and Privacy in Scots Law*, para. 2.32, suggesting that the criminal decision, *Drury* v. *HM Advocate* 2001 SLT 1013 in requiring proportionality in the response makes 'it seem doubtful whether provocation the form of sexual infidelity would now be accepted as a defence in a civil claim for assault'. (On the other hand, infidelity or a revelation thereof can still constitute provocation in criminal law: Chalmers and Leverick, *Criminal Defences and Pleas in Bar of Trial*, paras. 10.10–10.12.)

that words could not constitute provocation when in the past it operated as a complete defence, it has been submitted that case law treating it as a partial defence reducing damages in a civil case 'casts doubt upon the usefulness of any continuing formal distinction between physical and verbal provocation'.[263] However, that distinction does operate in criminal law, except where the words concern sexual infidelity. In those modern civil cases where there was verbal abuse it was combined with acts.[264]

The question has arisen but has not been determined[265] as to whether contributory negligence (as a partial defence) is available as a defence to an intentional delict. It has been tentatively suggested that if consent is not a complete defence in delict, it might be treated as contributory negligence reducing damages.[266] However, it has been held in England that contributory negligence is not a defence to the tort of assault (or battery),[267] and is not a defence to the tort of deceit.[268] Any argument[269] that the position in Scotland is different would need to be based on the fact that the Law Reform (Contributory Negligence) Act 1945 defines 'fault'[270] in a distinct way for its application to Scotland. It is not at all obvious, however, that this means there is in contrast to England some scope for its applicability to cases of intentional delict. Further if, as considered above, it is accepted that provocation is a partial defence to reduce damages for assault in Scots law, there is no practical purpose to be served in considering whether contributory negligence is a defence in an assault claim.

4. Conclusion

It might be assumed that a small jurisdiction with a generalist judiciary would provide ideal conditions for links between two areas of law to develop and flourish. Somewhat surprisingly, that has not been the case

263 Reid, *Personality, Confidentiality and Privacy in Scots Law*, para. 2.31.

264 *Ross* v. *Bryce* 1972 SLT (Sh Ct) 76 – verbal abuse and physical violence to the defender's dog; *Ashmore* v. *Rock Steady Security Ltd* 2006 SLT 207– verbal abuse and the pursuer hitting the defender with his head.

265 *McLaughlin* v. *Morrison* 2014 SLT 862.

266 Reid, *Personality, Confidentiality and Privacy in Scots Law*, para. 3.02.

267 *Pritchard* v. *Co-operatve Group Ltd* [2012] QB 320.

268 *Standard Chartered Bank* v. *Pakistan National Shipping Corpn (Nos 2 and 4)* [2003] 1 AC 959.

269 Such an argument was put forward in *McLaughlin* v. *Morrison* 2014 SLT 862.

270 Section 5(a).

in Scotland. A rigid procedural division has been maintained, and even where criminal procedure has incorporated elements of compensation, these have been limited in their ambit and appear to remain entirely secondary to the principal goals of the criminal process. No significant consideration has been given to the interaction of criminal and civil process. In part, this may be because the relatively limited volume of case law in a small jurisdiction mean that interactions arise less frequently than they otherwise might; in part, it may be because the stricter the separation at the outset, the easier it is to maintain thereafter. In that regard, it is particularly significant that Scotland – in contrast to its nearest neighbour – has for a very considerable time now regarded criminal prosecution as an almost entirely public matter, with very little room for private parties to pursue redress in the criminal courts.

A similar lack of interaction can be seen in the substantive law, itself affected by these realities. Modern criminal law, although it has and still reflects its early roots,[271] is very substantially the product of a more recent extensive case law and literature which began to develop after the identification of delict and crime ceased around the start of the nineteenth century. As in many English speaking jurisdictions the main focus in delict in the nineteenth century has not been on intentional delict. It came to be on the developing law of negligence, and in the courts also on workplace accident cases based on breach of health and safety legislation. There has been only a very limited case law on intentional delicts, and until recently little consideration in the literature. In a few contexts the pre nineteenth-century law of crime/delict can be seen as affecting the modern law (such as in assault cases the concept of 'affront' and the availability of the defence of provocation (though changed from being a complete to a partial defence). Very rarely it is possible to point to an occasional direct or tacit reference to civil sources in the context of criminal law today (in connection with causation) or to contemporary criminal sources in the context of a civil case (accessory liability). Even in those instances where there has been consideration of criminal law in the context of delict or *vice versa*, this has not given rise to a thorough consideration of where there is or should be a common body of rules and principles, where they are appropriately different, and why. Recent civil cases and literature imply that rather than looking to the equivalent in criminal law in considering

[271] As seen, for e.g., through the use still made of Hume, *Commentaries on the Law of Scotland, Respecting Crimes*.

uncertainties and voids in the law of delict, the source turned to is Anglo–American tort law. Nonetheless, a consideration of the substantive law in Scotland can bring to a wider comparative discussion not just a study of how and why the law has proceeded in separate compartments and the downsides of that. It also demonstrates especially because the material extends over a very long period of time that the position need not be forever thus.

8

The Dutch crush on compensating crime victims

IVO GIESEN, FRANÇOIS KRISTEN AND RENÉE KOOL

1. Introduction

In this chapter we set out to supply the reader with an integrated account of the law in the Netherlands as regards the interaction and interrelationship between tort law and criminal law, most notably criminal procedure. We analyse the different forms and modes of interaction, dependence and influence between (the rules on) tort and crime, focusing on the position of the victim of a crime of some sort who has suffered some form of harm. In particular, we pay attention to how and by which route, criminal law or private law, victims of crime can be compensated.

The chapter starts by mapping the three key components of the interaction between tort and crime (in Section 2) and continues by analysing each of these three components in more detail in Sections 3 to 5. For each of those three sections we will answer three basic questions: where, how and why tort and crime have interacted. After a brief comment in Section 6 on why tort and crime developed as it has, Section 7 rounds off the chapter with a short conclusion. As will become apparent, Dutch law seeks to handle cases efficiently while still observing coherence of criminal law and private law and maintaining the unity of the legal system.

2. Three key components of the crime and tort relationship

If one were to take a helicopter view over the daily activities of the Dutch legal system, one would see three major component parts in the interaction between crime and tort in the Netherlands:

(1) Crimes *are* torts and torts *may be* crimes;
(2) A criminal court is equivalent to a civil court when it comes to dealing with the victim's tort claim; and

(3) Criminal conviction is strong evidence for a later related tort claim filed in a civil court after the criminal case is decided by the criminal court.

These three components will be briefly discussed and thus provide a brief introduction to the Dutch system, before they are explored in more detail.

First, under Dutch law, contrary to some systems, particularly in the common law, an act prohibited as unlawful by the criminal law, is also an *unlawful act* for the purposes of Dutch tort law.[1] Article 6:162 BW (Burgerlijk Wetboek, the Civil Code) expresses this in paragraph 2 by defining an unlawful act as, amongst other things, 'an act or omission in violation of a duty imposed by written law'.[2] Since all criminal acts are contraventions of written law in the Dutch Criminal Code (Wetboek van Strafrecht, Sr[3]) or other (specific) acts with criminal offences, each criminal act is also a violation of a duty imposed by law.

To a certain extent this is also true in reverse: a tort can in criminal law amount to unlawful behaviour that meets the requirement of 'unlawfulness', one of the conditions for criminal liability. When the other elements of the criminal offence are also met, there is a crime and thus the tort is then a crime. Since criminal offences often require more than 'unlawfulness' (or an autonomous interpretation is given to the idea of 'unlawfulness' in criminal law), in most cases a tort does not coincide with crime and therefore the tort cannot be classified as a crime.

Second, consistent with the first general rule that each crime constitutes a tort in private law, Dutch law considers it efficient to let the criminal court that handles the criminal case also decide on the parallel tort claim if the victim of the crime so desires. If that court rules that a criminal act has taken place, it can immediately rule also on the tort law aspects of the behaviour in question, functioning, as it were, as a civil court and applying rules of tort law. This is the so-called *vordering benadeelde partij*, the 'claim by an injured party', as regulated by Article 51f Dutch Code of Criminal Procedure (Wetboek van Strafvordering, Sv) in conjunction with Article 6:162 BW. However, a precondition for this efficient approach to

[1] The other elements that are always needed to constitute a tort (an *onrechtmatige daad*), in the private law sense, still need to be established as well. Think of damage(s), causation, imputability and relativity.

[2] See Section 3.B for a complete quotation of Art. 6:162 BW.

[3] This common abbreviation lacks a reference to 'Wetboek' like the common abbreviation for the civil code, BW. The same applies for the Code of Criminal Procedure, the 'Wetboek van Strafvordering', Sv. The only reason for this usage we can think of is the wish to be so brief as possible.

the tort claim in the criminal trial is that the discussion of the claim by the criminal court does not cause a disproportionate burden and hinder the criminal trial. An example of an undue burden would be where tort liability, or quantum, are complex. In such cases, the criminal court declares the tort claim inadmissible, leaving it to the plaintiff to file a civil suit. In practice, anything 'out of the ordinary', anything that cannot be dealt with simply, is seen as a complicating factor so only the run of the mill tort claims are dealt with through the *vordering benadeelde partij*.[4]

Third, once a criminal court has decided in a criminal trial at which the defendant was present that a certain act is, in law, a criminal act, this ruling serves as compelling (but not conclusive) evidence in any ensuing civil proceedings. This follows from the Dutch Code of Civil Procedure (Wetboek van Burgerlijke Rechtsvordering hereafter, Rv), which states in Article 161 that a final criminal conviction is compelling evidence of the criminal act in civil proceedings. However, this compelling evidence can be challenged by counter-evidence produced by the convicted person in the civil proceedings. If so, the compelling evidence is not conclusive (see Article 151(2) Rv). In practice this will hardly ever be forthcoming. But there is much more to the evidentiary relationship between tort and crime, as will become clear hereafter.

Of course, our division into three component parts begs the question why these defining components are in fact so defining. These three factors touch upon the main characteristics of the Dutch law on tort and crime, they are not just technical details in the law. More importantly, the most basic starting point in the Dutch legal system is that an act that is considered so objectionable to be declared 'forbidden' by the legislature, after having gone through a democratic parliamentary process, and thus entailing the chance of criminal prosecution and sanctioning, should also be considered a (private law) tort. If not, one part of the law would permit that which another part would not. Hence, the unity of the legal system as well as its internal coherence is at stake. In this context we address with 'unity of the legal system' the way Dutch law as a system deals with illegal behaviour and how to provide for redress. We use 'coherence' to refer to the mutual connection of principles, concepts, norms and rules of criminal law and tort law in terms of contents, cohesion, consistency, scope and structure within their own area of the law as well as in the relationship between tort and crime. Both logic as well as the 'unity of the system' and

[4] See Section 4.C and M. ten Brinke, S. Habets and C. Noordam, 'Het nieuwe ontvankelijkheidscriterium in de praktijk' (2014) *Trema* 83.

'coherence' of the system of law seem to require this line of reasoning. Interestingly, Dutch lawyers seem to accept this unity and coherence without discussion or debate. This might suggest that the homogeneity of the legal system so reached is but a side-effect of a practice that has developed without any (generally accepted) concept of coherence in mind.

That same, rather 'unphilosophical' and practical approach is probably also behind the second key component: the choice to deal with two (in essence, distinct) cases at once, within one criminal procedure. If the criminal court is dealing with morally blameworthy, criminal acts, let it also decide on the private law consequences of those same acts. That is efficient. So too the third component: why not use the conviction in a later civil court since it is based on evidence gathered and already judicially tested? The question answers itself, or at least that is what the Dutch seem to think. At the same time, there are in Dutch law no 'transfers' of tort to crime or *vice versa*. Both remain separate areas of law, with different institutions (criminal versus civil courts, professional groups etc.) and with their own rules, norms, principles, doctrine, jurisprudence and case law. We have already shown how the exception to the second key component itself proves this: where there are complex elements in the civil claim, a criminal court will declare the claim admissible and the claimant must seek the expertise of a (separate) civil court.

We will now turn to elaborate on these three components, and their links to further issues across Dutch law.

3. Crime = tort and tort ≈ crime

A. *Introduction*

Criminal law and tort law both serve public interests. Both aim at controlling society by offering some form of redress to victims of behaviour which constitutes a crime and/or a tort and/or redress to society at large. To that end both offer the possibility of holding someone liable[5] for a certain act, behaviour or situation, although the consequences of this

[5] In our contribution we use the terms 'liable' and 'liability' in the sense of the attachment of legal consequences to someone's conduct, which is the result of holding someone accountable. We define accountability in a procedural manner; it is the process aimed at a subsequent public assessment of a person's conduct in a given case in order to evaluate whether this conduct was required and/or justified by this person's responsibility which follows from (unwritten) law and moral and ethical standards, and once this evaluation is executed, to establish who can be held liable and to what extent. See I. Giesen and F. G. H. Kristen, 'Liability, Responsibility and Accountability: Crossing Borders' (2014)

liability will differ between criminal law and tort law. Therefore, the substantive criminal law and tort law do have something in common. In this section we identify where tort and crime overlap and where they do not. To that end we compare the basic requirements of tort and crime: once we have established where tort and crime overlap (Section 3.B), we turn to assess how they do so (Section 3.C) before exploring why (Section 3.D).

B. Where is the overlap (or the difference)?

When an act or omission occurs which is considered to be reprehensible according to moral, social or other (policy) standards[6] the Dutch legal order offers, basically, two forms of redress: criminal or civil liability.[7] In both cases it is all about imputing the act (or the omission) to a person, which can be a natural person and/or a legal person according to Article 51 Sr.[8] Therefore, liability is a (re)construction of the facts in such manner that legal consequences can be attached to acts or omissions of a natural person and/or legal person. This process is governed by rules and conditions of substantive law. For tort the basic requirements are laid down in Articles 6:162–3 BW and for crime the requirements for establishing criminal liability follow from the description of the specific offence in connection with the doctrine of criminal liability.

Article 6:162 BW in conjunction with Article 6:163 BW reads as follows:[9]

3 Utrecht L Rev 1, 6 and R. S. B. Kool, '(Crime) Victims' Compensation: The Emergence of Convergence' (2014) 3 *Utrecht L Rev* 14, 16–20.

6 In essence this boils down to all crimes defined in the Dutch Criminal Code and in specific acts which set certain standards to protect, for instance, consumers, road-users, the environment, the financial markets. Of course, the legal order does not always offer redress for forms of reprehensible conduct. Obvious examples are having no manners, excessive billing, having a love affair during a marriage etc.

7 In places (like the supervision of financial markets) there exists also liability according to administrative law, such as the imposition of an administrative fine or other administrative sanctions. These are alternatives to criminal liability due to the *una via* principle and the *ne bis in idem* principle. Apart from that, some unlawful acts have been decriminalised (like some road traffic offences) and are only punished by administrative sanctions. As this chapter focuses on tort and crime, we will not address this issue further.

8 In Dutch criminal law, legal persons can be held criminally liable for the acts committed by natural person(s) in addition to the liability of those natural persons. The act or omission of the natural person(s) is then imputed to the legal person. However, for criminal liability of the legal person it is not required that the natural person who committed the crime is convicted or even prosecuted (see Art. 51 *Sr*).

9 Own translation, based on I. Giesen and E. F. D. Engelhard, 'Medical Liability in the Netherlands' in B. A. Koch (ed.), *Medical Liability in Europe* (Berlin: De Gruyter, 2011), 369–70.

(1) A person who commits a tortious act (unlawful act) against another person that can be attributed to him, must repair the damage that this other person has suffered as a result thereof.
(2) A tortious act can either consist of a violation of someone else's right (entitlement) or an act or omission in violation of a duty imposed by written law or of what according to unwritten law has to be regarded as proper social conduct, always as far as there was no justification for this behaviour.
(3) A tortious act can be attributed to the tortfeasor if it results from his fault or from a cause for which he is accountable by virtue of law or generally accepted principles.

Article 6:163 BW reads:

> There is no obligation to repair the damage on the ground of a tortious act if the violated standard of behaviour does not intend to offer protection against damage as suffered by the injured person.

The general definition of a criminal offence reads:

> A criminal offence consists of an act or omission which falls within the terms of the definition of the offence which is ex ante laid down in a statute or regulation and which is unlawful and blameworthy.

This definition of a criminal offence is not laid down in an act, statute or whatsoever and does not have an official status; it is the general accepted definition in the doctrine.[10] The elements of each crime are specified in the criminal offence, which is, as a consequence of the legality principle (Article 1 Sr), described in an act, statute or regulation (thus written law) and then interpreted by the courts.

When one compares both definitions of tort and crime important overlaps and important differences can be found. We will focus on two important differences but also provide an overview of the key similarities and differences in a table.

Both tort law and criminal law can establish liability for wrongs and harms. However, the kind of liability differs. In case of a tort, the law imposes on the tortfeasor the obligation to pay compensation to the victim. The Dutch Civil Code contains a group of seventeen articles which govern the legal duty to pay damages (Articles 6:95–110 BW). The basic principle is that financial loss, which covers the losses suffered as well as future losses and lost profits, must be compensated in full; on the other

[10] See, e.g., C. Kelk and F. de Jong, *Studieboek materieel strafrecht* (Deventer: Kluwer, 2013), 61.

hand, non-pecuniary damage is only recoverable if certain (restrictive) requirements set out in Article 6:106 BW (or specific legislation) are met. The latter provision offers victims, the right to financial compensation for their immaterial damage if the tort that gave rise to liability qualifies as an infringement to the victim's person. This is the case, for instance, if the victim suffers from a physical injury caused by the tort or damage to his reputation. In the case of a conviction for a crime the convicted person is held liable for the crime itself and sentenced: there are a variety of criminal sanctions, from imprisonment to the measure of paying a financial sum for illegally obtained profits to the state.[11]

However, tort law and criminal law are intertwined by a particularly Dutch phenomenon. Criminal courts can sentence the wrongdoer to pay compensation *to the state for the benefit of the victim of the crime*, the state collecting the compensation and passing it on to the victim. This criminal sanction, the compensation order of Article 36f Sr, is most commonly, but not in every case, imposed when the criminal court accepts the tort claim of the injured party. There are also a few other means in criminal law to effectuate compensation of the injured party, like the condition to pay compensation to the injured party as a specific condition to a conditional sentence or mediation. These instruments are significantly less frequently used than the compensation order. The compensation order's function is to insure that the victim receives compensation. The compensation order is, in a way, comparable to the responsibility of the tortfeasor in tort law to pay compensation to the victim. The result is the same: the victim of the crime is compensated for his damage caused by the crime. However, the way in which this obligation to pay compensation is executed differs. Since it is a criminal sanction, the state is responsible for the execution, which means that police and judicial powers can be used to force the convicted person to pay. More than this, if the convicted person does not have the financial means to pay compensation, the state has made itself responsible for compensating the victim. By contrast, in tort law the victim whose claim is granted by the court must enforce the court's order himself. This means that he must pay for a bailiff in order to make the tortfeasor pay and/or must use the procedures provided for in the Dutch Code of Civil Procedure. He also risks the defendant being unable to satisfy the claim.

[11] For an elaborate discussion of the Dutch sentencing system, see F. W. Bleichrodt and P. C. Vegter, *Sanctierecht* (Deventer: Kluwer, 2013) and for a brief overview J. F. Nijboer, 'The Criminal Justice System' in J. M. J. Chorus *et al.* (eds.), *Introduction to Dutch Law* (Deventer: Kluwer Law International, 2006), 399–444, at 421–4.

There is another important difference between tort and crime, which concerns the flexibility of the system. Due to the principle of legality in criminal law, enshrined in Article 1 Sr, the definition of an offence must be laid down in an act, statute or regulation. The Dutch principle of legality is in this sense a bit stricter than the minimum standard of the European Court of Human Rights, which allows for a definition in the law, a concept that also encompasses case law.[12] The principle of legality also contains a *lex certa* component, which demands that the legislature defines the criminal offence in a manner that is sufficiently precise and clear. So the act or omission (and any other relevant objective elements of the crime such as relevant circumstances) that constitute the offence must be defined clearly. This definition must be put in place in advance; it is the duty of the legislature to take care of a proper and adequate definition of the offence. For these reasons, offences can be found in the Dutch Criminal Code and specific acts, like the Road Traffic Act, the Act on Economic Crime and the Financial Markets Supervision Act. Tort law is more flexible. Article 6:162(2) BW provides for three criteria for unlawfulness, though admittedly these greatly overlap. Acts or omissions that belong to either one or more of these three categories are considered to be unlawful (unless there is a ground of justification). The three categories are:

(1) Breach of a legal right. Examples are breaches of real rights (rights *in rem*), like the property right, and personal rights, like the right to privacy.
(2) Acts or omissions that violate a statutory duty. These duties can be open standards in a statute like Article 7:453 BW: 'Medical practitioners must take all due care in the exercise of their profession in order to act as a good practitioner . . . '.
(3) Acts or omissions that violate a rule or norm of unwritten law pertaining to proper social conduct. This category concerns a breach of a particular duty of care which is formulated specifically taking all the concrete circumstances of the case into account; in other words, a general duty of care. The Hoge Raad, the Dutch Supreme Court, has formulated four questions which can be used in cases that concern dangerous or risky activities to determine whether the duty of care has been breached: (i) the likelihood that one can expect that others are not paying the required attention or exercising sufficient caution; (ii) the chance that an accident might happen due to the

[12] See, e.g., *Scoppola* v. *Italy No. 2* (2010) 51 EHRR 12.

defendant's actions; (iii) the severity of the consequences that can occur; and (iv) the extent to which it is either difficult or possible to take precautionary measures.[13]

The third category of unlawfulness particularly shows the open character of tort law and how Dutch tort law evolves through the work of the courts. Yet Dutch tort was not always arranged this way. This third category did not appear in the old Civil Code (1838) and the Hoge Raad interpreted the unlawfulness requirement narrowly: only a violation of a statutory rule could result in tort liability.[14] This approach, which shows some resemblance to the core of the principle of legality in criminal law, was heavily criticised by scholars. In 1919 the Hoge Raad introduced the general duty of care,[15] which was incorporated into the new Dutch Civil Code (Article 6:162(3) BW) of 1992. Since 1919, a huge body of case law with specific duties has been developed. This development is a manifestation of the structural tendency amongst Dutch courts to deduct the protected interests, standards of care and/or concrete rules in each individual case by identifying the relevant facts and putting a meaning on them. This process takes place in the interaction with already existing law. Subsequently, the courts decide the case on the basis of these interests, standards of care and/or concrete rules. In Dutch law, it is the courts, not the legislature, which are really establishing the boundaries of liability.

The first two categories for unlawfulness (legal rights and statutory duties) also require interpretation by the courts; they are not defined in Article 6:162 BW either. Over time, case law has set out more or less specific rules for unfair competition, defamation cases, liability in sports, traffic liability, employers liability, professional liability and other cases. It shows that this approach allows tort law to react in a made-to-measure fashion, with an opportunity to use 'local' knowledge and experience to identify and formulate the relevant standard of care on a case-by-case basis.[16] Furthermore, the standards are inherently adaptable to changing

[13] Hoge Raad 5 November 1965, *NJ* 1966, 166 (*Kelderluik*).

[14] Hoge Raad 6 January 1905, *W.* 8163 (*Singer*).

[15] Hoge Raad 31 January 1919, *NJ* 1919, 161 (*Lindenbaum/Cohen*). About this development: G. E. van Maanen, *De Zutphense juffrouw en de ontrouwe bediende van Lindenbaum* (Nijmegen: Ars Aequi Libri, 1995).

[16] In our view, this is similar to the common law with its judge-made law. However, in Dutch tort law the courts have to start from an act, statute or regulation and there is, strictly speaking, no principle of precedent (that forces courts to follow previous case law in subsequent cases).

circumstances, preventing rigidity. At the same time, since in these forms of wrongfulness the courts must start from an act, statute or regulation and their decision has to fit in existing (case) law, or at least, must explain why a new interpretation is given or a new rule is defined, they do not in principle breach the principle of legal certainty, even in cases where it concerns the general duty of care.

At the level of the elements of a tort and a crime the similarities and differences might usefully be summarised in Table 1:

Substantive Elements of Dutch Tort and Crime

Requirement	Tort	Crime	Evaluation
Separate definition in a statute	No	Yes	The legality principle in criminal law requires the definition of offences in statutes which is not the case in tort law
Who? (tortfeasor/ suspect)	Any person	In principle any person, but in some cases persons with a certain capacity or position	*De facto* the same
Act or omission	Yes	Yes	The same
Consequence of the act or omission?	Yes, damage	Depends on the crime: many crimes require specific consequence, but others do not (such as theft, which does not require proof that the proprietor has lost his property).	Not the same
Causality	Yes, the act or omission must result in damage	Depends on the crime: causality is required when the occurrence of a consequence is an element of the offence	The same in case of a crime with a causality requirement

(*cont.*)

(cont.)

Requirement	Tort	Crime	Evaluation
Unlawfulness	Yes	Yes, though in many crimes unlawfulness is implied by the conduct whilst in other crimes unlawfulness is an explicit element of the offence	More or less the same; criminal law seems to encompass more
Mens rea element	Negligence, intent or no *mens rea* requirement in case of strict liability	Each crime requires blameworthiness (which is normally assumed when the perpetrator fulfils all elements of the offence); many crimes require on top of that a specific subjective element (negligence, *dolus eventualis*, intent or even purpose). No strict liability.[17]	Different system, with different interpretations of negligence and intent
Relativity[18]	Yes, see Art. 6:163 BW	No	Relativity is necessary in tort law to compensate for tort's open character. In criminal law there is no such thing as relativity: the definition of the offences provides the limits and is itself a manifestation of a certain norm or standard that protects a particular or general interest

[17] Dutch criminal law does not accept strict liability but administrative law does, sometimes with regard to offences which formerly belonged to the domain of criminal law, like some road traffic offences.

[18] The rule that is violated should protect the victim's interests and the class of persons that he belongs to. E.g., road traffic rules only protect road-users, not someone who suffers a miscarriage from a sudden noise in the street.

C. *How are the substance of crimes and torts related?*

Crimes and torts are related on a substantive level. We distinguish three levels at which this relation between crime and torts manifests itself.

On the first level, the function of criminal law and tort law is to deal with reprehensible behaviour. Although both serve several functions, they have in common that in the end they aim to control society by offering some form of redress. In tort law this redress is primarily offered to the claimant; Article 6:162 BW allows for damage caused by unlawful behaviour to be compensated by the tortfeasor. However, this also serves the public interest. In criminal law the focus of the redress is primarily on society at large. However, the picture is more complex because, as noted, criminal law can also offer redress to the victim. It does so by considering the injured party's claim at the criminal trial and imposing the sanction of compensation to the state for the benefit of the injured party, the compensation order, (discussed in detail in Sections 2 and 4.C.7). The different focus of the redress offered by tort law and by criminal law explains why tort law belongs to the domain of private law, particularly the law of obligations, which governs horizontal relations between citizens and/or private organisations/businesses, whilst criminal law is part of public law and deals with vertical relations between the governmental bodies on the one hand and citizens and private organisations/businesses on the other hand. There are related major differences in the functions of criminal law and tort law. For example, the preventive effect of criminal law as such is generally accepted, although there is discussion about which kind of prevention criminal law can offer and its effectiveness,[19] while in

[19] In Dutch criminal law, a distinction is made between general prevention and specific prevention. The general preventive effect is the impact of actual and perceived enforcement of the criminal law on society at large. When other citizens notice that reprehensible behaviour is prosecuted and sentenced, it is expected that they are deterred from committing crimes themselves, because they fear punishment (deterrence). At the same time, that process of adjudication confirms the rules and norms set by criminal law, or even re-sets them if there has been a new interpretation of a rule or norm. The specific preventive effect is the effect of application of criminal law to the perpetrator in three ways. First, he may be prevented from committing new crimes due to incapacitation (such as imprisonment, which removes the perpetrator physically from society, so he cannot commit another crime). This aspect also encompasses the function of safeguarding society from crime. Second, it is expected that the perpetrator will learn from his sentence and will refrain from committing new crimes in the future (deterrence). Third, with measure-made sentencing to the needs of the perpetrator he can acquire knowledge, education and skills to give him a new start in life after sentencing (re-socialisation). Thus, the preventive effect of criminal law encompasses not only several aspects of deterrence, but also more. See J. Remmelink, *Mr. D. Hazewinkel-Suringa's Inleiding tot de studie van het Nederlandse*

tort law the preventive effect, through deterrence or otherwise, is heavily debated and the mainstream view is that prevention is not a function of tort law.

Second, crime and tort are related on the level of basic concepts and requirements. These similarities on the level of basic concepts and requirements also explain why a crime = a tort. The classic example is the interpretation of the causality requirement in offences as well as in tort. In the 1970s the Hoge Raad decided that causation in tort (1970) and crime (1978) should be found by means of the standard of *reasonable imputation.*[20] This standard entails that on the basis of grounds of reasonableness, it is considered to be fair that a specific consequence is attributed to a concrete act or omission. A second example is unlawfulness: one can say that more or less the same standard is used in criminal law and tort law. Where in tort law Article 6:162(2) BW provides for three overlapping categories of unlawfulness which are interpreted by the courts, in criminal law unlawfulness is only defined in the case law of the Hoge Raad. The Dutch Supreme Court uses the catch-all definition of an act or omission contrary to the law, which encompasses a violation of a written law (rule or norm) as well as a violation of unwritten law, like a rule or norm of unwritten law pertaining to proper social conduct.[21] The scope of this definition is at least the same as the scope of the categories for unlawfulness in tort law, perhaps a bit wider thanks to its open character and the principle of autonomy of the criminal law, discussed below in Section 3.D. For this latter reason, unlawfulness in criminal law cannot be interpreted exactly the same as unlawfulness in tort law.[22] However, one has to bear in mind that unlawfulness in criminal law is only one of the elements of a crime and that its open character is filled in the context of the specific elements of the crime in relation to concrete circumstances of the criminal case.[23]

The third level at which crime and tort are related, is how the elements which make up the offences and torts are interpreted. Interpretation is particularly important in criminal law, as interpretation by analogy or

strafrecht (Arnhem: Gouda Quint, 1996), 899–908; Kelk and De Jong, *Studieboek materieel strafrecht*, 26–27, 30–2.

[20] See for tort law Hoge Raad 20 March 1970, *NJ* 1970, 251 (*Doorenbos* v. *Waterleidingsgebied Leeuwarden*) and for criminal law Hoge Raad 12 September 1978, *NJ* 1979, 60 (*Fatale longembolie*). See Section 3.D for a brief discussion.

[21] Hoge Raad 9 February 1971, *NJ* 1972, 1 (*Dreigbrief*).

[22] J. de Hullu, *Materieel strafrecht* (Deventer: Kluwer, 2012), 190.

[23] Ibid., 191; Kelk and de Jong, *Studieboek materieel strafrecht*, 153–65.

even too extensive interpretation would breach the principle of legality. Many definitions of offences use terms which are also used in private law. If there is value in a uniform interpretation of a term across private and criminal law, the question arises whether the element of the offence which is defined with the same terms as used in private law should be interpreted in the same way as in private law. However, we will show in the next section that historically a clear distinction has been made between tort and crime, and that in criminal law the principle of autonomy exists, allowing criminal courts to give their own interpretation to terms which are also used in private law.

D. *Why are tort and crime so (un)connected?*

First and foremost it must be stressed that the 'relationship' between tort and crime is not dealt with in the Netherlands in terms of either 'equality' or 'hierarchy'. This terminology is basically not used at all. The tort system and the criminal justice system are considered to be two distinct areas of law that intertwine at some points. This follows from the principle of autonomy, discussed below. Given this context, the relation between the tort and crime is not further analysed in terms of a 'relationship' or 'what comes first'.

The foregoing sections show that tort and crime are not so connected as one would expect given the historical background of tort and crime. In Roman law and Medieval law there was no distinction made between crime and tort. A natural person could be held liable for reprehensible behaviour that was prescribed by statutes and rules, which also set out specific sanctions.[24] Slowly tort and crime developed into separate areas of law. One could pinpoint the opinion of Hugo de Groot, who in 1631 made a clear distinction between sentencing in criminal cases and paying damages in tort law cases, as a starting point for this development of tort and crime as separate areas of law.[25] This development expanded enormously with the codification of rules and norms of private law and criminal law in the Napoleonic Codes which were applicable during the French dominion over the Netherlands from 1810–13, which followed a period starting from 1795 where the Netherlands were a vassal state of the

[24] A. S. Hartkamp and C. H. Sieburgh, *Mr. C. Assers Handleiding tot de beoefening van het Nederlands burgerlijk recht. 6. Verbintenissenrecht. Deel IV. De verbintenis uit de wet* (Deventer: Kluwer, 2011), nos. 3–4.

[25] Ibid., no. 5.

First French Republic. The French Code Civil (1804), Code Pénal (1810) and Code d'Instruction Criminelle (1808) were shortly prolonged after the French dominion and gradually replaced by Dutch Codes in 1838, which, however, were at least inspired by the Napoleonic Codes. The Dutch Civil Code of 1838 and the Dutch Code of Criminal Procedure of 1838 featured the dogmatic distinction between tort and crime which is characteristic of the substantive Napoleonic Codes.[26] However, this dogmatic distinction began to unravel.

Already by 1838 the Dutch Code of Criminal Procedure offered the victim of certain crimes, which were only the crimes dealt with by the courts in correctional cases (the ordinary crimes like theft, the so-called *wanbedrijven*), the possibility to join the criminal proceedings if his claim for damage was below 68 Euros and not pending before a civil court (Art. 231 Sv 1838). These strict conditions were inspired by the distinction between tort and crime, according to which the criminal court does not have jurisdiction over issues of private law, while at the same time the criminal court should not be distracted from the principal issue, namely deciding the criminal case, so the tort claim must be very simple and was considered as something 'additional'.[27] This rationale must be seen against the background of the legislature's wish not to copy from the French Code d'Instruction Criminelle the right of the injured party to start prosecution. Only the Public Prosecutor's Service should have the (monopolistic) power to prosecute.[28] With the amendments of the Code of Criminal Procedure in 1886 the *offence limitation*, restricting the process to certain crimes was removed, thus all crimes (even serious offences or *misdrijven*)[29] were covered. In addition, the effective position of the injured party was improved (for instance with the possibility of

[26] See for this dogmatic distinction, e.g., J. de Bosch Kemper, *Wetboek van Strafvordering, Eerste deel* (Amsterdam: Johannes Müller, 1838), 47–54; J. Slingenberg, *De strafbare daad en de schadeloosstelling van den benadeelde* (Amsterdam: Delsman and Nolthenius 1896), 96–8. Compare the similar distinction in the French and German legal systems. Note the Burgerlijk Wetboek (BW) was revised in 1992, the Wetboek van Strafvordering (Sv) in 1926 after a partial revision in 1886. A following revision of the Wetboek van Strafvordering is planned and will be executed in near future.

[27] See J. de Bosch Kemper, *Wetboek van Strafvordering, Eerste deel*, 47.

[28] Ibid., 51–2.

[29] The new Criminal Code of 1886 abolished the distinction between very serious crimes like capital crimes (*misdaden*), ordinary crimes like theft (*wanbedrijven*) and minor or petty offences (*overtredingen*) and introduced the twofold distinction between crimes (i.e. serious offences) and minor or petty offences.

legal assistance). However, the same limitations to the admissibility of the claim for damages of the victim of crime in criminal proceedings, *claim limitation*, were kept on basis of the initial rationale.[30] Even on the introduction of the current Code of Criminal Procedure in 1926, the claim limitation of 68 Euros was retained for the same reasons; though the limitation that the claim was not yet pending at the civil court was removed.[31] The monetary limitation to claims with a maximum of 68 Euros, which had in 1954 been raised to 136 Euros, then to 226 Euros in 1963 and subsequently in 1978 to 680 Euros for cases pending at district courts,[32] was removed in 1995 with the coming into force of the Terwee Act. This Act introduced a qualitative criterion instead (see further Section 4.C).

It follows from the historical origins of the current procedure of the joinder of the injured party's claim for compensation in criminal proceedings that tort and crime have always been intertwined. In particular, based on a mix of compassion and efficiency, the victim, as an injured party, was (and still is) entitled to bring forward a (simple) civil claim for compensation to be handled by the criminal court.[33] Traditionally, this procedure is considered to be ancillary in two respects. First, the tort claim is dependent on the criminal law as only the victim who directly suffered damage as a consequence of a crime can use the procedure. Second, the handling of the claim is subordinate to the criminal proceedings.[34] However, there is a trend to focus on the position of victims of crime and to improve the victim's chances of obtaining compensation. We will discuss it in detail in Sections 4.A and 6.

An important explanation for the lack of connection between tort and crime is the principle of autonomy. According to this principle criminal

[30] See H. J. Smidt and E. A. Smidt, *Wetboek van Strafvordering met de geschiedenis der wijzigingen daarin gebracht bij de invoering van het Wetboek van Strafrecht, Deel I* (Haarlem: H. D. Tjeenk Willink, 1886), 583–4, 588–9.

[31] A. J. Blok and L. Ch. Besier, *Het Nederlandsche strafproces, Tweede deel* (Haarlem: H. D. Tjeenk Willink, 1925), 113–15.

[32] See the Act of 4 May 1954, *Staatsblad* 1954, 169, the Act of 20 November 1963, *Staatsblad* 1963, 485 respectively the Act of 10 October 1978, *Staatsblad* 1978, 528. The only reason for raising the monetary limitation was to adjust for inflation, see *Parliamentary Papers* 1962–3, 7101, no. 3, p. 6 respectively *Parliamentary Papers* 1977–8, 15 019, nos. 1–3, p. 13.

[33] R. S. B. Kool, 'Comment 2 at Arts. 51a–51h' (suppl. 178, November 2009) in A. L. Melai and M. S. Groenhuijsen *et al.* (eds.), *Het wetboek van strafvordering* (Deventer: Kluwer (loose leaf edition)).

[34] M. S. Groenhuijsen, *Schadevergoeding voor slachtoffers van delicten in het strafgeding* (Nijmegen: Ars Aequi Libri, 1985), 33–4.

law has its own functions and purposes from which it follows that criminal courts can and must decide on crimes themselves and this demands an autonomous interpretation of the elements of offences. It means that they have the discretionary power to abstract from rules, norms, interpretations and concepts of private law. When criminal courts would be bound by those rules, norms, interpretations and concepts of private law, it may hinder the purposes of criminal law and therefore harm the functions of criminal law. Criminal law should determine itself in which cases and under which conditions someone can be held criminally liable, which criminal sanctions can be imposed and by which criminal proceedings this is realised, thereby observing the principles, concepts, norms and rules of criminal law (such as the principle of legality and guilt principle). This also implies that criminal courts can decide on issues of private law that have to be decided in order to judge a criminal case.[35] The principle of autonomy stems from the development of tort law and criminal law as separate areas of law. Remarkably, the principle is generally accepted in criminal law, but not as such recognised in private law; private law is considered to be autonomous *in se.* As we will demonstrate below, there are provisions in Dutch law that express the principle of autonomy, like the rule of Art. 14 Sv that a criminal court can adjourn the proceedings in order to await the outcome of civil proceedings, but the criminal court is not obliged to do so and has thus the power to decide the private law issue itself (see Section 4.B).

The existing connections between tort and crime have often been triggered by reasons of pragmatism and/or coherence. For instance, the identical interpretation of causation in tort and crime amply demonstrates both reasons. First, it is very difficult to transform the concept of causality into a workable standard for the courts to establish whether the causality requirement is met in a concrete case. In the doctrine several theories about causation have been developed and continue to be. The legislator left it, for reasons of pragmatism, open to the courts to decide what the causality requirement should entail in tort as well as in crime. The legislature made clear by 1886 that it was not able to draw up a general criterion with which the causality requirement could be applied in tort and in

[35] H. A. Demeersseman, *De autonomie van het materiële strafrecht* (Arnhem: Gouda Quint, 1985), 565–79, 608, 610–11, 618–19, 643–4; F. G. H. Kristen, 'Comment 4.4 at Art. 14' (suppl. 118, October 2000), in A. L. Melai and M. S. Groenhuijsen *et al.* (eds.), *Het wetboek van strafvordering.*

criminal cases.[36] After a development in the case law, the private law chamber of the Hoge Raad first decided in 1970 that the causality requirement in tort should be decided with the standard of reasonable imputation.[37] Eight years later the criminal law chamber of the Hoge Raad followed and decided that the same test for causation should be used in criminal law.[38] Although the court did not made explicit for which reasons it followed the approach of the private law chamber of the court (it was not required to do so), it has been assumed that the standard developed by private law chamber was workable and it would contribute to the coherence between tort and crime to use the same standard in criminal law. Such coherence can also enhance legal certainty. However, it must be remembered that this only concerns the standard to be used to establish causality in criminal cases and civil cases; the law of evidence and particularly the standard and burden of proof are different in criminal procedure and civil procedure (see Section 5.B). This obviously affects the application of the causation standard.

4. Criminal Court ≈ Civil Court

A. *Introduction*

1. Context: increasing attention on compensation for victims of crime

Drawing up a clear description of the interaction between tort and crime in Dutch procedural law is rather a challenge. While there is, in practical terms, procedural overlap, there is at the same time a strong element of autonomy for each of the rules of civil and criminal courts. Recent legislative interventions to encourage the award of compensation to victims of crime and simultaneously provide for procedural justice show an increasing attention to this topic. These interventions bypassed the traditional opinion that no 'private' element whatsoever must be admitted

[36] See for criminal law H. J. Smidt and J. W. Smidt, *Geschiedenis van het Wetboek van Strafrecht, Deel I* (Haarlem: Tjeenk Willink, 1891), 138. The Minister of Justice remarked during the deliberations on the bill for the Criminal Code: 'It is incontestable that no legislator has it within his powers to prevent the variety of questions which raise in connection with criminal liability or civil liability by means of providing for a definition of causation' (authors' translation).

[37] Hoge Raad 20 March 1970, *NJ* 1970, 251.

[38] Hoge Raad 12 September 1978, *NJ* 1979, 60.

within criminal proceedings: the victim had, for instance, traditionally been barred from having a distinctive place the criminal trial. Nonetheless, compassion had driven the Dutch to allow victims to bring small claims through the adhesion procedure.[39]

It was in the 1990s that a shift of the penal paradigm became manifest. Except for the introduction of the adhesion procedure at the beginning of the nineteenth century (see Section 3.D), there had not been much of a debate with regard to victims' compensation.[40] Due to a rise of traffic accidents, debate rose in the 1960s, but the real trigger for the paradigm shift in the 1990s lies in the work of the Law Reform Commission on Financial Penalties (1969).[41] This committee, chaired by the penal abolitionist Hulsman,[42] recommended a fundamental re-orientation of the concept of sanctioning, focusing on conflict solving instead of the traditional aim of prevention and deterrence. The approach of the committee, however, was academic rather than immediately practical, focusing on behavioural aspects, pursuing re-socialisation by 'civilising' the criminal law. In the years to come, other law reform commissions would also addressed the victims' position, however but without yielding practical results.

Meanwhile, in the wake of secularisation and individualisation, the idea of 'citizenship' has changed. In the past decades, the Dutch society has fragmented, experiencing a decline of authority and individualisation. This has, amongst other things, been accompanied by a strong call for state protection, featuring a collective rejection of victimhood.[43] Self-help organisations were set up, ultimately leading to the formation of the Dutch Victim Aid Organisation that was founded in 1984. A year later

39 This position reflects the profile of the Netherlands as a 'high-trust society', featuring a 'politics of accommodations' (pursuing political consensus by negotiation), implying a high esteem in the authorities. E.g. A. Lijphart, *The Politics of Accommodation. Pluralism and Democracy in the Netherlands* (University of Berkeley Press, 1975); C. de Voogd, *Geschiedenis van Nederland* (Amsterdam: Arena, 2000).

40 See for a brief description Section 3.D above. For an overview: Kool, 'Comment 2 at Arts. 51a–51h' (suppl. 178, November 2009).

41 Commissie Vermogensstraffen, 'Het Strafrecht en de benadeelde partij. Tweede Interimrapport' in: *Eindrapport van de Commissie Vermogensstraffen* (The Hague: Staatsuitgeverij,1972), appendix IV.

42 Louk Hulsman was professor of criminal law at the Erasmus University Rotterdam. He was inspired by the work of Thomas Matthiesen and Nils Christie. Except for the report mentioned, his work has not deeply influenced the Dutch debate. Nevertheless, his work is reflected in the topical introduction of restorative justice schemes.

43 H. Boutellier *Solidariteit en slachtofferschap* (Nijmegen: SUN, 1993).

Groenhuijsen, who would become the key player in the academic victim's movement, published his thesis on victims' compensation.[44] Finally, the women's movement came into play, waging an active campaign against sexual violence. One aspect of this was arguing that women and minors were in need of adequate legal protection, including being entitled to redress for wrongs.[45] Subsequently, the Public Prosecution Service initiated ad hoc committees to consider victims' need and make recommendations, amongst others on compensation.[46] In the wake of these social and legal changes, a law reform commission, the Terwee Committee, was set up in 1985. This committee considered the convergence of tort law and criminal law, recommending, amongst other things, a raise in the value of the claim limitation, a simplification of the admissibility criterion and the introduction of a new form of punishment, the *schadevergoedingsstraf* (compensation penalty). The latter recommendation was innovative, as it suggested that a criminal offence can constitute both criminal and civil liability, to be assessed in the context of the criminal proceedings.[47] This proposal, however, was rejected: the legislature opted for a compensation order instead (Article 36f Sr). Since then, developments in the area have been concentrated on the legitimacy and consequences of upholding the crime victim's legal rights, including an improvement of the right to claim compensation. Yet this has not fundamentally altered the Dutch law's scope of the victim's formal position, in particular, victims still are not granted a procedural position on equal footing with the defendant or the Public Prosecution Service. To date, the victim is acknowledged as a participant, but not as a 'party'. The latter is a 'breaking point' within the Dutch scheme of justice. Indeed, although the Dutch government highly values the victims' interests, acknowledging the victim as a principal stakeholder having legal rights,[48] and is moreover showing eagerness to

[44] Groenhuijsen, *Schadevergoeding voor slachtoffers van delicten in het strafgeding*.

[45] A. C. Zijderveld *et al.*, 'De wisselende aandacht voor slachtoffers. Enkele cultuursociologische overwegingen', in Handelingen Nederlandse Juristenvereniging, *Het opstandige slachtoffer* (Deventer: Kluwer, 2003-I), 1–33.

[46] According to the case-law such recommendations count as substantive 'law' ex Art. 79 *RO* and must be pursued (Hoge Raad 27 May 2014, ECLI:NL:HR:2014:136).

[47] Note the Dutch criminal law uses a bifurcated concept of sanctions: punishment (*straffen*) and measures (*maatregelen*). Generally speaking, the first category is based on retribution, requiring a *mens rea* element; the latter is in pursuit of public protection.

[48] Title IIIA Sv provides an extended catalogue of victims' rights, covering a wide range of interest, e.g. with regard to treatment (Art. 51a Sv), disclosure (Art. 51b Sv) and legal assistance (Art. 51c Sv).

further the facilities with regard to compensation,[49] there is no intention to extend the formal position of the victim.

Indeed, the adhesion procedure – to be discussed below – must not be confused with the right to prosecute, for the Dutch system does not hold a right for private prosecution. The right to prosecute rests exclusively with the Public Prosecution Service. Moreover, the Public Prosecution Service is not obliged to prosecute (Arts. 167 and 242 Sv) rather they exercise a discretion, only prosecuting when they view it as being within the public interest. Double jeopardy, that is, initiating criminal proceedings more than once for the same fact, is prohibited in the Dutch system (Art. 68 Sr).[50] If, however, the Public Prosecution Service abstains from prosecution, the victim can request a review by the Court of Appeal of that decision to abstain (Art. 12 Sv). In cases where the complaint is upheld, the Public Prosecution Service must prosecute.[51] The reason to opt for the Court of Appeal as the reviewing authority, instead of the Court of First Instance (here, the District Court) is because of the position of the Public Prosecuting Service in the Netherlands: the Public Prosecution Service and the District Court are on the same level of seniority. Thus the legislature wanted to prevent a conflict of authority.[52]

2. The legal routing

Facts can be brought to court by using different routes. In general, conflicts of jurisdiction are settled within the relevant codes (Sv, Rv, Code of Judicial Organisation (RO)). There is, however, no formal hierarchy between the distinct sections for the legal issues ruled upon are autonomous

[49] The latter development, however, relates to furthering both the criminal law and the civil law facilities.

[50] As will be discussed under Section 4.C, the criminal courts are instructed to avoid ruling the claim to be unfounded, and to opt for an estoppel in order to grant the victim the opportunity to bring the claim before a civil court.

[51] Next, the victim (or his/her relatives) has the 'right' to request a second opinion regarding the judicial investigation. However, this is no legal right, but one based upon policy of the Public Prosecution Service (directives).

[52] Note the Public Prosecution Service is a hierarchical organisation, with different representatives associated with the different levels of courts. On the level of the Court of First Instance, the members of the Public Prosecution Service are called '*officier van justitie*', on the level of the Court of Appeal they are addressed as '*advocaat-generaal*'. Next, there is the '*advocaat-generaal*' and (one) '*procureur-generaal*' at the level of the Hoge Raad. The role of individuals in these last two categories differs, however, since they do not initiate public prosecution, expect for a limited category of offences. Their primary task is to advice the Hoge Raad.

(see Section 3.D). An earlier judgment does not bind findings in later courts, assuming that these courts operate in different fields of law. The point of departure is the 'claim': the claim for prosecution being of a different nature from the claim for compensation, the civil and the criminal procedures address different elements of legally relevant behaviour. Notwithstanding that there are mutual points of reference (for example, the prerequisite of an activity or omission and an element of blameworthiness),[53] the legal standards used to assess tort and crime differ (see in this respect the remarks about the different focus in functions of criminal law and tort law in Section 3.C).

Thus the criminal court can – but as a rule will not – ignore a relevant ruling of a civil court and *vice versa.*[54] Indeed, the Dutch Code of Criminal Procedure also offers a criminal court the discretion to postpone its decision in order to await a decision of a civil court on a matter which is of importance for criminal case (Art. 14 Sv). The aim of this technique is to prevent different interpretations of the law. In practice courts seldom apply this rule. Although this is no hard and fast rule in civil procedural law, a similar management technique exists for the civil law (see also Section 5.C).

Nevertheless, notwithstanding that the civil and the criminal court assess cases autonomously, procedural regimes regarding compensation for tort or crime can overlap. For example, as already noted, a tort can be subject to both criminal and civil procedure simultaneously though it rarely happens in practice. Another possibility, though very rare, is that the civil court might decide its case first. If this civil court accepts or rejects the whole of the claim, the victim will be estopped from bringing any later civil and criminal action because her interest will be extinguished.[55] However, there is also the more common situation in which a criminal court admits only part of the claim, rejecting those parts which were unduly burdensome (discussed further below, Section 4.C.2). In this case, a judgment from a criminal court on those elements would still leave some interest which the victim could pursue with

[53] We abstain from discussing compensation with regard to strict liability (Art. 6:169 BW); the criminal law does recognise such a category, but only for the minor offences (misdemeanours).

[54] F. G .H. Kristen, 'Comments 4 and 9 at Art. 14' (suppl. 118, October 2000) in A. L. Melai and M.S. Groenhuijsen *et al.* (eds.), *Het wetboek van strafvordering.*

[55] An interlocutory injunction, not being a final ruling, also allows the criminal court to rule on a civil claim brought before the civil court. (HR) 19 February 2010, ECLI:NL:HR:2010:BK9301.

a later civil claim. There is a pragmatic argument underlying this informal 'hierarchy': a criminal ruling provides compelling evidence in civil cases (Article 161 Rv).[56]

B. *Where is the overlap (or the difference)*

As is commonly the case in a civil law system, which place great importance on the principle of legality, it is the legislature who decides whether a particular rule in an act or statute will belong to the civil or criminal law. An offence by definition implies a contravention of a statutory rule; by virtue of Article 6:162 BW, the latter also qualifies as a tort. Of course, it should not be forgotten that a tort can also consist of a violation of another person's right, caused by an activity or omission that has, according to unwritten law, to be regarded as improper social conduct (see Section 3.B). As regards the creation of legislative rules, generally proposals to introduce statutory law come from the Ministry for Security and Justice (MSJ). However, there is a possibility for initiatives by Members of Parliament (Lower House only), though this is rare.[57] The MSJ has a specific section that prepares Bills, with subsections with regard to the specific legal areas. The civil servants assigned to develop and execute the government's policy are consulted. As a rule, the MSJ consults the State Council, as well as other advisory boards (e.g., the Board for the Judiciary, the Public Prosecution Service and the Bar Association).

Civil law, including tort claims amongst others civil wrongs, on the one hand and the criminal law on the other are traditionally separated areas of the law (see also Section 3.D). This separation already starts at the universities: most law faculties offer a bachelor programme in law with separate courses in private law, criminal law, constitutional and administrative law and European and international public law. The distinction between tort and crime is thus already set down before students graduate. This division flows from the legislator setting down requirements to enter legal practice as a solicitor/barrister, public prosecutor or judge: students must have what is known as *civiel effect*. This in turn requires a bachelor's and master's degree which included separate courses in at least private law, including civil procedure, *and* criminal law, including

[56] Nevertheless, the 'compelling evidence' needs to be put into perspective so that the defendant can try to rebut the evidence by bringing counterevidence (Art. 151(2) Rv). See also above.

[57] The Higher House does not have the right to initiate, nor does it has the right to make amendments.

criminal procedure, *as well as* one of constitutional law, administrative law or tax law.[58]

There are also separate branches within the District Courts, Appellate Courts and the Hoge Raad.[59] First, who can bring a claim? Anyone who has a justified interest can bring a claim before the courts. A justified interest implies the appellant claims to have had a right violated that was protected by the law (the procedural condition of relativity). As for who hears the claim: for the District Courts and the Courts of Appeal, these consist of a single professional judge (so-called *politierechter*), or three professional judges (*meervoudige kamer*).[60] Courts are divided into branches. The criminal branch of a court deals with crimes, while the civil branch of that same court deals with civil cases.[61] Nevertheless, particularly at the level of the District Courts, the judges circulate roughly every four years. However, they only alternate between two distinct law areas, such as criminal law and administrative law or criminal law and family law or criminal law and commercial law. The Public Prosecution Service can play a role in any of civil procedures but this is a rare exception indeed.[62]

The majority of the cases in the Netherlands concern private law disputes of all sorts (labour, rent, contracts, tort etc.). After that, criminal law

[58] See for instance Art. 2(1)(a) Act on Advocates (Advocatenwet) in connection with Art. 1 Besluit beroepsvereisten advocatuur, *Staatsblad* 2005, 48, which requires that the final exam of a bachelor's and master's programme must contain a criminal law course, which must also include criminal procedure, as well as a private law course, which must also include civil procedure.

[59] Note the Hoge Raad also has a tax chamber. Traditionally, the Hoge Raad functions as a court of 'third instance', however, not ruling upon the facts. An application to cassation thus can be filed after a case has been tried at first and second instance. In order to limit the case-load a selection-rule has been introduced recently: Art. 80a(1) RO allows the Hoge Raad to declare an appeal inadmissible if this does not serve an interest of the claimant, or would not benefit the development of the law. Note, victims whose claims have been rejected by the appeal court in the context of an adhesion procedure (see Section 4.C), are not entitled to appeal the Hoge Raad (Art. 473(3) Sv). If, however, the Public Prosecution Service and/or the defendant appeal(s), the victim's claim is allowed to follow.

[60] Note, in appeal the single judge is not called *politierechter*, but *enkelvoudige kamer* (single chamber).

[61] The civil law being wide, the civil court is organised in subsections (e.g., family law or commercial law). Next to the civil law and the criminal law sections, there is an administrative law section.

[62] The common denominator is that there is a 'public' interest to take care of, for instance placing a juvenile into civil care, or requesting a bankruptcy, followed by an annulment of a legal person. See: M. E. de Meijer, *Het Openbaar Ministerie in civiele zaken* (Deventer: Kluwer, 2003).

has become perhaps the next most significant major specialisation within legal practice. Since both fields are individually so large, not many people work in both fields. While practitioners tend to specialise in a specific area of the law, this is represented by an agreed list of skills and abilities particularly important for either tort or crime. Nevertheless, practitioners have to periodically apply for additional courses in order to be entitled to work as a barrister, prosecutor or judge. There are also associations for lawyers, associations which specialise in a certain field (and who impose a certain measure of expertise) but membership is not needed in order to take on a case in that field. There are, however, two situations which do require specialist training. First, cassation-procedures are executed by a group of specialised lawyers who have undergone specific training.[63] Second, due to the rise of the victim, the group of barristers handling tort cases, including in the context of a criminal procedure, has increased. Indeed, the LANGZS Foundation, a group of barristers specialised in providing legal assistance to victims of crime who seek reparation, was invited to develop a training programme, perhaps indicating a new branch of the bar. Barristers who have been assigned for legal aid assistance to crime victims must have undertaken this training programme.[64]

C. *How are tort and crime procedurally related*

Any overview of the procedural aspects of the relationship between tort and crime inevitably touches upon aspects of the substantive law. This follows logically from the systematic positioning of the claim for compensation *ex* Article 51f Sv: the victim lodges a civil claim within a criminal procedure, obliging the criminal court to deal with the criminal allegation and, within limits, civil compensation. This avenue for claiming compensation is the so-called adhesion procedure or joinder as injured party (*vordering benadeelde partij*). There are no accurate statistics available on in how many criminal cases victims use the adhesion procedure and

[63] For the criminal law section this training is not obligatory. However, in practice cassation-lawyers practicing criminal law do take such a training programme. Cassation is a process which focuses on appeals of law, not on the details of fact, and the superior courts may require more rigour, time-keeping and precision so this training is hardly surprising.

[64] Actually, there are two training programmes and only the first is obligatory: a basic one with four to five meetings and a specialised one with seventeen meetings. The first is required to be assigned legal aid cases; the second one is required to sign up as a specialised victim's barrister. Roughly twenty candidates will take these training programmes on an annual basis. After the initial start, however, these training programmes will probably be offered every two years.

what the outcomes of those procedures are. However, some (qualitative) studies show that in a significant number of criminal cases in which there is a victim, and which were decided by a district court at first instance, the adhesion procedure is used. In our interpretation of the available data it concerns approximately 31 per cent of such criminal cases. Of those cases, the court granted compensation, in whole or in part, in approximately 65 per cent of the cases.[65] This represents what we think of as Dutch pragmatism.

1. The adhesion procedure (Article 51f Sv)

If the case is brought before the court, Article 51f Sv allows the victim of a crime who suffered damage directly from the crime to bring a claim for that damage before a District (Criminal) Court. In that case the victim is joining criminal proceedings as the 'injured party'. While there is no longer a claim limitation on the amount of compensation, there are other limitations. In the first place, complex claims will be rejected. Thus, for instance, where he suffers a number of types of loss, he might select to bring only the part which relates to a simple part, bringing the complicated part in front of the civil court (see Section 5.C). In this way, the injured party pre-emptively seeks to avoid the risk that the claim will be grounded inadmissible by the criminal court due to the complicated nature of the claim. If the injured party does not do so, the criminal court itself can split the claim, ruling it to be partially inadmissible (Article 361(3) Sv). Although seldom used, the criminal court can also rule a claim to be inadmissible in advance, thus giving a preliminary ruling.

Nevertheless, there may be some overlap between how civil and criminal courts award compensation. Some judges are willing to award such a claim in terms of 'an advance', leaving it to the victim to start a civil procedure to claim the remainder. Nevertheless, this is not general practice. Moreover, the term 'advance' is not well chosen as the ruling by the criminal court is final, indicating this part of the claim cannot be subject

[65] The figures concern 2010. That year the district courts dealt in first instance with 110,000 criminal cases (source: CBS Statline, www.cbs.nl (last accessed November 2014)). In 54,000 cases there was a victim. In 17,000 cases the district courts decided on the claim and in 11,000 cases the court awarded the claim in whole or in part (source: W. Schrama and T. Geurts, *Civiel schadeverhaal door slachtoffers na strafbare feiten* (The Hague: WODC, 2012, no. 1), 70–2. For a qualitative study with comparable results, see M. R. Hebly *et al.*, 'Crime Victims' Experiences with Seeking Compensation: A Qualitative Exploration' (2014) 3 *Utrecht L Rev* 27. To put it in perspective: in 2010 there were 209,000 criminal cases recorded at the level of the first instance and almost 1,200,000 crimes (that is without the misdemaenours) registered (CBS Statline).

to a civil procedure. It was chosen to suggest the idea that the sum was, like a publishing company's initial payment towards a promised book, a way for the victim to be in a secure enough financial position to proceed with a civil claim for the full amount in front of a civil court.

The civil claim can be brought at any time once the indictment has been laid until it is presented by the public prosecutor in court. In practice, the *Slachtofferloket*, which forms part of the Public Prosecution Service, must inform the victim in advance about the right to lodge a claim, sending the victim a standard-form (Article 51g Sv).[66] As a rule, the *Slachtofferloket* receives information from the police, who, as a rule, inform the victim of his rights, including the right to claim compensation. The victim's wish to request compensation, is then reported to the *Slachtofferloket*, present at the level of the District Courts and Regional Courts. However, the victim is not obliged to use this form. Indeed, the victim can choose to attend the trial and bring the claim forward in person. Nevertheless, in practice the courts do have a strong preference for the use of the standard form, and the victim might be requested to use one. Although the majority of the claimants do use the form, and the idea is that the forms should be annexed to the dossier before the trial, in order to enable the defence, the public prosecutor and the court to prepare an opinion with regard to the claim, this tends to happen only a few days before the trial is scheduled. From the court's perspective, looking to the defendant's interests – this is rather late, causing a risk that the claim will be ruled inadmissible. In order to further the chances of success, however, the forms are reviewed before the trial by a controller, in service of *Slachtofferhulp* (Victim Support).[67] Although such a review is not obligatory, it is important. If that review finds that the claim needs further evidence, it gives the claimant more time to find it and present it at the trial. However, in practice such a review is limited to complex claims, and with regard to victims who do not have legal assistance. The court itself will not slow down the prosecution so the claimant can find it. That said, there is one situation where the court can and does adjourn, which is where a claimant has informed the Public Prosecution Service of his/her wish to attend trial in order to elucidate the claim, and the Public Prosecution Service has not given notice of

[66] The standard-form covers a range of items relating to the victim's interest, amongst others the victim's wish to claim compensation. Other topics are, amongst others, the wish to stay informed and the wish to make us of the right to make an oral statement in court.

[67] These controllers are posted within the local Public Prosecution Service office, located in the court building. *Slachtofferhulp* is an NGO, financed by the Ministry of Security and Justice; the controllers are on the pay-role of Victim Support.

the trial. Note the claimant is not obliged to pay a court fee, nor to be present or to be represented in court. If, however, the victim chooses to be represented by a barrister (Art. 51c Sv), the barrister must be paid[68] with the fees being based on the claimant's income.[69] Article 44, Wetop de Rechtsbijstand (Code on Legal Assistance), however, grants victims of sexual crimes or violent crimes, or, if the victim has deceased, his or her relatives, free legal assistance.

Quite remarkably, Article 51f Sv also allows claims to be brought to the court for acts that are not mentioned in the indictment, but which are related to it as subsidiary facts. If the defendant admits to having committed these offences (*ad informandum gevoegd feit*) they are added to the indictment, but they benefit from a sentencing reduction.[70] This legal construction is not without risk for the defendant, for although he is entitled to sentencing reduction, he also risks having to pay compensation for any harm proven. While his consent does imply a waiver of the right to oppose to these claims on the facts, any civil claim will not be dealt with in detail at trial so he will have limited opportunity to contest it.

2. Admissibility, the 'ten minute rule'

Whether the claim will be ruled admissible depends on its complexity. In practice, the judge uses the 'ten minute-rule': if the court is of the opinion that the handling of the claim will take more than ten minutes, it will be ruled inadmissible. This is in line with the criterion in Article 361(3) Sv stating that in case the handling of the claim will cause a disproportionate burden, hindering the criminal trial (*geen onevenredige belasting*), the court must declare the claim inadmissible. This means that the claim will only be considered by the criminal court when the tort claim is not complicated in any way. This qualitative criterion therefore functions as a barrier to the victim to have his claim for damages dealt with by the criminal court. It replaces the earlier requirement that the

68 The court fee and the cost for legal assistance are not part of the damage caused by the offence (Art. 361(2)(b) *Sv*). The ruling must mention a separate consideration; the criteria being similar to those used in civil proceedings (Arts. 237–245 Rv.)

69 Claimants will always have to pay a certain amount of the cost, however, there is a minimum of 196 Euros for single persons with an annual income of maximum 18,000 Euros and families, or single parent-families, with a maximum income of 25,200 Euros. Those who have an annual income above 25,600 (singles) or 36,100 (other categories) are not entitled to aided legal assistance. If the claim is awarded, however, the cost will be assigned to the tortfeasor.

70 Note the Dutch do not have plea-bargaining; the scheme of adding *ad informandum gevoegde feiten* is just another example of Dutch pragmatism. Such additional offences do not fall within the full scheme of truthfinding.

claim must be of a 'simple nature', which criterion was introduced with the Terwee Act in 1995 in order to restrict the complexity of civil claims.[71] In practice, the new criterion has not changed the evaluation of the complexity of the claims by the courts. Notwithstanding the legislature's wish to extend the range of the adhesion procedure, the courts still interpret the admissibility-criterion rather strictly.[72]

The 'ten minute-rule' is not a legal criterion, but was introduced by the judiciary.[73] In practice, anything out of the ordinary is seen as a complicating factor so only the run of the mill tort claims are settled in criminal court, that is, for instance, where that there is sufficient evidence that the defendant caused the requested amount of damages.[74] A hypothetical example of how the criminal court will probably apply the criterion of the disproportionate burden, hindering the criminal trial might help. Consider a victim of aggravated assault who files a tort claim for damages consisting of property damage (ruined clothes), pure economic loss consisting of the inability to work for a couple of years (loss of income) and non-pecuniary damages for his pain and suffering. The district court will probably award the property damage and a fixed amount of money as partial compensation for the non-pecuniary loss and will declare the remaining part of the claim for non-pecuniary damage inadmissible as well as the claim for pure economic loss. Of course, the criminal court can also declare the injured party's claim unfounded in case the victim did not provide enough proof for the claim (see further Section 5 below.).

There is another complication with the adhesion procedure. If the civil claim is ruled admissible but it is ultimately is dismissed, the avenue of the civil law is barred since there has been a substantive judicial review. This would be a particular risk for the claimant if the reduced time and perhaps less extensive experience and knowledge of the civil law made a criminal court less likely to uphold a civil claim. In any case, in order to preserve the avenue of the civil law, the criminal courts are instructed to prefer a ruling of inadmissibility instead of unfounded, leaving it to the plaintiff to file a civil suit. However, in practice, a substantive cohort of the

[71] See Section 3.D as well as Section 6.

[72] J. Claassens, 'Het slachtoffer in het strafproces' (2012) *Strafblad* 251; Ten Brinke *et.al.*, 'Het nieuwe ontvankelijkheidscriterium in de praktijk'.

[73] Landelijk Overleg Voorzitters Strafsecties, *Aanbevelingen civiele vordering en schadevergoedingsmaatregel*, October 2011, www.rechtspraak.nl/procedures/landelijke-regelingen/sector-strafrecht/documents/wet-terwee.pdf (last accessed 28 July 2014).

[74] J. Candido *et al.*, *Slachtoffer en de Rechtspraak* (Deventer: Lovs, 2013), para. 4.2.2.

crime victims whose claim was (partially or wholly) ruled inadmissible by the criminal courts do not seek recourse by the civil court.

Recently, it has been suggested that there is a need to improve this civil procedure. One target for reform has been a parallel route to claims, the so-called *kantonprocedure* (Article 117 Rv).[75] This is a more informal and faster form of civil justice, as opposed to the 'fully dressed' civil procedure. In particular, there is no obligation to pay court fees and to be represented by a barrister as both obligations are felt to deter claimants from seeking civil recourse. Moreover, since July 2011 the cantonal judge is competent to rule upon claims to a maximum of 25,000 Euros. Research, however, shows that victims still focus on the adhesion procedure.[76] Thus, the reforms to date have not achieved their purpose.

3. Clarification of the claim

After having dealt with the facts mentioned in the indictment, and the personal circumstances of the defendant, the criminal court deals with the civil claim. The claimant, or his legal representative, is given the floor to clarify the claim. Since the claim cannot unduly burden the criminal trial, the clarification by the claimant can only be modest and is time restricted (see further Section 5). Moreover, Article 334(1) Sv denies the claimant the right to call upon witnesses or experts to clarify his claim. Next, in his closing speech, the public prosecutor will include an opinion regarding the claim. Finally, the judge will address the defendant, or in case he is not present, his authorised defence counsel,[77] to hear the defence's arguments as regards the claim and to learn whether the defendant is willing and able to (fully or partially) pay compensation and has the means to satisfy any compensation order made in case the claim is awarded. Next, the defence is entitled to bring forward their arguments, particularly on quantum and proof of harm. Although the claimant is entitled to have the final comment at the end (Art. 334(3) Sv), this opportunity is seldom used.

[75] *Parliamentary Papers* 2013–14, 33 552, no. 7 (Victim Policy).

[76] Schrama and Geurts, *Civiel schadeverhaal door slachtoffers na strafbare feiten*; Hebly *et al.*, 'Crime Victims' Experiences with Seeking Compensation: A Qualitative Exploration'; R. S. B. Kool, M. R. Hebly *et al.*, *Schadeverhaal na strafbaar feit via de kantonrechter* (Den Haag: BJu, 2014).

[77] Note according to the Dutch rules of criminal procedure, the defendant is not obliged to be present at the trial. In order for the trial to qualify as an adversarial procedure in which defence counsel is able to provide for full defence on his clients' behalf if the client himself is not present, the defence counsel needs to be authorised by the defendant (Art. 279 Sv).

4. Ruling by the court

For minor cases, handled by a single judge, the oral verdict will follow immediately after the hearing. In the more complicated criminal cases, the written verdict must be presented within a two-week term. Where the court rules that a criminal act has been committed, it can also then rule on the tort law aspects of the behaviour in question. The court uses civil law to determine the question of tort damages, although as noted above (Section 3.B), many of the substantive components of the crime are similar to those of tort. Thus the criminal court rules as it were a civil court and applies the rules of tort law. The ruling will be recorded in the verdict as: (in whole or in part) inadmissible, (in whole or part) unfounded or founded. The ruling of unfounded will be given when the victim did not provide sufficient proof of his claim and did not clarify his claim adequately at the trial. That can for instance be the case when, in the hypothetical example mentioned in Section 4.C.2 above, the victim did not provide information about the price of the ruined clothes. Some criminal courts expect a receipt of the purchase of the clothes to be submitted, others accept an overview of pricing of similar clothes. But when there is nothing available about the price of the clothes, the victim's claim will be declared unfounded.

The ruling of the criminal court serves as compelling evidence in any ensuing civil proceedings (Art. 161 Rv) so potential civil claimants not part of the criminal proceedings usually wait for them to be complete (see further Section 5). The claimant is also entitled to a free copy of the ruling (Art. 554 Rv).

5. Appeal

As the aim of the legal procedure is to provide for redress, the legislature has granted the claimant a right of appeal against the amount of damages awarded but he can only join the prosecutor or defendant's appeals, not bring an autonomous appeal of his own. Where there is such an appeal already in motion, the claimant's appeal will be dealt with by the criminal court again, again acting as a civil court for that purpose. If the Public Prosecution Service nor the defendant appeals, the claimant must appeal to the civil court of second instance. He is, however, only allowed to appeal if the claim exceeds the amount of 1,750 Euros (Article 602 Rv).[78] Note a claim for compensation cannot be brought for the first time before the

[78] The rules of the Dutch BW are applied, requiring summons, court fees and legal representation; in practice this opportunity is seldom used.

Court of Appeal, nor can the claim made be altered (Article 421(3) and (4) Sv). Where claim was partially granted, however, the claimant can appeal for the part that has been rejected. Note also that an appeal in the criminal case defers the verdict of the criminal court of first instance, thus the compensation awarded by this court is not enforceable until the appeal has been determined.

6. Concurrent claims and additional support

A wrongdoer's activity may constitute tort and crime, giving way to both a civil and criminal procedure. As the claimant may bring a claim before the civil court (Article 6:162 BW) and the Public Prosecution Service simultaneously may start a criminal prosecution, rulings with regard to the substantive components of tort and crime can run in parallel (in the context of distinct procedures; see Section 4.A.2). Although there is no specific provision for civil courts similar to Article 14 Sv (whereby the criminal court may adjourn the trial in order to await the outcome of the civil procedure),[79] a civil judge may choose to suspend the civil claim. This possibility is rationalised in three related ways: first, the civil procedure is slower anyway, so why not take advantage of the faster criminal determination for assistance; second, a suspension makes sense, since a conviction is compelling evidence in civil cases (Article 161 Rv); and third, it promotes effective management of the court's case load. In practice therefore, concurrent trials and judgments seldom happen.

Nevertheless, there is room for manoeuvre, reflecting the Dutch preference for pragmatic solutions particularly where it might benefit victims. Indeed, the legislature, as well as the Hoge Raad, is prepared to remove legal barriers to the victim's swift compensation, giving rise to rather complicated, yet practical, legal constructions. In particular, a victim can change the route seeking compensation until the point at which that route has concluded with a substantive ruling. This means that if a civil claim has begun, until it has been concluded the victim can still bring a claim before the criminal court, if within the criminal court's time limits. If the criminal court subsequently rules the claim to be partially awarded, the victim must withdraw the other parts of the claim brought and take them to a civil court. If, *vice versa*, the civil court has partially awarded the claim, the criminal court's sentence will read inadmissible for this part

[79] Hoge Raad 23 June 1953, *NJ* 1954, 116 (the court is not obliged to adjourn the criminal trial in case of disputes with regard to a civil law issue); Hoge Raad 17 February 1957, *NJ* 1959, 356 (the criminal court is competent to rule on the dispute).

due to a lack of recognised legal interest to compensated. Next, where the victim can deliver proof that the defendant has not yet satisfied the order made against him by the civil court, the criminal court can – but is not obliged to – award a compensation order for the unsettled part, thus enabling the claimant to profit from the enforcement service of the Central Fine Collection Agency (Centraal Justitieel Incassobureau (CJIB); Art. 361 Sv).[80] In addition, if the victim was awarded compensation by a criminal court in a sentence which was then appealed, the whole sentence is suspended during the appeal and thus the compensation is unenforceable. If the claimant, for practical reasons, meanwhile seeks recourse by the civil court, his claim will be admissible for there has not been a final substantive ruling.[81] Finally, where the claimant has brought a claim before the criminal court in the context of an adhesion procedure, he can, request compensation in advance in a civil procedure. Valid reasons for requesting this advance include, for example, attempting to prevent further harm/costs stemming from the original wrong done. These rather complicated legal constructions reflect the autonomous nature of the ruling by the civil courts and the criminal courts.

7. Remedies: the compensation order and substitute detention

The criminal court's jurisdiction to hear a civil claim necessitates remedies beyond those available to a criminal trial alone. First, and most importantly, one remedy that a criminal court can impose once there is liability to pay damages to the victim of the crime according to the rules of tort law is the compensation order, the order to pay compensation to the state for the benefit of the victim of the crime (*schadevergoedingsmaatregel*; Art. 36f Sr). Criminal courts have a discretionary power to impose the compensation order; the legislature did not wanted to oblige the courts to impose the order. However, the criminal courts typically do impose one when the victim's tort claim in the adhesion procedure is awarded by the criminal court. This practice stems from a binding recommendation of the chairs of the criminal sections of the courts, an organ of the Board for the Judiciary. By doing so the courts want to serve the rationale of

[80] Hoge Raad 26 April 2011, *NJ* 2011, 205; Hoge Raad 19 February 2010, *NJ* 2010, 131; also: A. H. Sas, 'Strafrecht voor civilisten deel II: over de gewijzigde Wet schadefonds geweldsmisdrijven en nog enkele opmerkingen over schadeverhaal via het strafproces' (2012) *Tijdschrift voor Vergoeding Personenschade* 58.

[81] E.g., District Court Arnhem 16 September 2009, *LJN* BK0509.

the Terwee Act: to improve the position of victims of crime as well as to unify the application of the adhesion procedure of Article 51f Sv nationwide. Thus the criminal courts went one step further than the legislature because it was acknowledged that the compensation order is in pursuit of the execution of the civil claim, awarded in the adhesion procedure.[82] The imposition of a compensation order provides an executorial title to be executed by the Public Prosecution Service, on behalf of the victim (Article 572(1) Sv). In practice the CJIB (the Collective Debt Collection Agency) performs the enforcement on behalf of the victim. Since compensation orders represent a criminal sanction, the enforcement can be furthered by the use of police and judicial powers. Most remarkably, substitute detention (discussed below), can be used to force the convicted person to pay. Although the CJIB works closely together with the Public Prosecution Service, both are autonomous organisations in the service of the Department of Security and Justice.

The compensation order, being of a penal nature, can be made of the court's own motion, that is, even without the victim requesting it.[83] However, this seldom happens because it may not be clear whether the victim will appreciate receiving compensation from the perpetrator and, more practically, if the victim is not present or consulted in advance, necessary evidence about the harm suffered will be missing.[84] In addition, a compensation order can theoretically be awarded by the criminal court to support the enforcement of a claim already awarded by the civil court. Clearly, the victim having initiated a civil procedure, s/he is in pursuit of compensation. By awarding a compensation order, the criminal court grants the claimant the benefit of the executorial services of the CJIB. Such awards are rare, particularly due to the fact that criminal proceedings are mostly faster than civil proceedings and offer with the adhesion procedure a much cheaper and less formalistic way to file the tort claim. Nonetheless, the possibility is there, once again showing the pragmatic approach of nature of the Dutch legal system and the strong wish to provide for victim compensation.

The compensation order is strengthened by related orders, such as protective seizure: to prevent the defendant from embezzling his assets in

[82] Landelijk Overleg Voorzitters Strafsecties, *Aanbevelingen civiele vordering en schadevergoedingsmaatregel*, October 2011, 34–6, www.rechtspraak.nl/procedures/landelijke-regelingen/sector-strafrecht/documents/wet-terwee.pdf (last accessed November 2014).

[83] Ibid., 36. [84] Candido *et al.*, *Slachtoffer en de Rechtspraak*, 169.

an attempt to escape having to pay the victim compensation, the police and the public prosecutor can seize assets in advance (Art. 94a(3) Sv).[85]

If there are multiple defendants, the court will impose the compensation order on each of them individually for the full amount of compensation awarded (the so-called *hoofdelijkheid*). On the one hand, Dutch criminal law uses distinct categories of perpetrators (Arts. 47 and 48 *Sr*):

(1) the individual who commits an offence by himself (*plegen*);
(2) those who (more or less) act together, co-participation (*medeplegen*);
(3) those who merely assist the main perpetrator, complicity (*medeplichtigheid*);
(4) those who provoke someone else to commit the offence by making promises, using force or other means, incitement (*uitlokking*); and
(5) those who use another individual instrumentally to commit the crime, while that other individual is not criminally liable, acting via an intermediary (*doen plegen*).

These distinctions, however, are not relevant for the liability with regard to the obligation to compensate the damages caused, for the liability is based on the civil law. Again, the rationale lies in the legislature's wish to relieve the victim of the burden and risks of enforcement. Thus the risk of insolvency of the perpetrator(s) should not bother the victim: if one of them has not provided for full compensation, the victim – due to the executive efforts of the CJIB – can recover from one or more of the other convicted defendants.

As noted above, a remarkable fact of Dutch law is that a compensation order is accompanied by an order for substitute custody in default: the perpetrator must serve detention if he does not satisfy the compensation (Art. 36(8)f Sr). The obligation to impose substitute custody has met with criticism. In particular, it is particularly harsh since serving substitute detention does not dissolve the civil law obligation to satisfy the compensation ordered; the claimant still holds an executive title against the perpetrator. Indeed, substitute detention merely results in the dissolution of the enforcement by the CJIB and the Public Prosecutor's Service. Once the substitute detention has been fully executed, the victim is left to seek compensation via the civil route, by making use of a bailiff (Art. 554(2) Sv).

[85] *Staatsblad* 2013, 278. See E. Gijselaar and S. Meyer, 'Conservatoir beslag ten behoeve van het slachtoffer' (2014) 3 *Delikt & Delinkwent* 180.

Finally, a second remedy is that the criminal court can instruct the return of stolen property (Article 116 Sv). Such instructions are generally given where the property was seized by the police (Article 95 and 96 Sv) in the course of an investigation. As well as serving several aims, for example for the purpose of evidence, or public safety (e.g., possessing a weapon for which the defendant has no permit), seizure can also serve to return property (e.g. stolen goods) to those who it belonged to. In fact, the return of such property is not actually part of the adhesion procedure since the court will do so without a claim being formally made.[86] Nonetheless, the investigation of who might be entitled to property will tend to also reveal who might have suffered loss and therefore wish to bring an adhesion claim. Indeed, bringing a claim before the criminal court, might further an instruction to return the goods as it reveals the identity of the party entitled.

8. Advance compensation

In order to guarantee the victim of sexual offences and/or violent offences receive the compensation quickly, the legislature recently granted victims (or in case of death, his/her relatives) who were awarded compensation by the criminal court the right to receive compensation in advance, to be provided by the state (Art. 36(f)(7) Sr). Such an advance will only be granted if the perpetrator is unable to pay within an eight-month period. Moreover, the damages awarded must relate to crimes in the category of sexual offences and/or violent crimes which are summed up in an Order in Council.[87] In 2016, however, this offence limitation will be lifted, with the effect that advance compensation will be available for all offences, but will be capped at 5,000 Euros. While the state, who pays this advance up front, will have a right of recourse against the convicted person, it is foreseeable that a substantive cohort of perpetrators will be unable to pay the compensation.[88] Again, this illustrates how highly the victim's interest in receiving compensation is valued within modern Dutch legal policy.

[86] There is, however, one condition: the defendant must renunciate the seized goods.

[87] Art. 1(2) Uitvoeringsbesluit voorschot schadevergoedingsmaatregel, Staatsblad 2010, 311. The crimes are Art. 141, 239–253, 273f, 287–291, 300–303, 312 and 317 Sr.

[88] There are, however, also plans to introduce a so-called *slachtoffer-tax*, implying perpetrators to be obliged to pay a certain amount of money to cover for the cost with regard to State compensation; *Parliamentary Papers* 2012–2013, 33 552, no. 5.

D. *Why are tort and crime procedurally connected*

Why then are tort and crime procedurally connected in the Dutch discourse? First one has to bear in mind that the Dutch legislature traditionally has been receptive to the victim's wish for compensation. Indeed, as early as the end of the nineteenth century, at the time of the introduction of the first national code of criminal procedure, an adhesion procedure was introduced, albeit limited to small claims only (see Section 3.D). While this was criticised as being contrary to the parallel desire to ban the victim from criminal proceedings,[89] however, compassion overcame resentment.

Political intentions, however, changed over time. The right to prosecute still lies in the hand of the Public Prosecution Service, and although the possibilities to claim compensation have been widened, it still is qualified as a subordinated item that may not unduly burden the criminal proceedings. On the other hand, a clear shift in the victim's position in the Netherlands can be seen in other mechanisms, and developments are still pending. For instance, to date, the victim has only been acknowledged as a stakeholder, having participatory rights. This implies, however, not an acknowledgment as a 'party', on equal footing with the defendant. Nevertheless, in view of current proposals to introduce an advisory right for victims, indicating them to be entitled to advise the judge on the issue of evidence and sentencing, one can observe a nascent but important shift within the Dutch paradigm.[90] Victim's compensation, indeed, is highly valued within the present political discourse, however, so are the (overall inquisitorial) features of Dutch criminal procedural law and the dogmatic distinction between tort and crime. While trying to strike a balance but also pursuing an adequate response to victims' needs,[91] the legislature is

[89] For an historical overview: R. S. B. Kool, 'Uit de schaduw van het strafrecht' (1999) 9 *Justitiële Verkenningen*, 60–73.

[90] To date, the Dutch are on the cusp of an important change, which will have major dogmatic consequences: a draft bill has been introduced to award the victim an advisory right related to the evaluation of the evidence and the imposition of sentencing Parliamentary Papers 2014/15, 33176, no. 1–3. For a review: R. S. B. Kool, 'Alles naar wens? Observaties naar aanleiding van het conceptwetsvoorstel ter aanvulling van het spreekrecht voor slachtoffers en nabestaanden in het strafproces' (2014) 3 *Tijdschrift voor Herstelrecht*, 9 and R. S. B. Kool and G. Verhage, 'The (Political) Pursuit of Victim Voice: (Comparative) Observations on the Dutch Draft on the *Adviesrecht*' [2014] *Utrecht LR* 86.

[91] To provide for 'an adequate response' has become the slogan used by the legislature with regard to victim's policy. The slogan was taken from the research project Strafvordering

apparently willing to opt for convergence between tort law and criminal law, loosening up the dogmatic distinction and introducing pragmatic solutions to further victims' compensation.

This increasing focus on victims' need has not only been a feature of Dutch law. Both within Europe and on a worldwide scale, victims of crime are at the centre of political attention, urging national authorities to provide for an adequate legal procedural framework for compensation. Within the Dutch legal discourse, Book 2, Title IIIA, section 2 Sv, together with some articles mentioned in Title VI, section 2 Sv, provides such a framework. The rights related to the issue of compensation (Title IIIA, section 2, Art. 51f–h Sv),[92] however, are separated from other procedural rights focused on procedural justice (Title IIIA, section 1, Art. 51a–e Sv). Nevertheless, the latter can also be of benefit to the issue of compensation, for example the right to disclosure and the right to legal assistance (Art. 51b and c Sv). Moreover, the MSJ plans to simplify the civil procedures for awarding compensation. The aim is to lower the hurdles to a successful civil claim after a criminal court has ruled an adhesion claim inadmissible or has partially rejected it, for instance, by removing court fees, or the obligation to be represented by a barrister.

It seems highly likely that this search for an adequate modus to facilitate the victim's interest, especially his need for compensation, will lead to further 'procedural exchanges' between the civil law and the criminal law. Moreover, one can expect the measures to be introduced not to be restricted to the issue of how to further compensation and the relationship between tort and crime. Against the backdrop of the attention for procedural justice further convergence between tort and crime is to be expected, shedding new light on the traditional relevance of procedural differences.[93] This hybridisation, however, is firstly to be expected regarding sentencing. Already, Article 36f Sv provides a clear example. Next, the plan to introduce a new behavioural order can be mentioned (Art. 38z Sr). The intention is to introduce the possibility to impose a measure in order to subject certain convicted persons (mostly sexual and violent offenders) to long-term supervision, behavioural training and/or

2001, which set out the contours of contemporary victim's policy; M. S. Groenhuijsen and N. M. Kwakman, 'Het slachtoffer in het vooronderzoek' in M. S. Groenhuijsen and G. Knigge (eds.), *Dwangmiddelen en Rechtsmiddelen* (Deventer: Kluwer, 2002), 773–971.

[92] Note Art. 51h Sv to address mediation. The Public Prosecution Service is obliged to further mediation by instructing the police to investigate whether there is room for mediaition.

[93] Kool, '(Crime) Victims' Compensation: the Emergence of Convergence'.

other restrictions of freedom.[94] This instrument resembles the Civil Protection Orders, applied in the United Kingdom.

5. Criminal conviction = civil evidence

A. *Introduction*

As noted above in Section 2, Article 161 Rv establishes that once a criminal court has ruled an act to be a criminal act, in a criminal trial at which the defendant was present, this ruling serves as compelling evidence in any ensuing civil proceedings. This criminal conviction is however not conclusive since Article 151(2) Rv affirms, that it is always allowed for a party in a civil suit to bring counterevidence to rebut the evidence of the opposing party, even if the opposing party has brought forward evidence (in this case, by means of the former criminal conviction) which the judge must in principle rely on. The Civil Code of 1838 already contained a similar provision with Article 1955, so the origins of this doctrine date back to 1838.

In the Dutch system, such a rule makes sense. Since a criminal act is also considered to be a tort the civil judge who gets a case after it has been through a criminal trial will basically be answering the same questions since the component parts of the tort claim overlap with the elements needed for a criminal conviction. But in real life as in law, there is much more to the evidentiary relationship between tort and crime, as will be seen hereafter. We turn now to look at these rules in more detail, again looking at where, how and why it plays out.

B. *Where is the overlap (or the difference)?*

1. Substantive overlap, evidentiary differences

There are several points of 'overlap' between the substantive law with regard to tort and crime. However, the proof of the substantive points of overlap between tort and crime is evaluated by different standards. For instance, the concept of causation shows common ground (since the standard of 'reasonable imputation' is used in both areas of the law, see above at Section 3.D), but a key difference is that stricter standards of proof are applied in criminal cases.

94 *Parliamentary Papers* 2013–14, 33 815, nos. 1–2. At the time of writing (September 2014), the draft is still pending.

As for negligence, this is a prerequisite in tort law according to Article 6:162(3) BW, but within criminal law such negligence represents the lowest level of fault: usually more is required (for instance, intent). The different use of these points of departure for both areas of the law can be explained by the need for a restrained use of the criminal law as a tool of last resort. In particular, criminal law implies that prosecution is justified in terms of 'public benefit', whereas the point of entrance for tort law lies in the fair allocation of losses.

As for defences, for instance, self-defence, the Criminal Code provides for general provisions that apply to all offences, and these same defences are recognised and used (as unwritten rules) in tort law.[95] The standard of proof as regards such defences is, however, in criminal cases lower than usual: the defendant only has to put forward a plausible defence.[96] This standard seems to resemble the civil standard that will be set out below.

2. Standards of proof

What can be gathered from the above is that, although there is some overlap as to the evidential value of criminal convictions (a conviction is to be accepted as proof in civil cases if no rebuttal evidence is forthcoming), the elements of criminal law have a different standard of proof to those of civil law. Let us elaborate somewhat on that thought, starting with tort law (which serves as an example of private law more generally).[97]

The standard of proof in civil cases refers to the extent or degree of certainty or probability that the evidence delivered by the litigants must generate in the mind of the judge when deciding an issue of fact.[98] If the required degree is reached, the court can say it is convinced of the 'truth' (whatever that may be in a more philosophical sense) of a certain factual proposition and decide the case accordingly. Included in the foregoing description is the notion that in principle, but with exceptions, the courts in the Netherlands, as in other parts of Europe, are free to attach their own weight to different pieces of evidence. Whether they believe an eyewitness

[95] See Hartkamp and Sieburgh, *Mr. C. Assers Handleiding*, nos. 88 ff.

[96] If such a defence is not accepted, the criminal judge has to put forward a deliberate, written opinion giving the reasons for this choice (Art. 358(3) Sv). For civil cases, this rule is unknown; the usual standard for giving reasons in judgments applies.

[97] The following part is taken, with minor adjustments, from: I. Giesen, 'The Burden of Proof and Other Procedural Devices in Tort Law' in H. Koziol and B. S. Steiniger (eds.), *European Tort Law 2008* (Springer: Wien, 2009).

[98] See P. Murphy, *Murphy on Evidence* (Oxford University Press, 2007), 101.

or not, to give one example, is at their discretion. Related to that notion is the starting point that the standard of proof is decided according to the weight that the judge in question decides to give the evidence. It is thus in principle a subjective judgment, one which is objectified however by the obligation for a judge to give reasons for his decision.[99]

As to the degree or extent of evidence required to pass the standard of proof hurdle, it would seem that common law and civil law countries are divided.[100] In England[101] proof 'on the balance of probabilities' ('is it more likely than not?') would suffice for a civil claim, while elsewhere the measure to reach for civil claims is put (somewhat) higher, for instance at 'a reasonable degree of certainty' in the Netherlands or 'at a practical degree of probability or certainty that silences doubt without totally excluding it' as it is specified in Germany, which is an even higher standard, laid down in paragraph 286 Zivilprozessordnung (ZPO) and usually described as *sehr hoher Warscheinlichkeit* (i.e. a very high probability).[102] And in Austria, to give one more example, the required degree is that of *die hohe Warscheinlichkeit* (a high probability); this is based on paragraph 272 österreichische Zivilprozessordnung (öZPO) and case law.[103]

It is also noteworthy that in most systems the standard of proof can vary according to the type of case that is being dealt with. In Germany, for instance, the degree of certainty can and sometimes is lowered in certain private law cases when *Glaubhaftmachung*, or *überwiegende Wahrscheinlichkeit*, which translates as 'more probable than not', seems to suffice.[104] In line with that, Dutch courts lower the standard in

[99] For details, see I. Giesen, *Bewijs en aansprakelijkheid* (Den Haag: BJu, 2001), 49 f., at 53–5.

[100] See for instance E. L. Sherwin and K. M. A. Clermont, 'A Comparative View of Standards of Proof' (2002) *AJCL* 243. The ALI/Unidroit Principles of Transnational Civil Procedure try to bridge the gap by stating in Principle 21.2: '*Facts are considered proven when the court is reasonably convinced of their truth*'. See further on this 'divide' and on this Principle: M. Brinkmann, 'The Synthesis of Common and Civil Law Standard of Proof Formulae in the ALI/Unidroit Principles of Transnational Civil Procedure' (2004) *Unif L Rev* 875.

[101] Chapter 2.2.E.4. See also Murphy, *Murphy on Evidence*, 107. See also (in German) Chr. Schröder, *Das Beweisrecht im englischen Zivilverfahren* (Munich: Peter Lang Publishing Group, 2007), 222 ff.

[102] See Giesen, *Bewijs en aansprakelijkheid*, 50 and 55; H. -J. Musielak, *Grundkurs ZPO* (Munich: C.H. Beck Verlag, 2007), 281; BGH, 17 February 1970, Entscheidungen des Bundesgerichtshofs in Zivilsachen (BGHZ) 53, 245, 256 (*Anastasia-Urteil*). For Belgium, a degree of *redelijke zekerheid* suffices, see B. Allemeersch, *Taakverdeling in het burgerlijk proces* (Cambridge: Intersentia, 2007), 466.

[103] See the discussion (and further references) in C. Bumberger, *Zum Kausalitätsbeweis im Haftpflichtrecht* (Linz: Trauner Verlag, 2003), 45 ff., 49 and 182; OGH, 9 July 2002, *Juristische Blätter* (JBl) 2003, 249 f.; OGH, 17 November 2004, JBl 2005, 464.

[104] Musielak, *Grundkurs ZPO*, 283.

so-called *kort geding* procedures. These are very fast preliminary proceedings, issued at short notice, before a single judge, based mainly on oral arguments, in cases where a speedy decision is needed due to the nature of what is at stake. There, the standard is lowered to *aannemelijkheid*: 'is it probable?'[105]

The principle aim of the standard of proof is to have a certain measure to decide whether the burden of proof has been discharged and applied equally to all litigants in the same sorts of cases. In order to perform that function, the degree of evidence required as such could also be easily varied. A variation in the degree required would be feasible if in a given situation demanding that more evidence be supplied would be unjustified. For possible reasons why demanding more evidence might be unjustified, one refers to the general justifications for a court to accept a reversal of the burden of proof. For example, one party has in fact caused the evidentiary problems of the opposing party, or there is a substantive justification such as the need for the law to protect employees against employers to a certain extent.[106]

The standard of proof, however determined and set, will be of influence on the burden of proof; this in turn will affect how much work the concept of proof does in deciding cases. If a court is convinced of the existence of a certain fact, the required evidence apparently has been brought forward, allowing the judge to decide the matter accordingly. The risks associated with the burden of proof are then no longer at stake: it would be impossible to have a so-called *non liquet* situation, the situation in which the fact that needed to be proven has not been proven according to the standard of proof applicable.[107] From this it follows that if the required standard were to be lowered, the degree of evidence necessary to reach the standard would also be lower, making it less likely that the burden of proof will be decisive for that case at hand. Lowering the standard, as happens in *kort geding* proceedings, noted above, results in fewer cases being decided on the burden of proof.[108] The Civil Code, Article 6:97 BW, also provides, in some cases, for the claimant to estimate the amount of damage suffered, and use a lower standard of proof.[109]

[105] See Giesen, *Bewijs en aansprakelijkheid*, 56 ff.

[106] For elaboration, see ibid., 475 and 477 ff.

[107] See for instance G. Baumgärtel, *Beweislastpraxis im Privatrecht* (Berlin: Heymanns, 1996), no. 377 ff.

[108] C. Bumberger, *Zum Kausalitätsbeweis im Haftpflichtrecht* (Linz: Trauner Verlag, 2003), 42.

[109] Compare for Germany paragraph 287 ZPO. The same deviation from the regular standard applies, according to paragraph 252 BGB, for the determination of lost profits.

Within criminal law,[110] as already alluded to, the standard of proof is that the facts supporting a conviction must be 'legally and convincingly proven'. 'Legally' denotes here that proof must be delivered by means of the categories of evidence mentioned within Articles 339–44a *Sv*. As for the further evaluation of the evidence so presented, the Dutch criminal law also uses the so-called 'free system': assuming the minimum rule has been fulfilled (normally, that there is more than one) it depends on the personal, professional opinion of the judge whether he is convinced of the perpetrators guilt or not.

Turning to the application in practice of these provisions, for some years now, criminal law requires a reasoned and written explication in the verdict of the judge's evaluation of the facts in the indictment that needed to be proven (Article 359(2) Sv).[111] Although the law nowadays specifies that an acquittal needs to be reasoned as well (Arts. 359(2) and 352(2) Sv) courts are a bit reluctant in following this instruction except for high profile media-cases.

In practice, a judge will confine himself to making referrals to the specific pieces of evidence on which the verdict is based (police reports, witness statements, confiscated objects and so on), so in essence the standard of proof poses not too much of a burden. If the defence attorney has raised clear arguments that are rejected, the judge is obliged to explicitly provide for an answer to those objections.[112]

3. Compensatory mechanisms

When considering these rules on the standard of proof, one must be aware however that there might be other mechanisms to compensate for a difficult procedural position of one of the parties. For instance, at least in civil cases, it might be that the burden of proof can be shifted between parties, a so-called reversal of the burden of proof. Other private law mechanisms that could be used in just about any case where evidentiary problems arise include: presumptions of fact, including *res ipsa loquitur*; the duty to provide additional information and, as alluded to already, a lowering of the standard of proof.[113]

110 See on the following G. J. M. Corstens and M. J. Borgers, *Het Nederlands strafprocesrecht* (Deventer: Kluwer, 2011), 675–7.

111 These are the so-called *Promis* verdicts.

112 However, if the rejection of such an argument follows logically from the facts mentioned in the verdict, such an explicit answer is not required.

113 See Giesen, 'The Burden of Proof and Other Procedural Devices in Tort Law' in Koziol and Steiniger (eds.), *European Tort Law 2008* (Springer: Wien, 2009).

The rule in criminal cases is that the prosecutor has to deliver evidence to substantiate that the facts are 'legally and convincingly proven'. There's one exception: the procedure in cases of *ontneming van wederrechtelijk verkregen voordeel* (what might be called the dispossession of unlawfully obtained advantages). This is in many cases a separate procedure, following the main criminal procedure, aiming at getting a legal title to confiscate finances/possessions that are assumingly related to the criminal activities that the individual has been convicted for in the main procedure. The standard of proof differs here since it suffices to make such a correlation 'assumingly present', to use an ugly translation of the Dutch terminology. As for the application of exclusionary defences, such as self-defence, in criminal law, it is up to the defence to provide arguments for what might be called the 'assumingly presence' of such a defence. This is another example of lowering the standard of proof, the threshold for proving an element of the criminal case.

4. Means and production of evidence

When it comes to the means and production of evidence, the criminal and civil law rules diverge considerably, which is of great significance for legal practice. In criminal cases the Dutch system provides for a strict regime of evidence, at least as to the categories of evidence. This is exemplified by the use of the 'minimum rule' mentioned above: a person may not be convicted on the basis of a sole piece of evidence. There is however, one rather important exception to this rule and that is that a report, under oath, of a police-officer that is based upon the direct observation of the offence, can and will be accepted. This exception, and some less common ones, means that one must not have too high expectations of this minimum rule; in practice, the amount of evidence in the majority of the cases is in fact rather poor.

Experts or witnesses may present evidence, orally in court or in written form (if indicated, followed by further explication in court) and their statements may be used by the judge. Although the defendant has a right to present contrary expert evidence, he has to pay for the costs thereof himself, which is a significant impediment. Furthermore, to guarantee the use of qualified forensic experts only, the legislature has recently introduced an official register of forensic experts who may be called upon in criminal proceedings. That said, in some fields of forensic evidence the state acts as a monopolist, for example, in the field of DNA-evidence.[114]

[114] However, initiatives are employed to bring more competition to this field.

The defendant is not called upon as a witness; although he is questioned in court, he is cautioned and not obliged to testify. But, it must be stressed, adverse inferences can be drawn by the judge if the defendant decides to remain silent.

In regular tort cases, dealt with in civil courts, the claimant has to bring forward a plausible claim, providing sufficient evidence of the tortious act, the fault, the damage itself, as well as the causes of the damage which have to relate sufficiently to an act or omission by the respondent. If this body of proof supports a plausible claim – the 'minimum rule' from criminal law does not exist in civil law – the defendant needs to refute this by providing counter-evidence. The judge in a civil procedure will receive and then weigh the evidence but does not collect it himself. That is for the parties: they may in principle bring forward any piece or form of evidence they see fit (see Art. 152(1) Rv), such as witnesses, video and audio tapes, a party appointed expert and so on. In this regard the system is adversarial in nature.

As regards witnesses, there are some restrictions on their admissibility but these are rather trivial; an offer to bring in a witness testimony must in principle be awarded if the witness may have something to say about the factual position that needs to be proven. Even though the judge himself can order evidentiary measures (hearing witnesses, for instance) *ex officio*, this hardly ever happens. What does happen to some extent, however, is that the judge orders an expert opinion by a court appointed expert (see Arts. 194 Rv *et seq.*), usually because the party appointed experts seem to disagree.

5. Powers of investigation and disclosure

Of course, the gathering and presenting of evidence goes hand in hand with the questions as to the powers of investigation and the rules for disclosure for those involved in civil and criminal proceedings. When it comes to the powers of investigation, the Dutch civil courts take a rather passive stance towards the gathering of (evidence to prove) facts. A civil judge takes the case and the evidence as presented to him by the parties, even though he has *ex officio* powers. However, if required, the court can *request* further information from the parties, as set out in, for instance, Article 22 Rv: the disclosure of this information then rests on the parties themselves. It is also for the parties to name the proposed witnesses who are then obliged to testify. Forsaking this duty to testify may lead to the witness being brought to the court by force and even placed in custody, if needed.[115] Given these rules, the outcome of a civil case will not always equal 'the truth'.[116]

Be that as it may, the Dutch consider that criminal courts more actively search for the truth, the so-called 'substantive truth' (that is, what has in fact happened), as opposite to the 'procedural truth' (what seems to have happened given the formal restrictions of the proceedings as regards the fact-finding and gathering and admissibility of evidence) which features in more adversarial systems. Nevertheless, because the Public Prosecution Service is in charge of the investigative stage, and also of the composition of the dossier and the indictment, judges are rather reluctant to carry out any additional investigation. However, if the court is of the opinion that there is a need for more information, the trial will be suspended in order to carry out an additional investigation, for example, additional interrogations or forensic investigation. An order to complete this additional investigation can be given to an investigative-judge, but one of the judges on the bench of the case at hand may also be appointed.

It will not be surprising to learn that the rules for disclosure, as well as the compellability of witnesses, differ from those in a civil court setting. This is the case because in a criminal, more inquisitorial setting, the Public Prosecution Service is in charge of the criminal investigations, and thus also in charge of granting disclosure and compelling witnesses. Recently, the Public Prosecution Service has been given full charge of the investigative phase, but before the case is tried in court an investigative judge evaluates whether there is a need for further evidence. This provides the defence with an opportunity to put forward requests regarding disclosure or the hearing of witnesses. Once the decision to prosecute has been taken, the defence is entitled to full disclosure subject only to exceptions such as where disclosure would be a threat to public security.

6. Intermediate conclusion

Due to the application of stricter rules and standards of proof in criminal cases the substantive overlap in rules and terminology is in practice of limited importance. If a component of a crime or tort is substantively the same but in need of more convincing proof, there will be a relevant difference between a civil tort case and a criminal case.

[115] See Arts. 172 and 173 Rv. Taking a witness into custody is also known as 'an imprisonment for debt'.

[116] On this topic, see particularly R. de Bock, *Tussen waarheid en onzekerheid: over het vaststellen van feiten in de civiele procedure* (Deventer: Kluwer, 2011).

C. *How are tort and crime related in evidentiary matters?*

How can the relationship between tort and crime be classified and characterised, especially in terms of evidence? Are there cross-influences? Are these influences direct or indirect? As already noted in Section 3.D the relation between tort and crime is not analysed in the Netherlands in terms of a 'relationship' or 'hierarchy'.

Needless to say, however, there are, as we have already seen, some intersections between tort and crime. The most evident and direct influence, from the point of view of evidence, is marked by Article 161 Rv as mentioned before. A criminal conviction after a full-blown criminal trial provides the civil judge with all the evidence he needs to conclude that the act in question was tortious. But that is about all that can be said here, because that same civil judge will need to assess on his own as based on the evidence brought before him by the parties whether key tortious requirements have been met: that the act in question was imputable to the defendant (by way of guilt or risk allocation, see Art. 6:162(3) BW;[117] to be sure, in practice there is hardly any evidentiary hurdle as regards this imputation requirement[118]), that there was a legally relevant loss suffered and what the amount of damages might be for that loss, whether the unlawful act was a *condicio sine qua non* of the damage, and so on.

To the extent that there is some movement from one side of tort and crime to the other in respect of evidence, it is clear that it this movement is one-sided only. Criminally tested evidence has high standing in civil court, but that is not the case the other way around. If a civil judge has already ruled an act unlawful that does not mean that a criminal judge must then conclude that a criminal act was committed also. So, where the civil system shows some porosity or permeability, the criminal system shows none.

D. *Why are tort and crime so connected?*

As suggested in Section 2, the Dutch seem to have found – at least for the time being – an efficient way of handling the overlap between tort and crime that they recognise their system naturally generates (because of

[117] Quoted in Section 2.B. This is at least the case in theory, in practice there is hardly any evidentiary hurdle as regards the imputation requirement.

[118] To elaborate: if a criminal act that requires some element of intent (a form of *dolus* or *culpa*) has been established by the criminal court, the civil judge will also rule that the tortious act was imputable to the defendant in the civil sense. The law however, does not expressly oblige the judge to do so.

Art. 6:162 (2) BW). This way of handling the system turns particularly on reasons of unity and coherence. The evidentiary overlap and legislative permission to build on a criminal conviction as evidence in a civil trial is only a logical consequence thereof. And indeed, shows why the question 'why not let the civil judge use the evidence gathered and already judicially tested (to a high standard) and considered in criminal court if such evidence is indeed present' is truly rhetorical.

6. Tort and crime over time

It is interesting to note that – from a certain perspective – Dutch law on the interplay between tort and crime has been in place for decades without a lot of significant changes to the system. As much can be seen from the long history of some form of adhesion procedure set out in Section 3.D. The only truly interesting shift has been the growing amount of recognition and attention that the victims of crimes have received and the ensuing improvement of their position within the criminal trial.

This stability is due, perhaps, to the fact that the use of tort law within a criminal procedure – this is where in the Netherlands the actual interplay takes place – usually involves the relatively simple cases. Anything complex, from a tort law perspective, is thrown out of the criminal court immediately. The substantive components of torts and crimes have not generated much interest. A theft is always a tort, and physical abuse also constitutes both a crime and a tort. The substantive private law rules that the victims of crime would need to rely on – and thus, that politicians would be interested in – was therefore never in need of any change. Only the procedural aspect, relating specifically to the rules of criminal procedure, i.e. the place and role a victim of a crime might be given in criminal proceedings, was and is deemed politically interesting enough to gain and keep momentum. Since the 1970s the victim's position within the criminal procedure has become subject to continuous political debate. From then on, and in line with international developments, Dutch policymakers have shown themselves to be highly receptive to victims' needs. Subsequent coalition cabinets, being driven by electoral considerations and responding to the social call for legal protection of certain groups or interests provoked by the so-called 'risk-society' we (seem to) live in, have prioritised victims' issues, urging for both legal and policy changes. These changes, however, have been of a somewhat incoherent nature. Legal initiatives by Members of Parliament, failing to take into account the doctrine and system of private law and criminal law, set the political agenda, giving way to incident-based law reforms. As a result of all these factors, Dutch law has adopted a pragmatic viewpoint, especially on the procedural possibilities offered to victims of crime to obtain compensation and/or recognition (see Section 4).

In 2009, however, a coherent catalogue of victims' rights was introduced, including, amongst others, the traditional right to compensation. This legislative revision, however, did not end the quest for victims' rights. On the contrary, it provided a boost for further developments. The current Dutch Government even made the establishment of a crime victims' policy one of its objectives. This crime victims' policy aims at improving the position and the rights of victims of crime before, during and after the criminal trial.[119] One of its five objectives is to simplify and enhance the possibilities for victims of crime to actually receive financial compensation and other forms of redress. Or, to put it differently, according to the Dutch Government, in policy language: 'The victim's damage is to be paid by the perpetrator.'[120] This shows that policymakers seek to find ways to serve the victim's interest with regard to compensation and redress. Indeed, victims having high expectations of the legal possibilities, the policymakers are eager to live up to these expectations in order to prevent disappointment and related risk of legitimacy. Relying on the criminal justice system to do them justice, in particular with regard to compensation, victims of crime find their way to criminal courts with their tort claim and use the adhesion procedure. However, these victims are often proven disappointed: due to the subsidiary nature of the claim for compensation a substantial number of claims are ruled to be (partially) inadmissible (see Section 4.C). This concerns particularly the more complicated tort claims, due to the criterion of unduly overburdening the criminal trial, and this is often related to serious crimes. Victims can of course subsequently start a civil procedure, however, this seldom happens.[121] Being aware of the risk of secondary victimisation and related loss of legitimacy, Dutch policymakers are in continuous pursuit of ways to adapt the legal procedures in order to serve the interest of victims' compensation. These

[119] *Parliamentary Papers* 2012–13, 33 410, no. 15, 25.

[120] See *Parliamentary Papers* 2012–13, 33 552, no. 2, 6–7 respectively *Parliamentary Papers* 2012–13, 33 410, no. 15, 25.

[121] Very few cases are filed in Dutch civil courts in which damages are sought on the basis of an act which is also a crime. Even the civil parts of those criminal cases that are not dealt with in criminal court in the adhesion procedure, hardly ever go to civil court. See for facts and figures Schrama and Geurts, *Civiel schadeverhaal door slachtoffers na strafbare feiten* and Hebly *et al.*, 'Crime Victims' Experiences with Seeking Compensation: A Qualitative Exploration', (2014) 3 *Utrecht L Rev* 27 ff.

changes, however, have not (yet) destabilised the traditional distinction between tort and crime. Furthermore, these politics appear to have had a side-effect, academics already observing 'victim-fatigue'.[122]

The changes already accomplished, however, represent pragmatic solutions instead of a fundamental reassessment of the system, dogma and doctrine of the Dutch (civil and criminal) law. The criminal courts tend to apply the rules of tort law less strictly and, in case the claim is too complex to be handled, are willing to award 'compensation in advance', meaning a small part of the sum to be awarded, thus showing compassion with the victim.[123] Moreover, being aware of the complexity of the civil route, the legislature is considering the introduction of a so-called 'folding mechanism', implying an automatic transfer of the victim's claim to the civil court.[124] These developments seem to be, however, rather more symbolic than of a fundamental nature. However, no option should be discarded out of hand because we do not know what the future holds in terms of convergence with regard to tort and crime.[125] We expect that the political attention with regard to victims' rights, specifically the issue of compensation, will not cease. Bearing in mind the populist tune in today's Dutch victims' policy, 'pragmatism and efficiency' could serve as a breeding ground for more fundamental legal changes, giving way to a significant convergence of tort law and criminal law. Suggestions have been made to strengthen the enforcement function of tort law, in order to prevent tortious wrongs in the first place, rather than providing retrospective redress.[126] These suggestions imply that tort law is to become instrumentalised, serving – in its own way – the public interest. Moreover,

[122] M. S. Groenhuijsen, 'The Development of International Policy in Relation to Victims of Crime' (2014) 20(3) *IRV* 31.

[123] The legal basis of such an advance being unclear, one can hear criticism; e.g. M. J. Heemstede and A. H. Sas, "Rechter maakt van voorschotregeling een wassen neus", www.NJB.nl/blog/rechter-maakt-van-voorschotregeling-een-wassen-neus.11111.lynkx (last accessed 28 July 2014).

[124] Note this proposal initially comes from the Board for the Judiciary. The latter is an independent organ, established in 2002 responsible for the management and business of and allocation of budget to the courts. It also provides advice to the Ministry of Security and Justice on bills and policy issues which have implications for the administration of justice. It aims at improving the quality of the (legally independent) judiciary. See: www.rechtspraak.nl/english/Pages/default.aspx (last accessed November 2014).

[125] Kool, '(Crime) Victims' Compensation: the Emergence of Convergence'.

[126] W. H. van Boom, *Efficacious Enforcement in Contract and Tort* (The Hague: BJu, 2006); I. Giesen, 'Handhaving in, via door en met het privaatrecht: waar staan we nu?' in E. F. D. Engelhard, I. Giesen, C.B.P. Mahé and M.Y. Schaub (eds.), *Handhaving van en door het privaatrecht* (The Hague: BJu, 2009), 310–312.

a recent (28 May 2014) draft bill sent to consultation from the Ministry of Security and Justice seeks to introduce compensation for bereavement damages in tort law, as well as in criminal law, although with a system of tariffs.[127] It also seeks to offer certain family members and next of kin of the victim killed as a consequence of a crime the possibility of claiming bereavement damages in the adhesion procedure in criminal proceedings.[128] However, we do not suggest that these developments and proposals will result in a 'melt down' of the traditional distinction between tort and crime. Nevertheless, we do observe clear signs of convergence present within the Dutch discourse.

7. Conclusion

The Dutch are often considered to be more pragmatic than philosophical. Efficiency, or at least, searching for as much efficiency as possible, seems to go well with that. That might be the starting point for an explanation for the way the Dutch legal system handles the tort/crime connection. Referring back to what was stated earlier in this chapter, we can only conclude that when it comes to the relationship between tort and crime the Dutch legal system seems to be in search of – and has found, we think – a rather efficient way of handling the overlap between tort and crime. Let one court do all the work instead of bringing in more judges dealing with parts of the bigger problem. This manner of operation is consistent with legal standards and values like 'unity of the legal system' and 'coherence', but such 'big' words are seldom used in the Netherlands in this respect. This might suggest that the homogeneity of the legal system so reached is only a side-effect and not a sought-after purpose. It has only been by looking outside the Netherlands that we came to use such terminology and such a principled approach to something that works so profoundly pragmatically in everyday life in the Netherlands.

127 About a system of tariffs, see for instance J. Candido and S. D. Lindenbergh, 'Strafrechter en smartengeld: de civiele vordering in het strafproces al aanjager van een rechtsontwikkeling' (2014) 21 *NTBR* 173; (from a comparative perspective) I. Giesen, 'Normering van schadevergoeding in Engeland: een les voor Nederland?' (2001) *NJB* 120.

128 See www.rijksoverheid.nl/nieuws/2014/05/28/ruimere-schadevergoeding-voor-slachtoffers-en-hun-naaste-omgeving.html (last accessed November 2014).

9

Australia: a land of plenty (of legislative regimes)

KYLIE BURNS, ARLIE LOUGHNAN, MARK LUNNEY AND SONYA WILLIS*

1. Introduction

Australia is a common law-based federation of states and territories that derived its legal system from England. Australia has no national Bill of Rights but its federal constitution grants specific powers to the federal government with the remaining powers exercised by each state. Two states have created human rights statutes.[1] The federal powers to govern crime and tort are limited to crimes or torts falling within one of a number of narrow federal constitutional heads of power.[2] Therefore, most criminal law and tort law is state based and, hence, varies across Australia. On the one hand, each state legislature has ultimate constitutional power to alter the common law through legislation.[3] The federal constitution also enables the enforcement throughout Australia of tortious and criminal decisions by state courts.[4] On the other hand, the High Court of Australia is the ultimate arbiter of the common law of Australia as applicable in each state. The common law system of precedent applicable in Australia thus enables the High Court to bring significant uniformity to tort and crime law in Australia albeit constricted by potentially conflicting state legislation.

During the past few decades, statute-based law has proliferated in Australia in many areas including both the criminal and tort spheres.

* The authors would like to thank Matthew Dyson for his comments on an earlier version of this chapter, and Thomas Kiat and Isaac Morrison for their assistance in the preparation of the chapter for publication.

1 Victoria and the Australian Capital Territory.

2 E.g., the federal corporations power in the Constitution (s. 51(xx)) empowers the Commonwealth to create a federal corporations law code on corporate crime.

3 Although state legislation must be consistent with the exercise of federal judicial power; *Kable* v. *Director of Public Prosecutions (NSW)* (1996) 189 CLR 51.

4 Constitution, s. 51(xxiv) provides for 'the service and execution throughout the Commonwealth of the civil and criminal process and the judgments of the courts of the States'.

Much of this legislative reform has been driven by 'law and order' politics, public policy objectives and lobbying by a powerful insurance industry. Overall, the proliferation of statutes has increased the diversity of both criminal and tort law throughout Australia. Particularly in the area of tort, different states have adopted quite disparate statutory regimes for resolving high frequency disputes such as those involving motor vehicles and work place injuries. However, there remains a strong common law of both tort and crime with a unifying thread provided by the High Court of Australia.

There are eight state/territories in Australia of which New South Wales (NSW), Victoria and Queensland are by far the most populous (containing over 75 per cent of the Australian population between them). This chapter most commonly uses NSW as an example because over 30 per cent of Australia's population resides in NSW.

Tort and crime remain predominantly separate areas of law in Australia for litigation, legislation, professional practice, education and academic research purposes. However, there are important similarities and overlaps in the motivations, methods, substance and procedures in tort and crime both historically and in recent legislative and common law developments. We analyse these issues by dividing the remainder of the chapter into four sections. Section 2, Australian Legal Culture and Context, provides a brief background analysis of the legal culture and context that influences the development and practice of the law of tort and criminal law in Australia. The third section of the chapter looks at substantive differences between tort and crime, and the fourth at procedural differences. Although the distinction between substance and procedure is slippery and imprecisely demarcated, it is informative to separate conceptual and taxonomical discussions about tort and crime from the structures within the legal system that provide for enforcement of crime and resolution of disputes about tort law. The fifth section of the chapter, Institutions and Practices and Change over Time, examines the drivers of change in the law, including the influence of law reform bodies, industry groups and others on the laws of tort and crime in Australia.

2. Australian legal culture and context

This section considers matters of Australian legal culture and its context which have influenced the development, practice and interaction of tort law and criminal law in Australia. The intersection of tort and crime in Australia can only be properly understood by placing them within

Australian legal culture, and by recognising that the law (and its practice) in Australia has developed in response to certain social, institutional and legal contexts.

A. *The complexity of the law of tort and crime in Australia*

There are key commonalities in the laws of tort and crime (as well as recent divergence) within and between Australian jurisdictions. In Australia, criminal law is a mixture of Code (ACT, Queensland, Western Australia, Northern Territory, Tasmania and Commonwealth (Cth)) and statute, combined with common law (Victoria, NSW and South Australia). Tort law is partially governed by the common law and partially by legislation in each jurisdiction. The nine different jurisdictions (including the Commonwealth) within Australia and the proliferation of procedural legislation mean that procedural rules are complex and varied for both tort and crime. This complexity is exacerbated by the fact that the division of power between the Commonwealth and the states in the Constitution of Australia is sometimes disputed, and there are no borders within Australia limiting trade or movement. This means numerous crimes and torts engage multiple jurisdictions at once.[5]

Australian tort law is further complicated by a range of statutory compensation schemes for work-related injuries,[6] motor vehicle injuries[7] and criminally caused injuries.[8] Some of these state and territory based schemes remove common law rights in tort, and replace them with no-fault based benefits.[9] Others retain some common law rights (typically in

5 See, e.g., *Sweedman* v. *Transport Accident Commission* (2006) 226 CLR 362; which involved the 'no-fault' Victorian accident authority suing a NSW driver in NSW under the 'at fault' NSW law to recover compensation paid to a Victorian driver injured in a car accident in NSW.

6 For a discussion and comparison of the various schemes, see Safe Work Australia, *Comparison of Workers' Compensation Arrangements in Australia and New Zealand*, April 2012, www.safeworkaustralia.gov.au/sites/SWA/about/Publications/Documents/687/ComparisonWorkersCompensationArrangements2012.pdf (last accessed 10 June 2014).

7 For a discussion and comparison of the various schemes, see H. Luntz and D. Hambly, *Torts: Cases and Commentary*, 7th edn. (Sydney: Lexis Nexis, 2013), 53–6.

8 For a discussion and comparison of the various schemes, see Luntz and Hambly, *Torts*, 56–7.

9 See, e.g., Motor Accidents (Compensation) Act 1979 (NT). The benefits available under these schemes are typically capped and are much less than a successful plaintiff would receive in damages in an unrestricted common law tort claim.

a restricted form), and provide an alternate claim for no-fault benefits.[10] The introduction of tort law reform legislation across Australia in the last fifteen years has limited and restricted the law of torts further. This reform legislation does not generally completely override or abolish the common law of tort, but rather is a mixture of restatement, clarification, amendment and restriction of common law tort remedies.

B. *Legal education and the legal academy*

The laws of tort and criminal law in Australia are typically treated as separate and discrete areas of legal knowledge and practice. All Australian law students are required to study a specified list of knowledge areas, known as the Priestley 11, for the purposes of admission as legal practitioners.[11] These include the substantive areas of torts and criminal law as well as procedure.[12] The relevant legal admission standards (implemented in all states and territories) deal with these two areas of legal knowledge as discrete areas. They are typically taught in law schools as separate subjects or courses with little interaction between the two areas.

The areas of tort and criminal law are typically discrete areas of teaching and research within the Australian legal academy.[13] However, some academics (particularly those interested in intentional physical harm or medical injury) may research and teach in both areas.[14] Also, tort and crime are sometimes combined in university courses on procedure and/or evidence.[15] It is common for criminal law academics to engage with

[10] See, e.g., Workers' Compensation and Rehabilitation Act 2003 (Qld).

[11] Council of Australian Law Deans, *The CALD Standards for Australian Law Schools* (as adopted 17 November 2009 and amended to March 2013), www.cald.asn.au/assets/lists/Resources/CALD%20Standards%20As%20adopted%2017%20November%202009%20and%20Amended%20to%20March%202013.pdf (last accessed November 2014).

[12] Legal Admissions Consultative Committee, *Uniform Admission Rules 2008*, Schedule 1, www.lawcouncil.asn.au/LACC/images/pdfs/212390818_1_LACCUniformAdmissionRules2008.pdf (last accessed November 2014).

[13] E.g., they are the subject areas of separate interest groups in the Australasian Law Teachers Association. The leading Australian specialist journals are subject specific – e.g, the *Torts Law Journal*, *The Torts Law Review*, the *Criminal Law Journal*, and *Current Issues in Criminal Justice*. The leading academic textbooks are also subject specific.

[14] See, e.g., J. Devereux *et al.*, *Torts: A Practical Learning Approach*, 3rd edn (Sydney: LexisNexis, 2014); J. Devereux and M. Blake, *Kenny's Criminal Law in Queensland and Western Australia*, 8th edn (Sydney: LexisNexis, 2013).

[15] The University of Sydney, among other Australian universities, teaches 'Civil and Criminal Procedure' as a single subject and 'Civil and Criminal Evidence' is also commonly a single subject in Australian universities.

socio-legal disciplines such as criminology, and criminal law academics can often be found working in criminology departments in Australian universities and engaging in empirical research. Whereas, Australian legal academics working in tort law much less commonly engage with or carry out socio-legal or empirical research.[16]

C. *Australian legal practice*

Lawyers across Australia typically practice as either solicitors or barristers.[17] Judges are usually appointed from the ranks of senior practising barristers. Solicitors can appear in any court, however there remain barristers in all Australian states and territories who specialise in court work in both the civil and criminal spheres.[18] Solicitors and barristers (defence or prosecution) practising criminal law are assumed to have detailed knowledge of criminal law and sentencing (both of which have grown increasingly complex in recent decades), criminal procedure and evidence, and skills, such as negotiation and advocacy. This knowledge and these skills are particularly important for barristers who are the legal actors usually involved in more serious criminal matters in higher courts where imprisonment is a likely penalty. These skills remain of critical importance for solicitors practising in criminal law. Solicitors typically appear directly in lower criminal courts and in less serious criminal matters and deal with the bulk of criminal matters there. They also are involved in briefing barristers and preparing and managing serious criminal matters for trial. Solicitors and barristers practising tort law require detailed knowledge of the complex interactions between the statutes and common law applicable to varying kinds of personal injuries and other tort claims. Lawyers practising in Australia in personal injury law, in particular, require detailed knowledge of the array of different statutory schemes (e.g., workers' compensation and motor vehicle accident schemes)[19] and

[16] Although examples of this kind or research is increasing, see, e.g., G. Grant and D. Studdert, 'The Injury Brokers: An Empirical Profile of Medical Expert Witnesses in Personal Injury Litigation' (2013) 36 *MULR* 830; K. Burns, 'The Australian High Court and Social Facts: A Content Analysis Study' (2012) 40 *FLR* 317.

[17] See Office of the Legal Services Commissioner, *Admission to Legal Practice*, www.olsc.nsw.gov.au (last accessed November 2014) for a discussion of the admission regimes and requirements of the different Australian states and territories.

[18] Ibid.

[19] Safe Work Australia, *Comparison of Workers' Compensation Arrangements*; Luntz and Hambly, *Torts*, 53–6.

an array of different procedural regimes[20] dependent on the kind of injury suffered by the plaintiff.

In smaller metropolitan and regional legal practices across Australia, it is common for legal practitioners to practice in both tort and crime matters. However, specialist and boutique firms and specialist lawyers in these areas also exist. Large corporate law firms usually represent insurance company defendants in insurance/tort matters. There has also been the development in Australia of a section of the legal profession which is particularly interested in the litigation of personal injury matters for plaintiffs, including class action litigation.[21] Corporate firms do not usually practice in criminal law. State and Commonwealth governments typically employ lawyers in prosecutorial departments or services to carry out the prosecution of crimes.[22] There are also barristers who predominantly practise in criminal matters ('the criminal bar') and those who predominantly practice in civil matters ('the civil bar'). Some state law societies may also accredit practitioners as competent in certain areas – for example, personal injury practice or criminal law.[23]

D. The incidence of tort and crime in Australia: blame culture and crime explosions?

The development of the laws of tort and crime in Australia since the turn of this century has been influenced by popular cultural beliefs about the incidence of tort and crime, and the behaviour of plaintiffs and criminals. In the case of tort law, there has been a perception that the number of tort claims brought by injured plaintiffs is rapidly increasing, that injured people are very likely to unfairly 'blame' particular deep-pocketed defendants such as doctors and public authorities, and that the amount of damages recovered by injured plaintiffs is typically very large.[24]

[20] E.g., in Queensland, see the Personal Injuries Proceedings Act 2002 (Qld). In different states there are different procedural regimes dependent on the nature of the tort, whether a personal injury resulted and the nature of the personal injury.

[21] The Australian Lawyers' Alliance is a body that represents lawyers and law firms interested in the rights of individuals and justice for individuals including in relation to personal injury. See www.lawyersalliance.com.au (last accessed November 2014).

[22] States, territories and the Commonwealth have Offices of the Director of Public Prosecutions.

[23] E.g., the Queensland Law Society offers specialist accreditation in personal injury law and criminal law.

[24] See Luntz and Hambly, *Torts*, 6–8 and 20–1; E. W. Wright, 'National Trends in Personal Injury Litigation: Before and After "Ipp"' (2006) *TLJ* 233; K. Burns, 'Distorting the Law:

These prevailing, yet mistaken, beliefs were reflected in legislative tort reform, which substantially restricted the rights of Australian tort plaintiffs to recover for their injuries. Available empirical evidence about tort litigation suggests, however, that despite the significant rate of injuries in Australia, there is a comparatively low rate of personal injury tort litigation in Australia.[25] The claim rates and litigation rates for most personal injury torts have generally been static or falling over the last decade.[26] In the case of criminal law, there has been a popular belief that the incidence of crime, particularly violent crime, is increasing.[27] Empirical evidence suggests the incidence of crime in Australia, particularly violent physical crimes such as murder, is generally static or falling rather than rising.[28] However, the influence of law and order politics, discussed below, continues to result in increased criminalisation of activities via legislation.

E. *The critical relationship between tort law and tort reform and insurance in Australia*

The operation of the tort law system and tort law in Australia is inextricably linked to the existence and operation of insurance. Although Australian courts are reluctant to expressly recognise the existence of insurance as a factor that is relevant to the determination of tort law principles,[29] Australian tort law has developed in the shadow and influence of insurance.[30] For example, there is little doubt that the legislative reform of the law of tort, in particular negligence, which occurred in the first decade of the twenty-first century in Australia was the result of lobbying from powerful interest groups including insurers.[31] In the absence of the availability of liability insurance, it is almost always impractical for a plaintiff to bring an action against an uninsured defendant even where an arguable tortious action exists. Liability for the deliberate and

Politics, Media and the Litigation Crisis: An Australian Perspective' (2007) 15 *TLJ* 195; R. Graycar, 'Public Liability: A Plea for Facts' (2002) 25 *UNSWLJ* 810.

25 See Luntz and Hambly, *Torts*, 6–12.

26 See above n. 24 and 25.

27 See M. Lee, *Inventing Fear of Crime: Criminology and the Politics of Anxiety* (Cullompton: Willan Publishing, 2007). See also D. Weatherburn and D. Indermaur, *Public Perceptions of Crime Trends in New South Wales and Western Australia* (Sydney: NSW Bureau of Crime Statistics and Research, 2004).

28 Australian Institute of Criminology, *Australian Crime: Facts and Figures* 2012, 2013, iii, www.aic.gov.au/publications/current%20series/facts/1–20/2012/foreword.html (last accessed November 2014).

29 Luntz and Hambly, *Torts*, 23.

30 Ibid., 21–4.

31 See n. 24.

wilful infliction of criminal injury will generally not be covered under a defendant's liability insurance.[32] Unlike many European countries, legal expenses insurance (which would fund a plaintiff to bring a personal injury action or make a criminal compensation claim) is uncommon in Australia and most legal actions are personally funded by plaintiffs.[33] The availability (and lack of availability) of insurance influences who brings claims and against whom. It also creates one of the injustices of the Australian tort system.

The vast majority of negligence actions in Australia are against individuals in name only. Typically, under the terms of statutory and private liability insurance policies, insurers will control the defence of actions brought in tort.[34] It is insurers who will manage claims against their insureds, brief defence lawyers and determine the tactics and outcomes of claims. Insured defendants are required by the terms of their liability insurance policy to co-operate with and assist their insurer, although the insurer must act towards their insured defendant with good faith in relation to management and settlement of claims.[35] There is evidence that,

[32] D. Derrington and R. Ashton, *The Law of Liability Insurance*, 2nd edn (Sydney: Lexis Nexis, 2005), 114–26. Such liability will generally be expressly excluded under the policy. Courts are also reluctant, for public policy reasons, to interpret a policy as covering such liability, or enforce insurer liability for deliberate criminal wrongdoing. Compulsory motor vehicle insurance schemes may however provide compensation for injuries caused intentionally and/or criminally through the use of a motor vehicle, with a right for the compulsory insurer to then recover the compensation from the insured. See, e.g., Motor Accident Insurance Act 1994 (Qld), s. 58.

[33] Productivity Commission, *Access to Justice Arrangements: Draft Report*, April 2014, 562, www.pc.gov.au/__data/assets/pdf_file/0008/135296/access-justice-draft.pdf (last accessed November 2014). While there have been some experiments in Australia with legal expenses insurance it has not proved popular either with insurers or consumers. A number of factors are likely reponsible for this including difficulty pricing the insurance product due to unpredictable court costs in Australia, lack of response by consumers and the offering of stand alone legal expenses insurance products rather than, as in the UK and Europe, in combination with motor or house insurance. Larger law firms in Australia may offer conditional (no win, no fee) funding for personal injury actions. However this form of funding is dependent on the strength and size of a plaintiff's claim, and plaintiffs will still be responsible for outlays, and legal costs of the defendant if they lose. Corporate litigation funders are becoming more widespread in Australia, however only a very small percentage of tortious actions (typically class actions) are funded in this way at present.

[34] Luntz and Hambly, *Torts*, 22. Negligence actions may also be brought by an insurer subrogated to the rights of its insured under an indemnity policy where the insured has suffered tortiously caused property damage or economic loss.

[35] *Groom* v. *Crocker* [1939] 1 KB 194.

in most areas, damages serve as, at best, a limited deterrent of tortious behaviour.[36] This is due (in part) to the existence of insurance.[37]

F. *Coherence, individual responsibility and the Australian High Court*

It seems that, at a baseline level, concerns with 'fairness', 'certainty', righting of 'wrongs' and correction of the infringement of 'rights' such as the rights to personal bodily integrity and property, should be shared by both Australian criminal and tort lawyers.[38] In both areas however, there is reduced scope for these concerns. The increasing complexity of the criminal law (with the proliferation of different offences, including preparatory offences, and the multiplicity of sentencing regimes) means that there is reduced scope for legal argument about principles like 'fairness' other than in relation to (post-conviction) mitigation. The increasing effect of tort law reform legislation and the focus of Australian courts, including the High Court, on 'legal' rather than 'social' policy[39] have also reduced the availability and effect of 'fairness' or distributive justice arguments in tort cases. Arguments such as accident prevention and deterrence (which once found favour in Australian courts) are now given minimal weight in tort cases.[40] In the last ten years, arguments in tort cases which have found particular favour with Australian courts (and accordingly with lawyers) are arguments relating to individual responsibility[41] (particularly for plaintiffs) and the coherence of the claim with other areas of law. In addition, since 2002 many tort cases turn on issues of statutory interpretation of tort reform legislation rather than broader 'policy' arguments.[42]

36 See the review of the literature on deterrence in H. Luntz, 'Compensation Recovery and the National Disability Insurance Scheme' (2013) 20 *TLJ* 153, 186–201.

37 Ibid. As discussed above, n. 33, there are however circumstances where a compulsory insurer can recover the costs of compensation from an insured who has injured a claimant through intentional and/or criminal behaviour. This has a potential deterrent effect however likely has little practical effect due to impecunosity of most criminal defendants.

38 See the discussion of the rise of corrective justice and rights based theories in tort law theory in Section 3 below.

39 K. Burns, 'It's Not Just Policy: The Role of Social Facts in Judicial Reasoning in Negligence Cases' (2013) 21 *TLJ* 73.

40 *Neindorf* v. *Junkovic* (2005) 222 ALR 631, [21] (Kirby J).

41 M. Lunney, 'Personal Responsibility and the New Volenti' (2005) 13 *Tort Law Review* 76.

42 E.g, in cases which involve the interpretation of legislative provisions limiting liability for 'obvious risks' or 'dangerous recreational activities'. Broader policy arguments retain some

In recent times the High Court of Australia has repeatedly stressed that the principles of tort law, particularly negligence, must develop and be interpreted consistently and coherently with other areas of the law.[43] Coherence has emerged as part of the 'salient features' or multi-factorial approach the High Court has taken in negligence cases in the last two decades.[44] This has involved a shift away from single factor tests such as 'proximity'. In the tort/crime context, the High Court has refused recovery by tort plaintiffs where this would lead to an outcome which conflicts with, or is incoherent with, the criminal law, with existing legislation or with another area of law.[45] More generally, as Australian tort law has evolved, following tort law reform in the early 2000s, into a fusion of both common law principles and statute, the concept of coherence has informed both the development of remaining common law principles and the interpretation of tort reform legislation. The approach of the High Court has been described as symbiotic, with the common law providing an important context for the interpretation of tort reform legislation.[46] However, there is evidence that the approach of the High Court over the last decade in tort cases has favoured defendants, at the expense of plaintiffs.[47]

importance in determining issues such as duty of care and causation under the tort reform legislation. However the High Court has held that, generally, these arguments must be based on precedent or 'legal policy', see *Wallace* v. *Kam* (2013) 250 CLR 375, 385.

43 See *Sullivan* v. *Moody* (2001) 207 CLR 562, [42]. This concept of coherence may also apply to the relationship between the common law principles of contract law and legislation: see *Commonwealth Bank of Australia* v. *Barker* (2014) 88 ALJR 814, 8 (Gageler J).

44 M. Davies and I. Malkin, *Torts*, 6th edn (Sydney: Lexis Nexis, 2012), 257–60.

45 See, e.g., *CAL No 14 Pty Ltd* v. *Motor Accidents Insurance Board* (2009) 239 CLR 390; *Stuart* v. *Kirkland Veenstra* (2009) 237 CLR 215. In *Miller* v. *Miller* (2011) 242 CLR 446 a plaintiff who had been engaged in a joint illegal activity was allowed recovery (subject to a deduction for contributory negligence) where she had withdrawn from the activity shortly before the accident on the basis this would not be inconsistent with the relevant criminal statute. In the barrister (advocate) immunity case, *D'Orta-Ekenaike* v. *Victoria Legal Aid* (2005) 223 CLR 1, the accused pleaded guilty to rape on the allegedly negligent advice of counsel and sought to sue the barrister. The High Court of Australia upheld an immunity for advocates from an action in negligence in part because the ability to bring an action in negligence would call into question the finality of the criminal action.

46 P. Stewart and A. Stuhmcke, 'The Rise of the Common Law in Statutory Interpretation of Tort Law Reform Legislation: Oil and Water or a Milky Pond?' (2013) 21 *TLJ* 126.

47 See H. Luntz, 'Torts Turnaround Downunder' (2001) 1 *Commonwealth Law Journal* 95; A. Stuhmcke and P. Stewart, 'Lacunae and Litigants: A Study of Negligence Cases in the High Court of Australia in the First Decade of the 21st Century and Beyond' (2014) 38 *MULR* 151–97.

G. *The practical availability of litigation and prosecution in response to torts and crimes in Australia*

The limited empirical evidence that exists in relation to the Australian tort system suggests that most injured people with a potential claim, for a variety of reasons, do not pursue their claim in court.[48] Lack of affordable access to legal services, particularly for civil actions, remains a major problem in Australia and an impediment to the exercise of legal rights.[49] Where claims are pursued, the vast majority of those tort claims are settled prior to trial, typically for a discount of what might have been expected as full damages.[50] Procedural regimes across Australia encourage early resolution of civil tort claims. These regimes typically require that claims are processed through extensive pre-court steps including compulsory alternative dispute resolution prior to being eligible for determination by a court.[51]

Of all crimes reported in Australia, only some will actually be prosecuted in an Australian court, and, of those, a far smaller number will lead to a conviction.[52] This has implications for the ability of victims to obtain any compensation through compensation orders, discussed below, as these are available only upon successful criminal prosecution although state-sponsored schemes for paying compensation to victims of crimes of violence do not always require a conviction before payments can be made. Plea-bargains between prosecutors and accused people in criminal cases are an increasing phenomenon in Australia and can result in a lesser penalty for the accused, in return for a guilty plea or a guilty plea to a lesser offence.[53] This process has been criticised on the basis of lack of

[48] See Luntz and Hambly, *Torts*, 6–12, that suggests in some categories of claim (typically where there is a statutory insurance scheme) injured people are more likely to sue, e.g., motor vehicle accidents.

[49] Productivity Commission, *Access to Justice Arrangements: Draft Report.*

[50] Luntz and Hambly, *Torts*, 6–12. See also Productivity Commission, *Access to Justice Arrangements: Draft Report.*

[51] See, e.g., Personal Injuries Proceedings Act 2002 (Qld). Unlike Queensland, New South Wales did not proceed with its similar procedural regime originally in Civil Procedure Act 2005 (NSW), Part 2A.

[52] The so-called 'dark figure' of crime (the gap between victimisation and official crime rates) and the rates of conviction, vary from offence to offence, and over time. Regarding victimisation, see Australian Bureau of Statistics, *Crime Victimisation, Australia, 2011–12: 4530.0*, www.abs.gov.au/ausstats/abs@.nsf/mf/4530.0 (last accessed 10 June 2014).

[53] A. Flynn, 'Fortunately We in Victoria are Not in that UK Situation: Australian and United Kingdom Legal Perspectives on Plea Bargaining Reform' (2011) 16 *Deakin LR* 361. For

transparency and uncontrolled prosecutorial discretion to the detriment of victim rights,[54] and also has potential implications for the ability of victims to receive compensation orders.

3. Substance

This section considers the differences between tort law and criminal law as a question of substantive law. As we noted in the introduction, there is no rigid divide between 'substance' and 'procedure'. However, to understand the interaction between tort and crime, it is important to understand how the two areas of law are conceptualised and it is in this sense that we discuss substance. More theoretical questions, such as how and why lawyers construct the divide between tort, crime and other areas of law (taxonomy), how the theoretical justifications for tort and crime vary, and how the conceptual tools used to determine civil and criminal liability operate, will be used to unpack what is at the gist of these two areas of legal classification.

A. Classification

Tort is part of the private law of obligations. There is a range of recognised divisions within Australian tort law – typically these include intentional torts (e.g. trespass to person and property), nuisance, defamation and negligence. Criminal law is part of public law. In the academic realm, criminal law is not generally subdivided.

The classification of a wrong as tortious or criminal is not subject to any *substantive* limits on criminalisation. Where conduct that attracts a legal sanction is proscribed by statute, the legislation itself may *formally* specify whether that conduct is 'criminal', the most extensive examples being the criminal codes of Queensland and Western Australia.

For both crime and tort, state, territory and Commonwealth legislatures determine whether legal rules will be left to the common law or be subsumed by statute. Outside of this formal regulation, taxonomy is largely left to the academics. If conduct attracts a legal sanction but is not criminal, it will be classified under the taxonomy of private law where tort law is only one of a number of civil wrongs (contract and equitable

discussion of the limits of the role of the prosecutor in sentencing, see *Barbaro* v. *The Queen*; *Zirilli* v. *The Queen* (2014) 305 ALR 323.

54 Flynn, 'Australian and United Kingdom Legal Perspective on Plea Bargaining Reform'.

obligations are others). However, 'allocating' something as a tort makes little practical difference if the elements necessary to establish a legal claim remain the same irrespective of the classification.

For most of its history the tort law that applied in Australian jurisdictions was (like contract law) a creature predominantly of the common law, while criminal law in Australia was predominantly the creature of legislation (or codes). Having said this, common law states have often used statutes to consolidate rather than alter the common law. In any case, this formal distinction has significantly eroded in the last ten years with the growth of tort reform legislation across Australia with the result that legislation now intervenes into the common law of tort (especially the tort of negligence) in major ways. These reforms focus on modifying the existing law of tort rather than creating new domains of law which impact upon the conventional taxonomy of private law. There is no history in Australia of codifying existing law to create new classifications so as to alter the conventional taxonomy. New domains are created by legislation (e.g., trade practices legislation) but these domains are largely independent of the law of tort.

However, the creation of these new domains has had some impact on what is considered the law of tort. While in one sense, 'statutory' wrongs may be seen as hybrid, it is more common to divide them into the classification of existing common law tort rules, in which case the statutory remedy would be allocated to 'tort', or to place statutory remedies into their own new kind of (*sui generis*) civil liability. The best-known example of the former practice is the tort of breach of statutory duty.[55] The liability recognised in breach of statutory duty has conventionally been regarded as part of the law of tort although it is clear that the basis of liability lies in the judicial interpretation of the statute itself and on whether a legislative intention to create a private law right of action can be gleaned from the statutory language. Of course, this question is only relevant where the legislature has left it unclear whether breach of a statutory obligation gives rise to a private law claim. Paradoxically, where the legislature specifies that breach of a statutory obligation is actionable, the action thereby created is sometimes allocated to the law of tort, but is frequently treated as a *sui generis* civil claim.

The relationship between tort and statutory liability is largely uninfluenced by whether the statutory obligation creates a criminal sanction

[55] See, generally, N. Foster, 'The Merits of the Civil Action for Breach of Statutory Duty' (2011) 33 *Syd LR* 67.

for breach: statutory conduct criminalised by legislation remains within the domain of the criminal law.[56] Australian law does not, in the absence of specific legislative authority, create a civil claim to provide a remedy for conduct that is found to be criminal. Nonetheless, there are examples of such specific legislative duality. For instance, in consumer protection legislation many breaches of the legislation will give rise to fines or other penalties while simultaneously allowing a party adversely affected by the breach to bring a civil claim for damages.[57]

Perhaps the most significant example of legislative duality linking tort and crime is that criminal conduct that results in injury can result in compensation for the victim. The presence of a criminal offence can be the trigger for awards of compensation – an important goal of tort law – even if no tort is committed. Thus, the victim of a crime of violence can claim compensation under criminal injuries compensation schemes (state-funded schemes).[58] Payments under these schemes are not dependent on the victim establishing an independent civil claim nor, generally, on anyone being convicted of a criminal offence: it is sufficient that the injury was caused by violent conduct that could have resulted in conviction if a prosecution was brought.

Where there has been a conviction for a criminal offence, this can have impacts in tort law. In one Australian jurisdiction, a person in custody as a result of being convicted of a serious indictable offence requires the permission of the court before commencing any civil proceedings.[59] This limitation is a surviving remnant of the civil disabilities that historically attached to convicted felons (persons convicted of serious criminal offences) which included the inability to commence civil proceedings as well as forfeiture of property.[60]

[56] In fact, the presence of a criminal penalty may be a factor that *prevents* a court finding a legislative intent to create a private law action for breach of a statutory obligation as may its absence support the finding of an action: *Morgan* v. *Workcover* [2013] SASCFC 139.

[57] See Competition and Consumer Act 2010 (Cth) especially Sch. 2 (the Australian Consumer Law). For detail, see S. G. Corones, *The Australian Consumer Law*, 2nd edn (Pyrmont: Lawbook Co, 2013).

[58] All Australian jurisdictions have such schemes: see, e.g., Criminal Injuries Compensation Act 2003 (WA).

[59] Felons (Civil Proceedings) Act 1981 (NSW).

[60] See, generally, A. Freiberg and R. Fox, 'Fighting Crime with Forfeiture: Lessons from History' (2000) 6 *Aust JLH* 1; J. Goudkamp, 'Revival of the Doctrine of Attainder – the Statutory Illegality Defences to Liability in Tort' (2007) 29 *Syd LR* 445. The issue was of great significance in the early history of white settlement in Australia as a strict application of the rule would have prevented the vast majority of the population – who were convicted

More generally, criminal courts have power to make compensation orders against a person who is convicted of a crime in favour of the victim of that crime[61] as well as having power to make restitution orders for property that has been misappropriated or stolen.[62] These orders are not dependent on the criminal conduct amounting to a tort. In most jurisdictions, the powers granted to criminal courts to make these awards are discretionary and formulated in very general terms.[63] Importantly, jurisdictions within Australia vary on whether the ability of the person to pay is a factor to be taken into account. There is very little guidance as to what heads of damage can be claimed,[64] how awards are to be calculated[65] and what evidence is required to prove any damage for which compensation is claimed.

There are a variety of means by which a compensation order can be enforced. Some jurisdictions provide that the award is enforced in the same way as a civil judgment, some in the same way as a fine, and others leave it for the court making the order to determine. Two jurisdictions – Queensland[66] and the Northern Territory[67] – provide that the court making the order can determine that non-compliance with the order can be punished by imprisonment. These remarkable provisions demonstrate the ambiguity that surrounds these orders: while non-compliance with a penal fine can result in imprisonment, imprisonment for failing to pay a civil debt has not existed in Australia since the nineteenth century.

In practice, compensation orders in criminal cases are not widely made. This is primarily because of the impecuniosity of the persons against whom the award is to be made, a practical problem even where not a doctrinal one; as well as the judicial view that awards should only be

criminals – from using the civil courts. In practice, the rule was not consistently enforced and when it was it caused controversy: see B. Kercher, *An Unruly Child: A History of Law in Australia* (Sydney, Allen & Unwin, 1995), 36–9.

61 See, e.g., Penalties and Sentences Act 1992 (Qld), s. 35; Sentencing Act 1997 (Tas), s. 68.

62 See, e.g., Criminal Procedure Act 1986 (NSW), s. 43.

63 However, there is considerable and inconsistent variation between the jurisdictions. In NSW, the maximum amount that can be awarded is $50,000 (Victims Rights and Support Act 2013 (NSW), s. 94). In Western Australia, orders can only be made in respect of damage to property (Sentencing Act 1995 (WA), ss. 116–17) while in Tasmania an award must be made if the offence is burglary, stealing or unlawfully injuring property (Sentencing Act 1997 (Tas), s. 68).

64 The Victorian legislation provides the greatest detail: Sentencing Act 1991 (Vic), Part 4.

65 There is judicial authority that the common law approach to assessing damages for personal injury should be adopted: *R* v. *McDonald* [1979] 1 NSWLR 451; *R* v. *Babic* [1980] 2 NSWLR 743.

66 Penalties and Sentences Act 1992 (Qld), s. 36(2).

67 Sentencing Act 1995 (NT), s. 93.

made in simple cases for small amounts.[68] However, while it remains the case that complicated and contested issues are not suitable for resolution in these proceedings, it has recently been held that significant factual and legal issues can be considered when determining compensation orders.[69] While this was said in the context of Victorian provisions which expressly allow the court to call for additional evidence, statements and documents, the inherent flexibility attached to the process in other jurisdictions would seem to allow for additional evidence to be produced and hence allow more complicated cases to be heard across the board. In many ways, compensation awards in criminal cases are true hybrid awards; they have been justified as providing 'easy access to civil justice for victims in criminal proceedings'.[70] But this hybrid nature also presents challenges for consistency: given that some crimes will also constitute torts, it is desirable that any award seeking to compensate the victim is assessed in the same way irrespective of whether the award is in criminal or civil proceedings.[71] Consistency is also challenged by the differing standards of proof in criminal and civil actions. In statutory schemes for compensation for crimes of violence, it is not always necessary that there be a conviction for an award to be made. It may be sufficient for compensation that the offence be proved on the balance of probabilities[72] which is lower than the beyond reasonable doubt standard of the criminal law. This is an example of what may described as the penumbra of criminality: when we look to civil aspects of criminal behaviour the usual procedural protections of the criminal law seem to be discarded.

B. Theory

Despite some similarities in elements of the theories underpinning tort and crime, the theoretical underpinnings of these two areas of law

[68] *RK* v. *Mirik* [2009] VSC 14, [34]–[41].

[69] Ibid., [68], where the trial judge noted that changes to the relevant Victorian legislation meant that the principle that the power to award criminal compensation was meant for straightforward cases 'cannot be applied with its former force'.

[70] Ibid., [11]. In this case, a compensation award was described as civil compensation, not criminal punishment, so that the civil standard of proof was applicable ([14]). Presumably this means that determining whether the offence caused the injury for which compensation is sought must be determined by that standard.

[71] E.g., should defences be recognised in criminal compensation cases, and if so, should they mirror tort defences? See *R* v. *McDonald* [1979] 1 NSWLR 451.

[72] *L* v. *Carey* [2010] TASSC 54 applied balance of probabilities for the Victims of Crime Assistance Act 1976 (Tas). However, in South Australia, Victims of Crime Act 2001 (SA), s. 22 requires the underlying offence to be proved beyond reasonable doubt: *Puric* v. *State of South Australia* [2009] SASC 107.

differ significantly. Much though depends on what the theoretical underpinnings of tort and crime actually are, and this fundamental question remains in dispute. In tort law, for example, instrumental approaches founded on deterrence and compensation[73] compete with more theoretical justifications based on corrective justice and the protection of rights.[74] Adherents to this later theory place greater value on coherence by rejecting certain arguments that seek to evaluate the legal rule or application of that rule by reference to its consequences: they are concerned with theories of interpersonal justice.[75] Conversely, instrumental approaches to tort law look to a wider range of arguments to justify legal rules, and broad questions of distributive justice can play a role. While in one sense this is a 'public' dimension, it is difficult to see these concerns as akin to the concerns that underpin the public nature of criminal law.

By contrast, in the modern era, the role of the state in crime (embodied by the police and the prosecutor, acting on behalf of the public) has meant that theories of criminal law have been oriented around notions of 'publicness'. 'Publicness', howsoever defined, is generally regarded as an essential feature of criminal law. According to this idea, the criminal law is concerned with 'public wrongs' – wrongs that are of concern not just to the victim and perpetrator, but to the society or community *qua* society or community. In terms of positive law, this idea is used to legitimise offences such as so-called 'victimless crimes' (such as simple possession of illicit drugs), and, more abstractly, to provide an apparently neutral co-ordinate in a pluralistic social and moral context.[76] While this concern with 'publicness' should operate to limit criminalisation (the practice of making certain conduct criminal), as generally held to be appropriate in liberal political democracies, the exponential growth of criminal offences in jurisdictions in Australia (and elsewhere) suggests that 'publicness'

[73] In Australia, instrumental approaches to tort law trace their origins to the work of Professor John Fleming whose seminal textbook, *The Law of Torts*, was published in Australia in 1957.

[74] There is now a vast literature on corrective justice and rights-based approaches to tort law, but leading examples are E. J. Weinrib, *The Idea of Private Law* (Harvard University Press, 1995), A. Beever, *Rediscovering the Law of Negligence* (Oxford: Hart Publishing, 2007), R. Stevens, *Rights and Private Law* (Oxford University Press, 2007).

[75] Some theorists advocate for a modified corrective justice approach where distributive concerns can in limited cases override a result otherwise reached through applying interpersonal justice concerns: see A. Robertson, 'Justice, Community Welfare and the Duty of Care' (2011) 127 *LQR* 370, A. Robertson, 'On the Function of the Law of Negligence' (2013) 33 *OJLS* 31.

[76] For critical discussion, see N. Lacey, 'Community, Culture, Criminalization' in R. Cruft *et al.* (eds.), *Crime, Punishment, and Responsibility: The Jurisprudence of Antony Duff* (Oxford University Press, 2011), 292–310.

is a capacious concept.[77] Thus, while the 'publicness' of the crime may provide something of a theory underpinning the criminal law, it does this only in a general and loose way that has failed to constrain the states' resort to criminalisation only as a regulatory option of last resort.

In criminal law, at least in theory, fault (*mens rea*) is of vital significance for the legitimacy of the law. If 'publicness' justifies or legitimates criminalisation in general, then fault does the same for the imposition of criminal liability on an individual in a particular instance. In the current era, the cardinal idea of fault in criminal law is subjective, based on what the defendant himself or herself intended, foresaw or the risks he or she perceived as appropriate. But the requirement of a subjective fault element may not, in practice, apply in the new criminal offences created in the expansion of criminal law over the last few decades. Here, fault is often either objective (as with negligence based offences) or strict (in the sense that the defendant will have to discharge a duty to the court before the prosecution's duty to prove fault is enlivened at trial).[78]

The rationale usually given for lower fault requirements is that these offences are regulatory (to do with the good working of a social and economic system) rather than moral (conduct regarded as wrong in a moral-evaluative assessment). But it is perhaps just as significant that removing the fault requirement means that these offences are easier to prosecute and thus demand fewer resources on behalf of the police and the court. Viewed broadly, these distributive concerns share similarities with those that motivate the imposition of strict liability in the law of tort.

It is interesting to note that the rise of rights-based theories of tort law – which generally eschew arguments based on distributive justice – have challenged the legitimacy of strict liability as a basis for imposing tortious liability at the same time that the criminal justice system has been more willing to establish criminal liability on this basis. It is somewhat paradoxical, then, that at the same time as tort law is criticised for paying insufficient attention to the importance of agency in determining tort liability,[79] the basis of criminal liability has been widened so that the model

[77] See, for discussion, D. Brown, 'Criminalisation and Normative Theory' (2013) 25 *Current Issues in Criminal Justice* 605.

[78] While exact numbers are not known, there is general recognition that strict liability offences are increasing. See D. Brown, 'Constituting Physical and Fault Elements', in T. Crofts and A. Loughnan (eds.), *Criminalisation and Criminal Responsibility in Australia* (Oxford University Press, 2015).

[79] In the sense that corrective justice looks to the relationship between the parties, each as individual agents. Unlike the traditional criminal law, however, corrective justice is not

of the agentic, autonomous and reasoning responsible individual ceases to explain large sections of criminal law. These developments suggest that the theoretical bases of tort and crime share more than has conventionally been recognised.

C. *Concepts*

There is very little direct relationship between the substantive rules of tort and crime. As discussed below, tort and crime do share some concepts in determining liability but care must be taken here because the use of the same term does not guarantee the same meaning for that term in both areas of law. We consider this issue in relation to specific concepts below.

1. Capacity

There are few formal rules relating to the capacity to sue or be sued in the law of tort. Sometimes, the particular nature of the tort may limit the capacity of a plaintiff to sue (e.g., the limits on a corporation suing in the tort of defamation).[80] Other limitations arise not from formal limitations on capacity but from the need for a defendant to achieve certain levels of understanding to be able to satisfy any intention,[81] or, in some cases, any fault requirement. For example, although there is no discrete age limit below which an action cannot be brought, in practice it would be impossible to sue successfully a very young child in the tort of negligence because the reasonableness of the conduct would be judged taking into account the age of the child and, judged by that standard, it is extremely unlikely the conduct would be considered negligent.[82] Conversely, in some cases, such as where an adult defendant suffers from a mental incapacity, the law of tort in Australia may still assume the

concerned with individual agency: A. Beever, 'Corrective Justice and Personal Responsibility in Tort Law' (2008) 28 *OJLS* 475.

80 See the uniform defamation legislation, s. 9 (uniform because the legislation has been passed by every Australian jurisdiction). Only excluded corporations (a corporation whose objects for which it is formed do not include obtaining financial gain for its members or corporators and which employs fewer than ten persons and is not related to another corporation) which are not public bodies (as defined) can sue in this tort.

81 Hence a person who hits another under the delusion that he is kicking a piece of wood may not be liable in battery as battery requires that the defendant intend the contact *with the person* of another. See further K. Barker *et al.*, *The Law of Torts in Australia*, 5th edn (Oxford University Press, 2012), 2.7.2.

82 *McHale* v. *Watson* (1966) 115 CLR 199.

defendant has the capacity of an objective reasonable 'normal' person despite evidence to the contrary.[83]

By contrast, the criminal law has robust capacity rules. This reflects the development of criminal procedure as a protection against the power of the state. Like other common law systems, Australian criminal laws have a minimum age of criminal responsibility (ten years in all jurisdictions), which prohibits young people from being charged with criminal offences, *doli incapax* (protecting children aged ten to fourteen years to whom a rebuttable presumption that they are incapable of committing a criminal offence applies), and other rules – around unfitness to plead – which prevent defendants with mental or cognitive impairments from being subject to a criminal trial in which they cannot competently participate.[84] In addition, some criminal defences (such as insanity) relate to the defendant's capacity at the time of the alleged offence.

2. Fault

Fault plays an important role in tortious liability. The most common tort – in terms of number of actions brought – is the tort of negligence, an essential element of which is that the defendant has failed to exercise reasonable care in the circumstances. 'Fault' in this tort is judged objectively by reference to what a reasonable person would do or omit to do in the circumstances.[85] Many other torts require an element of intention although the meaning of this term varies across torts.[86] Although all torts based on intention require some element of fault – liability is only very exceptionally based on the bare fact that a defendant acted voluntarily – in torts with a weak intention requirement it must be admitted that liability is imposed in practice on a strict liability basis. Outside torts of intention and negligence, there are only small pockets of strict liability in the law of tort. One possible example is the tort of private nuisance where

83 *Carrier* v. *Bonham* [2001] QCA 234. For a contrary view see J. Goudkamp, 'Insanity as a Tort Defence' (2011) 31 *OJLS* 727.

84 On the age of criminal responsibility in Australia, see G. Urbas, 'The Age of Criminal Responsibility' (2000) 181 *Trends and Issues in Crime and Criminal Justice* 1–6. Regarding unfitness, in NSW, the test for unfitness to plead is contained in *R* v. *Presser* [1958] VR 45. A new test for unfitness has been proposed by the NSW Law Reform Commission. For discussion, see A. Loughnan 'Reforming the Criminal Law on Mental Incapacity' (2013) 25 *CICJ* 70.

85 *Glasgow Corporation* v. *Muir* [1943] AC 448; the issue is now governed by legislation in Australian jurisdictions (see, e.g., Civil Liability Act 2002 (NSW), s. 5B).

86 Barker, *Law of Torts*, 37–41.

it seems that the defendant can be liable even if he or she acted with all reasonable care. Even here, however, liability seems to be fault-based in some sense because a defendant is probably not liable if the defendant could not take the first step towards reasonable conduct, foreseeing that the plaintiff might suffer injury caused by the defendant undertaking the action in question.[87]

This notion of fault is in no sense a synonym for the mental element (*mens rea*) in criminal law, which is also known as the fault element of a criminal offence. There is no equivalent concept to *mens rea* in tort law. As mentioned above, fault in criminal law generally refers to the mental state the defendant must have at the time of committing the conduct comprising the offence (which is the *actus reus*). The cardinal fault requirements of the criminal law in the current era are the subjective mental states of intention and subjective recklessness. Here, these kinds of fault requirements have come to act as a lynchpin in the criminal law of the late modern era, legitimising the imposition of criminal liability (and exposing the defendant to punishment) on the basis that the defendant turned his or her mind to the risk he or she created, or intended to perform the conduct comprising the external element of the offence. This, in turn, reflects the central place of the idea of a rational thinking and choosing individual subject at the heart of criminal law (and academic theorising about it).[88]

3. Intention

As mentioned above, there are a considerable number of torts that have 'intention' as an element but the precise meaning of this term varies between torts.[89] Broadly, the meaning of intention varies between an intention to produce a consequence other than loss or damage to the plaintiff, and intention to cause loss to the plaintiff. In the latter category – where the relevant intention is an intention to cause a loss to the plaintiff – are the economic torts where the intention is to cause financial harm to the

[87] *Gales Holdings Pty Ltd* v. *Tweed Shire Council* [2013] NSWCA 382.

[88] For critical discussion, see N. Lacey, 'Responsibility and Modernity in Criminal Law' (2001) 9 *The Journal of Political Philosophy* 249, N. Lacey, 'In Search of the Responsible Subject: History, Philosophy and Social Sciences in Criminal Law Theory' (2001) 64 *MLR* 350, N. Lacey, 'Character, Capacity, Outcome: Towards a Framework for Assessing the Shifting Pattern of Criminal Responsibility in Modern English Law' in M. D. Dubber and L. Farmer (eds.), *Modern Histories of Crime and Punishment: Critical Perspectives on Crime and Law* (Palo Alto: Stanford University Press, 2007), 14–41.

[89] For discussion, see P. Cane, 'Mens Rea in Tort Law' (2000) 20 *OJLS* 533.

plaintiff.[90] Some of these torts will also constitute crimes, although usually not at common law but under legislation – for example, fair trading and competition legislation. Conversely, some torts have a very weak intention requirement in that the loss to the plaintiff does not need to be intended but merely some other consequence of the defendant's conduct.[91] The most common examples are the 'trespass' torts such as assault, battery and false imprisonment. In battery, for example, a defendant need only intend that the consequence of his or her conduct is an application of force to the body of the plaintiff.[92] Such an application of force is *prima facie* actionable if this is the intended consequence of the conduct even if done for non-harmful purposes (or even for purposes that are beneficial to the plaintiff). As noted above, this is effectively strict liability. The contrast with criminal law – which also recognises crimes of assault, battery and false imprisonment – is striking because much more in the way of fault or intention is required than simply an intention to produce a particular consequence.

Although the matter is not free from doubt, the better view seems to be that recklessness as to the consequences of conduct is sufficient to establish intention in an intentional tort. There is very little Australian authority and what little there is has tended to assume that recklessness suffices without exploring why it might or might not be adequate.[93]

In criminal law, intention forms the *mens rea* requirement of the most serious offences (such as murder and sexual assault). Generally speaking, it connotes aim, object or purpose. Intention can be contrasted with motive, which is generally not relevant to liability (but may be considered at sentencing where a 'good' motive may mitigate punishment). Orientating the question of criminal liability around the defendant's intention became possible with the growth of the so-called psy-knowledges,[94] which meant it was possible to regard a defendant's mental state as a question

90 Examples include the torts of lawful and unlawful means conspiracy, interference with trade and commerce by unlawful means and intimidation.

91 Some academics argue that these are not really intentional torts at all but are examples of strict liability: Cane, 'Mens Rea in Tort Law'; Beever, *Rediscovering the Law of Negligence*, 112.

92 Barker, *Law of Torts*, 37–41.

93 *Hall* v. *Fonceca* [1983] WAR 309; *White* v. *State of South Australia* [2010] SASC 95, [365]; *Carter* v. *Walker* [2010] VSCA 340, ([215](8)). See further A. Beever, 'Transferred Malice in Tort Law' (2009) 29 *LS* 400.

94 See, generally, Lacey, 'Responsibility and Modernity in Criminal Law'. On psy-knowledges, see N. Rose, *Inventing Our Selves: Psychology, Power and Personhood* (Cambridge University Press, 1996).

of fact. But, as mentioned above, pragmatic considerations of cost and police and court time, has generated momentum around other, lesser fault requirements. In addition, in relation to sexual assault, for example, concerns about justice and the difficulty of securing convictions have led to the inclusion of objective fault requirements alongside subjective ones.[95]

4. Causation

Causation is an essential element of tortious liability.[96] It consists of two, theoretically distinct, elements. The first is *cause in fact*, or, for many fault-based torts, 'necessary condition causation'.[97] Australian tort law uses 'but for' causation, like many other jurisdictions. By setting up a counterfactual, it is decided whether the plaintiff would have suffered the same injury if the defendant's tort had not been committed.[98] Special rules seem to apply where this enquiry is complicated such as where there is causal over-determination (e.g., if the injury was caused conjointly by a number of factors each of which on its or their own would have been sufficient to have caused the harm, such as two fires set on either side of a house, each being sufficient to destroy the house).[99] Second, even if the defendant's tort is a factual cause of the plaintiff's harm, liability may be limited if the *scope of the defendant's liability* should not extend to the harm that has been factually caused by the tort.[100] This is a complicated area and there is little consensus of what kind of factors are relevant to it.

95 See, e.g., Crimes Amendment (Consent – Sexual Assault Offences) Act 2007 (NSW).

96 Most theories, apart from economic analysis of tort law, see causation as at the core of tort law: see P. Cane, *The Political Economy of Personal Injury Law* (University of Queensland Press, 2007), 90–3.

97 Where the cause of action is based on the defendant failing to exercise reasonable care, this requirement is now found in legislation: see, e.g., Civil Liability Act 2002 (NSW), s. 5D(1)(a).

98 Some scholars argue that certain assumptions have to be made to frame the counterfactual enquiry: see Burns, 'It's Not Just Policy: The Role of Social Facts in Judicial Reasoning in Negligence Cases', 80–2; D. Hamer, '"Factual Causation" and "Scope of Liability": What's the Difference' (2014) 77 *MLR* 155.

99 A common solution to causal overdetermination is to adopt the 'NESS' test: that D's contribution was a necessary element of a set of sufficient conditions to cause the harm. The literature on the NESS test is vast, but for recent contributions see C. Miller, 'NESS for Beginners' in R. Goldberg (ed.) *Perspectives on Causation* (Oxford: Hart Publishing, 2011); R. Wright, 'The NESS Account of Natural Causation: A Response to Criticisms' in R. Goldberg (ed.), *Perspectives on Causation* (Oxford: Hart Publishing, 2011).

100 This was historically referred to as remoteness of damage or proximate cause. The scope of liability terminology is now used for torts based on a failure to exercise reasonable care (see, e.g., Civil Liability Act 2002 (NSW), s. 5D(1)(b)).

It seems to encompass concerns as to whether the type or kind of loss was reasonably foreseeable,[101] whether the duty which the defendant owed to the plaintiff extended to the loss caused in the particular way it was[102] and whether the fact that there were intervening events between the tort and the injury should negative the defendant's liability (although there are also arguments that this latter consideration should be dealt with through causal concepts rather than in scope of liability).[103] Torts based on intention generally have wider scope of liability rules than fault-based torts.

Causation operates in the same way in criminal law. It also has two elements: factual causation and legal causation, the terminology which tort law used until the twenty-first century and which broadly apply in the same way as in tort. Legal causation has been defined in different ways but can be captured by the idea that the defendant's action must be a substantial cause of the prohibited outcome.[104] However, as this suggests, causation is only relevant to what are called 'result crimes': offences which require a particular outcome (such as a death) to found liability. The most significant other category of crimes, conduct crimes, does not require causation to be established; similarly, inchoate crimes (such as attempt) clearly do not require any causation. Further, causation is rarely a live issue in court. For instance, liability for result crimes may be disputed where there has been a break in the chain of causation (such as an intervening act from a third party) after the actions of the defendant and before the prohibited consequence occurs. Other offences (such as sexual assault) do not have proof of a particular outcome as an element of the offence.

5. Secondary/accessory liability

The law of tort recognises extensive liability for torts committed by another through the mechanisms of vicarious liability and non-delegable duties. However these are not examples of true secondary or accessory liability, as liability is based on the relationship between the parties rather

[101] *Overseas Tankship (UK) Ltd* v. *Morts Docks & Engineering Co Ltd* [1961] AC 611 ('*Wagon Mound No. 1*').

[102] This is sometimes raised as the question whether P's loss fell within the scope of D's duty of care. For an example, see *Wallace* v. *Kam* (2013) 250 CLR 375.

[103] See Hamer, 'Factual Causation and Scope of Liability'.

[104] See for discussion, T. Anthony *et al.*, *Waller and Williams Criminal Law Text and Cases*, 12th edn (Sydney: LexisNexis, 2013), ch. 4.

than any involvement in the primary tortfeasor's wrong.[105] Apart from these examples, the law on secondary/accessory liability is relatively undeveloped. The predominant view appears to be that secondary/accessory liability is more limited in the law of tort than in criminal law.[106] It has generally been assumed that secondary tortious liability is limited to situations where the accessory has procured the commission of the tort or where there has been some kind of agreement or understanding between the accessory and the principal tortfeasor that the conduct constituting the tort will be committed. Strictly speaking, this basis for liability is not a secondary liability, as the accessory is considered to commit the tort along with the primary tortfeasor, that is, both are liable as primary tortfeasors.[107] True secondary liability, based on the accessory's assistance to the primary tortfeasor in committing the tort, has not been recognised as creating liability.

Accessory liability for crime is a well-established, if complex, part of criminal law in the Australian context. Still largely governed by the common law (in NSW at least), accessory liability has been the subject of several law reform reports and recommendations for legislative change. Relative to tort, criminal accessory liability is more extensive, as, at least theoretically, it covers all assistance or participation in crime, extending beyond 'knowing assistance' or conspiracy (agreement to commit an offence).[108] In practice, however, conduct that might give rise to accessory liability may be prosecuted as a substantive preparatory offence.[109]

The wider scope of accessory liability in criminal law, as opposed to tort law, has been criticised on the basis that, given the greater penalties and public opprobrium that criminal sanctions entail, it should be more, not less, difficult for accessory liability to be imposed in criminal law than in tort law.[110] Whatever the merits of this argument in principle, it ignores the possibility that compensation orders can be made in criminal cases

[105] J. Dietrich, 'Accessorial Liability in the Law of Torts' (2011) 31 *LS* 231, 235–6.

[106] P. Davies, 'Accessory Liability for Assisting Torts' [2011] *CLJ* 353.

[107] *Sabaf SpA* v. *Meneghetti SpA* [2003] RPC 14.

[108] See for discussion, NSW Law Reform Commission, *Complicity* (Report No. 129, 2010). The criminal defendant is liable as a principal (at trial and for sentencing): see *Gillard* v. *The Queen* (2003) 219 CLR 1.

[109] See B. McSherry, 'Expanding the Boundaries of Inchoate Crimes: The Growing Reliance on Preparatory Offences' in B. McSherrry, A. Norrie and S. Bronitt (eds.), *Regulating Deviance: The Redirection of Criminalisation and the Futures of Criminal Law* (Oxford: Onati/Hart Publishing, 2009), 35–58.

[110] Davies, 'Accessory Liability for Assisting Torts', 362–5.

(although, as we have noted, there is little authority on the boundary of such awards).

6. Defences: self-defence, illegality, duress

Self-defence is a defence to allegations of criminal conduct. It is available to all defendants, but, because it requires the defendant to have responded to a perceived threat to self, others or property with reasonable force, in practice, it is available only against alleged crimes of violence. Self-defence has been reformed in recent years. In NSW, the test for the defence is now whether a defendant genuinely perceived the need for force (a subjective test), and that the force was reasonable in the circumstances (an objective test).[111]

Self-defence has long been a defence in respect of torts of intention.[112] Its modern existence varies depending on whether the common law or statute is applied. At common law, self-defence is available if the tortious conduct is a reasonable response to the threat and is not excessive in the circumstances of the case.[113] Although the position is not entirely clear in Australia, it seems that a defendant need only show that the threat of death or injury was reasonably perceived, even if in reality there was no threat.[114] It has been argued that such an approach provides inadequate protection to the plaintiff in civil law.[115] It is certainly the case that for other defences

[111] See, e.g., Crimes Act 1900 (NSW), s. 418. As a matter of law, lethal force is not able to constitute reasonable force in defence of property: Crimes Act 1900 (NSW), s. 420.

[112] J. Goudkamp, *Tort Law Defences* (Oxford: Hart Publishing, 2013), 106–7. In theory, it may be possible that self-defence can apply to an action in negligence. Even though negligent conduct is by definition unreasonable but only reasonable responses attract the defence, 'reasonableness' in self-defence is considered in the relationship between the threat to D and D's response. It is not concerned with the manner in which the response is carried out. Hence if A threatens B with a knife and B runs to his car and, in attempting to escape, carelessly hits A causing him injury, it could be said that B was acting in self-defence. The response to the threat (escaping in the car) may be considered reasonable even if the execution of the response was careless. Other defences may also be applicable here, such as illegality and contributory negligence.

[113] *Hall* v. *Fonceca* [1983] WAR 309. As in criminal law, 'self-defence' is used to cover situations where the conduct is a response to a threat to oneself, one's property, to another person and perhaps also to another person's property: see Barker, *Law of Torts*, 67–9.

[114] This is the position in criminal law, as mentioned above, and it seems the same rule applies in civil cases: Barker, *Law of Torts*, 68.

[115] *Ashley* v. *Chief Constable of Sussex* [2008] 1 AC 962, [16]–[20] (Lord Scott). See G. Virgo, 'We Do This in the Criminal Law and That in the Law of Tort' in S. Pitel, J. Neyers and E. Chamberlain (eds.), *Tort Law: Challenging Orthodoxy* (Oxford: Hart Publishing, 2013), 101–4.

to intentional torts (such as consent) a reasonable but mistaken belief in the presence of the circumstances enlivening the defence is insufficient.[116] In New South Wales the defence (with modifications) has now been put on a statutory footing in respect of many tort actions.[117]

An important area where tort and crime interact substantively is the defence of illegality. When the plaintiff and defendant (and perhaps even only when the plaintiff) are engaged in criminal activities at the time the tort is committed, the defendant may be able to rely on the defence that the tort was committed in course of the plaintiff's unlawful activities. For example, in the tort of negligence a duty of care will not be owed to a plaintiff injured by a defendant in the course of joint illegal activity if this would be incoherent with the relevant criminal law or statue.[118] In addition, some Australian tort reform legislation specifically limits the ability of a person injured in the course of criminal activity to recover in negligence even where that person has never been charged with or convicted of an offence.[119] These rules are part of a wider concern to ensure that there is (or is seen to be) coherence and congruency between the civil and criminal law.[120]

Following England and Wales, duress is available in NSW as a defence to all criminal offences except murder and attempted murder, while in Victoria it has been made available in response to homicide charges by virtue of statute.[121] It is a common law defence, which requires the defendant to commit what would otherwise be an offence had he or she not acted out of fear that serious harm would be inflicted on him or herself, or another. In practice, it is difficult to successfully raise duress as a defence.

Apart from one context, there is remarkably little authority on the effect of duress in the law of tort. The exception is in relation to the defence of consent, where the general rule that a consent given under duress is ineffective, is well established.[122] Whether duress could vitiate conduct that would otherwise be tortious is a more difficult question. Certainly

[116] R. Balkin and J. Davis, *Law of Torts*, 5th edn (Chatswood, NSW: LexisNexis, 2013), 6.2.

[117] Civil Liability Act 2002 (NSW), s. 52. See further J. Goudkamp, 'Self-defence and Illegality under the Civil Liability Act 2002 (NSW)' (2010) 18 *TLJ* 61.

[118] *Miller* v. *Miller* (2011) 242 CLR 446. If a plaintiff is injured during the course of a criminal activity and is able to demonstrate a duty of care is owed, participation in criminal activity can affect whether a breach of duty can be shown, and may also constitute contributory negligence which will reduce damages.

[119] See, e.g., Civil Liability Act 2002 (NSW), s. 54.

[120] See Section 4.A below.

[121] In NSW, see *R* v. *Lawrence* [1980] 1 NSWLR 122; in Victoria, see Crimes Act 1958 (Vic), s. 9AG.

[122] Barker, *Law of Torts*, 71.

for many of the intentional torts – such as trespass to the person, where the tortious conduct may also amount to a crime – there seems no reason why it should not, as voluntariness is an essential element of the cause of action.

In NSW criminal law, provocation is available as a partial defence to reduce murder to manslaughter. It has long been a controversial defence, with critics arguing that it effectively permits the use of lethal force in response to perceived slights or harms.[123] In NSW, provocation was recently subject to a review by a select committee of the Upper House of Parliament, which issued a report recommending that the defence be reformulated as a defence of 'gross provocation' and significantly restricted. In response to this report, the NSW Government proposed to alter provocation such that it would only be available in response to actions which constituted serious offences, a change which, having been enacted, as a practical matter, renders provocation an otiose part of criminal law.[124]

Provocation plays a very minor role in the law of tort at common law. Provocation is not a defence to any tort and its only remedial effect is to reduce any award of exemplary or punitive damages that would otherwise have been made against the defendant.[125] The cases in tort law that have considered the issue have generally involved battery and the concern here is that allowing a defence of provocation would be inconsistent with the rule that contributory negligence is not a defence to battery.[126]

An important defence in both civil and criminal law is consent.[127] In criminal law, consent may be a defence (e.g., to charges of common assault) or its absence may be an element of the prosecution case (e.g., sexual assault).[128] In tort law, the presence of consent deprives the

[123] See for discussion T. Crofts and A. Loughnan, 'Provocation: The Good, the Bad and the Ugly' (2013) 37 *Crim LJ* 23.

[124] See s. 23 Crimes Act (NSW); see further T. Crofts and A. Loughnan, 'Provocation, NSW Style: Reform of the Defence of Provocation in NSW' [2014] *Crim L Rev* 109.

[125] *Fontin* v. *Katopodis* (1962) 108 CLR 177. There is authority that it also operates to reduce aggravated damages: *Whitbread* v. *Rail Corporation NSW* [2011] NSWCA 130.

[126] *Horkin* v. *North Melbourne Football Club Social Club* [1983] 1 VR 153, 162 (Brooking J). It is unclear whether the same rule would apply for a compensation order made in criminal proceedings.

[127] Although there is some debate as to whether lack of consent should be viewed as an element of a tortious cause of action, the better view is that consent is a defence in the law of tort: *Secretary, Department of Health* v. *JWB and SMB* (1992) 175 CLR 218 (*'Marion's Case'*).

[128] In criminal law, because the absence of consent may be an element of the charge (that is, for the prosecution to prove), consent may be considered a putative defence, or a 'defence',

interference with the plaintiff's interests of its wrongful nature. But consent must be real to be effective and there is considerable complexity around what factors will vitiate an otherwise effective consent. An area of particular complexity is the circumstances when consent will be vitiated when it is based on a mistake induced by fraud.[129] For example, sexual intercourse without consent amounts to the tort of battery (and in criminal law, to the offence of sexual assault). Whether a consent is based on a mistake (and hence exposes the plaintiff to being sued for the tort of battery) depends on the distinction between the core elements of the contact – for which there must be no mistake – and peripheral elements – mistakes about which, even if induced by fraud, will not vitiate consent.[130] Hence a man who deceives a woman into having sexual relations with him by fraudulently telling her that he is a millionaire commits no battery. Although the woman may not have consented to the contact if she had known the truth, there was no mistake as to nature of the contact (which is the core of battery) and she consented to that contact. Conversely, it is clear that mistake as to the identity of the person responsible for the contact will vitiate consent. In the context of medical treatment, it has been also held where a mistake as to the *need* for treatment is induced by fraud consent will be vitiated.[131] It must be admitted, however, that the boundary between matters going to the core elements of the contact and peripheral matters is not always easy to identify.[132]

Although criminal law and tort law use similar rules for determining whether valid consent exists, an important difference lies in the effect of a valid consent. In criminal law, valid consent may be ineffective for reasons of public policy (for instance, the 'consent' of an underage person to sex). This can be justified by the different functions of criminal law from tort law, which include a public protection element.[133] In tort law, however, it is difficult to see how a plaintiff could sue in battery if she had consented to the application of force. As between the parties, the

in that arguing consent undermines the prosecution case, rather than establishes an affirmative defence in itself.

129 Barker, *Law of Torts*, 71–3.

130 *Dean* v. *Phung* [2012] NSWCA 223, [65] (Basten JA). Although the distinction was made in the context of consent to medical treatment, in our view it is a useful general distinction in cases of this kind.

131 Ibid., [63].

132 P. W. Young, 'Is There Any Law of Consent with Respect to Assault?'(2011) 85 *ALJ* 23.

133 This public protection element is probably most prominent in relation to sexual offences. See for discussion Anthony *et al.*, *Waller and Williams Criminal Law Text and Cases*, Ch. 3.

defendant's conduct is not wrongful and does not infringe any interest of the plaintiff.[134]

4. Procedure and evidence

In many regards there is significant overlap in Australia between civil procedure (including tort) and criminal procedure. Perhaps the most extensive overlaps are in court structure, the judiciary and the rules and procedures for evidence. However, there are key differences which divide the procedures for tort and crime, such that the majority of participants in Australian cases are involved solely in one sphere. Australian criminal matters are always prosecuted by the state, while tortious disputes are between private citizens (with the state acting, in some tort cases, as a private party). Australian criminal procedure imposes a higher burden of proof and greater evidentiary obligations on the state in order to reduce the potential for erroneous convictions and innocent incarceration. The increase in statute-based law in Australia has sharpened the divide between tortious and criminal procedure with the advent of numerous specialist courts and tribunals of limited jurisdiction in either tort or crime operating under specific statutorily devised procedures often with expurgated rules of evidence.

A. *Court and tribunal structure for crime and tort cases: together but always apart*

In Australia, the courts (and often judges) at all levels in all state jurisdictions hear both criminal and civil matters, but not simultaneously. Within the Supreme Courts of each state, there is an appeal court hierarchy that may include a separate Court of Criminal Appeal or a division for criminal appeals. However, judges in Supreme and lower level courts commonly hear both civil and criminal matters, and hear both types of case in the same physical location.

Final appeal is to the High Court by special leave only and most leave applications are unsuccessful.[135] In crime and tort, only a small percentage of cases are appealed to the High Court. High Court tort cases

[134] There is conflicting Australian authority on this point: in support of the view in the text see *Bain* v. *Altoft* [1967] Qd R 32; see *Pallante* v. *Stadiums Pty Ltd (No. 1)* [1976] VR 331, 340 (McInerny J).

[135] Constitution and Judiciary Act 1903 (Cth), s. 73. Sections 3 and 35A enable High Court appellate jurisdiction from State courts (s. 122 of the Constitution for territories). Over

(particularly in negligence) were relatively frequent but are declining,[136] and few criminal cases are suitable for High Court appeal.[137]

The advent of specialist tribunals with specialist procedures potentially further separates tort and crime procedure in Australia by removing many matters from the courts and evidentiary processes that traditionally constituted points of procedural similarity. Many claims relating to accidental injury are heard by specialist tribunals governed by state specific legislative regimes rather than the common law of tort, some of which are 'no-fault' (hence removing them from tort law entirely).[138] The number of these tribunals, and their complicated nature, led several states, including Victoria and NSW, to introduce super tribunals that hear a wide range of claims including thousands of tortious claims (especially personal injury).[139] Such tribunals usually dispense partially or fully with rules of evidence and often utilise briefer, less onerous procedures for case preparation.[140]

the past decade, annual applications for High Court special leave have declined from 900 to below 500 compared with between 100 and 150 full court hearings. Many special leave applications are self-represented litigants with immigration claims. Over 50 per cent of special leave applications are heard without a hearing: see High Court of Australia, *Annual Report 2012–2013*, 13–16 and 33–4, www.hcourt.gov.au/assets/corporate/annual-reports/HCA-Annual-Report-2012-13.pdf (last accessed 8 June 2014).

136 Between 2000 and 2007, seventy-nine High Court of Australia decisions concerned personal injury according to H. Luntz, 'A View From Abroad' [2007] *University of Melbourne Legal Studies Research Papers* 2.

137 In 2012, the High Court determined nineteen criminal law cases throughout Australia whereas, just for NSW, the NSW Court of Criminal Appeal disposed of 336 cases in 2012 and 279,425 charges were finalised through the NSW Local, Children's, District and Supreme Courts in 2011; Supreme Court of NSW, *2012 Annual Review*, 54, www.supremecourt.justice.nsw.gov.au/agdbasev7wr/supremecourt/documents/pdf/annual_review_2012.v2.pdf (last accessed November 2014); NSW Department of Attorney General and Justice, *Annual Report 2011/2012*, 22 www.lawlink.nsw.gov.au/lawlink/Corporate/ll_corporate.nsf/vwFiles/AGJ_AR_2012_AttorneyGeneral.pdf/$file/AGJ_AR_2012_AttorneyGeneral.pdf (last accessed November 2014).

138 Luntz, 'A View From Abroad'.

139 The NSW super tribunal, NCAT, commenced in January 2014 following a Parliamentary enquiry which determined that the tribunal system prior to NCAT, which included over twenty different tribunals, was 'complex and bewildering': Legislative Standing Committee on Law and Justice, *Improving Access to Justice for Tribunal Users* (March 2012).

140 E.g., Civil and Administrative Tribunal Act 2008 (ACT), s. 8 states: 'To remove any doubt, the tribunal need not comply with the rules of evidence applying in the ACT'. See also M. Allars, 'Administrative Law: Neutrality, the Judicial Paradigm and Tribunal Procedure' (1991) 13 *Syd LR* 377 and Victorian Law Reform Commission, *Civil Justice Review Report*, 63.

Similarly, for criminal cases, there has been an increase (often with supporting legislation) of specialist tribunals to deal with specific types offenders in efforts to reduce incarceration and recidivism. For example, the Drug Court of NSW, which operates under the Drug Court Act 1998 (NSW) takes referrals from the Local and District courts in NSW of eligible drug dependant offenders to maximise the opportunities for diversion of such offenders from the prison system.[141] Some Australian courts have also embraced 'circle sentencing' that engages the Australian indigenous community in sentencing indigenous offenders.[142]

Conversely, however, use of tribunals and their inherent procedural flexibility can increase the interaction between tort and crime. Tribunals are the most common body hearing disciplinary trials relating to professional wrongdoing. Matters heard by such tribunals may have a criminal element (e.g. trust account fraud by lawyers or negligence occasioning death or bodily harm by doctors). Specialist tribunals may have authority to award financial penalties as well as to strike professionals from the roll of those entitled to practice.[143] They may also direct professionals to rectify wrongdoing or apologise to victims of wrongdoing.[144]

There is no procedural mechanism or practice to combine tort and crime disputes with the exception of criminal compensation orders.[145] Combination could not happen in Australia for both procedural and substantive reasons.[146] Tort and crime litigation flowing from the same event (e.g. a criminally negligent car accident occasioning death) would be run separately, quite possibly in different courts or tribunals, and would be initiated by different parties.

B. *Differing parties to crime and tort disputes*

Criminal cases are always run by the state as prosecutor against the defendant accused of the crime and in practice, never by a victim of the crime.

[141] www.drugcourt.lawlink.nsw.gov.au/drgcrt/dc_index.html (last accessed November 2014).

[142] R. Tumeth, 'Is Circle Sentencing in the NSW Criminal Justice System a Failure?' (2011) *Aboriginal Legal Service*, www.drugcourt.lawlink.nsw.gov.au/drgcrt/dc_index.html (last accessed November 2014).

[143] *Legal Profession Complaints Committee* v. *Detata* [2012] WASCA 2014.

[144] R. Carroll, 'Apologies as a Legal Remedy' (2013) 35 *Syd LR* 317.

[145] See Section 2 for detail on criminal compensation orders.

[146] The High Court decision of *Lee* v. *New South Wales Crime Commission* (2013) 251 CLR 196 discusses the fundamental protective and evidentiary bases for the separation of civil and criminal proceedings. The differing substantive law tests limiting combination are discussed above and the protective and evidentiary bases are expanded below.

Conversely, tort cases are always commenced in the name of the wronged plaintiff, with the defendant being the person or entity that committed the wrong. This is despite the fact that, as discussed in Section 2 above, many tort cases are actually run on one or both sides by insurers acting in the name of the plaintiff or defendant.

In Australia, there remains a circumscribed and largely unused right to bring a private prosecution.[147] Such prosecutions may be taken over or stayed by the government and are subject to strict limitations regarding the adequacy of the state/territory (through the Office of the Director of Public Prosecutions) actions in undertaking a prosecution (that is, that if the state has reasonably decided not to, having taken adequate means to investigate, the private person cannot either).[148]

C. *Different resolutions for tort and crime*

There is little overlap between the remedies available for tort and crime in Australia. Criminal courts can impose fines, imprisonment, home detention, community service, suspended sentences and a range of other penalties (including, in NSW, 'intensive correction orders' which are a mix of treatment, community service and supervision) and some state based legislation enables criminal courts to award victims' compensation.[149] There is no criminal compensation other than victims' compensation schemes, which provide limited damages, and the ability of criminal courts to award compensation in criminal injury cases where offenders are not impecunious.[150]

For certain 'white collar' crimes, such as high-level fraud, embezzlement or misuse of a public office, additional prohibitions (on being appointed a director of a company or holding trust funds, for instance) may be imposed as punishment.[151] Australian jurisdictions have not adopted the additional punishment of permanently disenfranchising individuals convicted of felony (serious) offences, although, as a matter of

[147] There is a tightly circumscribed right to private prosecution in some states: see, e.g., Criminal Procedure Act 1986 (NSW), s. 174.

[148] See, e.g., Commonwealth Director of Public Prosecutions, *Prosecution Policy of the Commonwealth: Guidelines for the Making of Decisions in the Prosecution Process* (November 2008), 13–15.

[149] See, e.g., Victims Rights and Support Act 2013 (NSW) and Victims Compensation Act 1996 (NSW).

[150] Refer to Section 2 above for more detail on remedies available.

[151] Corporations Act 2001 (Cth), Part 2D.6 (ss 206A–206HB).

practice, voting obligations of those in custody at the time of elections may be restricted.[152]

Conversely, in tort, compensation is the most common remedy. Access to punitive damages is very limited (to circumstances such as intentional sexual or criminal assault), there are no entitlements to moral damages and damages are often capped by legislative regimes, which, again, vary from jurisdiction to jurisdiction.[153] In some tort cases such as nuisance, defamation and trespass to property, injunctions may be available – usually to cease the offending conduct or, more rarely, to take positive action to ensure a wrong does not continue to be committed.[154] Tort reform in 2002 legislated for apologies to be given without constituting admission of liability (though not as a remedy *per se*).[155] In some jurisdictions no-fault compensation is available for certain kinds of injuries (e.g. work, motor vehicle). In some jurisdictions there is only no-fault compensation for injuries under the relevant schemes, and in others no-fault compensation exists alongside the right to pursue tort actions.[156]

There is minimal overlap in tort and crime resolutions in Australia. Criminal sanctions will usually not be reduced where an offender has paid compensation to a victim (although genuine remorse may be a mitigating factor in determining sentence).[157] However, as noted above, criminal courts may order compensation to victims of criminal offences, and defendants may be ordered to pay court costs in criminal cases.[158] In addition, the prior incurrence of significant criminal penalties will militate against the award of exemplary damages in subsequent tort proceedings.[159]

[152] Commonwealth Electoral Act 1918 (Cth), s. 109 requires notification of the Electoral Commissioner for those serving sentences over three years and s. 110 requires action upon this notification; cf. *Roach* v. *Electoral Commissioner* (2007) 233 CLR 162.

[153] E.g., aggravated damages are available for breaches of the Commonwealth Fair Work Act 2009: *Grant* v. *State of Victoria (The Office of Public Prosecutions) (No.2)* [2014] FCCA 991, but punitive damages are no longer available for defamation: see, e.g., Defamation Act 2005 (NSW) s. 37.

[154] *Australian Broadcasting Corporation* v. *O'Neill* (2006) 227 CLR 57; *Network Ten Pty Ltd* v. *Seven Network (Operations) Ltd* [2014] NSWSC 692.

[155] See P. Vines, 'Apologising to Avoid Liability: Cynical Civility or Practical Morality?' (2005) 27 *Syd LR* 483.

[156] J. J. Spigelman, 'Tort Law Reform: an Overview' (2006) 14 *Tort Law Review* 5.

[157] *Cameron* v. *R* (2002) 209 CLR 339.

[158] See, e.g., Victims Rights and Support Act 2013 (NSW) and Criminal Procedure Amendment (Court Costs Levy) Act 2013 (NSW). See further below, Section 5.

[159] *Gray* v. *Motor Accidents Commission* (1998) 196 CLR 1 (discussed further below).

D. *Separate procedural rules for tort and crime*

Although the same courts hear both criminal and civil cases, civil and criminal divisions operate pursuant to differing procedural rules. In addition, in criminal law cases, the police have a significant role in criminal procedure and there is no civil law equivalent for tort cases. For example, in NSW, tort cases from Local Court through to Supreme Court level are governed by the Civil Procedure Act 2005 (NSW) and the Uniform Civil Procedure Rules (UCPR) 2005 (NSW). On the other hand, criminal cases are governed by relevant state legislation (e.g., the Criminal Procedure Act 1986 (NSW) with the role of the police predominantly governed by the Law Enforcement (Powers and Responsibilities) Act 2002 (NSW)).[160] There are similar procedural acts in other Australian jurisdictions.

There are, however, significant procedural overlaps, as all Australian court procedure reflects an adversarial legal process. General procedural rules govern disclosure and compellability of witnesses in both kinds of proceedings. Failure to comply with a subpoena (a court order compelling court attendance or production of materials) may constitute criminal contempt of court whether the litigation is civil or criminal.[161] There are certain kinds of compelling orders for disclosure and compulsion that are available in both types of proceedings but are easier to obtain in criminal proceedings. Search warrants and orders freezing assets are more commonly obtained by police in criminal cases than by plaintiffs in civil cases where asset freezing orders ('Mareva Injunctions') and search orders ('Anton Piller orders') are considered an extraordinary remedy.[162]

1. Crime takes priority over tort

Criminal proceedings take priority over civil proceedings. Although there is no entitlement to stay civil proceedings due to concurrent criminal proceedings, the court has extensive power to stay proceedings in the interests of justice.[163] The court in *McMahon* v. *Gould* queried whether the civil

[160] Other procedural legislation also relevantly demonstrates the divide between crime and tort. E.g., in *Commonwealth Bank of Australia* v. *Salvato (No.5)* [2013] NSWSC 924, the NSW Supreme Court determined that the Crimes (Sentencing Procedure) Act 1999 (NSW) could not apply in relation to a contempt of court because contempt was not a criminal offence.

[161] *Markisic* v. *Commonwealth of Australia & Anor* [2007] NSWCA 92; and see, e.g., Criminal Code (Qld), s. 644D.

[162] *C.T. Sheet Metal Works Pty Ltd* v. *Hutchinson* [2012] FCA 17 ("*search order case*").

[163] *Websyte Corporation Pty Ltd* v. *Alexander (No 2)* [2012] FCA 562.

proceedings present '. . . such a real risk of injustice to the defendant that the court would be justified in denying the plaintiff his fundamental right to a hearing in ordinary course'.[164] In practice, the potential burden of preparing simultaneous criminal and civil defences can constitute sufficient risk of injustice to warrant staying the civil proceedings.[165] However, civil proceedings will not be stayed pending foreign criminal proceedings where there is no realistic possibility of miscarriage of justice in the foreign criminal proceedings as a result of the domestic civil proceeding.[166] In the unusual case where a civil trial has preceded a criminal prosecution on the same facts, the criminal case will not usually be stayed as the public interest in prosecution would be expected to outweigh the vexation or oppression to the defendant of repeat proceedings.[167]

The prioritisation of criminal proceedings is also subject to legislation; for example, in NSW, the state may bring a civil action to recover the proceeds of criminal activity even where related criminal proceedings are pending.[168] Although these proceedings are formally described as civil proceedings, the penalty strongly resembles a fine, a well-recognised criminal sanction, rather than tortious damages. Perhaps for this reason, there has been considerable controversy attached to legislative attempts to jettison traditional criminal law protections – such as the privilege against self-incrimination – and also more general concerns as to the prejudicial effects on the accused's right to a fair trial that any adverse finding in the civil proceedings would have in the later criminal trial.[169]

2. Similar evidentiary rules but standards and burdens differ between tort and crime

Evidence law, which is predominantly uniform throughout Australia, applies to both tort and crime but with significant variations between criminal and civil evidentiary procedure. The Evidence Act 1995 (Cth), which is substantially uniform throughout much of Australia, applies to

[164] *McMahon* v. *Gould* (1982) 7 ACLR 202.

[165] *Websyte Corporation Pty Ltd* v. *Alexander (No 2)* [2012] FCA 562. See also *De Simone* v. *Bevnol Constructions and Developments* [2010] VSCA 231.

[166] In *Alstom* v. *Sirakas (No. 2)* [2012] NSWSC 64 the NSW Court refused to stay its civil proceedings due to pending Romanian criminal proceedings.

[167] *Roberts* v. *The State of Western Australia* [2005] WASCA 37.

[168] Confiscation of Proceeds of Crime Act 1989 (NSW).

[169] However, it seems clear that, at least in some circumstances, this is allowed: see *Lee* v. *New South Wales Crime Commission* (2013) 251 CLR 196.

criminal and civil proceedings and governs the competence and compellability of witnesses, rules of giving evidence, examination and cross-examination of witnesses, and the admissibility of evidence at trial for tort and crime proceedings.[170] Procedural mechanisms such as discovery of documents and subpoenaing of witnesses also operate similarly in both criminal and tort cases to assist parties with obtaining the evidence necessary to meet the burden of proof obligations.[171] However, there are numerous provisions in the Uniform Evidence Act that are limited to either criminal or civil proceedings.[172] For example, there are special rules for vulnerable (e.g. child) witnesses and sexual assault witnesses and indigenous defendants that affect particular criminal evidentiary procedures.[173]

The primary evidentiary distinctions between tort and crime arise due to the existence of long standing common law protections for defendants in criminal law cases that derive from English common law. As the Chief Justice of the High Court of Australia recently stated: '[t]he presumption of innocence, the privilege against self-incrimination and the right to silence are important elements of the "accusatorial system of justice" which generally prevails in the common law world.'[174] These procedural protections do not exist for tortious wrongdoers and they impose significant differences in the evidentiary process of criminal trials as compared to tort proceedings. The major evidentiary distinction between tort and crime cases, arising from these common law protections, is the higher burden of proof imposed on the state in criminal cases (beyond reasonable doubt) compared to the balance of probability for civil cases.[175] Hence proving criminal liability is significantly more difficult than establishing

[170] The Uniform Evidence Legislation is exemplified by the Evidence Act 1995 (Cth). NSW, Victoria, (between them, the source of the vast majority of litigation) Tasmania and the ACT have mostly identical legislation to the Evidence Act 1995 (Cth). The Northern Territory, Queensland, South Australia and Western Australia retain non-uniform evidence legislation and some common law. See S. Willis, *Civil Procedure* (Melbourne: Palgrave MacMillan, 2012), 238–40.

[171] Compare, e.g., the Criminal Procedure Act 1986 (NSW) with the Civil Procedure Act 2005 (NSW) which provide similarly for preliminary disclosure of documents, subpoenaeing of witnesses and case management to reduce delay.

[172] Particularly the provisions on standards of proof discussed below but also provisions on compellability of witnesses and other matters.

[173] E.g., Evidence Act 1995 (Cth), ss. 17–19 limits the compellability of criminal defendants, their spouses and children.

[174] *Lee* v. *New South Wales Crime Commission* (2013) 251 CLR 196, [1].

[175] *Azzopardi* v. *R* (2001) 205 CLR 50; Evidence Act 1995 (Cth), s. 140; C. R. Williams, 'Burdens and Standards in Civil Litigation' (2003) 25 *Syd LR* 165.

civil liability. However, in practice, the criminal law burden of proof has been eroded for low level criminal offences (e.g., misdemeanours and fine based offences created by recent statutes)[176] and, more controversially, for recovery of assets allegedly held as a result of criminal conduct.

While the standard of proof varies between criminal and civil cases, the initiator of the proceedings generally bears the burden of proof for tortious and criminal cases. Traditionally, the presumption of the defendant's innocence in criminal cases (that is, innocent until proven guilty) ensures that the burden of proof rests with the prosecution even to the point of disproving the availability of certain defences raised by the defendant.[177] Increasingly, however, some burden has been placed on the defendant (e.g., to raise a substantive defence, rather than merely cast doubt on the strength of the prosecution case) and this shift in the division of labour in the criminal courtroom has also been felt in relation to the rise of strict liability offences (whereby the prosecution burden to prove *mens rea* is not enlivened until the defendant has discharged a burden relating to an honest and reasonable mistake of fact).[178]

Where there are defences in tort areas, there can be legislative shifts in the burden of proof to constrain the action (e.g., in some state tort reform legislation) and even in the common law.[179] There are also varied burdens of proof under some statutory regimes, for instance, motor vehicle accident cases and workers' compensation and dust diseases which affect a significant percentage of tort claims.

3. Use of evidence in parallel tort and crime proceedings

Evidence of criminal conviction is admissible in subsequent civil proceedings as a bar to awarding punitive damages, but the effect of, for example,

[176] R. Fox, 'Infringement Notices: Time for Reform?' (1995) 50 *Trends and Issues in Crime and Criminal Justice*, www.aic.gov.au/publications/current%20series/tandi/41–60/tandi50.html (last accessed November 2014).

[177] *CTM* v. *The Queen* (2008) 236 CLR 440; *Momcilovic* v. *The Queen* (2011) 245 CLR 1.

[178] *He Kaw Teh* v. *R* (1985) 157 CLR 523. Defendant burdens of proof, where they exist in criminal cases, require only balance of probability proof; Evidence Act 1995 (Cth), s. 141(2).

[179] E.g, (in line with English cases) in public nuisance cases, the onus of proving nuisance rests with the plaintiff but, once demonstrated, the onus shifts to the defendant to prove the defence of reasonable and proper steps being taken: *Onus* v. *Telstra Corporation Limited* [2011] NSWSC 33, [115].

suspended sentences or quashed convictions remains uncertain.[180] Findings of fact in criminal cases are not automatically transferable to related civil proceedings. No explicit factual findings are made in some criminal cases because findings, at least for indictable offences triable by a jury, are made by the jury (the general criminal verdict – guilty or not guilty – is infamous for its inarticulateness).[181] More generally, the extent to which criminal convictions can be used as evidence in civil cases (beyond the fact of their existence) varies between jurisdictions. In a number of jurisdictions, convictions cannot be used to prove the existence of a fact that was in issue in those proceedings.[182] Ambiguously, this does not prevent the admission or use of evidence that a party, or a person through or under whom a party claims, has been convicted of an offence. What use may be made of this remains unclear. In Queensland, the legislation goes further and provides a rebuttable presumption that the conviction is proof of the acts and state of mind that constituted the crime the subject of the conviction.

Similarly, there are limits on the extent to which a later civil trial can challenge findings of an earlier criminal decision: a later civil action must not amount to a collateral challenge to the earlier criminal decision.[183] It must be admitted that there is a fine line between legitimately re-litigating a matter that has been the subject of criminal proceedings, and improperly launching proceedings that constitute an unacceptable collateral challenge to the earlier decision.[184]

One instance where use may be made of criminal proceedings in a civil claim is where a criminal conviction is tendered as evidence of tortious breach. This is not conclusive of breach but is strongly persuasive. For example, breach of a requirement imposed on an employer under

[180] Evidence Act 1995 (Cth), s. 92(2) (equivalent to NSW, Victoria, Tasmania and ACT); *Gray* v. *Motor Accident Commission* (1998) 196 CLR 1: provided it can be shown alleged relevant conduct is the same. *Whitbread & Anor* v. *Rail Corporation NSW & Ors* [2011] NSWCA 130 called for High Court authority for the effect on civil proceedings of criminal proceedings where there was no conviction or sentences were quashed or suspended.

[181] *MFA* v. *R* (2002) 213 CLR 606.

[182] NSW, Victoria, Tasmania, ACT and the Commonwealth pursuant to the uniform evidence legislation, ss. 91 and 92. Conversely, the Northern Territory, Queensland and South Australia admit evidence of convictions in subsequent civil proceedings: P. Stewart, 'Tortious Remedies for Deliberative Wrongdoing to Victims of Human Trafficking and Slavery in Australia' [2011] 34 *UNSWLJ* 898, 935.

[183] *Carter & Anor* v. *Walker & Anor* [2010] VSCA 340.

[184] The finality doctrines of *res judicata*, issue estoppel and Anshun estoppel operate in Australia to prevent the re-litigation of issues already determined by the courts. See Willis, *Civil Procedure*, 119–24.

occupational health and safety legislation may amount to a criminal offence and also be strong evidence that the employer has failed to exercise reasonable care in the tort of negligence.[185] Certainly material used by parties in one type of proceedings may be tendered as evidence in the other type of proceedings.[186]

5. Institutions and practices, and change over time

The relationship between tort and crime in Australia has changed over time. In this section, we consider the three main factors influencing this change – change within each legal field, the influence of institutions (including appellate courts and law reform bodies), and the impact of external or non-legal factors (most notably, the prevailing political context, and the existence of industry lobby groups). The effects of this changing context have included an extended reach of state sanctioning power, increased complexity in the tort/crime relationship and the growth of concerns about coherence and congruence between the law of negligence, in particular, and the criminal law.

A. Change within legal fields

The most significant influences on the relationship between tort and crime in Australia have come from within each of tort and crime themselves, rather than wider external pressures. In relation to tort, it is clear that the demands of public policy as discerned by elected legislators have been the primary driver for change. This is graphically illustrated by the raft of tort (primarily regulating the tort of negligence) reform legislation passed in the first five years of the twenty-first century. This has resulted in further complexity within tort law and an increasingly ambiguous relationship between different pockets of tort (especially negligence) law[187]

[185] It may also constitute the tort of breach of statutory duty: see Section 2.A above.

[186] In the tort case of *XY* v. *Featherstone* [2010] NSWSC 1366, the court awarded damages for psychiatric injury following sexual abuse, using evidence as summarised by the Court of Criminal Appeal in earlier criminal proceedings (*Featherstone* v. *R* [2008] NSWCCA 71) on the basis that the evidence tendered at the criminal sentencing hearing was an agreed statement of facts and hence uncontroversial.

[187] Different rules may apply to fault-based liability depending on whether the accident happened at work, on the road, or elsewhere: see D. Ipp, 'The Politics, Purpose and Reform of the Law of Negligence' (2007) 81 *ALJ* 456, 461.

and between tort law and no-fault compensation schemes.[188] In relation to criminal law, as noted by several commentators and as is the case in England and Wales, there has been a marked growth in the number of criminal offences on the statute books, and thus in the size of the criminal field, across Australian jurisdictions over the last decades.[189] There has also been a change in the nature of the criminal field. Viewed as a whole, these new offences reflect the influence of 'law and order' politics or penal populism on Australian law, evident in the high maximum penalties applicable on conviction, as well as changes to the laws of evidence and procedure and law enforcement powers that have accompanied the creation of these new offences.[190] We discuss 'law and order' politics below.

Changes within the fields of tort and crime have made the relationship between tort and crime more complex, and blurred the boundaries between the two fields, which, as discussed above, have traditionally been regarded as separate. The Australian legal systems provide numerous examples of this blurring. Viewed from the criminal side of the relationship, a useful example is the expansion of the criminal law to encompass so-called regulatory offences. Viewed from the civil side of the relationship between tort and crime, the availability of punitive or exemplary damages in civil actions (albeit a restricted category of actions),[191] represents a blurring of the (at least theoretically) sharp distinction between the private and regulatory role of the civil law, and the public and expressive or symbolic role of the criminal law, as well as the compensatory function of damages, and the condemnatory and deterrent function of punishment.[192] As a

[188] Such as workers' compensation schemes.

[189] See, e.g., D. Brown, 'Criminalisation and Normative Theory' (2013) 25 *CICJ* 605; S. Egger, 'Criminal Justice Policy in Late Modernity: The Significance of Local Experiences in Global Trends' (2004) 28 *MULR* 736; B. McSherry, 'Expanding the Boundaries of Inchoate Crimes: The Growing Reliance on Preparatory Offences' in B. McSherrry, A. Norrie and S. Bronitt (eds.), *Regulating Deviance: The Redirection of Criminalisation and the Futures of Criminal Law* (Oxford: Onati/Hart Publishing, 2009), 35–58.

[190] See further A. Loughnan, 'Drink Spiking and Rock Throwing: The Creation and Construction of Criminal Offences in the Current Era' (2010) 35 *Alt LJ* 18.

[191] Exemplary damages are not generally awarded where significant criminal penalties have been incurred: *Gray* v. *Motor Accidents Commission* (1998) 196 CLR 1. In practice punitive damages are limited due to legislative tort reform in the negligence area. There is some availability of punitive damages for some categories of intentional tort dependent on the jurisdiction.

[192] See R. A. Epstein, 'The Tort/Crime Distinction: A Generation Later' (1996) 76 *BU L Rev* 1.

result, in Australia (as elsewhere), it is no longer straightforwardly the case that 'tort law prices, while criminal law prohibits'.[193]

This increasing complexity of the interaction between tort and crime has had a range of effects. In particular, as discussed in the first section of this chapter, it has generated concerns about coherence and congruence between the law of negligence, especially, and the criminal law. The idea of coherence and congruity between tort and criminal law has shaped elements of the law of tort but it has done so negatively. In other words, coherence with the criminal law has been used to limit tort claims. By contrast, the criminal law has rarely been called on to reinforce tort liability at common law (although the position is more complex in respect of statutory crimes that give rise to civil claims under the statute). Concern with coherence has informed the scope of the illegality defence in the law of tort and also the manner in which duty of care in negligence is determined. For example, in some situations, the domain of criminal law directly affects a related tort claim such that the tort claim is defeated by a defence that the tort arose out of illegal conduct. However, in the tort of conversion – which requires possession or the right to immediate possession – a plaintiff generally has a right to bring the tort claim against someone unlawfully depriving him of his possession even though the plaintiff's possession may be unlawful.[194] The common law's (in private law at least) concern with ownership as a relative rather than absolute right prevents the defendant's pleading of the *ius tertii* – that the better right to the property was in someone other than the plaintiff – even if the plaintiff cannot prove the possession was lawful. (Of course, if it is proved that the plaintiff's possession is unlawful then no possessory right may be present at all).

B. *Institutions: appellate courts and law reform bodies*

A range of institutions now influence the relationship between tort and crime in Australia. As is the case elsewhere in the common law world, the legal order is informed by a series of formal and informal discussions:

193 See J. Coffee, 'Does "Unlawful" mean "Criminal"? Reflections on the Disappearing Tort/Crime Distinction in American Law' (1991) 71 *BU L Rev* 193. See also P. Cane, 'The General/Special Distinction in Criminal Law, Tort Law and Legal Theory' (2007) 26 *Criminal Law and Philosophy* 465.

194 In the absence of proof that the possession is unlawful, mere suspicion that it might be does not displace the plaintiff's possessory title: *Flack* v. *Chairperson, National Crime Authority* (1997) 150 ALR 153.

law reform bodies, parliamentary committee enquiries, semi-government research bodies (such as the Australian Productivity Commission and the Australian Institute of Criminology), professional organisations and a wide array of other organisations influence changes in the legal order. Academics and the views of law reform bodies may be influential in both the arguments that counsel put before courts and, sometimes consequently but not always, in the reasoning adopted by the judges. These views may also be important when the legislature is seeking input on whether and how to reform the law. It is rare, however, for legislatures to implement wide-scale reform of tort or criminal law in accord with the views of law reform bodies or academics (although the latter rarely speaks with one voice in any case). Here, we discuss the influence of two sets of institutions: appellate courts and law reform bodies.

In Australia, as elsewhere in the common law world, appellate courts can have a decisive influence on the domestic legal order.[195] In the post-war era, the Australian High Court adopted a strict legalism, eschewing any political dimension to its decision-making; and, while it is now generally recognised that judicial deliberation is not value-neutral, the High Court continues not to be as politicised as the US Supreme Court, for instance.[196]

As a federal system, Supreme Courts in each Australian state exercise influence on interpretation of the law. In this context, Supreme Courts have had a significant influence on the development of the law. As a result, there is considerable variation across Australian jurisdictions. One of the most notable Australian examples of such influence arose in relation to sentencing in criminal matters. From the late 1990s, in NSW, guideline sentencing was championed and advanced by the Supreme

[195] The *Mabo* decisions (*Mabo* v. *Queensland (No. 2)* (1992) 175 CLR 1) which recognised indigenous native title by reversing previous findings that Australia was *terra nullius* before the arrival of white man, are well-known Australian examples of such decisive influence. Of course, adaptation of the law through judicial decisions as opposed to parliament is more restrained because of both the limits imposed by the doctrine of precedent and because of concerns over the appropriate role of the judiciary in 'making law'. This latter concern has been the subject of controversy in Australia and there remains current a debate about the appropriate limits of judicial activism. See M. D. Kirby, 'Judicial Activism' (1997) 23 *CLB* 1224.

[196] See M. Bhattacharya and R. Smyth, 'The Determinants of Judicial Prestige and Influence: Some Empirical Evidence from the High Court of Australia' (2001) 30 *JLS* 223. On the politics of the High Court, see B. Galligan, *The Politics of the High Court* (University of Queensland Press, 1987) and H. Patapan, *Judging Democracy: The New Politics of the High Court* (Cambridge University Press, 2000).

Court under Spigelman CJ,[197] and guideline sentences became part of the NSW Government's 'law and order' platform.[198] In relation to tort law, the tort reform legislation of the early 2000s has given state Supreme Courts some additional influence. Although much uniformity remains among the Australian jurisdictions – and in those areas, the High Court of Australia remains the ultimate decision-making court – there are now a considerable number of local variations. Although the High Court retains *de jure* supremacy in interpreting these variations, state Supreme Courts have some *de facto* authority in respect of these provisions due to legal and practical limitations on the circumstances in which appeals are made from state Supreme Courts to the High Court.

Law reform bodies have come to enjoy a high profile in Australian legal systems, although their systematising influence is variable, and subject to the political will required to implement their recommendations. Law reform commissions exist in each jurisdiction, including at a Commonwealth level.[199] Law reform reports often encompass criminal and tortious issues, sometimes within the scope of a single report.[200] In addition to Law Commissions, in the criminal context, a number of Australian jurisdictions have a sentencing advisory council or equivalent, which is engaged in research and policy development on behalf of state/territory government departments.[201] The politicisation of legal policy in Australia has affected the work of these committees,[202] indeed, political pressure

[197] See J. J. Spigelman, 'Sentencing Guideline Judgments' (1999) 11 *CICJ* 5.

[198] For discussion, see C. A. Warner, 'The Role of Guideline Judgments in the Law and Order Debate in Australia' (2003) 27 *Crim LJ* 8; D. Spears, 'Structuring Discretion: Sentencing in a Jurisic Age' (1999) 22 *UNSWLJ* 295. More generally, see A. Freiberg and P. Sallmann, 'Courts of Appeal and Sentencing: Principles, Policy and Politics' (2008) 26 *LIC* 43.

[199] Commissions generally comprise a number of (full or part time) commissioners, and law reform references cover both civil and criminal law.

[200] E.g., the Australian Law Reform Commission (ALRC), is the federal law reform body empowered by the Australian Law Reform Commission Act 1996 (Cth). In December 2013, the Attorney General announced an ALRC review of all Commonwealth laws for consistency with traditional rights, freedoms and privileges including laws which 'reverse or shift the burden of proof', 'exclude the right to claim the privilege of self incrimination', 'apply strict or absolute liability to all physical elements of a criminal offence', 'authorise the commission of a tort', 'retrospectively extend criminal law' and other elements relevant to tort and/or crime, www.attorneygeneral.gov.au/Mediareleases/Pages/2013/Fourth%20quarter/11December2013-NewAustralianLawReformInquiryToFocusOnFreedoms.aspx (last accessed 2 July 2014).

[201] The New South Wales Sentencing Council was the first such body in Australia, established in 2003. To date, no sentencing advisory body has been established in the Northern Territory or Western Australia, or at the Federal level.

[202] For a discussion of the political dimension of law reform in a civil justice context, see R. Graycar, 'Frozen Chooks Revisited: The Challenge of Changing Law/s', in R. Hunter

even led to some significant legal reforms having bypassed the existing institutional framework for systematised reform. For instance, recent reforms to the partial defence of provocation in NSW, referred to above, were the result of a special select committee of the NSW Upper House, not the product of a reference to the NSW Law Reform Commission. In addition, as discussed earlier in this chapter, major tort reform legislation was introduced across Australia in 2001–3. This occurred as a result of a co-operative state/Commonwealth inquiry, the *Review into the Law of Negligence*,[203] which operated independently of any extant law reform organisation. This *Review* is discussed further below in relation to the influence of insurance on the development of the tort law system in Australia.

C. *External or non-legal factors*

Unlike countries in Europe, there are no major supra-national organisations affecting Australian tort or criminal law. There are, however, numerous international treaties (mostly arising from United Nations) that have been ratified by Australia which potentially influence judicial decision-making, including human rights conventions (particularly for criminal cases in semi-codified areas such as anti-terrorism legislation where imprisonment often precedes conviction).[204] There are also treaties which potentially influence tortious claims with international elements.[205]

In relation to criminal law, the most significant external factor influencing the law is what has been called 'law and order' politics, or penal populism.[206] As the term penal populism suggests, this factor is not so much external to criminal justice, but operates across – and beyond – it, with David Garland suggesting that approaches to penal policy have

and M. Keane (eds.), *Changing Law: Rights, Regulation and Reconciliation* (Aldershot: Ashgate, 2005), 49–76.

203 D. A. Ipp *et al.*, *Review into the Law of Negligence: Final Report ('Ipp Report')* (2002). See also Section 2.B above. B. MacDonald, 'Legislative Intervention in the Law of Negligence: The Common Law, Statutory Interpretation and Tort Reform in Australia' (2005) 27 *Syd LR* 443.

204 See for discussion B. Saul, 'Terrorism as Crime or War: Militarising Crime and Disrupting the Constitutional Settlement?' (2008) 19 *PLR* 20.

205 E.g., the Trans Tasman Proceedings Act 2010 (Cth) which came into effect in October 2013.

206 See A. Freiberg, 'The Four Pillars of Justice: A Review Essay' (2003) 36 *ANZJ Crim* 223, an essay reviewing J. Roberts *et al.*, *Penal Populism and Public Opinion: Lessons from Five Countries* (Oxford University Press, 2003).

exerted influence over other areas of governance in liberal democracies.[207] As mentioned above, 'law and order' politics – summed up as a broad cultural and political trend toward increasingly punitive and populist penal policies that is evident in a number of jurisdictions, and facilitated by 'tough on crime' political rhetoric and widespread fear of crime – has contributed to a significant expansion of the criminal justice field.[208] At the same time, a growing victims' movement has come to exercise some influence over criminal justice law and policy.[209] In the Australian context, these developments are set against the backdrop of an increase in imprisonment rates from the early 1990s, a development that has seen the prison return to the centre of criminal justice policy.[210]

The influence of the broad cultural and political current of 'law and order' politics is particularly apparent at the state/territory level. A prominent illustration of the effect of penal populism on the criminal law is the criminalisation of association between members of 'bikie gangs'. Following a series of high profile offences by members of 'bikie gangs', and amidst media and public furore about organised crime, South Australia (and, subsequently, New South Wales, Queensland and the Northern Territory) enacted extensive legislative regimes to criminalise association between members of 'criminal organisations'.[211] Under these laws, which vary from state to state in Australia, judges acting in their individual capacities (*personae designatae*) are empowered to issue, on the application of the police commissioner, civil control orders limiting or prohibiting communication between members of declared organisations or associations.[212] The breach of these orders is an offence, which attracts significant criminal penalties, including imprisonment. These provisions are backed up with reverse burdens of proof (shifting the onus onto

[207] See, generally, D. Garland, *The Culture of Control: Crime and Social Order in Contemporary Society* (Oxford University Press, 2001).

[208] G. Appleby and J. Williams, 'A New Coat of Paint: Law and Order and the Refurbishment of Kable' (2012) 40 *FLR* 1.

[209] This is evident in relation to victim impact statements (VIS), for instance: see E. Erez and L. Roeger, 'The Effect of Victim Impact Statements on Sentencing Patterns and Outcomes: The Australian Experience' (1995) 23 *JCJ* 363.

[210] See, for discussion, M. Hall, 'Key Themes in New South Wales Criminal Justice' (2010) 22 *CICJ* 19.

[211] See Serious and Organised Crime (Control) Act 2008 (SA); Crimes (Criminal Organisations Control) Act 2009 (NSW); Criminal Organisation Act 2009 (Qld), and Serious Crime Control Act 2009 (NT) respectively.

[212] This strategy of backing up the criminal law with the civil law avoids both issues with the criminal standard of proof, on the one hand, and issues relating to proving direct harm, on the other.

the party seeking to defeat the order), and the ability of the prosecution to withhold evidence from the defence, as well as (in the broader legal context), wide-ranging civil forfeiture laws.[213] The first two legislative regimes were declared unconstitutional by the High Court, and newer regimes may also face constitutional challenge,[214] but political will to extend the criminal law in this way remains strong.[215] To a lesser extent, the influence of 'law and order' politics can also be detected at the Commonwealth level, evidenced by the harsh approach to the offence of 'people smuggling' (as an instance of a strict immigration and refugee policy).[216]

Turning to tort, as discussed in the first section of this chapter, the most significant external factor is arguably the insurance industry. The interaction between insurance and the tort law system is complex due to the nature of the Australian federated state, territory and Commonwealth jurisdictions. This complexity contributes to the lack of rationality and the 'patchwork' lottery nature of the Australian tort system. Insurers have had a profound impact on the shape and limits of tort law in Australia, particularly in the last ten to fifteen years, and particularly in negligence. Indeed, the existence of insurance is now said to be the 'driver' of Australian tort law.

Insurance interacts with, and is affected by, tort law and the tort system in different ways across the country. Insurance-based no-fault workers' compensation schemes, some of which exist alongside tort liability, have been in force for many decades. Motor vehicle injury insurance is compulsory across all Australian jurisdictions funding a mixture of fault and no-fault recovery,[217] and pseudo-compulsory medical indemnity insurance sits alongside torts liability.[218] This already complex situation is set

213 See, for discussion, A. Loughnan, 'The Legislation We Had to Have? The Crimes (Criminal Organisations Control) Act 2009 (NSW)' (2009) 20 *CICJ* 457. See also J. Ayling, 'Pre-emptive Strike: How Australia is Tackling Outlaw Motorcycle Gangs' (2011) 36 *American Journal of Criminal Justice* 250.

214 Regarding the SA legislation, see *South Australia* v. *Totani* (2010) 242 CLR 1; for NSW, see *Wainohu* v. *NSW* (2011) 243 CLR 181.

215 The most recent – and most extensive – version of this legislation was passed in Queensland in December 2013: see Vicious Lawless Association Disestablishment Act 2013 (Qld); see also *Kuczborski* v. *Queensland* [2014] HCA 46.

216 See A. Schloenhardt and C. Martin, 'Prosecution and Punishment of People Smugglers in Australia 2008–2011' (2012) 40 *FLR* 111.

217 See, e.g., Motor Accident Insurance Act 1994 (Qld), Part 3.

218 See, generally, B. MacDonald, 'Legislative Intervention in the Law of Negligence: The Common Law, Statutory Interpretation and Tort Reform in Australia' (2005) 27 *Syd LR* 443, 446–8.

to become more complex with the introduction of the National Disability Insurance Scheme and the possible introduction of the National Injury Insurance Scheme for catastrophic injuries.[219]

Tort law in Australia is also influenced by the existence of state-funded compensation schemes, which produce uneveness across the national field. Australian jurisdictions generally allow criminal courts to order compensation to victims of serious criminal offences.[220] It has been said that statutory schemes of compensation are the complement to the common law awards of damages,[221] and several such schemes exist in Australian jurisdictions. Schemes vary between states but typically award amounts well below what could be achieved in a common law action.[222] This has been important because the lack of insurance coverage for intentional tort actions means that plaintiffs who are intentionally injured are unlikely to have a pool of funds they can recover from without these funds. However, the prospect of large numbers of victims (arising from the historic cases of child abuse in church institutions, for instance) has put pressure on state resources, and it is in this context that caps on amounts awarded from these compensation schemes have been set.[223] In addition to compensation schemes, there have been moves in a number of Australian criminal jurisdictions to charge defendants greater amounts in court costs.[224]

Hence, external factors have, arguably, increased the disparity between the outcomes of crime and tort in Australia. Legislation driven by 'tough on crime' politics has increased criminal penalties for wrongdoers while legislation driven by financial constraints, both in private (insurance

[219] The Council of Australian Governments (COAG) Disability Reform Council communique from March 2014 suggests the development of these schemes remains, although they were developed before a change in the Commonwealth government: see mitchfifield.dss.gov.au/media-releases/76 (last accessed 2 July 2014).

[220] The power to do so is statutory; at common law there was no power to award compensation in criminal proceedings. Criminal sanctions will not be reduced where the offender has paid compensation to the victim (although genuine remorse may be a mitigating factor in determining sentence).

[221] M. McHugh, 'Introduction' (2005) 27 *Syd LR* (Torts Special Issue) 385.

[222] E.g., in NSW, as a result of the Victims Rights and Support Act 2013, the amount is capped at $50,000.

[223] K. Barker and S. Degeling, 'Private Law and Grave Historical Injustice: The Role of the Common Law' [2014] *UNSWLRS* 36.

[224] E.g. the Criminal Procedure Amendment (Court Costs Levy) Act 2013 (NSW) replaces the existing discretion of the court to order costs with a statutory court costs levy, which will apply to most defendants found guilty of an offence in summary proceedings before the Local Court.

industry) and government sectors, has reduced tortious compensation for many victims of wrongdoing.

6. Conclusion

This chapter has revealed the complexity of the relationship between tort and crime in Australia. Although Australia's common law heritage means that there are similarities between our law and that of England and Wales, the federal system and some idiosyncratic developments (such as those around tort law reform) have produced a distinctive tort and crime landscape. Tort and crime share some of the same terminology, and disputes are adjudicated in the same courts, according to substantially similar rules of evidence and procedure, and before the same judges. However, there are significant differences between the two fields, including in relation to the substantive law and remedies and regarding the drivers of change over time. At the same time, the primacy of 'law and order' politics has led to an extension of quasi-criminal remedies being imposed according to standards applicable to civil law, including tort law. Given the dynamic Australian legal context and the complexity of both tort and crime, relations between these fields seems likely to only increase with time.

10

Tortious apples and criminal oranges

MATTHEW DYSON

This concluding chapter will draw out some of the most important points about the relationship between tort and crime. The first, and largest, step will be to analyse where tort and crime have interacted, which will then be followed by picking out some points of how, why and when they have. Let us begin by examining first where tort and crime have been shown to interact: in particular, the institutions, reasoning, substance, procedures and resolutions.[1]

1. Where tort and crime interact

A. *Institutions*

Two broad questions are particularly important in respect of the institutions connecting tort and crime: what is the framework within which tort and crime operate and which legal actors are involved in the overlap between them. In the present study, each legal system recognises a category of tort and crime, so that antecedent question has already been answered.

1. What is the legal framework within which tort and crime operate

How does the legal system construct the relationship between tort and crime? The chapters show that for most systems, criminal law is most closely associated with public law, though it tends to be thought of as slightly different from constitutional and administrative law. On the other hand, tort is uniformly seen as part of the law of obligations, private and civil law. This is so even in Sweden, where the practical effect of much

[1] Cf. the slightly different arrangement in M. Dyson, 'Tort and Crime' in M. Bussani and A. Sebok (eds.) *Comparative Tort Law* (Cheltenham: Edward Elgar, forthcoming).

of tort law is actually performed by state and private insurance systems. The major exception to this arrangement is the position of criminal law in France. On the one hand, the key division within the French legal system, particularly its courts, is between the general law (including tort and crime) and administrative law, rather than between, for instance, tort and crime. That administrative law is so distinct affects how closely related the other parts of the system are. On the other hand, French academia also has its own pressures for jobs and other matters which affect the classification in Universities. The result is that criminal law is classified as part of private law for posts in French Universities, with 'public law' being reserved for constitutional and administrative law, and a few places each year for legal history.[2] In any case, French law, like the rest of our legal systems, acknowledges that there are links from tort/crime out to other areas of law, like contract, family law and property law. There are also links into newer and relevant divisions of the law, such as medical law and competition law.

Historically, less trouble was taken to divide between criminal and civil laws. To begin with, attempts to classify ancient laws are fraught with difficulty.[3] For instance, many of what might be regarded as ancient *civil* law systems contained *penal* elements and this is particularly evident in Roman law. In the early common law, 'crime' and 'tort', as we call them now, were equally valid ways for a victim to pursue justice for a wrongful act.[4] The choice seems to have been between *compensation* and *vengeance*, and this choice was one for the victim.[5] It is hard to be clear on when the need for a distinction, using the ideas behind 'tort' and 'crime', if not those terms, was recognised. Certainly by the end of the eighteenth century, Lord Mansfield felt confident enough of it to say: '[T]here is no distinction better known, than the distinction between civil and criminal law.'[6] However, even if the need for a distinction was known by then, its edges were uncertain.[7] Indeed, certain procedural rules governing the relationship between civil and criminal claims changed their

[2] Chapter 3.2.

[3] See J. Lindgren, 'Why the Ancients May Not Have Needed a System of Criminal Law' (1996) 76 *BULR* 29.

[4] Chapter 2.1; See, generally, D. J. Seipp, 'The Distinction between Crime and Tort in the Early Common Law' (1996) 17 *BULR* 59; J. B. Ames, *Lectures On Legal History and Miscellaneous Legal Essays* (Cambridge, MA: Harvard University Press 1913), Ch. II, III and IV.

[5] On Spain, see M. Roig Torres *La reparación del daño causado por el delito (aspectos civiles y penales)* (Valencia: Tirant lo Blanch, 2000), 32–8.

[6] *Atcheson* v. *Everitt* (1775) I Cowp. 382, 391; 98 ER 1142, 1147, per Lord Mansfield.

[7] As they were in *Atcheson* v. *Everitt*.

shape over time, such as the rule that a civil claim must be suspended while a criminal prosecution was pending. This was originally a rule that the 'private wrong and injury' was 'merged and drowned in the public wrong', but later developed into a suspension, rather than a 'drowning' and now trial judges even have a discretion whether to apply it.[8] As it developed, the rule clearly shows the language moving from 'private' and 'public' wrongs, to 'tort' and 'crime'. Similarly, French law did not at first make a distinction between civil and criminal.[9] Of course, modern language like *responsabilité* was not then known; indeed, in that period one might realistically speak of *repression pénale* and *réparation civile*, that is, on process or outcome, rather than doctrinal arrangement.[10] To some in Germany, the distinction between private law and criminal law is even said to be one of the great achievements of the nineteenth century.[11] Two smaller European legal systems recognised this distinction also quite late. Medieval Swedish law did not distinguish between tort and crime *per se*, but between wrongs to individuals and wrongs to society.[12] Wrongs to individuals were often remedied by the *bot*, a tariff system of compensation to the victim, but which also went in equal measure to the King and to the county. This system remained in the landmark Law Code of 1734, though academic literature began to refer separately to civil and criminal law and procedure. In reform projects of the nineteenth century, Swedish law contemplated a distinction between tort and crime, but did not directly implement it. Rather, that discussion ultimately led to the practical coupling of tort and crime, in that the rules on compensating for damage caused by criminal acts were put in the criminal code.[13] That arrangement, theoretically distinguishing between tort and crime but practically merging them (there being no civil code, only a criminal one) continued until 1972. It is only in the last hundred years or so that Scotland has developed completely separate jurisdictions, procedures and penalties for tort and crime, which in turn has led to some differences of substantive legal rules.[14]

[8] See, generally, M. Dyson, 'The Timing of Tortious and Criminal Actions for the Same Wrong' [2012] *CLJ* 85.

[9] O. Descamps, *Les origines de la responsabilité pour faute personnelle dans le Code civil de 1804* (LGDJ, Paris 2005), 204–13; J. Bell and D. Ibbetson, *European Legal Development: The Case of Tort* (Cambridge University Press, 2012), 72–3.

[10] See, e.g., G. Viney, *Introduction à la responsabilité*, 3rd edn (Paris: LGDJ, 2008), 162–3.

[11] Chapter 4.1.A. text to n. 7. [12] See, generally, Chapter 5.2.

[13] And theoretically, even by non-criminal acts: Chapter 5.2.B.4, n. 27.

[14] Chapter 7.3A, C.2, D, E, F and Chapter 7.4.

a) Markers of tort and crime today While legal systems run close together in theory, whether certain conduct is criminal or not varies from legal system to legal system. The predominant approaches can be generalised as four overlapping and contradictory indicia:[15]

(1) moral or natural description of the wrong;
(2) characterisation of the process of remedying the wrong being of public concern rather than merely private;
(3) the presence of 'penalty' or compensation;
(4) a positivist approach of some kind, focusing on the process of creating the legal classifications and form.

Moral or natural wrongs provide potent but imprecise markers. While, it may be sufficient, many of the well-known criminal offences comprise moral wrongs, *mala in se*; it is not necessary, since there are also *mala prohibita*, things prohibited for reasons other than their essential character, and which tend to be justified by legal positivism. In addition, this indicium says little about civil law: many serious wrongs are also remedied by tort, such as serious physical injury or death and sexual wrongs.

The *public* or *private* character of a wrong looks to the social or constitutional construction of that wrong. That analysis may include whether the wrong is morally or naturally prohibited, which can be hard to tell. For instance, in Australia, some of the leading theories of criminal liability attempt to hinge on 'public wrongs'.[16] Every legal system studied acknowledges the public character of the criminal law. Some legal systems highlight this link more than others. For instance, in Spain the *fiscal* is translated as '*public* prosecutor', with the same term used in Germany. In Sweden the prosecutor is *allmän åklagare* where *allmän* means both general and public (literally: 'every man's' or 'all men's'). In common law countries like England and Australia, perhaps as a throwback to the times when it was normally the victim who prosecuted,[17] the title is merely 'prosecutor'.[18] There, and elsewhere, where a prosecutor has discretion about prosecuting, one of the factors to weigh is whether the prosecution

[15] There are many ways to slice this particular cake. See, in particular, the helpful analysis in K. W. Simons, 'The Crime/Tort Distinction: Legal Doctrine and Normative Perspectives' (2007–8) 17 *Widener LJ* 719; Lindgren, 'Why the Ancients', 36; W. H. Hitchler, 'Crime and Civil Injuries' (1934–5) 39 *Dickinson Law Review* 23, 23–9.
[16] Chapter 9.3.B. [17] Chapter 2.2.E.2.
[18] That said, the state official in charge of the prosecution service tends to be called the Director of Public Prosecutions: Chapter 2.2.E.2 and Chapter 9.2.C., n. 22.

is in the 'public interest'.[19] Some countries, like the Netherlands, identify the 'public' element within tort law more explicitly, regarding tort law as a means to also promote public interests through the regulation of society.[20] Other legal systems do not stress this form of 'public' good nor put it on the same level as the 'public' interest within criminal law, but it seems likely all would accept the underlying argument for their systems too.

Penalties are usually within the realm of criminal law since most of our systems do not regard tort law as punitive. Even in the common law,[21] where tort can punish, it rarely does; by comparison, in Scotland punitive damages are not recognised at all.[22] This allocation of punishment to the criminal law is not, however, completely stable. A number of civil law jurisdictions are considering introducing punitive damages and/or assessing whether there may be a punitive function to some traditional civil awards;[23] at the same time, some common law jurisdictions have found new ways for the civil law to perform what are arguably punitive functions, such as ASBOs and confiscation orders.[24] Indeed, a number of legal systems have introduced new forms of remedies which blur the line between civil and criminal concepts by toying with the meaning of penalty, which is discussed below in Section 1.E.

The opposite indicium to a *penalty* is *compensation*, typically a marker of civil law. Sometimes known as reparation or restitution, compensation is generally agreed to be the paradigm activity of civil law, not criminal law. Sometimes a convicted criminal is colloquially said, by his wrong, to have created a 'debt' to society, language reminiscent of the reparatory effect of damages; at the same time, criminal theory rarely expresses it in compensatory or reparative terms.[25] Where a legal system's substantive criminal law awards compensation, such as in England, Scotland, Australia and more recently, France, it is harder to view compensation as a function solely of civil law. As the Australian authors noted, it is no longer straightforwardly the case (if it ever was) that 'tort law prices, while criminal law prohibits'.[26]

[19] E.g., Chapter 5.3.A, n. 44; Chapter 6.3.B.3. [20] E.g., Chapter 8.3.A.

[21] See, e.g., W .S. Holdsworth, *History of English Law* , vol. 8 (London: Methuen & Co., 1923), 306 referring to penalty and procedure for its enforcement; Chapter 9.4.C.

[22] Chapter 7.1.E, n. 40; the rule appears to be well established: Stair, *Institutions* (1693), 1. 9. 4.

[23] E.g., in France: Chapter 3.4.B.1; Spain: Chapter 6.2.B.2; Sweden: Chapter 5.3.B.4–5; Germany: Chapter 4.2.B.

[24] Chapter 2.3. and Chapter 2.2.E.1 respectively.

[25] R. A. Duff, 'Torts, Crimes and Vindication: Whose Wrong Is It?' in M. Dyson (ed.) *Unravelling Tort and Crime* (Cambridge University Press, 2014), 166–7.

[26] Chapter 9.5.A.

A *positivist* indicium is a subset of wider positivist legal theory, identifying the rule by the formal process and label given to objects. It is often seen as a form of constitutional protection to the use of criminal law: that only those who are constitutionally appropriate should create criminal liability. Closely related, criminal liability is also often subject to a form of legal certainty, in the civil law typically expressed as *nulla poena sine lege* or a related form, requiring any criminal offence and sanction to be clearly expressed and, in most legal systems, to be in the form of legislation or a code. In the past this might have been harder to state, such as before the French Revolution. Certainly in the common law, and Scotland, such certainty was not always the case: in part because judges could, in the past,[27] create new torts and crimes, and particularly because legislators did not take proper care to make clear of what kind some provisions were. Legislators might refer only to a 'penalty' for the breach of a statutory provision, rather than using an unambiguous term like 'offence' or prescribing a specific criminal penalty like imprisonment, leaving it unclear whether this was really civil or criminal.[28]

This discussion highlights how connected, or perhaps muddled, the indicia have been. Even looking to the location of the rules within the legal framework is too simplistic, as the Swedish and Spanish chapters prove. In the end, none of these tells the whole story. For instance, it was once concluded that the only reliable way to know what English criminal law was, was to sit in a criminal law court.[29] The implication is that there are people and contexts which drive certain areas of law, and that attempting to understand what they do, not merely what they say, is the safest course.

b) Justifying tortious and criminal liability A slightly different angle on the same question is *why* we impose 'criminal' or 'civil' liability. The indicia above provide a first step towards answering this: criminal law responds to moral, natural or public wrongs with a penalty and should be characterised by clear, certain and formal rules; tort law responds to many of the same moral and natural wrongs, but does so for private parties and tends to focus on putting the wrong right, rather than punishing. However, this is only a first step, since it describes rather than explains. Sadly many steps remain to be taken since the literature defining the relationship of tort to crime is not at all complete.

[27] Perhaps the most recent example being *Shaw* v. *DPP* [1962] AC 220.

[28] See, e.g., Chapter 2.2.E.1 cf. Chapter 2.2.D and Chapter 7.1.D.

[29] Glanville Williams, 'The Definition of a Crime' (1955) 8 *CLP* 107, 124, 130. Cf. P. A. Landon, 'Review of Winfield's The Province of the Law of Tort' (1931) 8 *Bell Yard Journal of the Law Society's School of Law* 19, 19–20.

German law, perhaps characteristically, does go into detail on the concepts and focal points of the justifications for criminal and tortious liability.[30] It may shed light on the reasoning of other jurisdictions as well. First, German lawyers will talk of the functions of both tort and crime, but in criminal law they separate out the abstract justification for punishment in general, from the specific reasons for punishing in any particular case. Civil lawyers might draw a similar distinction but it does not play such a significant role. This is probably broadly true for many other legal systems. Even where theories of tort law are developed, as they have been in the Anglo-American world in the last few decades,[31] they are neither as significant as the same discussions in criminal law, nor do they tend to have a direct influence on court practice. Second, in Germany, tort has both backward- and forward-looking functions: to compensate past harm and to regulate future behaviour. This latter element, the preventive function, has become ever more important within academic discussions, discussions which sometimes use law and economics reasoning concerning the most efficient solution. Again, other legal systems will be familiar with this, and the sometimes fine line between regulation through allocating future losses[32] and deterring behaviour with a punitive award.[33] The recent Anglo-American jurisprudence just mentioned considers further functions, particularly in obtaining redress through *civil recourse*, obtaining *corrective justice* and *vindicating rights*.[34] Third, German criminal lawyers have traditionally recognised three reasons to punish: retribution, special prevention and general prevention. English law, for instance, has developed similarly. It recognises retribution (or 'just deserts'), rehabilitation, incapacitation and specific deterrence (in Germany, all part of 'special prevention') and general deterrence (in Germany, 'general prevention'); in addition, criminal law is also sometimes used to set standards of conduct.[35] That said, the general principles are difficult to apply in practice. In a recent essay on the topic, R. A. Duff has doubted whether any such master principles or criteria to decide which wrongs should be criminal, and which (only) tortious, can be provided.[36] He notes instead that the purpose of tort law is perhaps the less certain, and that if or when it aims at the vindication of wrongs, rather than the allocation of costs, it will be brought inherently closer to criminal law. Similarly, the more the criminal law and its procedures allocates losses rather than only punishes, the harder it is to distinguish it from tort. It is hard to find a core of

[30] Chapter 4.2. [31] E.g., Chapter 9.3.B. [32] E.g., Sweden, Chapter 5.3.B.2.
[33] As in Germany: Chapter 4.2.B. [34] See generally, Duff, 'Crimes and Vindication'.
[35] Chapter 2.2.C. [36] Duff, 'Torts, Crimes and Vindication', esp. 173.

criminal law left, perhaps only some as yet undefined list of victimising wrongs, where the state should be interested in punishing the wrongdoer regardless of the victim's wishes.

Are there perhaps other purposes of criminal law and tort law? One candidate is that they both seek to establish the truth. Perhaps all court proceedings seek truth, at least, any court proceedings leading to an order based on facts the court considers proven, such as a conviction or civil liability. However, the extent to which the truth is a concern may vary in different areas of law. Criminal law would seem to be a prime example of an attempt to ascertain truth. Where the state punishes, it should do so only where there is a high degree of certainty about the events that constitute the crime. The level of certainty of allegations required for a conviction tends to be high, adding to the idea of the appearance of such a conviction being founded on truth. All this can, in the minds of the public, approach the establishment of truth, even while they accept that trials are fallible and some appeals will always be successful. Within tort law, on the other hand, there is a sense of relativity: that the dispute is between the parties and, at least on some level, it is up to the parties to prove what is relevant to the dispute.[37] This may mean that there is less certainty that all the facts have come to light, particularly facts helpful to no litigant in the dispute. Therefore, the outcomes of civil proceedings might not be thought to be founded on truth to the same extent as criminal law. A good example is Dutch law: there, though a civil judge might consider a fact proven to her satisfaction, it is understood that the search for truth is a greater concern to criminal courts than to her, and the limitations within the civil trial process may restrict what truth can be found there.[38]

Nonetheless, a claimant's aim to establish the truth of certain events might be a purpose supported, or at least not hindered, by tort law. For instance, in the English case of *Ashley* v. *Chief Constable*,[39] the claimant wished to proceed with a claim in trespass despite the defendant having admitted negligence to an extent that no further damages would be awarded. The House of Lords allowed the claim to proceed to trial, the majority doing so to vindicate the right not to suffer physical harm.[40] Two of the law lords did so on the basis that if a claim was arguable and legally

[37] E.g., Chapter 6.3.B.2–3. [38] Chapter 8.5.B.2 and 5.

[39] [2008] 1 AC 962, on which see Chapter 2.2.D.10.

[40] E.g., ibid., [18]–[22] (Lord Scott). This vindicatory purpose was also permissible where the claim was in fact brought by the estate and would not bring financial benefit to that estate, despite that being perhaps the primary purpose of the legislation allowing such a claim to be brought: e.g., [28]–[30]. Cf. [79]–[83] (Lord Carswell) and particularly [103]–[134] (Lord Neuberger).

unobjectionable, it was not for the court to enquire about the motive of the claimant in bringing it.[41]

However, our systems seek to establish the relevant facts, and thus perhaps, truth, in different ways. An important question is whose task it is to find the truth. English adversarial procedure acknowledges the search for truth in criminal law,[42] but even there, the burden of proof in a criminal case lies on the prosecution: should they fail, the court itself does not go out to seek truth.[43] The common law more generally may regard truth as a thing best found by two opposing parties fighting for it; that view may encourage courts themselves not to refer to truth, leaving the task to advocates. In Germany, on the other hand, and in many civil and typically inquisitorial systems, the court itself must be sufficiently certain of the facts, and should investigate of its own motion to attain that certainty.[44] As a consequence, German lawyers would not say that the prosecution have a burden of proof, only something like a *function*, to present evidence.[45] Indeed, one does not speak of burden of proof in German criminal law at all. By comparison, according to Swedish law, the burden of proof in a criminal case is on the prosecutor, and in Swedish legal thought this follows both from the view that an incorrect conviction is worse than an incorrect acquittal and from the presumption of the innocence of the defendant.[46]

In the end, it appears that there is no clear and comprehensive set of rules for criminalisation or the imposition of tortious liability across the jurisdictions, nor, indeed, within most individual jurisdictions.

c) **Importance of structural issues** What is the importance of structural issues, like how tort and crime are conceived? The shape of a legal system can strongly affect how reasoning within that system takes place. It can be difficult to find a new path of thinking once one has become

41 Ibid., [4] (Lord Bingham); [62]–[63], [71] (Lord Rodger).

42 Chapter 2.2.E.3., e.g., Criminal Procedure Rule 1A.1.

43 As in Scotland, Chapter 7.3.F., n. 256 and Australia, Chapter 9.4.D.2.

44 In France as well, Chapter 3.3.B.2., as in Spain, e.g., Chapter 6.3.D.3. and Chapter 6.6. (referring to 'investigating judge' and 'investigating court', and the Netherlands, Chapter 8.5.B.5., though there courts tend to be reluctant to do so.

45 It seems unlikely that the prosecution is truly under no burden at all, but it certainly seems not to be discussed in the way a burden of proof would be in, say, English law. For instance, there are obligations on the prosuection to present all appropriate evidence, whether in favour of the defendant or against him, and this could be described as a burden.

46 Reference R. Nordh, *Praktisk Process VII. Bevisrätt B. Bevisbörda och beviskrav* (Uppsala: Iustus 2011), 35.

established. Perhaps the most interesting example of the framework of tort and crime is the arrangement in Sweden for a hundred years until 1972 and in Spain from 1848 to today, whereby the rules for compensating harm where the wrong was a crime and a tort sit in the criminal code, not a civil code. Both countries brought this about for reasons of expediency, since civil codes were not being passed and in this specific area more contemporary rules were at least ones that could be combined with the criminal code to do some good without that much harm. Yet both arrangements have shown significant resilience to change. In the Swedish case, a historical connection between tort and crime through the *bot* predated this legislative formulation, but it is not a great stretch to think that the law today in Sweden has been strongly influenced by the period when the rules were in the criminal code. For Spanish law, the arrangement is even more significant, both because it continues to this day, and because it has had such a significant effect on the development of Spanish law. It was only recently that this *ex delicto* liability was clearly accepted as being a form of civil liability, turning on damage, rather than some kind of criminal liability, turning on the criminal wrong.

There are other points of structural importance. For instance, having a unitary court system with generalist judges plays a role in promoting coherence across the legal system. Perhaps the most advanced form of this is Sweden, where general courts determine most civil and criminal legal questions and the same judge might hear a civil case on Monday and a criminal one on Tuesday.[47] A similar arrangement exists in both the Sheriff Court (Sheriffs) and the Court of Session (in the form of Senators and of the College of Justice), the two tiers of the Scottish legal system; in the more senior Court of Session, judges sit roughly two thirds of the time in criminal cases, and one third in civil.[48] In systems where criminal courts award compensation, criminal judges will have to be familiar with civil law concepts, though to varying degrees. In the Netherlands, as an unofficial 'rule' they need only know ten minutes' worth of civil law, because this is about the amount of time usually spent on civil aspects of the case, while in France they must understand enough to deal with all compensation claims. The real exception is where the compensation

[47] Chapter 5.3.A. Some lower courts in other countries have some similar arrangements, e.g., younger judges and lower functions in France, Chapter 3.2. In Germany, judges will usually work in both civil and criminal law during their career, sometimes at the same time: Chapter 4.4.C.

[48] Chapter 7.1.B., though the UK Supreme Court generally has no jurisdiction over Scottish criminal cases.

determined by the criminal courts is not done using the purely civil rules, such as in Spain, and in compensation orders in the common law.

That said, the picture is different at the highest, and most influential, level of courts. In England, Scotland, Australia and Sweden the highest court is not divided into chambers, they hear all cases together. The same relatively small pool of judges[49] deals with the whole spectrum of cases. Aside from Sweden, which is exceptional in a number of ways, the fact that common law countries have unitary 'supreme' courts may reflect the lower importance of systematics and structure, as compared to procedure, in common law reasoning. This arrangement also has an effect on the number of cases that are heard. In common law countries, where appeal to the highest court is not by right, but by application, perhaps 100 cases are heard each year. By contrast, the highest court in France, Spain, Germany and the Netherlands is divided into chambers with at least separate chambers for tort and crime, and it appears, little movement of personnel between the chambers, they hear hundreds or thousands of cases per year.[50] Indeed, the extent to which judges specialise also seems to be significant.

More generally, the structural arrangements of a system can suggest that an object 'belongs' in one area of law, and thus, by extension, 'belongs to' the legal actors who operate that area of law. This is particularly apparent in Spain, where the criminal chamber of the Supreme Court has developed *ex delicto* liability differently from the civil chamber of the same court. For example, in 1995, during the most significant attempt for some time to remove the rules from the criminal code, it was the intervention of criminal judges, citing the inconvenience to them of the proposal, which ended it.

2. Legal actors

The form and content of legal rules is affected by the range of skills, experience and focus of the legal actors involved in it. Part of this issue is how specialised those actors have become. Specialisation tends, symbiotically, to encourage narrower and more intricate areas of law to develop and be isolated from the rest of the law.

a) **Actors in both tort and crime** To begin with, all the systems studied view knowledge of tort and crime as essential to the training of law

49 E.g., twelve standing Justices of the UK Supreme Court, Constitutional Reform Act 2005, ss. 23(2) and 38–39 and seven in the High Court of Australia, High Court of Australia Act 1978, s. 5.

50 Interestingly, the French Cour de cassation has five civil chambers, and one criminal: Chapter 3.2.

students.[51] Legal actors should, it appears, have once been trained in both areas of law.

After that, all systems have some legal actors playing important roles in both tort and crime. Specialisation plays a key role here, with the degree of specialisation is largely based on the ability of lawyers to make a living out of their work in that area. Absent private resources, that means lawyers require sufficient cases and commentary. This is highlighted in smaller jurisdictions particularly. Scotland has a much less specialised group of lawyers, including its legal academics. The same is true in Sweden. Given its size and structure, it is not surprising that the Swedish chapter can explore the impact of specific legal actors on tort and crime. It appears that Sweden takes a strong view on the unity of its law, that shapes the extent of separate categories within the law, and how any such categories 'overlap'. It does not appear the same view on unity is taken in Scotland, though historically the category of 'Scots Law' in Universities in part approximated this idea. The same principle applies in larger jurisdictions where the greater concentrations of work, and of specific types of work, will be in larger cities. Smaller towns tend to see lawyers offering services in many areas of law.[52] In some cases, such as in France, the majority of solicitors do not advertise themselves as having a specialisation,[53] whereas English barristers and solicitors tend to declare their particular competences to attract clients seeking specialisation.

Some systems deliberately place certain legal actors clearly on the border of tort and crime. Perhaps the most important is the prosecutor. Where 'public', in many systems the prosecutor also plays a role in securing compensation in some cases (England, Scotland, Australia, Germany, the Netherlands), whenever the victim wishes it (France) or in all cases as a duty where harm has been caused (Spain, Sweden). Where 'private', in those systems which allow it, the prosecutor tends to be the victim, clearly linking the civil and criminal interests recognised by the law. Judges can also straddle tort and crime, and all our systems give some adjudicative role to criminal courts in civil disputes under certain conditions, though of course, not the reverse. Only rarely do jurisdictions, like Sweden, create even more specialised legal actors like the aggrieved party counsel. We can, in fact, be slightly more specific. While the systems with procedures to allow civil claims to be joined to criminal claims naturally breed more

[51] Chapter 2.2A., Chapter 3.2., requring only civil law, public law, criminal law and criminal procedure, Chapter 4.4A., Chapter 5.3.A., Chapter 6.2.B.5, Chapter 7.1.A., n. 5, Chapter 8.4.B., Chapter 9.2.B.

[52] See, e.g., Chapter 7.1.C., Chapter 9.2.C.

[53] Chapter 3.2.

criminal lawyers able to deal with civil claims, the reverse, civil lawyers able to handle criminal prosecutions, is less common.

Another vitally important legal actor is the insurer. Private insurance is an incredibly significant factor in any form of compensation, and its importance is increasing. In many cases, it is the primary (and often the only) means for the victims to get compensation: *victims* do not have the funds to sue without it, or a similar mechanism like conditional fee arrangements; similarly, there is rarely much point suing *defendants* who do not have insurance. For that reason it is said to be the 'driver' of Australian tort law.[54] It is particularly important for civil litigation. In Germany, for instance, very many Germans have liability insurance as well as first party insurance, covering harms done/suffered as well as some litigation about those harms.[55] In civil cases, the potential downside to such insurance is that the insurer may have the contractual right to determine how the case should be run.[56] By contrast, legal expenses insurance is rare in Australia so claimants must have the money upfront (which is rare, perhaps from a trade union or other body) or find a lawyer who will take on the case on a 'no win, no fee' basis, or similar.[57] Finally, it is unclear how much the fact of insurance affects substantive liability. In Germany, such influence sometimes occurs in private law;[58] in other states, like Australia, the courts are reluctant to recognise the relevance of insurance to finding liability.[59]

Insurers are also significant for the litigation they bring. First, having *indemnified an insured*, an insurer can then subrogate a claim against the wrongdoer. In which case, it will not normally appear on the face of the court papers that the litigation is actually being brought by an insurance company.[60] In France, such an insurer can intervene, and even become a party, within certain more serious criminal prosecutions (manslaughter and more serious injury).[61] Second, having paid out *in the place of a wrongdoer*, the insurer, typically a state body, may then bring a recourse action against the wrongdoer to recover the amount paid. This is different to a claim in subrogation since it will follow a finding of liability which the defendant has been unable to satisfy. From the *state*'s perspective while all

[54] Chapter 9.5.C. [55] Chapter 4.1.B. [56] E.g., Chapter 2.2.D.10. and Chapter 9.2.E.

[57] Chapter 9.2.E, esp. n. 33. [58] Chapter 4.6.B. [59] Chapter 9.2.E.

[60] In Sweden, it is known that property damage or loss cases are often brought this way: Chapter 5.4.B.2. See also Chapter 9.4.B.

[61] Chapter 3.2. Cf. in Spain, where the insured is not classed as a directly damaged party, a *perjudicado*, as the loss is thought to flow from the contract not the defendant's wrong: Chapter 6.3.D.3, and see particularly Chapter 6.3.D.4.

the legal systems in this study have some form of victim's compensation from the state for violent crime,[62] it is not necessarily the case that there are effective means of recourse from those systems against the wrongdoer. In England, for instance, there is only a right to recover from the victim if that victim brings a successful tort claim;[63] while in Spain there are recourse actions for certain crimes.[64] In at least two cases, states go even further: in the Netherlands[65] and Sweden, there are systems for the state to pay the compensation awarded by a criminal court if the defendant does not (until 2016 the Dutch system applies only for serious crimes). The state victim compensation bodies will then seek recourse against the wrongdoer, with the Swedish success rate being around one third.[66] Particularly significant here are the mechanisms to cover harm caused by (typically criminal) *untraced* drivers and (always criminal) *uninsured* drivers.[67]

While it is clear that criminal sanctions are not risks against which one can insure, the line between sanctions and other risks is not always easy to draw.[68] It is similarly true that a common principle of insurance is that you cannot obtain insurance for intentional acts,[69] though there may be some instances where this principle is set aside to benefit victims, such as some instances of compulsory insurance. Insurance can also cross the state/private boundary. In Sweden, for instance, a 'pyramid' of compensation sources exists, with a state insurance system covering the base, topped up by optional private insurance, with any remainder open to tort claims.[70] This suggests a level of state solidarity for its citizens which exceeds the social security provision of even the more generous states in Europe, and certainly Australia.

[62] Council Directive 2004/80/EC of 29 April 2004 relating to compensation to crime victims OJ 2004 L 261/15 and Chapter 9.3.A., n. 58 in Australia.

[63] Chapter 2.2.E.4., n. 292. [64] Chapter 6.4.H.

[65] Chapter 8.4.C.8. Considered but rejected in Scotland: Chapter 7.2.C.2.

[66] Chapter 5.3.A.

[67] Mandatory in Europe: Directive 2009/103/EC of the European Parliament and the Council of 16 September 2009 relating to insurance against civil liability in respect of the use of motor vehicles and the enforcement of the obligation to insure against such liability, OJ 2009 L 263 / 11; see, e.g., Chapter 2.2.A.

[68] For instance, in France, punitive damages cannot be covered by insurance, Chapter 3.4.B.1., whereas in Australia being insured is no bar to punitive damages being awarded: *Gray* v. *Motor Accident Commission* (1998) 196 CLR 1. See also particularly, Chapter 6.4.H.

[69] E.g., Chapter 4.7.B.1., Chapter 5.3.C.4. and Chapter 9.5.C, highlighting that there are particular pinch points for these rules, such as sexual abuse cases, particularly where a state's rules on vicarious liability are restrictive.

[70] Chapter 5.2.B.4.

In addition to campaigns and links with law enforcement to reduce offending, insurers can be incredibly important legal reformers, though their preferred reforms may not appeal to all.[71] Perhaps the most famous example is the 'Insurance crisis' which led to the tort reform of Australian law in the early 2000s. Insurers managed to put sufficient pressure on legislators, by threatening to refuse cover for many activities, that tort liability itself was substantially curbed.[72]

b) Actors crossing tort and crime Specialisation is not only interesting when it concerns substantive knowledge: it might also relate to how legal actors perform multiple roles or work together to pool and share skills.

First, one person might perform a number of different roles. For instance, an important feature of the Dutch legal system is the participation of legal scholars as part time judges on the benches of Courts of Appeals and District Courts,[73] as well as at the higher levels of the judiciary, and therefore indirectly influencing the development of case law. Something similar has evidently been the case in Sweden in the past, and to some extent today.[74] In England, there have been some notable examples of academics being part time judges; some few have also become full-time judges, but will almost always have practised as a lawyer first.

Second, though specialised in what they do, legal actors might work synergistically with others. French law,[75] for instance, has professionally trained generalist magistrates, strong written procedures, investigating judges and advocates-general, a court of cassation hearing over 4,000 cases a year and a close connection between academics, practice and the judiciary, particularly at their highest levels. For instance, the academic's 'note' on a Cour de cassation judgment is a vital part of the dissemination of legal knowledge. Members of the Cour de cassation go on tour to the Courts of Appeals annually to explain their landmark cases. This is considered to be necessary due to the rather brief reasoning in the decisions of the *Cour de cassation.* This is in stark contrast to the traditional position of English law. It has long been practitioners, who later in their

[71] E.g., France, Chapter 3.2. [72] Chapter 9.1, Chapter 9.2.F and Chapter 9.5.B.

[73] E.g., Renée Kool and Ton Hol in Utrecht; at the Supreme Court, Jaap Spier.

[74] E.g., Ivar Strahl and Hjalmar Granfelt, Chapter 5.2.A., and today, Martin Sunnqvist, co-author of the chapter. Similarly, judges can play an important role in law reform, e.g., Erik Marks von Würtemberg and Johan Gabriel Richert, Ch.5.2.B.3.

[75] See, generally, M. De S.-O.-L'E Lasser *Judicial Deliberations: A Comparative Analysis of Judicial Transparency and Legitimacy* (Oxford University Press, 2004.

careers might become judges, who shape English law.[76] They do so as specialised advocates/lawyers in oral and written proceedings, though once on the bench those same advocates have to deal with cases further from their original focus. Academic writing has only generally been able to influence court practice in the last few decades, though there were some distinguished exceptions. In Germany and the Netherlands, and in Sweden since the 1970s, the tradition is somewhat different: the highest courts argue their decisions rather extensively and even refer to arguments developed in academic literature.

c) **Actors confined** Despite these points of contact there are many instances where legal actors are separated between tortious and criminal. For instance, all of the legal systems studied recognise the need for academic positions in both, though academics who work on the relationship between the two are rare indeed.[77] It has been said to be 'almost unthinkable for a French academic who specialises in administrative law to study – never mind say anything about – the private law (civil) courts'. There is a similarly rigid distinction between the '*pénalistes*' and the '*civilistes*'.[78] The same applies to a German academic, where almost no chairs in universities combine more than one of private, public and criminal law.[79] Given that other faculties and departments can have widely interdisciplinary approaches, this appears to be a phenomenon felt particularly in law. Many law reform bodies predominantly focus on non-civil law, especially criminal law, and only rarely make proposals which directly address the relationship between tort and crime.[80]

d) **Actors contrasted** Legal actors play a complex and under-researched role in many legal systems. The role of specialisation amongst such legal actors is particularly interesting because it feeds back into the categories into which the law is divided. It is difficult for a legal actor to describe herself as specialising in an area of law which her colleagues would not recognise as an area of law in the first place. A point which merits further research is the extent to which there are characteristics

76 Chapter 2.2.A.

77 E.g., Sandra Friberg is said to be one of the only people who studies the relationship between tort and crime on some level *as an academic*, for the last 100 years in Sweden: Chapter 5.3.A., n. 41.

78 Lasser *Judicial Deliberations*, 6, see also n. 12.

79 Chapter 4.4.A.

80 E.g., Chapter 2.2.A. and Chapter .2.2.D., Chapter 6.2.B.7., Chapter 9.5.B., highlighting ad hoc reform bodies, bypassing the established ones. Scotland may be becoming an exception.

which can be ascribed to these specialisations: what makes a good 'tort lawyer/civil lawyer' or 'criminal lawyer', and whether there are particular arguments or values that such actors respect. Answers to these questions are not obvious within the national discourses, at University level or higher. Nonetheless, it appears that legal actors think themselves able to describe a legal rule as, for instance, 'good tort law' by reference to objective standards, even if they do not do the same about each other with as much precision.

B. *Reasoning*

Are there forms of reasoning that are particular to, or dominant in, tort or crime? Answering this question is complicated since legal systems are naturally diverse, with a range of legal actors, each with a range of ideas, values and preferences. In addition, there may be national biases in reasoning or discipline, for instance, in favour of doctrinal work over socio-legal work. Nonetheless, three examples might assist us: the approach to unity of a legal system, the relative weight of certain principles, and whether certain principles are thought to be the exclusive domain of one area of law.

Most legal actors seem to view their legal system as being, on some level, unified and coherent. They would certainly promote those qualities.[81] However, it appears that the meaning of 'unity' or 'coherence' varies, from legal system to legal system, and perhaps even from legal actor to legal actor. English law, for instance, prefers vague terms like 'coherence' and 'consistency' to what might appear to be harder terms like 'unity'.[82] Two countries that do make use of the term 'unity' are France and Germany.

In France, the relevant focal point is the unity of civil and criminal fault, not the unity of the legal system.[83] Since 1912, fault has been held by the courts to be the same in both areas of law. This approach actually lowered the criminal standard of negligence to that of the civil law: 'the slightest departure from the ideal behavioural model of the *bon père de famille* (or the reasonable man) would constitute negligent behaviour, which could, under certain conditions, become a criminal offence'.[84] The principle of unity of 'fault' of course does not import strict liability, which civilian countries increasingly turned to in the 1920s and 1930s, into criminal

[81] E.g., Chapter 6.3.D.1 and Chapter 6.4.F., text preceding n. 135; perhaps admitting where it fails, e.g., Chapter 2.2.E.1. in respect of compensating victims of crime.
[82] Chapter 2.3–4. [83] See, generally, Chapter 3.4.A.1.
[84] Chapter 3.4.A.1, text following n. 70.

law.[85] In practice, this unity is not always rigorously enforced and it has arguably been broken by legislation passed in 2000. In particular, that Act undid the very mechanism that created unity in the first place: allowing a criminal judge to determine that there was no criminal negligence, but that there was civil negligence. However, this only applies in respect of indirectly inflicted harms, not directly inflicted ones.[86]

The German conception of 'unity' is more thoroughly worked out than most others. It is nonetheless a particular use of the word. It does not mean substantive unity, or resolutive unity, which might be the most obvious meanings. Instead:

> According to this principle the entirety of the legal norms forms a consistent system... The principle of unity requires that each legal norm is interpreted in such a way that the consistency of the legal system is preserved.[87]

This has been interpreted to mean unity demands consistency, not sameness.[88] This might be right as a matter of theory. Indeed, at some point the semantic difference between 'unity' of an object, and 'coherence' across norms might merge. What is particularly striking about German law is that the differences between tort and crime are said neither to go unnoticed nor cause much surprise.[89] The methodological, substantive and procedural differences are said to follow from 'the different theoretical foundations of, and differing policy considerations underlying, criminal law and the law of delict'.[90] The interactions noted are primarily procedural and for the benefit of victims. Yet there are interactions in the codes, such as the *Adhäsionsverfahren*, that is, the adhesion process,[91] which are not used in practice and this is strange. It appears they are not used in part because of practical disadvantages to the system. However,

85 Indeed, the French authors go so far as to conclude, Chapter 3.5: 'On the one hand, tort and crime each have their own distinct character in France. Academics have worked hand in hand with the *Cour de cassation* to develop two systems, each highly coherent within itself: an objective system in tort law, a subjective and moral system in crime law.'

86 See further Chapter 3.3.B.1.

87 Chapter 4.1.A, text preceding n. 2.

88 Ibid., text preceding n. 4.

89 See the conclusion, Chapter 4.9.

90 By comparison, in Spain the constitution requires not the unity of the system, as it in part does in Germany, but the unity of jurisdiction and the absence of exceptional courts: Chapter 6.3.A.

91 Chapter 4.7.B.1. The term adhesion seems to arise first in German. Interstingly, Swedish lawyers use *adhesion* for attaching a civil case to a criminal but *cumulation* as a wider concept. Adhesion is most often used for the principle that the criminal and the civil cases are cumulated, and cumulation is used when discussing the actual cases taken up together: Chapter 5.5.A.2, text to n. 132.

in addition, because of the perception of the legal actors as to what the divide between tort and crime should be, or how its rules should be used, rather than what that law in fact is. Tort and crime is also a rare example of an area of law which German scholars have, hitherto, not thoroughly catalogued and explained. Dedicated work on the relationship of tort to crime is rare, with the treatment in leading commentaries on civil law, criminal law and their associated procedural laws being regarded as largely sufficient. It may be for this reason that German law does not have a great deal of doctrine about how the parallel substantive rules in tort and crime compare with each other, just like most of the legal systems studied do not. At the same time, this seems not to concern German scholars: they expect differences when they look. But exceptionally, and importantly, when they look, they have a strong normative framework to which they can turn to explain the relationship of these substantive components. It is just that that analysis does not appear to be thought particularly necessary, or useful. It is an interesting question whether such a normative framework predicting and able to be used to explain difference may even discourage analysis of the relationship between the two areas.

Similarly, many legal systems seem to have an 'exit' from conflicts between tort and crime. For instance, in the Netherlands unity and coherence are said to be highly valued, though not well-defined or debated.[92] Nonetheless, the Dutch have a principle of autonomy to justify examples where criminal law diverges from, for instance, civil law.[93] In England, a similar feat is done by reasoning, openly or not, that criminal law is isolated from, or superior to, civil law.[94] Interestingly, in the chapters on the smallest and most general jurisdictions studied, Sweden and Scotland, neither 'unity' nor 'coherence' are referenced. They may simply be too obvious there to be worth mentioning.

The relative weight of certain principles may vary between tort and crime. It might be wondered, for instance, whether tort lawyers value fairness more, while criminal lawyers value legal certainty more. One thing is certain, criminal lawyers tend to require greater specificity in their legal rules than tort lawyers do in theirs. For instance, all the legal systems studied have a concept of legal certainty. Many of the continental systems refer to the Roman law principle of *nulla poena sine lege* or a related form of it. The English know the principle, but typically refer to legal certainty,[95] as, in fact, do the French.[96] Many other interesting

[92] Chapter 8.1–2. [93] Chapter 8.3.D. [94] Chapter 2.3.
[95] Chapter 2.2.B. [96] Chapter 3.4.A.1.

questions arise here, such as whether England's lack of a prescription period for most criminal offences offends legal certainty, while at the same time English law will not countenance a possible alternative, trials *in absentia*, while many other systems on the continent will. However, in practice the force of this 'legal certainty', howsoever phrased, is often diluted. For instance, in France, while criminal offences must, in theory, be precisely defined, some of them do resemble the general provisions found in Articles 1382 and 1383 Civil Code.[97] Similarly, in Spain, while fault is required in Spanish law, the Codes themselves don't define it, it has been left to academics to fill in the detail and a complete consensus has not been achieved.[98]

A final question to consider is if and why theories, principles and concepts used in one area of law are used in the other. There are many difficult questions, requiring further work. For instance, are there really 'criminal' principles, or merely core formants which are re-clothed and re-emphasised in different legal contexts? When do legal actors see the parallels between tort and crime, and call in aid a mutual comparison; perhaps more interestingly, when do they not, when they could or should? Can legal actors hold two separate concepts, one tortious and one criminal, in their heads, on the same matter, and not ask or challenge their separation? It is sometimes stated that some common law countries are exceptional in giving tort law a punitive function, through the award of exemplary damages, but we already know this is actually more complex. Some have argued that there are concepts which only apply to the civil law: for example, the blanket exclusion of defences of ignorance of the law and true strict liability have been said to all be concepts exclusive to civil law.[99] The former is beyond the scope of this study, but the second is difficult to sustain in the common law where criminal strict and perhaps even absolute liability exists. This *appears* to be a significant difference, since in the rest of our systems strict liability cannot be part of criminal law, as, for instance, has been highlighted in the German[100] and Spanish chapters.[101] However, much of the force of this provision is removed when one realises that in the common law criminal lexicon, a 'strict liability offence' is not necessarily, indeed, only very rarely, one without any fault. Rather it is one where at least one of the physical elements does not have a corresponding mental state. This difference in terminology seems

[97] Chapter 3.4.A.1. [98] Chapter 6.4.B.

[99] E.g., Christian von Bar, *The Common European Law of Torts* (Oxford University Press, 2000), vol 1, n. 7, [603].

[100] Chapter 4.6.B.3. [101] Chapter 6.4.B.

to be a result of criminal law breaking down wrongs into separate acts or results, often many of them, and them loosely describing the whole offence as strict, almost as a general heading. In addition, the civil law rejection of strict liability may be balanced out by other sub-divisions in the law. The common law uses negligence within criminal law only rarely, while it appears to be more common in civil law countries, including in those places where the common law might use strict liability for the relevant physical element. Furthermore, such alternative sub-divisions include, for instance, the creation of regulatory offences or administrative sanctions which might use strict liability. These, as their titles suggest, are indeed sanctions, or offences, but somehow are not criminal.

C. *Substantive content*

The substantive comparison between parallel rules of law across tort and crime is perhaps the least developed in all the legal systems studied. This is remarkable because such comparisons are so simple, once considered: a child is liable under different conditions, and a 'yes' means something different in criminal law than in tort law. However, such issues typically arise in one court which has no immediate need to make such comparisons. They are technical, doctrinal rules for the most part, not calling for practitioners to compare across areas of law unless something makes it obvious. For instance, the call to compare becomes more obvious where the civil claim follows a criminal trial and where the same defence was used but apparently with a different reasoning.[102] More specifically, comparison is encouraged where the legal framework jars in some way: there are 'right' rules which have been departed from, but are still in the minds of lawyers. This is particularly evident in Spain, where, particularly in the last few decades, *ex delicto* liability has been critiqued against the liability in the Civil Code. Unsurprisingly, the Spanish is one of the chapters where substantive (and other) comparisons between tort and crime come the most easily to the authors.

There are seven common areas of law which will be compared: general integrative techniques, capacity, consent, fault, causation, secondary liability and defences.

1. General integrative techniques

While a particular criminal wrong might mirror a civil wrong (whether in the form of a general clause, or a nominate tort such as in the common law

[102] E.g., Chapter 2.2.D.10, n. 179.

and Scotland), most of our legal systems all go further in integrating the two types of wrong. In England, Scotland and Australia some integration happens through the tort of breach of statutory duty. In Sweden there appears to be no 'gathering' provision, but as a matter of fact many criminal offences have parallel civil liability.[103] In France, deeper integration occurs through the unity of criminal and civil fault, a judicial doctrine tweaked by legislation in 2000. German law has §823(2) BGB which replicates the general provision (§ 823(1)) for anyone who commits a breach of a statute that is intended to protect another person. The difficulty then is to determine which statutes are intended to protect another, but that list will certainly include many criminal statutes. The Dutch and Spanish rules are the most integrative. Dutch law's key definition of an unlawful act is as, amongst other things, 'an act or omission in violation of a duty imposed by written law' and all criminal laws must be in written form (in addition, breaching social standards of due care also generates liability).[104] Spain makes its integration even more obvious: Article 109(1) of the Spanish Criminal Code provides that:

> The carrying out of an act prescribed by the law as *delito* or *falta* obliges reparation, according to law, for the damage and losses caused by it.[105]

That is, the law turns on damage being caused by what happens to be a criminal offence. This is quite a remarkable link between tort and crime, and in part, was what was thought to justify the placing of civil law norms in the Criminal Code in 1848, a situation that was originally intended to be temporary, until a Spanish civil code could be passed.[106]

2. Capacity

Tortious and criminal conditions for the personal imputation of liability, particularly age, differ in theory and in practice.[107]

Criminal law tends to rely on age as the fixed standard for imposing criminal liability. In England, it is ten, with an earlier rule requiring the prosecution to prove knowledge of the wrongfulness of the actions between ten and fourteen removed in 1998; in Germany it is fourteen;

[103] Chapter 5.3.C.1. [104] Chapter 8.3.B.

[105] *Delito* marks out the more serious crimes, *falta* the less serious ones. See also Art. 100 LECrim.

[106] J. F. Pacheco, *El Código Penal* (Madrid: Edisofer, 2000; reprint of 1867), 279.

[107] See, specifically, Chapter 2.2.D.1., Chapter 3.4.A.3., Chapter 4.6.B., Chapter 5.3.B.1., Chapter 6.4.D., Chapter 7.3.A., Chapter 8.3.B., Chapter 9.3.C.1.

the Spanish Criminal Code, Art. 19, sets the minimum age as eighteen, but from fourteen to eighteen there is a separate, and quite harsh, scheme under a Law of 2000;[108] in Scotland, the age is twelve;[109] in the Netherlands, twelve;[110] in Australia, ten. In Sweden, there is no official age, sentencing being impossible before fifteen, but liability can be established probably from the same age as in tort, three or four. French law is exceptional in having no discrete ages referenced. In France the prosecution must prove in each case that the defendants under eighteen had *discernement*: they were aware of their conduct. Other than age, there are specific defences for those suffering from mental conditions which reduce their individual culpability or responsibility, such as a defence of insanity.

Tort law applies a variable standard, if any standard at all. Children are sometimes sued in tort law, particularly where there is insurance but not all systems have felt the need to set a clear rule. The question seems to be a practical one, as there are pragmatic reasons against suing a child and a claimant tends to look more foolish in so suing the younger the child is. In addition, an action against the child will be more likely where the parent is not liable, particularly not strictly, for the wrongs of the child. For instance, in France, civil fault is now defined only by one objective component which ignores age: a behaviour deviating from that which would have been adopted under the ideal behavioural model of the reasonable person. In effect, they apply no rule of subjective imputation. Similarly, in England, as well, possibly, as Scotland and Australia, children can be liable without any defined lower age limit, though to establish liability the 'reasonable person' would likely be a reasonable child of the age of the defendant. The one country which uses only an age standard is the Netherlands, and it uses fourteen years old.[111] It does so by a somewhat opaque provision which obliquely refers to the capacity of children while stating that parents could be liable under that age. German law is more complex, combining age and a residual equitable discretion. Between seven and seventeen, a defendant needs to have had the ability to discern, in a general and abstract way, that he acted in a way for which one is accountable; but even when this is not established, German law has

108 Ley Orgánica 5/2000, de 12 de enero, reguladora de la responsabilidad penal de los menores.

109 At least, they cannot be prosecuted under that age (Criminal Procedure (Scotland) Act 1995, ss. 41–41A), but from the age of eight they can be referred to a children's hearing on the grounds that they have committed an offence.

110 Art. 486 Dutch Code of Penal Procedure, with special procedures available for juveniles: Art. 7a Criminal Code.

111 Art. 6:169 Dutch Civil Code: it is, at least, a clear rule.

a flexible jurisdiction to impose liability based on fairness under § 829 BGB. In Spain, the rules are unsettled, but there is no age in the codes and the jurisprudence varies; it is at least clear that over the age of fourteen the Law of 2000 regulates liability if the tort was also a crime.[112]

There are two other differences. First, in criminal law, the relevant term is *accountability* in Germany, the rest (some in translation) refer to *responsibility*. Tort law tends to refer, more broadly, to *capacity*. Second, there are also some variations of how this mechanism works: below the specified age children in the common law do not commit a crime: there is no wrong. In Germany and Sweden the issue is slightly different. There is a wrong, but there is no guilt and thus the individual cannot be punished. That is, a wrong can take place even though no person is guilty of it. This difference may be significant, for instance on whether an object 'stolen' by a child becomes stolen property or not. In tort law, a parent or other person vicariously liable for the incapable person is only liable if there was a tort, but there can also be primary obligations on the parent or other which do not require a tort by the child. In Scotland, between eight and twelve, the child commits a wrong but cannot be prosecuted.

Put generally, tort law seems to apply a wider definition of capacity, bringing more people into liability, than criminal law. A further example is that criminal law tends to regard insanity as a reason why individual guilt cannot be established while tort law tends not to do so. Neither of these facts are surprising, since criminal law still focuses on the guilt of the *individual* (even if it accepts objective measures of it) while tort law has broadly moved to an objective position and a focus on loss allocation. This attention on loss allocation, and the objective responsibilities of individuals, also explains the strong links between capacity and liability for others: when one potential defendant cannot be sued, others will be sought, such as parents or the guardians of the insane. The Spanish chapter notes the age of responsibility in passing in the section on liability for others, demonstrating how the matter practically comes before the courts.[113] This issue then highlights the need to insure and the importance of the insurance market in determining compensation.

3. Consent

Even once an individual has capacity to make valid determinations about their life, further limitations may be imposed on how that volition is

[112] See, further, M. Martín-Casals, *Children in Tort Law Part I: Children as Tortfeasors* (Vienna/New York: Springer, 2006).

[113] See also, 6.169 Dutch Civil Code.

recognised. In principle, no wrong is committed where the 'victim' consented, but it appears that in at least some jurisdictions, criminal law will set more limits on what can be consented to than tort law. This certainly appears to be the case in England and Sweden.[114] In both countries, for many wrongs one could be criminally but not civilly liable because the victim's consent was invalid in criminal law but valid in civil law. This position does not seem to cause much concern there. Perhaps the state's concerns extend sufficiently beyond the victim's own: the victim may factually consent but there is still a wrong to other interests of the state, such as in the preservation of the consenting party. However, in doing so, this paternalism also denies the victim's ability to determine their own lives. In Scotland, an extreme position has been stated, at least in theory: consent is not a defence to any criminal charge,[115] not even basic assault.[116] However, this exclusion has not been applied in serious cases and is open to doubt more generally. Finally, the determination of whether and why consent is factually valid, even if legal valid, is a further difficulty.[117]

4. Fault and intention specifically

As has already been noted, one of the general features of criminal law is a greater focus on the individual characteristics of the defendant. In tort, by comparison, objective liability is the norm, with some points of strict liability.[118] Intention does much less work in practice in tort. In part this is because proving intention requires further evidence than showing a lack of reasonable care without granting obvious benefit, and perhaps also because proving intentional acts will usually deprive the defendant of insurance cover.[119] Where intention is still used in tort, it may well require that the defendant intend a consequence which is not an injury (harm or injury being the normal focus in criminal law), or, perhaps in some cases, even merely intend an act, not a consequence.[120] Interestingly, in the common law, criminal strict liability is possible, indeed common, but negligence based criminal liability is rarer, at least in the traditional areas of criminal law.[121] In some cases, the relationship between civil and criminal concepts of fault has been of great significance. In France, the relationship of criminal and civil negligence was instrumental in

[114] Chapter 2.2.D.3., Chapter 5.3.C.1. [115] Chapter 7.3.F. [116] Chapter 7.3.C.1.

[117] E.g., Chapter 2.2.D.3. and Chapter 9.3.C.6.

[118] In Spain particular, a reverse burden of proof of fault has played a key role: Chapter 6.4.B.

[119] E.g., Chapter 5.3.C.6. [120] E.g., Chapter 2.2.D.4.; Chapter 9.3.C.3.

[121] E.g., Chapter 2.2.D.4–6.

creating the unity of civil and criminal fault, just as much as it was in arguably breaking that bond ninety years later.[122] Similarly, there are strong links between fault concepts in England;[123] while in Germany there is extensive theoretical work done distinguishing them, with criminal *guilt* and civil *fault* represented, respectively, by the cognate words *Schuld* and *Verschulden*.[124] Fault is one area where in some countries, for example, France and Spain, the principles of legality and certainty appear to be more generously interpreted, with both criminal and civil fault not always being precisely defined, at least not in legislation.[125]

5. Causation

Wherever the law seeks to respond to harm, it will have to establish that a particular person(s) caused the harm specified, but only in some systems do tort and crime use the same test.[126] Every system starts out with requiring 'but for' causation to prove the fact of an event being a cause of an outcome. This is potentially under-inclusive, so some systems accept causation even without it, particularly where proof is practically very difficult. It is also potentially over-inclusive, suggesting a further stage is necessary. It is at this further stage that significant divergence occurs. In the common law, the second stage might conveniently, though not completely accurately, be called 'legal causation': tort law tends to focus on *foreseeability* and *intervening acts*, while criminal law talks of a *substantial* and *operating* cause. The tests appear similar, though the use of different language appears to be deliberate. In fact, the criminal law test calls on 'common sense' and physical descriptions of events more, perhaps to aid jury decisions. A roughly similar position appears to be the case in Scotland. French law is quite distinctive, using a somewhat flexible concept of 'directness' as well as a number of presumptions about causation in both tort and crime. German law is particularly intricate. Criminal law requires objective attribution, including objective unforeseeability, objective unavoidability and for being covered by the protective ratio of the infringed norm. Civil law under § 823(1) BGB divides causation into (i) the causing of injury to the absolute right, and (ii) that that injury to the right caused harm; such a division is not necessary where the provision of the BGB does not protect such rights, as is the case in § 826.

[122] Chapter 3.3.B.1. [123] Chapter 2.2.D.4–6. [124] Chapter 4.6.B.3.
[125] Chapter 6.4.B. and Chapter 3.4.A.1.
[126] See, generally, Chapter 2.2.D.8, Chapter 3.4.A.2., Chapter 4.6.B.1.f, Chapter 5.3.C.5., Chapter 6.4.C., Chapter 7.3.E., Chapter 8.3.D. and Chapter 8.5.B.1., Chapter 9.3.C.4.

However, the civil methods to then restrict 'but for' causation (in Germany, the *Äquivalenztheorie*) are less extensive than in criminal law. In particular, it appears that the civil law rarely uses one of its ostensibly key doctrines, the *Adäquanztheorie* theory, to disprove causation: according to this theory damage which is highly unusual and which could not have been foreseen by an ideal observer will not count.

What is most interesting for present purposes is the number of legal systems who have expressly made causation formally the same in both tort and crime. In 1970, the Dutch Hoge Raad adopted the limiting condition of 'reasonable imputation' of the outcome to the event in civil law; in 1978, it said criminal law should use the same standard. In Spain, the adoption of a single limiting theory on causation happened the other way around: criminal law scholarship and jurisprudence adopted the 'objective imputation' theory first, followed some time later by the Civil Chamber of the Tribunal Supremo. This theory is technically a normative assessment of facts and their attribution to an individual, but seems to do work that might otherwise be done by a causation theory, at least to the eyes of a foreign observer. By comparison, it is hard to say exactly when Swedish law adopted broadly the same test for causation in tort and crime, but it appears well established.

In addition, it should be borne in mind that legislative rules could, in theory, adjust or remove causation requirements. Criminal law, rather than tort law, often criminalises conduct which does not have to be proven to have caused harm, such as inchoate offences like attempts liability. But there are also specific statutory provisions which specify new, or seen another way, adjust existing, causation rules in particular circumstances.[127] In Sweden they do so by lowering the standard of proof in tort cases, rather than changing the substantive rules.[128]

6. Secondary and accessory liability

In all the legal systems, civil accessorial liability seems to be much less developed than criminal accessorial liability.[129] Criminal law uses secondary liability extensively, while generally rejecting vicarious liability (even amongst common law countries). It also draws greater distinctions

[127] E.g., in England, *R* v. *Hughes* [2013] UKSC 56; France, Ch.3.4.A.2, text following nn. 116 and 122.

[128] Chapter 5.3.C.5.

[129] See, generally, Chapter 2.2.D.2., Chapter 3.4.A.3.b., § 830 BGB and §§ 26–27 and 29 StGB, Chapter 5.3.C.7., Chapter 6.4.D., Chapter 7.3.D., Section 6.1.2. Dutch Civil Code and Arts. 47–54(a) Dutch Criminal Code, Chapter 9.3.C.5.

between types of secondary party, such as an incitor and an assistor.[130] Civil law is less developed, or at least, less differentiated. Criminal law separates out its forms of wrongdoing far more, with specific offences and modes of accessory liability. Tort law often has general clauses, or general torts, even if it has also further niche torts.[131] In a similar vein, tort law can use joint tortfeasorship (including vicarious liability) and insurance to do much of the work in civil law that accessory liability does in criminal law.[132] Indeed, many legal systems have extensive liability for others, particularly parents. The Spanish regime is particularly extensive, and confusingly varies between tort and crime, as well as between tort and *ex delicto* liability. The *ex delicto* form even gives a criminal court jurisdiction to order that those who, without wrongdoing, have benefitted from a wrong provide restitution. French law has some similar complexities, focused especially on the liability of the employer. One country to watch in the future is Scotland: a very recent case seems to suggest that civil law will attempt to draw on the complex and quite draconian 'art and part' doctrine within criminal law.

Another reason for this difference in treatment may be that the decision-making about possible parties appears to be different. At a certain point, a claim in tort does not benefit from adding further defendants, but criminal law sees only a minimal further administrative or trial effort but many benefits in convicting all involved.

7. Defences

General defences are more developed in criminal law than in tort law.[133] For instance, while tort and crime typically both accept that there are *justifications*, it is not clear that every system's tort law accepts *excuses* while criminal law typically does. There are three approaches to the comparison of defences.

First, a system may have no sustained attempt to compare or link tortious and criminal law defence, examples being England, Scotland and

[130] The Dutch and German systems distinguish between five forms of participation, including principals and accessories.

[131] Some niche wrongs create liability for assisting wrongs where only specific people could be the principals, e.g., the English tort of inducing a breach of contract.

[132] An example of the link to joint tortfeasorship can be seen in Germany where the relevant provision is contained in the second provision under the heading 'Joint tortfeasors and persons involved', equating 'instigators and accessories' with joint tortfeasors: § 830 BGB.

[133] See, generally, Chapter 2.2.D.10, Chapter 3.4.A.3.c., Chapter 5.6.C., Chapter 5.3.A. and Chapter 5.3.C.2. , Chapter 6.4.F., Chapter 7.3.F., Chapter 8.5.B.1–3.,

Australia. As a result they are unsure, for instance, whether duress is a defence to a tort law claim (it is to most criminal offences) as well as mental defences like insanity.

Second, systems may have links which are variable or uncertain. The French and Swedish positions are quite nuanced, but it appears that while the same defences are recognised in tort and crime, there is no need to apply them in the same way in both areas. This is especially the case as they might not apply to no-fault tort liability, while they would in any parallel crimes. The position in Spain is also uncertain: the criminal code refers to a number of defences which the civil code does not, and commentators are divided about whether civil courts can refer to the criminal provisions by analogy. It seems many defences operate similarly in practice.

Third, a legal system may create some unity of defences across both tort and crime. This is the approach in German law, where criminal law uses defences from the BGB (the Civil Code) and tort law uses defences from the StGB (the Criminal Code), apparently in an example of a 'hard' use of the unity of the legal system:

> We find [reasons excluding wrongfulness] both in the BGB and the StGB. Those reasons which justify a wrongdoing and are regulated in the BGB, will, in general, be applied in criminal law; those in the StGB similarly apply in civil law. It is said that anything else would contradict the principle of the unity of the legal system.[134]

This sameness is also the Dutch solution, though there the criminal code sets out the defences and the civil courts recognise them, even if it is unclear whether they are bound to apply them identically in tort.

This variation is interesting. Where the defences have been specified in one or both of the civil and criminal codes, some unity or direct comparison of the texts might seem to be encouraged, as in Germany and the Netherlands, but interestingly without the same result, as in Spain. In defences, unlike other substantive areas, our systems which value the unity of the legal system are more likely to link their defences. For other systems, perhaps the practical cost in keeping up to date with any developments in the parallel defences is off-putting, though apparently not in the eyes of the Germans and Dutch. This is particularly interesting since Germans normally do not think unity requires sameness, but they do think it does in defences. By contrast, it is not surprising that the common law countries (including Scotland) should generally fail to link up tortious

[134] Chapter 4.6.C., text to nn. 172–3.

and criminal defences.[135] They do not link their substantive law much, are not as concerned about the unity of the system, and have fewer codified norms.

Systems also vary on how defences operate. A separate point is how these defences operate across different jurisdictions. In the common law there is probably no clear answer, indeed, somewhat shamefully it is sometimes still uncertain whether a particular set of facts is something the prosecution should prove, or a defence for the defendant to raise and prove (if only by raising sufficient evidence, not proving beyond reasonable doubt). By contrast, in French law, while

> [t]here is therefore a substantial link between the defences in tort and criminal law; . . . they operate differently within each area of law. That is, '*faits justificatif*' are used for their appropriate effect and as specific concepts in criminal law whereas the components of tort law themselves ask the questions that are answered by discrete defences in criminal law.[136]

A further interesting issue, and one of the points addressed in the case study in the appendix to this volume, is whether our systems have developed a defence of illegality to tort claims.

D. *Procedure*

Procedural law shows the greatest interface between tort and crime. This can be seen in the length and prominence given to procedure in the national reports.[137] Three jurisdictional, evidential and procedural areas will be discussed here: the victim's role in prosecutions, compensation in criminal courts and the rules of the trial process.

1. The victim's role in prosecutions

The decision to prosecute is a classic interplay between tort claimants and the status of the victim within the criminal process.[138] All our systems put the public prosecutor as the primary prosecuting authority, using the resources of the state to enforce the criminal law. This often involves formally recognised discretion on when to prosecute, such as in the common

[135] Rare examples seem to be very recent: Chapter 2.2.D.10 nn. 170 (2014) and 179 (2008).

[136] Chapter 3.4.A.3., text preceding n. 154.

[137] Even while following the questionnaire's structure in other ways: Chapter 2.2.E., Chapter 3.3., Chapter 4.7., Chapter 5.4., Chapter 6.3., Chapter 7.2., Chapter 8.4. and Chapter 8.5., Chapter 9.4.

[138] Some further insight can be gained from E. Hoegen and M. Brienen, *Victims of Crime in 22 European Criminal Justice Systems* (Nijmegen: Justitie, 2000).

law, Scotland, France and the Netherlands. Sweden is slightly unusual in having a rule requiring prosecutions, but allows narrow exceptions where the public interest in proceedings is not strong enough.[139] Two countries where there is a strong rule against any discretion in prosecution are Germany and Spain. There, the principle of legality is taken to mean that no state actor, neither prosecutor nor judge, can deviate from the clear rules for the commencement, scope and continuation of criminal procedure. That said, it would be possible for legislative provisions to grant discretion in specific areas, as indeed happens in, for instance, in Germany.

However, there must be some discretion, even informal, in determining whether there is sufficient evidence of a crime. Since reasonable people might disagree in assessing that evidence some review of prosecutors' decisions is now quite standard.[140] In Germany, this review is both at the level of the prosecuting authority and, if that fails, a court. This *Klageerzwingungsverfahren* seems to be an example of German thoroughness: perceiving the risk, however slight, that the public prosecutor might not assess the facts and evidence in the right way. On the other hand, in Spain, any such review appears to have a low profile, perhaps because the prosecutors seem to prosecute readily. It might be that any review of a prosecutor's decision not to prosecute could be folded into any other allegation of dereliction of duty. In any case, in 2012 the European Union passed a Directive, requiring victims to have some form of review of a decision not to prosecute, though this may be done by the same body that decided not to prosecute and might also be limited only to serious crimes.[141]

There are therefore four levels of victim involvement in the decision to prosecute:

(1) *No review*: in Australia there is no formal mechanism to review a prosecutor's decision not to prosecute.
(2) *Light*: in England there is now a right to request that the prosecuting authority review its decision not to prosecute. Swedish law allows the aggrieved party to request a review by a senior prosecutor. Scottish law is about to introduce an internal review process.
(3) *Medium*: a right to review by a court. In Germany, the first review is by the prosecuting authority, but this can be followed by a court

[139] Chapter 5.3.A.4, n. 43. [140] Chapter 6.3.B.3.

[141] Directive 2012/29/EU of the European Parliament and of the Council of 25 October 2012 establishing minimum standards on the rights, support and protection of victims of crime, OJ 2012 L315/57.

hearing. In the Netherlands, the victim can request a review by the Court of Appeal; that court is selected as it is hierarchically superior to the Public Prosecution Service, who are treated as equivalent to a first instance court.[142]

(4) *Strong*: a right to force a prosecution by becoming a civil party *par voie d'action* and, indeed, require the public prosecutor to carry out the prosecution, making French law quite exceptional. That said, there are safeguards: it is available only in the Police Court, the Neighbourhood Court[143] or the Correctional Court,[144] which excludes more serious crimes.

Of course, informal or political pressure, might be applied to encourage the public prosecutor to prosecute and perhaps even not to prosecute.

The alternative to affecting the prosecutor's decision whether to prosecute, is for the victim to prosecute. Such a right is rarely exercised in the common law, perhaps more commonly in England than in Australia, though it is practically unknown in Scotland.[145] In England, it has been variously described as a constitutional safeguard and as an anachronism.[146] However, in both England and Australia, the state can take over a private prosecution and then discontinue it, so the right is somewhat illusory.[147] In France, there is much less call for it given the *strong* right of review, but even so, in recent decades independent administrative authorities and sometimes even private persons have been given the right to prosecute.[148] The right exists in Germany in respect of minor crimes, but apparently not to enhance the position of the victim, rather to relieve the state of the burden of such prosecutions.[149] In Sweden, the *målsägande*, 'the person who owns the case', if she has been personally harmed, can prosecute cases, support the prosecution, appeal an acquittal against which the prosecutor does not appeal, and act as a party claiming damages; however in practice the *målsägande* rarely prosecutes, given the generous state provision for prosecution and assisting the victim.[150] In Spain, the right of every citizen to prosecute, the *acción popular*, is thought to be an important constitutional safeguard,

[142] Chapter 8.4.A, noting other related rights. [143] Art. 531 CPP.

[144] Art. 388 CPP. [145] Chapter 7.2.A.

[146] *Gouriet* v. *Union of Post Office Workers* [1978] AC 435, 476–7 cf. *Jones* v. *Whalley* [2006] UKHL 41, [16].

[147] Chapter 2.2.E.2, text to n. 241; Chapter 9.4.B. text to n. 148.

[148] Chapter 3.4.B.1., text to n. 161. [149] Chapter 4.7.B.4.

[150] Chapter 5.3.A.5., nn. 46 and 52.

but again is rare, being used in not more than 3 per cent of all criminal cases.[151] There is no right to private prosecution in the Netherlands. The high cost and investigative and evidential burdens tend to discourage the use of such a right. However, some administrative bodies and large corporations, such as media companies, are willing to turn to private prosecutions in sufficiently significant cases, particularly in England and France.

Finally, there are certain other rights to information and participation in the criminal trial in some legal systems. These might include information rights as well as appeal rights, such as in Sweden. Within Europe, many of these rights are included in the same Directive from 2012, such as Arts. 6–7 the right to receive information and appropriate translation and Art. 10 the right to be heard. These were not traditionally rights granted by the common law, and are not recognised in Australia. Germany allows victims to apply to be a *Nebenklage*, a private accessory prosecutor, who can then intervene in some ways, such as on evidence and narrowly in appeals. Effective use of these further rights will often require legal advice, which might be granted through legal aid, but often will not be. Here, Sweden goes a step further, giving victims an aggrieved party counsel to ensure that all their interests are protected.

It is difficult to trace and explain the impact of the 'victim'. The trajectories seem to be very different even in closely related legal systems: English law has seen an increased emphasis on the victim, in rhetoric and in some legal rules, which has been seen perhaps to a lesser extent in Australia (such as through Victim Impact Statements); German law has almost no practical status for the victim, but Dutch law has steadily been moving the victim towards the centre of criminal justice policy. French and Spanish law go a long way towards aiding the victim, but in part by and for the state, rather than the victim herself. Swedish law perhaps goes furthest, where another distinctive but small jurisdiction, Scotland, perhaps goes less far than English law. Even in France where victims have great power, the state limits their ability to dictate state action.

2. Compensation

One of the primary interests someone injured by a criminal wrong will have is to obtain compensation with the minimum effort, particularly where the state prosecutes the defendant. Five aspects of this interest will

[151] Chapter 6.3.B.3.

be examined: the nature of any such claim, how it is opened and closed, its limits, its enforcement and its international dimensions.

a) **Nature of the claim** The vehicle for obtaining compensation for the aggrieved party could take a number of forms, but its nature could be one of three things: criminal, civil or a hybrid.

An autonomous criminal compensation vehicle would be difficult to create and maintain, since direct comparisons with civil law would be so obvious and would need constant reasoned rejection. None of our systems use a pure criminal model.

A pure civil compensation vehicle is theoretically the case in many systems but it is hard to say that it will come to the same outcome as a civil court would. At the very least this is because of questions about the legal actors involved, timing, burden of proof and rules of evidence.

As for hybrid rules, like those in the compensation orders of the common law and Scotland, the links between tort and crime are unclear. It seems to focus on the practical utility of the order to criminal courts, not wishing to complicate criminal adjudication by having to get the civil law perfect.[152] One tricky example is Spain: it does not use the 'pure' civil rules from the Civil Code, but, at least in modern legal theory, it is or should be using 'civil' rules, albeit that they appear to deviate towards criminal goals or forms in some ways. A further difficult example is that it is theoretically possible for a Dutch compensation order to be awarded in support of a civil judgment, thereby using the state's enforcement mechanism to force the loser in a civil action to pay. However, this possibility appears not to be common in practice.[153]

b) **Opening and closing** Any vehicle for compensation must be opened, whether by the victim or not, and once triggered, include sufficient evidence of the harm. Here formal rules blend into practice, since even where an application by the victim is required the state may try to obtain it, such as through the police, prosecutors and victim support organisations. For this reason, the Spanish and Swedish vehicles might be thought of as *presumptive adhesion.* Criminal compensation is of course

[152] Other attempts to peg compensation to tort standards, like some state compensation funds, may have a similar problem, often leading to cheaper and more efficient tariff-based systems; Dutch and Swedish state guarantees for criminal compensative vehicles are similar.

[153] Chapter 8.4.C.7. text following n. 84.

linked to initiation of a prosecution, as Spain and France particularly show.

As for closing the compensatory process, there are again formal and informal mechanisms. Formally, it seems more likely that where it is a fully civil process, like adhesion or the *partie civile*, the claim might be settled and leave the criminal process. For instance, in Sweden, the aggrieved party can settle and that ends the civil claim within the criminal procedure, but the criminal procedure itself will continue. In Germany, uncharacteristically for a criminal court, the parties can suggest, or ask the court to propose, a settlement.[154] Conversely, in hybrid vehicles there may be less opportunity to do so, especially where the victim did not apply in the first place. In England or Scotland there is no such chance. However, the party aggrieved, or the prosecution, could decline to offer the necessary evidence and no order would be made. Doing so would not jeopardise a later civil claim, since it is a hybrid order, governed by statute. In addition, in the common law all the criminal court can do is acquit, not positively find that there was no crime.

c) **Limits** Limits on the vehicle for compensation are common. They can be divided into restrictions on bringing the compensation vehicle and costs and risks for using it. In both cases, there can be formal and informal limitations. In ascending order of limitations:

(1) Spanish law has the fewest limitations of any kind. Prosecutors must claim on behalf of the victim, the claim cannot be rejected once made and there are no cost or risk implications for making the claim. This open door policy has led to an over-reliance on the criminal law to solve what might best be characterised as civil disputes.[155] By comparison, the private prosecution through an *acción popular* does require a security deposit.
(2) French law freely allows all compensation claims, not other actions with civil ends, but does put some risks on *parties civiles* who tread close to malicious or unfounded claims: if the civil party forces an abusive or dilatory prosecution, he can be fined and is liable to pay damages.[156]
(3) Swedish law has light formal limits:[157] claims which are 'clearly unjustified' or where there is a 'significant inconvenience' for the prosecutor putting it forward will be rejected. Examples include where the

[154] § 405 StPO.
[155] Chapter 6.3.D.2. and Chapter 6.3.B.3. Remember also that the rules Spanish law use are special and in the Criminal Code.
[156] Chapter 3.3.A., text preceding n. 25.
[157] Chapter 5.4.A.3.

evidence is hard to obtain, multi-party claims and where the prosecutor and aggrieved party disagree on how to classify the crime. However, the criminal court is incentivised to hear the claim then, as otherwise it would simply be postponed to the same judges in a different capacity where the victim will only have free legal advice if an aggrieved party counsel had already been appointed in the criminal trial.

(4) Formally a German criminal court can reject a claim if inadmissible, without merit or if, after taking all legitimate causes into consideration, the claim seems inappropriate to be solved in criminal court (for instance, it would prolong the trial substantially).[158] The criminal court can also determine liability, and perhaps certain facts, but leave the exact quantification to civil courts. However, the informal limits are more significant. Lawyers resist using it because they maintain the strict separation between criminal and civil law instilled at University and prefer specialised civil judges to hear the claim; criminal judges might fear that they will be overburdened by having to deal with complex issues of civil law.[159] Furthermore, and more mundanely, the lawyer's fees will be lower.[160] Finally, there are fears about how insurance cover may operate, particularly because a finding of no civil liability will prevent another claim against the offender's compulsory insurance. That, of course, is a particular problem where the legal system does not automatically equate criminal wrongs with civil ones. German law, as already noted, only does so within the scope of § 823(2) BGB.

(5) The English, Australians, Scottish and Dutch have admissions limits but little risk. In England, only 'clear cases' will be dealt with by the criminal court, though the criminal court has developed its own more simple rules in some areas of law, like causation, which may help to keep cases 'clear'.[161] One important limit is that the order is set partly by the defendant's means so is unlikely to compensate fully. In addition, compensation orders require the judge to convict, therefore the standard of proof is 'beyond reasonable doubt'; it is slightly unclear

158 Chapter 4.7.B.1.

159 Eberhard Siegismund, 'Ancillary (Adhesion) Proceedings in Germany as Shaped by the First Victim Protection Law: An Attempt To Take Stock' in Hiroshi Iitsuka and Rebecca Findlay-Debeck (eds.), *Resource Material Series No. 56* (Tokyo, United Nations Asia and Far East Institute for the Prevention of Crime and Treatment of Offenders, 2000) 102, 108–9.

160 It is surprising that the fees are not simply increased as a means to get more claims, especially if they could be met by the defendant.

161 Chapter 2.2.E.1.

whether all the facts justifying compensation have to be proven to that standard, but it seems likely they will have been.[162] Beyond these points, the Australian position is more complicated,[163] given the diversity of jurisdictions. In Australia, some conceptually difficult issues might make orders unsuitable, but it has recently been held that complex factual issues should not hinder compensation orders. Given the low profile of victims within the justice system, and the lack of effective insurance, there may be other informal limits to such compensation. The Dutch have a similar formal rule to the Swedish,[164] claims will be rejected where they cause a disproportionate burden, hindering the criminal trial (*geen onevenredige belasting*). However, the judiciary have interpreted 'disproportionate burden' as a 'ten minute rule' for how long the criminal court can spend on the claim. In practice anything out of the ordinary or with insufficient evidence is rejected. This itself was an shift from a *claim limit*, of a rather low equivalent of 68 Euros in 1926, rising to 680 by the time of its removal in 1995 and the current system being set up; the limit replacing it was that the claim was 'simple', a limit itself now replaced. By comparison, since 2011 Dutch law has also had a power for the more informal and faster *kantonprocedure* to rule on claims up to 25,000 Euros, but aggrieved persons nonetheless still rely on the adhesion procedure.

Formal limits might have a stronger effect in practice: potential compensation requests might be abandoned, or curtailed because of uncertainty about whether it meets the limits, or fears about any *res judicata* effect on a later civil claim.

These limits seem to have been introduced for divergent reasons. Spain imposes no limits as part of its view of the obligations of the state to right wrongs and punish the guilty. French law accepts that the ability to force a prosecution is exceptional and should at least have protections against abuse, such as it only being available outside the most serious crimes and liability for abusive claims. It may also be a constitutional protection, to ensure that prosecutors exercise their discretion to prosecute properly lest a victim intervene and force them to do so. On the other hand, admissions limits are more generally justified by seeking to avoid overburdening the

[162] It is surprising that this point is not more controversial, but the 'clear case' requirement probably dispenses with most of the difficult cases, at least in England.

[163] Chapter 9.3.A., text from nn. 61–71.

[164] Chapter 8.4.C.2.

criminal justice system, or, to protect Dutch defendants' rights to justice. They can also be linked to a concept of constitutional or institutional competence: that criminal courts are not the best placed to determine all civil claims. Finally, systems which have a separate hybrid order, especially the English and Australian compensation order, have concerns about consistency since those orders typically need not match an underlying civil wrong.[165]

One very interesting procedural question which this book cannot go into in detail is the role of criminal courts in restoring property: some countries allow such claims, indeed, they are very significant;[166] other countries do not.[167] Such a remedy is particularly interesting because the definition of property and the role of property offences is controversial in some common law legal systems, such as the English,[168] while apparently not controversial elsewhere.[169]

d) Enforcement The person aggrieved by a crime is not only interested in a court order for compensation, she is interested in that order being satisfied.

Compensation orders in England and Scotland are hybrids but for the purposes of enforcement they are orders of the criminal court. This partly explains why the defendant's means are taken into account in most jurisdictions: the criminal courts do not want to be involved in using their extensive coercive powers to squeeze the little money that the defendant has from him, and then try to get more than he does have. In Scotland this is taken one step further, and the means of the defendant do not include post-sentence earning capacity. The position is far more complex in Australia, with the orders sometimes being classed as normal civil orders, to be enforced by the person aggrieved by civil methods, sometimes as a fine, and in two states, the criminal court can state that if the order is not satisfied, imprisonment will result (also a remedy in England). In the Netherlands the compensation order is regarded as a criminal sanction, comparable to but not the same as tort liability, and the state enforces it as a criminal order.

165 Whenever non-civil law limits are put on the compensation vehicle, it moves closer to being a hybrid, or a criminal vehicle.

166 However, see, e.g., Chapter 2.2.E.1. text following n. 229, Chapter 5.5., Chapter 6.2.B.3. and Chapter 6.3.D.5., Chapter 8.4.C.7; Chapter 9.3.A., text to n. 62.

167 E.g., Chapter 3.3.A.1., text following n. 28, Chapter 7.2.C.1, n. 73 other than through the action of 'spuilzie': Chapter 7.3.A, text following n. 102.

168 Chapter 2.2.D.9.

169 E.g., Chapter 6.2.B.3.

Of the states that treat the compensation vehicle as a purely civil claim, any resulting order is a civil one. Thus the burden is on the person aggrieved to enforce it and the risk on him that the enforcement fails, for instance, through the defendant's impecuniosity. Sweden and the Netherlands are exceptional in having the state guarantee certain instances of compensation, paying the victim if the defendant fails to and leaving the state to go after the defendant, perhaps over a longer period of time than could be expected of the victim.

e) **State and inter-state rules** Some states choose to take on greater moral and legal obligations to victims than others. This is particularly evident from the role of state actors, the social security system, legal aid for litigation, quasi-official bodies acting to support victims and the extent of state compensation funds to the victims of violent crime. However, the role of the victim in the legal process has long also been a matter of international concern,[170] though it is only recently that such concern has matured into domestic legal change. The Council of Europe and the UN took a particular interest in the 1980s. After some earlier measures,[171] International Recommendation (85)11 of the Council of Europe (1985) on the position of the victim in criminal law and procedure gave sixteen guidelines for promoting the victim's role in the justice system.[172] The UN victims' Declaration of 1985 covered a number of procedural and protective rights, including 'fair restitution' covering compensation and recovery of property.[173] The European Union has also been active, both through the European Court of Justice[174] and through legislation. Legislative efforts began with Decision 2001/220/JHA on 15 March 2001 on the standing of victims in criminal proceedings. This gave rights to information, protection, participation and compensation (specifically, under Art. 10, within a reasonable time, adequate and

[170] E.g., Howard Association, 'Paris Prison Congress: Summary Report' (London: The Howard Association, 1895).

[171] E.g., European Convention on the Compensation of Victims of Violent Crimes, 24 November 1983.

[172] For detail, see Hoegen and Brienen, 'Victims of Crime'; and more recently Recommendation Rec (2006)8 of the Committee of Ministers to member states on assistance to crime victims.

[173] General Assembly, Declaration of Basic Principles of Justice for Victims of Crime and Abuse of Power, A/RES/40/34 of 29 November 1985, Articles 8–11, and in default, the state should compensate, Articles 12–13; see e.g., UNODCCP *Handbook on Justice for Victims* (New York, 1999), 42–9.

[174] E.g., Case 186/87 *Cowan* v. *Tresor Public* [1990] 2 CMLR 613.

including the recovery of property). Implementation of this measure was unimpressive, so after the Lisbon Treaty gave the EU greater legislative powers over justice matters, a Directive was passed in December 2012. Many articles of the Directive are the same as the Framework Decision, such as those on compensation, but there are also more and more detailed rules. Member states have three years in which to implement the Directive, so minimally harmonising some of the law for victims. However, its high level of generality with respect to compensation makes it particularly unclear in the short term how much will change. Finally, the European Court of Human Rights has generally not applied Article 6(1) European Convention of Human Rights (right to a fair trial), to civil claims within a criminal process though it will do so in a limited way in certain circumstances.[175] Finally, there is EU Directive 2014/42 on freezing and confiscation of proceeds of crime,[176] Art. 8.10 of which provides that: confiscation shall not prejudice the rights of the victim to compensation of damages.

3. Trial process

The final aspect of procedure to be discussed is how trial procedure varies across tort and crime, and what that means. This is a vast area, involving narrow legal rules and complex questions of advocate, court and witness practice. Four examples will be briefly noted: legal frameworks, evidence and procedure in practice, suspension rules and *res judicata.*

a) Legal framework Civil and criminal procedures in the modern world tend to be clear, certain and collated in a code or similar collection.[177] This might seem natural in civil law systems, but it is somewhat surprising in the common law, particularly in England, where the codification movement has generally had less success. However, in the last twenty years a movement towards clarity in legal procedure has produced a number of new and consolidated legislative measures. While reforming its rules it has often compared and linked the civil and criminal rules.

175 See M. Chiavario, 'The Rights of the Defendant and Victim' in M. Delmas-Marty and J. R. Spencer (eds.) *European Criminal Procedures* (Cambridge University Press, 2002), 544–5.

176 OJ 2014 L127 / 39

177 Civil procedure rules seem not to sub-divide between tort, contract or other civil claims, though of course some rules do not apply to one area or another as a practical matter. Otherwise, it seems criminal law usually has its own rules, and the one other area likely to have its own rules is Administrative law, though they may be a sub-set of other rules.

For instance, Scotland has the Criminal Procedure (Scotland) Act 1995, almost a complete codification. As of 2013, it also has a Scottish Civil Justice Council which has already begun drafting civil procedure rules to replace the separate Councils and sets of rules for the Sheriff Court and Court of Session. The Sheriff Court has a civil and criminal jurisdiction, perhaps encouraging some fruitful comparison. Similarly, the relevant Act, the Scottish Civil Justice Council and Criminal Legal Assistance Act 2013 addressed in detail civil and criminal justice, which would be unlikely in England. In Australia, the Evidence Act 1995 (Cth) provides for almost all evidence and procedural questions for both civil and criminal legislation.[178] Many of those provisions are the same for tort and crime, though at the same time, a significant number are not. English law shows an even more developed linkage, with the Civil Procedure Rules 1998 being the model for the Criminal Procedure Rules 2013.[179] On the other hand, it is unclear that the well-established civil and criminal procedure codes on the continent have seen their rules exert a mutual or even one-directional influence. This is not surprising compared to England: there, in an age of austerity, the first criminal procedure 'code' looked to the recently passed and fully-researched civil rules for structure and even for some specific substance. What is remarkable is that the common law has much less trouble codifying, and linking its civil and criminal forms, for its legal frameworks for its evidential and procedural rules, than its substantive law.

b) Evidence and procedure in practice Similarity across evidential and procedural rules varies. In criminal law, there is an internal balance achieved in each system, between ensuring protections for the defendant in the trial, and ensuring the state's ability to enforce the law and, perhaps even, find the truth. In tort law, there is a difference between common and civil law traditions. In England, for example, the balance seems to focus slightly more on equality of arms between the parties with the judge taking on significant organisational case management authority since 1999. On the other hand, in civil law legal systems while the parties still lead in civil litigation, the role of the judge is more significant, especially with regard to obtaining evidence.[180] Three classic examples will be examined: the standard of proof, discovery and compellability of witnesses.

[178] Chapter 9.4.D.2.

[179] Chapter 2.2.E.3. para. preceding n. 263 through to the para ending in n. 272.

[180] E.g., Chapter 3.3.A. but cf. Chapter 6.3.B.2.

There is no doubt that all the legal systems in this study offer significant protection to the defendant, whether through common law or civil law traditions and, more recently, through the effect of the ECHR (excluding Australia). The protections include rights to a fair trial generally, the presumption of innocence, rights against at least some forms of self-incrimination and protections against certain forms of evidence being obtained or admitted. One matter that is not at all obvious is the standard of proof.[181] In the common law and Scotland, the criminal law requires facts to be proven beyond reasonable doubt, while the civil law requires the balance of probabilities. The picture in the civil law is more complex and what follows are going to be rough generalisations. It appears there is a similar standard of proof for civil and criminal law. However, it is not a legislative standard, indeed, Taruffo believes no civil law system has a legislative rule requiring civil courts to use the same standard as criminal ones.[182] In the civil standard greater focus may be placed on the personal belief of the judge rather than looking to an objective description of the likelihood of facts. It is hard to know in what contexts individual judges may require more certainty. It also hard for appellate review to intervene and show what is going on and set standards. It is also worth bearing in mind that in the common law, a standard of proof is usually closely allied with the obligation on parties to raise evidence to substantiate that proof. However, in civil law systems, shifts in that burden are more common.[183] Furthermore, the judge will often play a greater role in obtaining that evidence than in the common law, as might the prosecutor in providing evidence both for and against the defendant.[184] All legal systems face the problem of two competing versions of the facts, and courts will, whatever legal theory says, have some sense of the relative merits of the versions in mind.

Let us take some examples on the standard of proof from the civil law.[185] For instance, in France, criminal law and tort law admits evidence to prove facts under the principle of the 'freedom of proof', (as opposed to proof of a juridical act where written evidence is required). The Code of Criminal Procedure specifies that the guilt must be established to the judge's *intime conviction*.[186] In tort law like in criminal law, it appears also to be a question of the fact being proven according to the conviction of the judge. The civil

[181] See especially M. Taruffo, 'Rethinking the Standards of Proof' (2003) 51 *Am J Comp L* 659

[182] Ibid., 665. [183] E.g., Chapter 4.7.A., text to n. 193.

[184] E.g., Ibid., text to n. 188. [185] For a useful comparison, see Chapter 8.5.B.2.

[186] Art. 427(1) Code of Criminal Procedure.

standard, however, is somewhat unclear and is certainly not something that is discussed much in the literature. German law is slightly different, perhaps looking more to a conviction which can be supported by reasons. The relevant civil provision is §286(1) ZPO, giving the court discretion to determine the truth of an allegation. This should involve not just an assessment of probabilities, but also a personal process of the silencing of doubt.[187] The position in Spain seems a little uncertain, with a perception both that a higher standard of proof is required in criminal law and that in practice the difference will be slight.[188] There are two of our civil law countries which expressly have a different standard for civil and criminal law. In Sweden, in a criminal prosecution, the requirement is formulated as 'beyond reasonable doubt'. In a civil claim, it is required that the facts are 'shown' or 'proven' (a higher standard than 'clearly more likely than not' but lower than 'beyond reasonable doubt').[189] In the Netherlands, criminal cases require facts to be 'legally and convincingly proven' but in civil cases there need only be a 'reasonable degree of certainty' about them. It should not be forgotten that many legal systems have exceptional doctrines for adjusting the standard of proof in certain difficult cases, such as cases of the cancer mesothelioma caused by asbestos.[190]

As for gathering evidence in a pre-trial phase, comparisons are difficult as the nature and purpose of that phase is very different in tort and crime. For instance, in English law, civil disclosure is stronger than criminal disclosure, but there are more extensive powers to compel witnesses to attend in the criminal courts (albeit that even in civil courts witnesses can be fined, or, in the High Court, held in contempt of court, for non-attendance). By comparison, in Australia, both are largely the same in tort and crime. Yet both countries provide greater protection for vulnerable witnesses within the criminal law. Spanish law, though somewhat uncertain,[191] seems to have weak discovery proceedings in civil law, but when the claim is brought within a criminal prosecution, a range of powers like preliminary injunctions are much easier to obtain.[192] Dutch law puts greater obligations of disclosure and powers of compellability in the hands of the criminal prosecution and criminal courts, but an exact comparison with civil law is very difficult.[193] Swedish law does not

[187] C. Engel, 'Preponderance of the Evidence versus Intime Conviction: A Behavioral Perspective on a Conflict between American and Continental European Law' (2009) 33 *Vermont LR* 43, 40–1.

[188] Chapter 6.3.D.2. cf. Chapter 6.3.B.3., text following n. 51. [189] Chapter 5.4.D.

[190] Cf. Ch. 8.5.B.2. in the Netherlands with, e.g., Chapter 2.2.D.8., Chapter 3.4.A.2. and Chapter 8.5.B.2.

[191] Chapter 6.3.D.2. [192] Cf. Chapter 6.3.B.2. [193] Chapter 8.5.B.5.

recognise 'disclosure' powers, but does have rules to the effect that you can force your opponents to show documents that you know he has.

c) **Suspension rules** The majority of the systems studied have a formal rule to suspend a civil claim while a criminal prosecution is pending or ongoing. The suspension is mandatory in France,[194] Spain[195] and the Netherlands,[196] whereas there is a discretion to suspend in England, Germany,[197] Sweden,[198] and Australia.[199] That discretion is exercised commonly in the Netherlands but less so in Australia and even less so in England. The exception is Scotland,[200] where it appears that no rule on this exists. It is interesting that some states expressly note the link between a civil case suspending to allow a criminal prosecution to go forward with the reverse, a criminal court suspending in order for a civil matter to be determined. In Germany, for example, the criminal court does not need to suspend, but if it does, it does not need to follow the civil court's judgment.

In practice, criminal justice is typically faster than civil justice in any case, so even if brought first or soon after the criminal prosecution is begun, it is likely that the prosecution would conclude first. In any case, it will normally be in the claimant's interests to wait for the criminal prosecution to be complete: they might benefit from a compensation vehicle and they can at the very least use evidence and arguments deployed in the criminal trial and in some cases the conviction itself.

The reasons for such a rule vary. One reason is to avoid the risk of conflicting judgments: in France this is commonly put as 'guarantee[ing] compatibility', in Spain avoiding '*resoluciones contradictorias*'.[201] This is not a reason in the Netherlands, which seems to be more pragmatic, noting criminal justice is faster and might provide any desired compensation anyway, that a conviction would provide compelling evidence in any later civil claim and that it is effective case management. Another possible reason is institutional competence, in that matters of criminal law inherent in a claim should be decided by a criminal court. English law is exceptional. There (but not in Scotland) all a convicted felon's property was forfeited

194 Chapter 3.3.C.

195 Chapter 6.3.C.1; noting the interesting divergence between the civil and the criminal procedure rules.

196 Chapter 8.4.C.6. 197 Chapter 4.7.B. 198 Chapter 5.4.B.4.

199 Chapter 9.4.D.1. 200 Chapter 7.2.

201 E.g. Núria Reynal Querol *La prejudicialidad en el proceso civil* (Barcelona : J. M. Bosch, 2006), 141–2.

to the Crown until 1870; the state was therefore financially interested in private persons prosecuting as well as being interested for the sake of society itself. This all shifted in the twentieth century. First, the mandatory suspension rule, which had only ever applied to the more serious crimes, felonies, was abolished when the distinction between misdemeanour and felony was abolished in 1967. However, twelve years later, under the influence of Australian case law, a remarkable shift happened. A rule on the same question was created which gave a discretion to suspend in order to protect the defendant from having to reveal his defence in a civil case instead of saving it for the criminal trial. This ultimately brings the common law into the same balancing act as many other jurisdictions: a suspension should not be used as a tactical tool to pressure the defendant by extending litigation,[202] nor delay the criminal court from doing its duty.[203]

d) ***Res judicata*** Where a civil court is presented with a claim in respect of which there is a relevant conviction, it has five options:

(1) *Independence*: ignore the conviction and decide the matter entirely on its own. Only some Australian jurisdictions do this and even there the defendant's admissions in a criminal court are admissible.[204]

(2) *Evidential*: admit the conviction as evidence of the facts upon which it must have been founded. This is the (statutory) position in England and Scotland.[205] Since tortious and criminal wrongs are not normally substantively aligned, a conviction cannot normally bind a later court about liability itself. There is a further difficulty in jurisdictions, like England and Australia, which use juries in criminal cases since they do not specify what facts they find when they give their verdict. However, if the judge's directions are clear, it should be possible to establish what the jury must have found in order to convict. The conviction is normally strong evidence.

(3) *Persuasive*: the conviction represents a competent judicial investigation of the facts; comity and respect suggest the second court should have respect for the outcome of that investigation. The

202 Chapter 2.2.E.2., n. 257. and Chapter 3.3.C., paras. following n. 62 through to para ending with n. 68.

203 E.g., Chapter 4.7.B.5.: noting especially § 262(2) StPO.

204 Other jurisdictions in Australia adopt other solutions, such as Queensland's rebuttable presumption that the conviction proves facts and the defendant's state of mind: Chapter 9.4.D.3.

205 At common law a conviction is not even admissible: it is treated as a *res inter alios acta*: Chapter 2.2.E.2., text to nn. 253–7; Ch.7.2.B., text to nn. 64–9.

conviction will normally be followed (Germany),[206] or will have a 'very strong influence' (Sweden)[207] or serve as 'compelling evidence' (the Netherlands)[208] on potentially all the determinations of the civil court (substantive and factual).

(4) *Binding*: the conviction binds a later civil court, for instance, by *res judicata*. This is normally positive, as in France, but in Spain it can also be negative: a criminal court can determine that the defendant did not commit the crime or that the crime itself did not happen at all.[209] In France the conviction is binding in regard to substantive and factual elements: the existence of a causal link between the defendant's act and the harm to the victim, of intentional or negligent misconduct, of the specific harm and of various material facts. In Spain, only findings of fact are binding so the modern position is that their rules are not 'full' *res judicata*.

(5) *Differentiation*: whatever general position is adopted, have a different treatment for certain wrongs. For instance, in an English defamation case, a conviction is irrebuttably presumed to be proof of the facts upon which it must be founded while in other civil actions the conviction is only (strong) evidence.

Weaker effects tend to be supported by more practical reasons, such as the wasted costs of re-litigating, though they can include the risk of implied criticism of the criminal justice process should a civil judge find differently to the conviction. The decisive factor in the common law was how the public would perceive a civil judgment undermining a criminal conviction. Stronger effects tend to have further or other justifications, such as the pre-eminence of the criminal system and its methods, as in France, or perhaps the unity of the legal system or its cohesion and efficiency, as in the Netherlands.

In the reverse situation, should a civil case come before a criminal one, itself unlikely, the judgment is never treated as authoritative on the facts. Of course, in practice, the process of gathering evidence for the civil case may make a later criminal prosecution easier to substantiate. It also

[206] Chapter 4.7.B.5.: 'The judge in the civil procedure has to consider the legal relevance of the criminal judgment himself: § 286 ZPO. However, if the civil court does not have serious doubts about the accuracy of the judgment and especially the facts that it is based on, it must adopt the findings of the criminal court. Consequently a civil judge will normally follow his colleagues from the criminal court.'

[207] Chapter 5.4.C. [208] Chapter 8.4.C.4.

[209] Art. 116 LECrim, though it does so rarely; this is obviously far more than the mere acquittal, for instance, through failing to persuade the judge of the charge.

appears that procedural methods to prevent 'collateral attacks' on earlier convictions are a significant development of the common law, not other legal systems.[210]

4. Procedures compared

Procedure is the chief *locus* of tort/crime interactions in most systems for at least three reasons.

First, procedure is where any alleged interaction would have to be given form and steps must exist to deal with any disputes which arise. Such challenges will arise wherever legal actors see an advantage in attempting to link them, especially where any potential superiority of the criminal law rules can be exploited.

Second, as in substantive law, comparisons of procedural rules may be more obvious where those rules are seen to interfere with the established legal framework, or legal actors' perceptions of it. In France, the rules on the *partie civile* are expressly recognised as exceptional, and thus requiring a balance of rights against responsibilities. The German *Adhäsionsverfahren* is embedded in the criminal procedure code, but because it is practically less useful and, importantly, perceived as anomalous, it is almost never used. The Dutch have, in effect, created a new category of legal thought: the 'crush' on victims. This category has begun to transcend other established rules, though slowly and against resistance. In Spain, the substantive differences in *ex delicto* liability are perhaps more anomalous than the procedural interaction, but even there the pressure from victims seeking to use criminal courts has pushed towards even further over-criminalisation: in theory but especially in practice. This is highlighted by the use of a dedicated and derogatory term by some in Spain, to describe a civil claim filed within a criminal proceeding just to coerce the opposing party to a monetary settlement, a 'Catalonian criminal complaint'.[211] By contrast, in Sweden, the links between tort and crime are part of a long historical tradition and are less controversial, and also some of the most developed.

Third, procedure is a confluence of important principles. Some are pragmatic, such as the Dutch and arguably the French, Swedish and Spanish. Even the more minimal links in the common law and Scotland have been influenced by practical concerns. This practical concern meets

[210] Chapter 2.2.E.2, text to n. 256; Chapter 9.4.D.3. text to n. 183–4.

[211] Chapter 6.3.D.2., text to n. 68.

other important factors like the unity of the legal system, its coherence and it being free from 'contradictions'.

Germany is the interesting exception, where procedural rules do not strongly link tort and crime. There, pragmatic requirements and legal actors' perceptions of how the system does or should operate seem to push out procedural links. The normative framework for tort and crime is thought sufficiently to answer questions or problems which elsewhere might be dealt with by comparing or linking tort and crime. Though some of the detail of this answer is contested in the academic literature, it is even more disappointing to victims. In 2000, 1 per cent of Local Court cases had civil claims for harm appended to the criminal process, despite 97 per cent of victims saying they would like that to happen.[212] Of course, many lay people would like the law to do something it does not. Those same victims typically benefit from affordable civil claims, because of both low court fees and the extensive insurance cover available. That said, it is perhaps surprising that insurance companies have not been incentivised to encourage a cheaper solution than two separate court proceedings. That said, in many cases where there are insurers on both sides, an out of court settlement is much more likely in practice, a settlement which will not necessarily follow the rules of delict.[213]

E. Resolutions

There are different remedies across tort and crime and the outcomes have a significant effect on when each area of law is called in aid. For instance, if an aggrieved person can obtain satisfaction by criminal law as much as civil law, he will likely turn to the faster, cheaper and less burdensome process. To that end, criminal courts have a far wider range of resolutions than the civil law, giving them greater flexibility to deal with the interests of the state as well, potentially, as the person aggrieved. These resolutions include cautions, fines, community penalties, drug rehabilitation orders and suspended sentences through to imprisonment in various forms. By contrast, in civil courts the most common remedies are an order to pay a sum of money and an injunction to do or refrain from doing something, with the most severe sanction being a bankruptcy order. However, these orders are imbued with varying levels of meaning, sanction, censure and implications of risk making comparison more difficult: for instance, an

212 See, e.g., Siegismund, 'Ancillary (Adhesion) Proceedings', 108–9.

213 Chapter 4.1.B.

arrest may bar you from getting a visa to some states even if no charges were laid; even a County Court judgment might have implications for a credit rating for years. Finally, the impact of different remedies may in fact be counterintuitive. Sometimes the burden of compensating will far exceed the punishment the criminal law would apply.

The interaction of different remedies is also important. For instance, some of our systems, like the French and the German systems, formally reduce, defer or abstain from punishment where the defendant compensates the victim.[214] Many other states almost certainly have informal mechanisms to do so, whether within general discretions exercised by prosecutors or judges, hybrid remedies, or even in the post-sentencing phase through assessing parole or early-release conditions. Such a payment may even result in no claim being made where the victim must claim (or where, in Spain, it is renounced) or even where the civil part of the criminal proceedings is settled. Otherwise, where the criminal compensation vehicle is a civil order, it tends not to be *formally* related to the criminal orders of the court. That said, a defendant of little means who has been imprisoned for a crime has effectively lost the ability to earn money to pay off the civil award against him. This can be contrasted with Hybrid orders since they typically encourage specific rules about the priority of the claim. For instance, in England the compensation order takes priority over a fine and even a confiscation order; in Australia someone who has been convicted and suffered a substantial punishment should not be liable for punitive damages.[215] This is another example of hybrid orders, existing outside of, or indeed, in defiance of, the established legal order; it also shows how much more noticeable such hybrids can be and what special rules they often engender. Another example is the *sanction-réparation* introduced in France in 2007. The convicted defendant must compensate the victim, either by paying him damages by a certain date, or by making good the damage in kind. The victim must consent to this sanction and the chosen form of reparation. When imposing a *sanction-réparation*, the court also sets the maximum term of imprisonment (which cannot exceed six months), or the total sum of the fine (which cannot exceed 15,000 Euro) in case of default.[216] Similarly, in Sweden, 'discrimination compensation' (*diskrimineringsersättning*) was introduced in 2009 as a civil order. This *compensation*, rather than 'damages', was set up to encourage higher monetary awards in respect of discrimination by discouraging quantum being set by the (lower) levels of a crime victim.

[214] E.g., Chapter 3.4.B.2., Chapter 4.8.
[215] Chapter 9.4.D.3., text to n. 180.
[216] Chapter 3.4.B.2.

However, they combine the compensatory function with a punitive one, particularly one based on deterring further discriminatory behaviour.[217]

2. How have tort and crime interacted

Given the complexity of the 'where' in substantive and procedural law, it is no surprise that the national reports could devote less space to how, why and when tort and crime have interacted. The chapters, including this one, have therefore interspersed brief explanations with their descriptions of the law, from explanations of which four points are explored here.

First, it is important to understand exactly how tort and crime interact. There are three axes against which any interaction can be plotted to show how it has worked: *Equality/Hierarchy, Partition/Permeability, Directness/Indirectness.* Each describes a scale between two different characteristics of any interaction.

Equality/Hierarchy is one mode or axis, where objects within a legal system are given equal standing or ranked compared to objects in another domain of law. For instance, a common position on this axis is priority, such as a French or Spanish conviction binding all later courts, civil or criminal. By comparison, in England, convictions only became *admissible* as evidence in 1968 and are only conclusive of anything in a defamation claim.

Partition/Permeability describes the ability of objects to pass across the boundaries between domains of law. Partition is a pole of the axis Partition/Permeability which describes the use of a boundary between two domains. On the one hand, one domain could inhibit another from impacting it by setting up a boundary around the domain: a wall to keep things out. On the other hand, the same could be achieved by hardening the components within the domain so that any external influence is ineffective. Permeability is the absence of a boundary.

Directness/Indirectness describes the relationship between the place where the influence comes from and the place in which it is felt. For instance, a direct influence occurs where a rule of criminal law is integrated into the civil law in exactly the same place, such as where German (§ 823(2) BGB) and Dutch (Art. 6:162 *BW*) tort law imports criminal rules. An example of indirect influence would be where a substantive rule of criminal law is given effect through a rule of civil procedure, such as a rule suspending a civil claim while a prosecution is ongoing.

[217] Chapter 5.3.C.2., esp. para. accompanying n. 86 and Chapter 5.3.B.3.

The second point, drawing on these categories, is there are clear examples of rules and practices being 'transplanted' not only from legal system to legal system, but also within the same legal system. International transplants are common. Classic examples can be seen within the wider common law tradition: rules have spread from England (such as convictions being admissible as evidence in Scotland[218]) as well as to England from Australia (such as its modern suspension rules[219]). Others amongst our systems, for instance German, have also regularly been drawn upon conceptually and directly transplanted.[220] What might be called 'internal transplants' have also clearly taken place. They will tend to occur less noticeably where the object in question is legal reasoning, since the transplant will likely be adapted and re-phrased. Transplants within legal systems are therefore most obvious in the context of substantive rules. In a number of countries the general integrative techniques[221] are arguably methods of transplanting a rule from criminal law into tort law. We have also seen discrete transplants particularly in respect of causation rules in Spain and the Netherlands, described above[222] and there have been other examples.[223] Such transplants may seem simpler because both the object transplanted and the receiving location are within the same system. However, they can still raise difficult issues. For instance, other components, from donor or recipient area of law, may be required and thus complicate the transfer. An example might be where a criminal rule is transplanted even though it would, within criminal law, have a narrower interpretation than tort law would give it. The risk of such 'rooted' transplants is part of the reason for selecting hybridisation: by creating a chimaera you may make a monster, but one that at least can act independently. Furthermore, transplants may not entirely fit with the new area of law, even that area is part of the same legal system. As the Spanish example *ex delicto* liability shows, such transplants can remain 'irritating' for centuries.[224]

Third, the interactions between tort and crime occur through informal as well as formal means. For example, informal practices of legal actors in Scotland seem to have meant that certain rules do not need to have been laid down in significant areas of tort and crime. Sweden, by comparison, a larger but still small jurisdiction, does not have as many clear gaps in

218 Chapter 7.2.B.

219 Dyson, 'The Timing of Tortious and Criminal Actions', 99–101.

220 E.g., Chapter 6.4.C.1. 221 Section 1.C.1 above. 222 Section 1.C.5 above.

223 E.g., on defences, Section 1.C.7 above.

224 In Tuebner's language, see Chapter 1.4. text to n. 30.

its rules. In part that is because its system is designed to formally bring tort and crime closer together. Similarly, the Dutch 'ten minute' limit on adhesion claims is a rule of thumb created by judges to give flesh to the bones of the formal rule of preventing 'disproportionate burdens' on the criminal trial. In effect, a rule without legislative authority is the key limit on Dutch adhesion claims, in a country where the principle of legality forms the first article of their Criminal Code. There are also often rules to co-ordinate tort and crime, but which appear not to be used in practice. One important example is the bodies which exist in non-unitary court jurisdictions to settle disputes between different court branches, such as in France and Germany. It appears they are very rarely engaged across tort and crime, perhaps even less so than in other areas (but it is hard to be certain). There are also specific rules which appear to be rarely used, the German adhesion procedure being the obvious example.

Fourth, there may be important lessons by finding the pinch points where tort and crime come together most acutely in each system. For instance, mass product liability claims create significant difficulties of organisation and proof for civil litigation.[225] In Spain, mass product liability claims tend to be expressed through the criminal law, an obvious example of which is the *Colza Oil* case, important enough to be mentioned in that chapter's introduction.[226] Spanish civil law lacks effective rules for co-ordinating large numbers of claimants within the same procedure, while criminal prosecutors and courts are more able to do so, albeit by shifting problems elsewhere by making the criminal trial much more complex. This pinch point shows how the normal procedural reasons for interaction can be enlarged by one further benefit. Other pinch points are often remedial, for instance the range of mechanism employed to maximise the victim's chances of compensation from a convicted criminal.

3. Why have tort and crime interacted

A. Categories of reasons

Given the complexity of where and how tort and crime interact, it will come as no surprise that the reasons why they do are complex. The first step is loosely to categorise the reasons:

225 Hence, many national funds for contaminated blood victims.

226 Cf. also e.g., N. Coggiola and M. Graziadei, 'The Italian "Eternit Trial": Litigating Massive Asbestos Damage in a Criminal Court', in Willem H. van Boom and Gerhard Wagner (eds.) *Mass Torts in Europe: Cases and Reflections* (Berlin/Boston: de Gruyter, 2014).

(1) *Internal norms*: reasons which relate to the shape of the legal system. The most significant such reason is the importance attached to the homogeneity and intelligibility of the legal system. This can be expressed in a variety of forms, but is most commonly seen in some form of 'unity' or 'coherence'.
(2) *External norms*: calls to higher level principles in how specific interactions should take place. Classic examples of such principles include 'fairness', 'certainty' and 'intellectual robustness'.
(3) *Instrumental*: where the interaction is guided by the outcomes to be achieved. The most common forms of this are efficiency and regulation. Typically the law is used directly to achieve an end, but a side-constraint is the operative capacity of the law itself. This category therefore includes perceptions of non-legal actors of the law itself, a factor in how much it is esteemed and respected.
(4) *Institutional*: reasons why an institution, either a framework with associated norms or more commonly, a legal actor, is suited to a particular object. The most common form of this is competence, whether the framework or legal actor can process the interaction (cardinal competence) and whether it can do so better than alternatives (ordinal competence). There are other dimensions to competence, particularly against what qualities the competence is judged. The three most common are technical, cultural and resources. Overall, institutional reasons are practical, like instrumental ones, but they focus on the process, not on the outcome.
(5) *Political*: the law is shaped by its political implications. This clearly has legislative implications, such as what law can be passed in the first place. It also has non-legislative forms, such as the role of the victim and the political surroundings of judges.
(6) *Psychological*: reasons concerning the preferences and attitudes of the legal actors involved. The most commonly seen of these appears to be about power and authority, particularly in not wishing to lose power(s) already possessed.

B. *Balancing reasons*

How are these classes of reasons balanced in each interaction? The most common is to limit an interaction. For instance, French law accepts that the ability to force a prosecution is exceptional and should at least have protections against abuse, such as it only being available outside the most serious crimes and having liability for abusive claims. It may also be a constitutional protection, to ensure that prosecutors exercise their discretion to prosecute properly lest a victim intervene and force them to do so. The admissions limits known to other systems are more generally justified by seeking to avoid overburdening the criminal justice system, or, such as in the Netherlands, specifically in not delaying or burdening the *defendant.* They can also be linked to a concept of constitutional or institutional competence: that criminal courts are not the best places to determine all civil claims. Systems which have a separate hybrid order, especially the English and Australian compensation order, balance instrumental benefits against internal norms in the form of consistency, particularly where an order does not match an underlying civil wrong. By contrast, Spain's lack of balancing limits has been criticised: the focus on punishing the guilty in general misses the practical effects of too many prosecutions.

Three further issues merit future investigation. First, most of the information on each interaction comes from a subjective viewpoint, bound up in the same preferences and attitudes that are under scrutiny. The perceptions of the national legal actor guide their reasoning process. For instance, based on the way the chapters were written, it seems that some of our systems (particularly the German) reach for their norms early; others, like the common law, reach for them later, if at all. Second, such subjective perceptions will also cloud the process of balancing these reasons, but it is unclear whether they do so in the same way as they affect the individual reasons themselves. Third, some of these reasons may be combined in interesting ways. On the one hand, some may commonly be packaged together, for instance institutional and constitutional reasons. This packaging may be context-dependent just as much as actor-dependent.

C. *Patterns in practical reasoning*

Having identified what kinds of reasons are used in what ways, we might now turn to the kinds of patterns in which those reasons get expressed. Here we will pick up some recurring ideas: comparative structure, legal frameworks, path dependency, crucibles and feedback mechanisms.

First, to analyse these reasons we should not forget the comparative structure of how they occur. By plotting each interaction of tort and crime against these axes you can compare those interactions more meaningfully. In particular, it can help you push past the fact of the interaction, to see how and why it works. For example, in all but some of the Australian jurisdictions, a conviction is at least admissible in later relevant civil proceedings. A key everyday reason for this is to avoid wasting time and effort proving something that has already been proven to a high standard. In fact, in England the tipping point for the rules to change was cases in the 1960s where convicted criminals used defamation to sue anyone who said they committed the crime, using that tort's 'presumption of a good reputation' and the civil jury to undermine the conviction, since the defendant would have to prove everything from scratch. Only when the sanctity of the criminal law was challenged, did English law respond. By contrast, the French justify their rules (*res judicata*) on the pre-eminence of the criminal domain, not on its appearance to lay people or on the practical efficiency of the solution.

Second, while it is important to have a neutral set of standards against which to assess each system, the national framework, or 'mental map' can have a decisive influence on the interactions between tort and crime. This is certainly the case in Germany and Sweden while less comprehensive and/or unchallenged structures shape the law in France, Spain and the Netherlands. The framework in the common law and to some extent Scotland is less theoretical, focused instead on presumptive separation combined with practical solutions interactions. Whatever the structure, it seems to take a certain amount of pressure to shift from the established framework. One such tipping point is the relatively late build-up of victim-related pressure in the Netherlands, ultimately leading to very significant reform once the moral and political cases were made and given a practical form. By contrast, one example which has not yet reached enough pressure to tip over is punitive damages in France, Spain and the Netherlands. An important question is where such tipping points occur. In recent years legislators have made pinpoint changes, rather than anything as systematic as their forebears once did. These changes tend to focus on criminal law, affecting tort indirectly. This is even the case in the Australian jurisdictions, despite them having had significant tort reform in the early 2000s. The border of tort is being determined, in part, by the primarily legislative development of the criminal law. Other examples relate to courts, such as the tip in causation in Spain (crime to tort) and the Netherlands (tort to crime).

Third, as discussed in the introduction, path dependency describes how legal actors, faced with a new problem, avoid the cost and risk of innovative thinking by adapting ideas and techniques they already have. They rummage within their notional box of solutions, carrying out bricolage rather than going back to the drawing board. The common law has not seriously countenanced instituting an adhesion or *partie civile* procedure, but it was willing to create a new hybrid order, similar to a fine and to orders to restore property (as well as other niche orders to pay compensation in specific statutory provisions). While French law has seen some changes in the last fifteen years, they have not affected civil liability itself by and large. French law still allows the criminal courts to deal with civil claims but have restricted *parties civiles* from exposing the defendant to the risk of a large civil liability as a result of a criminal trial.[227] German lawyers do not find much doubtful or contradictory in their relationship between tort and crime, to an extent that is surprising even accepting that lawyers can tend towards the conservative. Scots and Australian law have developed their tort and crime relatively consistently. Even Dutch law, now so keen on promoting the welfare of the victim, has not done much more than tweak its remedies.

Sweden and Spain give us pause for thought. They both put their norms for regulating compensation within the criminal code, a novel step in the mid-1800s. However, we must examine this change further. Change itself was not unusual then: this was a period of significant legal change, with the codification movement sweeping across Europe. What is unusual is that these two countries did not follow the model of separate 'pure' civil and criminal codes that was unrolling across Europe. In Sweden, tort and crime were already closely associated, so the Criminal Code holding the compensatory norms until a Civil Code was passed was new, but only as new as having separate civil and criminal rules. Swedish law's links between tort and crime have evolved, from *bot* through to generalist lower courts and extensive civil adhesion and victim prioritisation. Nonetheless, in some ways, the closeness of the bond has not changed, even if court structures and the nature of the claim have changed. In addition, the changes that have happened have taken decades, even while the criminal code contained the civil provisions. Similarly, in Spain, the *Siete Partidas* had had some examples of civil and criminal rules interspersed. However, its rules linking the two were nascent at best and it was in the second criminal code, of 1848, by which time the civil/criminal distinction was better established, that the transposition took place, not the first of 1822. Nonetheless, the same reasons, the difficulty in passing a civil code and the belief in the importance of establishing at least these civil compensatory rules, was the same as in Sweden. However, this shift drew on the historical position in Sweden, whilst in Spain, against it.

[227] Such as the Acts of 2000 (in/direct causation), Chapter 3.3.B.1 and 2007 (suspension), Chapter 3.3.C.

Path dependency may be harder to measure the more complex the legal system is: the more inherent specialisation and variety, the more statements about a particular legal actor's path and his dependency on it lose context. There will be a greater range of paths, and the dependency to each becomes a relative statement. It would be quite possible for a solution from another specialisation to be both path dependent and path independent, depending on whom you were describing.

Fourth, there is the role of crucibles for the interactions of tort and crime. Much like the pinch points described in how tort and crime interact, there may be characteristics of where the reasons are mixed that affects how they are mixed. One key example is the role of the state. The state is the ultimate safeguard of the legal system itself, both civil and criminal courts, and in our systems it provides a broader safety net to prevent anyone who suffers loss from falling too far. It also plays a more specific role in the relationship of tort and crime. It punishes and coerces, sanctions and censures, prosecutes and in many cases aids substantially in how the victim's interests in the criminal trial are pursued. This is important because the state itself is a special nexus of different reasons for the interactions between tort and crime, particularly constitutional reasons.

Fifth, the law can develop in part through feedback mechanisms. There are a number of other procedural rules and practical implications which make the criminal justice system in Spain an attractive route for many civil claims, perhaps too attractive. This risk does not seem to have been acted upon by legislators. Similar fears, at least in a particular context, in France, led to the legislation of 2000 and 2007 to limit pressure on criminal courts. By comparison, when first introduced, English compensation in a criminal court required an application by the victim. However, by trial and error it was realised that the best way for criminal courts to ensure compensation is to inform victims and gather evidence from them and require a judge to give reasons if she does not give a compensation order where she could.[228] The new hybrid remedies of the last decade in France, Spain and the Netherlands show a similar pattern.

Feedback mechanisms are most easily effective where there is a process to respond to how rules work in practice. A judge is often the first to come across and potentially respond to such situations. This may make it more suited to tort law, almost uniformly a judge-made area of law; and, in the common law, perhaps within criminal courts as well. Legislative

[228] Chapter 2.2.E.1., text to n. 214–17.

mechanisms for feedback can also be effective, as the French and English examples show, but tends to take longer. It might be possible to have a detailed legislative regime for tort law, but so far such a regime has not taken root, certainly not in any of our systems.

D. The 'other' comparisons

There are three other comparisons to consider. First, why tort and crime have ignored each other may be revealing. This might be thought of as an interaction where the distance between them was created deliberately, or where path dependency turns the minds of legal actors away from comparisons or links without them realising it.

Second, we might consider what is distinctive about tort and crime: is tort/crime different to other overlaps of legal categories? How much have the developments affecting tort and crime stemmed from an underlying cause rather than something linked to one or other of them?

Third, we cannot compare the law of tort and crime without understanding where 'law' ends and something else begins. If the state reduces the amount it supports the victims of crime because a choice was made to put more money into education instead, is that a legal, economic or political decision? There may be a particular group of social, economic, philosophical and legal elements relevant to both tort and crime which we must understand to understand the law. The mystique surrounding 'the victim' in the last few decades has had an incredible impact within the laws of European countries particularly, re-orientating aspects of the legal system, sometimes to great lengths. Even in Germany, where the victim is not the focus of as great political and legal attention within criminal justice, the EU level rules are raising the profile of victims. Australia sits at the lower end of the spectrum, with a growing victim's movement, but one not yet as prominent as in many of our systems. What is interesting is that in Australia and England, perhaps elsewhere too, the 'victim' language was portrayed as inappropriate in tort law. If anything, in Australia insurers managed to portray themselves as the 'victims' of the tort system in the early 2000s, and that led to significant curtailments in the extent of tort protection.

4. When have tort and crime interacted

The volume is not an exercise in legal history, but it has highlighted a number of important historical points. Four points will be noted briefly here.

First, it can be revealing to probe why change happened *when it did*, and not earlier or later. There are numerous examples in the chapters of where pressures for change had not yet become strong enough to tip the law over into a new position. A particularly interesting example is why it was that French law shifted in 2000: why did the pressure on mayors coalesce in legal change then, not earlier or later. It may be a matter of political opportunity as much as the timing or a notorious case, perhaps with a key victim or indeed, the media interest relative to other events.

Second, some wider trends can be seen. Generally, a liberalising trend is evident in most legal systems over the last two hundred years: criminal law has given a wider role to the victim, even if France is still the only country where the aggrieved person can be a full party to the proceedings and can even force a prosecution. Recently, most of our systems have moved towards hybridisation. This has been where a new legal object has been created by blending existing ones to obtain the strengths of the originals without their limitations. This tends to take place as 'localised knotting', that is, greater complexity and overlapping ideas in one area of law. The law has become more specialised and some tort and crime locations, particularly remedies and resolutions, have been become hybridised. Such hybridisation usually takes place to achieve a particular end without the limitations of existing rules linked to 'pure' versions of the law.

Third, change will tend to be faster when effected within the established legal framework. The other possibility is that the framework itself might be adjusted or abandoned, a significant hurdle. However, frameworks vary in exactly how rigid they are or can be made to be. The German framework is perceived to be rigid, but in fact provides a great deal of explanatory power even for variation and change. Sometimes these changes map onto other trends in politics, society and intellectual movements. This is probably the case in the Dutch crush on victims from the 1990s, and in the institution of a compensation order in England and Scotland in the 1970s. Sometimes such movements are delayed, having needed time for political or social forces to build momentum to affect that change. It is harder to establish change from the other direction, that legal actors are able to originate that change, using law to change political or social forces.

Fourth, there may be a differential in the rate of change of tort and crime. For instance, English, Scottish and Australian tort law has shown a willingness to branch and adapt new torts, typically categorising them differently. French law has famously created new forms of liability, particularly for things under Article 1384. On the other hand, criminal legal change is led by legislation. It is an interesting question for future research whether the dynamics of legal change in each area, and each's effect on the other, leads to different speeds of development within them.

5. Conclusion

The purpose of this work has been to identify and analyse the comparisons and links that are made and that could be made between tort and crime. The introduction set out the methodological underpinnings of the work. The chapters told the national stories of tort and crime in eight significant legal systems. The questionnaire set out some of the key questions and gave shape to the conception of national stories, but each chapter is a distinctive approach to the one legal system. As a minimum, each asked where, how, why and when tort and crime have interacted, with a focus particularly on 'where'. This concluding chapter has analysed some of the most important findings across those chapters and sought to use them to understand the relationship between tort and crime better, both nationally and through frameworks to compare across jurisdictions. There is much more work to be done in unravelling the complex and important relationship between these two areas. The goal is that we can explain the nuance of 'tort' and 'crime' as much as we can 'English law' or 'French law'.

APPENDIX: CASE STUDY

1. Introduction

This case study was designed to provide a check on the method of the questionnaire and workshops by testing a practical case on the border of tort and crime. The issue for the case study was:

> *Two defendants, D1 and D2, steal V's car and drive off, being chased by the police. D1 tells D2 to drive faster and more dangerously to escape. D2 does, but loses control and crashes the car, injuring D1. D2 has limited financial resources, as does D1. The car is recovered by the police.*
>
> *Would the situation be any different if D1 and D2 tried to escape on a boat which then crashed in the same way?*
>
> *Or, would it be any different if D1 and D2 did not commit theft but punched V and broke V's nose, then tried to escape on foot?*

The responses below show interesting similarities and some noticeable differences. The problem is conceived of in similar ways, by and large, though some of our systems have specialised rules or approaches for road traffic accidents compared to river traffic. However, the systems do diverge on how redress will be granted for these wrongs. In particular, the national answers have demonstrated a further significant difference in the tort law defences of our legal systems. In the common law, a specific defence of joint illegality has been developed, but this does not appear to be the case in most civil law systems. In civil law systems, such claims might otherwise be dismissed, for instance, by an adjustment of the standard of care, causation or another defence, like consent or contributory negligence. Above all, the relatively simple question and its two alternatives help us to see how the problem is conceived and how it would work its way through our legal systems.

2. England

A. *First scenario*

D1 and D2 have committed various offences prohibited by criminal law. If they intended to take the car and deprive V of it permanently (broadly defined) then they have committed theft contrary to Theft Act 1968, s. 1(1). If they were using the car as a means of escape which they would later abandon, not intending that the owner lose it, they have committed the offence of vehicle taking, contrary to s. 12 of the same Act, or – given that damage and injury has been caused – the aggravated version of the offence under s.12A. Their driving dangerously is an offence under Road Traffic Act 1988, s. 2, and if D1's injuries were serious an aggravated offence under s. 1A of the same Act.

D1's claim in negligence is, absent the criminal offence of dangerous driving, simple. The mere fact that the car was stolen would not be enough to prevent a civil claim between D1 and D2, but relatively recent jurisprudence on joint illegality would likely bar the claim between D1 and D2. Perhaps the earliest clear example of this is *Pitts* v. *Hunt* in 1990.[1] The plaintiff was a pillion passenger on a motorcycle which was involved in a collision with an oncoming vehicle, killing the motor cyclist and injuring the plaintiff. Both the plaintiff and motorcyclist had been drinking prior to the accident, the plaintiff knew the motorcyclist did not hold a driving licence and was uninsured, and at the time of the accident he was encouraging the motorcyclist to drive in a reckless and dangerous manner. The plaintiff's claim in negligence was dismissed at first instance and on appeal to the Court of Appeal. The latter reasoned from the principle *ex turpi causa non oritur actio*, previously known well in contract but thitherto only hypothesised to apply in tort.[2] In addition to that principle, which could operate as a form of defence, there may be circumstances where no duty of care was owed between someone committing a crime and another person aiding and abetting that crime. Since 1972 the defence of consent, *volenti non fit injuria*, had been removed from motor vehicle situations, otherwise it might have applied.

Even if a claim against him were successful on these facts, D2 almost certainly does not have the means to satisfy it. It is unlikely that he held a policy of insurance with cover extending to driving another's (here V's) car, but even if there was a relevant contract of insurance in place, it would almost certainly contain a clause excluding cover for criminal activities like taking the car. In this way, the contractual reach of a criminal provision is broader than the approach taken within *ex turpi causa*, as there the wrongdoing must be sufficiently connected to the wrong done,[3] not merely creating its background as taking the car does. Thus D2 is likely to be uninsured. The Motor Insurers' Bureau has an agreement with the Government to cover uninsured and untraced drivers for

[1] [1990] 1 QB 302, affirmed [1991] 1 QB 24. This decision was recently applied by the Court of Appeal in *Joyce* v. *O'Brien* [2013] EWCA Civ 546; [2013] Lloyd's Rep IR 523.

[2] The only prior reported tort case where such a defence was mooted was *Ashton* v. *Turner* [1981] QB 137, 146–8. See however the earlier *obiter dictum* of Lord Asquith in *National Coal Board* v. *England* [1954] AC 403, 429.

[3] *Vellino* v. *Chief Constable of Greater Manchester* [2001] EWCA Civ 1249; [2002] 1 WLR 218.

the benefit of victims. They do so out of contributions from motor vehicle insurers in England. However, again this agreement limits cover for those committing crimes. Similarly, a claim V might have for any damage to the car would likely be unsatisfied, though the police would return the car to V.

B. Second scenario

In the alternative involving the boat, English law would make no substantial difference. Alternative criminal offences exist for the dangerous steering of a boat. English tort law uses the same basic principles for liability for negligent car driving as for negligent boat steering. However, no similar body to the MIB is known about for boats (or other vehicles).

C. Third scenario

In the alternative where no vehicle is taken, but V's nose is broken, tortious and criminal liability unsurprisingly remain. D1 and D2 are liable in tort and, depending on the level of harm, guilty of assault occasioning actual bodily harm contrary to Offences Against the Persons Act 1861, s. 47 or causing/inflicting grievous bodily harm contrary to ss. 20 and 18 of the same Act (if they had intended to break V's nose, they charge would be under s. 18, otherwise s. 20). It is unclear on the facts as stated whether they each committed the wrong, making them both principals, or one did so, while the other assisted or encouraged. So long as each party at least assisted or encouraged, English law draws no distinction between them as to their trial and possible punishment.[4] If convicted, a criminal court could make a compensation order against D1 and D2, but is required to take account of the means of the defendant and neither of them have the resources to compensate V. In tort the claim would be by V against D1 and D2 for trespass to the person, and more specifically battery. The tort is actionable *per se* so no harm need actually be shown, but serious physical injury has been suffered so recovery of general damages for pain, suffering and loss of amenity is possible, together with special damages in respect of medical expenses, lost income and related costs. Tort law also allows the possibility of a claim against another who encouraged a tort, but such actions are very rare.

However, what makes this situation different from the vehicle examples is that as the victim of a crime of violence, V could apply for monetary compensation under the Criminal Injuries Compensation Scheme. This state scheme will pay out compensation, based on a tariff rather than on *restitutio in integrum*. It is an administrative process with certain thresholds and hurdles, such as a minimum amount of loss or harm suffered. If V did not already know about the

[4] Accessories and Abettors Act 1861.

CICS, it is highly likely that the police would inform him when investigating the crime. This is the most likely avenue for V in the third scenario.

3. France

A. Procedure: how does this matter come before the courts?

The police officers who found the car and arrested D1 and D2 inform the prosecutor, who will take the matter before a criminal court. The facts in this case are straightforward and do not justify the involvement of an examining magistrate.

The prosecutor can use any one of the following methods to bring the matter before a court:

(1) A summons (Art. 550 et seq. CPP);
(2) A summons by police report followed by an immediate hearing (Art. 393 et seq. CPP);
(3) An appearance on prior admission of guilt: this is an option offered under Art. 495–7 CPP for those offences carrying a prison sentence of less than five years, as is the case in this particular set of facts. Where this option is chosen, Articles 495–13 et seq. CPP will regulate the civil party's claim.

The victim of the theft can join the criminal proceedings by claiming compensation for the harm suffered as a result of the theft; she is then described as acting 'by means of intervention'. Similarly, D1 can claim compensation for the harm he suffered as a result of the car crash.

B. Legal characterisation of the facts

The criminal court hearing the matter will characterise the facts of the case as follows:

(1) Theft of the vehicle (D1 and D2 are co-perpetrators);
(2) Direct exposure of another person to an immediate risk of death of injury by way of dangerous driving (which may be imputed to both D1 and D2);
(3) Involuntary injury to D1's physical integrity by D2. This classification is possible insofar as D1's own actions do not break the chain of causation between D2 and the harm to D1.

C. Compensation

The criminal court will then rule on the two civil actions:

(1) Regarding the civil action brought by the victim of the theft: the court may award compensatory damages and order the vehicle's restitution since it was recovered by the police officers.

(2) Regarding the civil action brought by D1: compensatory damages may be awarded whether D2 is convicted or not. Indeed, Art. 470–1 CPP allows the criminal judge to award compensation regardless of D2's potential discharge; the damage award will then be made on the basis of civil rather than criminal law rules.

Different (civil) rules will then apply depending on whether D1 and D2 were fleeing by boat or by car.

1. If D1 and D2 fled by car

The law of 5 July 1985 on road traffic accidents and compensation for personal injury applies. The claim may be brought either against the driver of the vehicle or its owner (both because he is the guardian of the vehicle and because it is a legal obligation for him to have subscribed to an insurance policy).

Can D1, who is both a thief and a passenger in the stolen car, claim compensation from the insurer on the basis of the 1985 statute? Initially the answer was yes according to a case of the first civil division of the Cour de cassation.[5] However, the situation has changed since a law enacted on 31 December 1993 amended Article L. 211–1 Insurance Code. A new paragraph was introduced, providing that: 'in the event of the theft of a vehicle, [the] said contracts shall not cover compensation for losses sustained by the perpetrators, co-perpetrators or accomplices.' It would therefore appear that D1 cannot bring a claim for compensatory damages against the insurer.

No compensation funds (such as the *Fonds de garantie contre les accidents* and the *Fonds d'indemnisation des victimes d'infractions*, which provide compensation respectively to victims of accidents and of criminal offences) will intervene, since there exists a cause of exclusion of compensation.

The driver, D2, remains liable to pay compensatory damages to D1. Under the law of 1985, a victim who was not driving the vehicle may recover damages in full irrespective of their own fault. Nevertheless, D2's limited financial resources will most probably prevent D1 from recovering in full.

2. Second scenario: if D1 and D2 fled by boat

The applicable law will be found in the ordinary principles of tortious liability developed in Article 1382 et seq. Civil Code, rather than the special traffic law. D1 may claim damages against D2 on the basis of the principles of either personal liability or liability for damage caused by a thing. In the former case, D1's liability arises on the basis of his error in the handling of the boat. In the latter case, D1's liability arises on the basis of his being treated as the guardian

[5] Cass. Civ. 1, 17 November 1993, n°91–15.867.

of the boat under Article 1384 Civil Code. In both instances, D1's contributory fault will limit the size of the damage award.

D. *Third scenario*

In this scenario, the legal characterisation of the facts would change. The wrong could be characterised under Article 222–11 Criminal Code as an act of violence causing a total incapacity to work (for a period of time most probably exceeding eight days). An aggravating circumstance of complicity would be recognised under Article 222–12, 8° Criminal Code insofar as the offence was committed 'by two or more acting as perpetrators or accomplices'. D1 and D2 would then be liable to a maximum penalty of five years' imprisonment together with a 75,000 Euro fine.

The three ways of bringing such a prosecution before the court would remain the same: summons, summons followed by police report followed by immediate hearing and an appearance on prior admission of guilt.

V's civil action would also remain unchanged. However, the local healthcare insurance body (*caisse primaire d'assurance maladie*) could bring a claim against D1 and D2 to recover the costs of any medical treatment received by V for the injuries sustained as a result of the criminal wrong. The claim would be made by the wider healthcare insurance rather than a private insurer because it is the latter that is primarily concerned in cases of bodily injury.

4. Germany

A. *First Scenario*

The first scenario involves a number of distinct questions: the delictual and criminal liability of D1 and D2 for stealing and crashing the car; the delictual and criminal liability of D2 injuring D1; the delictual liability of D2 towards D1 for his injuries.

1. Delictual and criminal liability for stealing and crashing the car

a. Delictual liability D2 as the driver of the car would be liable under § 823(1) BGB to V for all damages resulting from the damage to V's property. § 823(2) BGB would not be applicable because D2 crashed the car negligently only and because the closest criminal law provisions, §§ 303 and 15 StGB, require intent (see below).

The scenario involves a further, more tricky question: that of possible strict liability under the StVG (Straßenverkehrsgesetz – Road Traffic Act). In principle, it is the keeper of a motor car who is liable under § 7(1) StVG. Yet, if somebody uses the car without the knowledge and the will of the keeper of the car it is the user who is strictly liable under § 7(3) StVG. D2 has used the car without the knowledge and the will of V. Thus, D2 is liable for all damage resulting from the use of the car. This raises the question whether D2 is also liable towards V for the damage caused to the car itself? Case law has recently discussed a similar problem: is the keeper of a car which he kept under a leasing agreement strictly liable towards the owner of the car under § 7(1) StVG if the keeper damages it? So far the cases are against liability on the basis that the car itself does not fall within the protective purpose of § 7(1) StVG.

Even though D1 did not drive the car himself he is, according to § 830 BGB, liable under the same provisions as D2. § 830 BGB states:

> (1) If more than one person has caused damage by a jointly committed tort, then each of them is responsible for the damage. The same applies if it cannot be established which of several persons involved caused the damage by his act.
> (2) Instigators and accessories are equivalent to joint tortfeasors.

D1 and D2 are liable as joint and several debtors, as § 840(1) BGB makes clear:

> If more than one person is responsible for damage arising from a tort, then they are jointly and severally liable.

The liability of joint and several debtors is set out in § 421 BGB:

> If more than one person owes performance in such a way that each is obliged to effect the entire performance, but the obligee is only entitled to demand the performance once (joint and several debtors), the obligee may at his discretion demand full or part performance from each of the obligors. Until the entire performance has been effected all obligors remain obliged.

Thus, if D1 and D2 have limited financial resources V can see from whom it is more likely to receive his compensation. The internal adjustment between D1 and D2 will be done on the basis of § 426 BGB.

The fact that D1 and D2 have also stolen the car will be of no relevance for the delictual liability as the crash itself will make them fully liable.

b. Criminal liability In criminal law D1 and D2 will have committed theft as joint principals under §§ 242, 25(2) StGB. With respect to the crash both D1 and D2 did not act with intent but only negligently. §§ 303, 15 StGB require, however, intent. D1 and D2 will not be criminally liable for crashing the car. Furthermore, D1 and D2 may have committed a number of road traffic offences. The procedure of adhesion will not be made use of as the question as to the delictual liability for the crash involves findings of fact and law which are unrelated to the theft and the road traffic offences.

2. Delictual and criminal liability for the injuries of D1

a. Delictual liability D1 was injured in the car crash. The question whether D2 is liable towards D1 involves a number of problems. First, the causality between D2's act and D1's injury is not interrupted by D1 telling D2 to drive faster. Second, a German court will most probably hold that D1 cannot be said to have consented to his injury by telling D2 to drive faster. However, a German court would either apply § 254 BGB for contributory negligence or § 242 BGB and say that it is a *venire contra factum proprium* if D1 first tells D2 to drive more dangerously and then claims damages from D2 for an injury resulting from driving more dangerously.

The question whether D2 is liable towards D1 under § 823(2) BGB would depend on whether D2 committed a criminal offence by injuring D1 and thereby infringed a criminal provision for the protection of D1 (see below).

Again, the keeper of the motor car (V) is not strictly liable to D1 under § 7(1) StVG as the car was used without his knowledge and will: § 7(3) StVG. It is the user of the car who is strictly liable. Both D1 and D2 would count as users of V's motor car. Thus, D2 could be said to be strictly liable to D1 under this provision. However, a German court would most probably again apply § 242 BGB and the maxim of *venire contra factum proprium.*

b. Criminal liability In the case of causing bodily harm the offender is criminally liable both for intent under §§ 223, 15 StGB and for negligence under § 229 StGB. However, unlike a private lawyer a criminal lawyer will argue that D2 was acting lawfully when injuring D1 because D1 had given his consent by telling D2 to drive faster and more dangerously. Under the circumstances, it is unlikely that a court would hold that the consent violated public policy under § 228 StGB; the consent is therefore valid, rather than being null and void.

B. *Second scenario*

There is no strict liability of boat owners. Thus, the legal analysis of the second setting would be easier as it would not involve the provisions of the StVG or any comparable provisions. Apart from that, the legal analysis of the first scenario would apply.

C. *Third scenario*

D1 and D2 are joint debtors for V's damage resulting from his injury under §§ 823(1), 830, 840 BGB, under §§ 823(2) BGB, 224(1)(4), 25(2) StGB, 830,

840 BGB and under §§ 826, 830, 840 BGB. Both are criminally liable as joint principals for causing bodily harm by dangerous means under §§ 224(1)(4), 25(2) StGB. In this case the procedure of adhesion may be applied.

If D1 told D2 to run faster, D2 fell and injured D1 because he, for example, fell on him, then there would be no delictual and criminal liability for the same reasons as given in the first scenario.

5. Sweden

A. *First scenario*

The prosecutor would charge both D1 and D2 with theft according to the Penal Code, Chapter 8 Section 1 – at least if they were planning on keeping or using the car for more than a joyride; if, however, the two defendants have no intention of acquiring the car, the charge would be vehicle theft (Penal Code, Chapter 8 Section 7). If the car is of considerable valuable and the damage is severe (an amount of approximately 23,000 Euro is usually deemed to be 'considerable value'), D1 and D2 would be charged with gross theft. Furthermore, D2 would be charged with (aggravated) reckless driving while D1 would be considered to have abetted the crime. Finally, concerning the injury of D1, D2 would be charged with causing bodily injury or illness; the fact that D1 and D2 have jointly taken the risk might be taken into account when assessing D2's liability, the penal value of the offence or later in sentencing. However, consent in risk taking is never relevant when the harm involved exceeds minor bodily injury. Both D1 and D2 could also lose any driving licence each held.

The car owner, V, who most likely has his/her car insured, would report the theft and receive compensation from the insurance company. The insurance would most likely have a deductible part, which the company would not pay but which V could sue the defendants for in order to receive it (V always has the choice of suing the defendants for the whole amount of damages instead of using the insurance, but there is always a risk that the defendants could not satisfy the claim). The insurance company, who compensates V, subrogates their right from V to sue D1 and D2 for damages (i.e. the amount paid out to V).

As a starting point, D1 would according to the Motor Traffic Damage Act 1976, have a right to get compensation for his/her injury from the car insurance company. Compensation to drivers, passengers, pedestrians and bicyclists for bodily harm caused in traffic is almost always compensated; such compensation is paid out regardless of the circumstances forming the basis for the damage. This means that a thief who drives a stolen vehicle and gets injured while driving has a right to compensation from the car insurance. However, this compensation can be reduced if the injured person intentionally or by gross negligence contributed to the harm. If compensation is paid out to D1, the insurance company will take over the claim that D1 would have had against D2 by subrogation, if the harm has been caused intentionally or with gross negligence.

D1 can otherwise, in conjunction with the criminal trial, sue D2 for damages for the bodily harm (this can include costs, loss of income and non-pecuniary damages such as pain and suffering) and for the violation, although the court would most likely not award D1 any damages for violation due to the conscious risk taking. Any remuneration for bodily harm can be reduced or waived entirely due to contributory negligence on D1's behalf. Worth noting is that medical treatment is part of the social security system, thus free of charge. Since D2 has limited financial recourses, the possibility of D2 paying any damages that the court might (although not likely) award D1 seems slim. If it turns out that D2 does not have any financial means, D1 could apply to the Crime Victim Compensation and Support Authority for compensation. The Authority is however, even more likely to turn down the claim in consideration of D1's own behaviour leading up to the injury.

B. *Second scenario*

In the situation where D1 and D2 try to escape on a boat instead, the differences would be that instead of (aggravated) reckless driving (cf. (1) above), D2 would be charged with (aggravated) reckless maritime driving. Second, there is no equivalence to the Motor Traffic Damage Act 1976 when it comes to other vehicles. What has been said there above would therefore not be relevant. Otherwise, the solution would be very similar to the first situation.

C. *Third scenario*

When D1 and D2 does not commit theft but punch V and break V's nose, then try to escape on foot, the answer to how the Swedish legal system would deal with the situation is the following.

The prosecutor would charge both D1 and D2 with assault (the Penal Code Chapter 3 Section 5).

V, who most likely has a private insurance, can report the injury to the insurance company and receive compensation for the assault with a predetermined, fixed amount or the equivalent to what the court would assess the damage to be. The insurance company would then have a right of subrogation against D1 and D2.

V could, instead of turning to his/her insurance company or in the unlikely event that V doesn't have insurance that covers the damage, with the assistance of the prosecutor or a specially assigned aggrieved party counsel sue D1 and D2 for damages in conjunction with the criminal trial. D1 and D2 would, if found guilty, be held jointly liable to pay the damages.

If V doesn't get (full) compensation from the insurance company and/or D1 and D2, V could apply to get crime victim compensation from the Crime Victim Compensation and Support Authority.

6. Spain

A. *First scenario*

The theft will be prosecuted before a criminal court. If the defendants had no intent to keep the car, they could be held liable according to Article 244 Spanish Criminal Code (CP) and punished with the penalty of community service from thirty-one to ninety days, or a fine if they return it, directly or indirectly, within a term not exceeding forty-eight hours. Should the vehicle not be returned within the term stated or should they have had the intent to keep the car from the beginning, they could be held liable for larceny or robbery (Arts. 234 and 237 CP) and punished even with imprisonment.

The affected party (the car's owner, for instance) could reserve her claim in tort and file it at a later civil procedure, but this will rarely happen in practice and usually the civil damages will be decided in the criminal procedure. Both D1 and D2 could be held liable pursuant to public law rules for having driven the vehicle in a risky way (with infraction of the Road Traffic Circulation Code, entailing possible administrative sanctions) and this may even amount to other crimes besides the theft (for instance driving at an excessive speed, Art. 379 CP).

Regarding D1 and D2's civil liability in the hypothetical criminal proceedings, it is important to note that according to Art. 117 CP:

> Insurers that have underwritten the risk of monetary liabilities arising from use or exploitation of any asset, company, industry or activity when, as a consequence of a fact foreseen in this Code, an event takes place covered by the risk insured, shall have direct civil liability up to the limit of the legally established or contractually agreed compensation, without prejudice to the right bring an action for recovery against who such may be appropriate.

So, if an insurer has underwritten the risks originating from the theft of V's car, that insurer could also be a legal actor in the criminal proceedings. Depending on the specificities of the insurance contract, V could obtain compensation through the criminal proceedings even if D1 and D2 have no financial resources. On the other hand, if D1 and D2's financial resources are extremely limited, they will have access to free legal aid.

As regards the hypothetical claim of D1 against D2, the court would probably take contributory negligence into account.

B. *Second scenario*

Probably no difference in practice, although the rules on the Road Traffic Circulation Code would not apply.

C. *Third scenario*

V could again choose between filing a criminal claim plus requesting compensation at the same time or either reserve her action for a later tort law procedure. Damage could probably be assessed following the criteria laid down for motor vehicle accidents.

7. Scotland

A. *First scenario*

D1 and D2 have committed a variety of criminal offences.[6] Their taking of V's car almost certainly amounts to theft,[7] and may alternatively be charged as a statutory offence of taking a motor vehicle without authority.[8] They are also guilty of the offence of dangerous driving[9] and (if D1 has suffered 'severe physical injury') D2 is guilty of the offence of causing serious injury by dangerous driving.[10] If required, V can recover the car from the police.[11]

If D1 were to bring an action against D2 in negligence, D2 might be entitled to plead the defence of *ex turpi causa non oritur actio*. This defence may prevent A from recovering damages from B where A was engaged in criminal activity

6 Although the scenario uses the term 'defendants', the Scottish term is 'accused' or 'accused persons' (the archaic term 'pannel' is sometimes also seen). In civil cases, the parties are the 'pursuer' and the 'defender'.

7 According to *Black* v. *Carmichael* 1992 SLT 897, it is sufficient *mens rea* for this offence that they intend to deprive V of the car; and it is not necessary to prove that they intended to do so either permanently or a nefarious purpose, despite suggestions to this effect in earlier case law. In any event, the temporary use of a car in this way is clearly an offence at common law: *Strathern* v. *Seaforth* 1926 JC 100, although the name of the offence concerned, if it is not theft, is unclear. It is a peculiarity of Scots law that the prosecutor need not set out the name of the offence with which the accused is charged, provided that facts sufficient to amount to a criminal offence are alleged: Criminal Procedure (Scotland) Act 1995 Sch. 3 para 2.

8 Road Traffic Act 1988 s. 178. Unlike the other offences under the 1988 Act cited here, this offence applies only to Scotland, although there is a near-equivalent offence in English law under s. 12 Theft Act 1968.

9 Road Traffic Act 1988, s. 2.

10 Road Traffic Act 1988, s. 1A.

11 Enforceable through a civil process (*Chief Constable of Strathclyde* v. *Sharp* 2002 SLT (Sh Ct) 95).

at the time the injury was suffered. The Scottish courts have stressed that in this context the question of whether this defence is available depends on the particular facts of the case. While the Scottish case law discloses a reluctance to permit the defence where it is pled by the driver of a car against a passenger, it may fairly be said that the reported cases involve less serious criminality than suggested in this scenario,[12] though it is less serious than in one English case (which would be followed) where the defence was sustained.[13] The defence of *volenti non fit injuria* (that D1 consented to the risk) is statutorily barred in a road traffic case such as this one.[14] The court might prefer to take the pragmatic approach of holding D1 to have been contributorily negligent, thus reducing the damages which he could receive rather than excluding liability.[15] As noted, however, D2 has limited financial resources. While damages in motor vehicle accident cases are often met from insurance policies, any insurance policy held by D2 would almost certainly exclude the possibility of covering D2's liability while engaged in conduct such as this. While the Motor Insurers' Bureau scheme provides for compensation in respect of the negligence of uninsured drivers, it excludes liability in cases where the vehicle was being driven in the course of a crime, and so D1 would not be able to obtain compensation from the Bureau.[16]

In the alternative involving the boat, the criminal offence of theft would again almost certainly have been committed. If the manner in which the boat was controlled by D2 put third parties at risk of injury, this would amount to the common law offence of reckless endangerment.[17] The analysis of civil liability would remain unchanged, except that the defence of *volenti non fit injuria* would potentially be available and likely to succeed on the facts presented.[18]

In the third scenario, the punching of V's nose would amount to the common law offence of assault. It is assumed that only one of D1 and D2 threw the punch concerned. Assuming, however, that either (a) they agreed to do so or (b) that one of them threw the punch as a foreseeable part of a common purpose in which they were engaged, the other party is guilty of the offence 'art and part'. V may also seek damages from his attacker in delict, which would include

[12] See *Weir* v. *Wyper* 1992 SLT 579; *Taylor* v. *Leslie* 1998 SLT 1248 at 1250 ('his behaviour was essentially skylarking rather than criminal'); *Currie* v. *Clamp's Executor* 2002 SLT 196 at [20] ('Even if, technically speaking, there was a breach of the statutory provision, it could not, in my view, be considered as in any respect a serious breach.')

[13] *Pitts* v. *Hunt* [1991] 1 Q B 24 distinguished in *Currie* v. *Clamp's Executor* 2002 SLT 196 at [21].

[14] Road Traffic Act 1988, s. 149(3). See *Winnik* v. *Dick* 1984 SC 48.

[15] See, e.g., *Currie* v. *Clamp's Executor* 2002 SLT 196.

[16] See, e.g., *Delaney* v. *Pickett* [2012] 1 WLR 2149.

[17] See, e.g., *Quinn* v. *Cunningham* 1956 JC 22 (dangerous cycling); *Macphail* v. *Clark* 1983 SLT (Sh Ct) 37.

[18] See *McCaig* v. *Langan* 1964 SLT 121; *Winnik* v. *Dick* 1984 SC 48.

compensation for *solatium* (pain and suffering) as well as any financial loss occasioned by the injury.[19] It is likely that, dependent on the precise facts of the case, D1 and D2 would be jointly liable in delict to V, thus allowing V to seek damages from either or both.[20] Alternatively (or in addition), a court which convicted D1 or D2 of assault might make a compensation order in favour of V, or V could seek state compensation from the Criminal Injuries Compensation Authority.

8. The Netherlands

A. *First scenario*

Most likely, D1 and D2 would be prosecuted for theft of the car. Furthermore, D1 and D2 both could be prosecuted for dangerous driving. However, there will be no prosecution of the harm suffered by D1, it being no matter of public concern. Note that in the Netherlands the Public Prosecution Service will not prosecute unless the public interest requires to do so (according to the so-called 'expediency principle').

As for the harm brought upon D1 by D2's driving: D1 could of course lodge a tort claim against D2, but this would not be an easy case to bring and win for it was D1 himself who acted carelessly by urging D2 to act recklessly. This fact will lead at least to a reduction in the damage award because of contributory negligence, if the claim could be granted at all, which is doubtful. Indeed, his acts may even have been criminal, although that is not important *per se* for the civil court. Careless driving which leads to personal injury is a crime. Given the complexity of the case, the civil suit will probably also be considered to be too complex to be joined and dealt with in the criminal trial.

B. *Second scenario*

There no is difference between this case and the previous one. Of course there are lots of specific road traffic rules (as well as rules on the use of waterways) but under the more generally framed criminal and tort law rules that seem to be applicable, that would not matter a great deal.

C. *Third scenario*

A prosecution for maltreatment, as well as a possible civil claim for compensation based on tort by V against D1 and D2 is likely and possible.

[19] See, e.g., *Downie* v. *Chief Constable, Strathclyde Police* 1998 SLT 8.

[20] See, e.g., the example given by Lord Justice-Clerk Macdonald in *Hook* v. *McCallum* (1905) 7 F 528, 532.

V can thus lodge a claim as an injured party within the criminal procedure (assuming prosecution follows), or through a civil claim. Moreover, if V does not lodge a claim as injured party but makes clear that he values compensation, the criminal court may *ex officio* decide to impose a compensation order.

9. Australia

A. *First scenario*

This hypothetical raises issues in criminal and civil law. In the criminal domain, a variety of crimes, including theft and dangerous driving, and failing to obey police directions or being involved in a police pursuit (a specific offence in NSW), may have been committed. There may also be questions of accessory liability. The criminal prosecution would be launched by the relevant state authority in each jurisdiction responsible for prosecuting serious criminal offences (in many jurisdictions the Office of the Director of Public Prosecutions). The prosecution and (most likely) the accused would be represented by legal representatives (barristers) and, depending on the seriousness of the charges, would be tried either before a judge, or a judge and jury. The seriousness of crime would also determine the court in which the hearing took place. The two defendants may be tried together in this sort of case, although, if convicted of the criminal offences, D1 and D2 would be sentenced separately in order to take into account any differences between them (such as level of culpability, early guilty plea, and other mitigating or aggravating factors).

The civil law relating to motor vehicle negligence and motor vehicle accidents in Australia is complex. Each state and territory has its own regime. Some Australian states retain the common law of negligence, some have legislative pure no-fault schemes and have abolished the common law, and others have a mixture of no-fault schemes with rights to the common law retained for more serious or catastrophic injuries. Much will depend on where the accident occurred in Australia, where the vehicle is registered and/or where D1 and D2 are resident. An action in the tort of conversion will also lie against D1 and D2 as their conduct is inconsistent with the rights of the owner of the car (V). All Australian jurisdictions have procedures that would allow V to seek to recover possession of the car from the police if it was not voluntarily returned to V (for instance, the Law Enforcement (Powers and Responsibilities) Act 2002 (NSW) Part 17).

In those states where only a common law claim is possible, D1 and D2 will likely have no claim. Clearly, D2 as the driver at fault has no common law claim. D1 is likely to be unable to show D2 owed him/her a duty of care. In Australia, the common law position (following *Miller* v. *Miller* (2011) 242 CLR 446) is that a duty of care will not exist in such circumstances (i.e. passenger and driver in continuing joint illegal enterprise) where it would be in conflict with or incoherent with the relevant criminal law. Applying this principle would require the court to construe the criminal law of the relevant state. Even where a duty of care could be shown to exist, tort reform legislation in most states has introduced provisions which either defeat or severely limit a claim by a plaintiff who has been injured while engaged in serious criminal conduct: see Civil Liability Act 2002 (NSW), Pt 7; Civil Liability Act 2003 (QLD), s. 45; Civil Liability Act 1936 (SA), s. 43; Civil Liability Act 2002 (Tas), Pt 3; Civil Law (Wrongs) Act 2002 (ACT), s. 94; Personal Injuries (Liabilities and Damages) Act 2003 (NT), s. 10.

In those jurisdictions where a no-fault system exists, D1 and D2 may still encounter difficulties with their claims. The existing no-fault schemes in most states either disallow a no-fault claim by claimants injured in a motor vehicle during criminal activity or restrict the kinds of claims that can be brought (for example to medical or care costs only). D1 and D2 will be able to access publicly funded health care (if required) and social security disability income support if they are unable to work due to disability. In Australian states where the National Disability Insurance Scheme (NDIS) has commenced, if D1 and D2 were resident in trial areas and had suffered major and permanent disability, they may also be able to access future care costs such as the costs of rehabilitation, carer assistance and home help.

The fact that D2 had limited financial resources would not prevent a claim, in theory or in practice, because of the presence of compulsory third party liability insurance for motor vehicles (although, as noted above, it is very unlikely there would be any substantive claim because of the defence of illegality).

Although there is some difference between jurisdictions, most civil actions are now tried by a judge sitting alone without a jury.

B. *Second scenario*

Apart from the range of offences with which D1 and D2 might be charged, the criminal law analysis would not change. Assuming the boat was stolen, theft offences would remain applicable although the specific offences relating to motor vehicles would not apply. Other offences relating to the dangerous use of a maritime vessel could be substituted.

In relation to civil proceedings, the analysis above in relation to the common law motor vehicle position would apply in a similar way for boats. The only difference from the first scenario involving a car is that there is no compulsory third party liability insurance for recreational boats and currently no no-fault schemes for boating injuries. The majority of boat owners do have third party insurance as marinas and slipways often require it such that there may be a third party insurer to cover costs (unless excluded from the policy due to illegality).

C. *Third scenario*

The criminal offences will clearly be different in this case; the most likely charge is some kind of aggravated assault. In NSW, as in England and Wales, assault is aggravated both by *mens rea* (intent more serious than recklessness) and the level of harm caused (grievous bodily harm more serious than actual bodily harm). If only one of D1 or D2 actually punched V, questions of accessory liability would arise.

V would have a civil claim for battery against the parties who actually punched him/her. If only one of D1 or D2 punched V, a question of accessory liability would also arise although, as noted in the chapter, the requirements for accessory liability seem to be stricter in tort than in crime. Although, in theory, the civil claim for battery is available to V, this is very unlikely to occur in practice as both D1 and D2 have limited financial resources. Even if these individuals carried liability insurance, it would not encompass liability arising from criminal intentional acts. V would also have a claim under the relevant state or territory statutory criminal compensation schemes, although the amount that can be recovered under these schemes is limited. Similarly, a compensation order could be made at the criminal hearing however these orders are relatively uncommon and generally of limited amount.

INDEX